Driving DevOps with Value Stream Management

Improve IT value stream delivery with a proven VSM methodology to compete in the digital economy

Cecil 'Gary' Rupp

BIRMINGHAM—MUMBAI

Driving DevOps with Value Stream Management

Group Product Manager: Aaron Lazar
Publishing Product Manager: Alok Dhuri
Senior Editor: Rohit Singh
Content Development Editor: Kinnari Chohan
Technical Editor: Karan Solanki
Copy Editor: Safis Editing
Project Coordinator: Deeksha Thakkar
Proofreader: Safis Editing
Indexer: Rekha Nair
Production Designer: Ponraj Dhandapani

First published: July 2021

Production reference: 1290721

Published by Packt Publishing Ltd.
Livery Place
35 Livery Street
Birmingham
B3 2PB, UK.

ISBN 978-1-80107-806-1

www.packt.com

To my wonderful wife and children, who stood by my side through all the years of hard work, long hours, and often outrageous travel schedules that came with my career. And to my beloved grandchildren who have blessed me, their Papa Cecil, so dearly.

– Cecil 'Gary' Rupp

Foreword

For a while now, I've been referring to value stream management as the next evolution of DevOps. DevOps itself, of course, is an evolution of many software engineering and delivery practices that came before it. It builds on Agile's approaches to solving the problems we experienced with traditional Waterfall ways of working. It combines Lean and IT service management, safety culture, and learning organizations, and it cross-pollinates with site reliability engineering, systems, and design thinking. It addresses cultural aspects in a way we haven't before in the technology industry and has super-charged advances in automation. It undeniably stands on the shoulders of giants.

Value stream management's history goes back a lot further than DevOps' 12 years. It's inherently part of Lean. While some point back as far as the arsenals of Venice in the 1400s, most practitioners look to Toyota in the 1950s as the progenitors of the movement that not only has thrived up until 2021 but is poised to explode. The tipping point is here because digital disruption has raised the stakes for software delivery in all businesses worldwide in this technology revolution (the age of software). We can now connect all parts of our digital value stream; we can harness data to produce actionable insights. Teams are increasingly wanting and able to measure the flow of value they produce to their customers and the value they receive. Organizations can finally measure their progress on a DevOps journey by using value stream management. But we are at the start of the journey of applying value stream thinking to digital value streams.

This book is unique and timely. The first of its kind, it explains specifically how to combine DevOps and value stream management to best effect – to deliver optimum value to customers and assure organizational performance. Readers will experience a journey through the evolution of value stream management to the present day, learning how DevOps practices optimize flow and what it means to focus on customer value outcomes. With practical examples of the principles in action in the field, case stories, and insights from the leaders molding this market, this book promises to find its own place in our history of business improvement.

I met the author, Gary Rupp, when we launched the Value Stream Management Consortium in March 2021 and immediately invited him to join the consortium as a board advisor, so evident was the depth of his knowledge and expertise in this industry. It's been a pleasure to read his work and learn from him and his immense experience with both value stream management and DevOps.

For value stream management, as we move toward impact-driven development, insight-driven business, and continue to augment human intelligence with our machines, the time to act is now.

Helen Beal

Chair, Value Stream Management Consortium

Contributors

About the author

Cecil 'Gary' Rupp brings more than 30 years of practitioner and executive-level experience in applying the methods and tools of **information technology** (**IT**) for software development. His roles span IT professional services, executive management, business process re-engineering/improvements, CASE tool software product manager, and the sales and marketing of software development and middleware tools.

In addition, Cecil has directly managed more than 20 enterprise-class IT programs and projects, with the last 16 years having been focused almost exclusively on supporting large federal and commercial health IT programs. He is also the author of the *Building Our Digital World* (BODW) series of books on software and systems development practices and *Scaling Scrum Across Modern Enterprises*.

I want to thank the people who contributed their time and expertise to help make this a better book:

Steven Anderson, Ahmed Khan, and Jill Buhrfiend (Apptio, Inc.)

Helen Beal (VSM Consortium)

Richard Dunn and Ben Chicoswi (CloudBees)

Lance Knight (ConnectALL)

Richard Knaster, Mike O'Rourke, and Gaurav Rewari (Digital.ai)

Alec Newcomb (Highwire PR on behalf of GitLab)

Brian Muskoff and Al Wagner (HCL Software)

Kumar S Rajesh (Institute of Product Leadership)

Akshay Sharma (Kovair)

Kamana Jain and Chet Marchwinski (Lean Enterprise Institute)

Don Tapping and Todd Sperl (LeanFITT)

Christine Ewing (Micro Focus)

Charlie Ponsonby (Plandek)

Bob Davis and Jeff Keyes (Plutora)

Scott Ambler and All Shalloway (PMI)

Sean Harris, David Williams, and Colin Fletcher (Quali)

Adam Mattis and Marc Rix (Scaled Agile, Inc.)

RJ Jainendra, Richard Hawes, Yoav Boaz, and Anand Ahire (ServiceNow)

Naomi Lurie and Katherine Jeschke (Tasktop)

About the reviewers

Enrique Gomez is a Federal/Health Care IT expert with 20+ years' experience in full scale enterprise IT systems, software development, content/media development, and Agile/DevOps practices. His passion is problem solving for clients, with particular emphasis on creating memorable experiences, making IT work to improve health and quality of life, and leveraging emergent technologies to tackle the challenges of the human condition. He owns DevVinci Technica LLC. ("DevVinci"), a VA certified Service Disabled Veteran Owned Small Business (SDVOSB) and boutique consultancy serving federal, state, and healthcare IT industries in the US.

Joel Kruger is a Senior DevSecOps professional with experience architecting solutions that scale, reduce waste and increase visibility. He has enjoyed working with Configuration-as-code and Infrastructure-as-code to accelerate his client's business objectives for nearly a decade. Joel considers himself a hands-on and customer-service oriented person who loves to solve a challenge. Technology excites him, from computer servers, to embedded Raspberry Pi projects. He is passionate about being creative with tech and is not afraid to get some hot solder in his shoe laces.

Let's manage your business's value streams better, together.

Table of Contents

2

Building On a Lean-Agile Foundation

3

Analyzing Complex System Interactions

4
Defining Value Stream Management

5
Driving Business Value through a DevOps Pipeline

Section 2: VSM Methodology

6
Launching the VSM Initiative (VSM Steps 1-3)

7
Mapping the Current State (VSM Step 4)

8
Identifying Lean Metrics (VSM Step 5)

9
Mapping the Future State (VSM Step 6)

10
Improving the Lean-Agile Value Delivery Cycle (VSM Steps 7 and 8)

Section 3: VSM Tool Vendors and Frameworks

11
Identifying VSM Tool Types and Capabilities

12

Introducing the Leading VSM Tool Vendors

13
Introducing the VSM-DevOps Practice Leaders

14
Introducing the Enterprise Lean-VSM Practice Leaders

Section 4: Applying VSM with DevOps

15
Defining the Appropriate DevOps Platform Strategy

16
Transforming Businesses with VSM and DevOps

Assessments

Other Books You May Enjoy

Index

Preface

I started my professional career as a young engineering project manager at a high-tech manufacturing facility at **Texas Instruments**. I had no idea then that the basic concepts I learned about Lean production processes would serve me well throughout my career as a software product manager (*computer-aided software engineering – CASE and workflow* tools) and as a consultant and IT project manager in the development of business applications for business process improvements. However, my work in those areas was always about improving organizational value streams outside of the IT department.

Lean production concepts began to find their way into software development in early 2000 through the insights of people such as Mary and Tom Poppendieck in their book *Lean Software Development: An Agile Toolkit*. By 2010, the concepts behind Lean-Agile practices began to make their way into software development methodologies, such as the **Scaled Agile Framework** and **Disciplined Agile**. Finally, we began to see the practical application of Lean production improvement concepts applied to IT-oriented value streams in the form of modern **value stream management** (**VSM**) software tools and platforms.

As you will discover in this book, VSM is an approach to make Lean improvements across all development and operational value streams. A value stream is simply an end-to-end sequence of activities where work and information flow in a coordinated and streamlined manner to deliver value (for example, products, services, and results) most effectively.

In its modern reinvention, the software development industry applies VSM tools to integrate, automate, and orchestrate work across DevOps pipelines to improve the end-to-end activities involved in software deliveries across both the development and operations functions. Rather than manually collecting data, modern VSM tools capture critical performance metrics in real time and provide a common data model and analytical tools to assess both current and desired future state conditions.

In short, modern VSM tools offer a convergence of data and analytical capabilities that are necessary to make informed decisions to improve your software delivery flows. Implementing DevOps methods, configurations, and tools on an enterprise scale is not trivial or inexpensive. On the other hand, VSM tools provide the data you need to get the most out of your IT investments.

It's been an arduous journey to bring the thoughts and ideas together for this book, including input from the VSM Consortium, 16 tool vendors – with research on 24 software tool companies in all, plus the two leading Lean-Agile Framework companies and two of the leading Lean training and methodology companies.

Sometimes, it was like herding cats pulling all the information together from these disparate sources! However, the result, I believe, represents the most comprehensive source of VSM methods and tools to date. Moreover, this book also helps explain how DevOps and VSM go hand-in-hand to help drive competitive outcomes in a digital economy.

Recall that VSM is not a new concept, though more recently applied to help make lean-oriented improvements across IT value streams. Organizations that practice Lean production improvement concepts use VSM practices to improve all development and operational value streams. As a strategic enabler, VSM initiatives help discover and prioritize many potential improvement opportunities across the enterprise, to deliver value more effectively. And many of those identified value stream improvement opportunities are digital enhancements best realized through software applications.

For example, in our digital economy, businesses create software applications as commercial offerings or to deliver information or entertainment services as web-based services. However, software can also enhance physical products, such as the navigation and control systems in automobiles. Finally, businesses, government agencies, and non-profits use software applications to improve the flow of value across their critical business processes and value stream activities.

Through my research and discussions with many of the leading VSM, DevOps, and Lean organizations, I have concluded that organizations must integrate their IT-based VSM tool strategies into their corporate strategic VSM initiatives. While Lean is a relatively new concept in IT, the rest of the organization has likely been practicing Lean concepts for decades – or, at least, they should have been. That's not true just in manufacturing, as many service companies and healthcare providers have implemented Lean practices.

In this book, you will learn how to apply a generic VSM methodology that can help identify improvements in organizational development and operational value streams, not just IT. This approach was taken purposely for the reasons noted above. Organizations use VSM methods and tools to identify and prioritize improvement opportunities across all value streams, many of which require software to make the improvements.

In other words, VSM methods address two broad areas to make value stream improvements. First, modern VSM methods and tools help improve DevOps-based software delivery capabilities. Second, the same VSM strategies and techniques help identify digital improvement opportunities across other organizational value streams to direct the organization's improved software delivery capabilities.

So, VSM is not limited to making value stream flow improvements in DevOps. From the perspective of *systems thinking*, making value stream improvements to DevOps is a form of making *localized optimizations*. In other words, if software delivery is not the bottleneck in our business system, or if we don't know how to apply our improved software delivery capabilities, then the time and resources spent on the effort to improve our system as a whole may have little or no impact.

You have experienced this situation first hand if your organization has spent time and money implementing DevOps toolchains and platforms, but you have not seen a justifiable return on investment.

You may not know much about Lean practices yet, but that's OK. You will learn in this book that it's all about discovering and eliminating wastes that hinder flow, which in turn cause bottlenecks, delays, excessive work in process, and ultimately higher costs that your customers don't want to pay. For these reasons, Lean practitioners always have a cost and time to market or delivery advantage over their competitors.

The main point is that an enterprise can spend much time and effort on their DevOps and VSM tool initiatives but not see a justifiable ROI – unless they use those software delivery improvements to help improve the organization's other operational and development value streams. So, DevOps teams should align their activities to help make improvements across all organizational value streams. Moreover, it's the Corporate VSM initiatives, through their Kaizen Bursts (future state improvement opportunity scenarios), that help identify and prioritize the areas where the improved DevOps capabilities can have the most timely and beneficial impacts.

For these reasons, this book introduces the historical foundations behind the concept of adding value, Agile's values and principles, systems and lean thinking, and VSM and their modern context in IT. You will discover how to use VSM as a methodology to discover areas for improvement across all organizational value streams, while simultaneously using VSM tools to make Lean-oriented improvements in your DevOps-based software delivery pipelines. But ultimately, you will find that it's the integration of DevOps to support Lean-oriented improvements across all organizational value streams that help justify the time, expense, and effort associated with installing VSM tools and DevOps toolchains and pipelines.

The book logically divides into four parts, subtitled as follows:

- **Value Delivery** – what it means and how to go about it

  Chapters 1 – 5

- **VSM Methodology** – a Lean-oriented and proven approach to make **Flow** improvements across an enterprise

  Chapters 6 – 10

- **VSM Tool Vendors and Frameworks** – to improve your software delivery pipeline capabilities

  Chapters 11 – 14

- **Applying VSM with DevOps** – to drive digital business transformations

  Chapters 15 and 16

Feel free to skip around between the four parts of the book. Also, if you want to understand the issues organizations face when implementing DevOps platforms, start with a quick read of Chapter 15, Defining the Appropriate DevOps Platform Strategy, where you will hear from six experts on this topic.

I hope you enjoy this book as much as I've enjoyed writing it.

– Cecil Gary Rupp

Who this book is for

This book was written for corporate executives, managers, DevOps team members, and other stakeholders involved in digital business transformations to improve the flow of customer value through their organization's value streams.

What this book covers

Chapter 1, Delivering Customer-Centric Value, defines what constitutes the delivery of value.

Chapter 2, Building on a Lean-Agile Foundation, explains what it means to be a Lean-Agile enterprise.

Chapter 3, Analyzing Complex Systems Interactions, looks at software development activities as a complex system and explains the impact of interrelationships between participating elements.

Chapter 4, Improving IT Value Streams with VSM, explains the history and fundamentals behind value stream management.

Chapter 5, Driving Business Value through a DevOps Pipeline, assesses end-to-end activity and the information flows and integrated toolchains that make DevOps pipelines so complex and expensive to implement on an enterprise scale.

Chapter 6, Launching the VSM Initiative (VSM Steps 1–3), explains why an organization must commit to Lean, how to choose a value stream, and what VSM team members and other stakeholders need to learn about implementing Lean.

Chapter 7, Mapping the Current State (VSM Step 4), explains how to construct a current state value stream map using a CI/CD pipeline flow improvement use case as an example.

Chapter 8, Identifying Lean Metrics (VSM Step 5), explains the common Lean metrics used to identify waste that contributes to poor performance across value streams and those that most apply to assessing IT and DevOps-oriented value streams.

Chapter 9, Mapping the Future State (VSM Step 6), explains how to construct a future state value stream map and Kaizen Burst (production improvement opportunities) using a CI/CD pipeline flow improvement use case as an example.

Chapter 10, Improving the Lean-Agile Value Delivery Cycle (VSM Steps 7 and 8), explains how to develop and execute a Kaizen Plan that addresses the improvement opportunities identified in the future state value stream maps.

Chapter 11, Identifying VSM Tool Types and Capabilities, introduces the three primary types of VSM tools and their general purpose and capabilities.

Chapter 12, Introducing the Leading VSM Tool Vendors, offers descriptions of the capabilities provided by 16 leading VSM tool vendors, along with their individual strengths and areas of focus.

Chapter 13, Introducing the VSM-DevOps Practice Leaders, introduces the VSM Consortium and two of the leading Lean-Agile frameworks that promote VSM – Disciplined Agile and the Scaled Agile Framework®.

Chapter 14, Introducing the Enterprise Lean-VSM Practice Leaders, introduces two of the leading Lean training and certification organizations – the Lean Enterprise Institute and LeanFITT™.

Chapter 15, Defining the Appropriate DevOps Platform Strategy, provides interviews with six expert DevOps practitioners to explain the potential DevOps implementation pitfalls that organizations need to be aware of. This chapter also introduces four DevOps platform implementation strategies and the pros and cons of each.

Chapter 16, Transforming Businesses with VSM and DevOps, explains how to use VSM and DevOps tools and related implementation initiatives to transform businesses into viable entities to compete in our digital economy.

Download the color images

We also provide a PDF file that has color images of the screenshots and diagrams used in this book. You can download it here: `https://static.packt-cdn.com/downloads/9781801078061_ColorImages.pdf`

Conventions used

> **Tips or important notes**
> Appear like this.

Get in touch

Feedback from our readers is always welcome.

General feedback: If you have questions about any aspect of this book, email us at `customercare@packtpub.com` and mention the book title in the subject of your message.

Errata: Although we have taken every care to ensure the accuracy of our content, mistakes do happen. If you have found a mistake in this book, we would be grateful if you would report this to us. Please visit `www.packtpub.com/support/errata` and fill in the form.

Piracy: If you come across any illegal copies of our works in any form on the internet, we would be grateful if you would provide us with the location address or website name. Please contact us at `copyright@packt.com` with a link to the material.

If you are interested in becoming an author: If there is a topic that you have expertise in and you are interested in either writing or contributing to a book, please visit `authors.packtpub.com`.

Share Your Thoughts

Once you've read *Driving DevOps with Value Stream Management*, we'd love to hear your thoughts! Scan the QR code below to go straight to the Amazon review page for this book and share your feedback.

https://packt.link/r/1-801-07806-8

Your review is important to us and the tech community and will help us make sure we're delivering excellent quality content.

Section 1: Value Delivery

Chapters 1 through 5 introduce the core concepts behind adding value, Lean-Agile practices, systems thinking, and value stream management. They apply to modern IT practices and other value streams that deliver value across the enterprise. These concepts are also foundational to the knowledge you need to learn how to apply the concepts in section 2 of this book – *VSM Methodology* – a Lean-oriented and proven approach to make flow improvements across an enterprise.

In the first three chapters, you will learn how to focus on adding customer-centric value across an enterprise by blending Agile, systems thinking, and Lean development practices. Then, in *Chapter 4, Improving IT Value Streams with VSM*, you will learn about how value stream management (VSM) is an approach to improve Lean production capabilities across all value streams, including IT. Finally, in *Chapter 5, Driving Business Value through a DevOps Pipeline*, you will learn what a DevOps pipeline is and why it's the best approach to deliver value in a digital economy.

Modern VSM tools support implementing Lean improvements across IT value streams and improve DevOps pipeline implementations. In that context, these chapters help explain why the effective implementation of a DevOps pipeline – as an efficient software delivery system – is the necessary "table stake" that allow an organization to compete in our modern digital economy.

This section includes the following chapters:

- *Chapter 1, Delivering Customer-Centric Value*
- *Chapter 2, Building on a Lean-Agile Foundation*
- *Chapter 3, Analyzing Complex Systems Interactions*
- *Chapter 4, Improving IT Value Streams with VSM*
- *Chapter 5, Driving Business Value through a DevOps Pipeline*

1
Delivering Customer-Centric Value

This chapter introduces the many different definitions of value and explains how Agile, Systems Thinking, and Lean Development work together to deliver customer-centric value. With this base of understanding, **Value Stream Management (VSM)** and **DevOps(development-operations)** are also introduced as complementary **Information Technology (IT)** practices and tools to support **Lean-Agile** practices.

You will learn how VSM helps maximize the flow of customer value across an organization's software development and delivery processes. For example, VSM helps improve the flow of work across **systems development life cycle (SDLC)** processes when developing applications supporting business operations.

However, VSM cannot be just about improving software development and delivery practices for business systems in a digital economy. Many commercial businesses, government agencies, and nonprofits offer information-oriented products and services delivered as web-based services. Additionally, many physical products incorporate computing devices, software, and internet access to deliver new features and enhanced functionality on demand and throughout their life cycles.

For these reasons, the use of VSM methods and tools must go beyond IT to help improve workflows and information flow across operations and development-oriented value streams.

DevOps improves communications across IT departments in a complementary fashion, while integrating and automating IT processes to enable a continuous flow of customer-centric value across all organizational value streams. As a result, a modern DevOps team can deliver value orders of magnitude more efficiently, rapidly, and error-free than with traditional SDLC and Agile practices.

In this chapter, you will learn how these practices work in concert to deliver customer-centric value. The topics covered include the following:

- Defining the term *value* in its many forms
- Developing a value proposition
- Creating value
- Taking a Lean-Agile view of value
- Understanding VSM
- Understanding the role of DevOps in delivering value
- Integrating Lean, Agile, VSM, and DevOps

Defining the term value in its many forms

This book is fundamentally about creating digital transformations to deliver customer-centric value efficiently, rapidly, and at a lower cost. Such a strategy involves including and aligning IT with the value stream transformations occurring across the enterprise. VSM is a Lean production improvement strategy that's found new applications in IT. Since VSM is the primary focus of this book, let's start with definitions of value in a VSM context.

Viewing value from a Lean-oriented perspective

Value streams are a **Lean production** concept that describes the series of product life cycle activities required to guide product deliveries from ideation through creation, deployment, support, retirement, and sustainment. As the name *value stream* implies, the whole point is to ensure all product delivery activities add value. From the perspective of Lean, adding customer-centric value means going beyond the provisioning of features and functions to also eliminate all forms of waste that customers don't want to have added to their costs.

VSM is an approach to methodically eliminate waste and improve productivity and efficiency while lowering costs. More precisely, you will learn that VSM encompasses Lean-oriented methods to improve work and information flow across value streams. Modern VSM tools support the VSM methods initially developed by Toyota as an approach to map material and information flows, and then later introduced to the rest of the world in the early 2000s (Jones, Womack, 2003).

When we get to the sections on Lean-Agile views and VSM, you will also find there are two forms of value streams: **operations** and **development**. Let's take a quick look at the differences between these two types of value streams.

Differentiating development from operations

Operations-oriented value streams deliver products and services to an organization's external customers, while development value streams create things used or delivered by the organization's operations-oriented value streams.

Let's put this another way, as follows:

- Operations value streams include the work and information flow that define how your company—or its product lines or **lines of business** (**LOBs**)—conducts business, earns revenue, and delivers services to its customers.

- Development value streams include work and information flows to build and support the products, services, and other artifacts used by the operations-oriented value streams to deliver value.

Operations-oriented value streams enhance customer experiences by providing products, information, and services, either online or through personal contacts. In contrast, development-oriented value streams create products and services for either internal or external customers. In other words, development value streams build stuff, while operations value streams need to sell, deliver, and support the organization's customers.

Both functions are necessary and value-adding. However, making a distinction between development and operations is important in terms of purpose, planning horizons, and who controls and funds the activities. For example, LOB executives and product owners have accountability over investment priorities in their operations-oriented value stream activities. In contrast, portfolio management team controls investment priorities over development-oriented stream activities.

Another way to look at this distinction is the operations-oriented processes of selling, delivering, and supporting products. These are tactical activities that provide value to our customers, usually over relatively short planning horizons. Development value stream investments tend to be larger, are critical to the organization's long-term survival, and require longer planning and implementation horizons. In contrast, development-oriented value streams help ensure the organization has the infrastructure, products, and services to meet its strategic objectives.

At first glance, this distinction between development and operations seems to support the traditional IT organizational model. Development teams create software products for both internal and external customers or users, and operations teams exist to keep systems running, secure, and available, while also resolving customer and user issues via helpdesk services.

Later in this book, you will learn that an IT organization implementing Lean-Agile practices should consider moving traditional IT development and operations functions within dedicated product teams. But that is getting ahead of ourselves. We'll come back to that subject later in *Chapter 4, Defining Value Stream Management*.

For now, let's take a look at some examples of how an IT development-oriented value stream can develop and support software applications for use by other organizational value streams, such as a customer order entry or product fulfillment.

Developing applications to support organizational value streams

The following diagram displays three organizational value streams: *order entry, fulfillment,* and *software development.* Order entry and fulfillment are operations-oriented value streams, while the software development activity is a development-oriented value stream:

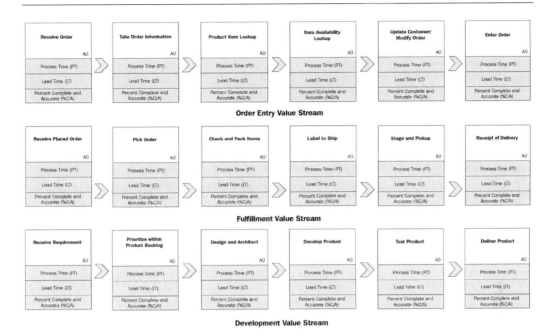

Figure 1.1 – Value stream examples

Each activity block identifies the activity's name, **process time (PT)**, **lead time (LT)**, and **percent complete and accuracy (%C/A)** metrics. You learn how to use these metrics later in *Chapter 8, Identifying Lean Metrics(VSM Step 5)*. The main point to understand is that IT is a critical development value stream that improves other operational value streams' delivery capabilities and efficiencies.

This book purposely opened with a discussion on operations- and development-oriented value streams. The current trend is to speak of VSM as a tools-based approach to improve DevOps pipeline work and information flows. DevOps pipeline flow improvements are a great application of VSM. However, your organization is missing the point if its VSM strategy is limited to DevOps. The discussion surrounding the value stream examples depicted in *Figure 1.1* clearly shows how IT-based development value streams help improve operational value streams.

This book provides instruction on integrating Agile, Lean, VSM, and DevOps practices to enable business agility on an enterprise scale. These are the methods and tools that allow organizations to provide the right set of products and services customers want rapidly, efficiently, and at the lowest cost. Those organizations that do this successfully, and enterprise-wide, have a leg up when competing in our increasingly digitized economy.

We discuss all these concepts later in this chapter and throughout this book. Before we do, it's essential that you first have a clear understanding of what it means to compete in a digital economy and IT role.

Competing in a digital economy

Don Tapscott introduced the term *digital economy* in his book *The Digital Economy: Promise and Peril in the Age of Networked Intelligence* (1997). The book's key focus is on how digital technology changes the way individuals and societies interact.

Later, in 2001, Thomas L. Mesenbourg, then Associate Director for Economic Programs at the **United States (US) Census Bureau**, delivered a paper titled *Measuring the Digital Economy*. The paper describes an effort initiated by the US Census Bureau to measure the economic impact of electronic devices as the basis of our then-emerging digital economy.

In his paper, Mesenbourg describes the digital economy as having three primary components, listed as follows:

- **E-business infrastructure**: This includes all participating computing, network, communication, security, and software systems.

- **Electronic business processes** that support the digital economy.

- **Electronic commerce transactions** that support the selling of goods and services online.

Building products for the digital economy

The term *digital economy* implies something much more significant than Mesenbourg's original e-commerce-centric views in a modern context. For example, digitally enhanced technologies now allow organizations to conduct business on the internet and mobile technologies while providing near-real-time and global access to information and knowledge-based services.

Moreover, digital technologies enhance physical products with new features not possible through simple modifications in materials or mechanical components. Broadly classified as the **Internet of Things (IoT)**, product features and capabilities can be updated, even after delivery to customers.

The key differentiator of an IoT capability is the ability to transfer data over a network without requiring human-to-human or human-to-computer interaction. At a conceptual level, IoT is a system of interrelated computing devices with **unique identifiers (UIDs)** that make them visible to other computing systems and digital devices via the internet and mobile connections.

IoT devices include mechanical and digitally enhanced machines and embedded objects within manufactured goods, people, or animals. As modern examples, your automobile gets factory updates to its computing and navigation systems via mobile connections. Telehealth-based IoT solutions enable real-time monitoring of patient health at long distances via external and embedded monitoring systems. As a final example, embedded biochips with transponders help identify animals and monitor their health and location in the wild and within farms, and can even identify your pets.

Connecting in the digital economy

Our modern digital economy is also more than the scope of e-commerce and digitally enhanced products. The internet has opened up extraordinary communication avenues, information sharing, and collaboration via social media tools and platforms.

Web-based social media tools enable people to interact and share information and experiences across multiple media formats (for example, audio, video, text, photos, images, and so on). Social media is all about leveraging content to drive *human-to-human* and *business-to-human* engagements.

Holly Gibbons, President of Gibbons Business Solutions, LLC., lists six categories of social media content that drive engagements (`https://gibbons-business-solutions.com/6-types-of-social-media-content-that-drive-engagement/`), outlined as follows:

- **Promotion**: Informing on products and services
- **Education**: Establishing expertise and enabling self-help
- **Connection**: Delivering an "insider" view of your business
- **Conversation**: Specifically targeted to engage customers
- **Inspiration**: "Feel-good" messages with quotes, facts, and personal stories of success that reflect the vision and values of the person or entity
- **Entertainment**: Connecting with audiences through sharing holiday wishes, jokes, comics, funny but informative videos, contests, and giveaways

Social media is a transformative capability that helps drive our modern digital economy. The following subsection lists other digitally enhanced business transformations.

Delivering value in a digital economy

Other names for the digital economy include the **internet economy**, **new economy**, or **web economy**. The evolution of the digital economy has forced traditional brick-and-mortar companies to rethink their business strategies or face being driven out of business by fierce competitive disruptors such as **Amazon.com** (retail), **Airbnb** (travel accommodations), **Google** (information searches), **Netflix** (home entertainment), **Lyft** and **Uber** (transportation services), **Tesla** (automobiles and aerospace), and **YouTube** (video-based information and entertainment content sharing).

Given their legacy investments in brick-and-mortar-based infrastructures, companies need to rapidly find creative approaches to leverage their traditional economies of scale to compete in the digital economy. In some cases, this means finding different ways of engaging with our customers. In other cases, a blended approach to integrating traditional and digital infrastructures may provide the most competitive advantage.

In any case, companies must define and execute their competitive value propositions. They must evaluate all their investments and activities to ensure maximal contributions to adding customer-centric value. Ultimately, this book introduces many interrelated concepts that help an organization deliver value in a digital economy, but before we get to those sections, we need a shared understanding of what *value* means. That is the topic of the following subsection.

Diving into the many concepts of value

Semantics is essential in computer science—so important that an entire IT discipline called **ontology** is devoted to the subject. If you look up the word *ontology*, you will find that the term's origins come from a branch of metaphysics that deals with the *nature of being* or *what exists*. Ontology is a compound word that combines *onto* (Greek ὄν) and "*being; that which is*" (*gen. ὄντος, ontos*). In other words, it's a discipline that seeks to discover *what is real*.

In the field of information science, Ontology deals with *semantic meanings*. The problem is that humans have this annoying habit of using the same terms but having very different views on what those words actually mean. Our life experiences, education, and intellectual capabilities greatly influence our understanding of the words we use. This is a primary reason why we humans so often get our communications wrong.

In contrast, traditional information systems must have a precise contextual understanding of the terms and values they employ; otherwise, they cannot correctly exchange information. The same issue applies to human-computer interactions. The words we want to use may not fit the computer's understanding of the term. This dichotomy is what drives much of the research in **artificial intelligence (AI)**. In other words, part of AI research seeks to help computers understand the contextual meaning of words in specific types of human-to-computer interactions.

The word *value* has many business meanings that support various business practices or desirable business outcomes based on contextual use (that is, the term *value* means different things, depending on the term's application). As an example that's relevant to this book, Agile, Lean, VSM, and DevOps all share the idea that organizations must deliver value from a customer's perspective. However, they have different strategies to achieve that goal. Moreover, IT specialists and business analysts need to understand that the folks they interact with within other departments may have entirely different thoughts on what the word *value* means.

Using an analogy, we have a situation a bit like the story of the blind men describing an elephant. Because they cannot see, the blind men have a limited understanding of what an elephant looks like, based only on what they can experience through touch, as shown in the following diagram:

Figure 1.2 – The six blind men and the elephant

For those not familiar with the story, the first blind man touches the trunk and exclaims, *"The elephant is like a thick snake"*; however, the next blind man touches the ear and says, *"No, it's like a fan"*. Next, another touches one of the elephant's tusks and says, *"I don't know what you guys are talking about; it's a spear"*. The next blind man in line touches the elephant's leg and proclaims, *"The elephant is like a big and stout tree trunk"*, but the blind man who touches the side of the elephant believes they have come up against a wall. Finally, the blind man who touches the tail believes he has caught hold of a rope.

There's only one elephant, but the blind men have different theories of what the elephant is, based on their particular "hands-on" experiences and their lack of a holistic view. The same issues face business analysts when they seek to understand what adds value to a business. So, before we can talk about how Agile, Lean, VSM, and DevOps improve value, we need to spend some time understanding the term's many contextual uses.

This chapter explores the many variants of value with that goal in mind, spanning ownership, accounting, marketing, supply chain, Agile, Lean, and DevOps.

Viewing value from the context of business assets

In its most straightforward context, the term *value* implies an asset's worth expressed from a monetary, material, usefulness, or personal view—for example, there are many ways to express public companies' business value, such as shareholder value, a firm's monetary value, value capture, fair value, and market value.

Shareholder value relates to the price of a company in terms of the value given to stockholders' shares. The shareholder's value fluctuates on the market's perception of its ability to sustain and grow profits over time. From this perspective, a company's value is roughly equivalent to the number of outstanding shares times the current share price.

Monetary value is an expression of the money an asset—such as a company, product, property, land, or service—would bring if sold. In other words, monetary value is an expression of how much money something is worth on a free and open market. Monetary value determinations come from the dynamics of *supply* and *demand*—for example, increasing the supply of a product relative to demand decreases its value. In contrast, limited supplies with high demand drive the price up.

If you talk to a **Master of Business Administration** (MBA) graduate or an accountant, they may use the term *value capture*. In their context, value capture describes a process to retain a percentage of the value provided in every business transaction, most often in the form of profit-taking. However, in matters related to public financing, value capture implies using public financing to develop infrastructure that improves a municipality's value as a whole and the value of adjoining commercial properties.

Fair value is an evaluation of business assets (and liabilities) for financial reporting in line with a country's standard accounting practices, often used to assess value in sales, mergers, and acquisitions. The **International Financial Reporting Standards Foundation (IFRS Foundation)** is a nonprofit industry standards group that defines globally accepted accounting standards, published as *IFRS standards*. *IFRS standard 13* (https://www.ifrs.org/issued-standards/list-of-standards/ifrs-13-fair-value-measurement/) defines fair value as "*the price that would be received to sell an asset or paid to transfer a liability in an orderly transaction between market participants at the measurement date (an exit price)*".

Finally, *market value* is a determination of what a company is worth under current market conditions. Market value is the estimated price that an asset has in the marketplace or the value that the investment community gives to the equity position—that is, the price a third party pays to obtain a position within a business or other asset in exchange for its stock or securities.

We now have a broad understanding of the term *value* as it applies to the ownership of businesses and other assets. But the term *value* can also have a contextual meaning that identifies the importance of specific business relationships, such as *value chains* and *value networks*. **Value-added (VA)** relationships are the topic of the next section.

Viewing value from the context of business relationships

The concept of value in terms of the ownership of business assets is straightforward in contextual use. People and businesses invest time, money, and resources to improve their business asset value, but businesses also gain value by leveraging relationships with suppliers and other partners.

In the most general sense, all external partners provide products or services to support another entity's business goals, though both partners receive value from the relationship. But here, again, we need to carefully define the types of partner relationships to understand the value each provides. For example, a business may have suppliers that deliver components and materials used in their products and deliver them to the consumer. Other partners may resell or rebrand another company's products. There are multiple variants of these relationships, such as reseller, **VA reseller (VAR)**, and **original equipment manufacturer (OEM)**.

A reseller is like a retail outlet that purchases and then resells products to its customers. A retail partner may be a traditional brick-and-mortar company, an online reseller, or a hybrid blend.

A VAR is a firm that enhances the value of another company's products with customizations or services. For example, a **recreation vehicle** (**RV**) manufacturer typically buys the bare truck chassis, engine, and tires from one or more primary automotive and truck manufacturers. It then adds the body and internal furnishings that make the vehicle fit for camping. VARs can also provide services around another company's products, such as installation and configuration services, consulting, troubleshooting, repair, or customer support.

An OEM firm typically takes another firm's products and rebrands and sells the original product under their company's name. The OEM can also provide product and service extensions, similar to the VAR type of business VA relationship. Regardless, the OEM procures the primary manufacturer's additional rights to rebrand its products as their own.

Establishing business relationships as value networks

A **value network** includes any set of connected organizations or individuals working in an integrated and collaborative manner to benefit the group as a whole. A business-oriented value network helps members buy and sell products, organize and distribute work, and share information. While there are many types of value network relationships, they all fall within two broad categories: internal or external value networks.

Internal value networks include people within an organization collaborating to achieve mutual or reinforcing goals. These internal value networks usually work within the bounds of established business processes or value streams. Both business processes and value streams describe structured approaches to work.

The term *business processes* tends to be associated with traditional cross-functional and bureaucratic organizational structures. The **value stream** concepts came out of the Lean and Lean Six Sigma approaches to product delivery. Later sections of this book provide much greater detail on the subjects of Lean production and value streams. For now, think of value streams as a series of activities that deliver products and services aligned with customer needs. Moreover, Lean production is an approach to improve product and information flows across value streams.

An organization that scales multiple but small agile-oriented teams, working in an integrated, coordinated, and synchronized fashion to develop and deliver large products, is another example of an internal value network. The Agile teams may also employ Lean product development concepts, often referred to as Lean-Agile methodologies or frameworks.

External value networks describe the cross-organizational interactions of third parties that lie outside the primary business entity's bounds but contribute to its success. In other words, the external value network has a mutual interest in supporting or benefiting from the goals of the primary business entity. In this context, external value networks include agents, business partners, customers, consultants, product users, stakeholders, suppliers, and any other person or entity participating in a value-adding relationship.

Internal or external value networks create value through their relationships, cross-functional or value-stream-oriented processes, and their specific roles within a business enterprise relative to products and services. The relationships must be mutually beneficial—in other words, all parties within the value networks receive value from their relationships. When this is not the case, the networks fail to meet their goals and expectations, and the relationships usually become disruptive. In extreme cases, the networks fall apart and the participants exit their business or employment relationships.

Additionally, participants within value networks must hold up their end of the deal. Ineffectual participants weaken the entire network, and others must step in to fill the void—assuming that is possible. On the other hand, one advantage of having a value network is that the participants can provide the resources, skills, experience, and redundancy to step in and help the weaker elements get up to speed or overcome their limitations.

This section concludes our discussion on value networks. In the next section, we look at a complementary concept referred to as value chains. Instead of looking at VA relationships as networks, value chains describe a company's activities to add value to its products and services.

Establishing business relationships as value chains

Value chains are the processes or activities by which a company adds value to its products and services. Value chains include product life-cycle activities, spanning product ideation, design, receipt of raw materials, and adding additional value through production processes at a more granular level. Value chain processes also include promoting a product, taking an order, and then selling the finished product to consumers.

Michael Porter coined the term *value chain* in his book *Competitive Advantage: Creating and Sustaining Superior Performance* (1985). Porter describes the primary value chain activities for adding value and competitive advantage in terms of the following five elements:

- **Inbound logistics**: Receiving, storing, and processing raw materials and inventories.
- **Operations**: Converting raw materials into a finished product.
- **Outbound logistics**: The distribution of products and services to customers.

- **Marketing and sales**: Including advertising, promotions, and pricing strategies, and managing all sales channels (online, inside direct, outside direct, indirect through resale partners).

- **Services**: These help maintain products and improve consumer experience— including customer support, product maintenance and repair, refunds, and exchanges.

Value chain analysis offers a strategy to use value chains for competitive advantage. Value chain analysis evaluates the activities involved in changing the inputs for a product or service into an output valued by a particular customer type. A value chain analysis starts with identifying every production step required to create a product and then discovering ways to increase the overall value chain's efficiency.

Michael Porter's view of **value chain management** (**VCM**) theories supports the traditional views of using business processes, best practices, organizational assets, and **human resources** (**HR**) to achieve a competitive advantage, driving further growth in the market. Michael Porter notes explicitly that his approach is to implement an activity-based theory to drive competitive advantage.

Though his approach sounds somewhat similar to Lean Development concepts, Porter's orientation is oppositional to Lean's initial focus on the customer. Porter advocates a strategy of building and delivering a product cheaper and faster than your competitors, which, in his view, automatically drives new customers and growth. However, Lean practitioners believe we must first focus on customer needs before refining activities to deliver what our customers want—otherwise, we'll miss the mark.

Now that we've made that point, let's explore value from a customer's perspective.

Defining customer value

Customer value is the value received by the end customer of a product or service. In the previous section, you learned that Lean Development strategies emphasize assessing activities to add value and eliminate those that do not add value.

Lean Development strategies make sense because, ultimately, customers are the sole arbitrators of what value means to them. Customers perceive value in terms of utility or usefulness, quality, and benefits. Our ability to deliver what they want is the determinant of customer satisfaction.

But customer value is a tricky thing. It would be nice if all our customers valued the same things. In such a homogenous world, we would only have to produce one variant of a product and be the most efficient producer. Of course, we would also have to be competitive across marketing, sales, delivery, and support processes. Such a market supports Michael Porter's view of using value chains to create a competitive advantage.

But that's not the world in which we live. Instead, customers have different budgets and different desires in terms of the features and functions they prefer. In a traditional mass-production model, marketing and sales organizations try to influence customer behavior by telling customers what they should like about their particular products and services. That strategy allows the producers to follow Michael Porter's guidance on improving value chains.

That strategy might work for a while, but only up to the point where other competitors start asking customers what they want and then deliver better offerings. As a result, customer-oriented value delivery strategies had to evolve. By the 1980s and 1990s, **customer relationship management (CRM)** and Lean Development strategies became mainstream practices, to focus on adjusting product development and delivery efforts to address customer needs for mass markets and profitable niche markets.

Lean manufacturing, also known as **lean production**, is a modern instantiation of production methods derived initially from Toyota's operating model, known as *The Toyota Way* and the **Toyota Production System (TPS)**. The term *Lean* did not come from Toyota but was instead coined in 1988 by John Krafcik, who was then studying management and performing research under the direction of James P. Womack. Krafcik's research was part of a 5-year study at **Massachusetts Institute of Technology (MIT)** on the automobile's future. Krafcik's research produced much of the data referenced in the book *The Machine That Changed the World* (Womack, Jones, Roos; 1991). But it was Womack's, Jones', and Roos' book that articulated Lean manufacturing concepts and introduced the term *lean production*.

The lean concepts defined by James Womack and Daniel Jones contain five fundamental principles, outlined as follows:

- Precisely specify value by specific product
- Identify the value stream for each product
- Make value flow without interruptions
- Let customers pull value from the producer
- Pursue perfection (Womack and Jones, 1996, p.10)

CRM is a data-centric approach to managing information and interactions with customers and prospects. Specifically, CRM methods and software tools apply data analysis techniques to customer data, to better understand their history with the company and improve customer relationships. CRM is primarily a marketing-oriented function supporting their objectives to improve customer retention and drive new sales growth.

With CRM and Lean, organizations have the tools to determine what value means from a customer's perspective and then align organizational activities and resources to deliver that value. Some other methods and tools aid in identifying customer perceptions of value—for example, marketing and product management functions may conduct focus groups and initiate surveys to collect customer data. In turn, that data helps support analysis across analytical techniques, such as the following:

- **Voice of the customer**: A term used to describe the process of capturing customers' expectations, preferences, and dislikes.

- **Customer utility map**: A map of six utility levers to deliver exceptional utility to buyers against six stages of various buyer-experience cycles.

- **Kano model**: A method to understand, categorize, and prioritize five customer requirements (or potential features) for new products and services.

- **Customer journey map**: A diagram to illustrate the steps your customers go through to engage with your company, be it a physical product, an online experience, retail sale, a service, or some combination of all of these.

- **Empathy map**: A method used by **user experience** (**UX**) designers to understand user behavior and also visually communicate findings to other stakeholders, to provide a shared understanding of the prospective user.

- **Customer value management (CVM)**: A method to assess the perceived value of an organization's product and service offerings. Value is assessed in terms of benefits, functions, and performance to the price, the cost, and profit margins.

This subsection concludes our discussion on the various definitions of value and why products and services must consistently deliver value from the customers' perspective. We've also learned how CRM methods and tools with Lean practices help us discover and deliver value to our customers. But how does a business entity know if they have a viable value proposition? That is the topic of the next section.

Developing a value proposition

Michael J. Lanning coined the term *value proposition* in his published writings related to his work as a consultant at McKinsey & Company. His work pioneered concepts in developing corporate strategies, goals, and business capabilities to customer needs. Lanning outlined his concepts in his book *Delivering Profitable Value: A Revolutionary Framework to Accelerate Growth, Generate Wealth, and Rediscover the Heart of Business* (Lanning, 1998).

Lanning views value from the perspective of customer experiences and therefore defines the term *value proposition* as follows:

> *The combination of resulting experiences, including price, which an organization delivers to a group of intended customers in some time frame, in return for those customers buying/using and otherwise doing what the organization wants rather than taking some competing alternative.*

In other words, the term *value proposition* implies an explicit relationship where targeted customers gain experiences from the products and services delivered by an organization, though bounded within an established time frame (that is, values can and do change over time).

The term also sets expectations that the customers must purchase, use, and otherwise do something the delivery organization wants instead of selecting a competitive option. A competitive option is not limited to the customer purchasing a competitor's products or services. The customer may choose to do nothing or to create the desired experience with their internal resources.

Note also that the value proposition definition does not directly address its use as a marketing and selling communications tool, though many people view the term's relevance from this perspective. Customers value the experiences they receive or not from using an organization's products and services. Therefore, the critical issue is to ensure an organization works in concert to deliver the desired experiences and not merely promote features or functions that may or may not be relevant.

Unfortunately, the term *value proposition* is most commonly used in a limited context by marketing and sales professionals as a statement of how to position a commercial product or service competitively. But that type of limited focus misses the point of Lanning's primary work, which is to align the organization with its corporate strategies to deliver profitable value. From this perspective, everyone within the organization plays a role in delivering profitable value.

That statement does not mean that marketing staff should not use value propositions to properly communicate their organization's value or for sales staff to use a value proposition to make sure they're selling the right experiences to the right customers. However, metaphorically speaking, there are two questions an organization must first address, outlined here:

- Who's driving the ship?
- Did the rest of the crew get on board?

Later sections of this book introduce value stream mapping techniques to identify and eliminate all forms of waste across an organization's value stream activities. But how would the value stream teams know which outcomes they need to align their activities to from a VA perspective? That is the proper goal of building compelling value propositions, accomplished by answering five simple questions.

Aligning business strategies through five questions

Value propositions answer five critical questions about how an entity plans to deliver value. These questions are listed here:

- Who or what are the target market customers?

- What is the planning and execution life cycle horizon for the value proposition?

- What do we want these target market entities to do in exchange for the experiences we deliver?

- Which competing alternatives do these customers have to obtain the desired experiences?

- Which resulting experiences do the customers receive (including price) versus the competing alternatives, assuming the customers do as we ask?

As a further note, Lanning makes it clear that resulting experiences must be *specific*, *actionable*, and *comparative*. He also notes that winning value propositions are trade-offs in that some experiences are inferior to the competitive alternatives. Therefore, what matters is optimizing experiences in total (Lanning, 1998, p. 62).

Creating a vision for the organization

Value propositions serve as strategic documents that help focus and integrate an entire business to communicate its purpose. A value proposition is a choice made by leadership that aligns with their organizational strategies, objectives, and mission. Most importantly, a value proposition expresses a vision that most benefits their target market customers.

In this context of value, the executive leadership is not responsible for deciding which products and services the organization must deliver to its customers, or even deciding how to create and deliver those products and services. To do so is an example of internal-facing product strategies that revolve around what leadership wants to do.

Yet the answer isn't to turn the question around and ask customers what your organization's value proposition should be. In that scenario, chasing customer opinions can quickly become futile as there are many different niches of customers who have different *experiential* preferences, and chasing specific customer preferences can inappropriately send the organization in the wrong direction from adding value to the broader or more lucrative target market clients.

Later, you will learn how to identify and prioritize customer needs as actionable work items in a product backlog. For now, it's essential to understand that an organization must eventually turn its attention to developing specific value-adding features and functions, but it's also dangerous to start such efforts until after the organization establishes its vision and can express it completely via its value proposition.

Successful leaders tend to be highly creative, and often visualize and articulate a vision for their businesses long before customers understand they need them. Examples include Steve Jobs and Bill Gates, who both saw an opportunity to bring the power of computers to the masses, forming **Apple** and **Microsoft**, respectively. Jeff Bezos, the founder of **Amazon.com**, imagined an online retail bookstore to change the way readers review and purchase books. Ultimately, Bezos dramatically changed the customer retail experience. Once he successfully figured out the online retail model for books, he imagined expanding the model to market and sell virtually anything and, in the process, became the wealthiest person in the world.

Elon Musk is another business leader who has used his creativity and brilliance to define multiple market opportunities. For example, he established **Tesla, Inc.** to mass-produce electric cars, **the Boring Company** to build underground tunnels to improve transportation in congested areas, and **SpaceX** to build reusable rocket ships that can land on their tails.

What's important to note with this latter example is that Elon Musk did not try to merge all these unique value propositions into one company. Organizations with multiple value propositions should create sufficient separation between disparate product lines to avoid confusing their customers.

Organizations may choose to separate product lines across departments, divisions, or companies. The degree of product-line separation is primarily dependent on the variances between their value propositions. The principle to appropriately differentiate products by their value propositions holds for both digital and physical products.

Delivering value

You learned in the previous section that successful chief executives are creative and often visualize new product ideas before prospective customers see a need for them. However, coming up with a creative idea is just the start. The organization's leaders collectively refine the initial vision by answering the five questions identified previously.

In the process, the leaders deliberate and articulate their shared vision within the value proposition document. In the end, the value proposition defines the business the organization is in, who their prospective customers are, and the types of experiences the business must deliver to gain their custom.

The title of Michael J. Lanning's book is *Delivering Profitable Value*. Organizations only survive when they obtain an adequate **return on investment** (**ROI**) to justify investments. Without sufficient funds, a business is unsustainable, so the profit objective is immediately apparent. The remaining part, *delivering value*, is equally critical. The ability to deliver value is what enables profitability.

In the context of value propositions, Lanning provides a set of expanded definitions for *value* and *value delivery*, as follows (Lanning, 1998, p. 316):

- **Value**: The net desirability customers perceive in some resulting experience(s) in comparison to some alternative—what those customers should be willing to pay accordingly

- **Value delivery**: Choosing, providing, and communicating some resulting experiences, including price

- **Value delivery chain**: The entities of relevance to a business—including suppliers, intermediaries, primary entities, customers, and offline entities—understood as delivering value to each other and as one interconnected set of relationships

- **Value delivery focus**: Understanding the business in terms of choosing, providing, and communicating a desirable set of resulting experiences to prospective customers

- **Value delivery framework**: The whole set of questions and corresponding actions of the primary and supporting **value delivery system** (**VDS**), understood in the context of the value delivery chain

- **Value delivery option identification**: Exploring a market space to discover which primary VDS is viable in contrast to conventional market segmentation

- **Value delivery system** (**VDS**): The **end-to-end** (**E2E**) business system working in collaboration and as a community to deliver a complete value proposition

This section concludes our discussion on value propositions. Before we end this chapter, you will learn about value from Agile, Lean, VSM, and DevOps contexts. But before we get to those topics, we need to take a quick look at the traditional business concepts related to creating value. This topic is addressed in the next section.

Creating value

Ultimately, this book is about value creation and an organization's ability to create value on demand, efficiently, and continuously. Most importantly, our efforts to deliver value must align with our customers' perspectives on what adds value to their experiences with our organization and our products and services.

The definition usually ascribed to the term *value creation* is relatively broad, and we need to understand what people mean when they use that specific term. In its simplest expression, value creation is any process or activity that creates *outputs* that have more value than its *inputs*.

Displays of the input-transformation-output process (a.k.a. **the input-process-output (IPO) model**) incorporate a functional graph that displays the inputs, outputs, and required processing tasks required to transform the inputs into outputs. See the following diagram for an illustration of this:

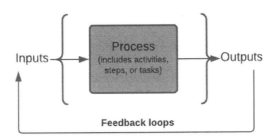

Figure 1.3 – IPO model example

The inputs represent the flow of information and materials into a process from external sources. The processing step includes all activities (steps or tasks) required to transform the inputs into something of value. The outputs are the enhanced data and materials flowing out of the transforming process.

The IPO graphic displayed in *Figure 1.3* demonstrates a value-adding activity. The value-adding process increases the value of goods and services and, by extension, improves the value of the business. The value transformation process only works if customers desire the outputs sufficiently to acquire them. It's the creation, delivery, and acquisition of value by customers that drives, in turn, shareholder value.

From a financial or management accounting perspective, we convert inputs to create outputs that drive monetary value across the value chain of an organization's products, services, and processes. However, the financial definition of creating value is limited and does not capture the full measure of the things that add value within an organization. Equally important are relentless and continual innovations, the labor and ideas of people, and branding.

As Lean-Agile and DevOps practitioners, you own the efforts associated with relentless and continual innovations, plus you provide the labor and ideas to generate value from digitally enhanced products and services. In addition, the product management and marketing functions are responsible for branding as part of their demand-creation efforts (that is, promoting the product's value proposition to create brand awareness and thereby generating customer demand to acquire the product).

Keep this simple IPO model in mind, as it forms a basic graphical approach to viewing most value stream activities. The primary difference is that we'll decompose the process function to show all associated activities and their value-adding interrelationships.

In the previous section on value propositions, you learned that our customers' experiential-based perceptions of value change over time. For that reason, value creation hinges on an organization's ability to create value on demand, efficiently, and continuously. In other words, an organization is under constant stress to change, and change is challenging in the best circumstances.

Change at a macro level occurs when an organization defines a new business strategy and potentially profitable value proposition. This type of change is much harder, especially when the organization needs to evolve from its traditional hierarchical and bureaucratic organizational structure.

Such change cannot occur solely through mandates, as any business transformation strategy of this magnitude fails without executive support and leadership, proper planning, and a controlled rollout. We'll table this topic for now and revisit it in *Chapter 6, Launching the VSM Initiative (VSM Steps 1-3)*

In the context of Agile's values and principles, change occurs at a micro level quite frequently, with every development iteration. This type of frequent change occurs because small, autonomous, and self-sufficient teams automatically self-organize to deliver the expected incremental value achievable within the planned time horizon— usually 1 to 4 weeks.

Moreover, at the end of each iteration, the teams conduct retrospective events to evaluate areas for improvements, and those improvements should begin in the next iteration. Teams operating with agility implement processes, such as Scrum, use change to their advantage when delivering customer-centric value in a repetitive and controlled fashion.

The following section describes the essential values and principles of Agile and Lean Development concepts.

Taking a Lean-Agile view of value

Lean-Agile practices blend the values and principles outlined in the *Manifesto for Agile Software Development*, more commonly referred to as the *Agile Manifesto*, with the Lean Development practices initially developed at Toyota and further elaborated by John Krafcik (Krafcik, 1988), James Womack, and Daniel Jones (Womack, Jones; 1990, 2013), and Mary and Tom Poppendieck (Poppendieck, 2003).

> **Note**
> My previous book, *Scaling Scrum Across Modern Enterprises*, provides much greater detail on the subject of Lean-Agile concepts and practices. This section provides a gentle introduction, sufficient to understand the applications of Lean-Agile practices described in later sections of this book.

Understanding the values and principles of Agile

In 2001, 17 software developers came together at a resort in Utah to discuss their software development views to see if there was common ground from which they operated. Though many of the participants were competitors or ascribed to different software development methodologies, they found common ground in their values and principles. Jim Highsmith described their result as the "*mushy stuff of values and culture*" in software development (`https://agilemanifesto.org/history.html`).

The *Agile Manifesto* established 4 values and 12 principles that articulate an agile software development approach.

The essential elements of the Agile Manifesto are its values, which are expressed as follows:

We are uncovering better ways of developing software by doing it and helping others do it. Through this work, we have come to value:

- *Individuals and interactions over processes and tools*
- *Working software over comprehensive documentation*
- *Customer collaboration over contract negotiation*
- *Responding to change over following a plan*

That is, while there is value in the items on the right, we value the items on the left more.

Kent Beck	*James Grenning*	*Robert C. Martin*
Mike Beedle	*Jim Highsmith*	*Steve Mellor*
Arie van Bennekum	*Andrew Hunt*	*Ken Schwaber*
Alistair Cockburn	*Ron Jeffries*	*Jeff Sutherland*
Ward Cunningham	*Jon Kern*	*Dave Thomas*
	Martin Fowler	*Brian Marick*

One of the signatories of *The Manifesto for Agile Software Development* is Jim Highsmith. He built and maintains the website that includes additional details of the event and the attendees' findings. The **Uniform Resource Locators** (**URLs**) for those pages are provided here:

- *Manifesto for Agile Software Development*: `https://agilemanifesto.org/`
- *Principles behind the Agile Manifesto*: `https://agilemanifesto.org/principles.html`
- *History: The Agile Manifesto*: `https://agilemanifesto.org/history.html`

These software developers represented or used lightweight software development practices to avoid the pitfalls of the traditional plan-driven and linear-sequential SDLC model (a.k.a. **Waterfall**). Since they used competitive methodologies, they did not find common ground across their disparate SDLC practices, but instead, found common ground in the written abstraction of their shared values and principles.

In a modern context, Agile-based software development practices have the following in common:

- Iterative and frequent development cycles.

- Incremental releases of customer-centric value.

- Small, autonomous, and self-contained teams that are nimble, adaptable, and able to self-organize to perform whatever relevant work comes their way (that is, we don't expect software development teams to perform marketing or sales-oriented work).

- Frequent interactions with customers to demonstrate the new increments of value and receive their feedback.

- Developers need the freedom to learn from experimentation, knowing they might fail, but also know to keep their failures small across brief development increments.

- Frequent retrospectives to assess areas for improvements and implement action plans to install those improvements in the next iteration.

- Technical excellence and good design enhance a team's abilities and agility.

- Diversity and respect among team members are critical elements for evolving and achieving ongoing success as a functional team.

Beyond these simple principles, software development teams are free to use whichever methods and tools they prefer. The 17 participants represented at least 7 lightweight software development methodologies. Of those 7 approaches, among others, Scrum went on to become the de facto standard for implementing small team agility.

This introductory section concludes our discussion of Agile. We'll now move on to introduce the concepts of Lean Development, and in particular, its modern relevance to Agile software development.

Reviewing the fundamentals of Lean Development

As noted in an earlier section, *Defining customer value*, Lean Development concepts evolved initially at Toyota. Toyota was not shy about sharing their ideas across their value chain partners and later—on a larger scale—to manufacturing companies across industries via the promotion of a booklet titled *The Toyota Way 2001*. They were committed to helping their value chain partners, as those efforts paid dividends in improving their value streams.

In 2004, Jeffrey Liker summarized his view of *The Toyota Way* via 14 fundamental management principles (Liker, 2004). I also provide examples of these principles in my book, *Scaling Scrum Across Modern Enterprises*.

As a quick introduction, the following list contains a summary of each management principle:

- Lean is a long-term management philosophy.
- Focus on establishing continuous flows to surface problems quickly and eliminating waste.
- Use a pull-oriented approach to order and materials entry based on demand.
- Eliminate all forms of batch processes.
- Build things right the first time, and stop production immediately when problems arise.
- Standardize tasks and processes across your value streams.
- Use visual controls such as Kanban boards to avoid hiding problems.
- Use only thoroughly tested and reliable technologies selected by your people to support their processes.
- Grow your future leaders, who already understand the work and organizational philosophies and who can teach it to others.
- Develop exceptional teams and people.
- Respect and help improve your extended network of partners and suppliers.
- Practice Gemba—go and see for yourself what's going on in the organization.
- Make decisions slowly, by consensus, and only after due diligence and consideration.
- Become a learning organization through reflection and continually improving.

Since this book is about Lean-Agile practices to improve an organization's competitive position in a digital economy, let's move on to discuss Lean Software Development practices.

Implementing Lean Software Development practices

Mary Poppendieck and Tom Poppendieck coined the term *Lean Software Development* in a book they wrote in 2003 by the same name. Their book was the first widely promoted example of employing traditional Lean Development practices to software development. Besides adopting and applying 7 Lean principles to software development, Poppendieck's identified 22 *Lean thinking tools* that aid in applying Lean to various Agile practices.

The Lean principles include the following:

- **Eliminate waste**: Remove anything from an activity that does not add value from the perspective of our customers.

- **Amplify learning**: Dedicate time and resources to learning and experimentation to improve skills, technologies, and processes.

- **Decide as late as possible**, to keep your options open.

- **Deliver as fast as possible**, through integration and automation of SDLC and operational support processes.

- **Empower the team**: Let the people doing the work make the most of their decisions, as they are most knowledgeable and closest to the work.

- **Build integrity in**: Build software systems with coherent architectures, usability, and fitness for purpose that are maintainable, adaptable, and extendable.

- **See the whole**: Avoid specialization of practices as specialists tend to optimize systems around their specific goals and interests.

The disciplines of Lean and Lean Software Development and the Lean tools recommended by the Poppendiecks are too broad to get into within this chapter. We revisit these topics throughout this book. But for now, let's move on to introduce the concepts of value streams, their purpose, their types, and how we define them.

Delivering value through value streams

James Womack, Daniel Jones, and Daniel Roos often get credit for defining the term *value stream* in their book, *The Machine that Changed the World* (Womack, Jones, Roos; 1990). Womack indeed discussed value streams in his later books, such as *Lean Thinking* (Womack; 1996, 2003) and *Seeing the Whole Value Stream* (Womack, Jones; 2003). However, James Martin was the first to define the concepts of **value streams** in detail in his book *The Great Transition: Using the Seven Disciplines of Enterprise Engineering to Align People, Technology, and Strategy* (Martin, 1995).

It's easy to associate value stream concepts with the concepts of *value stream mapping* in Lean, but that's an incorrect association. Martin briefly introduces lean manufacturing concepts in his book, but his association of value streams with lean manufacturing applies to reinventing workflows around customer value (Martin, 1995, p. 102). In contrast, value stream mapping is a visual technique to assess information and material flows. We'll talk more about value stream mapping in the following subsection.

Martin defines value streams as an "*end-to-end collection of activities that create a result for a 'customer', who may be the ultimate customer or an internal "end-user" of the value stream*". Martin also notes that a value stream must have a clear goal to satisfy or delight. Martin introduces value streams as an approach to reinvent business processes to support customer needs by developing products in the most "*simple, direct, and narrowly focused fashion*".

Martin wrote his book when **business process reengineering** (**BPR**) was a mainstream concept, and IT organizations worked with functional and cross-functional business organizations to streamline and automate critical business processes. Martin keenly observed that business processes traditionally evolved through successive changes driven by internal needs and not by customer needs. As a result, many business processes are bloated, inefficient, and anything but customer-centric.

Martin introduces his value stream concepts as an E2E redesign of business processes at the activity or task level to create better flows. Martin makes the point that too many business systems evolved to support then-existing business processes, and those underlying processes too often evolved to support dubious agendas and objectives.

A better approach is to eliminate the concept of business processes and instead have organizations reevaluate their enterprise as a collection of value streams, all of which likely need reinventing. This approach identifies what customers value and then assesses an organization's collections of activities that deliver the value (that is, value streams). The next step is to streamline the identified value streams. Only then should an organization consider developing information systems and automation to support their newly formed value streams.

In a modern Lean-Agile and DevOps environment, we can go faster, but the Lean-Agile concepts evolved after Martin's book came out. Today, value stream identification and value stream mapping are critical components of the Lean-Agile practitioner's toolkit.

Identifying value streams

Value streams are component processes of the broader and integrated business system that describe how stakeholders—either internal or external customers—receive value from an organization. A business value stream includes a series of steps or activities necessary to provide the products, services, and experiences our customers desire at a more fundamental level.

Value streams can support product development and delivery activities and any other customer-facing services. While development-oriented value streams can provide products and services directly to customers or resale partners, a more typical scenario is that they deliver products and services to operations or customer-facing value streams. Steps that do not add value represent waste in the eyes of the customer—in other words, customers do not want to pay for things that add waste without adding value.

It's easy to think our customers won't know about these extraneous activities, but in a competitive market, you will be quickly outed by your competitors who are paying attention and providing better customer-centric value for the money.

Lanning's concept of evaluating value as desirable customer experiences gives us a model to define our value streams. So, let's quickly look at the things customers commonly want from their product, service, and solution providers, outlined as follows:

- Open, available, and easy access to knowledge:

  a. About products and services

  b. Comparative information—from the company, trusted representatives, and industry experts

  c. Product and pricing information

  d. Procurement—How and where to acquire the products and services

- Simplified and possibly real-time order entry

- Products developed with desired quality, features, capabilities, and costs

- Upsell of product upgrades and services that may make their experience even better

- Fulfillment—delivered when and how the customer prefers

- Customer support—available on demand when needed; sufficient to answer their questions and resolve any problems they may be experiencing

- Ongoing product maintenance and enhancements

This list is incomplete but is a good starting point for this discussion. Various organizational departments collaborate to define and create value streams, though specific departments may lead efforts in defining selected value streams—for example, product management usually takes the lead in defining target markets and the customers' relevant needs. In contrast, the marketing department defines the value streams necessary to create customer awareness.

Mapping value streams

In the previous section, you learned that James Martin refined the definition of the term *value stream* and that the lean concept of value stream mapping is separate. Martin used the term *value stream* to articulate the need to reinvent workflows around customer value.

Value stream mapping, also known as *material and information flow mapping*, is a Lean method to map and assess the current *as-is* and desired *to-be* future states of activities across the life cycle of a product or service. In other words, value stream maps provide a visual aid to document and evaluate the flow of work from the initial request through development and delivery until it reaches the customer.

As an interesting side note, the concept of mapping the flow of information and materials predates Lean, dating back to a book written in 1918 by Charles E. Knoeppel, titled *Installing Efficiency Methods*. Today, value stream mapping is more commonly associated with Lean manufacturing and Lean Software Development practices.

Toyota applied value stream mapping as a standard practice within *The Toyota Way*. Mike Rother and John Shook studied Toyota and then published a book on what they discovered on this topic, titled *Learning to See: Value Stream Mapping to Add Value and Eliminate Muda*. Later, Mary and Tom Poppendieck introduced Lean Software Development, in their book by the same name. Their book made value stream mapping a mainstream technique in the Lean community.

The following diagram shows a value stream map example of current and future states. We will not get into any further details on value stream mapping here. Instead, we'll hold off until *Chapter 7, Mapping the Current State (VSM Step 4)*:

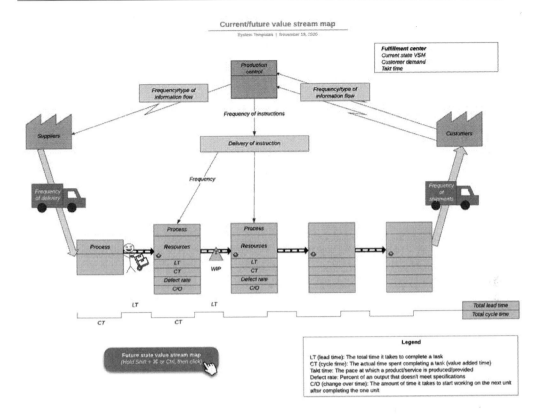

Figure 1.4 – Current/future value stream map

This section concludes the section on Lean-Agile concepts. The following section introduces VSM concepts, methods, and tools, and also introduces value stream mapping techniques and how they are used to identify the *as-is* status of a value stream and one or more desired *to-be* states that deliver value improvements. In the process, you will discover that development-oriented value streams feed operations-oriented value streams.

Understanding VSM

Section 2, Implementing Value Stream Management (VSM) - To Improve IT Value Streams, of this book provides comprehensive guidance on the methods and tools associated with VSM and introduces some of the leading VSM software products. We'll also introduce basic VSM concepts in *Chapter 6, Launching the VSM Initiative (VSM Steps 1-3)* Before we get to those subjects, this preliminary section aims to explain the relevance of VSM in helping organizations realize value.

Building on the foundations of Lean

If you only read recent literature on VSM, you may come away thinking VSM is an enhancement to Agile and DevOps practices that's limited to improving IT-related value streams. That's a mistake, as the practices originated Lean Manufacturing and Lean Development strategies that go back to the TPS evolution. Japanese industrial engineers Taiichi Ohno and Eiji Toyoda helped define these practices from 1948 and 1975. Toyota maintains and continues to refine its lean practices as part of its **The Toyota Way** initiative.

Toyota's Lean manufacturing and Lean production development practices created a significant competitive advantage that the rest of the world began to notice. By 1979, and under the guidance of James P. Womack, Ph.D., MIT initiated a multi-year **International Motor Vehicle Program** (**IMVP**) research program to study automotive value chains and Lean processes worldwide.

In 1991, James P. Womack, Daniel T. Jones, and Daniel Roos published the results of their work in a book titled *The Machine That Changed the World: The Story of Lean Production*, which helped make Lean production mainstream globally. Though their work focused on the automotive industry, in the epilogue of their book, the authors point out that they fully expect lean production to become the 21st century's standard global production system.

Business entities must adopt Lean production processes to compete effectively, while also leveraging IT to provide products relevant within our digital economy. The software industry was quick to see the advantages of implementing lean production concepts. Leading the charge were Mary and Tom Poppendieck, who wrote the famous book (at least in the Agile community), titled *Lean Software Development: An Agile Toolkit*.

Those of you who would like to learn more about Lean production and Lean software development can read my previous book, *Scaling Scrum Across Modern Enterprises*. Specifically, *Chapter 5, Driving Business Value through a DevOps Pipeline*, introduces Lean production concepts, while *Chapter 6, Launching the VSM Initiative (VSM Steps 1-3)* introduces Lean practices in software development.

VSM is about improving an IT organization's Lean value streams but does not replace Agile's values, principles, and practices. IT's current trend is to concatenate Lean and Agile practices as an integrated strategy, with VSM the glue that binds them together. Let's see why.

Building on Agile

VSM cannot be limited to merely installing a new discipline of agile software development. That strategy would be a bit of an overkill. For example, Dave Thomas wrote an important article titled *Agile is Dead (Long Live Agility)* (at `https://pragdave.me/blog/2014/03/04/time-to-kill-agile.html`) that suggests we've overly complicated the concepts of Agile software delivery. He's not wrong.

If we accept Dave Thomas's premise that we are already making agile software delivery too hard, what value does the additional overhead and complexity of VSM provide? It's a good question, so let's take a closer look at the origins of VSM concepts and processes and how they affect IT value delivery organizations.

Defining VSM concepts and processes

The term *VSM* did not originate as an IT-related acronym. For example, Peter Hines et al. use the term in their book *Value Stream Management: Strategy and Excellence in the Supply Chain* (Hines et al., 2000). Their book documents a research program involving nearly 20 manufacturing, retail, and service companies. Conducted by the **Lean Enterprise Research Centre** (**LERC**), the study's objective was to apply lean production concepts to understand value and waste in the supply chain environment.

The conglomerate's broader goals were to improve, expedite, and sustain development activities across supply chains, primarily in the automotive, electronics, and fast-moving consumer goods markets. The authors use the term *VSM* to communicate their findings that Lean enterprises must install and manage long-lived programs to reduce waste actively and continuously across their supply chain value streams (*Kaizen*).

In its modern context, VSM is a lean business practice to improve software value delivery and the efficient use of IT resources. Employing Lean Software Development concepts, VSM helps IT organizations improve the flow of value to their internal and external customers.

The modern context of VSM also centers on using software tools and integrated platforms to improve DevOps pipeline flows. However, organizations that employ Lean Software Development practices can achieve many Lean production improvements without using VSM tools. Always remember—methods come before tools!

Similar to how DevOps pipelines integrate and automate an IT organization's development and operations-oriented (development and operations) processes, VSM tools help integrate and automate Lean value stream improvement activities. Modern VSM tools also provide direct capture of metrics and analytics to guide improvement options. Modern VSM tools help integrate and automate value stream mapping, measuring, monitoring, and analyzing activities across DevOps pipelines. They also support the improvement of all organizational value streams.

Still, we need to build our foundation on proven VSM methods before leveraging the tools.

Learning methods before tools

Don Tapping, Tom Luyster, and Tom Shuker present a rigorous VSM methodology in their book *Value Stream Management: Eight Steps to Planning, Mapping, and Sustaining Lean Improvements (Create a Complete System for Lean Transformation!)* (Tapping, Luyster, and Shuker, 2003). Their book describes VSM as a data-centric and analytical approach to plan and link value stream initiatives.

The purpose of Tapping's, Luyster's, and Shuker's book was to simplify the Lean Development concepts of demand-based pull, flow, and production leveling as an eight-step process to help accelerate, coordinate, and sustain Lean Development practices, which they called **VSM**. In later books, Tapping and Luyster applied their VSM concepts to all organizational value streams, such as manufacturing, customer services, engineering, payables, and—of course—IT.

Both Don Tapping and Tom Luyster were kind enough to allow us to incorporate their eight-step VSM approach as the foundation VSM methodology for this book. However, from *Chapter 6, Launching the VSM Initiative (VSM Steps 1-3)*, through *Chapter 10, Improving the Lean-Agile Value Delivery Cycle(VSM Steps 7 and 8)*, this book applies their VSM methodology to improve flows across an Agile-based team's implementation of CI/CD concepts and tools.

Their eight VSM steps are listed here:

1. Commit to Lean.
2. Choose a value stream.
3. Learn about Lean.
4. Map the current state.
5. Determine Lean metrics.
6. Map the future state.
7. Create Kaizen plans.
8. Implement Kaizen plans.

Note that Tapping and Luyster's eight-step VSM process does not explicitly identify IT practices—that's because IT is just another value stream among many in the Lean enterprise. On the other hand, as noted previously, IT is a critical development-oriented value stream that supports virtually all other organizational value streams in a digital economy.

This book's central premise is that IT product requirements and Product backlog items can come out of any value stream across an organization, some supporting internal customers' needs while others support external customer needs. Similarly, some IT development teams may support individual internal or external value streams in a multi-team agile development environment. Nevertheless, VSM's foundational Lean-improvement concepts apply universally.

Chapter 6, Launching the VSM Initiative (VSM Steps 1-3) contains detailed descriptions of each of the eight process steps as a general approach to employing Lean practices organization-wide, including IT. But before leaving this section, let's take a quick look at how the IT industry currently views VSM.

Implementing VSM in IT

Chapter 6, Launching the VSM Initiative (VSM Steps 1-3), explains how to identify value streams before mapping the current and desired future states. Identifying value streams is the more challenging of the two tasks and the most critical, as everything related to making lean-oriented improvements starts from there.

Traditionally, software development teams think of instantiating functional and non-functional requirements as software features and functions. However, in the Lean/VSM model, the development and operations teams focus on improving activities to deliver a continuous customer value flow.

Customer requirements do not go away in software development teams operating as value streams. Functional and non-functional requirements, along with bug fixes and addressing technical debts, all become inputs to the development-oriented value streams. The outputs are developed features and capabilities. Those are important concepts to keep in mind when we get to *Chapter 6, Launching the VSM Initiative (VSM Steps 1-3)*.

In a modern context, VSM implements methods and tools that help organizations increase the value they deliver to customers by optimizing workflow across their value streams. Moreover, VSM often employs software technologies to integrate suites of tools to form robust **VSM platforms** (**VSMPs**).

One of the industry-leading VSMP vendors, **Plutora**, in their article titled *Value Stream Management Platforms* (at https://www.plutora.com/), lists nine key VSMP capabilities that help organizations to achieve their software goals, as shown here:

- Tool integration and interoperability
- Common data model
- Mapping people, processes, and data

- Governance and compliance
- Value stream **key performance indicator** (**KPI**) data capture and measurement
- Data analytics and analysis
- Dashboards and visualization
- Financials and budgets

In *Section 2, Implementing Value Stream Management (VSM)*, of this book, you'll learn how these VSM capabilities help an organization improve its value streams. Plus, you will learn the basic methods that implement these capabilities. But since this is the main topic of this book, let's first look at how industry analysts assess the importance of this emergent field in IT.

Promising VSM growth

VSM applied to software development practices, and especially VSMPS, are both considered emergent concepts. However, several leading IT industry analysts, such as **Forrester Research, Inc.** and **Gartner, Inc.**, now consider VSM a vital requirement and an exponentially growing trend.

For example, Forrester publishes a periodic *Forrester Wave*™ for VSM, with assessments of the leading VSM vendors by scores and weightings. The latest version, *Forrester Wave*™: *Value Stream Management, Solutions, Q3 2020*, provides assessments of the 11 leading VSM vendors.

Likewise, Gartner follows the VSM industry and recently released its Gartner Report titled [*Gartner*] *Predicts 2021: Value Streams Will Define the Future of DevOps*. Gartner states: *[to] accelerate development and enable continuous delivery of customer value, organizations need to reach the next level in their agile and DevOps practices. I&O leaders and application leaders must focus on value stream management to maximize flow, improve delivery efficiency and drive innovation.*

In the report, Gartner goes on to list its strategic planning assumptions for VSM, as follows:

- *By 2023, 70% of organizations will use value stream management to improve flow in the DevOps pipeline, leading to faster delivery of customer value.*
- *By 2023, the use of value stream delivery platforms to streamline application delivery will grow from 10% to 40%.*

- *By 2023, 60% of organizations in regulated verticals will have integrated continuous compliance automation into their DevOps toolchains, improving their lead time by at least 20%.*

- *By 2025, 60% of I&O leaders will implement chaos engineering to add resilience and velocity improvements to value stream flow, increasing system availability by 10%.*

- *Through 2025, 20% of enterprises will go beyond SRE by adding IT resilience roles to improve resiliency posture between product teams and traditional DR.*

(Gartner, Predicts 2021: Value Streams Will Define the Future of DevOps, Daniel Betts, Chris Saunderson, Ron Blair, Manjunath Bhat, Jim Scheibmeir, Hassan Ennaciri, October 5, 2020)

VSM appears to be growing in use and here to stay. Now, let's take a quick look at how VSM is complementary to DevOps practices.

Understanding the role of DevOps in delivering value

At this point, you should have a pretty good handle on what the term *value* means in the context of Lean-Agile and VSM practices. In this section, we'll explore how DevOps supports the delivery of value. We'll start with a quick introduction to the basic concepts behind DevOps and how it helps instantiate at least some of the values and principles of Agile.

Delivering value in IT

Mature IT organizations install the values and principles outlined in the *Manifesto for Agile Software Development* to improve their focus on the customer, speed of delivery, and efficiencies. Organizations do not need to integrate or automate their Agile-based SDLC and operations-oriented processes to achieve significant benefits. On the other hand, those organizations that do can rapidly accelerate their pace of delivering new value.

Moreover, IT organizations receive even more significant benefits by improving communications and integration between development and operations. The feedback from operations helps development teams create a more VA, sustainable, and higher-quality product. The collaborations also help the development teams deploy products that are easier to deploy, configure, secure, and roll back when necessary.

It's not wrong to think of DevOps as a reengineering of the IT function. How much reengineering is dependent upon the current state of the IT organization. Those organizations still practicing traditional *Waterfall*-type practices require more significant changes to their processes and culture than those who practice agile-based approaches such as *Scrum* or **eXtreme Programming** (**XP**). Agile-based methodologies already reengineer traditional SDLC processes from a linear-sequential development life cycle process to an iterative and incremental development cycle, from a practical standpoint.

At first glance, the individual activities of Waterfall and Agile look kind of similar. For example, both approaches include the following type of work:

- Planning
- Requirements gathering and analysis
- Design and architecture
- Development
- Testing
- Customer reviews and acceptance
- Product release and deployment

The primary difference is that Waterfall treats these activities across singular projects as a linear-sequential and plan-driven process. The traditional model lengthens the overall lead time to deliver previously identified value, which often creates a host of problems in finding and fixing bugs. Late deliveries may effectively deliver what customers thought they wanted but not provide what they need at the delivery time. The organization must justify, fund, and initiate new projects before adding new enhancements and correcting defects (previously unidentified customer requirements) in the product, which usually pushes the new work out into the next fiscal year. By then, it is too late.

In contrast, Agile treats SDLC activities as a cyclical process that does not stop until the ROI for continued development no longer supports the cost of adding new value. Agile-based practices release new value incrementally across multiple iterative development cycles as a frequent and repetitive pattern. Short delivery cycles keep the code small between testing, making bugs and defects easier to find and resolve. Frequent customer reviews and team retrospectives help ensure the team stays continuously focused on their customers' current needs, priorities, and requests for improvements.

Though the Agile Manifesto speaks to CD concepts, it does not promote an integration or automation strategy. Those ideas came later. Instead, the Agile Manifesto speaks about improving collaborations and communications across the development function. DevOps started as a strategy to improve collaborations and communications between development- and operations-oriented teams. In its current form, DevOps promotes IT agility through collaboration, integration, and automation across IT to rapidly deliver customer value, higher quality, and less stress.

Automating value across IT

DevOps extends the Agile model in two important ways. First, DevOps extends beyond the traditional SDLC processes to link the activities and people within IT operations. Second, DevOps evolved in lockstep with CI and automation capabilities, which further accelerated the ideation-to-value-delivery lead time while simultaneously improving the quality of delivery.

Business process improvement (BPI) and BPR specialists know that it doesn't make sense to automate a critical business process until after analyzing and implementing the desired process improvements. Ideally, the organization takes a lean approach to map their current as-is and desired to-be value streams to determine what the new process needs to look like and then executes the work to make the desired transformations.

An adage is that automating a flawed process simply makes it put out a lousy result more quickly. In other words, if an organization is already not delivering value, automating the process produces the wrong result more efficiently and more rapidly. In other words, automating a flawed process only generates more waste more quickly.

So, before any IT organization attempts to integrate and automate its SDLC and operations activities, they first need to understand which issues they need to resolve. We'll look at these issues in the next section.

Collaborating across IT development and ops

Conceptually, DevOps began as a strategy simply to improve collaborations between IT development and operations teams. The collaborations helped development teams see the issues operations teams faced when deploying their products. Here are some example issues:

- Without proper collaboration, engineering and test environments may not adequately mimic production environments, causing a host of problems, such as the following:

  a. Production environment configuration instructions may be inadequate.

b. Testing may not have the same applications installed as the production environments, making it difficult to see configuration, **application programming interface (API)**, and integration conflicts.

c. Performance testing in engineering and test environments may not adequately evaluate the loads and stresses encountered in production environments.

d. Rollback and failover instructions developed in engineering and test environments may not work correctly in production environments.

- Development teams may not pay sufficient attention to security concerns in production environments.

- Operations teams lack a practical way to make their concerns known and to make their needs a priority within development teams.

- Operations, through their helpdesk and customer support functions, have the most direct knowledge of customer issues and desired enhancements.

In effect, IT development teams have both internal and external customers they must support. However, when development teams focus only on external customers, they are unaware
of the significant technical debt accumulations that severely impact the operations teams.

Now that we've identified the communications and collaboration issues between development and operations, and the fact that development has two customers (internal and external), we can identify typical **IT value streams**. So, that is the topic of the next section.

Defining IT value chains and value streams

IT organizations are free to define IT value streams in any way they choose, so long as they identify their internal and external customers and take the time to organize and assess their activities to maximize customer-centric value. The VSM chapters provide detailed instructions on mapping as-is and to-be processes from the perspective of value and then monitor and analyze delivery performance against organizational improvement objectives.

On the other hand, an IT organization does not have to start from scratch—for example, the **Open Group** provides its **IT4IT Reference Architecture** (that is, *IT for IT*) as a standard reference architecture and value chain-based operating model for managing IT businesses. The Open Group subscribes to Michael Porter's definition of a **value chain** as a classification scheme for the complete set of primary and supporting activities that contribute to the life cycle of creating net value of a market offering. In the Open Group's vernacular, an IT organization is a value chain.

In this context, the Open Group defines a **value stream**, describing the critical activities for a discrete area within the IT value chain. The value stream activities create new net value units within the IT product or service as it progresses through its life cycle. In other words, each value stream activity within a sequence is value-adding. Otherwise, the activity shouldn't exist, or at least should not exist in its current form.

IT4IT defines four primary IT value streams, outlined as follows:

- **Strategy to portfolio**: Drive IT portfolio to business innovation.
- **Requirement to deploy**: Build what the business needs, when it needs it.
- **Request to fulfill**: Catalog, fulfill, and manage service usage.
- **Detect to correct**: Anticipate and resolve production issues.

Accelerating Agility

One of the Manifesto principles for Agile Development is that Agile processes promote sustainable development indefinitely and constantly. However, the practical reality is that those objectives are challenging to achieve. Customers always seem to have more immediate needs than the team can take on, and the team feels pressure from executives and marketing and sales staff to deliver everything at once and right now. Those pressures don't go away with Agile.

To be sure, development teams look like heroes when they incrementally deliver value that customers what, and when customers can see a timely result from their high priority requests. Still, the earlier sentence stands: "*Customers always seem to have more immediate needs than the team can take on.*"

The integration and automation capabilities employed in a mature DevOps environment substantially accelerate the pace of delivery. In their book *Accelerate: Building and Scaling High Performing Technology Organizations*, the authors (Forsgren, Humble, and Kim, 2018) compare the metrics of high-performing IT development teams, using DevOps capabilities, to the metrics of the low-performing teams that did not. The results are stunning, as we can see here:

- 46 times more frequent code deployments
- 440 times faster lead time from committing code to deployment
- 170 times faster **mean time to recovery** (**MTTR**) from downtime
- Five times lower change failure rate (one-fifth as likely for a change to fail)

This book addresses the fundamental mechanisms of DevOps. Specifically, *Chapter 5, Driving Business Value through a DevOps Pipeline,* introduces the complexities and challenges of developing CI/CD and DevOps pipelines. Then, in *Section 3, Installing DevOps Pipelines - To Compete in Our Digital Economy,* of this book, we'll dive into four strategies to develop your DevOps pipelines.

We have now completed our discussions on accelerating Agility and are now going to move on to understand why and how VSM and DevOps are complementary practices.

Integrating Lean, Agile, VSM, and DevOps

So far, you have learned that Agile's values and principles, Lean production practices, and the collaboration, integration, and automation capabilities of VSM and DevOps all support an organization's primary objective: to deliver customer-centric value. As a Lean-Agile practitioner, your job is to help blend these concepts and capabilities into a seamless way of working.

Industry research confirms that Agile and Lean-Agile practices are now mainstream. For example, Digital.ai's *14th Annual State of Agile* report (2020) found that 75% of their IT respondents are practicing **Scrum** or a hybrid of Scrum as their preferred Agile-based framework and that 35% of the respondents use the **Scaled Agile Framework**® (**SAFe**®) as their scaling Lean-Agile based framework of choice. Those numbers are 5% up from the previous year.

In the meantime, the installation of DevOps capabilities is increasingly viewed as table stakes to participate in our global digital economy. The high performers' metrics demonstrate that those organizations that effectively master DevOps have a significant competitive advantage over those that do not.

In contrast, VSM is still an emergent practice that is quickly evolving and gaining acceptance across the IT industry. However, given the large-scale success of Lean production concepts across the manufacturing and service industries, the fundamental lean concepts behind VSM bolsters the point of view that suggests continued adoption and success in the IT industry. This prediction stands because IT value streams must align with and support the broader Lean enterprise's value streams.

In her blog titled *How to Use Value Stream Mapping in DevOps* at `https://www.lucidchart.com/blog/`, Lizz Corrigan makes the following observation:

"*In a DevOps environment, VSM and lean methodologies are tailored to specific actions, such as moving work between teams to creating tangible deliverables and incident reports. DevOps VSM is a uniting visual representation of how IT and businesses build, deploy, and manage workflows. It should begin with the SDLC and move through quality assurance and release/operations.*"

In short, VSM provides the infrastructure to guide and monitor new requirements through the DevOps pipeline. By the end of this book, you should have a solid understanding of how to link these capabilities to marshal and accelerate value-oriented work across IT development and operations functions.

Summary

In this chapter, you've learned why the concept of value is critical when implementing Agile, Lean, VSM, and DevOps practices to get their full advantages. You've also learned that value is an expression of desired customer experiences and that an organization as a whole needs to work in lockstep to deliver those experiences.

Current IT methodologies often use the term *Lean-Agile* as their primary differentiator. However, both Lean and Agile are complementary concepts, and the amalgamation of both types of practices helps IT organizations deliver VA products rapidly, efficiently, and with higher quality.

You've also learned that VSM instantiates Lean practices across IT by integrating and automating value stream identification, mapping, analysis, measurements, and monitoring capabilities to support E2E product life cycle delivery of value. Finally, DevOps helps accelerate the delivery of value.

Later chapters in *Section 1, Focusing IT on the Delivery of Value*, of this book provide instruction on using value stream mapping to assess current and desired future state changes to improve your value streams. Then, you will learn how to use VSM capabilities to support, analyze, and monitor your value stream improvement activities. Finally, you will learn why DevOps is a critical enabler to rapidly, efficiently, and cost-effectively implement digital applications supporting your value stream improvements.

Before we get to those chapters, we need to explore how organizations link Agile, Lean, and Systems Thinking practices as an integrated set of practices. That is the topic of the next chapter.

Questions

1. The term *digital economy* originally described an e-commerce view to the application of IT. In a modern context, which other elements form our digital economy?

2. Why is the issue of semantics so crucial in information sciences?

3. What is a value proposition?

4. Who has responsibility for delivering an organization's value proposition?

5. Why is it important to pay attention to value?

6. What is a definition of value streams?

7. What is the difference between focusing on features and functions versus having a focus on value streams?

8. In a modern IT context, what is the purpose of VSM?

9. In the IT4IT Reference Architecture, what are the four IT-related value streams within the IT value chain?

10. Which two roles does the implementation of DevOps capabilities play in a modern IT organization?

Further reading

- *Krafcik, J. (1988). Triumph of the Lean Production System. Massachusetts Institute of Technology (MIT). Sloan Management Review. Vol 30, Number 1.* `https://www.lean.org/downloads/MITSloan.pdf`. Accessed November 16, 2020

- *Womack, James P., Jones, Daniel T. (1996, 2013). Lean Thinking: Banish Waste And Create Wealth In Your Corporation, Simon and Schuster, ISBN 9781471111006.*

- *Womack, James P., Jones, Daniel T., Roos, Daniel (1990). Machine that Changed the World. New York: Rawson Associates, ISBN 9780892563500.*

- *Poppendieck, Mary, Poppendieck, Tom (2003). Lean Software Development: An Agile Toolkit. Addison Wesley, Boston, MA. ISBN 0-321-15078-3.*

- *Rupp, Cecil G. (2020). Scaling Scrum Across The Modern Enterprise. Implement Scrum and Lean-Agile techniques across complex products, portfolios, and programs in large organizations. Packt Publishing. Birmingham, UK.*

- *Liker, Jeffrey K. (2004). The Toyota Way: 14 Management Principles from the World's Greatest Manufacturer. McGraw-Hill. ISBN 978-0-07-139231-0.*

- *Rother, M., Shook, J., (1999). Learning To See: Value Stream Mapping to Create Value and Eliminate Muda, Brookline, Massachusetts: Lean Enterprise Institute.*

- *Martin, K., Osterling, M. (2014). Value Stream Mapping: How to Visualize Work and Align Leadership for Organizational Transformation. McGraw-Hill. New York, NY.*

- *Tapping, D., Luyster, T., Shuker, T. (2002). Value Stream Management: Eight Steps to Planning, Mapping, and Sustaining Lean Improvements. (Create a Complete System for Lean Transformation!) 1st edition, Productivity Press, New York, NY.*

- *Tapping, D., Luyster, T., Shuker, T. (2003). Value Stream Management for the Lean Office. Productivity Press, New York, NY.*

- *Hines, P., Lamming, R., Jones, D., Cousins, P., Rich, N. (2000). Value Stream Management. Strategy and Excellence in the Supply Chain. Pearson Education Limited. London, England.*

- *Forsgren, N., Humble, J., Kim, G. (2018). Accelerate: Building and Scaling High Performing Technology Organizations. IT Revolution. Portland, OR.*

2
Building On a Lean-Agile Foundation

The IT industry undergoes constant evolution to deliver customer-centric value more quickly and efficiently and with higher quality. Some improvement concepts, such as Agile and DevOps, came directly from the software industry. However, Lean, Systems Thinking, and Value Stream Management all have their origins outside the software industry. Still, all these practices are now mainstream in the software and digital products and services delivery industries.

Though this book is about applying VSM and DevOps practices to accelerate digital value delivery, it's essential that each organization establishes a base of foundational practices. Specifically, IT organizations need to build their VSM and DevOps capabilities upon a solid value-centric foundation of Agile, Lean, and Systems Thinking practices.

This chapter will help Lean-Agile practitioners understand how to build this integrated foundation. We'll explore Systems Thinking in the next chapter. For now, in this chapter, you will learn how Agile and Lean practices work in concert to deliver customer-centric value.

In this chapter, we're going to cover the following main topics:

- Instilling the values and principles of Agile

- Gaining stakeholder support

- Implementing useful metrics

- Improving IT flows through Lean Thinking

- Eliminating waste in software development

- Creating the Lean-Agile foundation

- Accelerating flows across IT value streams

Instilling the values and principles of Agile

In the previous chapter, you learned that the Manifesto for Agile Software Development (also known as the Agile Manifesto, `https://agilemanifesto.org/`) laid out 4 values and 12 principles for improving software delivery. If you are new to Agile, you may not know that Agile is not a specific or single methodology. There is no guidance in the Agile Manifesto on how to instill Agile's values and principles, only a description of desirable outcomes or objectives.

Another way to think about the Agile Manifesto's values and principles is the notion of being Agile and not doing agile. In other words, while there are many things we can do to improve software development agility, the Agile Manifesto does not provide prescriptive guidance on how to do Agile.

Many methodologies claim to be Agile. For those who need a primer, I introduced Agile's history and the industry-leading Agile and Lean-Agile methodologies in my previous book, *Scaling Scrum Across Modern Enterprises*. At the time of writing this book, the leading Agile methodology at the small team level is Scrum – including several hybrid versions that enable multiple teams to work together in collaboration.

In contrast, the leading multi-team Lean-Agile methodology is **Scaled Agile Inc.'s Scaled-Agile Framework® (SAFe®)**. Another Lean-Agile methodology that's gathering traction is **Disciplined Agile**, offered by the **Project Management Institute (PMI)**. Later in this chapter, in the *Creating the Lean-Agile foundation* section, you will learn how Lean-Agile practices extend the basic Agile practices of iterative and incremental development.

For now, it's essential to understand that VSM and DevOps build on the concepts of Agile and Lean. Therefore, the organization must establish a base of Agile and Lean practices and allow the culture to evolve around these practices, before installing the process integration and automation capabilities that VSM and DevOps employ.

Integrating and automating flawed or poorly implemented processes only accelerates the undesirable outcomes of flawed processes. Undesirable outcomes include building products with features and functions that customers don't want, delivering inferior quality products, and delivering products with bugs and defects. Integration and automation won't fix those types of problems without reengineering the underlying development and operations processes.

Both Agile and Lean-Agile methodologies help organizations instill Agile's values and principles through the practices they implement. However, the scale and the level of sponsorship drive most decisions on which Agile methodology is the most appropriate and supports the needs of a software development team or program. We'll take a moment to quickly review the leading Scrum and Lean-Agile methodologies in the next section.

Leading Scrum and Lean-Agile methodologies

There's nothing that says an organization can't figure out on their own how to become Agile and Lean in their operations. On the other hand, why start from scratch when there are proven methodologies to help guide its efforts? The question then is, what methodologies and practices are most appropriate to the organization?

My previous book, *Scaling Scrum Across the Modern Enterprise* (Rupp, 2020), with Packt Publishing, presents detailed descriptions of many historical and currently leading Lean-Agile practices. Rather than repeating that information, this section will provide a short instruction to the current industry-leading Scrum and Lean-Agile methodologies and frameworks:

- **Scrum**: Developed in the 1990s, Ken Schwaber and Jeff Sutherland formalized their **Scrum Framework** as a **Scrum Guide** in 2010. Scrum implements a framework based on empiricism – a theory that all knowledge comes from experience derived from observations using our senses (that is, sight, hearing, touch, taste, smell, spatial, and so on). *Empiricists* value evidenced-based knowledge derived through experience, observation, and testing hypotheses through experimentation (that is, *the scientific method*).

Schwaber and Sutherland continue to update the Scrum Guide, with the most recent version being released in November 2020. Their latest version declares that the foundations of Scrum also include Lean concepts. However, they have not made this claim in their preceding versions of the Scrum Guide. And their discussion of Lean in the latest Scrum Guide is limited to the statement that *Lean Thinking reduces waste and focuses on the essentials.*

In a nutshell, the Scrum Framework implements iterative **Sprints** as a container to implement other practices and activities, all executed with agility, to deliver incremental value over short but frequent intervals. The container notion is essential as the IT industry employs countless technologies, methods, tools, and techniques. It makes no sense for a single Agile methodology to try to force a particular development strategy. Instead, the Scrum Framework guides the team's use of their preferred methods and tools in an Agile manner to deliver incremental value across each Sprint.

- **Scrum-of-Scrums**: The original scaling extension to Scrum, implemented as a team-of-teams structure, applies Scrum practices across multiple teams working in collaboration. The Scrum-of-Scrums model is generalized to coordinate small teams' efforts beyond the IT function, with all the teams cooperating to deliver the same product.

- **Scrum at Scale**: Jeff Sutherland's extension to the Scrum Guide scales the basic Scrum-of-Scrums concepts enterprise-wide and across business domains with **minimum viable bureaucracy** (**MVB**) via scale-free architectures.

- **The Nexus Framework**: Ken Schwaber's (Scrum.org) extension to the Scrum Guide implements **Network Integration Teams** (**NITs**) to manage cross-team dependencies, as well as integration and synchronization issues, on multi-team software product development efforts.

- **Large-Scale Scrum** (**LeSS**): This scaled Scrum approach, from Craig Larman and Bas Vodde, includes two Scrum scaling frameworks that help coordinate multiple teams' activities. The LeSS Framework coordinates multiple Scrum teams around *features*, while the LeSS Huge Framework coordinates the activities around *requirements areas*. Both frameworks support multi-team collaborations to develop large and complex software-enabled products.

- **Disciplined Agile (DA)**: This is a Lean-Agile approach to development that provides six product development life cycles, numerous process guides, and hundreds of potentially useful techniques. The DA approach allows teams to choose their preferred *way of working* to support their unique business and organizational needs and situations. Initially developed by Scott Ambler and Mark Lines, the **Project Management Institute (PMI)** acquired their firm in 2019 plus **FLow for Enterprise Transformation (FLEX)** from **Net Objectives**. Flex integrates with DA to implement Lean and Systems Thinking to improve organizational business agility.

- **Scaled Agile Framework® (SAFe®)**: With four configurations, SAFe is a Lean-Agile approach for big organizations working on large-scale product development efforts. SAFe helps large organizations leverage their economies of scale to provide greater efficiencies while incorporating Lean-Agile practices to enable business agility at enterprise scale. The four SAFe configurations are as follows:

  - **Essential SAFe®**: This is the foundational multi-team Lean-Agile scaling model, built around a team-of-teams concept called Agile Release Teams (ARTs). The size of each ART typically ranges between 50 and 125 people, constrained by Dunbar's number and derived from cognitive limitations regarding the number of stable relationships humans can actively maintain.

  Teams within an ART collaborate to support a single large product or individual value stream. Small teams within the ARTs situationally practice **eXtreme Programming (XP)**, Scrum, and DevOps, and all collaborate to deliver integrated and incremental value over time-boxed **Program Increments (PIs)**, which are typically 8 to 12 weeks long. XP, Scrum, and DevOps operate on smaller intervals and sync up with each PI.

  - **Large Solution SAFe®**: This extends to the *Essential SAFe* Lean-Agile foundation to coordinate and integrate the work of multiple ARTs supporting very large products or large volumes of products. *Large Solution SAFe* synchronizes any number of ARTs and hundreds to tens of thousands of team members.

  - **Portfolio SAFe®**: Aligns portfolio execution with the enterprise strategy by organizing the Lean-Agile Enterprise around the flow of value through its value streams. *SAFe Portfolios* are a collection of development and operations-oriented value streams that operate within a business unit. This SAFe configuration also adds **Lean Portfolio Management (LPM)** concepts to monitor and assess planned portfolio investment needs across time.

  - **Full SAFe®**: Links *Essential*, *Large Solution*, and *Portfolio SAFe* as an integrated and coordinated set of processes and activities.

Any of the previously discussed Scrum and Hybrid Scrum methodologies and frameworks can help your organization improve the agility of individual or multiple teams, working collaboratively to develop a single product or product line. Both DA and SAFe also include robust approaches to implementing Lean software development concepts and portfolio management processes to support strategic planning, funding priorities, and resource allocation across multiple product lines.

No matter which Scrum or Lean-Agile approach you choose to employ, its success is primarily dependent upon the level of sponsorship relative to the size and scope of the implementation. Leadership and executive sponsorship are the topics of the next section.

Leading the way

The implementation of Agile and Lean practices has organization-wide implications that impact the potential success of any implementation. Moreover, the larger the implementation, the broader the impact, and having the appropriate leadership and sponsorship levels is critical to its success. Ideally, the organization's Chief Executive leads the way.

Small software development teams can sometimes implement XP and Scrum practices at the small team level with minimal sponsorship. However, such implementations often find it challenging to obtain information on customer needs and priorities without a proper product owner leading those efforts.

Moreover, the development teams may not be allowed to break away from the project-oriented mindset under their organization's traditional funding and resource allocation practices. Agile practices have a product-oriented focus. Executives, customers, and other stakeholders may resist the organizational changes required to support the product-oriented model's iterative development and incremental release strategies. Frankly, Agile and Lean's product and customer-centric focus requires more effort on their part, and they may not see the value.

The value is there, but the impacted internal organizations and customers need to be educated and see results before buying. So, let's take a moment to discuss how to get their buy-in.

Gaining stakeholder support

Agile and Lean practices require more frequent and closer interactions across the business functions, and the participants must have a stake in the success of a new product or product enhancement. In the traditional software development model, management and customer interactions were limited to initial requirements gathering activities and then minimally across periodic milestone reviews, phase gates, and late-stage user acceptance testing. Lean-Agile methodologies are much more demanding.

Agility benefits come directly from the frequent and continuous team and stakeholder interactions, with complete, accurate, and up-to-date visibility on all critical information. But how do the early adopters encourage others within the organization and their customers to consider such a change?

The early adopters may have some success in educating their executives on the benefits of Agile and Lean-Agile practices. However, based on personal observations and experience, the least successful approach is to gain the ear of your executive managers and have them put out a mandate for immediate change. Without proper leadership, guidance, and resources, mandates tend to fail.

Instead, organizations can follow these practical steps:

- **Internal promotions**: Create educational materials on proposed Agile or Lean-Agile practices for distribution and review.

- **Executive sponsor**: Find a key executive sponsor with the authority, funding, and forward-thinking vision to see the benefits of delivering accelerated value.

- **Internal pilot**: Identify a product with high visibility and the significant potential to serve as an internal pilot and case study.

- **Pilot team**: Pull together a small team of like-minded early adopters who see the value of Agile and Lean-Agile practices, and who want to be on the leading edge of the change. Also, train the pilot team and other participating stakeholders.

- **Infrastructure**: Build the infrastructure necessary to support the pilot engagements. Ideally, agile teams operate from a single location with a dedicated meeting room, individual workspaces, laptops and servers, software development and testing tools, and network access.

- **Plan the pilot experiment**: Plan the activities and schedule to guide the initial pilot through a series of iterations, each delivering incremental value.

- **Run the pilot experiment**: Run the backlog refinement, plan, development, and test cycles as Agile-based iterations, with each cycle delivering incremental value. Equally as important, ensure the executive leadership, customers, and end users remain committed and actively engaged in each iterative review. Their guidance and input are critical to the team delivering incremental and customer-centric value.

- **Inspect and adapt**: Throughout the initial pilot engagement, the team and other stakeholders assess their performance through **retrospectives** and **product demos**, refine their activities for improvement, execute the planned improvements, monitor, and continue to adapt as necessary. This inspection and adaption process never stops.

- **New pilots**: After successfully completing the first pilot, find two to three new pilot projects to further prove and expand the organization's new development approach. Most people want to be part of something successful, and each new pilot success encourages other product teams to evaluate and adopt the approach for their development efforts.

- **Inspect and adapt**: Continuing with the additional pilot engagements, the new teams and associated stakeholders assess their performance through retrospectives and product demos, refine their activities for improvement, execute the planned improvements, monitor, and continue to adapt as necessary. The inspection and adaption process never stops.

- **Roadmap**: As the initial pilots prove the new way of working, the organization's executive leaders must create a detailed roadmap to guide its enterprise-wide deployment. It's impossible to accurately measure, monitor, and guide future deployments without an initial and updated plan from a practical standpoint.

  It may be necessary to redefine products and product lines under the new model to align with the new Lean value stream model. Such realignment does not affect just the software products. The business needs to evaluate all internal and external customer relationships from a value-adding perspective to define its operational and development-oriented value streams.

  Product teams need to be created, including hiring and mentoring people to serve as product owners and Scrum masters. Training, coaching, and mentoring resources and capabilities need to be developed and deployed to bring employees up to speed on the new Lean-Agile practices. It may be beneficial to establish one or more **Centers of Excellence (CoE)** to provide mentoring and coaching resources and guide the value stream transformations.

- **Rollout**: Execute the deployment plan outlined in the roadmap. Make sure that the appropriate metrics have been defined and monitor progress against those metrics.

- **Inspect and adapt**: Continuing with the rollout, the new teams and associated stakeholders assess their performance through retrospectives and product demos, refine their activities for improvement, execute the planned improvements, monitor, and continue to adapt as necessary. Here, again, this inspection and adaption process never stops.

As you can see, inspection and adaption activities prevail throughout the Agile and Lean-Agile transformations and across all product life cycles. Moreover, providing visibility is critical to the inspection and adaptation processes. Metrics and other forms of information help the organization visualize how they are doing against their plans and past performances.

In the previous chapter, we learned that the four most critical measures to evaluate team performance are as follows:

- **Deployment frequency**: A measure of team code deployment frequencies into test and production environments

- **Lead time**: A measure of the time it takes from developers committing their code in the shared repository to successfully running in a production environment

- **Mean time to repair or restore (MTTR)**: A measure of how long it takes to restore a service when a service incident or a defect that impacts users occurs (for example, an unplanned outage or service impairment)

- **Change fail rate**: A measure of the percentage of changes to production resulting in degraded or failed services (for example, lead to service outage), which then requires remediation (for example, a hotfix or rollback)

However, there are other useful measures and information each team may choose to maintain and make visible. For example, **Intellectsoft** identifies five categories for Agile measurements and 15 useful metrics that provide a good starting point (*15+ Useful Agile Metrics in Scrum & Kanban: Measure Quality, Productivity & Performance. 2018*, which you can refer to at `https://www.intellectsoft.net/blog/agile-metrics`). VSM vendor **Plutora** has a similar article titled *Agile Metrics: The 15 That Actually Matter for Success* (`https://www.plutora.com/blog/agile-metrics`). We'll take a quick look at the metrics presented in these two articles in the next section.

Implementing useful metrics

Not every Agile or Lean-Agile team needs the same metrics. Executives and customers will influence choices and likely request information not listed in this subsection. Additionally, product owners may need additional information to understand how the product's architecture, design, and technical depth issues can impact the delivery of identified and prioritized product backlog items.

The list that follows includes standard metrics that the product teams and their stakeholders may find helpful. The metrics broadly support the primary quality, productivity, and project objectives of Agile, Lean, and Kanban performance measures and software quality measures.

Agile quality metrics

The metrics described in this subsection support generalized quality improvement objectives in Agile-based development practices:

- **Product backlog**: This is a prioritized list of the new features, functions, enhancements, bug fixes, infrastructure changes, or other work items. The quality metrics in this measure deal with the degree to which identified work items are refined and prioritized based on value and delivery costs.

- **Escaped defects**: This is a measure of the defects that have been released into production that previously passed the team's definition of done. Since total defect prevention is an ideal goal, a high number of escaped defects indicates there are failures in properly defining our acceptance criteria or in our testing capabilities and procedures.

- **Failed deployments**: This is a measure of how often software deployments into production environments fail and require a rollback. Ideally, the development team's engineering and testing environments, as well as their testing tools and procedures, should capture and address problems that could cause system failures before they're deployed into production.

  Besides testing to find bugs and nonconformance with the acceptance criteria, the testing environments must accurately mimic the demanded loads against the same combination of applications and configurations within the production environments. Test environments may execute many performance tests, such as load, endurance, volume, scalability, spike, and stress testing. The ideal in DevOps is to automate these and all other tests.

- **Release Net Promoter Score (NPS)**: This is a measure that was initially defined to measure customer experience to predict customer loyalty and business growth. The release-oriented NPS uses directed questions to measure customer satisfaction on a scale of 1 to 10 on each new or major release. In the NPS model, **detractors** are customers who respond with a 6 or below on the scale; **passives** rank the release as a 7 or 8; **promoters** rank the release in the 9 to 10 range. The NPS calculation measures the percentage of detractors subtracted from the percentage of promoters:

  $NPS = \%Promoters - \%Detractors$

  Detractors are a problem as they are more likely to go with our competitors' offering and criticize our product. *Passives* tend to be neither supportive nor unsupportive of the new release. *Promoters* often tend to be more enthusiastic in promoting a company, product, or new release.

In theory, any ranking above 0 means the release had more enthusiastic promoters than unhappy detractors. However, organizations should strive to do much better than 0.

Agile productivity metrics

The metrics described in this subsection support productivity improvement objectives in Agile-based development practices:

- **Lead time**: As previously noted, this measure spans the time from code commitment to its release into production. It's one of the four metrics that helps assess the effectiveness of a software development team. However, in an Agile context, the lead time is a measure that spans when a user story or work item enters a product backlog to the end of a Sprint or the feature's release into production. The lead time includes the time the work item request waits in the product backlog, as shown in the following diagram:

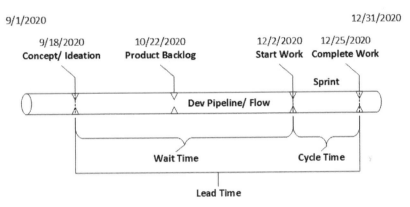

Figure 2.1 – Lead time/cycle time diagram

- **Cycle time (control chart)**: This is a subcomponent of the lead time and measures how long it takes to complete an activity or set of activities within a value stream. In other words, the cycle time is a measure of the time spent as work in progress, devoid of all previous wait times. The closer the lead time is to the cycle time, the more efficient the process.

  The following graph shows an example of a cycle time control chart. In our example, the VSM team collects data on cycle times for specific activities across their pipelines. In our example, the software development team may use VSM tools to capture metrics on how long it takes to conduct a set of end-to-end tests on new increments of code. Regardless, the cycle time control chart includes data points, averages, and established thresholds (limits) for control.

This type of testing automates the application's workflow from beginning to end, replicating common user scenarios through every possible permutation of operations to discover failures as the application interfaces with hardware, networks, external dependencies, databases, and other applications. The team believes an acceptable cycle time for this test is between 5 to 8 hours, and they usually run these tests at night to avoid software development downtime:

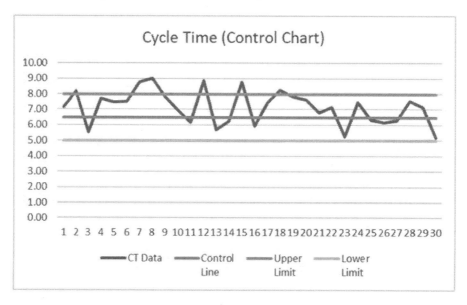

Figure 2.2 – Cycle time (control chart)

From the preceding control chart example, we can see that the performance over the past 30 days has not stayed within an acceptable range of 5 to 8 hours (6.5-hour average). Worse, the testing exceeded the allotted 8 hours on six occasions. With this information, the team has the data they need to explore what events caused the lengthy end-to-end testing. They can map this information with the test results from those dates to see what the team can do to prevent such problems in the future.

> **Note**
>
> In Agile and Lean/Kanban-based systems, the cycle time is a measure of time that a work item spends as a **work in progress** (**WIP**) once the stories have been refined and entered the *in-progress* stage. In this context, the cycle time does not include the time the work item spends in ideation through backlog refinements and waiting in the product backlog queue after that. Cycle time starts immediately when the work item is accepted as a work item in the Sprint backlog, or pulled into production in a Lean- or Kanban-based value stream.

Still, it's possible to have a cycle time that includes waiting times in Agile, Lean, and Kanban-based systems. The distinction is that the cycle time always includes both *touch* and *wait times* within Agile-based Sprints, but we'll want to break out and try to eliminate all wait times in a Lean-oriented software value stream.

- **Wait time**: The amount of time a product or material spends inactive in a *delayed* status before work begins. In Lean and Kanban-based systems, we seek to eliminate all wait times.

- **Sprint Burndown Charts**: A measure and visualization of team forecast velocity as the completion rate, usually in the form of estimated story points, from the Sprint Backlog across one or more Sprints. The primary purpose of a Sprint Burndown Chart is to show the team's progress against the Sprint Goal (see *Figure 2.2*).

  Teams initially forecast the level of effort required from each work item in the form of *story points*. A Sprint Burndown Chart tracks progress against the Sprint Backlog regarding the actual number of story points worth of work completed against the planned burndown. There are typically two lines on the chart: one to show the planned velocity and another to show the Sprint's actual velocity.

- **Epic and release burndown/burnup**: The same concept as the Sprint Burndown Chart applies to tracking work progress across defined Epics and product releases. Epics are an enormous scope of planned and interrelated work that's not been refined to smaller stories:

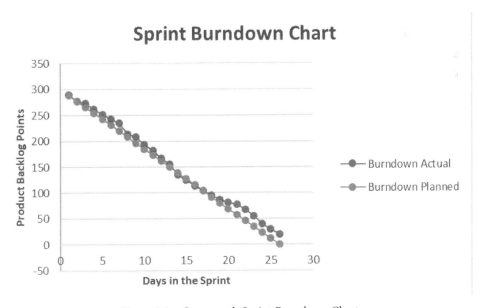

Figure 2.3 – One month Sprint Burndown Chart

The primary concern with using such metrics is not to use the charts to find faults with a team's progress. The longer the period and the less defined the requirements, the more difficult it becomes to estimate work with absolute accuracy. Epic and Product Release Burndown Charts merely show progress against initial plans and have nothing to add in the way of understanding why.

- **Burnup Charts**: Note that we can use the same data that was used to create a Sprint Burndown Chart to visualize the amount of work that was completed throughout the Sprint and how much work remains, as shown here:

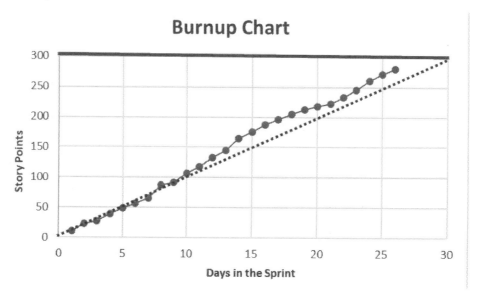

Figure 2.4 – Sprint burnup chart

Note that the smaller dotted line in the preceding diagram indicates the originally planned projection of work that's been completed. In our example, the team is on target to complete the initially estimated 300 points worth of work early.

- **Velocity**: This is the measure of estimated work a team or teams accomplish over time, usually measured across each Sprint in Agile:

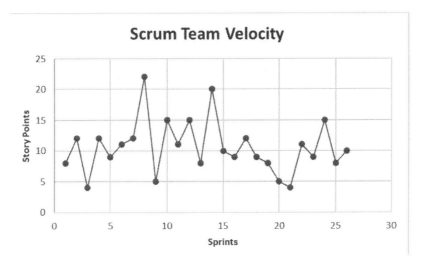

Figure 2.5 – Scrum Team velocity chart

The objective is to use the velocity chart to judge future performance. However, the more significant the variance in this number, the more difficult the team or teams will have estimating the scope of work within the product and Sprint backlogs, and the more difficult it will be to plan their deliveries.

In DevOps within large organizations, velocity measures the number of stories completed in days or even hours.

- **Control charts**: Also known as Shewhart charts (named after Walter A. Shewhart), this is a statistical process control tool that's used to determine if a process is in a state of control. In Agile and Lean development practices, teams use control charts to track the duration of tasks from *in progress* to *completion*:

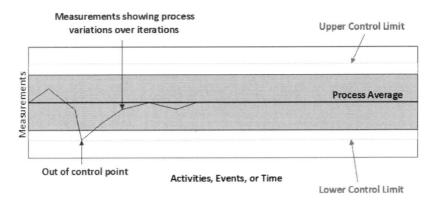

Figure 2.6 – Process control chart

In an ideal world, all activities would be very predictable and never vary from a desirable mean. However, that's rarely the case, and we use control charts to see if our processes are trending in the wrong direction. Control charts have upper and lower boundaries that define optimal durations and upper and lower control limits to indicate an out of bounds measurement. When the teams see their metrics trending toward the upper or lower control boundary limits, they know they have issues to address.

A typical use case for control charts is showing the rate of defects over instances of an activity or process. However, when used to measure activity durations, control charts help show the team's velocity and its trend in velocity.

Agile project metrics

The metrics described in this subsection support how workflows are managed in Agile-based development practices:

- **Kanban Boards and Cards**: Kanban is a "Pull" signaling system that was initially developed to support Lean-oriented and **just-in-time** (**JIT**) manufacturing concepts in Japan. Kanban stands for Kan (that is, card) and Ban (that is, signal), which, when interpreted together, mean *billboard* or *signboard*. In a Kanban system, no production process starts until receipt of the signal card indicates the desired quantity and type of parts or work required. The entire value stream process only kicks off on-demand with customer orders.

- **Visualize the workflow**: Teams can employ whiteboards with columns to indicate the team's defined stages of work. Using an IT example, those stages might include *Backlog*, *Refinement*, *Development and Test*, *Acceptance*, and *Delivery*.

  The following image shows an example of a Kanban Board with Kanban Cards indicating work in progress across the Story, To Do, In Progress, To Verify, and Done value stream activities:

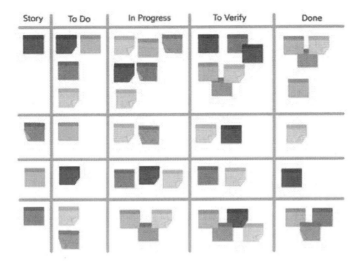

Figure 2.7 – Kanban Board with Kanban Cards

In the preceding image, the labels map to the Agile pipeline Kanban activities managed by the software development team. Stories are the user stories that are managed in the product backlog. The to-do list is the highest priority user story. In Progress includes the user stories under development. To Verify includes the user stories that are complete but need to be verified by their team members and product owner. Finally, Done represents the user stories that can be released into production.

- **Limit work in progress (WIP)**: Ideally, there should never be a queue of work or materials except in the initial product backlog. Downstream processes only pull work when they have the capacity to perform the work. Without this simple rule, work and materials accumulate at the slower processes within the pipeline, which we know creates waste due to excessive storage requirements and carrying costs. Additionally, excessive WIP hides bugs and defects in the queued products. These become increasingly challenging to find and expensive to fix later.

- **Manage flow**: Use Kanban Cards as signaling devices to indicate new requests from internal and external customers. These Cards enter a queue on the Kanban Board. As downstream capacity opens to take on work from the previous stage, the individuals taking on the work move the card they selected into the next column on the board to indicate they have accepted the work. In other words, work is only pulled into downstream processes when capacity is available; work is never pushed to a downstream process.

- **Make policies explicit**: Organizations must provide simple, clear, and visible policies describing desired work practices, approved technologies, procurement processes, and human resource management. The policies must evolve based on new learning that suggests better approaches.

- **Feedback**: Feedback in Kanban comes through collaborative meetings. Traditional Kanban practices implement seven types of meetings:

  a. **Strategy review**: These are corporate-level assessments of the business mission, goals, and objectives constrained by resources, time, competition, and technologies.

  b. **Operations review**: They help teams assess their Kanban practices, value stream activities, and resources to deliver value.

  c. **Risk review**: Identify risks and develop mitigation strategies and contingency plans.

  d. **Service delivery review**: Assessment of the services required to support product deliveries (also known as operational value streams).

  e. **Replenishment meeting**: This is a Kanban-based form of backlog management activity that's used to identify the tasks that must be pulled from the backlog. This is done by assigning the tasks to a **Class of Service** (**CoS**) and setting limits for the number of tasks that are pulled from each CoS. Examples of CoS tasks include emergency requests, fixed delivery dates, bugs, standard tasks, and maintenance tasks.

  f. **Kanban standup meeting**: This is similar in concept to the Daily Scrum Meeting, where team members meet briefly to discuss how the work is progressing, what work remains, and what's getting in the way of our work. The Kanban meeting's primary difference is managing work as a continuous flow, minimizing lead times by eliminating bottlenecks, and reducing WIP. Team members meet at their Kanban Board.

  g. **Delivery planning meeting**: This is required when organizations formally release products on fixed dates. The delivery planning meetings help teams address implementation concerns, support and maintenance hand-offs, data migrations, training development and delivery requirements, and other **service-level agreement** (**SLA**) issues.

- **Continuous improvements (Kaizen)**: Ideas for improvement come from observation, collaborations, retrospectives, and product demos. Use team-based retrospectives to review and analyze previous issues, implement immediate experiments to resolve those issues, and never stop these iterative efforts for continuous improvements. Moreover, use customer demos to help guide development priorities from their perspective.

- **Cumulative flow diagram (CFD)**: This is an analytical tool that's typically associated with the Kanban method. Similar conceptually to Agile's Burnup Charts, the CFD provides visibility on the amount of accumulative work across each stage of a value stream (for example, a software development value stream).

In an ideal world, work items flow through a sequence of activities in a synchronized and coordinated development pipeline with slight variance on activity durations, no rework, and no losses due to defects and bugs. But we don't live in that world, and stuff happens that causes work accumulations at various points of our development pipeline.

The following graph shows a CFD tracking work across the following four stages of a software delivery pipeline:

a. Work item requests (blue)

b. Requirements refined (orange)

c. Development and testing WIP (gray)

d. Delivery (yellow):

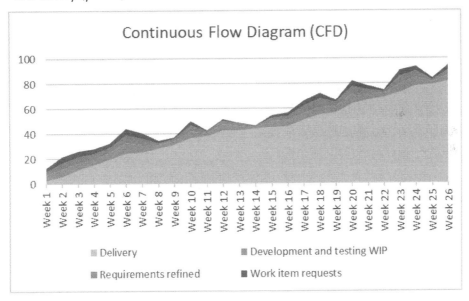

Figure 2.8 – Continuous Flow Diagram (CFD)

The CFD allows teams to visualize potential impediments in their value stream process and the most effective tool to observe the impacts across the value stream's activities. Instead of a relatively smooth graph with gentle rises and falls, sudden ascending or descending graphics indicate impediments.

- **Code Coverage**: This is a measure and visual display of how much of a team's product code is covered by unit tests or test suites. Typical code coverage metrics include method or function coverage, statement coverage, branch coverage, condition coverage, **multiple condition/decision coverage (MC/DC)**, parameter coverage, and cyclomatic complexity.

  The more extensive the code coverage in testing, the higher the software's potential reliability and quality. Any gaps in code coverage can result in software failures and bugs. And even if your team has high code coverage, there's always a chance something can slip through the cracks. On the other hand, with good code coverage, those instances should be few and far between.

Health metrics for Agile teams/Agile performance metrics

The metrics described in this subsection support employee satisfaction objectives in Lean and Agile-based development practices:

- **Employee happiness**: This is a somewhat subjective measurement but ultimately critical to keeping your employees in the long run. Happiness is measured through simple employee surveys, asking them to rate how happy they are with the company, what they like best, what they don't like, and what would increase their happiness. Of course, executive leaders need to proactively act on this information to produce positive changes that help keep and attract talented workers.

- **Team morale**: Measures of team-level morale often provide better indicators of job satisfaction. Again, surveys work best, but the questions are not open-ended. Instead, the surveys ask the team members to rate their agreement with the questions on a scale of 1 to 7. The questions ask whether the team member feels they are a good fit for the team, are proud of their work, enthusiastic about their work, and find meaning and purpose in their work.

Core Lean and Kanban metrics

The metrics described in this subsection support productivity improvement objectives in Lean software development practices:

- **Story lead time**: This lead time metric shows up again, but this time in the context of Lean and Kanban systems. Since Lean and Kanban implement value stream flows, the lead time for a story starts when it enters the product backlog and completes when completed. Thus, lead times always include the wait time when products and materials sit in a queue.

- **Story cycle time**: A component of lead time, cycle times measure how long it takes to complete the set of activities within a value stream. In a DevOps context, this is a pipeline flow measurement of the time it takes for work to flow through the team's development pipeline. Specifically, the lead time spans work item creation to completion, while the cycle time measures the duration a work item spends as work in process.

- **Feature lead time**: This is a variation on story lead time, where the focus is on implementing specific features. User stories represent a user or customer's desired capabilities, which can be quite granular in scope. For example, a user story for an online car buyer might state, "*As a car buyer, I want to view the color of the dealer's available automobile so that I can see any match my color preferences.*" From this example, it's clear that user stories are statements of requirements from the user's perspective.

In contrast, a feature implements a slice of business functionality that may encompass multiple user story requests. In this context, the dealer's online feature might include all customer online automobile lookup preferences, including make, model, year, price, color, and other differentiating options. In other words, a feature is the implementation of a piece of functionality from the point of view of the business.

Making the distinction between user stories and product features is essential as customers buy capabilities and may not know what capabilities and benefits a feature provide unless clearly stated. Recall our previous discussion on the need to clearly state a product's capabilities and benefits via its value proposition.

- **Feature cycle time**: Similar to the story cycle time, this is the total time involved when developers actively design, develop, and test the feature. In other words, cycle times measure the time of the work in progress.

- **Story wait time**: This is a measure of non-value-added time that a product requirement or work in progress sits in an idle state. The goal is to minimize wait times to the greatest extent possible.

- **Story throughput**: This measure of velocity calculates the number of stories running through development pipeline (or other value stream) over time. Smaller stories help improve throughput in two ways. First, smaller stories are quicker to implement because there is less work to complete. Second, smaller stories tend to be less complicated and, therefore, easier and quicker to debug discovered errors.

It is essential to keep your stories relatively consistent in size in a Lean- or Kanban-based environment. In a Lean-based system, the objective is to have matched activity durations to prevent queuing in slower activities. Of course, using a pull-based order entry system tied to available capacity also helps minimize queuing.

Also, recall that any value stream's ideal cycle rate is the available production time divided by customer requests within the same duration (also known as **TAKT time**). So, if your software development teams are receiving an average of 10 stories across each 8-hour day, the TAKT time is $\frac{10}{8} = 1.25\ stories\ per\ hour.$

In other words, the activities within your DevOps- or Kanban-based development pipeline need to cycle at the same rate as order entries. If you go slower than TAKT time, you won't deliver all your customers' orders; if you operate faster, you produce unrequested products.

- **Created-to-finished ratio**: This is a measure of the difference between the number of work items entering your value stream compared to the number of items completed over time. Queues develop when the number of work items entering that value stream exceeds the number completed, assuming the work is entered into the product backlog.

If the order entry level is stable, the dev teams may address the issues by streamlining their value stream activities or adding capacity. However, it may also be possible that some of the stories are not of sufficient priority or cost-justified to include in the product backlog queue. Regardless, an excessive created-to-finish ratio indicates lost opportunity when the work is a customer priority and has been cost-justified.

Measuring software quality in Agile

The metrics described in this subsection support software quality improvement objectives in Agile-based development practices:

- **Static code analysis**: This is a method that's used to debug software. It does so by examining source code against a predefined set of rules and standards without executing the program. Developers conduct static code analysis in the earliest code development phases, before unit testing, or before integrating with the source code repository's mainline code. The objective is to find and fix coding errors at the earliest time possible.

It's possible to run static code analysis as a manual test. But manual testing is time-consuming, laborious, and subject to human error. The better approach is to use a **static code analysis tool (SAST)** to scan and check compliance to coding rules such as syntax violations, undefined values, dead or unused code, programming errors, security, vulnerabilities, performance issues, and others. The output of a SAST is a summary report showing the health status of your code.

While there are numerous open source and commercial SASTs, modern compilers also perform syntactic or technical errors before running the code, catching many of the same types of errors.

- **Dynamic code analysis**: This identifies defects after compiling the code and running it across the product testing life cycle, including unit testing, integration testing, system testing, acceptance testing, and regression testing. Dynamic code analysis aims to check the system's response to variables that dynamically change within the application.

  The primary benefit of dynamic code testing is that the tests operate against many orders of magnitude greater numbers of permutations of data inputs than humans can manually implement, within the same time frame. For example, dynamic code analysis might involve tens of thousands or more data input configurations, operating against multiple components and integrated systems, in a batch run that lasts a few hours.

- **Quality intelligence**: Data analysis tools help improve software development processes that produce poor or undesirable quality outcomes. Static and dynamic analysis tools focus on identifying issues with code already under development. However, quality intelligence aims to discover the areas in the development process that consistently produce problems in terms of velocity, quality, and efficiencies. Quality intelligence tools help teams organize and analyze data from activities across the entire software development life cycle.

This section ends our discussion on useful Lean-Agile metrics. In the next section, you will learn how to improve IT flows by implementing Lean production and operations practices across the IT organization.

Improving IT flows through Lean Thinking

In the next chapter, you will learn how to apply Systems Thinking to reduce complexity across six potential value streams involving one to six sets of activities (See *Figure 3.2*, an image showing nodes, potential connections, actual connections, and network densities.) The graphic provided demonstrates how aligning value stream activities as streamlined flows reduces the number of possible connections and interactions across the activities. Thus, the linear-sequential approach is the most efficient way to operate within a value stream.

However, we can still mess things up by not reducing the setup and cycle times of lengthier activities and allowing work items to queue at those slower activities within the value stream. As noted previously, the ideal goal is to match each activity and the overall production rates to the rate of receiving customer orders or requirements. We can calculate this as the time to produce work items, divided by the number of items requested over the interval, otherwise known as **Takt time**.

Conceptually, Lean production eliminates all forms of waste that hinder our efforts to deliver customer-centric value. In the traditional view of Lean manufacturing, there are seven distinct categories of waste, as shown in the following list:

- **Waiting**: Delays in processing, including any time products spend waiting or in a queue.

- **Overproduction**: Producing more of something than you need or than your customer's currently want.

- **Extra-processing**: Over-processing or conducting any non-value-added activity.

- **Transportation**: Wasted time, resources, and costs moving products and materials from one location to another.

- **Motion**: Unnecessary movement, motion, or activities performed by people.

- **Inventory**: Carrying and storing any materials and products not undergoing a value-added activity.

- **Defects**: Any defects in the product or services produced.

The previous list of waste in Lean evolved primarily in the manufacturing industry, though it also supports services-oriented companies, such as software development companies. Waste in software development practices is the topic of the next section.

Eliminating waste in software development

In 2003, Mary and Tom Poppendieck released their book *Lean Software Development: An Agile Toolkit*, where they discussed applying Lean manufacturing concepts to software development. Their book maps seven forms of waste in software development back to the original Lean concepts of waste, as shown in the following table:

Seven Wastes of Lean Production	Seven Wastes of Lean Software Development	General Description of Waste
Inventory	Partially done work	Carrying excessive WIP
Extra Processing	Extra Processing	Performing non-value-added work, such as lengthy approvals or documentation that do not add value to the product.
Overproduction	Extra Features	Creating features that have relatively low priority and value from the perspective of the customer and users.
Transportation	Task Switching	Frequently jumping from one task to another, disrupting the developer's attention to the task, extending the time it takes to complete.
Waiting	Waiting	Time work items and resources spend waiting without value added work underway
Motion	Motion	Excessive movement - and therefore excessive time, people, materials, and work items spend moving between value stream activities
Defects	Defects	Not preventing, detecting, and fixing defects and other errors at the earliest time possible, making it more difficult, time intensive, and expensive to resolve at a later time.

Figure 2.9 – Mapping Lean Manufacturing waste to its software development equivalents

These definitions of waste in Lean production and Lean software development have been around for 3 and nearly 2 decades, respectively. Since then, a great deal of thinking has evolved around Lean practices, which I addressed in my previous book, *Scaling Scrum Across Modern Enterprises*. For expedience, I'll recap the primary concept here in this section. However, I encourage those who want a deeper dive to explore the two chapters from my previous book devoted to this subject: *Chapter 5, Driving Business Value through a DevOps Pipeline*, and *Chapter 6, Launching the VSM Initiative (VSM Steps 1-3)*.

As you read through the following list of Lean concepts, understand that they apply equally well to the development of physical, digital, and hybrid-physical-digital products and services:

- **Value**: Customers always define value. It doesn't matter how much experience we have or how bright we are; any idea we come up with is, at best, a risk until adequately validated by the target customers.

- **Continuous improvements (Kaizen)**: The goal is to make work more efficient and effective through teamwork, improved procedures, and employee and customer collaboration. The tools for continuous improvement include quality control mechanisms, just-in-time delivery, standardized work, fast setups, streamlined flows, more efficient equipment, and waste elimination. Additionally, improvements should help make the employee's jobs more fulfilling, less fatiguing, and safer.

- **Visual controls**: This involves controls such as Kanban Cards to manage the intake of work items to match value stream flows. Control charts are another form of chart that help us see when we are trending out of bounds on any metrics.

- **Built-in quality**: This means finding problems and fixing them immediately when they're introduced. In the continuous flows of a lean system, we may have to stop all the work in the value stream and focus everyone's efforts on resolving the problem quickly. Building in quality helps us eliminate the higher costs that result from product recalls, rework, and the lengthy process of finding and fixing bugs in the late stages of product development.

- **Improving knowledge**: This is an essential element of continuous improvements in Lean and Agile practices. Whether we learn from experience, by trial and error, or by learning from others, we can apply that learning to evolve new ways of working that are more effective and productive. Teams must make time for observations, analysis, and learning.

- **Delay decisions and commitments**: Though seemingly counterintuitive to lean principles, there are costs involved when making poor decisions due to insufficient information. It's better to delay decisions until we have enough information to mitigate our risks. In the long run, the organization saves time and money by building the products that customers want and value, not what we think they want.

- **Detect defects through automation (Jidoka)**: The Japanese Lean concept of autonomation means *Automation with a human touch*. Jidoka is a quality control principle that recommends using automated techniques to detect abnormalities, stop the process, fix the immediate problem, and then identify the cause and effects and explore ways to prevent or reduce future occurrences.

- **Eliminate mistakes (Poka-Yoke)**: This is also known as *mistake-proofing*. This approach to eliminating wastes prevents incorrect operations being performed by employees or product users. The objective is to design a process or mechanism that makes it impossible to perform a particular activity incorrectly. For example, a team's **continuous integration** (**CI**) practices might implement a build process that automatically performs static analysis and test-driven development instructions. The CI automation process helps ensure a developer's code meets the organization's coding practices and customer's acceptance requirements, before they are allowed to integrate their code with the main branch (also known as the master branch).

- **Eliminate waste**: Assess and eliminate the seven forms of waste, as identified in previously, for Lean production and software development.

- **Quit multitasking/task switching**: Because such activities break our attention and focus on what we are currently doing, this forces our brains to switch between tasks rapidly. In reality, multitasking is a form of task switching. In other words, when multitasking, you are not thinking about both topics at the same time. Instead, you are switching your attention back and forth between them.

Multitasking only works for a limited set of activities that split our cognitive activities across our brains' left and right prefrontal cortexes, such as talking while walking with a friend. Moreover, multitasking only works while performing a relatively autonomous motor skill with a cognitive task – and even then, you are likely to do both tasks slower.

When working across multiple cognitive tasks, our thinking involves a sequential switching process that creates a bottleneck when switching between cognitive tasks. While switching between topics, our brains require time and effort to reorient our thinking and pick back up where we left off, and we lose information in the process. As a result, we lose our train of thought, and it takes us longer to complete our thoughts and work.

But there are other undesirable effects of multitasking and task switching, including making mistakes, adding to your stress, disrupting your short-term memory, and missing essential details as you switch between tasks. Task switching also negatively impacts creativity, and you may end up revisiting a subject multiple times to get through the task.

- **Practice Gemba (that is, go to the source)**: This helps you see your current situation. When applied to Lean production, managers walk the manufacturing floors to review progress and talk to the workers to discuss their issues and concerns. In a software development context, we have collocated teams, and we use daily scrums and other events to communicate progress, issues, and ideas. Big charts are made visible in the development operations and updated frequently to simplify communications to anyone who needs or wants to know how things are going.

- **Implement single-piece flows**: This is ideal in Lean production and lean software development practices. This concept extends our discussions on why the most efficient value streams instill a linear-sequential set of activities to streamline workflows. The other killer of productivity is batch processing, which is made worse when batch processes between activities and activity durations do not match.

    Intuitively, it seems that large batch processes are less costly as they can work on hundreds of items in one batch. However, in real life, the cost savings are lost from lengthy wait times, excessive product changeover times across production equipment, and hiding bugs and defects in large batches.

    The ideal situation is to have the flow of one work item for each value stream activity. There should be lengthy setup or changeover requirements. Activity cycle times should be the lowest time possible and matched across all value stream activities. Finally, production throughput for the value stream should equal the rate of order entries (that is, takt time).

- **Level workloads (Heijunka)**: We must have a goal to prevent large batches of orders or requests from entering a system that causes waiting and other resulting problems. Heijunka involves leveling the type and quantity of production across a fixed time.

    In a Lean software development context, we can use an example of a product owner receiving requirements that vary from day to day, depending on sources and product management activities that provide information. However, for this example, let's assume that the overall demand stays relatively constant at approximately 25 new high-priority requirements a week, even if they don't come in at a constant rate of five per day.

Assuming our Lean development shop can handle the load of five work items per day, the product owner maintains a product backlog with a sufficient inventory to maintain a stable release of five work items a day. The volume of new requests may vary from day to day, but the goal is to maintain a steady flow of new work items into production.

- **Pull production systems**: Enforce rules to only produce goods in direct response to demand, instead of building products or features early and creating waste in the form of unsold inventories of products and features customers may never want. The lean value stream doesn't initiate work in a pull-oriented production system until it contains a customer order or requirement. The Kanban system is a method that's used to enforce the discipline of the pull-oriented production system across the entire value stream.

- **Just-in-time (JIT) deliveries**: This is another strategy that matches production rates to customer demand and eliminates all waste in activities that do not add value across the production processes. However, JIT initially dealt with inventory management problems. Rather than ordering and storing batches of materials, JIT only allows new procurement and material deliveries that match customer demands. Moreover, the producers schedule their materials to arrive just as they are needed to manufacture the ordered products.

  JIT works in a digital context in several ways. First, software development teams don't start work on new features or functions until there is customer demand. Moreover, when digital products support other organizational value streams, we need to make sure the deliveries align with the consuming value streams' needs.

- **Optimize the whole**: This is another way to aggregate the concepts noted in the single-piece flows, leveling workloads, pull production systems, and JIT subsections. The objective is to look at the entire value stream to simplify and reduce complexity and eliminate waste. Aim to make your production processes as efficient and streamlined as possible. Rather than fighting fires, only allow orders or requirements to flow into a system at the received rate. And never allow new orders to enter faster than your production system can handle the load as a continuous and uninterrupted flow without waiting.

Our value streams represent an approach to simplifying complex production and operations-oriented systems, while simultaneously ensuring we stay focused on adding or improving customer-centric value. In this context, a value stream is an end-to-end optimization of an entire (that is, the whole) complex development or operations-oriented system.

- **Reject unfinished work**: In a Lean software development context, this is any work in progress that's been promoted into production that's not yet met its *definition of done*. However, unfinished work creates havoc at all stages of a value stream. If developers or other workers feel pressured into sending their work before completion, the potential downstream effects include additional bugs, defects, failures, rework, delays, and unsatisfied customers. As a matter of policy, organizations should never allow downstream value stream activities to accept unfinished work from upstream activities.

- **Respect for people**: This should be an obvious requirement for building effective organizations. However, hierarchical and bureaucratic organizations often create hostile environments that do not encourage cross-team or cross-organizational communications and collaborations. In addition, such processes create stress when problems arise outside the bounds of the process and through the delays of getting appropriate responses and approvals across the hierarchy.

  Both the Agile and Lean practices promote the need for respect with accountability. These concepts are different than the "Golden Rule" concept you were taught as a child – *"Treat others as you would have them treat you."*

Let's quickly review how the Golden Rule plays out in Lean-oriented software development:

- Work regular hours, eliminate overtime, and maintain a sustainable pace.

- Help team members understand the value they provide to customers.

- Build compensation and incentives plans around continuous learning and skills.

- Challenge team members without belittling them.

- Hold teams, not individuals, accountable for their commitments.

- Implement safe working environments so that team members are not punished for seeking help when problems arise.

- Involve team members in analyzing problems, exploring cause and effect, and coming up with methods to resolve the issues at hand.

- Remove impediments to minimize frustration.

- While seeking stability, also provide variety to prevent boredom.

- Protect the organizational knowledge base by developing stable personnel, promotions based on demonstrable development of relevant knowledge and skills, and meticulous succession plans.

We have reached the end of this section on Lean Thinking. In summary, Lean Thinking is about organizing work around value (products, services, information) and streamlining work and information flows. So far, you have learned how to evaluate value streams through Systems Thinking with causal loop diagrams. This helps evaluate the interconnected relationships of nodes or elements participating in a value stream system.

In *Chapter 7, Mapping the Current State (VSM Step 4)*, and *Chapter 8, Identifying Lean Metrics (VSM Step 5)*, you will learn how to use value stream mapping to assess current as-is value stream activities and evaluate alternate to-be states to improve value across the value streams. But before we move on, let's take a quick look at how organizations blend Lean and Agile concepts.

Creating the Lean-Agile foundation

This section is about blending Agile and Lean concepts and practices. At first glance, both Agile and Lean practices have similar goals of improving customer value, but both development philosophies seem to approach that primary goal differently. So, the question then is, how do we blend the best of both approaches to make something better?

Earlier in this chapter, you learned that Agile is a set of values and principles, typically implemented as an iterative and incremental process, that deliver customer-centric value. The basic idea is that Agile teams create the most value for their customers when they have the flexibility to incrementally deliver small chunks of value with frequent customer and user reviews. This helps ensure the product stays aligned with current needs and priorities. You also learned that Scrum is an Agile-based methodology that implements a framework of empiricism. This encourages teams to try out different ideas and use their experiences and observations to uncover better ways of doing things.

In contrast, Lean seeks to improve customer-centric value by eliminating all waste forms and only doing what customers want. Some Lean practitioners like to think of the Lean concept of waste as avoiding spending time and effort on activities that customers don't want to pay. The challenge with that thinking is that it's a bit shortsighted. For example, an organization may spend money on infrastructure, training, and process improvements that indirectly provide more value for the customer, even though the immediate customer might not benefit from those investments.

Knowing that both the Agile and Lean methodologies primary focus on creating customer value, the primary difference is the development intervals. Agile practitioners tend to think in terms of small teams providing new value incrementally across small iterative releases. Though the iterative release may be relatively small and frequent, especially compared to the traditional Waterfall model, each Agile Sprint is still a batch process.

One effective way to make Agile practices leaner is to replace the Sprint iteration model with a Kanban-based pull model. This strategy limits the work in progress to a minimal number of work items and simultaneously replaces the Sprint batch process with single-piece workflows.

But Kanbans are manual processes, and we can do better. For example, we can make additional improvements by streamlining, integrating, and automating our IT processes to achieve the full benefits of Lean. That is the topic of the next section on accelerating flows.

Accelerating flows across IT value streams

In the previous section, you learned that Agile and Lean aim to improve customer value and manage product flows differently. You also learned that the quickest and simplest way to blend Agile and Lean practices is by moving away from the batch Sprint model, to a continuous flow model by using Kanban Boards and Cards. However, we can also streamline and accelerate our value delivery processes through integration and automation strategies. **Continuous integration (CI)**, **continuous delivery (CD)**, DevOps, platforms, and software factories help us achieve these goals.

First, CI and CD capabilities help the IT development teams streamline, integrate, and automate their **software development life cycle (SDLC)** processes. That's not to say that the entire set of SDLC processes should be streamlined, integrated, and automated all at once. Rapid adoption may not be possible for a small IT shop or a small team within a larger organization that has not implemented DevOps platforms or software factories. But the eventual end-to-end streamlining, integration, and automation of the software development value stream is the ideal goal from a Lean perspective.

With CI/CD capabilities, DevOps takes the Lean concepts as integrated value streams into the IT operation's functionality. Specifically, the IT organization can implement value stream management capabilities to integrate front and backend processes. Again, attempting to manage all these changes at once is not practical for most organizations. However, the ideal objective is to reach such a stage of integrated capabilities as quickly as possible.

Streaming, integrating, and automating end-to-end CI/CD and DevOps processes help the IT organization accelerate value deliveries. They also help improve the quality of the delivered products and services. In *Section 2* (*Chapter 6, Launching the VSM Initiative (VSM Steps 1-3)*, through *Chapter 10, Improving the Lean-Agile Value Delivery Cycle(VSM Steps 7 and 8)*) of this book, you will learn how value stream management helps marshal value delivery from concept through delivery and support, while simultaneously tying its business value delivery objectives to its software delivery capabilities.

Section 3 (Chapter 11, Identifying VSM Tool Types and Capabilities, through Chapter 14, Introducing the Enterprise Lean-VSM Practice Leaders) identifies the leading VSM tool vendors and methodologists. The VSM methodologists are split into two camps: those that implement VSM to support digital business transformations and those that support the general implementation of lean practices.

Finally, *Section 4 (Chapter 15, Avoiding DevOps Implementation Pitfalls, through Chapter 17, Conclusion – Enabling Lean Business Transformations)* of this book discusses using a DevOps platform or software factory strategies to expedite the organization's efforts to streamline, integrate, and automate DevOps processes as part of a business transformation. DevOps platforms are commercial offerings that contain integrated DevOps toolchains that development teams can use with minimal challenges. The potential downside is the limitations of the tools that have been adopted or developed by the platform provider.

An alternative approach is to have an internal or external IT development organization build software factories that implement fully configured DevOps toolchains as code. With modern tools and managed configurations as code, a team can download and stand up a fully provisioned DevOps environment on demand and in minutes.

With this, we will conclude our chapter.

Summary

In this chapter, you learned how Agile established values and principles to improve software development practices and how Scrum became the prevalent Agile methodology. Scrum implements an Agile framework that incorporates empiricism to help small teams evolve their development practices and products through observation and experimentation. We touched on Systems Thinking to understand the software value stream as a complex mixture of elements that form complex relationships. These relationships make it difficult to understand how the interacting parts respond to changes in variables within the system. Causal Loop Diagram (CLD) gives us a tool to analyze the system-wide impacts of those types of complex interactions.

This chapter also introduced you to the Lean Thinking and Lean software development concepts to add value by streamlining, integrating, and automating value stream activities and pulling in work matched with demands and production capacities. Finally, you learned how to blend Lean and Agile concepts and then accelerate value across your IT value streams.

In the next chapter, you will learn how to evaluate complex systems in terms of the participating elements and their interrelationships.

Questions

1. What is the leading Agile methodology?

2. What is the industry-leading Lean-Agile methodology?

3. What is the purpose of Lean Portfolio Management?

4. Name at least two Agile quality metrics.

5. How do Kanban Boards and Cards help improve the flow of delivery?

6. What is the purpose of Takt time, and how do we calculate it?

7. What is the least complex configuration of a system with multiple nodes?

8. How do we accelerate our value delivery processes?

9. What are the seven forms of waste in Lean?

10. Both Lean and Agile practices have primary goals to improve efficiency and add customer-centric value. What is the primary difference in their approach?

Further reading

- Beck, K., et al. (2001) *Manifesto for Agile Software Development.*
  `https://agilemanifesto.org/` accessed December 2, 2020.

- Rupp, C.G., (2020) *Scaling Scrum Across Modern Enterprises: Implement Scrum and Lean-Agile Techniques Across Complex Products, Portfolios, and Programs in Large Organizations.* PACKT Publishing. Birmingham, England

- Poppendieck, M., Poppendieck, T. (2003) *Lean Software Development. An Agile Toolkit.* Addison Wesley. Boston, MA.

3
Analyzing Complex System Interactions

IT organizations represent complex systems on several levels. First, the process of software development is a system, as are the operations and support functions. Second, the inclusion of team members extends the software development system's complexity, as does their computing equipment, networks, tools, and software applications.

Suppose the IT department supports multiple Agile or DevOps development teams working on a single product. In that case, each product team would function as both an independent system and as a component of a more extensive system – a "team of teams." In these scenarios, all the teams must collaborate to support the ongoing development of the software product or digitally-enabled service. This chapter provides guidance on assessing the complexity of these (and any other types of systems) by evaluating the elements that make up the system, their connections, and types of interactions.

An essential analytical tool of value stream management is a modeling and visualization technique referred to as value stream mapping. This technique is introduced in the next chapter as part of the introduction to value stream management. However, if a value stream team only examines their activities, they may miss the broader scope of elements that impact their value stream as a system. They may also miss how those elements impact their system. This type of cross-domain complexity analysis is the domain of **systems thinking**, which is the topic of this chapter.

In this chapter, we're going to cover the following main topics:

- Resolving IT complexity through systems thinking
- Analyzing cause and effects
- Calculating potential connections
- Limiting connections
- Learning the vocabulary of systems thinking
- Visualizing the interrelationships of system elements
- Reading **causal loop diagrams (CLDs)**

Resolving IT complexity through systems thinking

Systems thinking is an approach to evaluate the complexity of large systems not as a collection of individuals parts but rather the interactions between the elements that participate in the system. I discuss this subject at great length in *Chapter 4, Systems Thinking*, of the book *Scaling Scrum Across Modern Enterprises*, introducing 17 CLDs related to Scrum-based Agile practices. So we'll only touch briefly on the subject of systems thinking within this book.

Systems thinking also aids in analyzing other complex business processes, including the interactions of connected value streams. However, in this book, the primary focus is on using value stream mapping to evaluate and improve business processes. Still, systems thinking is a precursory activity to value stream mapping. As a result, Lean-Agile practitioners must understand the vernacular of systems thinking, analyze system-level cause and effects, evaluate approaches to reduce network densities, and use system visualization techniques.

Though both systems thinking and value stream mapping employ visualization and modeling techniques to evaluate flows, they have different objectives. Systems thinking aims to identify all the elements that intentionally and unintentionally participate in the system, determine which elements interact within the system, how the elements interact, and their cause and effects. In contrast, value stream mapping is a technique to assess the current and future state of how work is done, then find ways to improve it.

The impacts, causes, and effects of interacting elements are the most critical issues to address when evaluating complex systems' aggregate behaviors. Let's take a moment to find out why.

Analyzing cause and effects in systems

A key concept in systems thinking is that the whole is greater than the sum of the parts that participate within a system. This statement is true for both system capabilities and complexities. It's the interrelationships between the parts that create complexity within a system. But the interrelationships also are what allow systems to do both useful and useless things. If we don't understand the cause and effects of the underlying interactions across the system, we can't begin to understand how to control the interactions in useful ways.

Participant relationships and interactions can be accidental or intentional within the system. For example, we can evaluate a manufacturing ecosystem as representing a single system with any number of participating elements that interact, causing both desired (*intentional*) and undesired (*unintentional*) impacts. Some of the elements intentionally work to support the manufacturer's operations and delivery functions. However, the manufacturing system can also negatively impact other unintentional participants.

Within the manufacturing ecosystem, intentional participants include supply chain partners, distributors, employees, contractors, customers, and other stakeholders supporting the operations. Unintentional participants include people and other elements affected when the industry creates health or safety problems through unsafe environmental practices.

From a systems thinking point of view, we need to understand how organizations conduct their business at a more granular level. We also need to understand the interactions of the participating elements. An **element** is anything that makes up the system, including materials, people, processes, information, and technology. Elements within a system are also sometimes called **nodes**. In **CLD modeling**, we use nodes and arrows to construct directed graphic models of cause and effect relationships.

Technically, a directed graphical model includes the probability of random variables affecting the nodes in the graph. In other words, the cause and effects can vary across a range of values for each system interaction. However, we don't need to get into that level of detail in this chapter.

The challenge with understanding the interrelationships between elements within a system is that we may not know those relationships exist, nor how those interactions play out across the system, without detailed system-level analysis. We'll review how to visualize elements and their interactions via CLD modeling later in the *Visualizing the interrelationships of system elements* subsection. However, before we do that, let's take a quick look to see how the number of elements within a system dramatically impacts the number of interrelationships. Plus, we need to learn some of the terms used in systems thinking before getting to the *Reading a CLD* section. In the next section, you will learn how to calculate potential connections to demonstrate the exponential increase in a system's complexity through a geometric growth in participating elements.

Calculating potential connections

Systems represent interconnected networks. For example, the IT organization within a large enterprise might have several hundred or even several thousand employees and contractors working across its development and operations functions. Additionally, those employees and contractors work with and affect other departments, partners, employees, stakeholders, and customers. The IT system also includes computers, networks, applications, and a host of other elements that participate in the IT ecosystem.

The organization creates policies and processes to help coordinate business functions and people's activities in order to achieve desirable outcomes by producing value-added products and services at a profit or within budget. Every one of these process touchpoints represents an interaction within the more extensive business system. Of course, there is the possibility for any number of unintentional, unplanned, and potentially undesirable interactions.

By now, you may be getting a sense that the growth in connections in large systems might be a big problem. However, unless you are already familiar with the concept of managing network densities, you may not realize just how fast these interconnections and potential relationships grow.

Fortunately for us, there is a reasonably easy way to calculate the number of *potential connections* (PC in the following formulae) between elements that interact within a system. We can also calculate network densities as a percentage of actual connections to potential connections. Let's start with the potential connections algorithm; the highest possible measurement of interactions across a system.

The calculation for potential connections is $PC = \frac{n(n-1)}{2}$, where n is the number of nodes or element connections within the system. In any system, the participating elements are the nodes that create complexity through their interactions. The more nodes, the greater the complexity. Let's look at some examples:

If n=1, then the number of potential connections is 0, as there is nothing else to connect. Add another node, and the number of potential connections only grows by one, that is, $PC = 2(1)/2$. Add yet another node, 3 in total, and the number of connections grows to 3.

So far, the number of relationships and interactions looks very manageable. But now, let's grow the number of connections to 7, the size of a decent-sized Agile team. In this scenario, the number of potential connections is 21. As the team size grows, or we add more teams working together, the number of potential connections explodes.

Now, let's add the team member's laptops to our Agile team example. By adding laptops into our systems, we create equipment-related interrelationships in our IT team. The laptops grow the number of nodes in our Agile system to 14, and the potential connections to 91. In other words, the team and their laptops form 91 interactions that can impact how the team interoperates.

But the Agile team also works on delivering a Sprint Backlog item over each Sprint. For this example, let's use an average of 10 work items per Sprint. So, the number of connected nodes now increases to include 7 team members, 7 laptops, 10 work items – 24 elements in total, and the number of potential connections exponentially jumps to 276 potential connections in every Sprint.

Do you work in a multi-team environment? To demonstrate how that further adds to the complexity of managing an Agile team, let's add a second team of equal size to our IT product development system. As a result, the number of connected nodes now increases to include 14 team members, 14 laptops, and 20 work items, expanding our Agile system to 48 elements. As a result, the number of potential connections grows to 1,128.

We could include customers and other employees they must interact with, but I think you get the point. Every one of those potential connections is a potential point of failure or has the potential to create an undesirable outcome across every Sprint. The growth in system connections is shown in the following figure:

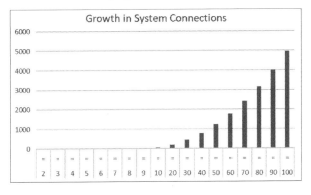

Figure 3.1 – Growth in potential system connections

As an example of how potential connections exponentially grow within a system, *Figure 3.1* provides a graphical depiction of accelerated PC growth from 0 out to 100 interconnected elements as an example of how potential connections exponentially grow within a system. A 10-person team has 45 potential connections, but an IT organization with 100 members has 4,950.

Before we leave this topic, it's important to understand that we can eliminate some potentially negative consequences by limiting the number of actual connections. That's the subject of the next section.

Limiting connections

Often, not all elements in a system are connected. The easiest way to reduce system complexity is to reduce the opportunity for elements to communicate or interoperate with one another. Another way is to reduce the number of elements that participate in a system.

If you have studied Scrum or Lean-Agile scaling strategies, you probably noted that they all leverage small team concepts. They do this even on very large product development activities, sometimes involving hundreds or thousands of people. Breaking up work across multiple small teams is one way to limit the number of interactions between the people working on the product.

For example, **Scrum of Scrums** limits cross-team interactions to a handful of team members, called Ambassadors. The **Nexus** approach to Scrum implements **Network Integration Teams** (**NITs**) to manage cross-team dependencies, coordination, and synchronization activities. Similarly, the **Scaled-Agile Framework**® (**SAFe**®) implements small teams in the form of **Extreme Programming** (**XP**) and **Scrum** teams, with a higher-level team, called the **Agile Release Train** (**ARTs**), to integrate and coordinate work across a large product development effort, or multiple value streams involving 50-125 people split into 5-12 XP/Scrum teams.

Regardless of their specific strategies, all scaled Scrum and Lean-Agile methodologies seek to minimize complexity by reducing the number of participant relationships and interactions. In other words, we want fewer actual connections in our system than the potential theoretical connections.

The ratio of actual connections to potential connections is called **network density**. The concept of network density is important as it offers a way to minimize the number of potential connections in large systems and reduce their potential for causing adverse impacts.

Figure 3.2 shows a set of six Lean value stream activities operating as sequential nodes connected along a single line. The graphic also shows the worst-case scenarios for each identified value stream, where all activities are interconnected. Each value stream includes metrics identifying the number of nodes (*n*), their potential connections (*PC*), actual connections (*AC*), and their network densities (*ND*):

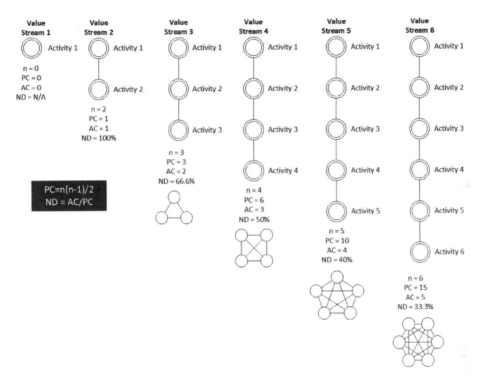

Figure 3.2 – Graphic showing nodes, potential connections, actual connections, and network densities

It should be clear from the graphic that the least number of interactions, and therefore the least complexities, occur in situations with value streams having linear-sequential processes or activities. In this book, you will learn that linear-sequential flows are the hallmark of lean production practices and CI/CD and DevOps pipelines. When we reduce network density by lowering actual connections, we lower the number of potential failure points.

Drawing on our previous example, ways to decrease the network density include having backup laptops and access to alternative software products. Another way to improve outcomes in a complex system is to improve policies and processes that reduce the impact of or repair failed connections. For example, an IT support group that can rapidly reprovision laptops and software can reduce the downtime from losing access to those resources.

We can also reduce the number of interconnections between team members and the work items. For example, if our team members have broad skills, they can split the work items to reduce the number of dependencies across the work items. We can also limit the number of inter- and extra-team member interactions. This issue is critical within cross-team interactions. It's the reason so many scaled Scrum methodologies implement **ambassadors** or **network integration teams** to minimize cross-team interactions.

In a lean system, the ideal goal is to create a streamlined set of activities across a value stream, much like an assembly line, enabling work to flow through a set of independent activities in one direction and without the need to recycle back to a previous activity. It should be clear from the examples shown in *Figure 3.2* that the linear-sequential flows are much less complicated and more streamlined. It should also be clear that network density issues become increasingly necessary to resolve with the increasing growth of activities (nodes) in a value stream system.

So far, our sample system interactions are quite simple. Life is much more complicated in that each system interaction can have different types of impacts. Complex system interactions between elements are modeled and analyzed as **causal links**. But, before we get to that topic, let's take a moment to introduce the vocabulary of systems thinking.

Learning the vocabulary of systems thinking

The vocabulary of systems thinking is unique and not directly tied to Agile or Lean practices. But the concepts behind systems thinking are powerful and useful in helping teams collaborate in analyzing the elements and interrelationships within their large and complex business systems. The following list includes the basic terms of use in systems thinking and causal loop diagrams:

- **Systems**: These are complex structures of tangible and intangible things, principles, procedures, and social and political environments that collectively serve some purpose or function.

- **Elements**: This term refers to the collection of parts that make up a system. These could be tangible and intangible things, principles, procedures, or social and political environments that participate in and guide the system's behaviors.

- **Interconnections**: The relationships—including physical, informational, formal, or informal linkages—that bind elements together within the system.

- **Function**: The purpose, goal, or objective of a non-human system.

- **Purpose**: The purpose, goal, or objective of a human-based system.

- **Stocks**: These are tangible, quantifiable, and measurable variables within a system, subject to dynamic changes over time through a flow's actions. The term *element* implies a type of thing at any given time; the term *stock* implies attributes of the elements with observable values at specific points in time. For example, an element might be a value stream activity, and its stock might be work items or materials.

- **Flows**: These actions dynamically change the directions of stock within a system, as inflows and outflows.

- **Inflows**: These indicate a direction of flow that serves to increase the measurable amount of stock. Inflow displays have lines with arrows that point to the elements accumulating stock.

- **Outflows**: These indicate a direction of flow that serves to decrease the measurable amount of stock. Outflow displays have lines with arrows that point away from the elements with decrementing stocks.

- **Delays**: These occur when inflows are greater than outflows, resulting in an accumulation of stock. Displays of delays are indicated by writing the word *delay* on the arrow connecting elements, or a double hash mark striking through the connecting arrow.

- **Feedback loops**: These are mechanisms that adjust flows to either stabilize a system or reinforce a particular trend within the system.

- **Balancing feedback loops**: These provide information or resources that bring a system or elements into equilibrium and maintain them within the desired range.

- **Reinforcing feedback loops**: These provide information or resources that support a trend within a system, or support elements within a system. The trend can be either positive or negative.

- **Causal Loop Diagram (CLD)**: A method to visualize the interrelationships of elements (a.k.a. *variables*) within a system as nodes and linkages between nodes (a.k.a. *edges*).

- **Positive causal link**: This means that the cause-and-effect impact of two linked nodes changes the observed attributes in the same (positive) direction, increasing the value of the monitored attributes.

- **Negative causal link**: This means that the cause-and-effect impact of two linked nodes changes the observed attributes in the opposite (negative) direction.

- **Open systems**: These are characterized by having inflows and outflows external to the system—that is, things that can enter or leave the system.

- **Closed systems**: These are characterized by having no net flows in or out of the system—that is, the system is fully self-contained and balanced.

- **Labels**: Use labels on everything displayed within your causal diagrams so that reviewers know what the elements and links represent within your system model.

Now that you know the basic terms of systems thinking and causal loop diagraming, let's take a quick look at using them when analyzing an Agile-based development team as a system.

Visualizing the interrelationships of system elements

This section uses an example CLD from the previous book – *Scaling Scrum Across Modern Enterprises* – that describes a Scrum-based Sprint planning process (see *Figure 3.3*). This exercise aims not to explain the Sprint planning process but rather to show how the CLD modeling process works, using an Agile point of reference. Again, for those of you who want a more detailed understanding of using systems thinking and CLD techniques to evaluate the Lean-Agile process, I refer you to Scaled Scrum Across Modern Enterprises.

A Sprint Planning example is shown here:

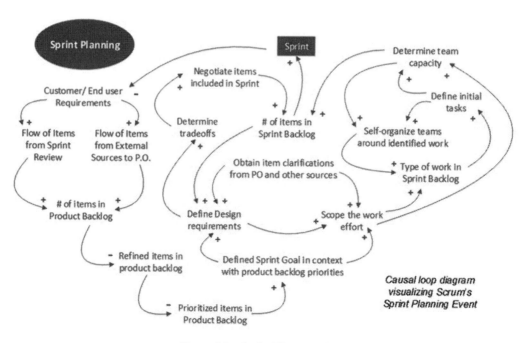

Figure 3.3 – Sprint Planning CLD

It's important to note that CLD arrows always close system cycles to show a reinforcing or balancing feedback loop. In other words, all CLD nodes connect back to the entry point to form a loop, no matter how large or complex the system, creating a reinforcing or balancing effect.

A reinforcing loop is a cycle in which changing a variable propagates through the system to increase or decrease a trend. In contrast, a balancing loop is a cycle in which the effect of changing a variable propagates through the loop and forces a response to counter the new trend. Our example of a CLD for the Scrum-based Sprint Planning process is a form of reinforcing loop, as work items entered into the Sprint Backlog decrements the number of work items in the Product Backlog.

In a CDL, we use lines to represent flows, and the arrows indicate the impact of these flows. For example, a positive arrow (+) indicates a *positive causal link* relationship that trends in the same direction, while negative arrows (-) indicate a *negative causal link*, or opposing trend.

In this model, the customer and end user requirements flow from a Sprint Review (a demo of the previous increments) or directly from external sources. The relationship is a positive causal link, as the trend is in the same direction. In other words, as customers and end users develop new requirements, they increase the flow of prospective work items.

In contrast, note the link between the number of items in the product backlog and the number of refined items in the product backlog, a negative causal link. This relationship suggests that the refinement process has a general trend to reduce the number of work items that flow out of the backlog.

Reading a CLD

Before we end this chapter, let's work our way around the Sprint Planning Process (displayed in *Figure 2.10* in the previous chapter). This exercise will help you understand how to assess the relationships described across the CLD model.

Sprint planning is part of Scrum-based Agile methodology. I previously noted that there are 17 CLD models in my previous book. However, the 17 CLD models span 3 distinct processes:

- Sprint Planning
- Project-to-product team transformations
- Enterprise implementations of Scrum

All three CLD models are related to analyzing IT functions, but each has a very different scope and set of objectives. For example, the Sprint Planning model is composed of five separate CLDs. The five CLDs break out loosely around specific areas of focus that the teams might want to analyze. These areas include the following:

- A CLD model of analyzing Product Backlog priorities

- An open CLD model of Product Backlog refinement activities

- A CLD model of design and work clarifications

- A CLD model of analyzing work against team capacity

- A CLD model of negotiations and trade-off activities

There is only one resulting Sprint Planning CLD model, but the team may prefer to break the work out along the lines of concern and build the Sprint planning CLD model incrementally. Let's now look at each of these sub-CLD models briefly.

CLD model of analyzing Product Backlog priorities

The goal of this CLD (see *Figure 3.4*) is to understand the elements involved in building a backlog of customer and end-user requirements. The model is shown here:

Figure 3.4 – CLD model of analyzing Product Backlog priorities

Customer and end-user requirements flow into or through the Sprint Review process and external processes beyond the scope of this Sprint Planning CLD model. The arrows *with* the positive (+) signs indicate a positive causal link, which indicates that the trend or impact moves in the same direction. In other words, the addition of requirements adds to the stock of items in the product backlog.

But note that this positive causal link does not mean the flow is only an additive process. The (+) and (−) signs on the arrows do not imply a mathematical addition or subtraction process, only whether the flow is reinforcing a trend, or not. As a result, the positive (+) flow as a relationship between elements also means a reduction in requirements. This leads to a reduction of the stock of items in the Product Backlog.

Open CLD model of Product Backlog refinement activities

The goal of this CLD (see *Figure 3.5*) is to understand the elements involved in refining the work items listed in the product backlog. To clarify, this means decomposing epics into user stories and understanding the development tasks. We can see this in the following figure:

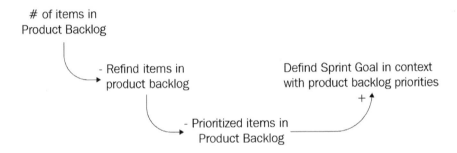

Figure 3.5 – Open CLD model of Product Backlog refinement activities

The example shown in *Figure 3.5* includes arrows with negative (-) trends, which means the relationships between elements are negative causal links between the number of items in the backlog and the number of refined product backlog items. There is a similar negative causal link between the number of refined product backlog items in the product backlog and the prioritized items in the product backlog.

It may be a bit difficult at first glance to understand what's going on, particularly for those who don't understand the details. The negative causal links indicate that as the node in which a link starts increases, the other node decreases, and vice versa. In other words, both the refinement and prioritization activities have an opposing effect on the stock of work items. This oppositional effect happens because there are limits on how much work the teams can take to refine and prioritize.

Suppose, for example, a customer wants a new feature included in the next release. The item is included in the product backlog as an epic or user story. The item must be refined to ensure the team fully understands the requirements, and whether they are a priority. The negative links indicate the number of refined item trends in the opposite direction from the number of initial items that go into the backlog.

The same trend occurs as the product owner decides which of the refined work items have a high priority. However, those items that have a high priority inform the Sprint Goal in the same direction. So, in other words, an increase in the number of high-priority work items increases the scope of the Sprint Goal. Likewise, if stocks of refined and prioritized work items dwindle, the scope of the Sprint Goal becomes smaller.

CLD model of design and work clarifications

The goal of the next CLD (see *Figure 3.6*) is to understand the elements involved in the CLD model of design and work clarifications. This CLD is a visualization of the work item design and scoping activities. Note that all relationships between elements have positive causal linkages:

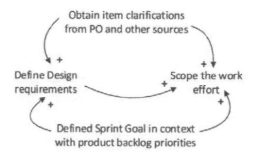

Figure 3.6 – CLD model of design and work clarifications

In this CLD, the team requires clarifications from the product owner and other sources, such as customers and end users, on the details of the requirements. Improved clarifying details improve the design and ability to scope the effort, and vice versa.

Note that we also have a positive causal linkage from another part of the model that describes the Sprint Goal in terms of priorities in the product backlog. Understanding the Sprint Goal leads to a better understanding of the design requirements and scope of the effort.

Finally, there is a positive causal link between the *Define Design requirements* element and the *Scope the work effort* element. As the team better understands the design, they can better understand the work scope in the upcoming Sprint.

CLD model of analyzing work against team capacity

This CLD (*see Figure 3.7*) aims to understand the elements involved in the CLD model of analyzing work against team capacity. Though this is a larger and more complex CLD, the concepts remain the same, and we just have to work our way through the linkages:

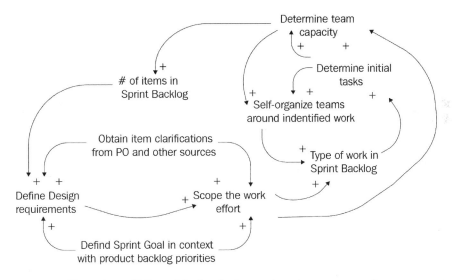

Figure 3.7 – CLD model of analyzing work against team capacity

Without seeing this part of the CLD in context with the entire Sprint Planning CLD, it isn't easy to see where we should start. However, we should start with the element titled *Defined Sprint Goal in context with product backlog priorities*. In the next subsection, we'll see how the interactions in this CLD exit to another CLD via the *# of items in the Sprint Backlog node*. Also, note that this CLD includes several smaller CLD loops. The activities are linked through their participation in evaluating team capacity against the desired product backlog priorities.

The importance of this CLD is that it defines the elements and interactions necessary to define the initial tasks in the context of team capacities and their ability to self-organize around the work planned for the Sprint. Ultimately, these relationships lead to decisions on the number (and type) of work items added into the Sprint backlog. Note that the items also reinforce the design criteria for the product's development within the Sprint.

CLD model of negotiations and trade-off activities

The goal of this CLD (see *Figure 3.8*) is to understand the CLD model of negotiations and trade-off activities. The elements and interactions in the previous CLD – analyzing work against team capacity – impacted design-related decisions. But note that the team has added a CLD loop to analyze design-related impacts against their capacity to determine whether trade-offs are required and need to be negotiated with the product owner. For example, there may be technical debt issues that need to be addressed before taking on some of the higher-priority work items:

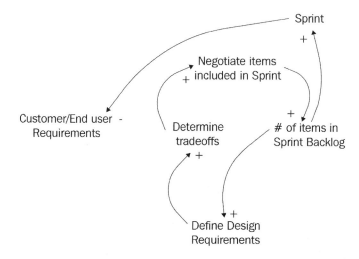

Figure 3.8 – CLD model of negotiations and trade-off activities

We've now completed our review of the entire Sprint Planning CLD and the topics for this chapter. The critical thing to know about CLD modeling is that there is no universal truth. What works in your value stream may not be appropriate or work in another organization's value streams, even when they have similar purposes.

We'll dive into value stream management basics as a Lean-oriented modeling and visualization tool in the next chapter. But, before we do that, let's summarize what you learned in this chapter. Then, take the quick test to see if you have any areas you need to review.

Summary

In this chapter, you learned that systems are much more complicated than the sum of their parts. The number of potential connections and interactions explodes with a geometric increase as the number of participating elements increases. You've learned how to use systems thinking to analyze the complexities of the elements and their relationships. You've also learned the vocabulary of systems thinking and how to use CLD as a modeling and visualization technique to work through complex interrelationships. Next, you got to use your newfound knowledge in systems thinking and CLD visualizations to review the Sprint Planning process. Finally, you learned that systems thinking takes a different approach to modeling and visualizing flows than value stream mapping.

With this knowledge, you now have the skills to assess the participating elements and their relationships within a system – relationships that contribute to complexities through their interactions. Systems thinking is an analytic approach to understanding the impacts, causes, and effects of interconnected and interacting elements. In contrast, value stream mapping is a technique to assess the current and future state of how work is done, then find ways to improve it.

Where systems thinking gives us the tools to discover and assess the impacts of interrelating elements, value stream mapping gives us the tools to improve work and information flows. We'll explore the components of value stream management in the next chapter.

Questions

1. What is the value of systems thinking?
2. What are the two types of relationships elements have within a system?
3. Why do we model the connections and interactions of elements within a system?
4. What is the purpose of closing loops in causal loop diagraming?
5. What is the least complex configuration of a system with multiple nodes?
6. What is the equation to determine the number of potential connections in a system?
7. Why do we try to reduce the number of actual connections?
8. What is the equation for calculating network densities?
9. What is the purpose of the arrows in a CLD diagram?
10. What is the difference between positive and negative causal links?

Further reading

- Rupp, C.G., (2020) *Scaling Scrum Across Modern Enterprises: Implement Scrum and Lean-Agile techniques across complex products, portfolios, and programs in large organizations*. Packt Publishing. Birmingham, England

4
Defining Value Stream Management

Value stream management (**VSM**) is fast becoming an essential capability in the **Information Technology** (**IT**) community, specifically as a means to assess and eliminate non-value-adding activities (waste) in your software delivery process. However, VSM is not a new concept. In this chapter, you will learn about the origins of VSM and its application to Lean-based production, supply chain, office, and IT-oriented processes.

VSM provides an approach to evaluate all organizational development and operational value streams systematically and continuously. VSM practices and tools help improve all value streams, not just those in IT. A VSM initiative aims to ensure that our value streams are most efficient, align with corporate strategies, and add customer-centric value with minimal waste, but there is no reason to learn multiple VSM strategies.

In this chapter, you will also learn the basic methods and tools of VSM. Specifically, you will learn about a generic eight-step VSM approach to plan, map, and sustain Lean improvements. Rather than learn an approach that's highly tailored to a specific set of VSM tools, this book aims to teach a proven approach, regardless of the value stream application or tools.

The VSM eight-step approach is summarized in the following screenshot:

1. Commit to lean.	6. a) Map future state – customer demand.
2. Choose value stream.	b) Map future state – continuous flow.
3. Learn about lean.	c) Map future state – Leveling.
4. Map current state.	7. Create Kaizen Plans.
5. Identify lean metrics.	8. Implement Kaizen plans.

Figure 4.1 – VSM eight-step approach

The reason for taking this generic approach to VSM is that, in our digital economy, IT solutions often support other organizational value streams, becoming inseparably linked in the process. Therefore, understanding the fundamentals of VSM is critical, as every IT-based VSM initiative must support an organization's broader objectives to build and sustain a Lean enterprise across all value streams.

Later, in *Part 2* of this book, we delve into actual case studies of IT-based VSM initiatives. Here, in this and the following two chapters, our focus is on learning the fundamental elements of VSM, regardless of the application.

In this chapter, we're going to cover the following main topics:

- Implementing Lean concepts
- Identifying value streams
- Applying VSM methods and tools
- Defining the eight steps of VSM

Technical requirements

There are no specific requirements for this chapter.

Implementing Lean concepts

VSM fundamentally involves implementing Lean concepts within an organization and making the Lean development and delivery processes a way of life. VSM is applied to streamline development and operations-oriented work to deliver customer-centric value more efficiently in modern Lean practices. In this context, IT-based development and operations activities are organizational value streams that similarly benefit from employing VSM capabilities.

Specifically, VSM supports an IT department's efforts to become Lean through the implementation of **continuous integration** (**CI**) and **continuous delivery** (**CD**) capabilities, often as part of a larger **DevOps** process integration, automation, and collaboration strategy. Put another way, the use of VSM to drive DevOps development and delivery capabilities is essentially an organization's Lean value stream implementation strategy for IT value delivery.

In their book *Value Stream Management: Eight Steps to Planning, Mapping, and Sustaining Lean Improvements*, the authors define VSM as follows:

"*Value Stream Management is a process for planning and linking initiatives through simple data capture and analysis.*" (Tapping, Luyster, Shuker, 2002, p.2)

Note that their definition of VSM is not limited to making Lean production improvements across IT value streams. In fact, these authors collaborated on three books that apply a reusable VSM methodology to manufacturing, to Lean administrative offices, and across healthcare value streams, and it is their eight-step methodology that is applied in *Part 2* of this book, *Implementing Value Stream Management (VSM) Methods and Tools*, to analyze, plan, and execute Lean improvements in a CI/CD pipeline flow use-case scenario. We'll introduce the eight steps of VSM in a later section within this chapter, *Applying VSM methods and tools*.

In our modern digital economy, IT supports virtually every organizational activity. Therefore, VSM practices cannot focus simply on improving IT value streams. Instead, IT-oriented VSM helps improve all value stream activities enterprise-wide. Moreover, since organizational value streams are often linked, we must improve customer delivery flows across all connected value streams.

Let's look at a quick example. A customer is interested in purchasing a customizable product in our scenario, so they go online to a vendor's website to check out the available options. While on the site, they decide what they want to purchase and submit the order. The order triggers other value stream activities to place the order, make and receive payments, update accounting systems, order replacement materials, execute production, and eventually execute the organization's downstream fulfillment or provisioning and support processes. Along the way, IT systems are initiating the processes from start to finish while ensuring the correct information and materials show up at the right time and in the right place. Thus, all organizational value streams are linked to some degree, with the IT value stream serving as an essential enabler.

In the *Further reading* section of this book, you can see a listing of books devoted to applying VSM to Lean production processes in manufacturing, Lean offices, Lean supply chains, and Lean IT value streams. In a truly Lean enterprise, all organizational value streams need to be improved continuously and coordinated with other linked value streams. That is the premise of VSM.

Implementing information flows

In a digital economy, every value stream has an information flow. In many cases, the digital value streams' materials are information elements (forms, graphics, **business intelligence** (**BI**), raw data, or information support services). In the previous paragraph, you learned that information flows are vital to support Lean production processes, but information flows are equally vital to support all frontend and backend value stream processes.

Frontend processes directly help the customer, while backend processes include all internal support activities that don't require face-to-face interactions. For example, frontend processes include sales support activities, either by people or via an online product information system. Likewise, an organization's customer support processes are examples of a frontend process. In contrast, examples of a **backend process** include supply and partner management practices and fulfillment.

So, in other words, the terms *frontend* and *backend* have nothing to do with their order within a product's life cycle. Instead, think of the term *frontend* as implying those processes are conducted in front of a customer, while *backend* processes occur behind the scenes.

However, in the lexicon of Lean terms, we use the terms *upstream* and *downstream* to indicate the relationships of activities in a product's life cycle, as illustrated in the following diagram. In Lean, the customer is always our focus, so the delivery of a product or service is the ultimate Lean process destination:

Figure 4.2 – Upstream versus downstream value stream activities

In this context, Lean value always flows downstream toward the customer, and any preceding activity is upstream. The same concept applies across each value stream. The activities furthest from the customer are always upstream from those performed closest to the customer.

Expanding on the upstream and downstream example depicted in *Figure 4.2*, the flow of value includes a combination of materials and information that accumulates with each succeeding value stream activity until it's ready for delivery as a product or service to a customer.

Defining types of value streams

The term *value stream* has expanded to include all value and non-value added activities within the business enterprise in a modern Lean context. Some value streams contribute directly to the development of products and services, while others focus on operations-oriented activities to deliver products and services.

The **Lean Enterprise Institute, Inc. (LEI)** defines value streams in this manner:

"All of the actions, both value-creating and non-value-creating, required to bring a product from concept to launch (also known as the development value stream) and from order to delivery (also known as the operational value stream). These include actions to process information from the customer and actions to transform the product on its way to the customer."

– From the Lean Lexicon, 5th edition

Note that the value stream definition includes the actions necessary to process information from the customer. Also, recall that Toyota originally referred to value stream mapping as *materials and information flow mapping*. In Lean, we strive to improve the flow of materials and information to deliver customer-centric value efficiently. In this chapter, you will learn why an IT-based strategy to facilitate VSM plays a critical role in implementing and sustaining Lean initiatives across an enterprise.

Modern VSM systems offer a set of methods and tools to map as-is and to-be activities, define the metrics for improvement, and monitor our progress against our performance objectives. In addition, analytical tools provide capabilities to evaluate cause and effect and simulate alternative business improvement strategies before making commitments and investments.

We will come back to understand better how VSM helps identify and improve value streams later in this chapter. But before we do that, let's first take a moment to understand the original and still important concepts behind value streams and VSM.

Employing VSM

VSM as a concept has been around for a while. Interestingly, James Martin, one of the IT leaders of the 1990s, applied the term *value stream* to software development practices in his book *The Great Transition: Using the Seven Disciplines of Enterprise Engineering to Align People, Technology, and Strategy* (Martin, 1995). Martin's book was published less than a year after James Womack and Daniel Jones initially coined the term in a *Harvard Business Review* article, *From Lean Production to the Lean Enterprise* (Womack and Jones, March-April 1994).

On page 104, Martin defines the term *value stream* as "*an end-to-end collection of activities that result from a 'customer', who may be the ultimate customer or an internal 'end-user' of the value stream.*"

> **Note**
>
> The **VSM** acronym for **value stream management** is identical to that used for value stream mapping. This duplication of acronyms is an unfortunate coincidence, as value stream mapping is a subset of the overall VSM process. The **VSM** acronym, as used in this book, always means value stream management, to maintain clarity. To further minimize the potential for confusion, this book will always spell out the term *value stream mapping* or shorten it to *VS map* or *VS mapping*.

While James Martin defined the term *value stream*, he tended to use the term *value stream reinvention* when describing the activities' processes to improve value streams. Martin took issue with using the term *process* and the notion of **business process reengineering** (**BPR**).

In the first case, Martin believed the word *process* is too generic and too far removed from the Lean concepts of adding customer-centric value. His primary issue with the term *BPR* was that he felt most of his era's processes were never *engineered* in the first place. Instead, most business processes evolved to support hierarchical business structures, where the activities often had more to do with protecting organizational fiefdoms and authorities than improving efficiencies.

Other authors later introduced the term *VSM* in their books, including the following:

- *Value Stream Management. Eight Steps to Planning, Mapping, and Sustaining Lean Improvements. Don Tapping, Tom Luyster*, and *Tom Shuker* (*Lean Production, 2002*).

- *Value Stream Management for the Lean Office. Eight Steps to Planning, Mapping, and Sustaining Lean Improvements in Administrative Areas. Don Tapping* and *Tom Shuker* (*Lean for the Office, 2003*).

- *Value Stream Management. Strategy and Excellence in the Supply Chain. Peter Hines, Richard Lamming, Dan Jones, Paul Cousins, Nick Rich* (*Prentice Hall/Pearson Education. Harlow, England, 2000*).

Tom Shuker was kind enough to grant the rights to use their eight-step process for this chapter as an example of how to implement a VSM strategy across an organization. The eight-step VSM process helps organizations simplify the fundamental Lean concepts of demand, flow, and leveling via Lean planning, and helps implement the overall process to accelerate, coordinate, and sustain Lean efforts.

Yes—this is a book about the application of VSM-to-IT transformations. But ask yourself this: in a digital economy, which business value stream exactly are we improving? To answer this question, let's revisit James Martin's original and seminal writings on this subject.

Identifying value streams

James Martin fundamentally understood why a business organization invests in IT to implement and sustain superior business processes that support its value streams. Martin was ahead of his time, but his ideas persist—for example, **The Open Group Architecture Framework** (**TOGAF**) still employs James Martin's value stream concepts in their *Business Architecture* standard (*Open Group Guide, Value Streams*, January 2017).

But what exactly did James Martin mean when he employed the term *value stream*? Martin was not merely looking for ways to improve IT development and operational processes. Instead, his goal was to help organizations restructure their value streams and implement software applications to support, sustain, and continuously improve value delivery across all value streams.

In his book, James Martin cites research from a study published by T. H. Davenport titled *Process Innovation*, which identified an average of 14 value streams across 5 large enterprise companies. The companies included **IBM**, **Ameritech**, **Dow Chemical**, **Xerox**, and a major—though unidentified—insurance company (Harvard Business School Press: Boston, 1993).

Martin synthesized the works found in Davenport's paper to identify 17 typical value streams (Martin, 1995, page 107). His list of 17 conventional business value streams includes the following:

- **Customer engagement**: Acquiring customers, determining their needs; selling, ensuring that they are pleased

- **Order fulfillment**: Receiving orders, fulfilling orders, collecting payment

- **Customer services**: Providing customers with services such as help using the product, planning, and consulting

- **Manufacturing**: Production of goods, maintenance of inventory, interaction with suppliers

- **Procurement services**: Assistance in supplier selection, contracting, and management

- **Product-design engineering**: Designing products and facilities for manufacturing them

- **Research**: Exploration of potentially valuable science and technology

- **Marketing**: Determining what customers need, which products to build, which features are needed; advertising

- **Market-information capture**: Acquisition of information about sales; locating intelligence about the competition

- **Product maintenance**: Repairing products and preventative maintenance on customer sites

- **Legal department**: Solving legal problems; writing contracts

- **IT- application development**: Developing and modifying systems and software

- **IT infrastructure**: Building the corporate-wide network, database, and facilities for distributed computing

- **Human resources (HR)**: Assistance in recruiting, training, compensation, care planning

- **Leased and capital asset management**: Management of buildings and capital resources

- **Financial management**: Accounting, negotiating with banks, cash management

- **Enterprise engineering**: Designing, implementing, and improving value streams; engineering the enterprise learning processes

Now that we have a better understanding of typical business-oriented value streams, it's essential to understand how we establish their boundaries and their interfaces.

Establishing value stream boundaries

Each value stream has specific starting and ending activities that establish its boundaries. This concept is so important that some in the **business architecture** community refer to their value streams by their start and end activities (for example, **Prospect to Order** and **Order to Delivery** value streams). James Martin provides examples of start and end activities for selected value streams.

The following table shows a list of value stream naming conventions from Martin's book (Martin, 1995, page 108, exhibit 7.3):

To clarify what the value stream is, its start and finish activities can be named.		
Order acquisition	Prospect, lead	Order
Order fulfillment	Customer order	Delivery
Procurement	Requirements determination	Payment
Mortgage request	Inquiry	Resolution
Manufacturing	Procurement	Shipment
Product design	Concept	Prototype
Software application	Concept	Cutover
Strategy development	Market requirements	Business strategy
Customer communications	Customer inquiries	Customer interest in products
Claims processing	Accident report	Claim payment

Figure 4.3 – VS naming conventions

Now that you understand how to apply value stream boundaries and naming conventions, let's look at how value stream improvements help deliver business value.

Improving business value

It's important to remember that James Martin wrote his book *The Great Transition* when virtually all businesses were still in the early stages of employing IT to support their critical business processes. Don Tapscott coined the term *digital economy* in his book titled *The Digital Economy: Promise and Peril in the Age of Networked Intelligence* in 1995, which was the same year *The Great Transition* was published. But James Martin and others in the BPR and **business process improvement** (**BPI**) community already understood the importance of redesigning or incrementally improving business processes to take advantage of IT's new capabilities.

Companies must develop more efficient, faster, and responsive organizational value streams in a digital economy, and Martin understood that its IT function had to support those efforts. Martin's view of value stream reinvention was to replace traditional cross-functional and siloed business processes "*with a new workflow that is fast, simple, automated where possible, and performed by a small team (or person) sharply focused on pleasing the customer*" (Martin, 1995, page 64).

James Martin further notes that value stream reinvention is an improvement strategy that seeks to answer several fundamental questions, such as the following:

- What are the organization's value streams?
- Who are the value stream's customers?
- What do those customers want?
- What do we need to do to delight those customers?

As IT specialists working in a digital economy, we must ask ourselves this fundamental question: *How do we employ IT and software applications to support an organization's customer-centric value streams as efficiently, cost-effectively, and quickly as possible?*

From the perspective of Lean, the answer is multifaceted and not extremely difficult to understand at a conceptual level: *An IT organization supports the automation and integration of organizational value stream activities while also improving the accuracy and timeliness of value stream information flows. In many cases, IT also supports the implementation of digital features and functions within physical products.*

We now understand the importance of leveraging IT to improve the delivery of business value. Let's now move on to understand why an organization's chief executives must drive the effort.

Leading the change

Lean strategies are not easy to implement. Lean development and delivery activities often require some degree of structural changes to an organization and its facilities, the implementation of new business processes and equipment, the development of new skills, and investment in IT. Only the organization's chief or **line-of-business (LOB)** executives can authorize such changes.

In support of enterprise-scale Lean initiatives, making informed IT investments in skills and tools is a primary topic of this book. Unfortunately, changing organizational structures, developing new skills, and investing in new IT methods and tools remains difficult. There are innumerable technology and product options to investigate, most requiring additional time and resources devoted to configuration and integration tasks.

These are the areas where leadership must step up. As with other enterprise Lean initiatives, only executive leadership can direct a VSM strategy and make the necessary tooling, infrastructure, integration, and configuration investments. Adding DevOps into the mix increases those investment costs. We'll get to that topic (that is, investments in DevOps tools, infrastructure, integration, and configurations) later, in *Chapter 6, Launching the VSM Initiative (VSM Steps 1-3)*.

CI, CD, and DevOps capabilities have evolved to the point where an IT department can better support the ideas promoted by James Martin back in the 1990s; plus, VSM offers a set of methods and tools to guide and help sustain an organization's Lean transformations. Nevertheless, all these capabilities require investments, and executive leadership must gain sufficient knowledge to make informed investment decisions.

You may not be a chief executive or a LOB executive, but you can still help provide education, thought leadership, and support in whatever position or role you have within the organization. An organization's success with its Lean initiatives depends on everyone's participation and support.

For the sake of argument, we'll assume the organization has executive-level support and the willingness to make the necessary structural alignments, install trained mentors and coaches, and invest in the necessary technology and tools. The next question, then, is: *How to initiate and execute a continuing VSM strategy?* That is the topic of the final section of this chapter. But before we get to that subject, let's take a quick look at an essential VSM visualization and analysis tool, **value stream mapping**.

Mapping the value stream

The purpose of this section is to explain the importance of value stream mapping. Later, in *Chapter 7, Mapping the Current State (VSM Step 4)*, you will learn how to create a value stream map, a technique to assess current (*as-is state*) and future (*to-be state*) processes. Value stream mapping helps the VSM team evaluate the scope of work required to transition to a desired future state of streamlined value stream activities, minimal waste, and customer-centric value. We will continue to use value stream mapping to help guide and prioritize our CI activities.

Toyota originated value stream mapping techniques, but they referred to the practice as *materials and information flow mapping*. In other words, Toyota understood that even when analyzing manufacturing processes, the improvement of information flows was every bit as important as improving material flows.

Timely and accurate information is required to support the material flows within a manufacturing organization. If information is not flowing correctly, production processes are delayed when the right materials do not arrive at the right time and in the right amounts to support the Lean production processes. Of course, customer order information must flow with the materials to ensure the fabrication of the correct set of products for each customer.

James Martin was also an early proponent of mapping value streams, and he devoted an entire chapter to the subject of value stream mapping in *Chapter 8* of his book *The Great Transition* (Martin, 1995). However, Martin's approach precedes the modern value stream diagramming techniques introduced by Mike Rother and John Shook in their book, *Learning to See* (Rother, Shook, 1999).

This book teaches the modern value stream mapping approaches set down by Rother and Shook and later updated by Karen Martin and Mike Osterling in their book *Value Stream Mapping: How to Visualize Work and Align Leadership for Organizational Transformation* (Martin, Osterling, 2014). Modern value stream maps provide a combination of activity and information flow data necessary to assess the state of Leanness across the value stream. In contrast, James Martin's value streams incorporate a fairly traditional process flow diagramming technique.

Whichever modeling techniques your organization may prefer, make sure it's a standardized approach and that everyone is trained on the techniques employed. Otherwise, the VSM team can expect issues in their communications, interpretations, and analysis.

At this point in our discussions on value streams, it's essential to understand this fundamental concept: **all value streams represent an end-to-end flow of value across an organization**. In this context, a Lean value stream operates similarly to the mass production concepts behind Henry Ford's first Model T assembly lines. A critical difference is that Lean incorporates pull-oriented production and order management production processes versus a push-based production control strategy. Forgetting the concepts of push-versus-pull production control strategies for a moment, mass production and Lean production share the notion of synchronizing and automating flows.

For example, a customer order documents a new requirement, which initiates the production or delivery of a product. The construction follows a value stream flow around an initial component, such as the frame of a car in the previously mentioned Model T car production example. Another example is the construction of a frame or chassis for a laptop or server at the start of a computer-system assembly process. In either example, as the frames traverse the activities along the production line, additional components of value are added to the product in the form of materials, parts, and information. In the lexicon of Lean, we add value to a product at every step along the value stream process.

The following screenshot depicts a display of a modern automobile assembly line. Despite the use of robotic technology and other automation capabilities, the basic concepts behind Henry Ford's original mass production concept as an end-to-end and synchronized process remain:

Figure 4.4 – Automobile assembly line

This book is not about how to implement Lean processes in manufacturing—there are many other good sources for that type of information. However, we will discuss the application of VSM to development-oriented processes, of which an assembly line is an example. Additionally, we will also discuss the use of VSM to support operations-oriented value streams, which have more to do with front-office and back-office processes.

As noted previously, front-office operational processes are customer-facing, while back-office operational processes are typically administrative. As with development and operations-oriented value streams, all business processes can be made Lean and improved by applying VSM methods and tools.

Having used the terms *front office* and *back office*, please note that you may very well decide there is no such thing in your organization to evaluate the activities that add value from your customers' perspective. Value streams are not bound by organizational hierarchies, skills, or business functions. Value streams are an end-to-end set of activities required to deliver value from an initial request through delivery. Their customers can be either internal or external to the organization.

In the next chapter, we explore how to implement VSM practices as a structured process consisting of eight steps. However, before moving on to that chapter, let's first take a quick look at the eight VSM steps for planning, mapping, and sustaining Lean practices.

Applying VSM methods and tools

Every VSM tool vendor has its unique VSM process, usually tailored to its business origins and its software tools' focus or strength. We don't need software tools to implement VSM capabilities, though they are a huge enabler. Still, before we invest in VSM tools, we must first learn the basic concepts and approaches behind the implementation of VSM practices.

VSM implementations, as described in this book, follow an eight-step process outlined by Don Tapping, Tom Luyster, and Tom Shuker in their *Value Stream Management* books (Tapping, Luyster, Shuker, 2002; Tapping, Shuker, 2003). Specifically, the eight steps walk an organization through a VSM process to plan, map, and sustain Lean improvements.

The following screenshot introduces the eight VSM steps:

1. Commit to lean.	6. a) Map future state – customer demand.
2. Choose value stream.	b) Map future state – continuous flows.
3. Learn about lean.	c) Map future state – leveling.
4. Map current state.	7. Create Kaizen plans.
5. Identify lean metrics.	8. Implement kaizen plans.

Figure 4.5 – Eight-step VSM process to plan, map, and sustain Lean practices

In contrast to Tapping's, Luyster's, and Shuker's books, whose focus lay in Lean management, Lean healthcare, and Lean offices, this book focuses on applying VSM to IT. However, *please note* that IT touches on everything going on within an organization in a digital economy. Moreover, as James Martin indicates, IT's role is to support an organization's process and value stream reinvention through Lean initiatives. Therefore, *any VSM initiative is likely to include planning, mapping, improvement, and sustainment activities as a participatory value stream, but not necessarily as the primary value stream.*

The preceding paragraph makes a critical point. Almost all modern VSM tools focus on modeling the DevOps process to show concepts. Improving the DevOps value stream is important. However, the more considerable benefits of VSM come from linking DevOps activities in support of enterprise Lean initiatives outside the IT function, including both operations and development-oriented value streams.

Defining the eight steps of VSM

Tom Shuker was kind enough to allow me to incorporate their **eight-step VSM process** for this book. Before we end this chapter and get into the details of executing their VSM strategy, we'll take a quick look at how Tapping and Shuker defined their eight steps for planning, mapping, and sustaining Lean improvements, as follows:

1. **Commit to Lean** (*Step 1*): A successful Lean initiative requires executive leadership and buy-in from employees and stakeholders. Everyone involved in the VSM initiative must understand the importance of Lean practices to provide a more sustainable business through value delivery. The goal of Lean is to extend the value of HR and not eliminate jobs or take shortcuts.

2. **Choose value stream** (*Step 2*): We can't implement and improve Lean practices organization-wide overnight. It takes time and effort to identify and implement value stream improvements, with priorities based on the work that adds the most value for the lowest costs. Moreover, the VSM team keeps identifying and working on new improvement priorities across the product's life.

3. **Learn about Lean** (*Step 3*): VSM is all about improving Lean practices across the organization's value streams. So, all VSM team members and the employees assigned to work within a value stream must have superior knowledge of the day-to-day practices of operating Lean production systems.

4. **Map current state** (*Step 4*): It's dangerous to begin to adjust a system before fully understanding how it operates. We need to understand how our work flows across the value stream, how much of our work is value-adding, and how much time is spent on value-added activities versus waiting. Finally, we need to identify other forms of waste that add to our costs without adding value. These are the goals when mapping the current state of our development or operations-oriented business practices.

5. **Identify Lean metrics** (*Step 5*): With the current value stream map completed, the VSM team turns its attention to identifying metrics that can help the organization achieve its business goals. We can't evaluate our future VSM efforts' success if we don't first identify our customers' needs, potential areas of waste, and our value stream's productivity goals. Meeting customer needs and eliminating waste provides the surest path to lower costs and obtaining a business-sustaining product price.

6. **Map future state** (*Step 6a*)—**Customer demand**: This is the first of three phases to build our plan for a desired future state. The goal is to assess customer demand for our products and services. In this mapping exercise, we input the previously identified Lean metrics for acceptable quality, demand in terms of units, and desired lead times.

7. **Map future state** (*Step 6b*)—**Continuous flow**: This is the second phase in future state mapping. The goal here is to standardize how work is performed and figure out how to organize the flow of work, materials, parts, and information to move continuously. In many if not most cases, it may be necessary to move equipment and office cubicles to affect better flows. Information systems are another critical enabler to help establish the efficient flow of information across value stream activities. Steps should also be taken to level the flow of work by minimizing variances between activity setup, changeover, and cycle times. Finally, we should decide which production control strategies to implement, such as **Just-in-Time (JIT)**, **First In, First Out (FIFO)**, and Kanban.

8. **Map future state** (*Step 6c*)—**Leveling**: This is the final phase of future state mapping. At this stage, we should have installed Lean practices across our value stream and minimized the more critical elements of waste affecting our productivity. We now need to implement strategies to level the flow of customer demand. This VSM work involves implementing pull-based strategies to minimize excessive queuing and waiting, reduce lot sizes to minimize queues and wait times associated with batch processes, and implement our value stream's delivery and pickup systems—that is, Kanban Cards or Kanban folders, and work items.

9. **Create Kaizen plans** (*Step 7*): VSM implements Lean-oriented changes, both large and small in scale. A Kaizen plan outlines our strategies for continuously improving our development and operations-oriented value streams, but many of the Lean-oriented investments require significant investments that the VSM team cannot authorize. Moreover, the scope of planned changes may require multiple planning horizons to implement, and their Kaizen plans may evolve over time. Therefore, the VSM team needs to create a change plan (Kaizen plan) to make visible and manage the planned scope of change.

   A key differentiator between Lean and Agile is that Lean evaluates all potential areas for improvement, regardless of the investments, authorities, time, and resources required. In contrast, Agile retrospectives tend to focus on what the small Agile team can authorize and accomplish over the next Sprint iteration.

   Both Lean and Agile practitioners understand the importance of continuous change. Still, VSM emphasizes much longer-term planning horizons and potentially includes changes that require more capital investments than those contemplated in Agile-based retrospectives.

   Finally, requirements, issues, and priorities change over time, therefore Kaizen plans need to be periodically reviewed and updated. Creating and modifying your Kaizen plans are the primary activities of this step.

10. **Implement Kaizen plans** (*Step 8*): Finally, we need to implement whatever Kaizen plans we created. Additionally, we need to review and update them as necessary, but frequently. One constant in business is continuous change, so we need to continually improve our Lean practices and maintain alignment with our customers' needs. We also need to continually evaluate how we plan to improve our value stream activities by discovering and eliminating additional waste.

Now that we've introduced the eight essential steps to plan, map, and sustain Lean improvements, let's take a closer look at what goes on in each step, starting with the commitment to Lean. That is the topic of the next chapter.

Summary

This ends the introductory chapter to VSM. You have learned that VSM provides an approach to evaluate all development and operational value streams methodically and continuously. The goal of VSM is to ensure an organization remains in alignment with corporate strategies and adds customer-centric value.

You've also learned VSM is not a new concept and that the concepts and practices support the implementation and sustainment of Lean production practices across an organization's value streams. Organizations typically have many value streams. James Martin, an IT leader, provided a comprehensive discussion on the need for an end-to-end reinvention of business processes in the form of value streams. Martin was also an early proponent of value stream mapping, though his approach preceded the modern format we'll use in *Chapter 6, Launching the VSM Initiative (VSM Steps 1-3)*, on mapping and improving value streams.

Finally, you can now identify the eight VSM steps to plan, map, and sustain Lean improvements across your value streams. In the next chapter, we move on to learn how to execute the steps associated with VSM planning, including making a commitment to Lean, choosing a value stream for your VSM initiative, and learning about Lean.

Questions

To enhance your learning experience, please take a few moments to answer these 10 questions:

1. What is the primary or fundamental purpose of VSM?

2. How did Toyota refer to its value stream mapping activities, and what's the significance of this?

3. What is the difference between upstream and downstream in a Lean production context?

4. True or false: Value streams always include both value-creating and non-value-creating activities.

5. How did James Martin define value streams?

6. What are the two types of value streams?

7. What are the eight steps of VSM?

8. What are the five elements critical to establishing a solid foundation when committing to a VSM initiative?

9. Which well-known principle or law helps guide your VSM decision-making process?

10. What is a good naming convention standard and approach for identifying value streams?

Further reading

- *Martin, J. (1995). The Great Transition. Using the Seven Disciplines of Enterprise Engineering to Align People, Technology, and Strategy. American Management Association, now a division of HarperCollins Leadership. New York, NY.*

- *Womack, J. P., Jones, D. T. (March-April 1994). From Lean Production to the Lean Enterprise. By James P. Womack and Daniel T. Jones. Harvard Business Review.* https://hbr.org/1994/03/from-lean-production-to-the-lean-enterprise *Accessed June 26, 2021.*

- *Open Group Guide. Value Streams (January 2017).* (must register to access) https://publications.opengroup.org/downloadable/download/link/id/MC45NDQ2MjkwMCAxNjA4MzM2NjcwNzM2ODYwNzU1OTU2MjUx/ *Accessed December 2020.*

- *Tapping, D., Luyster, T., Shuker, T. (2002) Value Stream Management. Eight Steps to Planning, Mapping, and Sustaining Lean Improvements. Productivity Press. New York, NY.*

- *Tapping, D., Luyster, T., Shuker, T. (2003) Value Stream Management for the Lean Office. Eight Steps to Planning, Mapping, and Sustaining Lean Improvements. Productivity Press. New York, NY.*

- *Tapping, D., Koslowski, S., Archbold, L., Speri, T. (2009) Value Stream Management For Lean Healthcare. Four Steps to Planning, Mapping, Implementing, and Controlling Improvements in all kinds of Healthcare Environments. MCS Media, Inc. Chelsea, MI.*

- *Gregory, L. (September 2018). Toyota's Organizational Structure: An Analysis.* http://panmore.com/toyota-organizational-structure-analysis *Accessed 28 December 2020.*

- *Ohno, T., Bodek, N. (1988) Toyota Production System: Beyond large-scale production. Productivity Press. Routledge/Taylor & Francis Group. An Informa Business. London, England.* (Originally published in Japan in 1978)

- *Hines, P., Lamming, R., Jones, D., Cousins, P., Rich, N. (2000) Value Stream Management. Strategy and Excellence in the Supply Chain, Prentice Hall/Pearson Education. Harlow, England.*

- *Martin, K., Osterling, M. (2014) Value Stream Mapping: How to Visualize Work and Align Leadership for Organizational Transformation. McGraw-Hill Education. New York, NY.*

- *Rother, M., Shook, J. (2003) Learning to See. Value-Stream Mapping to Create Value and Eliminate Muda. The Lean Enterprise Institute. Cambridge, MA.*

- *Jones, D., Womack, J. (2011) Seeing the Whole Value Stream, 2nd Edition. Lean Enterprise Institute. Cambridge, MA.*

- *Brenton, F. (2019) What Is Value Stream Management? A Primer For Enterprise Leadership.* `https://www.forbes.com/sites/forbestechcouncil/2019/07/08/what-is-value-stream-management-a-primer-for-enterprise-leadership/?sh=50a0be77b678` Accessed December 2020.

5
Driving Business Value through a DevOps Pipeline

In the previous four chapters, you learned there are many different ways to define the term *value* and the importance of understanding its use in context. Therefore, we spent some time learning about these terms to ensure that we have a common semantic understanding when communicating about using **value stream management** (**VSM**) and DevOps to deliver customer-centric value.

You learned how Lean and Agile practices complement each other to help an organization deliver customer-centric value. You also learned why we need to take a systems-thinking view to improve value delivery within large and complex organizations.

This chapter explains how and why IT organizations represent very complex systems across two primary functions: **development** and **operations**. In a traditional IT shop, the development and operations organizations function as separate departments with different activities, and each has a different focus and culture. This type of separation of people and responsibilities only adds to the complexity of the IT organization.

This chapter will explain why this functional split in the IT organization can become a problem. You will also learn about a collaboration and integration strategy that can be used to resolve such issues. That strategy is called **DevOps**, which is a concatenation of development and operations.

The topics presented in this chapter are a necessary precursor to our discussions on the implementation of VSM tools and methods, which we'll cover in *Section 2* of this book.

In this chapter, we're going to cover the following topics:

- Breaking down barriers
- Improving flows with DevOps pipelines
- Understanding virtualization
- Defining **continuous integration (CI)**
- Defining **continuous delivery (CD)**
- Enabling CI/CD and DevOps pipeline flows
- Understanding the scope of DevOps
- Integrating **IT service management (ITSM)**
- Moving beyond projects and into products

In this last chapter of *Section 1* of this book, you will gain an appreciation of the disparate technologies, portfolio-level investments, and genuine complexities involved in developing a competitive DevOps pipeline capability. Let's start this introduction to DevOps by understanding the business drivers that led to its evolution in the software industry.

Breaking down barriers

Nowadays, with a quick search on the internet, you will find many industry analysts and other commentators who will agree that DevOps has become the table stakes to effectively compete in our modern digital economy (Dietrich, 2019). Those organizations that master the integration and automation of tools of activities across the IT value streams of development and operations have orders of magnitude better velocity in software delivery and better quality and efficiency.

Just as Lean practices transformed the competitive landscape in manufacturing and other services-based companies, DevOps has similarly transformed the IT industry. Specifically, DevOps pipelines implement a software development strategy that is equivalent to the Lean production flow concepts in manufacturing and other industries. As a result, those organizations that effectively implement DevOps pipelines have significant competitive advantages when responding to new market opportunities, evolving competitive pressures, and changing customer needs.

Moreover, DevOps is an amalgamation of Lean and Agile practices or, for short, Lean-Agile. Agile provides values and principles to guide customer-centric software development practices; Lean production concepts provide proven approaches to eliminate waste and achieve efficient software value delivery. As you will learn in *Section 2* of this book, modern VSM methods and tools enable organizations to implement Lean transformations across their IT value streams.

DevOps concepts began to emerge in 2008. Specifically, Andrew Shafer and Patrick Debois were given credit for initially discussing these concepts in a private meeting during the Agile Conference held in Toronto that same year. DevOps then became popularized a bit later when Patrick Debois organized the first *DevOpsDays* conference, held in Belgium in 2009.

It's important to note that DevOps began as a collaboration strategy in **Agile systems administration**. The goal was to overcome conflicts between Agile-based software development teams, who could now deliver new software products and features with increased frequency (that is, increased *velocity*), and the traditionally risk-averse system administration organizations.

CI capabilities, which we'll introduce later in this chapter (see *Defining CI*), allowed developers to increase the velocity of application delivery to the IT operations' function. However, there was very little in the way of integrated processes or cultures of collaboration to facilitate the frequent releases of new software products into an organization's test and production environments.

In a traditional IT organization, development and operations are two separate functions. They have different goals and objectives. They also have different mindsets. Software developers thrive in a world of change, delivering new features and capabilities continuously. That's a good thing because customers and users want new features that add value, and the sooner the better.

On the other hand, systems administrators don't care for change because they are responsible for ensuring all networks, systems, and applications are running, stable, and secure. In short, changes can break their systems, infrastructures, and security. And their hesitancy is a good thing, as we need our networks and software to work and be secure.

Think of the difference in cultures like this: developers thrive in making changes, and they are rewarded when they release new functionality that supports the needs of customers and users. In contrast, any changes in operations are scary – as those changes can break their deployed networks, systems, and applications. Even worse than this is that the systems administrators will receive the blame when the systems go down, and they alone feel all of the pressure until the systems are back up and running.

Sharing accountability

First and foremost, DevOps is a communications and collaboration strategy. In this context, DevOps' objective is to get the two teams working together in a coordinated manner, with information flowing both ways. Developers need to know why their new releases fail in production. In contrast, an operations team needs detailed information regarding installation configurations, system administration and support information, and whether the product releases have been thoroughly tested via systems testing, security testing, performance testing, load testing, and stress testing. However, such collaborations are nearly impossible when the development and operations teams remain separated by responsibilities, desired outcomes, and their differing measurements of success.

Development teams frequently want to put out new releases that they've built and tested and believe are ready for release. But since the operations team traditionally works apart from the development team, the operations group will be reluctant to put out a new release until they have confirmed the product won't fail or cause other issues with systems configurations, performance, or security in their production environments.

While the development team implements the new changes, the operations department is held accountable for ensuring everything works properly in deployment. For example, the operations team might conduct tests, such as **user acceptance testing (UAT)**, that should have been completed earlier in development. If the software fails, the operations team has to go back to development with bug and defect lists, and then try to make them a development priority.

Other tests, such as **performance testing**, **load testing**, **stress testing**, and **systems testing**, require the duplication of the organization's production environments. If the development team cannot fully replicate the production environments in their testing environments, they might fail to discover potential problems with scaling the applications. That means performance and integration issues might not be uncovered until after the application has been moved into production. Even then, it could take some time before a set of events triggers a failure. As a result, it might look to be a failure of the operations team when, in fact, it was a failure to thoroughly test the system in a production-like environment.

Ideally, the development or operations team will build a preproduction or staging environment to mimic its production environments. When that's not possible, the operations team could be forced to run a limited set of tests directly on their production environments, and by doing so, hope for the best but be prepared for the worst.

All of the operation team's testing takes time to plan and execute. In addition to this, those tests won't occur until after the development team has already moved on to develop new features and functions during their next set of sprints. Any bugs or defects discovered by the operations team have to flow back into the product backlog for reprioritization and scheduling, potentially delaying the release of new features that customers are expecting. Moreover, the responsibility and blame for any failed releases tend to shift to the operations department.

This cultural logjam cannot be fixed if the development and operations teams remain separated in any fashion. Leveraging the Lean-Agile concepts you learned in *Chapter 2, Building on a Lean-Agile Foundation*, the organization needs to integrate, streamline, and orchestrate the flow of work and information across both the IT development and operations groups.

Organizations must remove the barriers that keep these functions apart. For smaller organizations, eliminating communication barriers can be as simple as getting the two teams to communicate together well before each release. However, larger organizations might have multiple product lines, multiple software product development teams, and even different operations support teams. In those situations, communication, integration, and synchronization challenges grow exponentially. The only practical way to remove the wedges between development and operations in larger organizations is to integrate the two functions within product teams or product lines and have everyone on the product teams be equally responsible for each release's velocity and quality.

The practical ramifications of such a strategy are that the activities across development and operations must be linked, streamlined, and synchronized to each product under development. In other words, development and operations need to interoperate as a single product team.

Product team members share accountability for each new feature release from ideation to delivery. The product teams are also accountable for effectively supporting operations-oriented activities across the product's life.

Another set of issues arises from the two IT organizations – development and operations – having different velocities. Traditionally, an operations team requires more time to manage the risks associated with deploying a new release into the organization's production environments. This mismatch in velocities creates a bottleneck that slows down the release of new features into the organization's production environments.

In the next section, you will learn how modern **CI** and **CD** capabilities address these issues.

Improving flows with CI/CD pipelines

In *Chapter 6, Launching the VSM Initiative (VSM Steps 1-3),* through to *Chapter 11, Identifying VSM Tool Types and Capabilities,* we will use the concepts you learn in this section as a use case to introduce how you can use an eight-step VSM methodology to improve work and information flow across a CI/CD pipeline. However, before we get to that use case, we need to have a basic understanding of the purpose of a CI/CD pipeline, its component activities, and the complexities of implementing a fully integrated and automated toolchain. Those are the topics that we'll cover in this subsection.

CI/CD toolchains enable the pipeline flows of work items and information during the software development life cycle. Another helpful way to think about CI/CD pipelines is that they enable the implementation of Lean-oriented production concepts across IT value streams. Before we discuss the components of a CI/CD pipeline, let's review the purposes of its two constituent elements:

- **CI**: This provides the infrastructure that allows several software developers or even different development teams to implement and test code changes to a software product under development.
- **CD**: This enables the automated provisioning of development, test, and production environments as **configurable items**.

There are three critical capabilities and related tools that support the implementation of CI/CD pipelines. These include the following:

- **Configuration management (CM)**
- Task management/automation
- Containerization

Let's take a look at these three enabling technologies and tools in more detail.

Tooling to establish CI/CD pipelines

CM helps us to track and manage the proper versions of CI that make up each software release. A configurable item is a system component or associated information artifact that has been uniquely identified for version and change control and identification purposes. **Source control management** (**SCM**) tools help developers maintain version control of source code and other CIs.

Git and GitHub are two of the better-known SCM tools. But there are other tools, such as **Apache Subversion** (**SVN**), Azure DevOps Server (formerly Team Foundation Server), Bazaar, Bitbucket Server, CVS, GitLab, Gerrit, Kallithea, Mercurial, Monotone, Perforce Helix Core, Rational ClearCase, and **Revision Control System** (**RCS**).

Task management tools facilitate the automation of CI/CD and DevOps workflows. In both CI/CD and DevOps platforms, the software industry refers to automated workflows as pipelines. Typically, a CI/CD workflow automates the pipeline activities of planning, designing, developing, testing, provisioning, and delivering software releases. In addition, task management supports tracking a work item's progress, monitoring and analyzing key metrics across the pipeline, and reporting the results.

One of the better-known task management tools is Jenkins, which lauds its community as providing the industry-leading open source automation server. Jenkins is used to automate software build, test, and deployment processes in a CI/CD environment. Though free, Jenkins is considered by some to be outdated and cumbersome to use. There are alternatives to Jenkins, including AutoRABIT, Bamboo, Bitrise, Buddy, Buildkite, CircleCI, CruiseControl, FinalBuilder, GitLab CI, GoCD, Integrity, Strider, TeamCity, UrbanCode, and Werker.

Containerization is a mechanism that is used to package an application's code and its related configuration files, libraries, and other dependencies to run an application in its target hardware environments. Conceptually, containers implement a virtualization strategy to maximize the utilization of computing resources.

Before virtualization, organizations had to dedicate servers to run specific applications, such as email, web-based applications, and backend business applications. Having dedicated application servers is extraordinarily inefficient and inflexible.

Two of the better-known container technologies are **Docker** and **Kubernetes**, and they work together. Docker is a software tool that developers use to build and deploy containers, while **Kubernetes** (that is, **k8s** or **Kube**) orchestrates and manages multiple containers in clusters. Orchestration is necessary to schedule and automate the deployment, management, and scaling of containerized applications.

As with SCM and task management, there are alternative tools available in the industry for both Docker and Kubernetes. Docker alternatives include Canonical (Ubuntu), **Linux Containers (LXD)**, CoreOS rkt, **Open Container Initiative (OCI)**, LXC Linux Containers, Mesos Containerizer, and OpenVZ. The Kubernetes alternatives include **Amazon ECS (Elastic Container Service)**, AWS Fargate, AZK, **Azure Kubernetes Service (AKS)**, Cloudify, Containership, **Google Kubernetes Engine (GKE)**, OpenShift, Marathon, Minikube, Nomad, and Rancher.

If you think the number of tools available to support these three technologies is daunting, just wait until we examine the larger tool options that are available to support the entire DevOps toolchain. These tools are a small subset of the DevOps pipeline tools that are available as commercial and open source offerings. Later, in *Chapter 11, Identifying VSM Tool Types and Capabilities*, you will learn that there are 17 categories of tools and more than 400 offerings available to support the full scope of a DevOps **value stream delivery platform** (**VSDP**).

We'll revisit all three of these technologies later in this chapter. However, before we get into the details of containerization, you need to understand the basic concepts behind virtualization.

Understanding virtualization

IT organizations, especially larger ones, need to maximize their computing resources' flexibility, utilization, and scalability. These goals are difficult, if not impossible, to achieve without virtualization. Virtualization is an approach taken by IT organizations to simplify their operations and respond faster to changing business demands.

Virtualization offers a practical approach to distribute an application across any number of computing devices. For example, in many cases, one computing device is not sufficient to run a business application due to the high demand loads. In a related example, application demand loads can vary over time across the organization's applications. Virtualization offers an approach to reapportion loads across servers as demands vary, enabling high availability for demand-critical applications while also streamlining the process to deploy and migrate applications.

Additionally, modern data centers employ servers deployed in racks to maximize their computing resource utilization. Virtualization makes it possible to coordinate the use of rack-mounted servers to utilize those resources maximally. These rack-based server strategies reduce power consumption for the computing devices and air conditioning needs; additionally, they reduce the land and facility space requirements of the data centers.

Virtualizing data center resources

Virtualization creates a logical (virtual) computing environment that sits on top of a physical computing environment. Each virtualized environment mimics the hardware, **operating systems** (**OSes**), storage devices, and other system and security components that are necessary to run a specific software application.

Virtualization allows IT organizations to partition a single physical computer or racks of servers into **virtual machines** (**VMs**). Each VM operates independently and can run different OSes or applications while sharing a single host machine's resources.

The primary benefit of virtualization is that each physical computing system can manage multiple virtual environments, thereby maximizing its utilization. Moreover, the IT department can automate building and taking down virtual environments to match demand loads and business application needs, maximizing the IT organization's responsiveness and flexibility.

Virtualization concepts employ a specific semantic description to distinguish between physical versus virtualized environments, as hosts versus guest machines. Host machines are the physical machines used for virtualization, and guest machines are the VMs. The host versus guest machine terminology makes it easier to distinguish the OS that runs on the physical machine from the OSes that run on its VMs.

Employing hypervisor software for virtualization

Figure 5.1 shows a traditional application server architecture on the left and a virtualized server on the right. The diagram clearly shows that the traditional model requires a separate computer as a server for each application requirement. In contrast, the virtualized host machine shares its resources among all the virtualized guest machines and their applications:

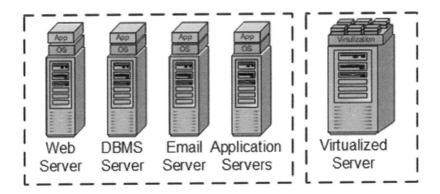

Figure 5.1 – Traditional (left) versus virtualized (right) servers

In the original virtualization model, **hypervisor** software (that is, *virtual machine monitor, VMM*, or *virtualizer*) is installed on a host machine to enable multiple VMs to operate as guest machines on one physical server. The hypervisor software is a lightweight OS that serves as an abstraction layer separating the applications and their required OS from the server's OS.

Hypervisors work in two types of operating modes:

- **Bare-metal hypervisors** run multiple OSes on top of one hardware server.

- **Hosted hypervisors** are installed on top of the hardware's standard OS but isolate the virtualized applications' OSes.

Figure 5.2 depicts the two standard hypervisor software implementation models, that is, bare-metal and hosted:

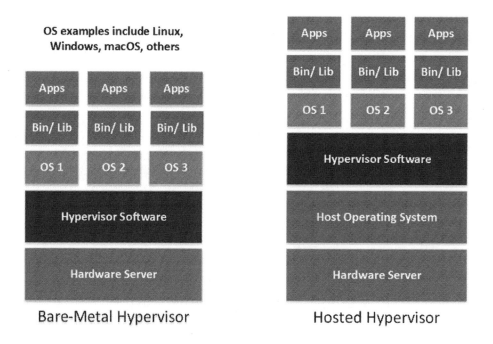

Figure 5.2 – Hypervisor software implementation models

The benefits of using hypervisor software for virtualization include the following:

- It offers greater speed, efficiency, and flexibility in provisioning VMs instead of installing one or more physical servers for every software application.

- It allows multiple OSes to reside on the same host machine. Therefore, software applications do not need to be rewritten to run on the host machine's OS.

- All virtualized applications share the same virtual computing, storage, and memory resources, thereby reducing computing equipment needs, computer room space, energy costs, and equipment maintenance.

- It improves disaster recovery by making it simpler and faster to create and recover snapshot images.

- It simplifies the process of creating test environments as VMs.

To put the virtualization's power into perspective, it's not unusual to have thousands of servers dedicated to supporting just one critical business application in large enterprises. Indeed, the largest commercial data centers might have more than a million servers deployed on tens of thousands of racks running any number of applications for any number of customers.

These data centers offer a network of remote servers hosted on the internet as a cloud-based service. Over time, the data centers could employ different technologies. The virtualization of servers is critical to the efficient storage, management, and processing of data for external customers regardless of the underlying physical environments.

However, as it turns out, hypervisor-based virtualization is not a perfect solution. Since the hypervisor software emulates virtual hardware, the hypervisor must include all the guest machines' application OS and system functionality, making them relatively inefficient.

In the following subsection, you will learn how containers resolve these issues by sharing a lightweight OS.

Using containers for virtualization

Both containers and hypervisors make applications faster, more portable, and more efficient to deploy. However, they achieve those objectives differently. You've already learned that hypervisor software implements a light OS over a host machine's environment. In contrast, a container's OS is smaller and more efficient than hypervisor software. Containers package an application and its dependencies and run them as an OS process on the host machine.

A container package can run anywhere a container engine is installed. For example, please refer to *Figure 5.2* for a graphical depiction of the container-based architecture, and then compare it with the hypervisor virtualization architectures shown in the following figure:

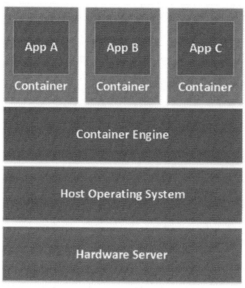

Container-Based Virtualization

Figure 5.3 – Container-based virtualization

At first glance, the container-based virtualization model looks relatively similar to the hosted hypervisor model. They both provide an abstraction layer between the host OS and the applications. However, VMs with hypervisors isolate the hardware and its OS to run the virtualized applications' full OSes. In contrast, the container engines provide an abstraction layer on top of the hardware's OSes in order to run the applications directly with their OS of preference without utilizing the OS installed on the VMs.

A commercial OS, such as Linux, Windows, or macOS, needs to provide numerous common services to support computer applications that are running on the hardware where the OS is installed. However, most of those services are not required by any single application. Therefore, containers do not contain a complete OS – only the bare-bones elements that are necessary to run the application it supports.

The container-based virtualization approach is much more lightweight and flexible than hypervisor-based VMs. For example, where a VM might take up tens of gigabytes of space, a container might only require tens of megabytes. Additionally, containers tend to be more secure since each container's OS is self-contained, thereby offering fewer entry points for malicious actors (for instance, through malware or intrusion attacks).

Metaphorically, containers serve a transport function that mimics the shipping containers used to move physical products by ships, trains, and trucks (for instance, one container type from the origin to the final destination). In the software-based analogy, developers build products and deploy them to their target host environments via their containers. But in our software-based variant, the containers transport the application together with just the resources it needs to execute during runtime as virtualized guests on the targeted host's physical environment.

These resources include the code, runtime, system libraries, system tools, and configuration settings. The containers are constructed as *images* that are separate from their runtime environment. Thus, they can be deployed anywhere – just as long as the target environment has a container engine installed, such as Docker Engine.

A modern approach to software development, especially in DevOps-oriented pipelines, defines and creates very small pieces of code as independent services, called microservices. The microservices-based development strategy allows the rapid coding, testing, and deployment of new functionality into production – often, this can be multiple times per day. Conceptually, the microservices approach mimics the concept of single-piece flow concepts in Lean production practices.

You will learn about the value of implementing single-piece flows in *Chapter 7, Mapping the Current State (VSM Step 4)*, and *Chapter 8, Identifying Lean Metrics (VSM Step 5)*, of this book. For now, it's essential to understand that single-piece flows represent the most efficient Lean development processes.

Container engines perform two critical services: **clustering** and **orchestration**. Clustering connects two or more servers as a single virtualized computer. The clustering of servers allows them to operate in parallel, and the container engines manage load balancing and fault tolerance activities across the cluster of servers.

Container orchestration automates the deployment, management, scaling, and networking of containers. Orchestration is critical when scheduling between hundreds or thousands of individual containers consisting of microservices that operate across multiple clusters.

When using software containers, software developers do not need to worry about deployments across multiple types of production environments nor the virtualization of hardware resources; the containers have everything they need to run the application on a desktop, an organization's backend servers, or computing environments available in the cloud.

Having it both ways

Still, an IT organization could deploy both hypervisor and container-based virtualization strategies to maximize their flexibility when deploying and managing applications. Both hypervisors and container engines can live on the same physical server.

Containers do well in cloud-based environments and when developers want to build fine-grained services, called microservices. IT shops without many legacy applications might prefer to go down this route right from the beginning as microservices offer the greatest speed and flexibility to build, test, and deploy new IT services.

On the other hand, VMs provide all the management capabilities and security tools available within a mature OS. VMs provide a **hardware abstraction layer (HAL)** that eliminates software application compatibility issues with the underlying hardware. VMs effectively utilize memory capacities and multiple cores in CPUs that allow the consolidation of numerous applications and tasks across each physical system. In fact, VMs are optimal for running applications requiring persistent and high-transaction volume workloads. For example, applications with large transactional databases – think of bank ATMs that require resilient and persistent backends – cannot lose data, and have high **input/output (I/O)** transaction requirements. Finally, some third-party applications have not and might not adopt the container model.

Now that you understand the necessary tooling required to support CI/CD, we can introduce the types of activities included in CI and CD processes. We'll start by defining the activities of CI.

Defining CI

Fundamentally, CI is a development approach that speeds up the velocity of software development. CI enforces a discipline that merges all developers' working copies of their code to a shared repository several times a day on a technical level. The purpose of this is to verify each incremental code integration's functionality through software build and test processes when developing the code. The goal is to ensure the main software code is always in a working and potentially deployable state.

A mature CI pipeline includes automated build and automated test capabilities; though, these two capabilities were not part of the original definition. Today, CI workflows encompass the process of taking each new code *commit* from the main branch (that is, the mainline code, trunk, or master) and running the appropriate steps to verify that commit.

A basic CI pipeline spans the following software development activities, as shown in *Figure 5.4*:

Figure 5.4 – CI pipeline flow

The preceding diagram is a high-level view of a more complicated process. As an example of the complexities, the following tasks are usually marshaled via a CI automation server, such as Jenkins:

- Move the source code to the version control system.

- Manage the version control system's push, pull, and merge functions.

- Execute the software build process (for example, compiling the source code, linking the object files and libraries, and packaging the libraries and tools).

- Execute static code analysis.

- Run automated unit tests.

- Execute code coverage analysis.

- Provision test servers.

- Set up test fixtures (for example, code that sets up the test environment and then returns it to its original state once the test is complete).

- Run automated tests.

- Publish logs and reports.

- Send information to the developers.

The CI process appears to be a lot of work and a highly complex process – and it is when implemented as a manual process. However, as an automated CI process, the complete feedback loop should run for less than 10–20 minutes. The goal is to make the process so quick and straightforward that developers won't hesitate to initiate the process several times per day.

The CI strategy addresses two fundamental problems. The first is to make sure every new piece of code implements its functionality correctly, according to its requirements and acceptance criteria, before making the change part of the main code. The second is to ensure the newly integrated code doesn't cause problems or bugs in the application's mainline code.

Encouraging frequent testing

It should be pretty clear that, fundamentally, CI is a process used to develop and test small increments of new software functionality rapidly and frequently. This strategy supports the first and seventh principles of the *Manifesto for Agile Software Development* (Beck et al., 2001).

> **The Agile Manifesto principles 1 and 2**
>
> 1) Our highest priority is to satisfy the customer through early and continuous delivery of valuable software.
>
> 2) Working software is the primary measure of progress.
>
> Please refer to `https://agilemanifesto.org/principles.html` for more details.

While the first principle is valuable, it turns out the seventh principle is often more important, at least in terms of the benefits of CI. Let's take a moment to understand why.

In the traditional waterfall model, software developers create all of the code that is necessary to implement all identified requirements before initiating any testing. A significant problem with that development strategy is that the source of the software bugs becomes increasingly challenging to locate and resolve in larger code sets. A much better strategy is to test small increments, or units, of new code every step of the way. The advantage of this is that the developers know more precisely what they changed in the code when an error or bug shows up in testing.

Additionally, frequent code updates can help identify code merge conflicts, diverging code strategies, and duplication attempts. In other words, with CI and automated testing, developers are forced to address these issues as they arise and not wait until they become exceedingly complex, time-consuming, and expensive to fix.

This section ends our discussion on CI. Next, we will learn how CD capabilities both augment and improve the velocity of the CI phase of software delivery.

Defining CD

CD capabilities allow product teams to stand up new environments to test new code updates with minimal manual labor and rapidly. CD's primary goal is to turn new updates into routine and high-velocity tasks that a development team can perform on-demand.

Just as CI has a sequential sequence of steps, so does the CD process, as depicted in *Figure 5.5*:

Figure 5.5 – CD pipeline flow

The CD pipeline view depicted in the preceding diagram provides a high-level view, and similarly to the CI pipeline, it can be decomposed into a lengthier list of related activities. These activities might include the following:

- Conducting static code analysis
- Conducting unit tests
- Conducting API tests
- Staging to test environment(s)
- Parallel testing (for instance, useability/accessibility, exploratory, UI, and performance testing)
- Staging to preproduction environment
- Executing application tests (for example, acceptance, exploratory, capacity, load, and stress testing)
- Executing software and network security tests
- Conducting UAT
- Deploying the application to production environments

Again, this list is not meant to be an exhaustive summary of all the possible tests that a team might need to execute.

One final comment is that there is no definitive place where CI as a process ends and CD begins. For example, some analysts put the merge code process – a source code integration activity – in the CI pipeline, while others view it as a CD pipeline activity. In reality, CI/CD pipelines represent a continuous flow across the entire **systems development life cycle (SDLC)**. There's no reason to make the distinction except to communicate the type of work that occurs in each section of the pipeline.

Once the development team determines which tests to run and which tools they require, they can automate the tests' execution by writing configuration instructions in machine-readable code.

Automating configuration tasks via code

Before the advent of CD methods and tools, development teams had to ask the operations staff to set up testing and preproduction staging environments. Then, the operations staff manually followed the instructions in the configuration documentation to set up networks, computing equipment, and software. Such manual processes are expensive and time-consuming.

In a modern CD environment, developers can deploy software and systems configuration instructions as machine-readable code. Moreover, these configurations can be managed in a source control repository and made available for rapid deployment as a self-service offering. The infrastructure and software resources are provisioned on demand in a cloud environment and are made available within minutes after executing the machine-readable code.

The term used in the software industry to describe automated deployment configurations is Infrastructure as Code (IaC). However, you might have also come across the term Configuration as Code (CaC), which individual IT practitioners and vendors use to connote the general implementation of configurations as source code. We'll discuss the semantic differences between IaC and CaC later in this chapter.

For now, it's essential to understand that IaC and CaC implement configuration instructions as machine-readable code to stand up and configure environments and software on demand. Before we get into the details of IaC and CaC, first, let's understand why CM is so important and why some configuration items cannot be deployed as code.

Both infrastructure and software configurations broadly fall under the discipline of **software configuration management**, as described in the following subsection.

Protecting our software assets

Complex software releases involve deploying and configuring a lot of hardware, network and application security, software components, and other related information artifacts. CM ensures that we have a complete understanding of the state and artifacts that make up each unique software release. Without that information, it's challenging, if not impossible, to go back to fix bugs and defects, sustain the product, or enhance previous software releases.

As the software evolves, each new release has a unique configuration. With each release, some of the components will have changed, while others will not. Although all the components might start with the same version control number, those version control IDs will vary across the software components and other information-oriented artifacts over time. Therefore, assigning a version control ID to the release is not enough. We need to know the specific versions of each of the information artifacts and software components that make up the release.

Modern version control repositories, such as Git (a local repo) and GitHub (a web-based collaboration SCM platform and repository), use a tree structure as a metaphor for managing the configuration items associated with each software release.

Getting back to the tree metaphor applied to SCM repositories, developers create (and evolve), integrate, and test components as separate *branches* of an application before merging them with the main *trunk* of code. The main code is the closest code set available for release at any given time. That's not to say the main code is releasable, but it is the furthest along in terms of integrated capabilities and testing.

However, besides tracking our source code, we also need to track all the other information artifacts that go with each release, which is the purpose of SCM.

Information and software artifacts under SCM encompass the entire SDLC processes, including the following:

- **Software requirements**: This includes functional and nonfunctional requirements specified in specifications, use cases, epics, and user stories.

- **Environment**: This includes network switches, firewalls, routers, servers, OSes, cybersecurity systems, databases, and other critical infrastructure elements.

- **Software builds**: This includes instructions to compile, link, and otherwise convert source code files into a standalone software artifact(s) so they can run on a computer.

- **Software release plan**: This provides instructions on how to release the product into production, its timelines, delivery dates, and production-oriented testing requirements such as **UAT**, QA testing, preproduction testing (for instance, stress, load, and performance), and field testing, as applicable.

- **Software reviews**: This could include peer reviews, **software quality assurance (SQA)** reviews, or **independent verification and validation (IV&V)** testing by third parties.

- **Version control**: This includes information on the current and past versions of all software system components and related artifacts, which are usually managed within a source control repository.

- **Configuration items**: This includes all the software components and artifacts, as identified by their independent names and version control IDs and belonging to a specific release.

- **Testing information**: This includes test cases, test scripts, test scenarios, and test results associated with each software release.

- **User support**: The support team's information provides user assistance guidance and helps troubleshoot user problems during the product's implementation and use.

- **Documentation**: This can include training aids, systems administration documentation, and architecture and design documentation.

- **Issue tracking**: This is used to document information related to bugs and defects. A bug results from a coding error, while a defect is an identified deviation from the requirements.

- **Task management**: This is used to maintain information on activities across the development and delivery life cycle.

Most of the preceding information-based components that go with a release are not part of the application's source code. Therefore, the product team must implement processes and systems that will record and maintain this information for each product release. We need to manage all this information by release to ensure operability and sustainability in the production environments, fix bugs or defects upon discovery, and enhance the product over its life cycle.

Now that we understand the more significant software configuration issues, let's examine the differences between managing and executing CaC and IaC. We'll start with a description of CaC.

CaC

CaC is a broad term that implies implementing configuration files in a source code repository, but the term is more generally applied to application configuration information. The purpose of CaC is to facilitate the versioned migration of application configurations between different environments.

CaC configurations are implemented as machine-readable code via configuration files that focus on the settings and parameters that are required to install software applications, servers, and OSes. Developers specify configuration settings in CaC with parameters that can be changed to affect the target information system's remote hardware, software, or firmware components. These configuration settings and parameters affect the security levels and functionality of the system.

A virtually unending list of potential configurations must be implemented and maintained across IT products, especially for those in which security-related configuration settings can be defined. The US **National Institute of Standards and Technology (NIST)** *Special Publication 800-53 (Rev. 4)* documents the following examples of configurable items:

Mainframe computers, servers (for example, database, email, authentication, web, proxy, file, domain name), workstations, I/O devices (for example, scanners, copiers, and printers), network components (for example, firewalls, routers, gateways, voice and data switches, wireless access points, network appliances, sensors), OSes, middleware, and applications (`https://nvd.nist.gov/800-53/Rev4/control/CM-6`).

The NIST publication also lists standard security-related parameters, as noted in the passage that follows:

> *Security-related parameters impact the security state of information systems, including the parameters required to satisfy other security control requirements.*
>
> *(i) registry settings,*
>
> *(ii) account, file, directory permission settings,*
>
> *(iii) settings for functions, ports, protocols, services, and remote connections.*

Established settings become part of the system's configuration baseline parameters. In a manual process, the software developers create security configuration checklists, lockdown and hardening guides, security reference guides, and security technical implementation guides. The operations staff follow these guides to configure the systems and applications properly. The value of CaC is that it automates and streamlines the process of establishing the configuration settings and parameters.

In contrast with CaC, IaC is about configuring IT infrastructures, including servers, networks, load balancing, and security, as described in the following subsection.

IaC

As its name implies, IaC allows developers to use a programming or scripting language to generate a repeatable set of code or scripted instructions to provision IT infrastructures. With IaC capabilities, developers do not need to manually provision or change the configurations of infrastructure components, such as servers, OSes, database connections, storage, networks, VMs, load balancers, and network topologies.

Without IaC capabilities, the developers must manually set up and configure new system environments every time they want to develop, test, or deploy a software application. From the perspective of Lean, and therefore our customers, these activities are unnecessarily repetitive and non-value-added. That's not to say they are not necessary. However, automating such processes improve cycle times and eliminate waste in the form of human, or other errors.

The issue of human error is especially concerning as the accumulation of configuration errors leads to **environmental drift** where each new environment configuration becomes uniquely different to previous configurations. Developers call the new configurations *snowflakes* because they share a similar characteristic in that each is unique from the others.

Managing environmental drift

The problem with environmental drift is that each new change in the system's configuration can affect previously deployed assets. Recall that the function of operations is to maintain stable, secure, and available environments and applications. However, let's suppose a developer fails to communicate a new configuration change to the infrastructure or applications. In that case, those modifications cause the production environments to fail or expose them to security-related risks.

The same situation is valid for engineering and test environments. Changes in configurations make it increasingly difficult to isolate and fix errors that result from the configuration changes, as opposed to bugs or defects in the code. Again, each new configuration change can introduce waste in the form of defects that are time-consuming and expensive to resolve.

There are innumerable issues that contribute to environmental drift. However, most often, these configuration changes result from improper documentation, communication, or the implementation of new or modified parameters when setting up servers, configuring networks, or other computing resources.

The preceding examples show human error as the root cause. Computers are better at executing rote instructions with accurately described configurations defined via code. But those types of errors can be discovered during the testing process, thereby avoiding any negative consequences and limiting any risks when new releases move into production.

Avoiding configuration errors

As with the CaC concepts, development teams employ IaC write scripts or code to describe the configuration settings and parameters. Each configuration file represents a single and authoritative source of defining and setting up an environment or updating an environment over time.

The code or scripts are saved as standalone configuration files and checked into the development team's version control and SCM systems. The advantage of managing IaC files in an SCM system is that the executable routines become freely available to all developers and operations staff via a self-service model.

In other words, both CaC and IaC help to improve the velocity of software deliveries while simultaneously reducing errors.

Improving velocities while reducing errors

With CaC and IaC, IT staff can download and execute configuration files on demand and set up a new environment in minutes without introducing manual errors. The self-service model means that developers don't need to involve the operations team to stand up and provision new testing environments. Moreover, the operations team can ensure the code and configurations for new releases are appropriately tested before releasing new updates to the production environments.

IaC enables high velocities for CD to match the same types of velocities developers have available via their CI tools. With a CI/CD pipeline, developers can change both the code and configurations on the fly and stand up test environments to quickly determine that everything is working correctly. Moreover, high-performing shops can deploy new functionality multiple times per day with lead times of less than 1 hour (Forsgren et al., Accelerate, 2018).

IaC is the critical enabler for specifying CI/CD and DevOps pipeline configurations and flows. Manual configuration processes are simply too slow and too inefficient. As you will discover in the chapters on VSM, CI/CD and DevOps pipelines implement Lean production concepts across all IT value streams when they are adequately implemented.

However, before we get to those chapters, we need to understand how CI/CD and DevOps pipelines support work and information flow across all IT value streams.

Enabling CI/CD and DevOps pipeline flows

This book makes a clear distinction between CI/CD and DevOps toolchains and pipelines:

- A toolchain is a combination of tools that collectively perform a specific set of IT tasks or functions. This term may or may not imply an integration or automation strategy and is somewhat vague.

- DevOps pipelines and CI/CD pipelines include a series of integrated tools to streamline and automate IT tasks or functions across an IT value stream. Pipelines are more equivalent to the Lean and VSM concepts presented later in this book. For now, let's understand CI/CD and DevOps pipelines as improving the speed and reliability of software value delivery.

The term **toolchain** specifies a scope of tools that support IT value stream activities. Again, by itself, the term toolchain does not necessarily imply an integration or automation strategy. Although not ideal, developers can manually set up the following tool in line with the previous tools' outputs.

A better strategy is to improve efficiencies by integrating and automating the toolchains to coordinate and streamline work and information flows. In this context, the word **pipeline** connotes a flow. In the case of Lean-oriented production philosophies, we want streamlined and efficient flows of both work and information across our IT value streams.

CI/CD and DevOps toolchains are integrated and automated to support the efficient and streamlined flow of work and information across all IT value streams. CI/CD and DevOps toolchains are called *pipelines* when the tools are integrated and automated to support streamlined and efficient work and information flows.

Improving pipeline flows

The distinction between toolchains versus pipelines is an important one. For example, an Agile-based software development team can procure a set of tools that collectively make up a toolchain. However, when chartered under a project-based operating model, it is unlikely that the team has the time or budget to implement an integrated or automated toolchain.

In such scenarios, Agile teams never achieve the same production efficiencies that are available to the product-oriented teams that implement a complete pipeline. Since the product team lives across its product's life cycle, they can justify and amortize the CI/CD and DevOps pipeline toolchain investments.

However, there is a workaround for Agile teams. For example, the Agile team can access an integrated and automated toolchain as a cloud-based service via a commercial or internal DevOps platform provider. You will learn more about those options in *Section 3* of this book. For the remainder of this chapter, we will go beyond the CI/CD activities to look at the full scope of DevOps-related activities.

Understanding the full scope of DevOps

CI/CD activities only take us as far as traditional SDLC processes, that is, from concept to deployment. But the IT organization must also maintain and support its software applications. For the remainder of this chapter, you will learn that DevOps goes beyond software development and delivery to ensure the proper life cycle support of deployed software products.

While DevOps still includes the base CI/CD activities you've learned so far in this chapter, the overall scope of work in DevOps expands to encompass all software life cycle stages. These include the following:

- Build automation and CI
- Test automation
- CD and provisioning
- Deployment automation
- Operating, monitoring, supporting, and providing feedback
- Release coordination and automation

Let's discuss what these activities are beyond the CI/CD phase of software development and delivery. In the following subsection, we will begin to define the boundaries between CI/CD pipelines and DevOps pipelines.

Defining CI/CD and DevOps pipeline boundaries

As you learned at the beginning of this chapter, DevOps began as a collaboration strategy to enable Agile systems administration. The primary goal was to improve information flows between IT development and operations teams as a risk management strategy. However, DevOps necessarily evolved to address the issues related to mismatched velocities. In other words, the velocity of operations-oriented services needs to match the velocities of the Agile-based development teams.

In traditional IT vernacular, we use the term SDLC to refer to IT value stream activities and tools implemented by the development teams. In contrast, the operations team uses the term **ITSM** to describe all the activities and supporting tools involved in designing, creating, delivering, supporting, and managing IT services-related activities.

It should be no surprise that the term **DevOps pipeline** encompasses both SDLC and ITSM activities and tools, ultimately forming an integrated DevOps pipeline. In the following subsection, we'll take a look at how the CI/CD model is expanded to become a DevOps pipeline.

Expanding the CI/CD model

The CI/CD model spans the activities customarily performed by a software development team spanning an iterative SDLC. DevOps expands the CI/CD pipeline concepts to include the IT operations team's activities. In other words, DevOps seeks to merge the activities of development and operations, ideally at the product team level.

In an article titled *8 CI/CD best practices to set you up for success*, Taz Brown created the following diagram to show the larger complexities of implementing and supporting Lean value streams across the IT function. This diagram breaks the value stream into three distinct flows, that is, **Software Development**, **User Support**, and **Incident Management**:

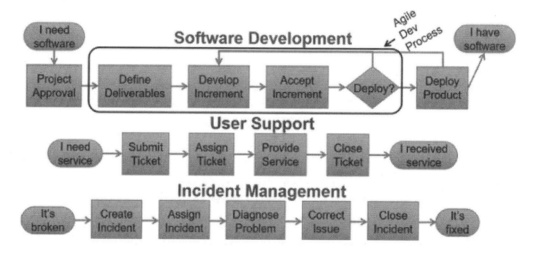

Figure 5.6 – IT value streams

https://opensource.com/article/20/5/cicd-best-practices (Taz Brown, CC BY-SA 4.0)

This diagram simplifies the view of the activities needed to build, deploy, and support a product. While this model is incomplete from a DevOps perspective, it does highlight the separations between development and support-related activities.

The first line of the diagram, which is within the boundary line, depicts a standard CI/CD pipeline set of activities. Note that there is a decision point within the boundary to decide whether the development and operations teams are ready to deploy the software into the organization's production environments.

Given its presence outside the boundary line, the **Deploy Product** node suggests a manual decision and process. However, that doesn't have to be the case. With a mature CI/CD pipeline capability, the software release is automated.

The development and operations teams might still prefer some manual review process before release. However, even that requirement becomes unnecessary when releasing tiny increments of new functionality with increased velocity, using automated testing capabilities, and perhaps automating UAT across a small segment of users before deploying the releases to the larger community of users.

Looking at lines two and three in *Figure 5.6*, we move into the operations team's traditional IT support and incident management functions. These activities fall under the ITSM processes.

However, this model is still missing the operations-oriented **IT operations management (ITOM)** processes. ITOM spans IT operations' control and facilities management but also overlaps with technical management and application management. A very mature DevOps pipeline integrates and automates these activities at the product team level.

We will dive into ITOM and ITSM in the last part of this chapter. But before we get to those topics, let's examine how the mismatched velocities between development and operations became the driver for evolving DevOps strategies and, later, DevOps toolchains and pipelines. That is the topic of our following subsection.

Resolving issues of mismatched velocities

As noted in the previous subsection, the speed of development often exceeds the ability of operations to manage the risks associated with effectively deploying new releases frequently. However, all of these issues can go away with CD and continuous deployment capabilities.

Many Agile-based IT developers employ innovative practices to deploy small increments of new functionality frequently using CI methods and tools. CI capabilities automate the frontend SDLC development processes to perform automated code integrations, builds, and integration tests every time developers check their code into the source code repository.

CD initially evolved to support automation testing needs, which sits at the boundaries between development and operations. Development teams should thoroughly test all new software releases before deployment, including systems, acceptance, load, stress, performance, and other critical tests. It takes time, computing resources, and human effort to manually set up the test environments to support these testing requirements.

Put simply, manual testing processes cannot approach the velocities of CI. CD automates the activities that are required to read application and infrastructure configurations in code, provision testing servers, install and configure the applications, and then run all of the necessary tests.

Continuous deployment takes the provisioning process one step further to automate the deployment process in the production environments. Moreover, continuous deployment can automate infrastructure resource provisioning in near real time to meet changing production demands.

The operations function can match the Agile-based development teams' velocities using CI methods and tools with CD and deployment capabilities. With its emphasis on the rapid delivery of high-quality products and services and just-in-time deliveries, Lean production processes offer a way to integrate the IT DevOps pipeline activities within a single IT value stream.

When you get to *Section 2* of this book, which is on *implementing VSM*, you will learn how to implement Lean production concepts across the IT value stream to create Lean pipeline flows. But before we move on to that part of the book, we need to look at the full scope of DevOps activities.

Scoping DevOps pipeline activities

As it turns out, a fully evolved DevOps pipeline encompasses quite a few integrated activities beyond CI/CD pipeline flows. In this section, we will explore the higher-level activities and how they operate as a continuous iterative and incremental development and support process.

As you read this section, bear in mind what you learned in *Chapter 1, Delivering Customer-Centric Value*, about organizations having two types of value streams: development and operations. As a reminder, operations-oriented value streams deliver products and services to an organization's external customers, while development value streams create things used by the organization's operations-oriented value streams.

The DevOps acronym is confusing as the term implies operations and development are part of the same value stream, and they are. But the semantic meanings of development and operations in the DevOps acronym are different from Lean's contextual meanings. The DevOps paradigm includes the iterative SDLC activities associated with CI/CD pipelines, plus the operations activities include the product's ITSM activities.

Figure 5.7 is a standard display for a DevOps pipeline. Although a DevOps pipeline can be displayed as a linear-sequential flow, the more common approach is to show it as an infinity loop. The infinity loop implies that iterative and incremental DevOps delivery activities operate as a continuous flow:

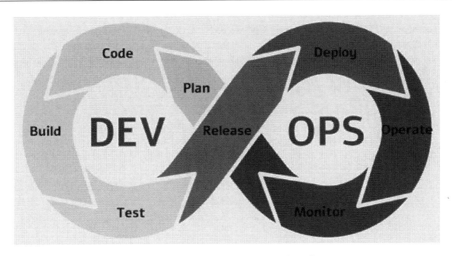

Figure 5.7 – Infinite DevOps pipeline flows

Modern Agile and Lean-Agile practices both implement iterative development cycles that deliver frequent increments of customer value. DevOps simply expands the iterative and incremental development model to encompass the IT service's management activities.

This DevOps model is overly simplistic, as its focus is only on conveying high-level pipeline processes. Just as we discovered with the CI/CD pipeline activities, the DevOps pipeline's ITSM portion includes many more activities than portrayed in the DevOps infinity loop diagram.

You already know how to implement CI/CD activities as pipelines into the DevOps pipeline model. In the next section, we will take a look at the activities associated with ITSM and their flows.

Integrating ITSM

In *Chapter 1, Delivering Customer-Centric Value*, you learned that organizational value streams support development or operations and are often linked. You also learned that IT-based development-oriented value streams often create software products that support the operations-oriented value streams.

For example, an insurance company's internal software development team might create web-based services to support the company's insurance products' promotion, sales, and delivery. Similarly, health care software providers have development teams supporting multiple value streams. These can include patient registrations, claims management, financial management, accounting, diagnostic and billing codes, patient health data, appointment scheduling, compliance, and reporting.

However, as you already know, IT value streams go beyond the implementation of software development and delivery activities. Besides these capabilities, the IT organization or software product team must install ITOM capabilities and ITSM processes and platforms.

ITSM focuses on how IT teams deliver services. In contrast, ITOM focuses on the activities and tools used for event management, performance monitoring, and the operations processes depicted in the **OPS** portion of the DevOps pipeline (please refer to *Figure 5.7*). Ideally, the IT organization installs ITOM and ITSM activities at the product team level as part of their DevOps pipeline flows.

Conveniently, ITIL 4 already addresses ITOM and ITSM from a **service value system** (**SVS**) perspective. If the organization has implemented ITIL 4 practices or equivalent, the VSM team needs to assess the operations-oriented work within the DevOps pipeline.

Delivering service value

In the previously displayed *Figure 5.7*, the DevOps pipeline's **OPS** portion includes **Release**, **Deploy**, **Operate**, and **Monitor** as its primary activities. Two of these activities, **Release** and **Deploy**, are transition activities that require support from both the development and operations side of the product teams.

However, in this section, you will learn that these 4 operations-oriented processes decompose into at least 34 separate ITSM domains spanning 3 management practices. The word domain implies a specified area of activity or knowledge. In the context of ITSM, you can presume the term domain includes specific areas of knowledge and related sets of activities.

The term service management broadly describes the practices and activities designed to improve a company's customer service processes. Service management includes activities spanning strategy, design, development, integration, operation, and service improvements. ITSM then includes the practices and activities to support customers using software and related infrastructure and security components produced or acquired by an IT organization.

There are multiple ITSM frameworks that a product team can choose to use, such as ISO/IEC 20000-1, ITIL 4®, COBIT 5, FitSM, **Microsoft Operations Framework** (**MOF**), The Open Group IT4IT Reference Architecture, VeriSM™, SIAM®, and YaSM®. Given its leadership position, this chapter evaluates how ITIL 4® defines its **service value chain** as part of its best practices to deliver ITSM in the context of DevOps, Agile, and Lean approaches.

ITIL 4® defines a *service value chain* as a set of "joined-up practices, activities, and actions used across the ITSM value stream." In other words, the ITIL 4® service value chain represents a flow. Of course, we know an ITSM value stream is only a component of the larger IT value stream work and information flows that are encompassed within a DevOps pipeline.

Before we get into the service value chain activities and flows, first, let's quickly take a look at the four dimensions of ITSM that help deliver value.

Encompassing the four dimensions of ITSM

ITIL 4 describes four dimensions of service management as the foundations of an ITSM provider's capabilities. From a systems-thinking perspective, these four dimensions are elements that participate in value-based ITSM deliveries. They include the following:

- **Organizations and People**: This is to build the right organizational structures and competencies.

- **Information and Technology**: This is to build IT systems and infrastructures with the right technologies to support service deliveries.

- **Partners and Suppliers**: This is to implement third-party service delivery contracts that are financially and technically appropriate.

- **Value Streams and Processes**: This is to develop efficient and customer-centric service value delivery capabilities.

All four dimensions of service management help the product team deliver service value. Software product teams must coordinate their service value chain responses to involve all four dimensions. If not, the service delivery function does not operate optimally and will fail to deliver value to its customers and product users.

As a final note, external factors such as the following can impact a service delivery's four dimensions: economic, environmental, legal, political, social, and technological. All of these factors must be considered when deciding how to deploy the four dimensions of service management.

Now that we understand the foundational elements of service management, let's explore the activity flows associated with ITSM.

Defining ITSM delivery flows

As with any value stream, the ITIL 4® service value chain represents an activity flow; although it is described at a high level, as we'll see in the following subsection. The service value chain includes six primary activities to respond to the IT service demands from a value delivery perspective:

1. **Plan**: This is to define an as-is/to-do assessment of the service capabilities, requirements, and policies to develop a common vision of what services are required and how they will be delivered.

    Value delivered: New service identification and provisioning plan.

2. **Improve**: This is to ensure the continual improvement of all products, services, and practices across all four dimensions of service management.

    Value delivered: Attainment of service-level targets.

3. **Engage**: This is to confirm our understanding of stakeholder needs, plus ensure timely engagement and positive outcomes with our stakeholders.

    Value delivered: Managing and resolving a user's complaint.

4. **Design and transition**: This is to ensure that new releases of products and related services repeatedly meet stakeholder expectations for quality, cost, and time to market.

    Value delivered: Enable upgrades to the next version of a business application.

5. **Obtain/build**: This is to ensure that service components are available when and where they are needed and that they meet agreed specifications.

    Value delivered: Timely and accurate fulfillment of a user request.

6. **Deliver and support**: This is to ensure services are delivered and supported according to the agreed specifications or service-level agreement while meeting stakeholder expectations.

    Value delivered: Successful resolution of all incident reports.

These six activities express the general flow of work to define, create, and deliver customer-centric services. So, just as software development has a flow that defined ideation through delivery, ITSM provides a value stream flow to define and deliver IT services. In DevOps, we need to integrate the two flows, as shown in *Figure 5.7*. Now, let's define the total potential scope of work involved in delivering value-based ITSM.

Delivering ITSM value

Earlier in this section, we mentioned, though not explicitly attributed to ITIL 4®, the service value chain document's 34 separate ITSM domains spanning 3 management practices. Again, the term domains refers to both knowledge areas and related sets of activities. The scope of this book limits our abilities to dive deeper into describing each domain. However, ITIL 4® provides detailed guidance on planning, managing, and improving these management practices and domain-related activities.

The three groups of management practices include the following:

- **General Management Practices**: This group spans 14 service management domains from general business management that helps support work or accomplishing specific objectives. The domains include the following:

• Architecture management	• Portfolio management	• Service financial management
• Continual improvement	• Organizational change management	• Strategy management
• Information security management	• Project management	• Supplier management
• Knowledge management	• Relationship management	• Workforce and talent management
• Measurement and reporting	• Risk management	

- **Service Management Practices**: This group spans 17 domains to ensure that services deliver agreed availability levels to meet customers' and users' needs. The domains include the following:

• Availability management	• Monitoring and event management	• Service design
• Business analysis	• Problem management	• Service desk
• Capacity and performance management	• Release management	• Service-level management
• Change enablement	• Service catalog management	• Service request management
• Incident management	• Service configuration management	• Service validation and testing
• IT asset management	• Service continuity management	

- **Technical Management Practices**: This group spans three domains to implement service management practices that expand or shift the focus from technology solutions to IT services. The domains include the following:

• Deployment management	• Infrastructure and platform management	• Software development and management

It should be apparent that ITSM brings in a much broader host of practices and activities to implement, improve, and support in a DevOps-oriented value stream. However, it's not necessary to go into the details of ITSM in this book. This chapter's primary goal is to introduce the scope of work involved in building and streamlining DevOps as orchestrated pipeline flows.

We are approaching the end of this chapter. By now, you should appreciate the complex challenges that lie ahead in developing a streamlined DevOps production flow. There are investments required in toolchains and innumerable activities to implement, integrate, automate, and orchestrate.

This book does not attempt to solve your specific CI/CD and DevOps pipeline flow issues but instead gives you the tools to do so. Specifically, *Section 2* of this book introduces an eight-step VSM methodology, modern VSM tools, and their capabilities. In this context, VSM encompasses the methods and tools you can use to improve Lean production flows across your CI/CD and DevOps pipelines.

Before we finish this chapter and this part of the book, there is one other topic we need to address, which is moving from a project-oriented development paradigm to a product-oriented development strategy.

Moving beyond projects and into products

The traditional waterfall model for software development is project-based. In the industry's early days, the project-oriented approach seemed to make sense due to the high costs, complexities, and risks involved in software development.

Let's review the type of work that is best suited to traditional project management practices. For example, the characteristics of project-based work include the following:

- Projects have definable *deliverables* or outputs in the form of *products*, *services*, or *results*.

- Project-based deliverables are relatively unique, and, therefore, the work has significant risks.

- Project constraints are defined in project charters, approved by customers or executive sponsors, with specific boundaries on authorized *scope*, *schedule*, *costs*, and *quality*.

- Project-oriented work is highly tailored to support each product's unique requirements, and, therefore, the work is relatively non-repetitive from one project to another.

- Given that software product requirements are relatively unique, the work's full details and scope might only become apparent as the project progresses (this is also true for Agile-based work).

- Project teams employ formal change management practices to minimize scope creep, budget shortfalls, and schedule overruns.

- Schedules help enforce the temporary nature of projects with defined start and delivery dates and predefined activities, dependencies, and durations.

- Project-based work often crosses organizational boundaries, thereby involving multiple skills.

Managing highly customized work under a dictated set of constraints seems like an odd dichotomy – and it is. That said, we should understand why customers place constraints on project-related work. Specifically, our paying customers establish project constraints to ensure the projected ROI is achievable in the timeline and at a cost at which the investments make economic sense.

Nevertheless, developing software under project-based constraints creates a host of problems, three of which are critical. First, given each software product's unique nature, the development team cannot foresee all of the issues they might encounter. Second, customers and users often don't know what they want or need until they have a version of the software product in hand to evaluate. Third, customer needs evolve, and their priorities change over time.

The bottom line is that no matter how much time and effort the project team applies to project planning, it will be outdated before it can be executed.

Modern software methods and tools have evolved to support the unique needs of software development, such as being responsive to customer demands and changes in priorities. That type of responsiveness was not possible under the traditional waterfall project management model. With fully developed CI/CD and DevOps pipelines, the most mature software development teams can iteratively, incrementally, and rapidly deliver new functionality, perhaps multiple times per day. Therefore, the CI/CD and DevOps pipelines have the functional equivalence of modern manufacturing facilities.

In *Section 2* of this book, we'll explore how VSM helps improve Lean production flows across DevOps pipelines. But before we get to that, first, let's take a moment to understand why a product-based development and delivery model is superior to the traditional project-based waterfall model in software development.

Funding product teams

There is no need to constrain software development activities to a specific scope, schedule, cost, or quality metric. Instead, just as a manufacturing plant operates for as long as they have new customers' orders, the modern software factory continues to operate for as long as their customers have evolving product needs.

Physical products tend to wear out, forcing customers to replace them. In contrast, software products do not physically wear out. On the other hand, the requirements that drove the initial software development objectives tend to have a shelf life. In that context, customers eventually need to replace or update their software applications.

For these reasons, it makes sense to move beyond the project model to implement a product-oriented development model. In a product-oriented development model, product teams replace project teams, and the teams stay together for as long as customers use the product.

The composition of the teams could change over time to support evolving requirements. At the beginning of the product's life cycle, development has an outsized role in efforts and costs. Toward the end of life, the development resources could dwindle, and the resource emphasis moves toward operations-oriented support.

A product-based funding model is different than a project-based funding model. Project-based funding builds on projected future returns on investments. The risk of project-based funding is twofold. First, there is a question of whether the product can be built within the authorized constraints. Second, there is a question of whether the market will exist in the future to support the investment.

Product-based funding is less risky as it turns the project-based model upside down. Instead of asking whether the product will eventually pay back the investment, product-based funding models evaluate current costs and revenues to assess how much money to invest in development and operations support.

There is still risk in the initial development cost investments. However, those risks move to the portfolio level, where corporate executives determine what investments they need to make to best position the company for future business. Those investments can develop new products or investments as enhancements to existing products to attract customers in new market niches. Portfolio-level investments are strategic, while ongoing adjustments to product team budgets are tactical decisions based on actual costs compared to actual revenues.

This section completes our final chapter of *Section 1* of this book. We'll close with a summary section and a set of 10 questions that will help you to analyze your comprehension of this chapter's content.

Summary

This chapter introduced the complexities of implementing CI/CD and DevOps pipeline flows. The information is a precursor to *Section 3* of this book, where you learn how to employ the methods and tools of VSM to implement and improve Lean production flows across your IT value streams.

Specifically, in this chapter, you learned the complexities of implementing mature CI/CD and DevOps pipelines. You learned that virtualization, primarily through container-based technologies, is crucial in order to support the efficient use of IT infrastructure resources and enable the rapid delivery of small increments of new software capabilities. Finally, you learned that CI/CD pipelines integrate and automate the traditional SDLC processes, but DevOps extends the CI/CD pipeline to include service management functions.

With this knowledge, you are now well prepared to understand how to use VSM methods and tools to implement and improve DevOps activities as Lean production-oriented flows. VSM methods and tools form the next part of this book's subject – *Section 2, Implementing Value Stream Management (VSM) Methods and Tools* – to improve IT value streams.

Questions

1. What drove the development of DevOps concepts and later its methods and tools?

2. What are the three critical capabilities and related tools that support the implementation of CI/CD pipelines?

3. What is CI, and what is its purpose?

4. What are the significant cultural differences between a software development team and an IT operations team?

5. What is CD, and what is its goal?

6.   What is the difference between IaC and CaC?

7.   What is the primary difference when using the term "toolchains" compared to "pipelines"?

8.   Using two terms only, what is the best way to describe the IT value streams that make up a DevOps pipeline?

9.   How can you differentiate ITOM from ITSM?

10. How are project-oriented teams funded differently from product-oriented teams?

Further reading

- Dietrich, E. (June 2019) *DevOps Table Stakes: The Minimum Amount Required to Play the Game.* DZone/DevOps Zone. `https://dzone.com/articles/devops-table-stakes-the-minimum-amount-required-to`. Accessed 2nd February 2021.

- **US National Institute of Standards and Technology (NIST)** Information Technology Laboratory. NATIONAL VULNERABILITY DATABASENIST. Special Publication 800-53 (Rev. 4). *Security and Privacy Controls for Federal Information Systems and Organizations.* `https://nvd.nist.gov/800-53/Rev4/control/CM-6`. Accessed 2nd February 2021.

- Forsgren, N., Humble, J., Kim, G. (2018) *Accelerate. Building and Scaling High-Performance Technology Organizations.* IT Revolution. Portland, OR.

Section 2: VSM Methodology

This part of the book introduces value stream management (VSM) as a generic methodology that can be applied to help identify, prioritize, and plan value stream improvements across the enterprise and any value stream. It is also the largest part of the book, given the scope of the work involved when implementing and improving Lean production capabilities across IT and other organizational value streams.

In a modern context, VSM tools support Lean improvements across an organization's IT value streams, intending to improve software delivery capabilities via DevOps-based pipelines. But tools are only part of the industry's VSM solution's needs. The IT industry also needs to adopt a proven VSM methodology to get the most value from their VSM tools.

With this goal in mind, chapters 6 through 10 introduce a robust and proven VSM methodology and apply it to an IT-based CI/CD pipeline implementation strategy as a sample use case.

VSM is not a new concept, and the techniques have been applied to implementing Lean improvements in manufacturing, supply chain administration, office administration, and healthcare administration. But the application of VSM to address productivity and value delivery issues across IT value streams is a relatively new concept.

Despite its new adoption by the IT community, VSM concepts and tools are gaining traction rapidly in the IT community. For example, Gartner reports that by 2023, 70% of organizations will use VSM to improve flow in their DevOps pipeline, leading to faster delivery of customer value.

In our modern digital world, IT touches nearly every aspect of the business. Therefore, improvements to an organization's IT value delivery capabilities also help improve nearly all aspects of the business.

This section contains the following five chapters:

- *Chapter 6, Launching the VSM Initiative (VSM Steps 1-3)*
- *Chapter 7, Mapping the Current State (VSM Step 4)*
- *Chapter 8, Identifying Lean Metrics (VSM Step 5)*
- *Chapter 9, Mapping the Future State (VSM Step 6)*
- *Chapter 10, Improving the Lean-Agile Value Delivery Cycle (VSM Steps 7 and 8)*

6
Launching the VSM Initiative (VSM Steps 1-3)

In the preceding chapter, you learned that **value stream management** (**VSM**) provides an approach to systematically and continuously evaluate all development and operational value streams. A VSM initiative's objective is to ensure that the organization remains aligned with corporate strategies while adding customer-centric value. You also learned the eight essential steps that support a VSM team in their efforts to plan, map, and sustain Lean improvements.

Understanding the fundamentals of VSM is critical as every **Information Technology** (**IT**)-based VSM initiative must support the organization's broader objectives to build and sustain a Lean enterprise. This chapter instructs how to apply the first three VSM steps. You will learn how to conduct the remaining five VSM steps in *Chapter 6, Launching the VSM Initiative (VSM Steps 1-3)*, through *Chapter 10, Improving the Lean-Agile Value Delivery Cycle (VSM Steps 7 and 8)*, where you will learn how to map, analyze, and improve your value streams.

This part of the book incorporates a **continuous integration/continuous delivery (CI/CD)** pipeline flow use case through *Chapter 5, Driving Business Value through a DevOps Pipeline* through *Chapter 10, Improving the Lean-Agile Value Delivery Cycle (VSM Steps 7 and 8)*. The use case will help you visualize how to employ the VSM methodology in a practical IT-oriented value stream application. Here, in this initial chapter, the focus is on learning the fundamental elements of preparing to initiate a VSM activity.

In this chapter, we're going to cover the following main topics:

- Committing to Lean—VSM Step 1
- Choosing a value stream—VSM Step 2
- Learning about Lean—VSM Step 3

Committing to Lean – VSM Step 1

VSM is about making Lean improvements across organizational value streams. Most VSM initiatives impact investments and decision-making at the strategic and portfolio levels of planning. Therefore, we need executive and stakeholder commitments to Lean to be successful with VSM. That is the topic of this first section.

It should be evident that an organization cannot be serious about employing VSM if they are not serious about implementing Lean production (development) and delivery (operations) practices. If your VSM initiative is only about improving the DevOps value stream, the organization has missed the point. VSM is about implementing and sustaining Lean practices across all value streams, and ultimately on an enterprise scale.

Before we decide to commit to Lean, we should understand something about its origins and purpose. That is the topic of the next subsection.

Navigating the origins of Lean

The origins of Lean trace back to Henry Ford's early automotive assembly lines and early mass-production concepts. Henry Ford's approach significantly improved productivity and quality with lower costs, but his assembly-line approach did not allow product-line variants.

For example, his early assembly lines limited his automotive products to just one color (black), one model (the Model T), and only one specification for each assembled part. There was no accommodation to assemble different types, body styles, colors, chassis, or other automotive parts.

Later, and through the efforts of Kiichiro Toyoda, Ohno Taiichi, Sakichi Toyoda, and Shigeo Shingo, Toyota improved Henry Ford's assembly-line and mass-production concepts to maintain continuous flows while supporting multiple product-line variations. Toyota's contributions to Lean production concepts are manifold, have evolved over decades, and continue to evolve.

The efforts started in 1930 when Kiichiro Toyoda implemented the concept of **Just-In-Time (JIT)** to improve the utilization of scarce and costly resources and eliminate waste that does not add value to the production process. Put most succinctly, JIT is about making only what's needed, only when it's needed.

Ohno Taiichia, Sakichi Toyoda, and Kiichiro Toyoda improved the JIT concept and implemented the concept behind **Jidoka**, roughly translated as **autonomation**, based on autonomous and automation. JIT and Jidoka form the two pillars of the **Toyota Production System (TPS)**. Shigeo Shingo worked for Toyota, implemented its **Single-Minute Exchange of Dies (SMED)** and **Poka-Yoke** (mistake-proofing) concepts, and published the first detailed assessment of Toyota's production processes. That book is titled *A Study of the Toyota Production System* (Shingo, Dillon; 2005—English translation).

In its modern form, the TPS, now known as the *Toyota Way*, involves JIT manufacturing, elimination of waste, and continuous improvement (Kaizen), but Toyota did not come up with the term *Lean*.

John Krafcik gets credit for defining the term *Lean* in his paper, *Triumph of the Lean Production System*, published in *Sloan Management Review* (1988). The paper describes his research while working on his **Master of Business Administration (MBA)** at **Massachusetts Institute of Technology's (MIT's)** Sloan School of Management and simultaneously working at the MIT **International Motor Vehicle Program (IMVP)** as a Lean production researcher and consultant.

Under the direction of James P. Womack, John Krafcik and the IMVP team researched more than 90 auto manufacturing companies across 15 countries to understand how Lean practices could help Western manufacturing companies compete with their Japanese counterparts employing Toyota's TPC concepts. Womack published the results of the IMPV research in his book *The Machine That Changed the World* (Womack, Jones, Roos; 1990).

Linking Lean to value delivery

The Lean enterprise seeks to achieve world-class value-delivery capabilities. Lean organizations reduce costs wherever possible, produce the highest-quality products in the industry, meet delivery requirements, and eliminate all waste from their customers' value streams.

VSM team members understand their responsibility is to help improve organizational value streams and simultaneously help the organization meet its customers' needs better than anyone else in the industry. They achieve these goals by facilitating Lean-oriented improvements across organizational value streams.

Lean companies are more competitive than others by continuously improving their business operations. Lean enterprises are more employee-friendly by showing respect for their work and delegating responsibilities to the people doing the work. These employee-friendly strategies help minimize the bureaucracy and hierarchical organizational structures that get in the way of productivity and that ultimately cause employee stress and burnout. Similarly, Lean management makes commitments to employee training, recognition, communications, and the use of Lean tools.

World-class organizations operate on a cost reduction principle that never approves passing on higher costs to customers, as operations are streamlined and made more efficient. The goal is to make it impossible for other competitors to take market share through better pricing. World-class organizations strive to produce zero defects and eliminate all waste forms from their value stream activities, further reducing their costs while increasing their competitiveness.

Lean organizations do not allow managers to push work into a production or operations function until there is available capacity to perform the work. Pushing orders and materials into a production environment faster than its production flow rate only causes waste in the form of inventory carrying costs, waiting, and hidden defects. Therefore, Lean enterprise executives know their employees must pull work into their value streams only when capacity becomes available and that materials, parts, and information must arrive just in time to support the operations, and no sooner.

Improving production flows without compromising flexibility

The significance of Toyota's work to improve production flows while maintaining flexibility in product variations cannot be understated. Yes—Ford's early assembly lines were efficient and produced high-quality automobiles, but a lack of flexibility in product-line variations left the company open to their competitors, who found ways to achieve efficient flows while still adding customer-centric value. Delivering customer-centric value means we must deliver the product features and capabilities our customers want, when they need them, and at a competitive price.

Those same lessons apply to our modern IT **development-operations (DevOps)** practices. Modern CI/CD and DevOps pipelines enable efficient production flows without compromising the organization's ability to build the right products when and as they are needed. Fully automated CI/CD and DevOps pipelines do not constrain the creative aspects of software development, but they do take the drudgery out of performing repetitive and non-value-added activities.

This section's remaining subsections stress the importance of ongoing communications, management participation, and setting up the proper starting conditions for long-term success. Lean stresses CI in the development and sustainment of production flows. The methods and tools of VSM support the Lean product life cycle commitment process. While this Lean commitment step is just the start of your VSM journey, it's critical to get off to a good start.

Installing the right operating system for VSM

It's important to note that Toyota never saw the need to move away from their classical hierarchical organizational structures. Instead, as Toyota grew into a global conglomerate, they established regional and product-line divisions with increased decision-making authority granted at the division level. The creation of regional divisions allows each geographic business unit to tailor products and services to meet local market needs. In contrast, the product-line divisions help Toyota develop and maintain its product brands.

The preservation of executive and functional management positions at the **line-of-business (LOB) level is not consistent with Lean philosophies**, but Lean production practices also move decision-making to the lowest practical levels of the organization.

For example, local operators and supervisors best know how things work and areas that can be improved. Value stream teams have the authority to make improvements at a local level that do not involve investments beyond their levels of authority or undue delays in production.

That does not leave management and executive levels out of decision-making. In *Chapter 7, Mapping the Current State (VSM Step 4)*, you learn the practice of **Gemba** (this translates as *the "actual" or "real" place*) as a practice for managers and VSM teams to walk the production floors to see what's going on. The value of Gemba is that the managers and executives are already aware and informed of the issues when decision-making needs elevation to higher levels of authority.

Lean value streams are superimposed across all business functions in hierarchical organizations, and the product lines operate as independent business units. The ideal situation in Lean is to have open communications and constant collaboration among executives, managers, and operators. In a Lean enterprise, communication flows both up and down the hierarchical or divisional business structures.

It may seem that the preservation of hierarchical organizational structures violates Agile's approach to operating small teams or scaling with **teams-of-teams** as fully self-contained and mostly autonomous production-delivery structures. However, taking a closer look, Lean value streams have dedicated resources that operate with similar independence and autonomy.

In Lean, functional management structures, when they exist, support value delivery across all development and operations-oriented value streams. Each value stream may have smaller independent teams that work as semi-autonomous units. Still, they must always remain aligned with supporting Lean-oriented work and information flows across their larger value stream and other interconnected value streams.

Another critical aspect of making Lean improvements is that executives and managers cannot be the only people coming up with ideas or making decisions in isolation. The people performing the work often have the best ideas on how to improve it. Free-flowing communications and respect for all team members allow those ideas to quickly gain support and propagate up to the decision-makers.

In his book *Building Strategic Agility for a Faster-Moving World* (2014), John Kotter suggests we need two business "operating systems." The dual operating system takes advantage of the large enterprise's economies of scale, not by taking down the functional hierarchies but by superimposing Lean value streams across the management structures.

The concept of overlaying hierarchical structures with value streams supports digital transformations by aligning resources along value streams. The functional structures help develop and maintain the resources for growth. The development and operations-oriented value streams help improve agility and responsiveness to customer demands and promote investment in emerging business opportunities.

You now know that VSM is an approach to make Lean improvements continuously, and you know why Lean is such an essential strategy for delivering optimal value from the customer's perspective. Let's now dig in to understand how to initiate and support a VSM initiative.

Managing a VSM initiative

Executives and managers play a critical role in guiding the Lean enterprise. They are ultimately accountable for a VSM initiative's success, and therefore bear full responsibility for the results. Their role is to ensure their value stream organizations deliver more value by working more efficiently, smarter, and leaner than the competition.

Executives develop and guide strategies, governance policies, and investment decisions. They have a fiduciary (trust) and legal responsibility to oversee these functions. They also develop the mission and vision for the enterprise and guide organizational values.

In contrast, managers translate strategies, missions, vision, policies, values, and investment decisions into actionable work. Put another way, managers can facilitate and guide the work that tactically implements the strategic plan's goals and objectives.

At a tactical level, managers review customer orders during monthly, bimonthly, or quarterly meetings to review customer status and complaints, suppliers, and pricing information. Managers evaluate and escalate requests for new investments in facilities, equipment, and tools necessary to meet customer needs.

Whether or not, as a formalized role of Product Manager or Product Owner, managers also review competitors' offerings and pricing and share that information with all product-team members and other interested stakeholders. LOB managers recognize employees for their efforts, plus they support the implementation of value stream process improvement activities.

When assisting in VSM efforts, executive managers identify the VSM champion and the initial core team members. The sponsoring executives establish a VSM charter that guides the VSM initiative and chooses a VSM manager to lead the effort.

If a value stream already exists, the sponsoring executives, VSM team lead, and the value stream managers should already practice **Gemba** (that is, walking around *the actual place* where value stream work occurs), but they must certainly do this once the VSM initiative kicks off. Their goal in Gemba is to break down any communications and hierarchical barriers that hinder cross-functional collaborations. The VSM leads also review any continuous improvement (Kaizen) plans if they exist.

At the beginning of the VSM initiative, the VSM team leads should create a checklist to ensure their team achieves its objectives. There is nothing wrong with having checklists, as they are simply another form of a *to-do* list so that we don't forget things we need to do. However, checklists quickly lose their value if they become directives that force unnecessary work because that's the way things are done and are used as a hammer to bludgeon people for not doing assigned work.

As an example, the checklist might include the following activities:

- Ensure a VSM charter is developed and approved by executive sponsors
- Develop an initial VSM initiative plan outlining goals, objectives, metrics, and resources
- Plan and facilitate kick-off meetings
- Allocate time and resources for training
- Create incentives for VSM team members and employees that support meeting VSM objectives and goals
- Create a communications plan and maintain diligence in executing and updating the plan
- Monitor team activities against a set of metrics mapped to desired outcomes
- Work with the VSM team to identify and eliminate roadblocks to their Lean initiatives
- Allocate sufficient funding to support the VSM initiative
- Allow flexibility on dates and times but not on driving toward Lean objectives
- Stay involved, participating in kick-off and review meetings, and keep informed

There is one final note regarding the role of the VSM lead. VSM teams must work together as a collaborative and respectful group and not fear retribution from an overbearing or authoritarian leader.

As an example, the team members must have the authority to stop work and ask for assistance to resolve any issues that impact the quality of their deliveries. This concept is called **Andon** in Japanese. The word means *lantern*, and the implication is that workers can turn on a light as a signal to stop a production line when they discover a quality issue. Any person, regardless of their rank or position, would be respected for taking this action, with no fear of repercussions.

As in Agile practices, the VSM leader is a facilitator and a servant leader to the VSM team, helping remove impediments that hinder their work. The VSM team leader also coaches, guides, and otherwise mentors the VSM lead on Lean production processes.

One of the reasons for integrating Lean-Agile practices in the IT community is because the fundamental ethos (that is, philosophy and culture) is very similar for both, as we can see here:

- Work as a team

- Respect all team members and stakeholders

- Focus on adding value in terms of the needs of the customer

- Collaborate as a team to immediately solve problems even if it means stopping other work

- Find and address the root cause to prevent problems from recurring

- Eliminate all forms of wasteful activities

- Solve problems iteratively, incrementally, and through experimentation

- Never quit looking for ways to improve

Now that we know the roles of executive sponsors, managers, and VSM team leads in the VSM initiative, let's move on to look at the VSM team startup requirements.

Starting a VSM initiative

Before choosing a value stream for a VSM initiative, we must establish the right environment for conducting a productive VSM project. This topic is our learning objective for this section.

Before selecting a target value stream for Lean improvements, we need to ensure that the target VSM project links back to a corporate strategic plan. We may also require the VSM initiative to support a portfolio investment objective.

In other words, the VSM team must have a clear understanding of why corporate investment in their project is justified. There is little value in improving value stream activities that do not positively support the organization's mission and strategies. Of course, traditional **return on investment** (**ROI**) criteria are equally important when making VSM investment decisions.

The executives and managers need to make sure that appropriate resources are approved to work on the VSM initiative. Those resources need to be committed to the effort and participate fully in the planning, mapping, and improvement initiatives.

VSM initiatives share the iterative and incremental aspects of Agile-based development projects. The following diagram shows the eight VSM steps as an iterative and incremental value delivery cycle to represent this concept:

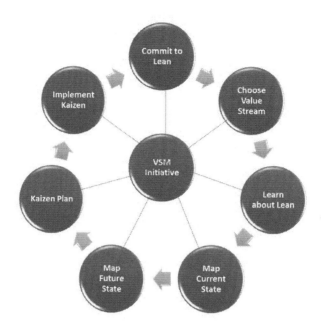

Figure 6.1 – Eight VSM steps as an iterative and incremental value delivery cycle

Each complete execution of the eight-step VSM planning, mapping, and improvement cycle is an iteration, with each iteration incrementally providing new value delivery capabilities.

Note that the VSM team may bounce back and forth between the eight VSM steps, usually to obtain additional information within an iterative VSM cycle. The main goal of having VSM cycles is to ensure continuity of work toward desired Lean value stream improvement activities.

As with Agile-based concepts, each VSM iteration incrementally adds value to the organization's efforts to implement Lean capabilities. For that reason, the organization's executives must resist the temptation to define and dictate a specific outcome as justification for the VSM effort. The VSM team initiative lives for as long as it's cost-justified to continue investments in their work.

To ensure the VSM initiative has long-term sustainability, the executives must dedicate a project manager or a VSM champion, or—in an Agile context—perhaps a Scrum Master to guide the team's efforts. During the VSM effort, the VSM team lead, VSM team members, and the value stream managers must be fully engaged, devoting their time to their value delivery improvement efforts, and be willing to sustain their Lean efforts across the life of the VSM initiative.

Anything worth doing is worth spending some time on in terms of preparation and planning—not a lot of time, but a couple of weeks might not be out of the question. Initially, organizational executives or their designates must develop a VSM charter. The charter formally approves and funds the initiative. The VSM charter also outlines goals and objectives, as well as the broad scope of work, and identifies the VSM team lead and the high-level metrics and outcomes for success.

Developing and having the executives sign the VSM charter helps ensure the VSM initiative has one or more executive sponsors supporting and hopefully driving the initiative. The organization's executives must be on board with supporting and leading the effort to get the funding and approvals the VSM team requires to support their identified improvement initiatives.

Once the VSM charter is approved, the VSM team develops the initial VSM plan. The plan should not be overly unwieldy or overbearing in terms of outlining the work of the team. However, at a minimum, the VSM plan needs to identify the following:

- VSM team members
- Resources available or needed for training and coaching
- Funding for the VSM team's work and their proposed Kaizen improvements
- The steps applied by the VSM team to guide the organization's Lean improvements, such as the eight steps outlined in this book
- Available VSM software tools
- Guidance on the ongoing team and stakeholder communications

After a VSM charter and plan are created and approved, the VSM team lead initiates a kick-off meeting to ensure everyone is on the same page and understands their respective roles and responsibilities. At a minimum, the VSM team lead, all VSM team members, the sponsoring executive (that is, the executive who owns the budget), and critical stakeholders must attend.

With the VSM kick-off meeting, the VSM initiative is formally in place and ready to start its work.

Sustaining the VSM initiative

While Lean concepts are relatively simple to understand, they are challenging to implement and much more challenging to sustain over time. It's human nature to want to move on to something else or begin to let things go.

VSM has several elements in common with Agile practices—for example, communications and respect for people help ensure difficult information is shared and acted on productively. As with Scrum, Lean practices encourage experimentation and observation (that is, empiricism) and small iterative and incremental steps to improve value, and the VSM teams must be willing to show their findings (**transparency**), examine their findings (**inspection**), and be flexible in responding appropriately and aggressively where change is needed (**adaptive**).

Most importantly, the executive sponsors and team leaders must remain fully engaged in leading the effort. Folks working within the value stream quickly realize when the leaders are not taking their improvement ideas seriously, and they back off their improvement efforts in frustration.

Visualization of value stream improvement activities is an essential component of VSM sustainment activities. Again, similar to Agile concepts, VSM employs visual aids with updated team information and metrics to continuously inform executives, managers, and other stakeholders on their work's goals and status. We'll discuss visual aids in more detail in the *Learning about Lean* section of this chapter.

This section concludes the discussions on the need to commit to Lean. Now that you know the importance of committing to Lean, let's look at the tools that help support this objective.

Committing to Lean – tools

The tools discussed in this section help us to achieve our objective of committing to Lean. These tools include the following:

- VSM charter
- Kick-off meeting
- VSM storyboard

Each of these tools will be discussed in detail in the next subsections.

VSM charter

A **VSM charter** is an essential tool that helps ensure you have executive commitment. A charter is a formal commitment by both management and the VSM team members on what they hope to achieve. A VSM charter should cover the following topics:

- VSM initiative title
- VSM charter's mission
- Deliverables
- Expected scope/approach/activities
- Strategic alignment factors
- Timeframe/duration
- Team resources
- Team process
- Expected results
- Key customers and suppliers
- Assumptions
- Risks
- Internal issues
- External issues

Appendix A includes an example of a **VSM charter**.

Kick-off meeting

A **kick-off meeting** is an important meeting to ensure that everyone is prepared to start the VSM initiative and knows their roles and responsibilities. The VSM initiative champion should attend this first meeting to explain why the team was assembled and how they were selected. The VSM champion explains to the VSM team why executive management sponsored and funded the VSM initiative. For example, the VSM project may address competitive pressures, emergent or niche market customer demands, lead-time reductions, improvements to quality, or other concerns over waste.

Critically, the VSM champion must reinforce the importance to the VSM team members that they take the time to learn the principles and tools of Lean, which we'll address a bit later in this chapter.

VSM storyboard

A **VSM storyboard** is one of the essential tools presented in this book. It serves as a guide throughout your VSM project, taking you through the eight-step process of planning, mapping, and improving your selected value stream.

A VSM storyboard includes the following sections:

- Date originated
- Identified value stream
- VSM champion
- VSM team members
- Problem categories
- Primary Lean tools
- Current (as-is) state map
- Future (to-be) state map
- Metrics
- Kaizen proposal/plans

Appendix B includes a diagram of a **VSM storyboard template**. Take a few moments to review this diagram, as we revisit the template frequently in this and other chapters within this book.

> **Note**
>
> For this initial VSM step, *Committing to Lean*, the VSM champion completes *Sections 1* and *2* of the VSM storyboard, indicating the initial project state, prospective value streams (if identified), the name of the VSM initiative's champion, and the VSM team members.

With this, we have completed the section on committing to Lean. Now, with the commitment made, it's time to discuss how the VSM team determines the best organizational value stream to support its efforts.

Choosing a value stream – VSM Step 2

This section deals with the activities that help a VSM team choose a value stream for its Lean improvement initiative. In the long run, the initial VSM team may go on to assess other value streams. However, it's also likely that larger organizations will initiate multiple VSM teams to support Lean improvement initiatives in other value streams.

VSM initiatives must have a sense of urgency that justifies investments in resources and time. We already know that organizations typically have numerous value streams and probably don't have the time and resources to work on all of them at once. So, we need to prioritize the team's efforts.

The question then becomes: *Which ones should we start improving?* In conformance with the **Pareto principle** (a.k.a. the **80/ 20 rule** and **Pareto's Law**), some value stream improvements are more critical to the organization's immediate success than others. The organization's executives may have already identified areas that are inefficient or costly, or not making products customers want, or exhibiting some other aspects of waste, but we still need to do the work to identify our value streams and prioritize areas for improvement. For example, the VSM team can do the following:

- Evaluate the degree to which the organization has identified its value streams
- Evaluate the degree to which each value stream maps to customer-oriented value delivery
- Conduct studies to discover which value streams have the highest costs and delays
- Conduct customer surveys to find out how well the organization is meeting their needs
- Use Lean metrics to identify value streams that have the highest levels of waste
- Discuss with employees their observations about value stream issues that need resolution
- If available, conduct a competitive analysis to determine how well the company is performing in the industry
- Identify critical benchmarks metrics, both inside and outside the company, to see how they compare with others in the company and businesses with similar value streams
- When making VSM investment decisions, employ the acronym **SMART**—**S**pecific, **M**easurable, **A**ttainable, **R**elevant, and **T**ime-based

Regardless of the steps taken, the VSM team must always address their work in terms of delivering customer-centric value and doing so in the leanest way possible in both the short and long run. So, to make those kinds of determinations, let's take a moment to revisit the subject of value, but in a VSM context.

Defining value in a VSM context

This section revisits the concept of **value** as it relates to VSM. You already know that, from the perspective of Lean, the term *value* implies the delivery of value in the form of a product, service, or result that you are creating for an internal or external customer. Moreover, the concept of value implies the activities are providing results your customers are willing to purchase.

In reality, our value streams always include elements of waste to one degree or another. Activities that produce results that are irrelevant to your customers' needs are forms of waste, and we need to make our best efforts to eliminate them—and that is the point of *Kaizen*, the Japanese term for continuous improvement.

The term *value* in Lean applies to the work we do in our value streams and our VSM activities. But you may have asked yourself what the term *stream* implies. It's literally as straightforward as you might think. Metaphorically, the term *stream* refers to a sequential flow of activities that create value, therefore VSM improves the flow of value across our organization.

Conceptually, work items flow downstream across the value stream activities, just like water flows downstream in a creek or river. Metaphorically, as water in streams and rivers ultimately flows to the oceans, Lean-oriented value flows to our customers.

Lean practitioners understand that value streams include both value-added and non-value-added work activities. In the long run, we want to eliminate the non-value-added work activities, though it may not be practical to do so in the short run.

The following diagram provides a graphical display of a generic **activity workflow model** showing the cycle times and wait times associated with four activities within a value stream:

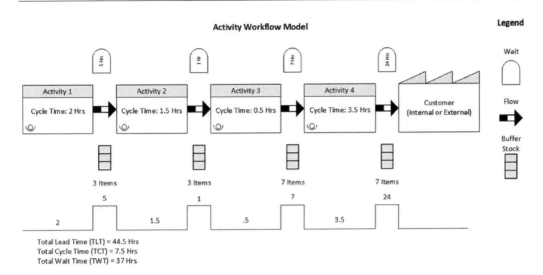

Activity Workflow Model

Legend

Wait

Flow

Buffer
Stock

Total Lead Time (TLT) = 44.5 Hrs
Total Cycle Time (TCT) = 7.5 Hrs
Total Wait Time (TWT) = 37 Hrs

Figure 6.2 – Activity workflow model

This model begins to introduce some of the icons used in value stream mapping, but we'll come back and revisit this subject in more detail later in the following chapter on current- and future-state value stream mapping. For now, use the legend to interpret the information contained in the diagram.

For example, let's say that our engineers know how to improve **Activity 2** to bring the cycle time down to 1 hour. At first glance, that seems a reasonable thing to do. However, the problem is that the system's major bottleneck is at **Activity 4** because it has a significantly greater cycle time of 3.5 hours. Improving the upstream activities' speeds only means more products queue at the entry to **Activity 4**, and the flow is not improved.

This example is elementary, as there are other variables to consider when improving flows. We might have setup times that can be improved through better tooling. We may have high levels of defects that cost the organization more than the slow output of **Activity 4**. So far, our value stream map doesn't say anything about the lot or batch sizes or buffer stock limits, all of which can significantly change the throughput and queuing across each of the identified activities.

All we know so far is the activity cycle times and the basic flow of materials. However, we can already see that this model does not indicate a Lean value stream. Instead, it's probably much more like the situations you find in organizations that have not yet made the transition to Lean. For example, the arrows indicate the materials are pushed to each downstream activity, and there are buffer stocks between each activity to contain overflow due to the mismatched cycle times.

Note that the overall wait time is 37 hours against a total lead time of 44.5 hours. In other words, only 7.5 hours of work is included in the overall lead time. The most likely cause is the mismatched cycle times and lot sizes, but we need to analyze the flow across the value stream to confirm the actual cause and effects.

There is another issue the Lean organization must consider, and that is the integration or touchpoints between value streams. This topic is the subject of the next subsection.

Integrating value streams

Value stream interactions occur whenever one value stream adds value in the form of products, services, or information that other value streams need. For example, in the IT community, we often see this when the IT development-oriented value streams produce software products that are then delivered by operations-oriented value streams to internal or external customers.

We also see value stream interactions occur when product and marketing management value streams conduct activities that help identify customer needs for product design, development, and delivery-oriented value streams. For example, organizations may develop or procure software applications to assist their product and marketing management functions, such as the following:

- Strategic planning
- Market analysis
- Product planning
- Go-to-market activities
- Sales enablement

In a digital economy, all value streams are integrated and supported by IT to enable infrastructure, computing equipment, software, networks, and security components. Many physical products and services have computing, networking, and software components built in as features to enhance the products' capabilities. The value of using digital features is that product updates can be streamed live to the products, enhancing existing products without costly maintenance or service calls.

But let's simplify things for a moment and get back to the subject of using digital services to support the value streams associated with product and marketing management. As our example, *Figure 6.3* displays an **adaptive productizing process** that includes three **product management subprocesses—Strategic Planning**, **Product Planning**, and **Market Analysis**—and two **marketing management subprocesses—Go To Market** and **Sales Enablement**.

Each of the five subprocesses includes multiple workflows, as indicated by the spokes of the wheel, that deliver value within the adaptive marketing process. Ideally, each workflow is streamlined to deliver value with minimal, if any, waste. In this context, each spoke is a form of value stream. Also, based on the unique needs of every product, and the variety of needs across a product's life cycle, the execution of these processes will vary over the life of each product.

The processes are depicted here:

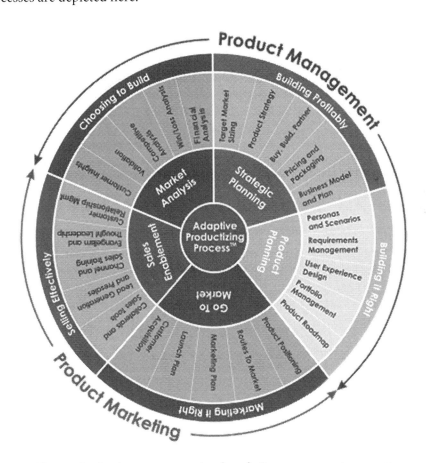

Figure 6.3 – Product management and marketing management processes

Product and marketing management value streams are operations-oriented—in other words, they do not develop products for our external customers, but they do support our ability to assist and deliver value to our external customers. We'll take a closer look at how operations-oriented value streams function in the next section, using the adaptive productizing process as an example.

Operations-oriented value stream integrations

By definition, operations-oriented value streams directly interface with internal or external customers but are not directly involved in product development. Very often, the operations-oriented value streams gather, analyze, and deliver information for their customers. The operations-oriented value streams may also be involved in delivering products and services directly to the organization's customers.

This subsection introduces operations-oriented value stream activities supporting product management and marketing management functions, and we are going to use the Adaptive Productizing Process as our example.

An adaptive productizing process is a customer-centric approach that helps an organization track and respond to customer demands. Adaptive product and marketing management approaches evolved to support emergent business models such as **Software as a Service (SaaS)**, new promotional and sales routes to markets through Web 2.0, and selling to customers via **business-to-business (B2B)** and **business-to-consumer (B2C)** industry segments.

A vital element of the adaptive productizing process is the utilization of social media-based marketing. As a result, the adaptive productizing process is well suited to work within our digital economies.

Adaptive marketing processes take advantage of digital enablement to support the organization's value chain—in other words, product and marketing management value streams have evolved to support what we develop and how we sell and deliver products in our modern digital economy. The product and marketing management subprocesses add value in the form of market and customer information to determine product requirements from a customer-centric perspective.

Figure 6.3 graphically depicted the adaptive productizing process as a **hub-and-spoke** process model—in other words, work artifacts and information moving across the adaptive productizing processes can flow in any direction. Therefore, when we design our product management and marketing management value streams, and associated information systems, we need to take these concerns into account.

Using an IT analogy, we need a value stream integration approach that mimics the work performed by a hub-and-spoke message broker to simplify communications, data flows, and asynchronous transformations. Unfortunately, a point-to-point process and information integration strategy won't work, as there are too many points of integration. Plus, there is no way the development team can account for every possible information flow or activity interaction across the adaptive productizing process.

A better approach is to assess each set of activities within each spoke as potential elements of the overall value stream. Each spoke of the hub represents a standalone activity or subprocess. Moreover, each subprocess can be invoked by other subprocesses as the need arises. For each product or product family, evaluate the overall product management and product marketing value streams to identify where the flow constraints form bottlenecks and where waste hinders the overall process.

The hub-and-spoke analogy is not meant to imply that work is pushed from one marketing value stream to another in the adaptive productizing process. In Lean-oriented production processes, work is always pulled on demand when it's needed by the upstream customer or succeeding activity.

Still, the hub-and-spoke analogy is useful because the flow of work through the identified adaptive product management and product marketing tasks is highly dependent upon each product's needs across their life cycles.

Taking the **Go To Market** processes as an example, **Product Positioning**, **Routes to Market**, and other associated subprocesses are potential value stream workflow components. Each workflow component potentially includes multiple activities and techniques. The component subprocesses have different cycle times and wait times. They all likely have a mix of value-adding and non-value-adding activities and other forms of waste that should be cleaned up over time.

Always prioritize improvement activities to eliminate the current constraint in the overall value stream process. If you have time and resources to work on more than one value stream improvement initiative, always make sure you place your priorities on resolving the leading flow constraints or highest-cost drivers. Later in this chapter, you learn how to use current (*as-is*) and future (*to-be*) value stream maps to help you make these assessments.

The adaptive productizing value streams represent a more complex view of the product and marketing-oriented value streams than those identified initially and outlined by James Martin. Nevertheless, the many subprocesses depicted in *Figure 6.3* are no less relevant. The diagram also does a better job of showing the complexity of activities and the potential for interactions across product and marketing management value streams. With this analogy, you should gain insights into why VSM and DevOps are critical enablers to improve Lean value streams across the organization.

Development-oriented value stream integration

Conceptually, a development-oriented value stream includes all the value-added and non-value-added actions necessary to produce a product or service, from the initial concept through development to receipt of the payment. Development-oriented value streams produce products for external customers or to support the organization's operations-oriented value streams.

In manufacturing, each product family follows a separate value stream. Product families typically group parts or part numbers that share a similar process sequence. The overall objective is always to make sure the right parts and materials arrive just in time, as they are needed to support the development process, and at the right location.

Conceptually, this means information related to a product order must flow across all upstream development-oriented value stream activities to match parts with products and their associated development activities. The parts and materials must arrive in the proper sequence at the buffer stores to their specific production activities to support the customer order. The customer order information flows back to the inventory management system to trigger new parts and materials replacement orders to supply-chain partners.

And each product area has three primary value streams that overlap and flow together, as identified here:

- A **concept-to-launch** value stream—Includes all the activities required to take a concept or idea through product design and engineering, determine competitive pricing, establish a supply chain and processes for the procurement of materials, design customer ordering and quoting activities, and determine the control plan release process

- A **raw-material-to-finished-product** value stream—Contains all the manufacturing materials and information activities to deliver a product to a customer with the highest possible quality at the lowest possible cost, with the shortest possible lead time

- An **order-to-cash** value stream—Begins with an incoming customer order and ends with a payment receipt

Concept to launch and **order to cash** are operations-oriented value streams, while **raw materials to finished products** is a development value stream. The naming convention for the three aforementioned development-oriented value streams follows the strategy identified previously to specify the name's start and ending activities. You don't have to name your value streams in this manner, but this approach makes it easier to conceptualize the work performed within each value stream and the deliverables.

Just as described for operations-oriented value streams, development-oriented value streams have multiple processes and activities. The activities vary across industries and companies, therefore an essential element of VSM is to define those activities that give you a better competitive advantage.

This issue bears repeating: never attempt to improve individual processes without having a complete picture of the value stream. Without a map of the current value stream, you cannot know where your bottlenecks and wastes are. Improving an individual process may have little or no effect if it's not the main bottleneck, and there is always only one main bottleneck at any given point in time.

Following the Pareto principle (that is, the 80/20 rule), once you fix the current main bottleneck, other activity cycle times pop up as relatively lengthy in the value stream, creating new bottlenecks. The same principle is true for resolving any form of waste across your value streams. It's the primary reason we must always practice Kaizen (that is, continuously improving our working practices to eliminate the next-highest constraints and other forms of waste).

In their book, *VSM for the Lean Office*, Dan Tapping and Don Shuker note that between 60% and 80% of all product development costs are non-production costs. In other words, the highest costs accumulate from the **concept-to-launch** and **order-to-cash** value streams. Since these are primarily information-driven value streams, VSM and DevOps are critical enablers to all Lean implementation activities (Tapping, Shuker; 2002, 2003).

Before we end this subsection, let's take a quick look at the tools that help identify which value streams have the highest opportunity to improve our value delivery capabilities.

Choosing a value stream – tools

At the start of every VSM initiative, the VSM team members should conduct four activities to help them choose the appropriate value stream for their next initiative. These activities include the following:

- Identifying immediate customer needs and concerns that aren't adequately addressed

- Performing a work-unit routing analysis

- Prioritizing targeted value streams in terms of the most significant net positive impact

- Updating the team charter and continuing brainstorming ideas

The primary tools available to the VSM team to assist with these four activities include a **product-quantity (PQ)** analysis, a **product-routing (PR)** analysis, a work unit routing analysis, plus updates to the VSM storyboard. These are outlined in more detail here:

- **PQ analysis**: This involves creating a Pareto chart containing the list of parts or work items produced over the previous 6 months. Each line item includes the part numbers, quantities produced, cumulative quantities, percent of production, and cumulative percent of production. This analysis helps the VSM team quickly see which product lines contribute to and have the highest impact on improving production volumes.

- **PR analysis**: If PQ analysis has a PQ ratio of 40:60 or greater (40% or more of products account for 60% of the total quantity of parts), use PR analysis to help choose your value stream. In other words, we want to form product families around the highest volume of products that have a similar set of value stream activities.

  Using a matrix or table format, list the products and their volumes in the first columns, and then list their product activity sequence horizontally. Next, group products with the same process sequences and analyze the mix of process routes. Your analysis should include evaluations of the highest-volume products, highest-cost products, most inefficient flows, and current and future customer demands. See the following screenshot for an example of this:

Volume	Product	Activity A	Activity B	Activity C	Activity D	Activity E	Activity F	Activity G
2500	1	A	B	C		E	F	G
1200	2		B	C		E		G
1000	3	A	B		D	E	F	G
800	4		B	C	D	E	F	G
150	5	A	B	C	D			G

Figure 6.4 – PR analysis table

In this example, the product team creates a PR table and can quickly see that the highest-volume products **1-3** all have activities **C**, **E**, and **G**. Also, products **1** and **3** both have a requirement for activities **A** and **F**. Thus, it probably makes sense to create a value stream with activities **A** through **C** and **E** through **G** as dedicated workstations. However, only product **C** in the list of the highest-volume products has a requirement for activity **D**. Further analysis is required to see whether adding activity **D** is cost-justified to add as a dedicated workstation to the value stream flow.

- **Work unit routing analysis**: This is the services-oriented equivalent to PR analysis, but instead of listing product lines in the matrix, you list families of work units or customers involved in the area you are targeting for improvements.

The following screenshot shows an example of a work unit routing analysis in a worksheet format:

Work Unit Routing Analysis						
Work Item Types	Average Monthly Volume	Activity/ Process A	Activity/ Process B	Activity/ Process C	Activity/ Process D	Activity/ Process E
WI_1	100	X	X	X		
WI_2	350		X	X	X	X
WI_3	25	X	X			
WI_4	125	X	X	X		
WI_5	150		X	X	X	X
WI_6	500		X	X	X	X

Figure 6.5 – Work unit routing analysis

The first column lists the work-item types produced for customers, while the second column lists the average volume of work performed for each identified work item or customer over time. The next set of columns lists across the matrix the sequence of processes or activities supporting the work items in production across the matrix. In the grid formed in the matrix, mark the activities or processes required to produce each product type. Finally, group work units with similar process flows and then rank all the flows according to their volumes.

Our example shows that work item types **1**, **5**, and **6** have similar workflows, with a combined volume of 1,000 work items. We'll call this *Group A*. Also, work items **1** and **4** have identical flows for a total volume of 225 work items, which we'll refer to as *Group B*. Work-item number **3** stands alone, with a mere **25** units required.

It should be pretty clear that *Group A* represents the most significant amount of work for the company, followed distantly by *Group B*. The production requirement for work-item number **3** is comparatively minimal and probably doesn't bear much analysis unless it's exceptionally profitable or causing bottleneck issues for the other product lines.

- **Updated VSM storyboard**: You should now have a definitive idea of which value stream(s) your VSM team plans to focus on for its Lean-oriented improvement activities. Update the VSM storyboard to reflect the identified value stream(s) in *Section 2*.

So far, you have learned the first two steps of the eight-step VSM process for planning, mapping, and sustaining Lean improvements. *Step 1* included the activities to identify and initiate the core VSM implementation team. Next, the activities in *Step 2* helped identify the highest-priority value stream for their VSM initiative. Now, it's time to examine *Step 3*.

Learning about Lean – VSM Step 3

In *Step 3*, the VSM team must make sure they have a strong understanding of Lean concepts, and they must make sure that the team members working in the value stream understand the concepts of Lean production.

There are many sources available to learn about Lean production practices. This section serves as a quick primer for those who are just starting their Lean learning journey. What's most important is that the VSM team members learn the basic concepts of Lean and then apply them. It's the application of Lean principles that helps build the skills for all future VSM initiatives.

Developing a learning plan

To ensure all team members develop sufficient skills and understanding of Lean concepts, the VSM team should start their learning initiative by building a **Lean learning plan**. Developing a training plan typically includes the following six steps:

1. Document required skills and knowledge.
2. Perform current skills and knowledge assessment.
3. Conduct skills and knowledge gap assessment.
4. Design training methods (that is, instructor-led classroom training, interactive group sessions, hands-on training, computer-based and e-learning training, video training, coaching, and mentoring).
5. Schedule and conduct the training.
6. Evaluate the effectiveness of the training and make the necessary adjustments.

Benchmarking

Suppose this is your team's first VSM initiative. In that case, they may not understand what looks good yet in terms of best practices and metrics for installing Lean production capabilities across their industry. In such cases, it's often useful to spend some time gathering information from similar enterprises or departments to develop a set of benchmarks for comparative analysis. This type of activity is called **benchmarking** and typically involves analyzing competitive practices using quality, time, and cost metrics.

The VSM team should start the benchmarking activity by being very clear on what they want to improve. Frankly, the team should be doing this from the start, as that's the whole point of the VSM initiative. As the team reaches out to potential benchmarking organizations, they need to understand this is a big ask, and they must be humble about it.

You're not likely to get your competitors to share this information, so the team's first order of business is to identify organizations and industries similar to the type of work performed in the VSM team's value stream.

As the VSM team reaches out to their targeted benchmarking partners, they should take the time first to understand their partner's business. You'll have a hard time convincing a potential partner to spend their time with you if you haven't taken the time to know anything about them. Besides, it's essential to let them know that your objective is to create a relationship where both parties win from sharing information—not just in the short run, but potentially over time. In that way, both organizations can continue to evolve and improve together, plus the benchmarking partner is not likely to feel they are being used.

Once you know what your goals of the VSM initiative are, use that information to develop a set of questions to ask your benchmarking partner. This work should be done in advance of meeting with them or even contacting them. Again, this type of preliminary activity will show them you've done your homework, and then you bring something to the partnership.

When you meet with the benchmarking partners, have more than one person from your VSM team in attendance. You don't need to overwhelm your partners by taking the entire VSM team, but you need at least two people to go to the meeting—one to take notes, and the other to ask questions.

The questions you might ask can be imposing in terms of encroaching on confidential and proprietary information. Therefore, you need to be sensitive to their concerns and respect their privacy.

Having a face-to-face meeting is almost always best for seeing people's reactions and responding appropriately to their concerns. Your partners might even be willing to show your team examples of their activities while you are visiting their site. However, especially in this day and age of COVID-19, online conference calls are certainly workable and appropriate.

After finishing the meeting, thank your benchmarking partner for their time and consideration, and make sure you follow up with the promised sharing of information. Specifically, you should share the outcomes of the VSM practices you put in place within your value stream.

The purpose of a benchmarking exercise is to have a set of metrics and procedures that you can compare to your own. Suppose you have chosen your benchmarking partners because they have demonstrated superior competencies in the areas you are measuring. In that case, you will have a sound baseline to gauge your current state and to define expectations for your desired future states.

With the Lean training plan in place, the VSM team needs to ensure all participants and active stakeholders take advantage of the training. Specifically, there are six areas of Lean they must understand. We'll discuss these six fundamental concepts in the next subsection.

Learning the fundamental concepts of Lean

There are six fundamental concepts that you need to understand to create a Lean system. These six concepts include the following:

- The cost reduction principle
- The seven wastes of Lean
- Two pillars of Lean—JIT and Jidoka
- The 5S system
- Visual workplace
- Three stages of Lean application—demand, flow, and leveling

We'll briefly review each of these six Lean concepts, in turn, in the next subsections.

The cost reduction principle

The **cost reduction principle** in Lean is oppositional to mainstream pricing practices where we calculate the price of a product by adding up costs and then applying desired profit margins. The problem with this strategy is that the focus is neither on the customer nor on how to improve. Without understanding how our customers assess value, we can't know what price they are willing to pay. Moreover, if we don't focus on optimizing value delivery and price this accordingly, we open ourselves to losing business to our competitors.

Instead, the Lean organization allows the customer to set the selling price, and the costs and profits become variables. In other words, the Lean organization analyzes to determine an acceptable price and then evaluates what must be done across the value stream to eliminate waste, such that they can deliver the product and service at an acceptable price.

The seven deadly wastes

The **seven Lean wastes** add cost and time delays or hinder quality without adding value to the customers. The seven wastes of Lean include the following:

- **Overproducing**: This occurs whenever we produce too much of something without a customer order or historical demand for external customers to justify the investments in time and resources or before the work items are required by our internal customers.

  Overproducing also occurs when we acquire or develop batch processes or high-speed equipment mismatched with the rate of flow across other value stream activities. Recalling the ideal of single-piece flows, we already know that batch processing causes queues to form and creates excessive inventories. Additionally, spending money, time, and resources to expedite one activity may cause wait times, bottlenecks, and queues to form across the value stream.

  Recalling the **80/20 rule** (**the Pareto principle** or **Pareto's Law**) always improves performance on the top 20% of your efficiency problems, as this probably represents 80% to 90% of your current waste and inefficiencies. By fixing your current bottlenecks, you improve flow and capacity across the value stream as a whole.

- **Waiting** (**Q time**): This is when anything—including people, materials, equipment, or information—spends time waiting without value-added work performed. The waste comes from hidden bugs and defects, inventory carrying costs, and extra storage facilities.

- **Transport**: Includes having to move something further than necessary to perform the next activity, representing a waste of time and energy. Transport applies to materials, people, and paper-based information flows.

  Transport-related waste often forms before moving to Lean, when value stream activities are located within or across disparate facilities by function or by department, or given to external suppliers, and do not support an efficient flow for a given product line.

  Transport as waste also occurs when items are temporally filed, stocked, stacked, or otherwise moved out of the way.

- **Overprocessing**: This occurs when we load a product with features and functions customers haven't requested. They may not be valued, and we shouldn't develop or deliver any product capability until we know there is a customer need to justify the work. Furthermore, we won't know this until the product managers or product owners conduct business opportunity assessments to know if there is a cost-justified market for the enhancements.

  Overprocessing is a critical form of waste as we can't get our time and resources back, and we have to eat the costs of something our customers don't value. Even if a market is identified, the features or functions may not have the highest priority, and they may not be cost-justified. Our customers may not want to pay the price that it takes to justify the costs of development and delivery.

- **Inventory**: This is an excess stock of any materials or products, or even resources, that are not immediately needed. We only need enough materials to balance flows, and no more.

  Remember that the ideal is single-piece flows with equivalent cycle times across all value stream activities and no changeover times. If we can obtain that ideal, including material deliveries under JIT, there is no justification for inventories.

  In the meantime, inventories take up space, may impact safety, can expire in specific circumstances, or hide bugs and defects in inventoried lots. Inventories are also expensive to purchase and store, and worse—they may not be what you require when you finally match the inventoried materials to customer orders (that is, wrong part number, model, or type).

- **Motion**: This includes any movement not necessary to complete an operation. Motion is a form of waste that results from ineffective job processes or facility layouts and often causes more walking, reaching, or bending than necessary. In the context of digital enablement, this can be seen as excessive process overhead and lag, or built-in push-type systems and workflows.

This form of waste is similar to transport but on a smaller scale. Think of transport as movement across facilities or geographies, while motion is limited to the range of movement within or across linked value stream activities.

- **Defects**: This is a hidden form of waste from defective work in physical products or bugs in software development. Although sometimes used interchangeably, the word *defect* in software development refers to situations where a product enhancement is missing a customer-requested feature. In contrast, bugs are defects in the software's code.

  Defects usually require rework or destruction of materials and products. In either case, defects are quite costly.

Though not included as part of the original seven deadly sins of waste, some Lean thought leaders describe another form of waste identified as **non-utilized talents**. Human beings have both intellectual and physical attributes that add value to an organization. In particular, our employees' intellectual attributes can grow by their gaining relevant experience, knowledge, and skills.

Suppose we don't initiate programs to improve our employees' intellectual potentials. In that case, we allow waste to form by limiting human capital growth and the innovations our people can bring to the workplace. Human capital is an economic view of our employees' contributions and evaluates their skills, knowledge, and experience as contributing both value and costs to our organization.

One final note to make in this section is that all forms of waste within our value stream are included in the product's overall cost, and therefore its price. This Lean concept is essential, as eliminating waste represents opportunities to improve our value streams to deliver customer-centric value. In this case, waste occurs because we are not taking advantage of unutilized human talent.

This section concludes our discussions on the elimination of waste. Let's now move on to understand the importance of the two Lean pillars behind the TPS: JIT and Jidoka.

Two pillars of TPS

Recall our earlier discussions on the TPS. In his books, Ohno claims TPS is based on two primary concepts, or pillars: **JIT** and **Jidoka** (which translates as autonomation).

The TPS aims to make vehicles ordered by customers as fast and efficiently as possible and deliver value as quickly as possible. Let's take a quick look at how JIT and Jidoka contribute to those goals, as follows:

- **JIT production**: This is an ideal state of continuous flow where materials reach their correct point of assembly, in the proper order, and just at the time of need. When a customer order comes in, signals propagate along the production line, or value stream, to indicate the new material requirements at each production stage. Under a **first-in, first-out** (**FIFO**) order entry system, the orders and materials utilized within the value stream trickle forward to meet up with the right product, at the right stage of production, at the right time.

  In other words, JIT systems replenish parts in a pull-based system driven by customer orders. The ideal scenario is to refine your Lean processes and value stream activities to enable a single-piece flow to replenish materials at the point and time of need. For example, JIT triggers third-party suppliers' parts and material deliveries upstream in a manufacturing line upon receiving a customer order upstream. In an IT-oriented value stream, we implement the same concepts via Kanban boards and cards.

  JIT is the heartbeat of Lean production systems, establishing its pulse to ensure the correct pacing in delivering information, materials, and parts when and where they are needed.

- **Jidoka** (a.k.a. **autonomation**)—This uses automation to perform repetitive and dangerous tasks. The goal is not to use automation to replace humans. Instead, the autonomation capabilities help free up workers' time to perform multiple tasks within their value streams that require flexibility and thought.

  To accomplish this goal, we must distinguish between work that needs human guidance from work that is repetitive, hazardous, or subject to human error, and therefore best performed by automated machinery. Autonomation includes developing defect detection and prevention devices and automation capabilities for all assembly and testing processes.

  Note that Jidoka applies equally to automating tasks such as testing, configuration, and provisioning in a software development context. In other words, the automation capabilities employed in CI, test automation, and CD allow the developers to stay focused on their value-adding tasks associated with requirements analysis, architecture and design, coding, and problem-solving.

The goal of Jidoka is to make workplaces efficient and safe while minimizing the possibility of delivering low-quality or defective products. Ultimately, Jidoka helps mistake-proof your value streams while providing efficiencies and throughput to deliver products at a rate that matches your customers' demands (that is, Takt time).

There are four basic concepts associated with Jidoka, outlined as follows:

a) Simplify or automate the discovery of abnormalities

b) Immediately stop all failed or failing activities, even if it means shutting down the entire value stream, as we don't want queues to form

c) Fix the problem before restarting the line

d) Investigate and solve the root causes of the problem

These four processes ensure that problems are discovered and addressed quickly. Moreover, the objective of Jidoka is to prevent problems from getting out of hand by producing more waste. Ultimately, we need to find out the root causes so that we can prevent future mishaps.

Now that we've discussed the concepts behind JIT and Jidoka, let's discuss the 5S system, a Lean production tool that helps improve workplace efficiency by eliminating waste.

The 5S system

As with the two pillars of Lean discussed in the previous section, the **5S system** was developed in Japan as part of the TPS manufacturing method. When first starting out on a Lean improvement initiative, it's not unusual to find that value stream processes are misaligned, cluttered, and inefficient, if they exist at all.

This situation often occurs in manufacturing lines that produce multiple product lines and in operations-oriented value streams with unorganized paper-based systems, files, supplies, tools, equipment, and books. The primary intent of the 5S system is to eliminate the clutter and improve the flow of our value stream activities in a structured approach.

The origin of the 5S term came from the Japanese words *Seiri, Seiton, Seiso, Seiketsu,* and *Shitsuke*. Conveniently, we have five English terms that also start with the letter S to stand in for the originals. The 5S system includes, as you might imagine, five steps, each starting with the letter *S*, as shown in the following screenshot:

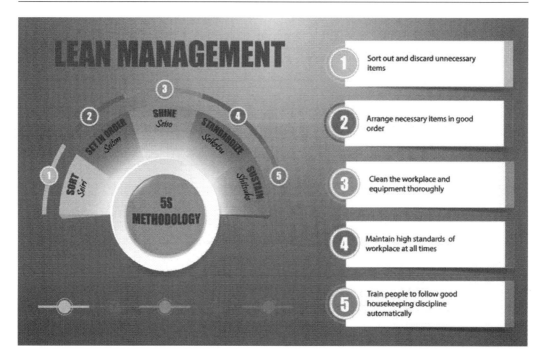

Figure 6.6 – The 5S system

Each of the five letters indicates a step in a process to improve and sustain our Lean practices. So, let's take a few moments to review the work associated with each step, as follows:

1. **Sort**—*Seiri* (tidiness): Start by reviewing all inventories of materials and parts, equipment, files, documents, books, or any other paraphernalia and get rid of anything no longer needed in the revised or new value stream.

2. **Set in order**—*Seiton* (orderliness): Organize whatever remains to support efficient workflow, including identifying and storing inventory and buffer stock storage areas. Arrange all necessary items to make them easy and efficient to access. Most importantly, strive to maintain orderliness going forward.

3. **Shine**—*Seiso* (cleanliness): As part of the first two steps, take the time to clean the areas and inspect equipment to make sure everything works properly. Clean and inspect each work area regularly. The process of regular cleaning helps ensure that your work area and equipment are adequately maintained, reducing the potential for creating waste or unanticipated work stoppages.

4. **Standardize**—*Seiketsu* (standardization): The goal here is to standardize activities to maintain the work environment across your value stream—in other words, create a 5S standard operating procedure to maintain orderliness, cleanliness, and maintenance of your work environment. Make your 5S standards visual and evident within the work area.

5. **Sustain**—*Shitsuke* (discipline): Maintenance of the 5S standards does not happen accidentally. It takes constant attention to detail and discipline to ensure the value stream team stays on top of their tasks. Value stream champions or leaders must assign responsibilities, track their progress, and continue the cycle. They are also responsible for educating and informing team members on the 5S processes and standards to ensure continued compliance.

The concepts behind the 5S system are quite simple to understand but challenging to implement and maintain. Due diligence and constant attention must be built into the value streams we are working for. The payoff is worth eliminating waste and keeping waste from coming back into the value stream system.

Since we have already introduced the notion of making your implemented 5S system and standards visual to help maintain the discipline, let's move on to talk about how visual aids improve other aspects of VSM.

Visual workplace

If you are an agile practitioner, you will already be very aware of the importance of creating visual aids within the workplace environment to provide relevant and timely information on your team's work. These visual aids take the form of **big visible charts (BVCs)** and **information radiators**. Though the concept of having large visual displays originated within the TPS, it was IT innovators Kent Beck and Alistair Cockburn who made the practice of using visual aids widespread within the IT community of Agile practitioners.

Kent Beck coined the term *BVC* in his book *Extreme Programming Explained* (1999), while Alistair Cockburn coined the term *information radiator* in his book *Agile Software Development* (2001). *Information radiator* is a generic term for any handwritten, drawn, printed, or electronic displays placed by an Agile or Lean-Agile team in readily visible locations, usually within their co-located work areas.

Having large visual displays aims to make it easy for all product team members, managers, and other stakeholders to quickly find and review updated information on product backlogs and work items under development. Regarding the visualization of production data, recall the old adage: *A picture paints a thousand words.* The information radiators can include Kanban boards, burndown charts, burnup charts, status and counts of automated tests, incident reports, CI status, and any other information relevant to understanding the product team's goals, progress, and priorities.

Now, let's move on to discuss the three phases of Lean application, including the concepts of demand, flow, and leveling.

Three stages of Lean application – demand, flow, and leveling

It's tempting to want to implement Lean practices across the value stream all at once, but that's likely not to work out too well. It's better to break up the analysis and implementation into three phases that focus initially on customer demand, followed by continuous flow, and—finally—leveling.

The phases should also occur in this order: demand, continuous flow, and leveling. We'll see how this works in the next chapter on value stream mapping, and in particular, mapping the future state. But before we get to that topic, let's take a look at the activities occurring in these phases, as follows:

1. **Customer demand phase**: This includes a set of activities to determine who our customers are and their requirements. The tools used in this phase include Takt time calculation, pitch calculation, buffer and safety resources, 5S for the office, and problem-solving methods.

2. **Continuous flow phase**: This includes a set of activities to help establish continuous flow across your value stream to ensure the correct units arrive at the right time in the required amounts to support your customers' orders, both internal and external. The tools used in this phase include in-process supermarkets, Kanban systems, FIFO line balancing, standardized work, and work area design.

3. **Leveling phase**: This includes activities to distribute work evenly and effectively across the value stream. This phase's tools include a visible pitch board, a load-leveling (heijunka) box, and a runner system.

The preceding descriptions should make it evident that each future state mapping phase includes a unique set of activities and tools. As mentioned previously, there is also an implied flow to the future state mapping work. We need to understand how customer demand impacts our value stream before improving the flow of work, and we need to improve flow before we can level the load of work as new customer orders come into our value stream system.

The guidelines for implementing the eight VSM steps provide a solid foundation for implementing Lean practices across your targeted value stream and sustaining and improving your Lean improvements. Still, it's also essential to learn how to implement the demand, flow, and leveling phases of Lean practices to achieve your desired future state goals.

The following screenshot shows the three phases of Lean application: demand, flow, and leveling, along with the tools of each phase and the sequence of the phases:

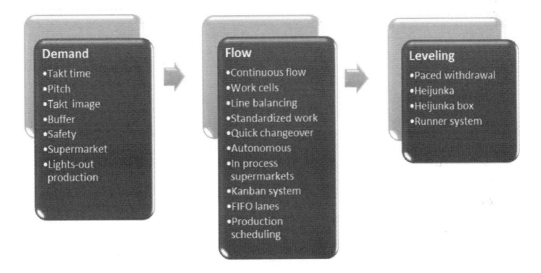

Figure 6.7 – Three phases of Lean application: demand, flow, and leveling

Executive managers cannot mandate the implementation of Lean practices—it's an all-hands activity involving all team members supporting the VSM activities, plus the employees who work within the value stream. The involvement of employees is the topic of the following subsection.

Total employee involvement

Employees are encouraged to make positive contributions to improving their work areas through continuous improvement activities, otherwise known as **Kaizen**. Note that in Lean, Kaizen events are synonymous with the concepts behind Agile retrospectives. In both cases, the product team sets aside time to assess what's working and not working so well. The objective is to explore ways to improve the things that aren't working well.

The term *Kaizen* comes from the Japanese conjunctions of *Kai* (to take apart) and *Zen* (to make good). So, we want to take apart the problem, explore the cause and effects, and then figure out how to change what we do to eliminate our problems' root causes.

The outcome of a Kaizen event or an Agile retrospective is to build an action plan of immediate activities the team can take to improve their performance. In Kaizen and retrospective processes, the focus must be on improving the work and not blaming people. The latter approach only causes finger-pointing and disfunction among the team members. As with any system, a team is much greater than the sum of its parts, but a dysfunctional team no longer operates like a well-oiled machine.

Every team member must share a vision for the work in front of them and view the value stream as a whole. If one part of a value stream breaks down, the value stream as a functional system breaks down. When this happens, all hands need to share ideas, encourage feedback, and obtain buy-in to identify strategies to address the problems.

Know that those good ideas come from all organizational areas, including managers, stakeholders, and employees. Therefore, all ideas require careful consideration, regardless of the source. Everyone needs to feel that they have ownership in the outcome and are encouraged to improve the flow of materials and information across a value stream and eliminate costly waste.

A good friend of mine, and technical reviewer of this book, Enrique Gomez, offered this story about how he was taught, during his Six Sigma training, that Kaizen events can be quite aggressive. The example he was given allegedly occurred at a Japanese manufacturing plant. The production at a specific workstation suffered from a disorganized execution of the production tasks. However, rather than iteratively improve the station, the managers took the tools and threw them all on the floor—a rather vivid example of the take-apart piece. Then, as a team, the operators rebuilt the station, putting things back where they needed to be, removing tools that were not needed, and replacing any tools or equipment that were not functioning optimally.

In this manner, the Kaizen event was rather disruptive but highly effective in fixing the root problems that hindered their production output. In short, not all Kaizen events are conducted like friendly Agile retrospectives. They can employ highly disruptive actions to force a needed improvement.

By analogy, we can also use the flipping of a house as another example of the need to sometimes make disruptive changes. For example, in order to make the kitchen in a house more functional, it's better to rip out the existing walls, equipment, countertops, and cabinets to get a better and more functional work environment. The long-term benefits outweigh the short-term disruptions.

This topic concludes the section on learning Lean concepts. Just as you need to know what Lean looks like, you also need to know what Lean doesn't look like. That is the subject of the following subsection.

Knowing when you are not Lean

Now that you know what Lean production concepts look like, let's discuss how we assess the state of Lean practices implemented within a value stream. To do this, we're going to want to look at the development and operations-oriented processes within an organization, and we need to ask ourselves a series of questions. The questions center on flow, order processing, lot size, customer demands, cleanliness, inventory management, and activity changeovers.

Before we go any further, please note that the terms *Lean*, *Lean production*, and *Lean product development* are used interchangeably in this book. All three terms imply the implementation of Lean concepts across both operational and development-oriented value streams.

The first set of questions deals with the flow of work, parts, materials, and information.

Flow questions

Questions related to flow help assess the extent of wasteful transport, motion, and waiting. Specifically, you want to ask questions to discover the extent to which your organization has done the following:

- Changed the layout of the facilities to support the continuous flow of work
- Eliminated batch processing that causes excessive inventories and bottlenecks and queues to form
- Taken steps to minimize the variance in changeover and cycle times across all value stream activities
- Taken steps to minimize the distance of transport of goods across value stream activities
- Taken steps to reduce travel distance, motion, heavy lifting, and bending required to perform each value stream activity

Next, we'll look at questions that help us assess the leanness of our order management activities.

Order management questions

Once we've addressed the area of flow, we need to evaluate how orders are processed, including the arrival of parts, materials, and information. These are the questions you should ask regarding order processing within your operations:

- Are parts and materials ordered and supplied only when they are needed to support existing customer orders?

- Are orders pushed into production on receipt, whether or not there is the capacity to take on the work?

- Are orders received and processed as a batch or handled individually?

- Can operators pull work only when they have capacity?

- Are value stream operators working on more than one work item at a time?

- Do the right materials show up at the right place and at the right time across the value stream activities?

- Is all order and process information available on demand at each activity to perform the current work?

At this point, we should have a pretty good idea of the efficiency of our processes in terms of flow and order processing. Now, we need to evaluate how orders are handled across the value stream in terms of lot size.

Lot-size questions

VSM practitioners attempt to match value stream inputs, outputs, and intermediate activity durations in sync with customer demands. In other words, the rate at which product orders enter the system and flow through each activity should match the rate at which our customers want the products delivered.

For example, if a customer wants 40 products delivered every week, the ideal production rate is 40 items per week, or one item every hour. To meet these customer demands across our value stream pipeline, we might introduce a new work order for one item into our production system once every hour. Likewise, each intermediate activity would cycle once every hour, and the output would be one item every hour. Production control gets much more challenging when we must move products in batches, and the durations between production and transport activities vary.

Conceptually, the production control manager "orchestrates" the flow of work, much like a conductor orchestrates a band to stay in tempo. Lean practitioners use the term T*akt time*—or, more simply, *Takt*—to refer to the production tempos required to meet customer demands. Takt is the German word for the baton that conductors use to regulate an orchestra or band's tempo.

Therefore, the ideal goal in Lean production is to orchestrate the flow of all materials and parts in single-piece lot sizes across all value stream activities at a constant rate of speed equal to Takt time. With that goal in mind, these are the questions you should ask regarding lot sizes within your operations:

- What is the batch size of work items running through your development and operational value streams?

- Has your organization identified the batch sizes for each activity across the value stream (that is, some equipment may optimally handle larger batch sizes than others, which can cause bottlenecks and waiting to form both upstream and downstream)?

- Has the organization taken efforts to move toward single-piece production across all value stream activities?

- What does the organization need to do to achieve single-piece production across all value stream activities?

With the questions of flow, order processing, and lot size answered, we need to assess the Takt time for the value stream in terms of known or projected customer demands.

Customer demand questions

In this section, we need to understand the frequency of customer orders. This issue can be particularly challenging in industries with seasonally-adjusted demands, such as a Christmas rush. These are the questions you should ask regarding customer demands within your operations:

- Have you calculated your value stream's Takt time?

- Do you have historical data to show Takt time trends over time?

- Do you have to make seasonal adjustments to your Takt time?

- Do you have specific customers who place larger orders all at once in a batch?

- Do your value stream production rates match your Takt time?

- What can you do to ensure your value stream production rates equal Takt time?

- How well does the organization manage flow across varying customer demands?

- What is the organization's process for managing order entry with varying customer demands?

Lean production seeks to match production capacities to meet customer demands. The objective of asking the preceding questions is to discern how well the organization can adjust production rates to meet customer demands without losing its efficiencies in production or causing other forms of waste to accumulate.

You learned earlier, in *The 5S system* section, how important it is to maintain a state of cleanliness and orderliness. Making such determinations is the focus of the next set of questions.

State-of-cleanliness questions

By now, you should already have a decent understanding of how well materials, parts, and information flow across the value stream, but it's always a good idea to ask specific questions to help discern the cause of any issues with flow, especially related to the facility's cleanliness and orderliness. These are the questions you should ask regarding cleanliness and the degree of order within your operations:

- Is the work area for your value stream messy or unclean?

- When was the last time the work area was cleaned?

- When was the last time the workers went through and removed any excess materials, supplies, files, folders, documents, and other paperwork?

- Is the work area for your value stream disorganized in terms of supporting optimal flows?

- What processes within the value stream exist to maintain cleanliness and organization?

- Is there a visual display of the cleaning and maintenance processes?

- Is there a checklist to ensure compliance with the cleaning and maintenance processes?

It may seem overkill to develop cleaning and maintenance processes and then display and comply with them, but investment in such efforts significantly reduces the risks of shutdowns, delays, defects, and ultimately higher costs in the longer run, which leads us to the next set of questions, which are on inventory management.

Inventory management questions

Organizations often allow queuing of materials as safety and buffer stocks. Buffer stocks allow the accumulation of materials and parts to maintain flow in abrupt changes to customer demand. Safety stocks exist within a value stream or production line to support upstream and downstream processes mismatched in cycle times and batch or lot sizes, but both safety and buffer stocks represent costly waste in terms of holding costs, delays, and their potential to hide defects and bugs.

With those concerns in mind, here are the questions you should ask regarding inventory management within your operations:

- Does your value stream work area allow queueing of parts and materials?

- Does your value stream work area have defined storage buffers?

- Does your value stream implement strict rules on storage buffer limits?

- Are their production activities where materials and supplies naturally tend to accumulate and queue?

- Does your organization know why stocks are queuing at certain stages of their operations?

- Has your organization found hidden bugs and defects accumulating within their stocks and buffers?

- Do you have historical data on cycle times versus wait times and total lead times across your value stream?

- Does your value stream have processes in place to minimize queuing, wait, transport, and motion times for inventories of materials and parts?

We are almost done with our questions. The one area we have not addressed is the impact of setup and part changeover times. That is the topic of the next set of questions.

Activity changeover questions

Equipment setup and part or work item changeover requirements seem to be a built-in necessity, but lengthy setup and changeover events impact the sizing of inventory and stock buffers needed to store materials and work in process. Therefore, from a Lean perspective, they are another major cause of waste in the form of delays and waiting, plus their potential to hide defective work items and materials.

We need to make investments to reduce, if not eliminate, setup and changeover requirements across our value stream, but first, we need to know how big a problem we might have. To answer that higher-level question, we need to look for potential causes by asking a series of questions regarding equipment setup and part changeover requirements within your operations, such as the following:

- Do you have equipment that requires periodic shutdowns to set up for changes in orders, materials, or part numbers?

- Do you know the time required to change over equipment across your value stream activities with changes in part numbers or customer orders?

- What information is required to support the equipment setup?

- Which tooling and dies are required to support your equipment changeovers?

- How often do your equipment, setup procedures, or configurations fail?

- Is a process in place to ensure you have backups quickly available when your tooling and dies fail?

- Do you measure the amount of time spent in setup and changeovers along with your lead, cycle, and waiting times?

- Do your value stream team members have active programs to evaluate and improve excessive changeover times?

- Which changeover activities cause the most problems in waiting and queuing parts and materials and delays in processing?

The preceding questions help the VSM team evaluate the state of Lean within the target value stream. Many of these questions relate directly to development-oriented value streams building physical products, but given the dependencies between operations and development-oriented value streams, problems in one value stream often create negative and unexpected consequences in their connected value streams.

You should now have a pretty good understanding of what you need to know about Lean production processes across both development and operations-oriented value streams, to prioritize and make future improvements. But before we leave this section entirely, let's take a few moments to review the tools that assist the organization's efforts to learn about Lean.

Learning about Lean – tools

In this subsection, you will learn about the various tools an organization can implement to assist team members and other stakeholders in learning the basics of Lean production processes. The primary tools include the following:

- Training plan
- Benchmarking checklist
- Demand-stage tools
- Flow-stage tools
- Leveling-stage tools

We'll start this discussion with a review of the Lean training plan components.

Training plan

A training plan is an essential tool that helps guide an organization's efforts to build skills and knowledge among its employees and other stakeholders. A Lean training plan should include the following sections:

- List of required skills and knowledge areas
- Plan to assess existing skills and knowledge levels across affected team members and their training needs
- List of available or desired training sources and materials, to include the following:

  a) **Microlearning**: This involves developing and deploying short and precise units of content for teaching key Lean concepts or practices. The modules must be easily discoverable, engaging, and contextually useful.

  b) **Audiovisual**: This involves integrating both sight and sound formats, typically as slides or video content and recorded speech, to demonstrate Lean concepts. May have overlays of music to make the content more engaging.

  c) **Interactive content**: This can be web-based or part of a multimedia presentation. This instruction approach asks employees to complete specific tasks, such as taking a quiz or poll, engaging in community boards, or employing gaming approaches to test students' approaches to solving specific problems.

d) **Images**: Photos, infographics, and diagrams provided in context with text-based instructions help illustrate Lean concepts and activities.

e) **Podcasts**: Audio or audio-visual content can help employees find time to learn Lean concepts from the organization's mentors and coaches in non-traditional learning environments—that is, outside the classroom or office.

- Training content development plans

- Training delivery schedule

- An evaluation process to discern training effectiveness

Benchmarking checklist

Benchmarking is a powerful tool to collect information about how other organizational value streams—or even other organizations—employ Lean practices, but to take full advantage of this approach, the benchmark assessment team must prepare their list of questions before meeting with the organization they are benchmarking. The benchmark checklist should clearly define the information you seek to obtain.

You must identify an organization that you believe represents world-class capabilities in the Lean value stream area you wish to emulate, and it would help if you made sure that the benchmark organization is sufficiently motivated to work with your team. This task can be challenging, as you need to figure out what's in it for them to support your efforts. It also helps to know something about the benchmark organization before meeting with them so that they know you have done your homework and are not wasting their time.

It's usually best to send your proposed questions in advance of your meeting to give them time to prepare. When you meet with the benchmark organization, it's best to have more than one person attend from the benchmarking team to divide and conquer, with one person asking questions and the other taking notes. Likewise, you may want to ask the benchmark organization to include more than one member, to sufficiently provide the expertise to cover the topics you wish to discuss.

Now, let's move on to discuss Lean demand-phase tools.

> **Note**
> The terms *phase* and *stage* are used interchangeably across the three Lean application processes of demand, flow, and leveling.

Demand-phase tools

In this chapter, you learned about three Lean application stages: **demand, flow,** and **leveling**. This subsection introduces the tools of the demand-phase stage, as follows:

- **Takt time**: This is the pace of customer demand. Takt time is a measure of available production time divided by the total quantity required in that same period (that is, seconds, minutes, hours, days, weeks, or months). In short, Takt time is a measure of time divided by volume.

- **Pitch**: This is the amount of time, based on Takt time, required for an upstream operation to release a predetermined quantity of work in process to a downstream customer. The issue is a concern when the upstream process must bulk-deliver a batch of items all at once.

For example, your customer may order products in bulk, shipped by the boxload, or a truckload, or in a shipping container. Bulk orders are often cheaper and become part of the customer's purchase decision even when the arrivals don't match the company's ideal goal of a single-piece flow. On the other hand, as a producer, you may prefer the certainty of knowing your customer is willing to place an order for 1,000 widgets every month, and therefore you want to ship them most cost-effectively.

The way to resolve this issue is to calculate a **pitch** rate equal to the Takt time multiplied by the bulk pack quality. If your Takt time is 6 minutes and the ideal shipping size is 100 widgets per container, your pitch is 600 minutes. Therefore, you should be able to release 100 widgets every 10 production hours. This pitch also means you can release 100 of the customer's monthly widget orders every 10 hours to the value stream. The formula is illustrated here: *6 minutes (Takt time) X 100 widgets = 600 minutes.*

The pitch concept applies in reverse too—for example, perhaps your value stream is unable to produce single-piece flows. Let's assume a value stream has a Takt time of 30 seconds but must produce in batch sizes of 20 pieces. In this scenario, the value stream's pitch is 300 seconds, which means 10 new orders are released every 5 minutes. The formula is illustrated here: *30 seconds (Takt Time) X 10 pieces = 300 seconds.*

- **Takt image**: This is a visualization process where the value team members must have a vision of achieving single-piece flows and have eliminated all forms of waste. The ideal is never fully obtainable. Following the 80/20 rule (that is, the Pareto principle), there is always something we can improve—and that's the whole point. Never stop visualizing ways to improve your value stream activities, and always seek to obtain Lean ideals.

- **Buffer and safety inventories**: Buffer stocks and safety inventories are forms of waste and are highly discouraged. However, in the short run, until reaching your improved future state, you may need buffers and safety inventories to meet customer demands.

  Buffer inventories are stocks of finished goods that are available to ensure delivery when customer demand suddenly increases—in other words, to protect against large variances in Takt time.

  In contrast, **safety inventories** are stocks of finished goods to protect against internal issues that slow down or prevent work in progress (that is, labor problems, material availability, quality problems, equipment reliability problems, and changeovers).

- **Finished-goods supermarket**: Conceptually, imagine customers pulling orders off your value stream shelf when they need them, just as customers pull products from grocery store shelves when they need them. In a supermarket, staff periodically replenish items on shelves as a batch process, but customers pull the items off the shelves in smaller lots on demand.

- **Lights-out manufacturing**: Conceptually, this includes any Lean production process that can run in an automated fashion without an operator in attendance. In DevOps, for example, we may run automated testing processes overnight to check for bugs and defects that the software developers can fix when they come back into the office the following day.

  If part or all of your value stream operates in this manner, here are some factors to consider:

  a) How durable is the automated process?

  b) How reliable are the materials and information needed to execute the process?

  c) How complex are the material and information flows needed to execute the process?

  d) What is the optimal lot size to run in automated mode?

This section completes our introduction to the Lean demand-phase tools. We'll move on to introduce the tools that support the Lean flow-improvement phase.

Flow-phase tools

This subsection introduces the tools of the flow phase or stage. First, we'll start with an introduction to continuous flows, as follows:

- **Continuous flow**: This is also known as one-for-one manufacturing. A continuous flow is an ideal state; each activity within a value stream pulls one work item from the upstream activity and only works on that one product. But continuous flows also work in a less ideal state, where each activity pulls one small lot from the upstream activity and then works on that small lot to completion. It's unnecessary to have everything across the value stream moving in lock sync, but that is the idealized goal.

- **Work cells**: The layout of working facilities is critical in both Agile and Lean practices. When time and space allow, it's best to arrange workstations and equipment sequentially to support the workflow. It's often useful for labor-intensive activities to have counterclockwise flows that support the efforts of predominantly right-handed workers as they move through the cell—that is, studies show that anywhere from 70% to 90% of people are right-handed.

  Move equipment and workstations close together while considering safety factors to minimize motion and transport between stations. While we want our work to flow sequentially, we do not need to have a linear flow. Instead, it's often better to locate the last station in the value stream close to the first station, which means a U-shaped working environment is often the most optimal. However, other shapes can work, such as C-shaped, L-shaped, S-shaped, or V-shaped cells. Equipment and resource constraints and availability most often dictate the best shape for the design of a cell.

- **Line balancing**: Try as hard as we might, very often, the cycle times for the activities that participate in a value stream vary. Continuous flows are difficult to achieve in such environments, causing excessive queuing and wait times. One strategy to overcome this problem is line balancing.

  Line balancing is a process in which we combine work activities to distribute the flow of work to create roughly equal cycle times (a.k.a. processing times). By definition, cycle time is the time from the start of an activity until its completion. We would love our cycle times to have the same duration as Takt time, but that's seldom the case. That's especially true when Takt time varies over time.

The following diagram provides an example of a U-shaped value stream that has grouped activities to balance flow in terms of matching cycle times. The goal is to have each grouping have a cycle time of around 30 seconds, which matches the cycle times for the lengthiest activities **A1**, **A4**, **A7**, and **A12**:

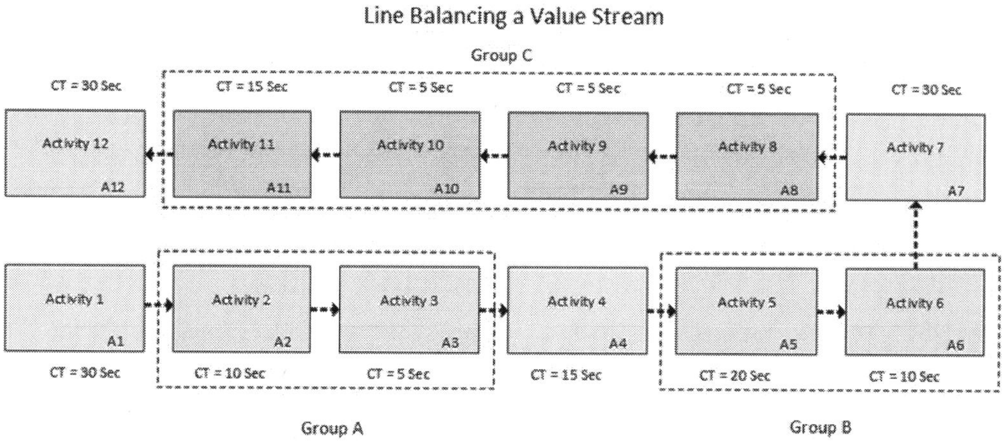

Figure 6.8 – Line-balancing example

Also, note that the total cycle time across all 12 activities is 210 seconds, including 7 cells times 30 seconds each. Of course, we have not included wait times. Since we have balanced our line, we would hope there would be no waiting times in this example.

Unfortunately, we seldom get such an ideal world as that displayed in *Figure 6.8*. For example, very often, value streams produce multiple variants of a product, service, or result. Each product variant may require different processing times and have a different setup or changeover requirements. They may even traverse the value stream in different work patterns and utilize labor in different ways.

Analyzing methods to balance a value stream in such circumstances is beyond the scope of this book. However, if you find yourself in such a situation, it can help to develop an **operator balance chart** as a visual display of work elements, time requirements, and operators for each activity.

The development of an operator balance chart is a two-step process. First, we want to create a quick table to show each product-line activity's cycle times. We also want to show how many operators are required for each activity and how many operators must support the entire set of value stream activities.

The following screenshot provides an example of a preparation table for an operator balance chart:

Activities	A	B	C	D	E	Total CT
Product A (CT)	50	10	47	30	65	202
No. Operators	1	1	0	1	1	
TAKT Time						60
Operators Needed (TCT/TAKT)						3.37

Figure 6.9 – Operator balance chart preparation table

Next, we create a bar chart showing the activities and their cycle times, with a line showing takt time. The next step is to evaluate ways to balance flows by combining activities with faster cycle times and methods to share resources across the activities.

The following screenshot shows an example of an operator balance chart for a single product. Similar charts need to be developed across product lines:

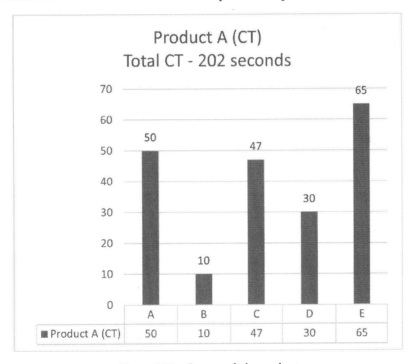

Figure 6.10 – Operator balance chart

Now, let's turn our attention to a visual display that helps ensure workers perform their activities in a standardized approach via a standardized worksheet.

- **Standardized worksheet**: This kind of worksheet is a visual aid in chart form that displays the sequence of operations across the value stream. A standardized worksheet should display activity cycle times, quality checks, safety precautions, standard working processes, number of pieces as **work in progress** (**WIP**), takt time, total cycle time, and the number of operators.

The following screenshot shows a standard worksheet in this type of format:

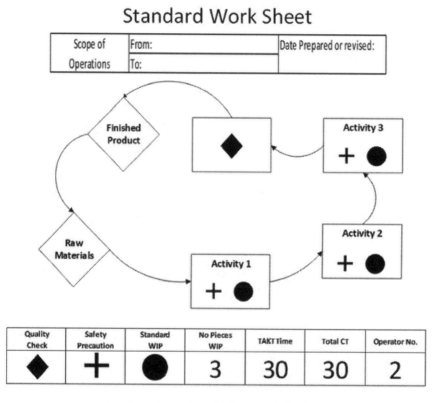

Figure 6.11 – Standardized worksheet

Another display approach is to create a worksheet in tabular form to display information on activity sequences, activity descriptions, and activity durations. The following screenshot shows a **standard work combination sheet** employing this format:

Standard Work Combination Sheet

Part #	Process Name		Date prepared:	mm/dd/yy	Required per shift	1000/ shift	Manual ++++++++++		
	Process Description						Auto -------------		
Process Name			Dept.		TAKT Time		Walk ~~~~~~~		
Step #	Description of Operations	Time			Operation Time (in seconds)				
		Manual	Auto	Walk	5 10 15 20 25 30 35 40 45 50 55 60 65 70 75 80 85 90				
1	Activity 1 Description	3	0	2					
2	Activity 2 Description	2	30	1					
3	Activity 3 Description	5	47	3					
4	Activity 4 Description	4	15	2					
5	Activity 5 Description	2	0	2					
6	Activity 6 Description	1	0	3					
	Total =>	17		13					

Figure 6.12 – Standard work combination sheet

The next item we'll discuss is the quick changeover method, which can keep changeovers to a single minute or less.

- **Quick changeover**: As the name implies, this method is all about ensuring we can quickly change over from one activity to another, even when the product type changes. The concept comes from the work of Shigeo Shingo at Toyota to develop methods to enable SMED.

  The time and effort spent to change over equipment and materials between activities are all wasted from a customer's perspective. They want to pay for finished goods, not activities to set up equipment or retrieve information. The latter concern (retrieving the correct information promptly) most affects IT specialists assisting in value stream improvements.

- **Autonomous maintenance**: In a manufacturing context, autonomous maintenance activities seek to eliminate potential equipment failure causes. In other words, we can think of these strategies as preventative maintenance. We have similar community needs, particularly in operations-oriented value streams, to implement appropriate maintenance, security, rollback, and failover capabilities.

- **In-processed supermarkets**: As introduced previously, supermarkets provide a finished goods inventory buffer from which clients can pull products on-demand. However, when it's challenging to achieve a continuous flow across a value stream, in-process supermarket strategies allow queues to build midstream so that upstream activities have WIP to pull as their capacity becomes available. This strategy helps alleviate production shortfalls when there are multiple demands made against a single machine or activity.

- **Kanban system**: This is a signaling-based pool system that uses cards attached to containers of materials to indicate standard lot sizes. When the container's materials are depleted, the card indicates which materials need to be replaced, as well as how many items.

  Kanban systems have become popular in the IT-based Lean-Agile community, though the approach differs slightly from the original Lean production concepts. The IT-based Kanban system usually employs a whiteboard with vertical lines segmenting the board into columns mapped to the team's development process's activity steps. Team members write the product backlog item names on sticky notes to allow placement across the columns. As team members become available to take on new work, they look in the upstream activity column to see the work items available for them to work on next, and they make their work selections from those items.

  The IT-based Kanban system's value is that it facilitates a continuous flow of work across software development activities. In traditional Agile processes, such as Scrum or **extreme programming (XP)**, work items are pulled as a batch into the Sprint backlog, and duration of the Sprint constrains the flow of the batch of work items.

- **FIFO lanes**: FIFO is a production control strategy used in Lean value streams when there is a great deal of variability between work items and where multiple value streams meet for final assembly or customization of products. In such cases, we need to make sure parts don't get stuck in the queue because nobody wants to work on them or make the required changeovers. A FIFO strategy ensures that products waiting in the queue the longest always have the highest priorities.

- **Production scheduling**: This has to do with scheduling parts and materials to support the flow of work across a Lean value stream. You can also throw information scheduling into the mix to ensure the information on customer order requirements also shows up at the right time and in the proper context with each activity within the value stream. The main point is that, in a pull-oriented system, production schedules and inventory control systems must coordinate upstream activities to support the needs of the downstream operations closest to the customer.

It can admittedly be challenging to get your head around pull-oriented production processes. Intuitively, it seems to make sense that when a new customer order comes in, we should immediately push it out to the production floor and allow each succeeding stage of production to push the product through the manufacturing process. But as you now know, pushing products through the production process only creates queues and waiting times, hides bugs and defects, and creates other forms of waste that hinder productivity while increasing costs.

As practiced within Lean enterprises, a better strategy is to conceptually have each downstream activity pulling the order through the production process. Implementing pull-oriented production-scheduling strategies exposes problems immediately, as downstream activities become starved of work due to impediments upstream. Moreover, the organization needs to refine its information systems to ensure parts and materials arrive in the proper sequence, to the right locations, at the right times.

The IT departments within Lean organizations must work in concert with the value streams to develop business information systems that support the new Lean process.

This section completes our introduction to the tools that support continuous flows. Next, we'll move on to introduce the Lean leveling-phase tools.

Leveling-phase tools

We can't move on to improving production load levels until we've addressed customer demands and flow issues, but now that we've done so, we can look at the tools that help us level the flow across our value streams to make them most productive and efficient. This subsection introduces the tools of the leveling phase or stage, outlined as follows:

- **Paced withdrawal** facilitates delivery of products when customers want deliveries made in standard pack-out quantities instead of one-at-a-time deliveries. However, paced withdrawal only works when you have no product variability in the value stream. In other words, production flows are stable, there is little or no changeover between product lines, and cycle times are roughly equivalent.

The timing of paced withdrawals is equal to pitch. Recall that pitch is equal to takt time times pack-out quantity. Paced withdrawal helps level production flows by dividing the total downstream customer's requirement over a specified duration of time into batch sizes equal to the pack-out quantity.

- **Heijunka (load leveling)** is a better and more robust approach to level-production schedules in value streams having mismatched activities in their production processes. Heijunka uses the paced withdrawal method of production leveling based on the pitch but breaks it out into Kanban units based on the volume and variety of production products.

Figure 6.12 shows an example of a Heijunka load-leveling table. Let's assume this Lean value stream can produce 500 units of a product per day across five basic product line variants (that is, products **A** through **E**), and we'll assume our downstream customers have the same batch delivery requirements of 25 units per batch.

Additionally, our value stream only operates one shift per day for a total available production time of 28,800 minutes. Therefore, our takt time equals the available time of 28,800 minutes divided by our production volume of 500 units, or 57.6 seconds, while our pitch equals takt time multiplied by our lot size of 25, or 1,440 seconds (24 minutes). In other words, every 24 minutes, we need to be able to ship another lot of 25 units of product.

But now, we need to decide the frequency of deliveries by product line. To do this, we need to know the daily production volumes of each product type. By dividing the daily demands by product type by the pack-out size, we can determine how many Kanbans we can form and release each day for each product type. The following screenshot shows the number of Kanbans required for each product type:

Product Type	A	B	C	D	E
Daily demands	150	200	100	25	25
Pack-out quantity	25	25	25	25	25
No. of Kanbans	6	8	4	1	n

Figure 6.13 – Heijunka load-leveling table

We can also see that we need a total of 20 Kanbans of 25 units each produced during the shift. Finally, the Heijunka table helps us evaluate how the Kanbans divide out across the product types (as shown in the bottom row of *Figure 6.13*).

Now that we've figured out how many Kanbans we need for each product type, we can figure out how to schedule them into production. A Heijunka box, as discussed next, is a good approach.

- A **Heijunka box**, as initially conceived, is a physical box to hold the Kanban cards in slots mapped to specific periods during the day. The objective of a Heijunka box is to level the load across fixed periods. However, we can schedule and level our Kanbans similarly in an electronic chart or table format. The following screenshot shows such an example:

Product Type	7:00 AM to 7:24 AM	7:24 AM to 7:48 AM	7:48 AM to 8:12 AM	8:12 AM to 8:36 AM	8:36 AM to 9:00 AM	9:00 AM to 9:10 AM	9:10 AM to 9:34 AM	9:34 AM to 9:58 AM	9:58 AM to 10:22 AM	10:22 AM to 10:46 AM	10:46 AM to 11:16 AM	11:16 AM to 11:40 AM	11:40 AM to 12:04 PM	12:04 PM to 12:28 PM	12:28 PM to 12:52 PM	12:52 PM to 1:16 PM	1:16 PM to 1:40 PM	1:40 PM to 2:04 PM	2:04 PM to 2:28 PM	2:28 PM to 2:52 PM	2:52 PM to 3:16 PM	3:16 PM to 3:40 PM	3:40 PM to 4:04 PM
A	1	1							1	1		1	1										
B			1	1							1	1				1	1		1	1			
C					1	Break									Lunch					Break	1	1	1
D																						1	
E																							1

Figure 6.14 – Heijunka box

Sometimes, we have to resort to brute force to get things done promptly. That approach to production scheduling and leveling is the topic of the following method.

- **A runner** is a person who moves from one activity location to another to move materials and address production issues on the fly. The primary objective of a runner is to ensure that pitch is maintained. They usually traverse a designated route within the pitch, picking up Kanban cards, supplying tools and materials, and delivering them to the right place at the right time.

A runner can't be just anybody or a new employee who has a strong understanding of the value stream production activities and requirements. They must have excellent communication skills and be able to recognize problems and report any abnormalities that are hindering flow. They must understand Lean concepts and the importance of takt time and pitch. Finally, they must be able to perform their work efficiently and accurately.

VSM storyboard updates

Another tool that you need to have ready to use in your learning Lean VSM step is a VSM storyboard. Recall that a VSM storyboard is a visual tool that provides updates to your VSM project's information, metrics, and value stream maps. This phase's primary update to the VSM storyboard documents the problem categories or issues your VSM team may choose to address.

If you haven't already done so, you should create your VSM storyboard now. All you need to get started is a simple large whiteboard with markers located in a shared or colocated space. You can use the VSM storyboard provided in *Appendix B* as an example to help guide your VSM team's efforts to build their storyboard. Note that the example VSM storyboard in *Appendix B* has numbered icons to indicate the information updates required across each of the VSM steps.

With the information you've learned in this chapter, you are now ready to start mapping your current-state value stream map, the next chapter's topic.

Summary

This section ends our chapter on planning and preparing for your VSM engagement. At the start of this chapter, you learned that VSM is a Lean business approach to improve the flow of value across an organization and manage and monitor the development and delivery life cycle from end to end. You've learned that VSM is not a new concept. There are eight traditional steps to planning, mapping, and improving Lean production processes across development and operations-oriented value streams.

Most importantly, you learned that VSM could not be merely about improving IT operations in a DevOps paradigm. Instead, VSM serves as a force multiplier within our digital economy that leverages Lean and DevOps capabilities to improve, monitor, and manage all the organization's development and operations-oriented value streams.

In the next chapter, you will learn how to map both your value stream operations' current and future states. You will also learn how to implement Lean Kaizen (that is, continuous improvement) processes sustainably. But before we get to that chapter, let's take a moment to review what you've learned in this chapter.

Questions

To enhance your learning experience, please take a few moments to answer these 10 questions:

1. What is VSM fundamentally about?
2. List three reasons why Lean practices are critical to an organization.
3. What is a viable strategy to determine the degree of "Leanness" within your selected value stream?
4. What are the three stages of Lean application?
5. Why is benchmarking an important Lean assessment tool?
6. What is the purpose and goal of Heijunka?
7. How is the relationship between VSM and the organization?
8. What are the three primary value streams that overlap and flow together?
9. List the six fundamental concepts that you need to understand to create a Lean system.
10. What are the seven deadly wastes of Lean?

Further reading

- *Toyota, Corporate (2013) Just In Time – Philosophy of complete elimination of waste* (http://www.toyota.com.cn/company/vision_philosophy/toyota_production_system/just-in-time.html)

- *Shingo, S., Dillon, A. P. (2005). A Study of the Toyota Production System: From an Industrial Engineering Viewpoint (Produce What Is Needed, When It's Needed) 1st Edition, English Translation. CRC Press, Taylor & Francis Group. Boca Raton, FL.*

- *Krafcik, John F. (Fall 1988). Triumph Of The Lean Production System. Sloan Management Review, Fall 1988; 30, 1; ABI/INFORM Global, pg. 41.*

- *Kotter, J. (2014) Accelerate (XLR8): Building Strategic Agility for a Faster-Moving World. Harvard Business Review Press. Boston, MA.*

- *Martin, J. (1995). The Great Transition. Using the Seven Disciplines of Enterprise Engineering to Align People, Technology, and Strategy. American Management Association, now a division of HarperCollins Leadership. New York, NY.*

- *Tapping, D., Luyster, T., Shuker, T. (2002) Value Stream Management: Eight Steps to Planning, Mapping, and Sustaining Lean Improvements. Productivity Press. New York, NY.*

- *Tapping, D., Luyster, T., Shuker, T. (2003) Value Stream Management for the Lean Office: Eight Steps to Planning, Mapping, and Sustaining Lean Improvements. Productivity Press. New York, NY.*

- *Gregory, L. (September 2018). Toyota's Organizational Structure: An Analysis.* (`http://panmore.com/toyota-organizational-structure-analysis`) Accessed December 28, 2020.

- *Ohno, T., Bodek, N. (1988) Toyota Production System: Beyond large-scale production. Productivity Press. Routledge/Taylor & Francis Group. An Informa Business. London, England.* (Originally published in Japan in 1978)

7
Mapping the Current State (VSM Step 4)

In the two preceding chapters, you learned the purpose of **value stream management** (**VSM**) and how to plan a VSM initiative. We're now going to get into the details of the type of analysis performed during a VSM initiative. Specifically, you will learn how to create value stream maps to describe your current processes. This is *Step 4* in our eight-step VSM methodology.

While it may be tempting to jump right in and start work to implement changes to eliminate perceived areas of waste, the problem is that, without proper analysis, your efforts may not get the results you and your VSM team expect. Without a current state value stream map, you may not be aware of the system-wide impacts associated with your current value stream activities. Specifically, we need to document our existing activity flows, order entry system, production control system, cycle times, equipment setup and product changeover times, lot and batch sizes, quality levels, defects, and unsynchronized material and information flows.

In this chapter, we're going to cover the following main topics:

- Evaluating the current state of Lean practices
- Getting started with mapping
- Beginning the map
- Creating an **Information Technology** (**IT**) value stream map

With the instructions provided in this chapter, you will have the ability to create a current state value stream map in virtually any type of value stream. Moreover, the **continuous integration/continuous delivery** (**CI/CD**) use case employed in this exercise will help you visualize how to use value stream mapping to assess your software development-oriented value streams.

Evaluating the current state of Lean practices

In classic business process analysis techniques, a common practice is to analyze the current way things are done (*as-is state*), then assess areas for improvement to achieve a desired future state (*to-be state*), conduct analysis to understand the full scope of work to make the desired changes (*gap analysis*), and finally create and execute a transition plan. You will find that VSM practices follow a similar pattern. This chapter introduces how to use value stream mapping to assess the current *as-is state* of our CI/CD activities from a Lean-oriented perspective.

As noted previously in *Chapter 4, Defining Value Stream Management*, the concept of **value stream mapping** has been around for a while. However, it is primarily attributed to an analytical approach used at Toyota, referred to as materials and information flow mapping. As the term *materials and information flow* suggests, value stream mapping provides a graphical technique to simultaneously model the flow of materials and information across value stream activities. But before we get into the details of value stream mapping, let's first understand how this technique differs from other business modeling techniques.

Contrasting business process modeling techniques

Those involved in **business process improvement** (**BPI**) or **computer-aided systems engineering** (**CASE**) tools are probably familiar with business process modeling techniques. For example, the **Object Management Group®** (**OMG®**) **Business Process Model and Notation** (**BPMN**) specification is a standard specification for business process modeling within the IT community.

Other standards for process modeling include activity diagrams from the **Unified Modeling Language (UML)** and the **Integrated DEFinition for Process Description Capture Method (IDEF3)**. The UML was initially created by Rational Software but is now an OMG standard, while the **United States (US)** Air Force developed IDEF3 under the **Integrated Computer-Aided Manufacturing (ICAM)** program. Additionally, IT specialists may also be familiar with various workflow modeling tools and techniques, such as the **Web Services Business Process Execution Language (WS-BPEL)**, which is often shortened to simply **BPEL**. BPEL is a standard executable language for specifying business process actions within web services.

With so many formal standards for modeling business processes, you may be wondering why we need a different standard for modeling Lean business practices. The answer lies in the focus of each type of modeling technique.

Value stream maps provide a high-level view of the flow of information and materials and provide an ideal infographic design to document, communicate, and ultimately eliminate waste that affects efficiencies and an organization's ability to deliver customer-centric value. As its name implies, value stream mapping forces an organization to isolate activities that add value from other activities and wasteful practices accumulated from bureaucratic bloat. The overall objective of value stream mapping is to identify and eliminate waste that hinders productivity—from ideation through the delivery of products and services—and hinders an organization's ability to deliver customer-centric value.

Another important aspect of value stream mapping is to provide a vehicle for visual collaborations among VSM and value stream team members and other stakeholders. The maps allow participants to communicate their understanding of the current operations better and later assess and communicate alternative change scenarios.

In contrast, business process improvement and workflow-oriented process modeling techniques focus on identifying the coordination of workflows with detailed information on data and data flows as part of a business process automation effort. BPMN is a classic approach to facilitate BPIs via software applications. In contrast, BPEL is a modern approach to model and improve business process data and information flows via web-based applications.

Business process models provide detailed visual displays of the interactions of technical and organizational activities in cross-domain and cross-function business environments, underscoring complex interactions and decision points. Business process models are often used to support business process reengineering and improvement activities and create business systems to automate those improvements.

In other words, standardized business process modeling techniques used within the IT community and BPI analysts focus on modeling business processes to automate them. In contrast, value stream mapping techniques model the flow of work and information across value streams to eliminate waste as part of a Lean improvement initiative.

As a quick side note, in the early-to-mid 1990s, as the product manager leading the CASE tool and workflow strategies at **AT&T Global Information Solutions** (**AT&T GIS**), I worked with Gloria Gery, the author of the book titled *Electronic Performance Support Systems* (Gery, 1991). Our collaborations' objective was to ensure the **Electronic Performance Support Systems** (**EPSS**) built by our professional service organizations supported the needs of both the expert and the novice practitioners of our customers' business processes.

One of the biggest concerns I had then, and still have today, is that too many business systems do not help support the flow of work from a value stream perspective. For example, suppose your business system does not help enforce the desired to-be state of both work and information flows. In that case, you will have difficulty achieving the goals and objectives of your VSM initiatives.

The automation of business processes is not inconsistent with Lean practices, as you will see in the next section. So, both types of modeling—a mix of value stream mapping and process modeling—are essential to achieve the broader efficiency goals of the VSM initiative.

Automating business processes

It's not inconsistent in Lean practices to employ process modeling tools (especially BPEL) to automate business processes, as such activities are consistent with the **Toyota Production System** (**TPS**) concept of **Jidoka**, a.k.a. **autonomation**. But it also makes no sense to automate a business process until and unless we know it's efficient and value-adding.

True—it may be possible to employ automated and digital information systems, perhaps as a mix of **commercial-off-the-shelf** (**COTS**)-based solutions, to make our processes more efficient. But the danger of moving too fast is having a process that is so mismatched in throughput or hiding defects, or bloated with non-value-adding work, that we end up automating waste. Moreover, even COTS-based solutions often require a high degree of customization to implement business processes that make the organization efficient, value-adding, and competitive.

Having laid this groundwork, let's get started with our value stream mapping exercise.

Getting started with mapping

For this section, let's assume your organization and VSM team are fully primed and committed to Lean practices. You've also chosen your value stream and have learned the fundamentals of Lean practices. Now, it's time to start doing the work to begin your transition to a Lean enterprise. There's no reason to delay any further. In the immortal words of Taiichi Ohno:

Just do it!

Since this is a book on VSM driving **development-operations** (**DevOps**) capabilities, our examples follow Lean improvements across the **continuous integration** (**CI**) and **continuous delivery** (**CD**) sections of an IT value stream. As you learned in *Chapter 5, Driving Business Value through a DevOps Pipeline*, CI/CD practices are a subset of a more extensive DevOps pipeline. Therefore, our CI/CD VSM use-case example aims to simplify the scope of analysis to focus on employing VSM methods and tools.

Don't forget that DevOps is a critical enabler of virtually all value stream improvements in a digital economy. Nevertheless, the principles and techniques presented in this book apply equally well to all VSM initiatives, regardless of the value stream undergoing improvements.

One final note: please take a moment to review the VSM Storyboard in *Appendix B*. It is the primary tool for documenting both current and future state value stream mapping activities.

Building a value stream mapping icon standard

An essential component of value stream mapping is sticking to specific icons to describe your value stream system elements—for example, *Figure 7.1*, which you will see shortly, shows the most common value stream mapping symbols as icons. Of course, your organization or VSM team may elect to use other icons. That is OK, as there is no definitive standard body governing the iconology of value stream mapping.

However, make sure everyone fully understands the definition of the icons used in your value stream maps, and do not allow people to create non-standard icons without appropriate agreement and communication. Without standards, communication and understanding quickly deteriorate among VSM team members and other stakeholders who review the maps. The value stream mapping icons used within this book are organized into separate categories, as identified in the following list:

- **Process**: Identifies work activities spanning customers and suppliers, dedicated and shared processes, activity work cells, and data boxes to show critical information and metrics.

- **Materials**: Indicates how materials are handled at various stages of the value stream, including inventories and buffer stocks, and production control strategies such as supermarket, pull, and **First In, First Out** (**FIFO**).

- **Shipment**: Includes all identified mechanisms for transporting materials, parts, and products, including air, forklift, truck, boat, or ship. But your organization might also include transport icons to show movements conducted by rail, automated lines, robots, or third-party shipping companies.

- **Information**: Capture metrics to inform our current state (as-is) and desired future state (to-be) analytics and provide information to support the flow of work across our development and operational value streams. The icons displayed in *Figure 7.1* indicate information gathered from several sources, such as the following:

  a) Gemba (*go to see*) activities or verbal communications

  b) Information maintained in **enterprise resource planning** (**ERP**)/**materials requirement planning** (**MRP**) systems

  c) Information from production control data or strategies

- **Value stream map**: Used to show specific points in the value stream where the team wishes to point out specific areas of interest on the map, such as Kaizen burst (that is, **a Rapid Process Improvement** (**RPI**) initiative requirement) operators, timeliness, or quality problems.

- **Kanban arrows**: Show the flow of materials and information across shipping and production processes. Note that straight arrows typically indicate push-oriented product control strategies, while curved arrows indicate pull-oriented strategies. Kinked arrows indicate electronic information flows.

You can see the most common value stream mapping icons in the following screenshot:

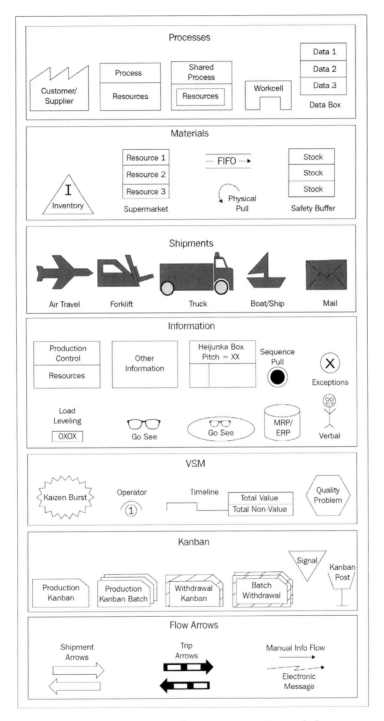

Figure 7.1 – Common value stream mapping symbols

Note that the common value stream mapping symbols shown in *Figure 7.1* contain 41 standard Lean icons used throughout this book. The graphic displays symbols across the previously identified seven VSM icon categories.

Every VSM tool provider provides a value stream mapping tool with its own set of icons. While most modern VSM tools have a value stream mapping capability, many graphical tools offer easy-to-use **graphical user interface** (**GUI**)-based tools with predefined icons to map value streams, often at a considerably lower price.

The VSM team can map the work and information flow across their target value stream with the standard set of value stream mapping symbols. However, another step precedes mapping, and that is gathering data to understand the flow of work and information across the value stream's activities.

The level of understanding required to create an accurate value stream map won't come from reading specifications and documentation. Instead, they must walk the floors, meet with the people doing the work, ask lots of questions, and see for themselves how work and information flow across the value stream.

Going to see (Gemba)

The current value stream mapping exercise's primary objective is to identify the activities that add value while eliminating those that add waste (Muda). Therefore, before starting the current state mapping exercise, our VSM team must *go to see* (Gemba) and understand how the value stream operates before mapping and recommending changes.

Some books make it appear that a Gemba walk is a simple one-time event. That's unfortunate because one tour of a value stream will not get the job done. For example, as a young manufacturing and industrial engineering project manager at Texas Instruments, I spent a much larger portion of my time out on the shop floor than I did at my desk. My job involved planning and guiding three large factory improvement programs involving two geographically separated manufacturing facilities. The production information I needed was not at my desk; it was out on the shop floor and mainly in the heads of the people performing the work.

The Gemba and current state mapping activities provide insights into the waste areas that hinder material and information flows. Another way to think about waste is that it almost always leads to further administrative overhead and processing time. Our focus always has to be on the customer, and such administrative tasks are mostly overheads and non-value-adding.

There are three fundamental rules when practicing Gemba, outlined as follows:

- **Go and see** what's going on for yourself.
- **Ask why** multiple times to get to the root cause of an issue
  (that is, **5 Ws** or **5 Whys**).
- **Respect people**: Your job is to help resolve problems, not find faults.

When VSM team members conduct Gemba walks, they need to do so in an organized fashion. The following steps outline a sensible Gemba Walk strategy:

1. Identify goals and objectives.
2. Let the value stream team know you are coming and the reasons for the visit.
3. Go as a team of two or more VSM team members.
4. Follow the value stream's flows.
5. Focus on identifying issues with value stream processes and work activities, not people.
6. Document findings.
7. Ask questions—that is, 5 Ws (who, what, when, where, and why) or "Why" five times to fully understand problems and identify root causes.
8. Listen—don't recommend changes in the initial walks. Your goal is to learn.
9. Follow up with the value stream employees at a later date with your observations and recommendations.
10. Gemba again to confirm the results of implementations and improvements.
11. Gemba again to start the new Kaizen improvement cycle.

A synchronized and organized value stream virtually automates itself from the perspective of flow. There is a natural and straight-line order to the flow of work in a well-organized value stream. Information and materials flow without impediments or bottlenecks. The correct information and materials are immediately at hand when needed, and not before or after. That is the idealized future state. Use your Gemba walks to identify the areas and reasons why these things are not happening in the current state.

Finally, the VSM team must understand the need to collect accurate and real-time information on actual work activities and information and material flows, whether the existing activities are **value-added** (**VA**) or full of waste. Failure to document all unsynchronized flows and waste makes it impossible to evaluate the value stream as a holistic system. Furthermore, without a holistic view of the value stream as a system, it is impossible to understand the dynamics that affect its performance.

Starting our map with the customer in mind

Start your current state mapping exercise from final customer deliveries and work your way upstream (backward) through the various processes. Remember—the goal is to deliver a product, service, or result that your customer wants. Your VSM team runs the risk of missing how beginning or mid-stream activities negatively impact value delivery if you don't start your current state assessments without the customer's needs and expected outcomes in mind.

The following diagram graphically depicts how value flows downstream to the customer:

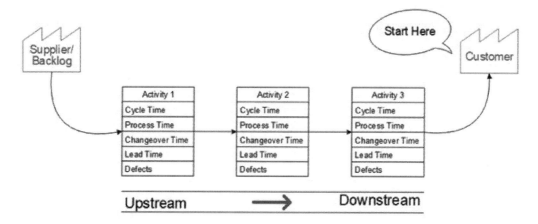

Figure 7.2 – Value stream maps start with the customer

In traditional process models, we tend to start with the first activity and work our way forward, mapping workflow across activities and work locations. In value stream mapping, we collect data from the point at which the customer receives value and then work our way backward (upstream). At each step, we ask ourselves whether the current activity is aligned with our customers' needs or is adding waste in some form.

The order of analysis doesn't mean we plan to resolve issues of waste in that order. Instead, the VSM team must prioritize improvements in terms of the highest-value impacts. We'll get to that subject in *Chapter 9, Mapping the Future State (VSM Step 6)*, but for now, it's essential to know that there are several reasons for mapping our way backward through the value stream, including the following:

- It keeps the focus on the needs of the customer.

- It orients our minds to think in terms of pull-based flows.

- We can better work our way through complex flows in production environments having multiple assembly branches.

The later issue, managing multiple branches, creates a bit more complexity in terms of managing flows. In push-oriented production scheduling systems, it's nearly impossible to synch the materials' flow to be available when needed and avoid queuing and waiting. However, as you will find out in *Chapter 9, Mapping the Future State (VSM Step 6)*, it's much easier to prevent bottlenecks with pull-oriented production schedules and **Just-in-Time (JIT)** material and information deliveries.

Here, you can see a value stream map with multiple branches:

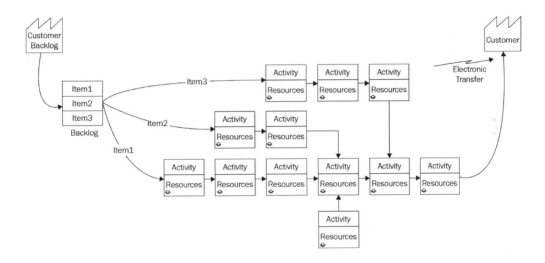

Figure 7.3 – Value stream map with multiple branches

Now that we understand that we need to start our VSM maps with our customers in mind, let's understand what we need to do to prepare for the current state mapping exercise.

Preparing to map

You've already learned the essential steps of Gemba to collect information for your current state map, but let's take a closer look at the preparation work required before the current state mapping exercise. There are four common steps the VSM team can take before mapping, outlined as follows:

- Determine VSM team member assignments
- Draw a rough sketch of the value stream flows
- Begin your Gemba exercise
- Discuss the data

The VSM team needs to assign individuals to specific roles that streamline their data capture and mapping activities in any current state mapping exercise. While the VSM team can use an electronic tool or flip chart to create their maps, it's better to start with an erasable whiteboard. You'll update this regularly throughout the exercise, and a larger whiteboard is more manageable for everyone to get around to see and participate in the discussions. It's also helpful to either assign someone as a scribe or, better yet, rotate that role among the team members.

Someone else needs to be responsible for facilitating the mapping activity, keeping folks focused on the goals at hand, and monitoring the time. Teams find it easier to focus their attention and accomplish the work if they keep to a schedule and have time for breaks—more time can be scheduled later to come back and finish up the work, if necessary. And it may even be beneficial to allow time between mapping updates for the team to rest and reflect on the work they have completed and review the map to identify any information they may be missing.

We also need someone to act as a timekeeper during the Gemba walks. Their responsibility is to record the cycle and changeover times for the value stream's activities, as observed during their Gemba walks. They should also record other important information discovered during the walks, such as issues, causes, effects, delays, or other waste areas discovered during the walks.

Let's stop for a moment to discuss the nature of creative work versus standardized work. Developers who create software architectures and designs and who write code perform creative work. No two business requirements are the same, and the developers must think through the work involved to design an appropriate approach. In contrast, standard work includes repetitive tasks that should not significantly vary in a controlled environment.

Standardized work is the whole point of Lean, eliminating waste and thereby improving the predictability of outcomes. Unfortunately, standardized work practices are often frowned upon in Agile practices, as many Agilists do not want to be bound to specific ways of doing things. But there is added risk when an organization attempts to build and maintain continuous flows across CI/CD and DevOps pipelines, or any other Lean value stream, without standardized methods and tools.

For example, suppose we've spent the time, effort, and money to design streamlined value streams, including procurement of tools. In that case, we should not haphazardly make changes without thoroughly assessing our needs and objectives and assessing the potential negative consequences of changing our activities and flows. VSM is the appropriate approach to evaluate ongoing improvements across our Lean enterprise.

Whether using Agile or Lean concepts, we still want to maintain a production flow that matches our takt time. In other words, ideally, our production rates (Takt) match our customers' demand rates. The one area where this is challenging is in the frontend of the **software development life cycle** (**SDLC**), where the product owner and the team identify, prioritize, and refine requirements. Next, the software team must evaluate the work involved to design and implement the requirements as software features and functions. Finally, there is a creative nature to product backlog refinement that makes it more challenging to predict work scope and duration.

Once a work item enters the development cycle as refined tasks, the flow of work can follow a standard set of time-bound activities that are reasonably standardized and predictable. However, it's much more challenging to force arbitrary time-bound restrictions on a product backlog refinement's creative endeavors. Instead, the best strategy to improve design-related work predictability is to break the initial high-level requirements down into the smallest bites possible.

Microservices-based architectures decompose requirements at the smallest level of scale to describe unique business services at their most granular level. Besides better design predictability, other benefits from microservices-based architectures include the ability to create highly maintainable, testable, and independently deployable units of functionality as loosely coupled business services.

The objective of drawing a rough sketch of the current state map before Gemba walks is to make sure the VSM team members understand the work within the value stream. Therefore, it may be helpful to have someone familiar with the value stream guide this effort.

The rough map helps improve the VSM team's understanding of the value stream activities before a Gemba walk, making their time on the walks much more effective. Moreover, the draft drawing helps the team later identify the value stream areas that do not reflect their original expectations of how the process should work.

When a team begins their Gemba walk, they should be prepared to capture the following information:

- Total work time per shift or day
- Planned downtimes and breaks within the value stream
- Available time to actually perform work
- The number of employees and contractors or partners supporting the value stream
- Quantity of work performed by each value stream worker
- Frequency of delivery for each activity within the value stream

- Cycle time for each activity, from start to finish

- Waiting (queue) times and quantities at each value stream activity

- Any exceptions to the standard processes

- Other relevant information items unique to the value stream

Before they begin Gemba walks, the team should respect the value stream workers' time and efforts. As a matter of courtesy, the VSM team members need to seek out the value stream managers' approval and plan their walks around the VA managers' and employees' schedules to minimize their work impact.

Take time to communicate where you plan to conduct your walks and what you want to accomplish. Then, when you show up for the Gemba walk, make sure you and your team members introduce yourselves and remind the team of the purpose of your visit. Answer their questions honestly, and don't hold back on explaining the objectives and benefits of Lean production practices.

Remember that you need to get their buy-in to support your efforts. While you are walking the area, be respectful of the workers' time and their work areas. Above all, remember that they are the experts in the work performed in the value stream.

The VSM team can now begin their Gemba walks. The VSM team members should not attempt to analyze the data they collect until they return to their meeting room. That will only take valuable time away from the value stream's workers and hinder the VSM team's data gathering objectives. There will be plenty of time to reflect on and analyze the data after the Gemba walks.

Now that we've conducted our Gemba walk and returned with the data, it's time to begin our current state mapping exercise.

Beginning the map

So far, you have performed the following steps to prepare for the current state mapping exercise:

- Determined customer needs and priorities

- Put a value stream mapping plan together

- Assigned roles and responsibilities

- Conducted information-gathering Gemba walks

- Developed a rough pre-draft of the current state map

Now, it's time to use this information to put our current state value stream map together. Again, use a large whiteboard or poster board for this purpose, and use erasable markers or pencils, as the case may be, so that you can correct any errors or omissions. Again, you can use a software tool to create your maps, but make sure you have a large enough screen for everyone to gather around and see.

While digital VSM mapping tools make better-looking and easier-to-read drawings, they can also slow the mapping process down, though some tools are easier to use than others. It may make more sense to create a manual drawing until the team is ready to show and distribute their work. The team needs to use their judgment to decide which approach works best for them.

Drawing the current state map in eight steps

There is no single best approach to drawing a value stream map. However, it's best to have a common strategy to guide the process from start to finish, ensuring nothing is left out. With that goal in mind, the following eight steps, applied in this order, provides a practical approach to current state mapping.

1. **Draw customers and suppliers**: Identify external or internal customers who provide requirements and receive the deliverables. Note that in *Figure 7.3*, the map identifies the product backlog from the customer's perspective. Also, note that *Figure 7.3* shows the customer icon twice, which isn't necessary. In this case, using the icon twice—once for requirements and the other time for delivery—indicates that the product backlog contains all customer requirements, while the deliverables go to specific customers. Finally, identify any suppliers, contractors, or partners who contribute materials, products, or parts to the value stream.

2. **Draw the entry and exit activities**: In an IT development-oriented value stream, the entry point might be the backlog refinement or identifying of Sprint goals. In contrast, the exit point might be a deployment activity. Since activities represent work, a good practice is to use verbs and verb phrases when naming your activities. Also, since our activities' expected outputs are tangible things— in the form of products, services, or results—a good practice is to use nouns and noun phrases to name the outputs.

3. **Draw all activities between entry and exit processes**: While you initially collected your data from the customer backward, you can map the activities starting with the furthest downstream (that is, from left to right). This approach makes it easier to depict the flow of work graphically. Make sure to use activity boxes with segmented fields to record essential data, such as cycle and changeover times, waiting times, resources, lot or batch size, defects, and other essential details.

4. **List all activity attributes**: These include lead times, cycle, changeover times, waiting times, resources, lot or batch size, defects, and other essential details.

5. **Draw queues and waiting times between activities**: Use separate icons to indicate the type of queues, such as waiting materials, safety stocks, buffer stocks, and anticipation inventories. **Waiting materials** are queues that form between work cells due to mismatched production rates. **Safety stock** is a store of materials to ensure we can continue to work during unanticipated material shortages. Buffer stocks help hedge against customer-induced variations or spikes in demand. Finally, **anticipation inventory** includes finished goods kept on hand to support expected spikes in demand, such as holiday demands.

6. **Draw all communications that occur within the value stream**: Use different arrow types to indicate whether communications involve verbal, mail, or electronic information flows.

7. **Draw push or pull icons to identify the type of workflow**: Use straight arrows to indicate push-oriented flows. Use circular arrows to indicate pull-based flows. Use different arrow types to indicate external shipments of materials and products versus the value stream's movement of materials and products.

8. **Document all other collected data**: Use the value stream storyboard shown in *Appendix B* to illustrate the type of information you may need to collect— that is, date of the map, value stream name, VSM champion, team members, problem categories, and other important activity- and flow-related information.

It may be tempting to move through the current state map exercise quickly—but don't. The team will make mistakes and omissions that can later impact the team's credibility and the accuracy of their future state maps and recommendations.

Also, don't be tempted to apply existing information on standardized practices within your current state value stream maps, such as shop processes or guides. Those sources typically represent an idealized approach and expected metrics, but may not be indicative of actual practices. Again, this issue is why we use Gemba to go and see for ourselves.

Creating an IT value stream map

VSM has become a critical capability to implement and improve Lean practices across IT-related value streams. Commonly, organizations that employ VSM methods and tools may have already established Agile practices and perhaps implemented CI/CD toolchains. But now, their goal is to move to implement CI/CD practices as Lean pipelines. The VSM team's primary goals are improving collaborations and synchronizing information and workflows across development-oriented value streams.

None of those activities guarantees the IT department has taken the effort to eliminate waste from the customer-centric perspective of Lean. However, VSM helps us do just that. Also, for this mapping exercise, assume executive management working with the VSM team has selected a software development program as its targeted value stream for improvement.

More precisely, in our examples of using the standardized eight-step VSM methodology for this book, we assume the organization has one or more software development teams using Agile practices and purchased toolchains to implement CI/CD capabilities. We do not assume any efforts to integrate or automate SDLC processes using the purchased tools.

Additionally, our corporate executives have approved or even mandated DevOps practices, but may not completely understand the issues involved in executing such a significant value delivery transformation. The resolution of that issue is beyond the scope of this CI/CD use case, but we address this in *Part 3 of this book, Installing DevOps Pipelines to Compete in Our Digital Economy*.

Before they begin their work, the VSM team members must receive all the instructions in Lean practices—assuming this is their first VSM initiative. After receiving their Lean training, the team meets again before conducting their current state mapping exercise to prepare for the mapping exercise. As part of that preparation, they assign roles and responsibilities and develop a rough sketch of the IT development processes they expect to see. Finally, they conduct Gemba walks to collect the necessary data.

At this stage, the VSM team discusses the data they have uncovered and constructs their current state map. During the mapping exercise, the team discusses the data and builds their current state map over several meetings. They may have also conducted additional Gemba walks to collect more data and verify previously collected data that later seemed incomplete or inaccurate.

Documenting our Gemba walk findings

Before we start drawing the current state map, we need to gather sufficient information for our map. For our example, the VSM team must document the following activities, from front to end of the program's IT value stream:

- **Planning**: Tasks include user story refinement, updating backlog priorities, conducting architecture and design reviews, making team assignments, and updating release schedules.

- **Coding**: Tasks include developing tests, developing software code and configurations, checking in the source code under version control to the source code repository, performing static code analysis, and conducting automated and peer reviews of code.

- **Building**: Tasks include compiling code, conducting unit tests, reviewing code metrics (size, complexity, coupling, cohesion, and inheritance), building code containers or packages, preparing or updating deployment configurations, and monitoring dashboards. However, the VSM team notes that the build process varies significantly, depending on the programming language and tools used.

- **Testing**: Tasks include—but are not limited to—smoke/build verification, regression, performance, load, stress, **user interface (UI)**, **end-to-end (E2E)**, and systems testing, and—depending on needs—perhaps other unique tests.

  Tests can be executed manually, or preferably by running automated testing scripts to provision the servers and initiate the tests. Ideally multiple tests run in parallel on separate test servers or containers. But that's a future state concern. Instead, the VSM team needs to learn how the IT organization sets up their testing environments, the types of required tests, and how the development teams conduct their testing activities for the current state map.

- **Merging**: Tasks to create branches and push, pull, and merge code in the **source code management (SCM)** repository.

- **Provisioning**: Tasks include setting up or updating the infrastructure configurations to include, as appropriate, development/engineering, **quality assurance (QA)**/test, staging, and production environments.

  As the VSM team conducts their Gemba walks, they note that the development team re-executes their smoke tests on all new testing instances, including staging and production environments. Their objective is to verify that the latest software installations are stable and conform to all acceptance criteria.

- **Deploying**: Part of the formal release process, and includes tasks to prepare the release notes, plus decisions to freeze the code, configurations, and features, plus the development of **system administrator (sysadmin)**, user, and process guides and training aids (as necessary).

- **Operating**: Tasks include monitoring performance and security through dashboards and error logs. The monitoring tools usually include capabilities to trigger alarms when the networks, servers, or applications become unstable, fail, or malfunction in prespecified performance and security metrics. **Security information and event management (SIEM)** is another critical component of operations monitoring.

During their Gemba walks, the VSM team also notes that the operations department has implemented **Information Technology Infrastructure Library (ITIL)**-based practices for **IT operations management (ITOM)** and **IT service management (ITSM)**. However, for the initial VSM engagement, the team has elected to focus on documenting the development team's IT value stream work and information flows to improve their CI/CD pipeline flows.

The VSM team plans to address the operations-oriented team's work and information flows later. The current issue is that the development and operations teams are not operating as an integrated IT value stream. Though the implementation of DevOps capabilities as a strategy is a stated objective of the organization's executive management team, the VSM team decides that value stream improvement work is beyond their approved scope and requires a separate charter.

As the VSM team observes these activities, they monitor and record activity lead times, VA time, **mean time between failures (MTBF)** and **mean time to recovery (MTTR)** times, and the percent of activity-related work that is complete and accurate at each value stream stage. In addition, the VSM team has observed work and information flows across the value stream and documented exceptions to the IT organization's standard software delivery process.

Mapping the IT current state value stream

For this section, please turn to *Figure 7.4*, displaying the final picture of the VSM team's current state IT value stream map.

Note that the IT value stream map in *Figure 7.4* includes monitoring activities, which is fundamentally an IT operations-oriented task. The VSM team elected to show the monitoring activities as a source of information and backlog items for the product backlog. The product backlog is shown as an activity to document the refinement process, but you could show an inventory or waiting queue of desired customer backlog items.

The current state map depicted in *Figure 7.4* seems relatively detailed and complex; however, it's not that detailed. The information provided is relatively high-level, and the VSM team would need to expend additional efforts to decompose these activities further.

For example, Karen Martin and Mike Osterling, in their book *Value Stream Mapping*, depict the **change request (CR)** process within a Scrum-based IT development organization, which is a tiny subset of the overall IT value stream. Their current state map for the CR process includes ten distinct activities and six information systems to manage work and information flows (Martin, Osterling; pages 181-186, 2014).

Take a moment to review *Figure 7.4*, shown next, including the metrics that the VSM collected. **LT** (denoting **lead time**) is a measure that sums both the cycle times and waiting times at each activity within the value stream. In contrast, **VA** is the amount of time the developers perform the work associated with the activities, enhancing the value of the work items across each activity. Finally, **%C/A** (for **percent complete and accurate**) is a metric for the percentage of work items that pass through this activity without having to come back for rework of some sort:

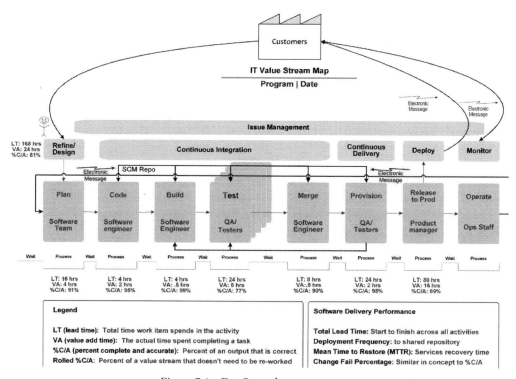

Figure 7.4 – DevOps value stream map

These are the standard Lean metrics monitored across any type of Lean improvement initiative, but there are many more. The following section takes us forward to *Step 5* in the VSM approach to Lean improvements—*Identifying Lean metrics*, but before we get to that section, let's take a moment to review the tools we used in mapping the current state.

Mapping the current state – tools

This section summarizes the tools used in current state mapping, most of which we have already identified in this chapter—for example, the tools used for current state mapping include the value stream mapping symbols identified in *Figure 7.1*. You also need a large poster board or whiteboard so that everyone can view the information and participate in the mapping exercise. As shown in *Appendix B*, a value stream storyboard is another vital tool used to record value stream data and your current value stream map. Whiteboards are best for team collaborations, but a value stream storyboard provides a more permanent record of VSM mapping activities and analysis.

Before heading out to perform your Gemba walks in the value stream work areas, your team should develop a checklist of activities and key metrics (that is, attributes) that you wish to record. Then, your team documents the metrics directly on the value stream map. A good strategy is to develop a bullet list of activities and related attributes to record the information you uncover during your Gemba walks.

When you and your VSM teammates get back from your Gemba walks, you can begin to draw your current state map.

This section introduced another eight-step mapping process as a tool to draw your value stream map and document critical attributes and activity information, completing our discussion on conducting a current state value stream mapping exercise, the fourth step in our VSM methodology.

Summary

In this chapter, you learned how to create a map of the current state of a value stream to evaluate work and information flow from the perspective of Lean production concepts. You also learned how value stream mapping differs from other process modeling concepts such as UML, IDEF3, and BPEL.

As part of the mapping exercise, you learned how to employ a standard set of Lean symbols as graphical icons. This strategy aims to simplify your value stream maps while also ensuring others understand what the map indicates.

Perhaps the most crucial aspect of mapping is getting valid information, which has nothing to do with constructing the map. In this chapter, you learned how to employ Gemba walks to see what is going on in work locations for yourself. In addition, you learned that the operators who perform the work are your best sources of information on how work is performed and for ideas on improving the flow of work and information.

In the next chapter, you will learn the value of using metrics to analyze a value stream's performance, both in the current and desired future states.

Questions

1. Why is it not recommended to jump straight into mapping the desired future state of a value stream?

2. How does value stream mapping differ from process modeling techniques?

3. Why shouldn't we automate a business process until we have made improvements to work and information flows?

4. Once the VSM team, value stream operators, and other critical stakeholders learn Lean processes, is there anything else they should do before executing their VSM plan?

5. What is the reason for having a standard set of symbols and icons for value stream mapping?

6. Collectively, what is the purpose of conducting Gemba walks as part of value stream mapping?

7. What are the three fundamental rules when practicing Gemba?

8. In which direction do you start to draw your current state map, and why?

9. In which order does a VSM team implement Lean improvements to a value stream?

10. What are the eight steps to draw a current state map?

Further reading

- Gery, G. (1991). Electronic Performance Support Systems. How and why to remake the workplace through the strategic use of technology. ISBN 978-0-9617968-1-5. Weingarten Publications, Inc. Boston, MA.

- Tapping, D., Luyster, T., Shuker, T. (2002) Value Stream Management. Eight Steps to Planning, Mapping, and Sustaining Lean Improvements. Productivity Press. New York, NY.

- Tapping, D., Luyster, T., Shuker, T. (2003) Value Stream Management for the Lean Office. Eight Steps to Planning, Mapping, and Sustaining Lean Improvements. Productivity Press. New York, NY.

- Tapping, D., Kozlowski, S., Archbold, L., Sperl, T. (2009) Value Stream Management for Lean Healthcare. Four steps to Planning, Mapping, Implementing, and Controlling Improvements in all types of Healthcare Environments. MCS Media, Inc. Chelsea, MI.

- Martin, K., Osterling, M. (2014). Value Stream Mapping. How to Visualize Work and Align Leadership for Organizational Transformation. McGraw-Hill Education Books. New York, NY.

8
Identifying Lean Metrics (VSM Step 5)

Having completed the current value stream map, we now turn our attention to evaluating potential future state opportunities to synchronize our flows and eliminate waste, in order to increase value for our customers. But first, we must identify our objectives in the form of quantifiable and measurable Lean metrics, which will be the fifth VSM step and is introduced in this chapter.

It's difficult to improve things without having measures of the current state and desired future states. It's like driving in a car to a new destination without an address or a map. Without these items, you don't know which roads to take, how far you have to go, or even how to know when you have arrived. This chapter helps you identify the key metrics that will inform your decisions in building the value stream maps that define your desired future destinations.

After reading this chapter, you will know the basic Lean metrics that help organizations and VSM teams assess areas for improvement across virtually any value stream. You will also learn the metrics that most apply to assessing the performance of modern DevOps-based software delivery teams and pipelines. Finally, you will learn about the tools that support the gathering of Lean metrics.

In this chapter, we're going to cover the following main topics:

- Defining universal Lean metrics

- Assessing Lean performance

- Measuring key software delivery metrics

- Adding flow metrics and analytics to VSM

- Implementing the tools of Lean metrics

Defining universal Lean metrics

We've already introduced some Lean metrics in the previous chapter on current-state value stream mapping. However, we did not take the time to define Lean metrics other than metrics explicitly related to software delivery performance. Additionally, there are many traditional Lean metrics that you and your VSM team need to understand how to use, as identified in the following list:

- **Cycle time** (**CT**): The CT is the timespan between starting and finishing a process or a value stream activity. The CT is actually a measure of throughput (units per period of time). So, if we can produce 40 widgets in a 40-hour work week, our cycle time is $\frac{400}{40} = 10\ widgets\ per\ hour.$ The VSM team only includes working time and does not include **work in progress** (**WIP**), nor the waiting time between value stream activities. However, the CT is not always all **value-adding time** (**VT**). There can be elements of non-value-adding work within the activity in the form of waste. This waste includes defects, inventory, motion, over-processing, overproduction, transport, and waiting.

  For example, suppose an operator pulls a work item but must wait to retrieve information, materials, or reviewing information to start their work. In that case, that type of waiting is still part of the activity's CT. Additionally, time spent setting up equipment or changing materials is part of the CT.

  Using a real-life example, I recently had some landscape work done in my backyard. The materials vendor dropped the items off on pallets in my driveway. I had to pay the landscaping contractor for their team's labor hours to break down pallets and manually move the materials into my backyard. As a paying customer, I preferred that the pallets were dropped off directly in my backyard. As a result, the CT I paid for included the value-adding landscaping work, plus the non-value-adding work of moving the materials, this being a Lean-oriented waste in the form of motion.

- **Days of inventory on hand**: This is the amount of material, parts, or products stored and quantified in daily production usage. For example, if we use 20 widgets per day and have 100 widgets in inventory, we have 5 days of widget inventory on hand.

- **Defects per million opportunities (DPMO)**: This is a measure of how many defects occur in every million opportunities to have a defect. For example, we might have 40 defects per every one million activities. Or, we might have 40 defects per every one million lines of code produced. Therefore, we need to be concise in explaining what type of defect ratio the DPMO is measuring.

  Our quality objective is always to strive to eliminate all defects and causes of errors or failures. We want to monitor and record defects against a control chart with min and max levels in any highly repetitive and continuous flow to see when our processes are beginning to fail. As our measures trend toward the upper or lower limits, we still have time to correct the problems before the issues become catastrophic.

  For example, Lean production practitioners often employ a Six Sigma calculation measure in Lean production processes as a desired quality goal. A Six Sigma quality goal is a measure of 3.4 defects per million opportunities.

- **Downtime**: This is the opposite of uptime. Downtime is a ratio that measures the percentage of unplanned time during which equipment is not available to perform work when compared to the total time.

- **First-time-through capability** (also known as **first-time-through yield**, or **FTT**): This is a measure of how many products are produced correctly without defects, bugs, or rework required, expressed as a percentage of total units produced across the value stream. An FTT of 80% means 80 products out of every 100 produced do not have bugs or defects that require rework.

- **Inventory or work item turns**: The number of times that materials, parts, or products are used or sold over a specific period. This metric is an essential measure as more frequent turns correlates to better flows, higher returns, and reduced inventory carrying costs.

- **Lead time (LT)**: This is the sum measure of total cycle times and waiting times from when an order is received until it reaches its internal or external customer. In this context, LTs technically apply to entire value streams, business processes, or even between one or more activities within a value stream. Regardless, LTs include the sum of both waiting and cycle times for the span of work measured.

- **Mean time between failures (MTBF):** This is a time-based measure of the frequency at which an activity or process fails, usually measured in hours. For example, an MTBF of 89 indicates we can expect the activity or equipment to fail once, on average, every 89 hours.

  Of course, things are never perfect. We should also measure the variances and probability distributions to gain better insights into our failure frequency. We also want to look at the causes of our failures to see how we can reduce or eliminate them.

  The VSM team should assess MTBF metrics for value stream equipment, software releases, and downtimes due to security breaches and network or computing system failures.

- **Meantime to recover/repair (MTTR):** This is a measure of the time between discovering a problem or failure and the point at which we have a working remedy that allows us to keep working. MTTR values often apply to our value stream's equipment, but they also apply to the availability of our software products and our IT infrastructures and security.

- **On-time delivery:** This is a measure of how well we are meeting our customer demands, expressed as the percentage of finished goods or services across all orders delivered to customers on time, as complete orders, and without errors or omissions.

- **Overall equipment efficiency (OEE):** This is a quantifiable expression of the percentage of effectiveness of industrial machinery or equipment in a Lean value stream consisting of quality, speed, and availability measures. Precisely, OEE calculates equipment efficiencies by multiplying the metrics as percentages for quality, speed, and availability, as we can see here:

$$OEE = quality(\%)xspeed(\%)xavailability(\%)$$

As an example, an OEE of 100% means that an operation produces good parts with 100% favorable quality, at 100% of the operation's maximum production rate and without interruption 100% of the time. But note what happens if quality, speed, and availability all drop down to 90% each. In that scenario, the OEE drops down to 72.9% (giving an OEE of .729).

In other words, even though all factors achieve a 90% efficiency rate, the measured value stream activity or equipment efficiency drops down to an overall productivity efficiency rate of just 73%.

- **Queue (waiting or wait) time**: This is the amount of time that materials, parts, products, or information spend waiting on a downstream process. Waiting occurs in both push- and pull-oriented production control systems when there are mismatched batch sizes and cycle times across value stream activities.

  Pull-oriented production processes help reduce waiting and inventories so long as the operators are disciplined in limiting buffer sizes and pulling in new work when they are ready to perform the work. Any waiting time that occurs is expressed as delays between activities until the work items at upstream activities are pulled into the next downstream activity.

  You can expect to have significantly higher waiting times and queues with push-oriented production scheduling processes. Having value streams with mismatched cycle times and batch sizes makes it more difficult to reduce inventories and waiting times. Having product lines with different flows across the same work cells or equipment further exacerbates these problems, as it becomes exceedingly difficult to predict which work items will show up at which work stations, and at what times.

- **Reportable health and safety events**: In the United States, the **Occupational Safety and Health Administration (OSHA)** implements health and safety regulations. But it's not just the law we are concerned with, as any safety issue represents productivity, financial, and legal liabilities to the entity. If an event is so egregious that it needs to be reported, then we should measure it and take actions to reduce, if not eliminate, the causes.

- **Total value stream WIP**: In Lean, the ideal state is to have one work item flowing between our activities across our value stream, in what is known as *single-piece flow*. If we have 10 distinct activities in our value stream, the preference is to have no more than 10 work items in total as WIP. That objective may not be possible in the short term, but our objective is to monitor, control, and limit WIP across our value stream.

- **Total cycle time (TCT)**: This is the sum of all cycle times for all activities across a value stream. As with activity-specific cycle times, we do not include the time work items spend waiting between activities, but we do include the time associated with non-value-adding work.

- **Total lead time (TLT)**: This is the sum of all cycle times and queue times across the value stream. This metric gives you an idea of how long your value stream takes to deliver a customer order, from receipt of the order to delivery. TLTs can be measured across value streams for internal or external customers.

  Note that the TLT value may also encompass the LTs across multiple developments and operations-oriented value streams that participate in the delivery. Whatever the case, it's essential that the map clearly states the span of the value streams and activities associated with the specified TLT measure.

- **Uptime**: This is an expression of availability, calculated as the ratio of the total time that equipment is available to conduct work across the desired time. Note, the measure of available time does not include planned downtimes (also known as nonproductive activities), such as preventative maintenance, equipment setup, or work item changeovers. Whether the planned work is value-adding or nonproductive is not the concern, just whether or not the equipment is available.

- **Value-adding time (VT)**: This is the CT of a value stream activity or process minus all time spent on waste elements. The idealized goal is to have an activity CT that is 100% VT. (This would mean designing an activity without defects, inventory, motion, over-processing, overproduction, transport, and waiting.) Unfortunately, we can rarely achieve that ideal goal, but we continuously try to improve our efforts to eliminate all waste forms.

The previous list of standard Lean metrics applies reasonably well to any Lean improvement initiative, regardless of the value stream type. However, four critical metrics tend to best predict an IT organization's software delivery value stream's performance. We'll discuss this in the section titled *Measuring software delivery performance*. But, before we get to that topic, let's review the concerns a VSM team needs to keep in mind when evaluating and gathering Lean metrics.

Gathering Lean metrics

As your VSM team reviews which Lean metrics best support your current VS mapping exercise, keep the following in mind:

- Review your team's charter for the strategic direction and desired outcomes.

- Assess the value stream from the perspective of eliminating waste and delivering customer-centric value.

- Determine which Lean metrics you need to collect.

- Get management buy-in for the metrics your team chooses.

- Calculate the best possible outcomes based on standardized processes or activity data.

- Make your metrics visible and readily available to all team members, operators, and stakeholders.

Now that you know the standard metrics that are useful to assess all value streams and strategies for gathering them, let's look at those that have proven to be most effective in evaluating IT value stream performance.

Analyzing current value stream map metrics

Back on our current state VS map in *Chapter 7, Mapping the Current State (VSM Step 4)*, depicted in *Figure 7.4*, we included metrics for LTs, VTs, percentage complete and accurate, and rolled complete and accurate. Now let's begin to use that information to analyze the performance of the value stream.

The following table displays the **total lead time (TLT)**, the **total value-adding time (TVA)**, and the rolled complete and accurate percentage across the value stream:

Metrics	Refine	Dev	Release	IT VS
TLT	168	80	80	328
TVA	24	17	16	57
RolledC/A	81%	56%	89%	41%

Figure 8.1 – Table of TLT, TVA, and rolling C/A

The table is divided into three data rows, these being for TLT, TVA, and rolling C/A values across three parts of the IT value stream. The first section of data in the table shown in *Figure 8.1* spans the product backlog's refinement and design of work item activities. The second data column spans all the development activities, from planning through provisioning. The third data column includes the activities related to releasing products into production environments.

Now let's take a closer look at the details across the IT value-stream delivery activities. *Figure 8.2* summarizes the Lean metrics and information captured by the VSM team, which spans all the activities across the entire IT value stream for software deliveries. The values and information are broken separately into work-related categories spanning backlog refinement, development, and release, as shown in the following figure:

Metrics	Backlog Refine	Development Plan	Code	Build	Test	Merge	Provision	Release Release
LT (Hrs)	168	16	4	4	24	8	24	80
VA (Hrs)	24	4	2	0.5	8	0.5	2	16
%C/A	81%	91%	95%	99%	77%	90%	95%	89%
Rolled C/A	81.0%	73.7%	70.0%	69.3%	53.4%	48.0%	45.6%	40.6%
Notes =>	Product backlog items spend on average three weeks in the backlog, and require 3 days to refine and design.	The Agile team meets over two days to develop Sprint Plan. Only 4 hours of VA time.	Dev team members have 4 hours to code new reqmts, but only take ~2 hours to write tests and dev code.	Dev team members have 4 hours to Build code and run Unit tests, usually takes half hour for build and 2.5 hours to run tests and fix code.	QA Team has 3 days to run tests and return the results. It typically takes 8 hours to set up and run the tests, when the servers are available.	Pull, Push, and Merge requests are quick and simple. But, getting prior approvals for merges takes the most time.	The QA team takes in test, pre-prod, and prod. server config requests and provisions the servers when they have time. They have a three day max limit.	Production releases are approved on a bi-weekly basis. The value added work to prepare guides and training aids is ~16 hours.

Figure 8.2 – Table of Lean metrics across the IT value stream

It's possible that some of the release tasks, such as developing guides and training aids, can be performed in parallel. But the IT value stream also accumulates features into planned bi-weekly releases, which is the reason for the 80-hour lead times. In effect, the release process is a transition or integration point between IT development and ops staff. It involves people from both sides of the IT organization, but the work is more operations-oriented and broken out accordingly.

Note that the TLT from planning through to release is 328 hours, or a little more than 8 weeks in duration from when a requirement comes into the product backlog until it's released into production as a feature or function. Yet, the total value-adding work time is only 57 hours (or roughly 1.5 weeks). While we don't know why yet, there is too much waiting built into our IT value delivery system.

Much of the non-value-added time for the work items accumulate at the product backlog – 168 hours in total. This is where the items wait in a queue based on their priorities. Recall the previous statement that the refinement and design processes are challenging to estimate and control due to that type of work's creative aspects. That may account for some of the delays. However, the large discrepancy between TLT and VA times for the product refinement and design activities suggests we have throughput issues in the downstream development and release activities.

Still, the lead times for work items in both the development and release segments of the IT value stream add another 80 hours each, or nearly a month, to the overall product lead times. So, we have a lot of built-in waiting in those activities as well. Based on this date, it appears we may have some built-in constraints that are hindering our flows in development and release. Perhaps we have equipment and resource limitations and approvals that hinder our flows.

We now leave the topic of analyzing current value stream map metrics to look more closely at the time elements that form the CT metrics.

Breaking down CTs

Looking across our VA times for the entire IT delivery value stream, we can see that Refine activities account for the largest amount of effort, followed by Release and finally Test activities. Those are three areas we need to improve to reduce costs and increase flow.

As we begin to look more closely at the VA times, we'll want to explore several non-value adding activities that contribute to waste, such as the following:

- **Time spent waiting**: This includes the times where materials or work items sit in queues waiting to be processed. Waiting can occur for a variety of reasons. One prominent reason for waiting is when production control pushes more products into the value stream or a value stream activity than it can handle. Another reason for time spent waiting is when multiple activities feed into a single activity faster than the single activity can handle. And, waiting occurs when a given value stream activity is slower than the upstream activities.

- **Time spent walking**: This is a Lean form of waste referred to as motion. Motion is non-value-added time and effort. The goal is to eliminate motion as much as possible. Ways to accomplish that goal include moving work activities closer together and possibly reconfiguring the layout of work cells within the value stream's location.

- **Time spent entering data**: This is non-value-added work but often necessary work. Using bar codes, image scanners, and **radio frequency identification (RFID)** tags and readers can dramatically shorten the time required for data entry.

- **Time spent retrieving files**: This is another form of waiting. It is also non-value-added work. However, both materials and operators are waiting on the information necessary to complete the activity in this situation.

- **Time spent sending and reviewing email, or other messages**: This is precisely what it sounds like – the information needed to conduct value-adding work is not available when and where it is needed. This problem is similar to the issues associated with lengthy file downloads.

- **Value-adding work:** This is, unlike all the previous list items, the only effort that adds value to the product.

We've now looked at the lead times and cycle times for our current VS map. Now, let's look at the percent complete to accurate metrics.

Improving percent complete to accurate (%C/A) metrics

One final issue that we need to look at is the rolled C/A values. The %C/A values in *Figure 8.2*, at first glance, all appear relatively reasonable across each activity. But take a closer look at the impact testing. The 77% C/A ratio has an oversized impact on the final rolled average (in this case 41%). The percent **complete to accurate (%C/A)** metric, more simply put, is a measure of the number of times out of 100 that a work item or information is reprocessed through an activity, or a series of activities, without requiring rework or error corrections.

Each activity has a %C/A value, while the rolled %C/A measure multiplies all %C/A figures across all the series' activities. As a result, just one outlier can have a tremendously negative effect. Additionally, a low %C/A value in testing is another area we need to look at in our future state mapping exercise.

Now that we've reviewed the metrics used in our current value stream map, let's review the tools needed to assess Lean performance across our value streams.

Assessing Lean performance

The Lean metrics identified so far help us evaluate the efficiencies of flow across our value streams and act as a means to identify areas of waste. But we also need methods to assess the areas that require the most attention in order to eliminate waste as part of our ongoing Kaizen efforts. A practical way to do this is by developing a **Lean assessment radar chart**.

The Lean assessment radar chart maps specific Lean objectives that you've already learned to a grid, radiating outward like spokes from a central hub. A completed radar chart looks a bit like a spider's web, as depicted in *Figure 8.3*. This figure contains a graphical display of an example Lean assessment radar chart:

Figure 8.3 – Lean assessment radar chart

A radar chart implements scales to rank capabilities ranging from no commitments at the center of the hub to a level representing world-class capabilities at the outer radius. The example in *Appendix C* starts at 0 (no commitment) and radiates outward across four improved capability levels.

In our Lean assessment radar chart example, shown in *Figure 8.3*, the spokes have the following rankings:

0: No commitment.

1: Beginning to implement Lean.

2: Changes are becoming visible.

3: Results improving at all levels.

4: World-class status.

A quick look at the radar chart in *Figure 8.3* shows our most significant improvement needs lie in continuous flows, quality, and visual controls. In contrast, implementation of the five S's system and training seem to both be well in hand.

Without Lean metrics identified as goals, the measure becomes subjective. The VSM team must strive to determine what world-class performance looks like across each of the assessed Lean practices. The Lean assessment metrics evaluated in our sample radar chart include the following:

- **Continuous flow**: This represents the degree of synchronization and efficiencies in flow with the ideal goal of achieving single-piece flows.

- **Five S's of Lean**: This is the degree to which the value stream's work area is clean, uncluttered, safe, well organized, with the 5S practices implemented, scheduled, and visually displayed.

- **Order leveling**: The degree to which the organization employs Heijunka and other Lean leveling practices.

- **Quality**: The degree to which the value stream meets its established quality metrics, while always working toward the ideal goal of no errors, defects, rework, or failures.

- **Training**: All value stream members have completed Lean training and have access to coaches and mentors, plus access to Lean training aids on demand.

- **Team member involvement**: The degree to which VSM team members and VS operators participate in following the value stream's standard lean practices, participate in Lean assessments meetings, apply 5S practices, participate in Lean training programs, and support continuous improvement objectives.

- **Visual controls**: The degree to which the VSM team and VA operators and managers maintain and display their Lean metrics, 5S standards, and standard activity information.

- **Work unit movement**: The degree to which the value stream limits waiting, applies just-in-time and pull-oriented scheduling concepts, and matches flow to Takt time.

Before their Gemba walks, the VSM team should discuss and decide what the values 0 through 4 should look like for each Lean assessment category. They also need to determine what things they plan to look at to assess each category properly.

For example, let's say that for the 5S category, each positive observation of the five "S" practices within the value stream earns .8 points toward the total possible 4 points. As a result, the VSM team obtained multiple numerical values for each category, and the averages, therefore, end up with decimal point values.

These Lean assessment metrics are an essential basis behind our Kaizen efforts. As with Agile teams, Lean teams must strive to improve their value stream activities and flow continuously. The Lean assessment metrics help us see where the team can improve their activities.

We are just about finished with the Lean metrics section. But before we leave, let's quickly review the tools associated with gathering and applying Lean metrics.

Measuring key software delivery metrics

So far, the metrics assigned to the activities are relatively traditional Lean metrics, applicable across any organizational value stream. However, Nicole Forsgren, Jez Humble, and Gene Kim, in the book *Accelerate: Building and Scaling High Performing Technology Organizations*, identified a shortlist of key metrics that predict software delivery performance (2018, pages 17-19). Based on their detailed statistical analysis, spanning 23,000 survey responses across 2,000 unique organizations, they found that the following four measures are most critical in measuring software delivery performance:

- Delivery lead time
- Deployment frequency
- **Mean time to restore (MTTR)**
- Change fail percentage

Their work continued under the direction of the **DevOps Research and Assessment (DORA)** team. This Google research group conducted a 6-year program to measure and understand DevOps practices and capabilities across the IT industry. DORA's research was presented in the annual State of DevOps Reports from 2014 – 2019 and is available at `https://cloud.google.com/devops/state-of-devops`.

We'll take a closer look at each of these metrics in the four subsections that follow.

Delivery lead time

Delivery lead time is the total amount of time required to take a customer requirement from ideation to customer satisfaction. In software development, satisfaction means the product enhancement meets its *definition of Done*. In other words, both the team and the customer have agreed a deliverable item meets its defined acceptance criteria.

But the calculation for a delivery lead time as a Lean-oriented metric is tricky. In *Chapter 7, Mapping the Current State (VSM Step 4)*, and specifically in the *Preparing to map* section, you learned that the activities to define and validate requirements and designs are creative tasks. The time and effort required to perform creative endeavors are challenging to predict compared to the relatively standardized work of developing and testing code, provisioning, and deployment. When we speak about using a delivery lead time to measure software delivery performance, it's usually best to start the clock when a requirement within the product backlog is sufficiently refined to begin coding efforts.

High-performance software delivery organizations can develop, test, and deliver a new requirement as working code into the main branch of their repository in less than one hour. In contrast, the lowest performers deploy working code into their main branch only once per week to once per month in the most recent data (2017), and as much as once every 6 months in previous years.

Deployment frequency

The **deployment frequency** is how often code is released into a production environment or sent to an app store. As noted previously, coding and testing smaller increments of functionality is superior to building and deploying large-scale code changes all at once. The lowest performers tend to take on bigger bites of functionality, increasing the complexity of their coding, testing, and debugging activities and thereby delaying their deployment frequencies to a range of 1 to 4 weeks. In contrast, the highest performers take in new requirements on demand, build functionality in smaller incremental chunks, and release multiple deployments per day.

Note that software development value streams are equivalent to the idealized production flow concept of *single-piece flows*. Single-piece flows occur in software delivery when the organization automates the DevOps pipeline from *code* to *release-to-production* activities. Single-piece flows are the ultimate goal of CI/CD pipelines. In other words, each commit of software code into the SCM repository can automatically flow through the pipeline and into the production environments without manual intervention.

In theory, it's still an example of continuous flow to stop at the preproduction environments for final approval. But if that step also involves staging and releasing multiple features, that part of the process now becomes a batch process. Regardless of the reason or merits, all batch processing impedes the flow of value to our customers.

Mean time to restore

Mean time to restore is a critical metric as it represents the amount of time an application or system has failed and is not providing service to its customer(s). Usually, when a system or feature fails, we have no choice but to roll back the changes until we can identify and fix the problem. So, the key is to rapidly discover the failures and execute a rollback to the previous working release. Ideally, we want to see this MTTR number in under one hour. Low performers take between a day and a week to restore failed services.

Change failure rates

Change failure rates specify the percentage of time taken until a change to the code results in a failure, usually detected in the form of a bug or a defect. With modern pipeline deployment capabilities, a new release may only involve rolling back new releases of functionality. But a failure can also take the form of a system-wide crash and loss of services. Regardless, low performers had change failure rates of 31% to 45%, while the highest performers had 0 to 15% (Forsgren et al., 2018). Improvements in writing test scripts, such as test-driven development and test automation capabilities, help lower change failure rate numbers.

You now have a thorough understanding of both common value stream metrics and the four metrics that most often define the performance level for software development organizations. In the following subsection, we'll explore how to use state value stream metrics to analyze the current state.

Adding flow metrics and analytics to VSM

Beyond the **DORA Four**, the trend in software development is to implement **flow metrics and analytics** capabilities to provide visibility to business leaders, product managers, and value stream teams to continuously improve their processes. Suboptimal processes and team performance can negatively impact the organization's Lean-Agile transformation efforts.

Alternatively, organizations can guide improvement activities and coaching when they have access to accurate and consistent metrics visibility of their business operations and value streams. The metrics must be available, up to date, and visible to all stakeholders at all times.

Modern VSM tools make it easy to capture value stream metrics. This is because they act as automated activities, devoid of human manipulations and reporting that might cloud the findings. Automating data capture makes the information increasingly available, timely, accurate, and usable. Business leaders, team members, and other stakeholders must have confidence in the data and its accuracy.

Data may come from many disparate tools or systems that participate in a value stream pipeline flow. Modern VSM tools apply a **common data model** that normalizes the data to provide an end-to-end view of the data across a value stream pipeline. In addition, analytical tools, some employing artificial intelligence capabilities, make it easier for executives and VSM team members to evaluate the flows across current-state activities, then assess alternative future-state scenarios.

Additionally, portfolio managers and product owners can use these same flow metrics and analytical capabilities to assess progress against their product and release roadmaps. Therefore, business owners and stakeholders will therefore have increased visibility on the delivery status of products and their related production costs.

Going beyond the DORA Four

The DORA Four metrics are beneficial because they help identify the critical metrics that define best-in-class software delivery capabilities. They also provide a valuable set of metrics as targets for the software development team during their transformations to Lean-Agile practices.

Still, in a Lean-Agile enterprise, there are many other metrics an organization should track to identify areas for continuous improvements and verify the achievement of its improvement goals. For example, Gartner analyst Bill Swanton identifies 18 flow metrics in the **Gartner Report** titled *How Software Engineering Leaders Can Use Value Stream Metrics to Improve Agile Effectiveness*. These areas are shown in the following figure:

Technical	Product	Business
Code change size	Lead time	Product cost
Code delivery speed	Cycle time	Product value
Code refactoring rate	Throughput	Return on investment
Code review churn	Work in progress	Product quality
Code quality	Flow efficiency	Net Promoter Score
Technical debt	Work profile	Customer satisfaction

Figure 8.4 – List of Gartner-identified flow metrics

Swanton says these are some examples of flow metrics that should be considered, noting: "*Much like the metrics in a lean manufacturing process, they measure how smoothly work is flowing through the system and how responsive teams are to changing demand.*"

He further points out that: "*Vendors are starting to offer systems that integrate with your software development, infrastructure and monitoring tools (version control, work management, test management, etc.) to collect, calculate and present the metrics continuously.*"

One company that has done a great deal of work in this area is Tasktop, with their **Flow Framework**®, under the leadership of Mik Kersten, the company's CEO.

Implementing the Flow Framework

Tasktop VSM tools are introduced in more detail in *Chapter 12, Introducing the Leading VSM Tool Vendors*. However, given the Flow Framework's relevance to this section, we'll take a moment to explain how modern VSM tools can help capture and analyze Flow Metrics.

The concepts behind flow metrics and the Flow Framework were initially introduced in the book *Project to Product* by Dr. Mik Kersten (2018). IT leaders have since adopted these concepts worldwide in order to bridge the gap between technologists and business stakeholders. Specifically, the Flow Framework provides both a methodology and vocabulary to systematically discover and eliminate bottlenecks that slow down software delivery and negatively impact business results.

The goal of the Flow Framework is to ensure that business-level frameworks and transformation initiatives are connected to technical ones associated with implementing Agile and DevOps, as well as future methodologies still to arrive. The Tasktop's Flow Framework scales the **Three Ways of DevOps** – **flow** (accelerate delivery through the development, operations, and on to the customer), **feedback** (create safer systems of work), and **continuous learning and experimentation** (fostering trust and a scientific approach to organizational improvements and risk-taking) – to the entire business. These concepts were introduced in the book *The DevOps Handbook* (Kim et al., 2016).

With modern VSM tools, every organization can gather hundreds of valuable metrics to evaluate improvements in process, productivity, quality, cost, revenue, and adherence to standards. The trick is to make sense of it all. Unfortunately, organizations often lack visibility into their end-to-end pipeline flows, making it difficult to answer the questions shown in the following figure:

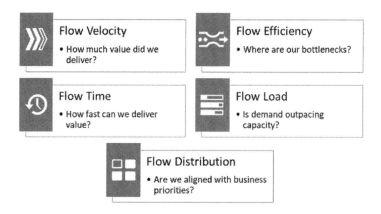

Figure 8.5 – Flow Framework flow metrics

Flow metrics help identify and solve a system's bottleneck, eliminating the inefficient local optimizations that may be present when visibility is limited to siloed, in-tool data. They also provide a historical view of your performance, so you can understand how choices and changes impacted your flow.

Four flow items constitute a unit of business value pulled by a stakeholder through a product's value stream. These are **features**, **defects**, **risks**, and **debts**, as shown in *Figure 8.6*. Flow metrics are measured for each of these flow items both individually and as a collective. The following figure shows these items:

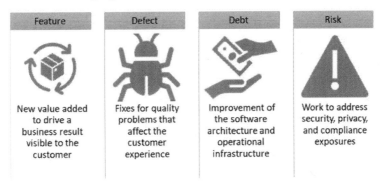

Figure 8.6 – Four flow items

Flow items represent items of value to the organization. In other words, how we address the prioritization of features, defects, technical debt, and risks affects our ability to deliver customer value. Therefore, business and technology leaders must work in concert to analyze the flow, speed, and prioritization of all four value types.

For example, frequently features have priority, but other times we need to fix bugs, reduce our technical debts, or address critical risks and issues. Eventually, we pay a heavy price if we don't balance the work associated with these four flow items.

Despite the complexity and intangibility of software delivery work, the Flow Framework makes flow metrics (and the daily practice of VSM) attainable for any organization in any structure, by defining how the necessary data can be extracted from the execution tools (**integration model**). These are abstracted into flow items and flow states (**activity model**), presented in a view that is aligned with the business (**product model**).

Thus presented and analyzed, flow metrics can then be used to inform the decision-making of leaders and teams to deliver targeted business outcomes. Tasktop's VSM platform provides these capabilities out of the box, through a point-and-click interface. *Figure 8.7* provides a poster view of the Flow Framework:

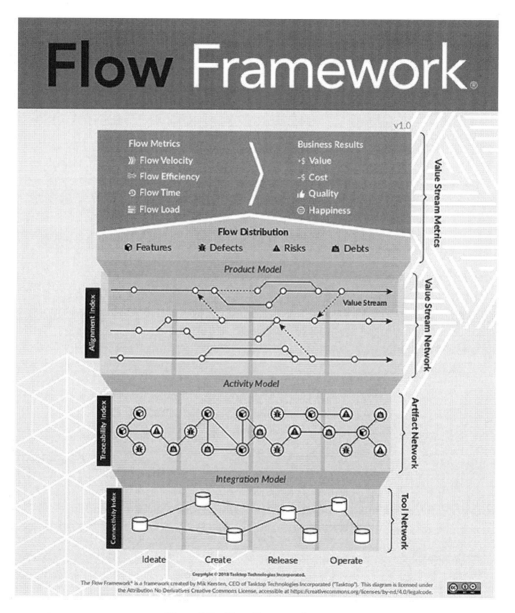

Figure 8.7 – Flow Framework poster

Tasktop makes the point that there are other important frameworks (such as **Disciplined Agile (DA)**, the **Scaled Agile Framework® (SAFe®)**, **Large-Scale Scrum (LeSS)**, and Nexus) that help organizations scale Agile and connect those practices to the goals of the business. You will recall that Agile is a set of values and principles that help an organization align its resources and activities around adding customer-centric value and nimbly responding to changes.

In contrast, VSM can increase the flow of business value, from the initial customer request to customer delivery. The Flow Framework is a structured, prescriptive approach to value stream management in software delivery organizations, created to provide a business with customer-centric view of flows across the entire software delivery process. Therefore, Agile helps ensure we deliver the correct customer-centric value at the right time, while VSM helps ensure we deliver that value rapidly and efficiently.

Creating a safe work environment

Remaining consistent with the values and principles of Agile, we must never use the flow metrics as a tool to punish or even reward individuals and teams. Instead, their purpose is to help guide our continuous improvement efforts.

Lean-Agile practices emphasize team-based performance, and when things go awry – which inevitably they will – we need an all-hands approach to resolve the issues at hand. If teams and individuals fear punishment, you can expect that they will avoid speaking out and may even hide critical information about issues that impact their ability to deliver software value effectively, rapidly, and efficiently.

Therefore, when our value stream flows are interrupted, we need to stop everything and have all team members work together to solve the problem. Attempts to keep production flowing lead to queuing, activity waiting, product delays, and possibly the accumulation of more defects, all of which can only serve to increase our costs.

The benefit of having access to real-time flow metrics is that we can spot issues immediately when they arise. This allows us to address them sooner and therefore reduce our lost production times and other waste. In addition, these metrics and analytics help the team evaluate problems and root causes, as well as brainstorm alternative resolution strategies.

Implementing the tools of Lean metrics

In this chapter on Lean metrics, you learned about metrics commonly applied to measure Lean production practices. You also learned about the four specific metrics that give the best prediction of a software delivery teams' performance. Traditional VSM practices implemented manual tools to capture and analyze value stream metrics. In addition, you also learned how modern VSM tools, flow metrics, and analytics help improve the speed and efficiency of software delivery, while ensuring software development stays in alignment with the goals and objectives of the business.

As regards manual tools, you learned how to use a large whiteboard or chart, or electronic screen, to make your metrics highly visible. You also learned how to make updates to your VSM Storyboard in order to keep all your VSM team data contained and available from a single source. Finally, you learned how to assess a value stream's Lean practices. These span eight categories and are displayed in a Lean assessment radar chart format. These are all manual tools that evolved concurrently with VSM practices.

The advantages of modern VSM tools are their ability to capture end-to-end pipeline information and provide analytical tools that work across a common data model. In their modern rebirth, VSM tool vendors implement capabilities to capture and analyze metrics to support CI/CD and DevOps pipeline flows, using the very same concepts and types of metrics employed across all other organizational value streams. Therefore, analysts can evaluate the performance of the pipeline activities, in part or whole, no matter how many third-party tools become integrated into the CI/CD or DevOps pipeline.

But the modern VSM tools go beyond data capture and analysis. They also support the **integration**, **automation**, and **orchestration** of pipeline flows. We'll start to get into these topics in the next chapter on future state mapping and delve into much greater detail in *Section 3* of this book on VSM vendors.

This section ends our discussion on Lean metrics, the fifth step in our VSM methodology. In the next chapter, *Chapter 9*, *Mapping the Future State (VSM Step 6)*, we'll start to map the desired future state in three phases: evaluating alignment with customer demands, implementing continuous flows, and production flow leveling through production control and orchestration strategies.

Summary

This chapter provided instruction on the critical metrics that help us evaluate the effectiveness of our value streams from a Lean-oriented perspective. You also learned how to go about gathering useful Lean metrics (step five in our generic VSM methodology).

While VSM teams can gather and analyze metrics manually, this is a labor-intensive process. In contrast, modern VSM tools have become increasingly important, in large part because of their ability to capture and display such information in real time. Moreover, the analytics and what-if capabilities of VSM tools support future state analysis.

In the next chapter, you will learn how to conduct future state mapping exercises across three distinct phases spanning customer demand, continuous flows, and leveling. Before we get to that chapter, take a couple of moments to answer the following questions. Don't worry if you don't recall the information or quite understand all of the questions. Going back to find the answers will help both your understanding and ability to retain the knowledge.

Questions

Please answer the following 10 questions:

1. Why is the identification of Lean metrics such a crucial concern?
2. What is **cycle time (CT)**?
3. Is CT the same as **value-adding time (VT)**?
4. What is the relevance of Six Sigma?
5. What are the four most important metrics in Lean software delivery?
6. List the types of non-value-adding activities that contribute to waste.
7. What is the relevance of change failure rates?
8. What is the essential Lean assessment tool?
9. What are the typical radials on the Lean assessment radar chart?
10. In its modern rebirth, VSM tool vendors implement platforms with metrics and analytics to support what three functions?

Further reading

- *Tapping, D., Luyster, T., Shuker, T. (2002) Value Stream Management: Eight Steps to Planning, Mapping, and Sustaining Lean Improvements. Productivity Press. New York, NY*

- *Tapping, D., Luyster, T., Shuker, T. (2003) Value Stream Management for the Lean Office: Eight Steps to Planning, Mapping, and Sustaining Lean Improvements. Productivity Press. New York, NY*

- *Tapping, D., Kozlowski, S., Archbold, L., Sperl, T. (2009) Value Stream Management for Lean Healthcare: Four steps to Planning, Mapping, Implementing, and Controlling Improvements in all types of Healthcare Environments. MCS Media, Inc. Chelsea, MI*

- *Forsgren, N., Humble, J., Kim, G. (2018) Accelerate: Building and Scaling High performing Technology Organizations. IT Revolution. Portland, OR.*

- *Kim, G., Humble, J., Debois, P., Willis, J. (2016) The DevOps Handbook: How to Create World-Class Agility, Reliability, & Security in Technology Organizations. IT Revolutions. Portland, OR*

- *Kersten, M. (2018) Project to Product: How to Survive and Thrive in the Age of Digital Disruption with the Flow Framework. IT Revolution. Portland, OR*

9

Mapping the Future State (VSM Step 6)

In the previous chapter, you learned how to map the current state, perform a Lean office assessment, and observe and record critical Lean metrics for the value stream. You also learned how to document important information relevant to the flow of work and information across the value stream. Most importantly, you learned how to visualize work and information flows from the perspective of Lean.

The work that's been performed in the current VS mapping exercise is documentary in nature. It does not involve much imagination – just accuracy in discovery (through Gemba walks), recording, and mapping. Now, we will enter the creative phase of Lean value stream mapping and design an improved future state. **Future state mapping** occurs in three sequential phases to help evaluate methods and improve the value stream's ability to meet customer demands, establish and maintain continuous flows, and level the distribution of customer orders to maximize operational efficiencies.

In this chapter, we're going to cover the following main topics:

- Modeling three future state objectives
- Phase 1 of future state mapping – customer demand
- Phase 2 of future state mapping – continuous flows
- Phase 3 of future state mapping – leveling

Specifically, you will learn how to develop your skills by combining Lean and Agile practices to implement continuous improvements, and incorporate the concepts of Lean Thinking in your CI/CD and DevOps pipeline implementations. You will start this learning journey by covering an introduction to the three phases of future state modeling: the customer demand phase, the continuous flow phase, and the leveling phase.

Modeling three future state objectives

This section provides instructions on conducting future state mapping exercises across three phases, involving analyzing customer demands, continuous flows, and leveling. The following list contains quick descriptions of the work involved in each phase:

- **Customer demand phase**: This includes analyzing customer demands for your products or services so that they include quality objectives and lead time.

- **Continuous flow phase**: This helps improve flows so that our customers receive the right products or services at the right time and with the right features and quantities.

- **Leveling phase**: This helps distribute work evenly across product lines, reduce waiting times, and eliminate batch processing (that is, the goal is to achieve single-piece flows).

While there is likely to be overlap between the three phases, the initial analysis will follow these three stages.

Value streams operate as pipeline flows that have inputs, a sequence or work activities, and outputs. In more complex environments, we can expect integrated branching with other value streams or even activities. For these reasons, it is virtually impossible to understand what our optimized and continuous activity flow targets need to be, if we don't understand how demand flows into our value stream.

As we identify and coordinate demand flows inputs, the VSM team can then analyze how to improve activity and information flows to match demand rates. Finally, we can expect customer demands to vary over time, so we need to understand how to balance production workloads to minimize bottlenecks, waiting, and other forms of waste on an ongoing basis.

Since the future state phases follow the aforementioned sequence of analysis, we'll start our introduction to the three phases in the same order, starting with analyzing customer demand.

Phase 1 – customer demand

This phase of the future mapping exercise is expressly set up to ensure the VSM team starts its Lean improvement objectives with the customer's needs firmly in mind. But we're not talking about understanding customer requirements in terms of features and functions, as that type of analysis lies with the product management function. In other words, work item identification, selection, and prioritization are part of the Agile product management and product backlog refinement processes in an IT context.

In this phase, you need to answer the following questions:

- What are your customers' demands for this value stream?
- How many customers do you have?
- What are the types of customers or market segments, or niches, that are supported?
- What is the predictability of orders, including seasonal adjustments, across all customers or types of customers by product line?
- Are you overproducing, underproducing, or meeting demand?
- Does your ability to meet your customer demand vary over time? If so, why?
- Can you meet your customer delivery dates with your current resources and capabilities? If not, why not?
- Do you need to carry buffer or safety inventories? If so, which type, why, and how many?
- What problems need to be solved right now?
- How clean and organized is your value stream's facilities and operations? If lacking, what are the negative impacts and what do we need to do to reduce clutter and disorganization?

In Lean, the focus of meeting customer demand lies in the area of fulfillment. In other words, the VSM team works to help the value stream improve its rate of deliveries. Improving the ability to meet customer demand in the future state is a multi-step process of addressing the following concerns:

- Calculate Takt time.
- Establish pitch.
- Adjust buffers and inventories.
- Improve the working environment.
- Resolve immediate problems.

The VSM team starts their future state – customer demand-related analysis – by calculating the value stream's Takt time.

Calculating Takt times

Understanding Takt is the first order of priority as it is a measure of how often the value stream needs to deliver its products or service to meet customer demand. We can't find out how much we need to improve our deliveries if we don't know our demand targets.

Takt time is the pace or rate at which customers demand delivery of our products or services. We calculate Takt time by dividing *net available operating time* by the *number of products required over time*. **Net operating time** is the work hours available over a specific period (that is, 7 hours in a shift, 14 hours of operation in a day, or 2,240 hours per month).

When calculating the net operating time, make sure to reduce the total time to account for meetings, health breaks, lunch breaks, and other non-value-added activities. So, in an 8-hour shift with two 15-minute health breaks, a 30-minute lunch break, and a 15-minute Daily Scrum or standup meeting, the net operating time is 405 minutes:

Net operating time=((8 hrs*60 min) – 15 min – 15 min – 30 min – 15 min) => 405 min

If our daily customer demand rate is 810 units per day, our Takt time can be calculated as follows:

405 min – 810 units/day=.5 minutes per unit

In other words, with a Takt time of .5 minutes per unit, you need to produce two units every minute. Manufacturers of large commercial aircraft or ships don't typically have a requirement to deliver multiple times per day. However, automotive and electronic equipment manufacturers usually do.

In the traditional Waterfall-based systems or the **software development life cycle (SDLC)** model, software development teams often released new products annually – usually initiated as time-bound projects aligned with fiscal year budgets. Unfortunately, the strategy didn't work out very well for many reasons. In contrast, modern Agile practices allow software development teams to deliver new functionality over 1 to 4 weeks.

However, even with Agile practices, software product managers may choose to release software into the production environments much less frequently. For commercial products, delivery activities may have to align with marketing and sales promotions. In a BPI context, new software enhancements affect business processes that require ancillary activities to create and deploy sysadmin support guides and training aids to go along with the software, to the operations staff and users.

On the other hand, **continuous integration and continuous delivery (CI/CD)** tools and practices enhance Agile practices and make it possible to deploy new software releases much more frequently. IT development shops may start by integrating software engineering tools to form integrated toolchains that help automate and accelerate flows across portions of the overall SDLC process.

With increased maturity, the IT organization implements an integrated and automated toolchain that supports the flow of work and information across both the software development and operations functions. Otherwise known as **DevOps pipelines** or **DevOps platforms**, these integrated and automated tools significantly improve the speed and reliability of software delivery.

For example, a modern DevOps environment's continuous deployment capability allows new features and functionality to be released into production environments multiple times a day. Moreover, a mature DevOps pipeline allows a development team to stand up multiple test environments on demand and rapidly check functionality, system load, performance, and stress capabilities before deployment.

The rapid pace of competitive change among the major online retailers, insurance companies, manufacturing firms, and healthcare providers helps justify the investments in the DevOps pipelines and platforms. As noted previously, DevOps capabilities are the table stakes that are necessary to compete in our digital economy and meet our customers' evolving demands. And Takt time sets the pace.

Establishing pitch

Pitch is the amount of time needed for a value stream to make one container of products. In an ideal world, customer orders would arrive one at a time, in lot sizes of one, at a constant rate of speed, and we'd be able to process those orders as single-piece flows at the same rate of speed. But that's seldom the case for most producers. Moreover, our supply chain partners may not be able to deliver materials and parts just to satisfy one customer order, if for no other reason, due to the fact that the cost of shipping physical products in bulk is usually cheaper.

Transport costs are not a concern in software delivery when they're deployed via internet connections. But software delivery does become an issue when it's packaged as a CD ROM or as part of a physical product.

For these reasons, it's challenging to match production rates to exact Takt time, and production schedulers must find ways to accommodate for these variances efficiently. That is the goal of establishing pitch – to make sure the organization can handle changes in demand in the most efficient manner.

Before learning how to calculate pitch, we need to understand **pack-out quantity** because it's part of the pitch measurement. Pack-out quantities are the number of items a customer (internal or external) wants to be delivered together as a lot, usually moved in a container during transport.

The easiest way to think about pack-out quantity is to imagine building enough parts to fill shipping cartons or shipping containers bound for a customer. If we can produce single-piece flows and ship our parts one at a time, our pack-out quantity is one. However, if we supply products to fulfill our retailers' orders, the pack-out quantities might vary by time of year, product type, and each customer's sales volume.

The calculation for pitch is fairly simple, which is *Takt time multiplied by the pack-out quantity*. If, for example, our optimal pack-out volume for product *A* is 100 parts per shipment, and our Takt time of 400 releases of Product *A* per day, our pitch can be calculated as follows:

Pitch=400 parts per day X 100 parts/ shipment = 4 shipments per day

In other words, the value stream must ship four lots of 100 products per day.

As you think about what pitch represents, it's essential to understand that Takt time is customer-driven, but pack-out quantity may or may not be. Therefore, there are several factors you must consider when considering your pitch.

Customers may not choose to purchase or receive one product at a time. Some customers may request shipments of varying lot sizes, perhaps due to seasonal adjustments. Also, the organization may not have the ability to produce products most efficiently as single-piece flows yet, due to lengthy setup and changeover times and batch processes.

Instead, it may be preferable to allow the value stream flows to proceed in larger lot sizes to minimize part and material changeovers. Finally, the cost of shipping is often an essential factor when determining optimal delivery lot sizes.

In software delivery organizations, pack-out quantity and pitch become factors in Agile shops that release across **Sprints**. For example, an Agile **Scrum** shop evaluates their pack-out quantity as the number of user stories completed per Sprint, which is their pitch.

Many IT organizations have infrastructure constraints that may limit the number of testing servers they can stand up in parallel. In those cases, the pack-out quantity is the number of parallel tests they can run, and their pitch is the duration of the testing activity.

Finally, customers may not be willing to receive new features one at a time in production, especially when those features impact business processes and the need to inform and train staff. Each release has a pack-out quantity of features in this context, and the pitch is the period between releases.

Understanding production controls

When organizations must process work items in larger lot sizes, the schedulers should implement a **production control** mechanism. Examples include **Kanban bins** or **Heijunka boxes** to level the flow of work items by volume and the types of work items that are produced.

The value stream operators still pull work items into their workstations. But they pull the entire lot, not just one part. For example, in manufacturing, the parts might come in a bin, and the operators complete their work at a piece rate that the design of their specific activity allows. Then once the bin has been refilled, the next operator in line can pull the entire lot into their workstation when they have available capacity.

In software delivery value streams, the software engineers pull the work items from the **Sprint Backlogs** and complete their work to implement and test the related user story's functionality. In effect, Sprint Backlogs serve as types of Heijunka boxes to manage the flow of a collection of user stories that flow together through the development and test activities.

The following diagram shows a Sprint Backlog portrayed as a container for the user stories undergoing development within an upcoming Sprint:

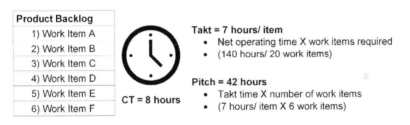

Figure 9.1 – Sprint Backlog as a type of Heijunka box

The team has selected the six highest priority items for the upcoming 2-week Sprint. However, the product owner releases an average of 20 new requirements into the product backlog every 4 weeks. Due to this, you need to manage your development team's ability to support your customer's demand.

Let's assume that the development team members, after breaks and meetings, work 7 hours per day for a total of 140 net operating hours per 4-week month, or 70 hours throughout a 2-week Sprint. Therefore, no matter which duration you choose, your Takt time will be 7 hours per work item. In other words, a new work item comes into our IT value stream, on average, every 7 hours.

Since the development team selected six items for their Sprint Backlog, the pitch for this lot size is the *Takt time multiplied by the number of items selected for the Sprint*, or 42 hours. In other words, the development team must initiate a new lot of six work items within 42 hours to match the Takt time delivery rates.

Since there are 70 net operating hours available in every 2-week Sprint duration, it's tempting to think that you should have no problems meeting the demand. But hold on – the VSM team's work is not done yet. For one, we need to evaluate the pitch in terms of how long it takes to process a lot of six work items across the entire value stream.

If we had a proper automated and continuous flow across our IT value stream, we may not be concerned about this. However, under Scrum-based Agile practices, the development team can only work on those six items over the next 2 weeks.

Review the metrics displayed in the current value stream map shown in the preceding diagram, and the metrics tables in *Chapter 8, Identifying Lean Metrics (VSM Step 5)*, in *Figure 8.1 (Table of total lead time, total value-added, and rolling C/A)* and *Figure 8.2 (Table of Lean metrics across an IT value stream)*. We know the **total lead time** (**TLT**) across the entire IT value stream is 328 hours, which is a little more than 8 weeks in duration. Most of the time is spent waiting in the product backlog queue or waiting on a new release as a feature.

On the positive side, our **total value-added time** (**TVT**) time is 57 hours across the entire IT value stream, which is well within the 72 net operating hours available within a Sprint. On the negative side, there are 80 hours of lead time in the development-related activities and another 80 hours of lead time in the release-related activities.

The VSM team has some work to do to resolves issues related to waiting and mismatched cycle times. For example, the work items may end up queuing again at testing if the infrastructure is not set up to handle testing on demand in single-piece flows. Similarly, the tested software work items, now available as tested features, may sit yet again in a queue, waiting to be released to the customer's production environment.

In Agile environments, product releases into production may occur with every Sprint, but they are more often released in less frequent and formalized product releases. The formalized releases give us time to implement marketing promotions and sales campaigns for commercial deliveries, and socialization and training when software deliveries impact critical business processes.

Waiting is a major problem in the sample IT software delivery value stream. Since we've already noted that queues sometimes become necessary or unavoidable, let's discuss how to manage them.

Managing buffers and safety inventories

So far, you've learned how to use Takt time and pitch to manage flows to meet customer demand. But we also need to manage our buffers and safety inventories to ensure there's always **work in progress** (**WIP**) to support our customers' needs. However, we cannot have so much inventory that we introduce problems artificially, creating product delays and increasing our carrying costs. We already know that **WIP** waiting is a problem in the sample IT value stream, so let's start there.

Eliminating work in progress queues

Before we go any further, it's essential to understand the need to eliminate all **work-in-process buffers** of work items and materials. WIP queues simply hide problems and don't, in any way to help improve flows. WIP queues are merely mechanisms to hide problems with flow. The only inventories Lean allows is for carrying finished goods, but even then, within strict limits.

It's also important not to confuse the concept of inventories with the processing work items in lots, as described in the previous section on establishing pitch. The word inventory connotes the total number of materials, work items, or products contained within our value stream pipelines, or in sections of our value stream pipelines. In contrast, a lot size is a mechanism that's used to flow some number of work items (materials or products) together through the value stream to improve flows.

For example, when a software development team selects a list of work items from the Product Backlog, the resulting Sprint Backlog is, in effect, a lot size that the team judges most appropriate for completion during the upcoming Sprint.

Flowing work items in Sprint Backlogs

In the short run, until we can achieve single-piece flows, it may be more efficient to flow work items in larger lot sizes. This limitation is due to uneven flow rates across value stream activities with mismatched cycles, setup times, and batch processes.

Such is the case in our IT value stream example. We gain productivity improvements by implementing Agile practices for iterative and incremental development while minimizing WIP lot sizes of work items via the Sprint Backlogs. Effectively, this is the purpose of Sprint backlogs in IT-related value streams: to control product development flows in manageable bites. But flowing work items in lots is not the same as allowing those work in progress items to queue and wait between activities.

In an Agile environment, a common approach is to select a "lot" of work items from the product backlog for an upcoming Sprint, and then manage the flow across the Sprint using a Kanban Board. Later, when the IT shop implements a mature CI/CD or DevOps Pipeline – to streamline, integrate, and automate their SDLC processes – the IT value stream can implement single-piece flows against work items queued in the product backlog.

Managing flows with Kanban Boards

Another strategy is to eliminate Agile-based Sprints altogether and instead move to a pure **Kanban-oriented** production control strategy. In a Kanban system, the development team members pull refined and prioritized work items directly from the product backlog. The team members work on each item from start to finish across the development pipeline.

It takes a reasonably mature CI/CD capability to implement a Kanban-oriented IT production control strategy effectively. Without integration and automation of SDLC activities, the team spends a great deal of their time on non-value-added work associated with setting up and configuring development, testing environments, and waiting on test results.

In a proper Kanban system, all work items in the Sprint Backlog must flow through the **SDLC** before the Agile/Scrum team takes on new work. In other words, Kanban and Agile practices do not eliminate the traditional SDLC activities of coding, building, integrating, merging code, configuring, provisioning development and test environments, performing unit, integration, system, and a host of other critical tests.

But these activities are performed more frequently to accommodate the production of smaller increments of new functionality across each iterative development cycle. **Integration** and **automation** improve flow and help eliminate waste across an SDLC, and value stream management helps prioritize and drive those IT value stream improvements.

The following image shows the Kanban production control strategy implemented within an IT value stream. Note that the Kanban Board does not reference specific SDLC tasks in the development pipeline. Instead, these activities are all encapsulated within the **In Progress** and **Verify** phases of the Kanban-oriented product workflow:

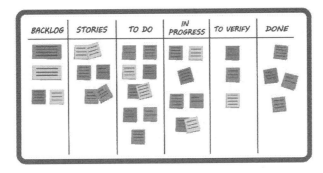

Figure 9.2 – Kanban Board for an IT value stream

In the meantime, the **pull-oriented production control strategy** of Kanban prevents the Scrum team from taking on new work until they've finished the user stories in the Sprint Backlog.

The only recourse is for the Scrum team to split the user stories across team members and work each user story from front to end across all relevant SDLC activities, up through the system, including load, stress, and performance testing. If they occur at all, those types of testing activities tend to be run in batches, just before the product is released into the production environments.

Improving flows with CI/CD pipelines

Unfortunately, pushing testing to just before the product's release brings up problems associated with batch processing. Any defects or bugs hiding in the code will be found when the IT department is planning to release the software product, which will push back the release date. Moreover, the integrated code's complexity at that late stage makes it difficult to isolate and debug the offending code, APIs/ web services, queries, security, computing, or network-related problems.

In short, Kanban and Scrum are inconsistent practices unless the development team has a mature CI/CD pipeline. With CI/ CD capabilities, the development team can work on each user story and feature individually from end-to-end without delays. At that point, the team needs to evaluate the length of their Sprints and how many work items they want to queue in a Sprint Backlog. Remember, your goal in Lean is to achieve single-piece flows ultimately. The same goal is valid for Lean-Agile practices.

Now that you know that it is not a Lean practice to allow WIP queues, let's look at where allowing queues and waiting does make sense.

Allowing finished goods inventories

In Lean, there are two types of inventories to manage within our value stream: **buffer inventories** and **safety stocks**. Both are examples of finished goods inventories. The term finished goods simply means that the products have completed development and passed QA/testing but are being held for some reason prior to sale.

In software development, the release of software components and products can be delayed (stored) after meeting their acceptance criteria for the Definition of Done, and the products are technically ready to be shipped to a customer, a retail or app store, or installed within a production environment. A primary reason for making such delays is to make sure other elements of the delivery are in place.

For example, software products may go out as part of the release in a physical product or be delayed as part of a larger release of capabilities. Software deliveries may also be delayed so that they coincide with marketing and sales promotions, or with the deployment of new business processes.

Buffer inventories are extra stocks of finished products that the organization carries to meet customer demand when customer demand rates change; that is, changes in Takt time. In contrast, *safety stocks* are inventories of finished goods that are used to meet ongoing customer demand when the value stream's flow is disrupted, such as equipment failures, power outages, labor issues, and unexpected quality issues. Buffer inventories and safety stocks are stored and independently managed as they serve two distinctly different purposes.

However, it's also important to understand that the concept of *finished goods* does not merely include the completed work items that are produced by your value stream. Finished goods can also include materials and parts that have been procured from your supply chain vendors. It may make sense to carry some of these types of inventories to prevent the starvation of your value stream if your value stream partners, or their transport or distribution services, run into delivery problems.

These concepts are particularly relevant when your software products are embedded in physical products, such as control systems in manufacturing equipment and automobiles, or to support IoT-based value delivery capabilities.

> **Internet of Things (IoT)**
>
> IoT is a term that describes a network of physical objects that have embedded sensors, software, and other technologies that enable internet-based connections and data to be exchanged with other connected servers, devices, and information systems. Moreover, IoT capabilities allow us to deliver product feature enhancements, such as updating the navigation systems in automobiles, trucks, aircraft, ships, and other transport systems.

With software products powering so many of our modern-day products and services, organizations must carefully manage inventories of work items (that is, software, hardware, and other physical products and components). However, organizations must also manage their resources across all organizational value streams to support variations in customer demand.

Managing buffer and safety resources

The inventories concept is not limited to merely managing stores of parts, materials, and completed work items. The value stream may require buffer and safety resources to ramp up production in periods of high demand or when our value stream operators call in sick. Buffer and safety resources include the use of overtime hours, hiring temporary workers or retirees, or borrowing staff from other departments.

Similarly, we may need to install excess capacity in equipment or tools to manage flows across varying customer demand loads, or to make up for lost time when the value stream unexpectedly shuts down for whatever reason. It's also possible to hand off excess work to other value streams or partners or contractors with excess equipment and human resource capacities. In the latter situations, the organization must take proactive steps to ensure the partners/contractors can deliver equivalent quality and costs.

Employing finished goods supermarkets

Inventories help maintain flow with disruptions in demand and availability of parts, materials, and products. But we can also use inventories to help enforce our pull-oriented production control strategies. Inventories that are used for this purpose are called **finished goods supermarkets**.

The idea here is that products are pulled on demand from finished goods inventories to fulfill customer orders, and the value streams quickly replenish those items. Conceptually, finished goods supermarkets operate in much the same way your local grocery stores operate. Customers pull products off the grocery store shelves, and stocking clerks replenish those inventories from their finished goods buffer stores.

Supermarkets work across value streams and value delivery chains. Customers pull products from the organization's finished goods inventories, even if the physical pull process involves the shipping department and freight company. The value streams replenish the finished goods inventories following the production and operations flows upstream. Similarly, supply chain partners replenish component materials and parts as the delivery organization's value streams pull them.

Supermarkets are the essence of JIT production concepts. Customers trigger the flow of work, information, and materials as the most downstream activity. All other preceding (that is, upstream) value stream and value chain activities replenish their value-adding work in a synchronized fashion and JIT to meet the next customer's demands.

The closest equivalent to carrying finished goods occurs when we accumulate features prior to a release in an IT context. But the purpose of having software finished goods inventories is not that different, as the goal is still to have products ready for release when the customers are ready to accept them.

By now, your VSM team has calculated Takt times for all the product lines and customers, and they have established a pitch or set of pitches to improve flows in line with customer delivery demands. You can also make improvements to your work environment to help the value stream meet customer demand.

Improving the work environment

Lean organizations use **the 5S system** to improve their work environments. We don't need to spend much time discussing this topic since we introduced how it improves workspaces in *Chapter 6, Launching the VSM Initiative (VSM Steps 1-3)*. The 5S system's objective is to create a functional and clean environment that improves the work environment's efficiency, effectiveness, and safety.

An essential element of the 5S system is that it provides an ongoing mechanism to observe and address disorder and clutter issues that can impede flow, cause delays, and otherwise hide problems. In Lean, we always view problems in terms of the seven forms of waste: transportation, inventory, motion, waiting, overprocessing, overproduction, and defects. Recall that the seven wastes of Lean were introduced in *Chapter 6, Launching the VSM Initiative – The Seven Deadly Wastes*.

As a quick review, the following table provides a list of the 5S system and **areas for potential waste** methods, as well as the seven wastes of Lean:

THE FIVE S SYSTEM	THE WASTES OF LEAN
1. SORT	• Defects
2. SET IN ORDER	• Overproduction
3. SHINE	• Waiting
4. STANDARDIZE	• Unused human talents
5. SUSTAIN	• Transportation
	• Inventory
	• Motion
	• Extra processing

Figure 9.3 – Methods of the 5S system and areas of potential waste

The 5S system is listed numerically as these activities' execution tends to follow this sequence. The types and extent of the wastes of Lean will vary across organizations and across every value stream. We attack wastes in the order they impact our ability to deliver value, from highest to lowest. The main point to be made here is that the 5S system helps the VSM team, VS operators, and other stakeholders eliminate any waste that hinders Lean production processes. If you need a further review of the 5S technique, please refer to *Chapter 6, Launching the VSM Initiative (VSM Steps 1-3)*.

Now, let's move on to the last area of work necessary to evaluate how to improve our ability to meet customer demand. In the next section, you will learn how to employ problem solving methods to improve value stream performance so that you can meet customer demand.

Resolving demand-related problems

Since customer demand often vary over time, both in terms of volume and product needs, demand-related issues are a continual problem that value stream operators and managers must address. From the customer's perspective, demand-related issues arise when it's difficult to place an order, or they can't get the features and functions they want, the quality is unacceptable, or delivery dates extend beyond their desire to wait.

There are many problem-solving models that the VSM team can use to address their customer demand issues. One that I like was published by the *Iowa University Human Resources Department*. Let's take a look at it.

The following is the **8-Step Problem Solving Process**:

Step 1 – define the problem

To understand this method, you must think about the following questions:

- What is the problem?

- How did you discover the problem?

- When did the problem start, and how long has this problem been going on for?

- Is there enough data to contain the problem and prevent it from getting passed to the next process step? If yes, contain the problem.

Step 2 – clarify the problem

Before attempting to solve a problem, we need to make sure we truly understand the scope of the problem. We can avoid this problem by asking the following questions:

- What data is available or needed to help clarify or fully understand the problem?

- Is it a top priority to resolve the problem at this point?

- Are additional resources required to clarify the problem? If yes, elevate the problem to your leader to help locate the right resources and form a team.

- Consider a Lean event (Do-it, Burst, RPI, or Project).

- Ensure the problem is contained and does not get passed to the next process step.

Step 3 – define the goals

In software development, we always want to know what capabilities a new feature or function must deliver to meet our customers' needs. In Agile, we call this our **Definition of Done**. The same concept applies here in resolving demand-related problems. We need to define goals that define the desired state for the future state's improvement:

- What is your end goal or desired future state?

- What will you accomplish if you fix this problem?

- What is the desired timeline for solving this problem?

Step 4 – identify the root cause of the problem

We mustn't focus on the symptoms and fail to fix the root cause of whatever problems we need to resolve. Having a focus on resolving symptoms is like taking aspirin for a headache – it provides temporary relief, only for the headache return because we haven't addressed its root cause. The following list provides a strategy for finding the root causes of customer demand-related problems:

- Identify possible causes of the problem.
- Prioritize possible root causes of the problem.
- What information or data is there to validate the root cause?

Step 5 – develop an action plan

Often, customer demand-related issues are complex and require a host of activities and people to address properly. In such cases, the VSM team should create an action plan that defines the required activities, time frames, and roles and responsibilities, as shown in the following list:

- Generate a list of actions required to address the root cause and prevent recurring problems
- Assign an owner and timeline to each action.
- Status actions to ensure completion.

Step 6 – execute the action plan

Of course, creating a plan of action is not the same thing as executing a plan of action. Someone needs to be responsible for ensuring the work is completed to satisfaction. Consistent with Lean and Agile practices, the **value stream mapping** (**VSM**) team may review progress and results, but someone needs to track and guide the effort, as noted in the following list:

- Implement an action plan to address the root cause.
- Maintain and display a visible chart of progress.
- Verify the completion of all action items.

Step 7 – evaluate the results

This step validates the attainment of the goals listed in step 3 and captures lessons learned for the actions. First, we need to ensure we achieved our action item goals before leaving an activity. But we also don't want to reinvent the wheel, if we have already performed similar discovery and analysis work in the past. In fact, we may already have a solution to our current problems if we paid attention and maintained accurate historical records. The following list includes activities for evaluating our findings and results:

- Monitor and collect data.
- Did you meet the goals you defined in step 3? If not, repeat the 8-step process.
- Were there any unforeseen consequences?
- If the problem has been resolved, remove activities that were added previously to contain the problem.

Step 8 – Continuously improve

This last step helps catch and address any loose ends. For example, do we have sufficient data to address and resolve the customer demand problem fully? Can we do better? If so, how can we do better? Step 8 involves the following activities:

- Look for additional opportunities to implement a better solution.
- Ensure the problem cannot come back, and communicate lessons learned.
- If needed, repeat the 8-step problem-solving process to drive further improvements.

To learn more, please refer to *Iowa University Human Resources, Organizational Effectiveness*:

```
https://hr.uiowa.edu/development/organizational-development/
lean/8-step-problem-solving-process
```

Mapping the customer-demand map

We now have enough information to develop a **future state map** that will address our improvement ideas for improving our ability to meet our customers' demands. The future state map for the demand phase uses the same VA mapping symbols, but the mapping process is different. The following list describes the sequence of steps necessary to support drawing the future state's demand phase map:

1. Start the new future state customer demand map on a whiteboard, poster board, or electronic system while using the VSM Storyboard as a guide.

2. Start by drawing the customers and suppliers (if they're different from the customer) at the top of the board.

3. Record the customer requirements and demand fulfillment requirements in terms of Takt time and pitch.

4. Place the last activity (that is, the most downstream activity) toward the drawing area's far-right edge.

5. On the board's left-hand side, draw the upstream process that initiates the customer request or demand.

6. Draw a manual or electronic communications link between the customer and supplier.

7. Draw the buffer and safety inventories with the appropriate VA symbols.

8. Draw where the value stream operators need to implement their 5S systems for improvement. Use the Kaizen Burst icon, which represents an improvement activity.

9. Determine where problem-solving projects need to be implemented.
    (Use the Kaizen Burst icon for this.)

The following diagram shows the future state's map of customer demand phase improvements, which might look like your future state IT value stream:

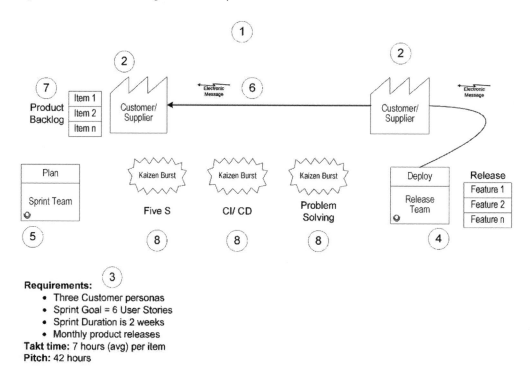

Figure 9.4 – IT value stream future state map – demand phase

The numbers on the future state map indicate the mapping steps noted in the previous list. In our example, the VSM team has decided that there are three critical areas they must focus on to improve the IT value stream's ability to respond to customer demand. The first planned Kaizen Burst uses the 5S system to discover low-hanging fruit that can improve flow and eliminate wastes. The second improvement activity is to help guide the development team's integration efforts on the software development and testing tools they have to implement more effective CI/CD toolchains. The final Kaizen Burst they have planned is to use problem-solving techniques to help the development team implement a Kanban system. This strategy enables a more rapid response to incoming requests.

This section completes our discussion on future state customer demand mapping. Before moving on to the future state customer flow phase, let's review the tools that are used in the demand phase of future state mapping.

Future state – customer demand tools

The tools that are used in this phase of future state mapping help the VSM team improve the value stream's responses to variations in customer demand. We started by calculating *Takt time* across customers and products, and across variations of holiday or other seasonal adjustments, as required.

Next, the VSM team established *pitch* for the value stream, which calculates the Takt time times the number of work units. Pitch's objective is to determine the most appropriate lot sizes to move work items through our value stream.

Next, you learned how to incorporate *buffer inventories and safety stocks* of finished goods and resources to ensure fluctuations in demand and flow don't starve your value stream, and prevent them from doing value-added work. You also learned how to employ finished goods supermarkets to enforce the pull-oriented production control strategies across your value stream, and even across your value delivery chains.

Another essential tool for improving the value stream's response to variations in customer demand is the *5S system*. The value stream operators use the 5S system to remove clutter, organize work areas to improve the flow of work and efficiencies, and generally improve the operators' health and safety. In addition, the 5S system helps the value stream team evaluate and eliminate the sources of waste.

In this phase, the VSM team starts to assess the problems that hinder the value stream's response to varying customer demand and analyze each problem's cause and effects. In this section, you learned how to employ the *8-step problem-solving process* to resolve demand-related problems.

Finally, you began developing your *future state map* to visually display the desired changes to the value stream, as well as updated your data on Takt time and pitch. The VSM team draws the future state map on a large whiteboard or poster board, or any electronic tool that's displayed on a large screen. Ideally, the VSM team should use the VSM Storyboard format (shown in *Appendix B*) to keep all their critical information in one place.

This section concludes our discussion on mapping the future state to make improvements to meet customer demand. Next, we'll learn how to develop the future state so that we can analyze and display improvements in order to implement and sustain continuous flows across the value stream.

Phase 2 – continuous flow

Now that the VSM team has addressed issues of customer demand, they can start figuring out how to improve production flows to meet our customers' demands. In this section, we will continue our future state mapping activities and address issues related to establishing and maintaining Lean continuous flows.

Continuous flow is a Lean strategy that's used to achieve the ideal goal of moving a single work item through every step of your value stream activities instead of grouping and moving *lots* of work items collectively as batches (also known as **Make One**, **Move One**; **One-Piece Flows**; **Single-Piece Flows**). The objective is to produce and move one work item at a time, or at least the smallest practical number of items, through a series of value stream activities as continuously as possible. As part of a pull-based production control strategy, each activity produces only what is necessary to fulfill the next activity's request.

What establishes Lean continuous flows is the value stream's mechanism to ensure its internal and external customers receive the right work unit, at the right time, and in the right quantities. It's not uncommon to focus our efforts initially on improving individual work activities, apart from the other activities in our value stream system. Inevitably, that type of limited focus leads to problems with the overall flow of work. Instead, we need to take a systems-thinking view to our value stream.

In this section, you will learn various ways to improve continuous flows across your value streams.

Evaluating the value stream as a complex system

Organizations focus on individual activity improvements because the improvement efforts are handed over to subject matter experts or engineers with deep skills in the activity. And to some degree, those skills are needed to improve the activities. But it's impossible to calculate throughput for a given activity and understand its impact on the system as a whole – recall our previous discussions in *Chapter 3, Analyzing Complex System Interactions*.

Instead of looking at each activity independently, we need to take a system view of our value streams to understand and control the mechanisms that impede the flow of work, materials, and information across the value stream. Across the value stream activities, variances in customer orders, cycle times, batch or lot sizes, setup times, and part changeover times all impede continuous flows.

The VSM team must look at the value stream as a complex system of integrated parts to work through these issues. Their job is to determine how to control the flow of work across the value stream in the most efficient manner. They must evaluate mechanisms to level the flow of work so that increased demands don't bog the system down, and periods of low demands don't starve the system.

They also need to work with the value stream operators to implement standardized work processes. This helps eliminate variances that impede flow and reduce productivity and consistency of quality. In many cases, the VSM team needs to design more efficient facility and workstation layouts and obtain funding and approvals from executive management to make the desired changes.

Applying the concepts of continuous flow

At a conceptual level, the ideal state of a continuous flow is replenishing a single work item every time a customer pulls another work item from our finished goods inventory. As shown in the following diagram, this concept is sometimes referred to as *Make One, Move One*:

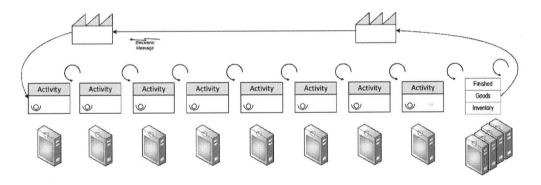

Figure 9.5 – Continuous flow – "Make One, Move One"

Value streams synchronize work in progress across multiple activities to continue the replenishment activities, as shown in the preceding diagram. In other words, the replenishment process must continue across all upstream activities in a coordinated and synchronized fashion.

The preceding diagram uses the curved *physical pull* arrow instead of the straight *push* arrows to indicate that this value stream uses a pull-oriented production control system. The pull-oriented production scheduling methods control how upstream activities are coordinated to achieve both synchronized and continuous flows.

The speed of the continuous flow is a separate matter. So long as everything flows together, it doesn't matter if the flow rate is once every 5 minutes or once every 5 hours. It also doesn't matter if one part flows across each activity or if 10 parts flow together as a single lot. If the flows of parts and materials are synchronized and they can move together at the same rate, you have a continuous flow.

In the future state for continuous flow, we most care about improving the value stream's overall efficiency in terms of increased throughput and fewer bottlenecks (that is, eliminating mismatched production rates, queuing of work items, and waiting). Therefore, improvements to flow always come from eliminating waste in all its forms.

Evaluating the impediments of flow

Most VSM teams cannot expect to make sweeping changes in one fell swoop. That was the original goal of **business process reengineering (BPR)**. But few organizations can afford the investments and disruptions associated with making radical changes all at once. Instead, most companies gain better results by making incremental changes with priorities based on cost-benefit assessments of identified improvement opportunities.

It is possible to implement radical change all at once through a future state value stream improvement initiative, but it's not recommended for the same reasons BPR fell out of favor. Unless the organization faces a **burning platform** situation to stay in business, the better alternative is to make improvement changes incrementally.

Fact

The term *Burning Platform* comes from a real-life story of a horrible situation that occurred on July 6, 1988, on the **Piper Alpha** oil rig in the North Sea. The oil platform exploded and caused a massive fire that claimed 167 lives. However, three men, who initially locked themselves in a room away from the fire, eventually made their way outside, where they were faced with a choice of jumping into the frigid waters or perishing in flames. Two of the men jumped and, though seriously injured, managed to survive and were rescued. Unfortunately, the third man, who stayed on the burning didn't make it.

In such cases, the VSM team evaluates the most impactful opportunities to eliminate waste and implementation costs and prioritize the change initiatives accordingly. Following *Pareto's Principle*, those change initiatives that offer the most significant improvements to flow and return on investment should always have the highest implementation priorities.

The VSM team evaluates the flows across the value stream by working their way through a series of questions, as follows:

- Which value stream activities, equipment, and systems need to be linked to obtain a synchronized and continuous flow?

- Can the existing value stream activities support a single-piece flow?

- If not, what is the optimum lot size until we can optimize flows better?

- Which work cells or activities act as bottlenecks, and why? (That is, lengthy cycle, setup and changeover times, batch processes, excessive movement, or travel times.)

- What is the order of priority in addressing identified bottlenecks?

- What can we do in the work cells or activities causing bottlenecks?

- What can we do to reduce the delays causing bottlenecks?

- How can we improve our facility's layout to improve workflows?

- How can we improve our information systems to improve information flow?

- What actions can we take to improve material flows internally?

- What process and contract changes must be made with our supply chain partners to align better incoming materials and parts with our customers' demands?

- How can we control upstream work so that it matches and synchronizes with downstream demands?

- Can we employ a Kanban system, and what changes are required to support the Kanban system?

- Should the value stream employ a **first-in, first-out** (**FIFO**) production control strategy?

- If any, do we need to place in-process supermarkets and buffer and safety stock inventories to address variations in customer demand or lengthy supplier lead times?

- What other issues impact our ability to support continuous flows?

The questions in the previous list guide the VSM team, VS operators, and other stakeholders through a process of discovery to find the impediments of continuous flow across the value stream. Each impediment leads to an improvement opportunity that is noted as a Kaizen Burst on the future state map. Much like the process associated with Product backlog refinement, the VSM team refines the list of improvement activities to define and prioritize the work tasks necessary to make the improvements to flows.

Note that the preceding list includes three production control strategies (that is, Kanban, FIFO, and supermarkets) that can help sustain continuous flows across our value streams. Let's take a moment to review them in this context.

Implementing production control strategies

Our value stream's workflow control strategies must support continuous flows. We introduced three workflow control approaches in the previous sections, and the VSM team may elect to include all three strategies within a single value stream. These workflow strategies are as follows:

- **Supermarket**: This is a pull-based workflow strategy that helps enforce JIT rules by allowing downstream customers to pull items from a limited work item buffer. Upstream activities replenish those inventories as the stores fall below their defined lower limits.

Kanban Boards or other control mechanisms prevent operators from pushing work into downstream activities in software development scenarios. Instead, the Lean-Agile teams pull work into their workstation from the Sprint or Product Backlog, but only when they have completed their previous work and have capacity to take on new work items.

In CI/CD and DevOps pipelines, integrating and automating toolchains links the activities to improve flow rates and implements pull-oriented production control orchestrations to minimize WIP.

- **FIFO**: This enforces a rule where the first item in a queue always has the highest work priority in the order of work. The FIFO workflow strategy is useful when delays can cause problems with a work item's quality deteriorating or unique customer orders not being fulfilled.

- **Kanban**: This implements a pure pull-oriented workflow that uses signals to indicate work requirements across value stream activities. These signals are in the form of instructions displayed on cards, sticky notes, signs, electronic signals, or folders. These work items can flow independently or in lots, and they are usually stored and pulled from a storage bin that moves with the lot.

The Kanban signals tell each downstream activity what to produce and how many. In a manufacturing value stream, the Kanban Card may include any or all of the following information:

- The Part/Item number and Part/Item description
- Bar codes for pulling additional order and shop process information and drawings
- The number of items or parts required
- Kanban bin or box capacity
- Origin (downstream) and subsequent (upstream) activity names or locations – used in job shop situations without sequential flows
- Material or parts supplier(s)
- Safety stock locations and quantities
- Replenishment triggers and quantities
- Lead time (that is, the duration before the items are due)
- The person who is responsible
- Order and due dates
- Other important information

In an IT-oriented value stream, the Kanban Card typically lists the User Story and its acceptance criteria. If the Kanban Card originates from operations, the card should include a ticket number, a description of the problem (defect or bug), the date of the issue, and the person who reported it.

Finally, the Kanban Card should also include information on any issues or bugs (also known as *blockers*) that were discovered during development or testing that prevent work from being carried out.

Weighted Shortest Job First (**WSJF**): This queueing model has gained acceptance in the Lean-Agile community, particularly among SAFE practitioners. The method was initially defined by Don Reinertsen in his book *Principles of Product Development Flow* (Reinertsen, 2009).

The WSJF prioritization model is used to sequence jobs (for example, Features, Capabilities, and Epics) to produce maximum economic benefit. In SAFe, WSJF is estimated as the **Cost of Delay** (**CoD**) divided by job size.

For example, let's assume we have three work items in our product backlog, and the product owner needs a way to assess priorities among them for the upcoming development iterations. The following table identifies the estimated durations as lead times in weeks, the cost of delays in lost revenues, and the adjusted weights for each work item:

Work Item (Features)	Duration (Lead Times)	Cost of Delay (CoD)	Weight = CoD/ Duration
A	12	$120,000	10,000
B	4	$400,000	100,000
C	8	$1,200,000	150,000

Figure 9.6 – Weighted Shortest Job First (WSJF) example

The preceding table shows that each week of delay in releasing Feature A costs the organization $10,000/ week, while Feature B has a cost of 100,000/ week, and Feature C will cost the company $150,000/ week. Assuming our CoD and duration estimates are reasonably accurate, Feature C should have the highest priority, followed by B, and then A.

Besides managing how work items flow through a value stream system, we also need to level the flows to maintain continuous flows. This topic will be discussed in the next subsection on line balancing.

Balancing our value stream flows

Implementing a pull-based production control system is of little value if there are no work items to pull in the preceding value stream activities. We need to instill **line balancing** techniques to prevent the starvation of upstream activities. To achieve this, we must optimize the distribution of work in progress across our value stream so that it matches our Takt time.

In a fully automated system, **line balancing** is a function of the system's design. For example, automobiles progressing through an assembly line are tied to a belt so that everything moves simultaneously, at the same rate of speed. However, the work stations in many development and operations-oriented value streams are not integrated, nor are they automated. Moreover, the operators may move between workstations and equipment to support multiple work activities across the value stream.

Line balancing is a strategy that's used to optimize the utilization of people within a value stream. The goal is to ensure our operators are not overburdened or underutilized. The VSM team uses the following equation to determine the number of workers needed to operate any given activity within the value stream:

 # workers needed=total_process_cycle_time/takt time

Recall that our Takt time for the IT value stream in *Figure 9.1* was 7 hours per work item. The VSM team has already identified each activity's total cycle times in our IT value stream, as identified in the following table. So, we have the data we need to determine the number of dev team members to support our IT value stream.

The following table uses the previously identified line balancing equation to calculate the number of workers required to support the IT value stream across the entire IT value stream:

Metrics	IT VS
TVA	328
Lot Size	6
Takt Time	42
No. Workers	7.8

Figure 9.7 – Line balancing equation to determine the number of required operators

Our total value-added times were a measure of all the cycle times across the IT value stream activities. But the value-added times (cycle times) are measures for processing one work item at a time. Because the development team works as a Scrum-based Agile team, we have to adjust the Takt time by a multiple of six to account for the total time required to produce six items, which – at 42 hours – is our pitch for this value stream.

Therefore, with these measures, the VSM team concludes that they need 7.8 development team members to staff the IT value stream. But things are never this easy. For one, the development team members process the entire lot of six work items at once in the *Refine*, *Plan*, and *Release* processes, but independently in the *Code*, *Build*, *Test*, *Merge*, and *Provision* processes.

The following table shows the lot size adjustments that have been made to adjust the hours so that they match work item's throughput, and then calculate the number of workers required across each IT value stream activity:

Metrics	Refine	Plan	Code	Build	Test	Merge	Provision	Release
VA (Hrs)	24	4	2	0.5	8	0.5	2	16
Lot Size Adj.	1	1	6	6	6	6	6	1
Adjusted Hours	24	4	12	3	24	1.5	6	16
Takt Time	7	7	7	7	7	7	7	7
No. Workers	3.4	0.6	1.7	0.4	3.4	0.2	0.9	2.3

Figure 9.8 – Adjusted cycle times per work item to calculate the number of required workers

The following table reevaluates the number of workers against the adjusted total value-added time of 90.5 hours. The adjusted TVA of 90.5 hours divided by our original Takt time of 7 hours indicates the IT value stream requires 12.9 workers to support the load:

Adjusted TVA	90.5
Takt Time	7
No. Workers	12.9

Figure 9.9 – TVA and labor adjustments

However, let's go back and look at Figure 9.7. It should be evident that the labor levels across the individual value stream activities vary significantly, from as few as 0.4 workers to as many as 3.4 workers. We would run into resource allocation issues if we tried to operate this value stream with single-piece flows.

To continue our assessment, let's carve out the development-related activities from the refine and release-related activities. Other people in the organization typically perform release-related activities, and a subset of the development team conducts refinement activities as a group before each Sprint iteration.

The VSM team creates a current state worker balance chart to start assessing the development stream, as shown in the following diagram. This chart shows us that if we were to dedicate resources to each activity, working at the rate of Takt time, there would be a lot of wasted time for all the workers waiting on new work, except for those dedicated to testing. This is because the testers don't have enough hours to conduct their tests within the Takt time of 7 hours per work item:

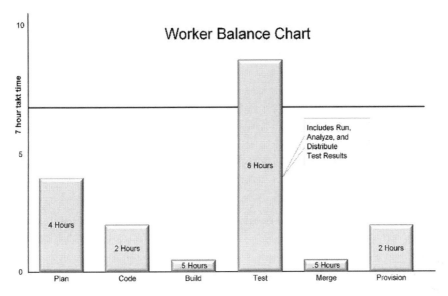

Figure 9.10 – Current state worker balance chart

It should be evident that you don't need to dedicate a worker to each activity. The whole point of Agile is to build cross-functional and self-contained teams where all the development team members can perform most, if not all, tasks in the software delivery value stream:

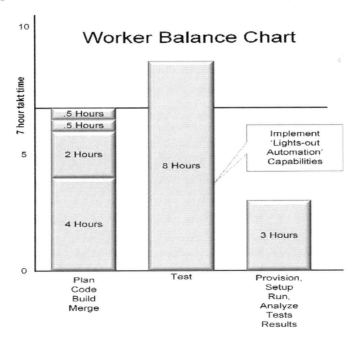

Figure 9.11 – Future state worker balance chart

As we can see, there are three logical areas to break down work by combining tasks. Within the team, one or more individuals can work on the plan, code, build, and merge activities. At the same time, other folks provision the servers and set up, run, analyze, and distribute test results.

Note that the software tests can run in a **lights-out automation** fashion. Once the tests have been set up and initiated, the tests run in an automated fashion without human attendance. Babysitting computers is not a value-adding activity and is one of the reasons why test automation is so important.

Stabilizing work practices

This section touches on a subject – creating standard practices – that some IT professionals may find questionable. The idea of implementing standardized work practices, at first glance, may seem restrictive, especially to those who view software development as much an art as it is a science. However, as we'll see later in this book, a mature DevOps pipeline – one that integrates and automates SDLC practices – only works when we have standardized processes.

Standardized work is an agreed-upon set of work procedures that establish the best current method and sequence of activities to complete each defined value stream process. In other words, standard practices implement the best, easiest, safest, and fastest way to perform work within the value stream.

Note that the concept of standardized work in Lean appears to deviate from the ideals espoused in Agile, where teams are generally free to experiment freely with new ways of working. The focus of Lean is to eliminate waste and improve continuous flows, whereas Agile's focus is on being adaptive and supporting the creative aspects of turning requirements into actionable architectures and designs prior to each new product release.

The issue is really one of demarcation between innovation and production. Innovation tends to be a creative process, also called the fuzzy front end, that is difficult to scope. In contrast, production development processes work best when they're standardized for optimal value delivery.

Fuzzy Front End (FFE)

The term **fuzzy front end** describes the *"innovation phase"* of each new product or feature development life cycle. Specifically, the FFE includes the initial phase of creating new products or features, where opportunities are identified, architecture and design concepts are developed, and construction and delivery strategies evolve prior to entering the product development phase. The FFE phenomenon exists in both Lean- and Agile-based development scenarios.

Once software development gets to the production stage, it makes no sense to automate an integrated process where the individual activities have such variability that it's impossible to control the flow of work or eliminate defects and errors. The whole point of implementing a CI/CD or DevOps pipeline is to improve work and information flows to improve value delivery. And we cannot improve flows without standardized processes and activities.

The VSM team needs to work with the engineers, domain experts, and operators to fix them first. Later, we can employ technology to help integrate and automate the underlying activities.

The VSM team may find it useful to use the **Standard Work Combination Timesheet** shown in the following image to capture this information during their Gemba walks. The worksheet provides rows to record the steps across a linked workflow within a value stream. In other words, an operator is expected to complete all these steps before starting work on another work item or a "lot" of work items. The VSM team records the amount of time required to complete each task and specifies whether the work is a manual or automated task, or whether it is related to moving or transport.

In our example, the VSM team identified the following nine high-level steps (activities) that define the CI/CD pipeline flow for the software development team. The team lists the activities in the order they're carried out:

Requirements analysis: Define the user stories and their acceptance criteria.

Feature design: Determine the software feature implementation requirements and development tests.

Write test scripts: As part of test-driven development practices, develop the test necessary to demonstrate code compliance with the requirements.

Develop code: Create the source code that implements the desired features in accordance with their acceptance criteria.

Unit testing: Conduct tests on each segment of code before you conduct integration tests to ensure they meet the requirements specified in the user stories and acceptance criteria.

Merge code: Integrate the source code after passing unit tests in with the mainline code in the source control repository. Ensure there are no errors with the integration.

Provision the pre-production server: Execute **Infrastructure as Code (IaC)** configuration instructions that automate standing up the pre-production server test environments.

Initiate pre-production tests: Execute the automated test in the pre-production test environments, as defined in the product's test plan:

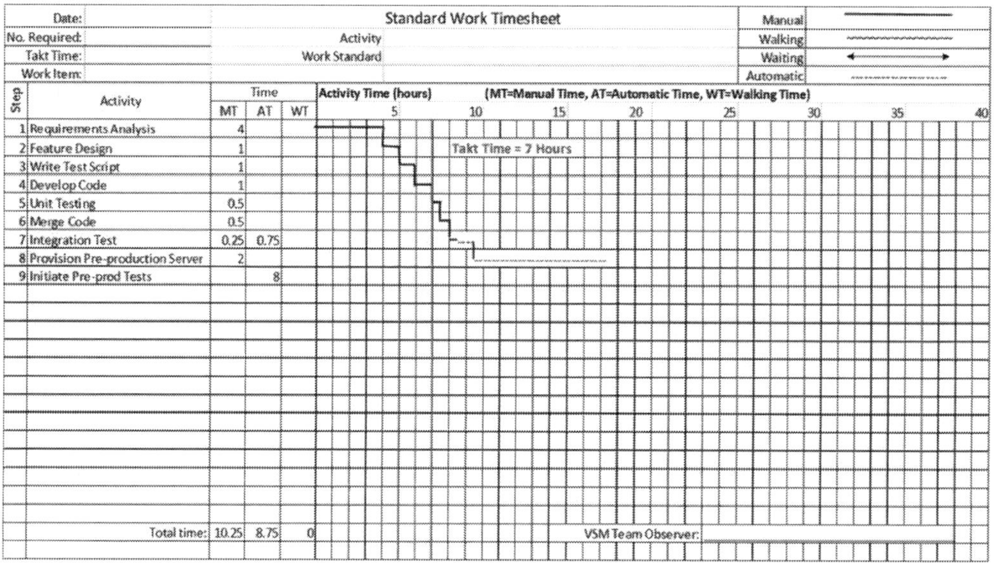

Step	Activity	MT	AT	WT	Activity Time (hours)
1	Requirements Analysis	4			
2	Feature Design	1			
3	Write Test Script	1			
4	Develop Code	1			
5	Unit Testing	0.5			
6	Merge Code	0.5			
7	Integration Test	0.25	0.75		
8	Provision Pre-production Server	2			
9	Initiate Pre-prod Tests		8		
	Total time:	10.25	8.75	0	

Takt Time = 7 Hours

Figure 9.12 – Standard Work Combination Timesheet

The standard worksheet also provides space to display the flow of work over time visually. A vertical line displays the Takt time for the work items in the context of the overall time associated with the workflow. When the overall workflow time exceeds the Takt time, we know that the value stream segment cannot meet customer order demands, as currently designed.

The Standard Work Combination Timesheet example shown here records the entire set of tasks for a work item flowing through the development work associated with the IT value stream. The worksheet tells us that it's impossible to move a work item through all the development and testing tasks within the Takt time associated with our customer's demands. We can evaluate ways to fix these issues by integrating and automating SDLC processes by implementing CI/CD toolchains and DevOps pipelines.

This concept is fundamentally what modern CI/ CD and DevOps toolchains and pipelines are about – eliminating variances across system development and operations-oriented activities. In both the Agile and Lean practices, the teams employ their workers' creativity via their product delivery skills and via Kaizen or retrospectives to make continuous improvements to their standardized processes. The objective of Kaizen is to make improvements that minimize risks, not increase them.

To summarize, standardized work does the following things:

Minimizes variances in work procedures
Establishes best practices to maintain quality.
Improves training and cross-training of employees.
Improves safety, and helps workers meet their customer demands.
Never accept a situation where your value stream cannot achieve takt time, as you are otherwise leaving the business to your competitors.

With the information we've gathered to complete the *Standard Work Combination Timesheet*, the VSM team can start evaluating ways to eliminate waste and improve flows. One common form of waste is motion; that is, having activities and work stations placed so far apart that we increase not-value-added time and resources simply moving people and materials between work areas. In the next section, you will learn how to improve work areas to eliminate waste from excess motion.

Changing work layouts

Whether your VSM team is working with a value stream to build physical products or software products, or to support administrative operations, facility layouts are critical to improving flow. The critical issue is to eliminate waste in the form of excessive transport and movement. These issues result from inefficient facility layouts or locating departments, business functions, or operations across disparate sites or geographies.

The VSM team needs to work with executive management to obtain funding and approvals, co-locate value stream activities, and change its layout to implement Lean production flows. In *Chapter 3, Analyzing Complex Systems Interactions*, you learned that optimum Lean flows in a diagrammatic form display a **linear sequential flow** for the work. However, in an actual physical work environment, a linear sequential flow might not be the best.

Instead, it's often better to have the workflow wrap back around to reduce waste related to the operator excessively transporting materials and motion within the value stream. Therefore, an optimal flow within a facility might have *U, C,* or *L*-shaped work areas, as shown in the following image:

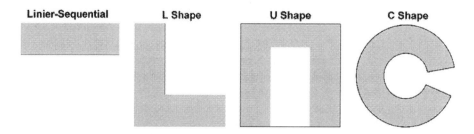

Figure 9.13 – Facility layout designs

As the VSM team evaluates alternative layouts, they need to overlay the flow of work. That is the topic of the next subsection.

Displaying standardized work

As the VSM team works to improve standardized work methods and flow, everyone working in the value stream must understand how to perform the work across multiple activities. This strategy provides the greatest flexibility in moving people to maintain flow across all activities.

The organization may employ detailed documentation or shop processes describing the work in both development and operations-oriented value streams. In many cases, all the operators need is a simple visual reminder of the standardized work tasks. A **Standardized Work Chart** is an example of such a display, as shown here:

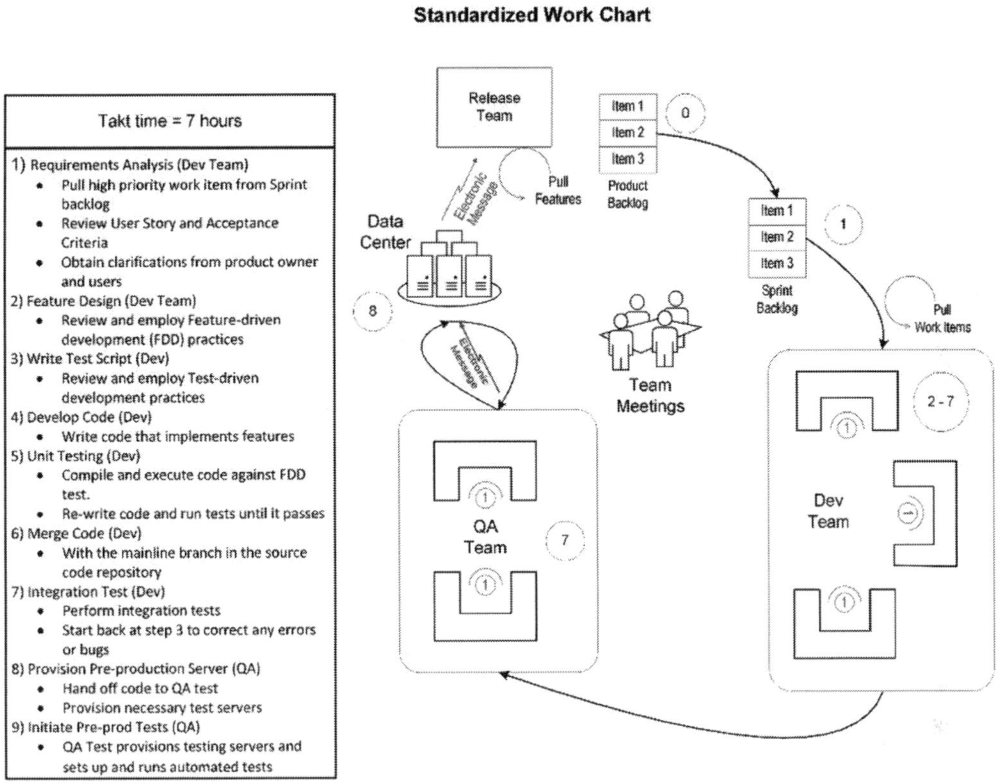

Figure 9.14 – Standardized Work Chart

At this point, the VSM team has analyzed the elements of work that can improve customer flows. Now, let's move on to developing the value stream's future state map of continuous flows.

Drawing the continuous flow phase map

Before the VSM team starts to draw their **future state map of continuous flow** improvements, they should review the analysis work:

1. First, the team must go back and review the current state map and the demand-phase maps.

2. Then, the VSM team members must go through the flow questions, and the information they obtained on their Gemba walks, that answer those questions.

3. Next, if they haven't done so already, the VSM team members must draw the current and future state **worker balance charts**.

4. Finally, they must go back and review the value stream symbols that we identified in *Figure 7.1*.

As with the previous maps, there is a preferred sequence of activities that aid in producing future state – continuous flow map – as shown here:

1. Use the demand phase map as the starting point.

2. Using the Standard Work Timesheet and Standardized Work Chart for guidance, draw the work locations in the map's proper sequence.

3. In the VSM Storyboard (see *Appendix B*), enter the number of workers in the proposed cycle times of work areas on the map.

4. Enter all the identified attributes in the appropriate work area locations.

5. Determine the tasks that support continuous flows.

6. Indicate on the map where to initiate pull-oriented production control strategies.

7. If required, display the placement of supermarket inventories.

8. Display where FIFO workflows occur.

9. Determine where Kanban signals are required.

10. Identify other improvement activities required to improve flows (for example, Kaizen Burst icons).

11. Display all necessary communications links on the map.

As the VSM team begins to draw the future state continuous flow map, they need to keep the following in mind:

- Implementing a continuous flow means that queues and waiting are eliminated.

- Evaluate work area designs and make change recommendations.

- The team needs executive approvals and funding to make significant changes.

- Lean production control pulls upstream work so that it's in sync with customer demand.

- Communicate reasons and benefits for all change recommendations.

The following diagram shows the VSM team's future state map of proposed continuous flow improvements across the IT value stream:

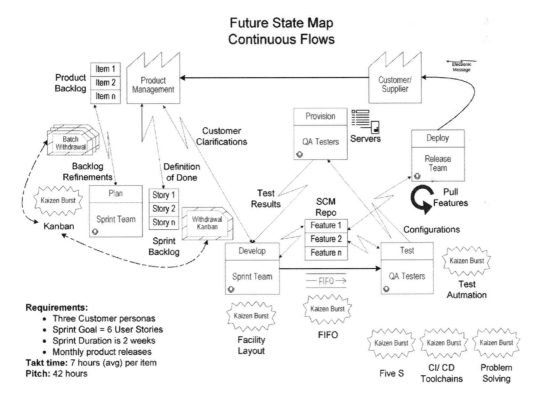

Figure 9.15 – Future state map of continuous flow improvements across the IT value stream

As you review the future state map, note how the map now indicates numerous communications links, as follows:

- Backlog refinement.
- Creating Definitions of Done for each user story.
- The development team obtains clarifications on requirements during development.
- Communicating test results from the automated tests.
- Moving code in and out of the source control management repository.
- Communicating server configurations for provisioning.

The VSM team has also identified four new improvement initiatives, identified by the Kaizen Burst icons for implementing Kanban signaling at two locations, as Kanban withdrawals associated with the Product and Sprint Backlogs:

- A new design for the development team's facilities
- A Kanban signaling and visualization production control system
- A FIFO production control strategy between development and test
- Implementation of test automation capabilities to enable testing to operate in a "lights out" capacity

Finally, note that we have replaced the individual development steps with two areas of activity – one for development and the other for testing. Technically, there is a third area associated with provisioning, which is the data center. However, all interactions with the data center are done through electronic communications to help implement infrastructure changes via code. This is also known as **Infrastructure as Code (IaC)**.

The release process is also separated from development since those activities fall outside the IT development stream domain. That's not to imply the development team members are not involved in release activities. The VSM team has elected to review those activities at a later date in a separate mapping exercise.

This section completes the future state - continuous flow improvement mapping section. Before we leave this section altogether, let's quickly review the tools that we used in this section.

Future state – continuous flow tools

In this section, you learned to ask several questions that help the VSM team assess the state of continuous flows across a value stream. Then, you learned the importance of using *pull-oriented production control strategies* to manage continuous flows. The three pull-oriented production control strategies include using *supermarket inventories, FIFO workflows, and Kanban-based signaling*.

You learned the importance of establishing standardized work as a prelude to enabling integration and automation of value stream activities. The two primary tools that are used to evaluate work activities are the *Standardized Work Timesheet* and the *Standardized Work Chart*.

Another important consideration in improving the flow of work and materials is the facility's *design and layouts*. Lean processes can implement linear-sequential flows with minimal waste associated with motion and travel. However, in many instances, it makes sense to redirect the linear sequential flows so that they wrap back to the front, such as via "U" or "C" shaped cells, or off to the side via an "L" shaped work cell.

In many value streams, the operator's most efficient use of time allows them to move between work cells or equipment. To leverage our human talent in this manner, they must be cross-trained in several – if not all – value stream activities. Moreover, the U- and C-shaped cells offer less movement between work locations.

In this section, you also learned how to employ the **Worker Balance Chart** to balance operators' utilization across a value stream's activities.

Finally, as we have been doing throughout the value stream management chapters, you learned how to update the VSM Storyboard to show the future state changes governing improvements to continuous flows. You also used several *flow-phase symbols* (Icons) in this exercise.

This section completes our discussion on developing future state maps to assess areas for improving continuous flows across the value stream. Now, we'll move on and learn how to use future state mapping to improve leveling work. This allows us to efficiently utilize our value stream resources while simultaneously meeting customer demand.

Phase 3 – leveling

At this point, the VSM team has conducted a series of Gemba walks to collect information they used for their value stream mapping exercises. They have built a current state map and future state maps to guide improvements in meeting customer demand and implementing continuous flows. The last future state map they will construct helps guide improvements in production leveling.

Leveling is a strategy that's used to distribute the work required to support our customers' demands over time. Our goal is to continuously feed our value stream with new customer orders, at the rate of the Takt time, so that we don't lose production time while waiting for new orders to arrive and have other times where the value stream contains more work than it can take on.

In an ideal state, production leveling aims to produce the same number of items consistently and just at the rate of the Takt time. Unfortunately, customer orders don't often come in as a continuous flow. They may come in batches, and the number of requested items can vary with each customer request. So, we have to implement strategies to flatten demand curves that match our value streams' production rates.

The time increments that are used depend on the total value added and total lead times associated with our products. In some cases, we can level work over hours, days, or weeks. However, we might need to level work over months or even years if we're constructing large buildings, aircraft or ships.

Leveling flows by analogy

By analogy, you can think of trying to flow water through a hose. Let's assume we have a garden hose that can hold one gallon of water at any given moment. If we try to flow 10 gallons of water all at once, the hose's size restricts flow, plus the hose can only contain one gallon of water at a time.

Unless we have a very flexible hose, allowing the water to bulge through the pipe, the 10 gallons of water only moves through the hose incrementally at a rate the hose can sustain without bursting; that is, the rate at which one gallon can traverse the hose from end to end.

Also, if we divide our hose into eight equal sections, each section will contain exactly one-eighth of a gallon of water at any given time. To complete our analogy, water must flow out of the hose's last section before the water in the upstream sections can flow into the linked downstream sections. Lean value streams operate in precisely this fashion, as continuous and equal flows.

We use the term **pipeline** to refer to the flows across our value streams. As an example, the following diagram shows the DevOps processes as a linear-sequential flow of work across eight primary activities:

Figure 9.16 – DevOps pipeline shown as a linear-sequential process

Of course, in real life, the monitoring activities obtain information that's been fed back to the development team as input for future planning activities. For that reason, the DevOps pipeline is more often displayed as an infinity loop, as shown here:

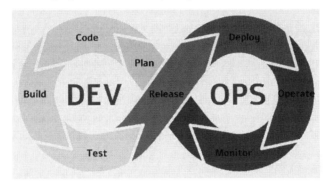

Figure 9.17 – DevOps pipeline displayed as an infinity loop

Neither graphical model is ideal, as new requirements come in from multiple sources. We'll discuss this issue in the leveling production flows subsection. Before we get to that topic, let's look at what questions the VSM team asks in this phase of the VSM initiative.

Assessing leveling needs

As with the previous future state mapping exercises, the VSM team can ask questions to help assess the needs for production leveling. Let's take a quick look at such questions:

- Do customer orders arrive more or less at a constant and predictable rate?
- Are the value stream's operators experiencing high and low peaks of activity as a result of changes in customer demand?
- Can we group incoming orders to level demand loads?
- Can we predict future orders sufficiently, in both volume and type, to build ahead of demands? If so, how far in advance can we build with minimal risks?

- Can we group orders in lots to improve the flows?

- When materials or parts must flow into various stages of our value stream, how will we distribute Kanban Cards to accurately flow the materials so that they sync with the work items?

- Where in the value stream should we schedule production/work requirements?

- Can we use **paced withdrawal** or a Heijunka box to manage the flow of lots?

- Do we need to employ runners to keep materials flowing and in balance?

- What other methods and tools can we employ to improve production leveling?

Now that we know what questions we need to answer, let's describe the concepts behind production leveling while using our IT value stream model as a reference.

Leveling concepts

At this stage of future state mapping, we need to concentrate on drawing the elements that help the value stream in leveling production. The problem this phase addresses is that customers seldom predictably bring us orders. When we have too many orders all at once, we may not have the production capacity to work through them quickly. At other times, the orders may come in at a slower rate that doesn't fill our capacity, which means our value stream is starved for work.

The objective of production leveling is to distribute our work over time to meet our customer demand. In high-volume production environments, we may need to level the flows once a shift or possibly even more frequently. On the other hand, retail manufacturers may have a much higher sales volume during the holiday seasons, which forces them to build in advance.

The VSM team waits until this late stage to manage leveling issues, because they need to understand the Takt time and optimal pitch for their value stream to match customer demand. Additionally, the VSM team needs time to work through the value stream activities to optimize flows to the greatest extent possible. In other words, there are more gains to be made in productivity by addressing issues with meeting customer demand and improving flows. Production leveling is more of a fine-tuning exercise than a significant change initiative.

In our previous IT value stream example, we noted that the Product Owner introduces, on average, 20 new requirements into the product backlog every 4 weeks. The Product owner receives these requests from multiple sources, including the IT shop's operations staff, directly from customers, industry sources, and product and marketing management teams.

It's doubtful that the product owner receives exactly one new requirement every day. Instead, they come in randomly and often in spurts – especially after the product marketing groups have conducted customer interviews and focused group sessions. When the new requirements arrive in batch, they are added to the product backlog to sit in a queue until the development team can start working on them.

Under Scrum-based agile practices, the development team evaluates how much work in the product backlog they believe they can take on and complete within the sprint's duration. In our example, the team pulls a batch of user stories from the product backlog as one lot of six work items to work through the Sprint. Once the work items have been selected, the team divides the work among the team members, and the team members work on each user story from start to finish.

All dev team members have all the skills necessary to work the item through the entire SDLC process in an ideal world. But that's not always the case. Moreover, depending on the complexity of a work item, the team may assign more than one team member to implement the capabilities outlined in a single user story.

The Scrum team example here is a method of production leveling across a Sprint. The items are taken in as a lot and worked on independently through the SDLC processes. But there is a problem since the team is working on six work items over 10 days. In that same 10-day period, the product backlog is likely to receive 10 new work items. In other words, the IT value stream is ignoring four new customer demand throughout every 2-week Sprint. Not only does this represent lost business, but it also opens the doors to your competitors to fill the void.

Production leveling alone is not going to solve this problem. The VSM team needs to work with the system engineers to implement the CI/CD and DevOps toolchains and pipelines to expedite workflows. In the long run, the VSM team should work with the IT department to implement capabilities that match the Takt time of one work item's completion per day. Faster flow rates provide surge capacity and the ability to make up for lost time if the IT systems go down.

Referring back to in *Figure 9.15*, with a mature DevOps pipeline, one work item leaves the pipeline every day, and other work items flow at the same speed throughout the pipeline. This means that one new work item can enter the DevOps pipeline every day. But since customer requirements come in haphazardly and often in batches, the development team still needs an incoming buffer, in the form of a product backlog, to store and manage the new requirements until they've been refined, prioritized, and pulled into the IT value stream.

While the IT department is implementing the new CI/CD toolchains, the VSM team begins to work out their production leveling strategies for the new development and testing environments. Let's take a look at the methods they can use to level production volumes.

Leveling methods

There are several methods the VSM team can explore for production leveling. In this section, you will learn about the 5S methods for leveling, including **Kanban Boards**, **paced withdrawals**, **Heijunka boxes**, **visual controls**, and **Kanban folders**.

Not all of these strategies work in every value stream. Moreover, Lean-Agile production has sufficient uniqueness to drive the evolution of a relatively new variant of Kanban that uses sticky notes and whiteboards to level flows across a Sprint. Known as a **Kanban Board**, we'll start with a description of that scheduling and leveling method first.

Kanban Boards

The product owner will usually bring new work items to the development team's attention in an IT environment. Each requirement's new work item instructions are typically noted on a sticky card and placed in the *Product Backlog* column on a whiteboard. The sticky notes are the Kanban signals, and the whiteboards are called Kanban Boards. Refer back to *Figure 9.9 – Kanban Board for an IT value stream*.

However, the initial requirements, expressed as business and user requirements, may be too broadly defined to develop as a succinct set of functional and nonfunctional capabilities. The development team members work with the product owner to refine the requirements into distinct and smaller user stories, representing the smallest work units that results in a definable capability.

User stories most often express the requirements from the customer's point of view. With this point of reference, a typical format for the user story is as follows:

As a (type of user), I want to (describe capability desired), so that (reason).

The user story should also define the acceptance criteria, which ultimately specify the story's Definition of Done. The following format helps define the acceptance criteria for a user story. Note that each user story may require multiple acceptance criteria statements to define all potential scenarios:

Given [a scenario] when [something happens] then [describe expected result].

The product owner then collaborates with the development team to determine priorities for the identified user stories. However, the development team makes the ultimate decision regarding the amount of work involved with each user story and the pace they can sustain.

This refinement work occurs during the planning phase of each Sprint, and the output is a Sprint Goal plus selected user stories that support the achievement of the Sprint's goal. The development team moves the Kanban Cards, one for each user story, into the *Sprint Backlog* column on the Kanban Board.

The user stories may need further clarification before the development team members can start developing and testing the functionality associated with each user story. Once the stories have been sufficiently developed, the Kanban Cards are moved into the **To Do** section of the Kanban Board. The development team members pull Kanban Cards from the **To Do** column and place them in the **In Process'** column, while they are developing and testing the functionality associated with that card's user story.

Once the developers have completed their work, they move the Kanban Card into the **To Verify** column. The verification process has another set of eyes review the work to ensure the new code implements the desired functionality and meets the standards set in its acceptance criteria. Once they have verified the new code's functionality, the Kanban Card is moved into the **Done** column to indicate that the work meets the acceptance criteria for the user story.

Some teams may elect to implement additional columns on their Kanban Boards to track the work they perform at a more granular level. That's OK. The critical issue is not to get into such small levels of detail that the tracking effort becomes overly burdensome.

Paced withdrawals

The Kanban Boards we previously described best support leveling of work for teams that work close by, often in the same room. Therefore, Kanban Boards are useful in software delivery or other administrative or operations-oriented types of value streams. In contrast, the paced withdrawal method of production leveling works in environments that are developing physical products, and where the workstations and equipment are spread out over a large area.

Paced withdrawals use a **human handler** (also known as **Runners**) to move information and work items along a value stream's activities, following the value stream's flow sequence. The handler sets the pace for the value stream as they move from operation to operation, moving parts and information from one work location to another.

The following diagram shows the paced withdrawal method of production leveling:

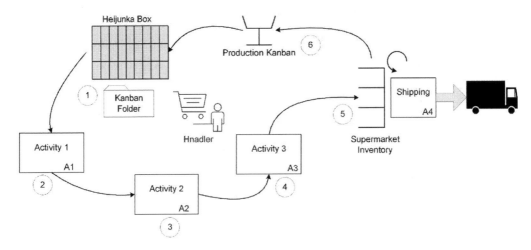

Figure 9.18 – Paced withdrawal leveling method

Let's take a closer look at how production flow leveling works using the preceding diagram:

1. The Runner (handler) starts a cycle by picking up the current production Kanban from a Heijunka box. A production Kanban is simply a detailed list of all items that need to be completed by a specific time. The Heijunka box has slots that map to specific time increments throughout the day. Each slot can hold a folder that contains the customer orders scheduled for that period.

2. The Runner takes the production Kanban to the most upstream work area to hand off the new orders.

3. The Runner later picks up the WIP goods at the location for activity 2 and moves them on to the next work area, to conduct activity 3.

4. When the work at activity location 3 is complete, the Runner moves that part to the workstation for activity 4.

5. When the Runner reaches the most downstream activity, they move the finished goods into a supermarket to hold the inventory until the products are picked up by or shipped to the customer.

6. At that point, the handler picks up new customer orders (that is, in the form of production Kanban information) and moves those documents to the value stream's Heijunka box.

This completes the original cycle, and the handler starts the cycle again. The key is to match the handler's cycle time to the pitch rate. This strategy limits production quantities as WIP while simultaneously matching flows to meet customer demand.

You may be wondering why you are learning about leveling strategies for value streams that build physical products. The short answer is because we all operate within a digital economy. IT teams often support the improvements in manufacturing and other types of development-oriented value streams, so IT specialists must understand how Lean processes work in other organizational value streams.

For example, the IT department may implement changes to the organization's **Enterprise Resource Planning (ERP)** or **Manufacturing Requirements Planning (MRP II)** systems to support evolving customer needs and business opportunities. Such modern business applications help integrate and automate business processes spanning inventory management, warehouse management, accounting and financial management, order management, scheduling, purchasing, shipping, **customer relationship management (CRM)**, and e-commerce. These functions operate as value streams within the organization, and most Lean improvements across these value streams require associated changes to be made to the enterprise business systems.

Heijunka boxes

As mentioned previously, the Heijunka box is essentially a slotted cabinet that holds production Kanban folders. The following diagram shows two examples of a Heijunka box:

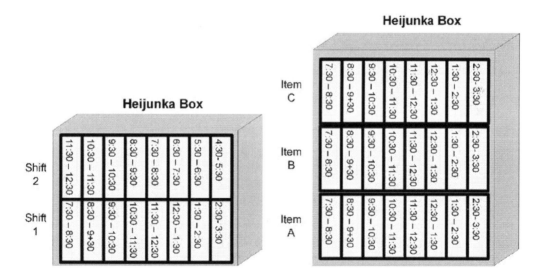

Figure 9.19 – Heijunka box

Each folder holds the production Kanban instructions for the work items produced by the value stream in that lot. The slots within the Heijunka box indicate the times within which the production items should be produced.

The Heijunka box on the left is slotted to support two shifts with 1-hour time periods scheduled between starting each new batch. In other words, each slot contains a Kanban folder with the production Kanban instructions to build the desired lot of work items within a 1-hour pitch.

The Heijunka box on the right is slotted to support three product types across one shift. The scheduler that's determining production capacities in a value stream with multiple product types. This determines how many items of each type can be produced within each slotted time frame.

Though we mentioned the Heijunka box as part of the paced withdrawal leveling method, the Heijunka box can stand alone as a leveling tool. In such cases, the Heijunka box is a visual workflow control method. Instead of using a Runner in a co-located space, such as in an administrative office, the employees can pull work directly from the boxes.

Visual controls

Instead of a Heijunka box, the VSM team may elect to implement a Visual Pitch Board to guide production flows across the day. The Pitch Board is a table that displays the number of each operator's work assignments across the pitch times within their shift. This a useful mechanism for operations-oriented value streams to level the flow of work within an administrative area.

For example, let's assume a value stream receives, on average, 20 new work item requests per hour and that four operators have been assigned to work on these tasks. This visual aid type works in both development and operations-oriented workstreams, where everyone can easily see the visual Pitch Board display. In other words, we don't need a runner, and the operators can pull their production Kanban Cards directly from the production control system.

The following is a sample Visible Pitch board for an administrative department:

Visible Pitch Board - Order Management Department (Order Entry)									
Time =>	7:30 AM	8:30 AM	9:30 AM	10:30 AM	11:30 AM	12:30 PM	1:30 PM	2:30 PM	3:30 PM	Average
OE Clerk A	5	4	5	5	5	5	4	5	5	4.8
OE Clerk B	5	5	4	5	5	5	5	4	5	4.8
OE Clerk C	4	5	4	5	5	5	5	4	5	4.7
OE Clerk D	4	5	5	5	5	4	5	5	4	4.7
Pitch	18	19	18	18	20	19	19	18	19	19

Figure 9.20 – Visual Pitch Board – order entry value stream example

In this example, the average pitch is 19 customer orders every hour, but with a low of 18 and a high of 20 customer orders. The scheduler has distributed the work so that no single order entry clerk has excessive orders every hour.

With a maximum order entry rate of five orders per hour per operator, the cycle time for each order entry activity is 12 minutes. But, in every 1-hour slot, one or two order entry clerks only need to work on four customer orders, giving them 12 minutes of open time. In addition, however, these individuals can work on other value-adding tasks, such as answering customer calls or emails.

The number of work items (pitch) assigned to individual workers can vary based on their skills and other duties they may perform. Also, note that the Pitch Board distributes workload by volume only and does not include instructions on the required work. In this case, the clerks receive colored Kanban folders that contain such instructions.

Kanban folders

Kanban folders contain production Kanban information. They are used in paced withdrawal systems, or in standalone Heijunka boxes, or distributed to team members who get their work assignment notifications via a Visual Pitch Board. For example, the production Kanban contains information on the performance of standardized work and the customer order requirements. In addition, the Kanban folders may be color-coded to indicate which operator the work has been assigned to or indicate the type of standardized work that's being performed.

In the paced withdrawal system, the Kanban folder flows with work and is moved by the Runner. In the standalone Heijunka boxes, the operators pull the work from the slots associated with the type of work they perform and the time of day. Typically, when a Visual Pitch Board is used, the local manager distributes the Kanban folders directly to the operators at a standard interval. The intervals set the pace, and the folders help break out and distribute the work across the operators.

This section concludes our discussion on leveling methods. After evaluating and choosing the appropriate leveling methods, the VSM team can move on and draw the future state value stream leveling map.

Drawing the leveling phase map

The VSM team now has the information they require to develop the future state value stream map for the leveling phase. As with the other phases, the team evaluates leveling opportunities by working their way through a series of related question, as follows:

- What are the minimum work item group sizes for optimal flows?
- What type of Kanban signaling methods work in the value stream's work environment? (That is, Kanban Boards, Kanban Cards, Kanban bins, or Visual Pitch Board?)

- How will Kanban Cards or folders be distributed? (That is, manager distribution, Heijunka boxes, or Runners/handlers?)

- If appropriate, what type of Heijunka box or visual aid is required? (That is, showing work that's been assigned to value stream operators or by part type?)

- If runners are required, what route and pace should be optimal for leveling flows?

Before drawing the leveling phase map, the VSM team should decide on what icons they plan to use to portray the production leveling requirements for FIFO, Runners, Heijunka boxes, Kanban Cards, Kanban folders, and Visual Pitch Boards.

The VSM team builds upon their previously evaluated future state – continuous flows map to add the elements necessary for assisting with leveling the flows. In the previous continuous flows exercise, the VSM team assessed the need for a Kanban-based system to help establish better product flows. They have refined their thinking and have decided to implement a Kanban Board with sticky notes as the ideal signaling method.

The following diagram shows the Kaizen Burst associated with implementing the Kanban Board-based leveling with sticky notes:

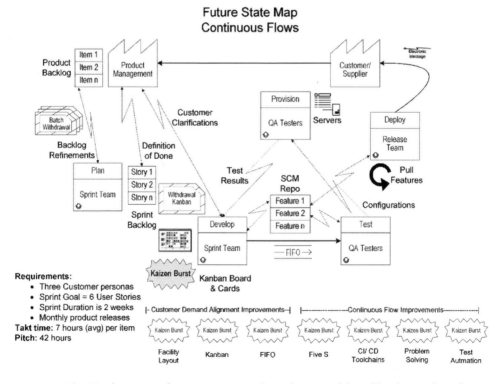

Figure 9.21 – The IT value stream future state map with Kanban Board-based leveling with sticky notes

The Kanban Board helps the IT value stream manage the cadence of their flows while simultaneously leveling the WIP at any given time. The developers still conduct Sprint planning sessions to refine user stories within the product backlog, and they work with the product owner to prioritize work items.

Many of the selected items support development customer-requested enhancements. However, some user stories address issues of technical debt, security, and architectural and design improvements. The VSM team annotates the proposed change on their future state maps by adding the Kanban Board Icon at the development stage. The VSM team also adds an associated Kaizen Burst to indicate the continuous improvement activity.

Throughout this chapter, we have discussed how to implement Lean-oriented concepts as an overlay to software development practices. But if the software development team has implemented Agile practices, we may have to undo some of the batch-oriented practices implemented by the Sprint Backlogs. Batch processing causes waste in the form of waiting and excess WIP.

If a software development organization has implemented Agile practices around Scrum, they may want to address a change to Kanban-based production scheduling concepts during their future state mapping exercises. So, before we leave our future state mapping activities, let's take a moment to address how we can improve Agile-based practices to eliminate the negative aspects of batch processing work items across Sprints.

Eliminating Agile-based batch processing

Sprint Backlogs are inherently a batch production process. The Agile teams pull work items as a "lot" from the product backlog and then hold them in a queue until the development team members have time to work on them. Queuing work items can lead to excessive waiting and WIP in queues, as well as task switching. All three practices are forms of waste.

Some organizations implement Kanban Boards to both visualize and manage WIP within their Sprints. In this manner, Kanban Boards help the development team level production flows across each Sprint duration.

However, Agile team implementations of Kanban Boards are not an example of a strategy that supports optimized continuous flows. The team is still moving work items across Sprints in lot sizes greater than one. However, with the implementation of CI/CD and DevOps pipelines, work items can flow as single-piece workflows across the value stream. Moreover, the development team can also use their Kanban Boards to level customer demand directly at the product backlog level, so long as the work items have been fully refined and prioritized.

Yes, Lean can be made part of Scrum and other Agile practices. But it's important to understand that using Sprints as a mechanism to control the flow of requirements then becomes a batch process, which is inconsistent with Lean philosophies on implementing the ideal of single-piece flows.

Does that mean that Sprints and other forms of developing on cadence – such as in SAFe? In a word, no. Sprints and other forms of development cadence force the value stream teams to take the time to plan their upcoming activities. The teams provide product and solution demos to customers and other stakeholders. They also inspect and adapt their work and perform Kaizen or Retrospective-based reflections to support their continuous improvement objectives.

This section completes our discussion on future state (phase 3) mapping to improve customer demand-flow leveling. Before we leave this section altogether, let's review the tools we identified that support leveling.

Future state – leveling tools

In this section, you learned who and when to employ a Kanban Board to manage work in progress flowing across a value stream. Kanban Boards work well in IT-oriented value streams and in other administration or operations-oriented value streams.

A value stream manager may employ a material handler or "Runner" to move materials and parts that must be manually moved across significant distances. The Runner can set the value stream's pace as they move the WIP components and production Kanban Cards or folders from one work location to another. The Runner follows the flow of the value stream, setting the cadence with each cycle they make.

Heijunka boxes offer a method to store production Kanban Cards and folders in slots within a box. The Heijunka box serves as a visual aid indicating the day's scheduled work over specific periods of time. The Hiejunka box may indicate which individuals are responsible for performing the work, or the type of products to be manufactured.

Another visual aid form is the *Visual Pitch Board*, which, like the Heijunka box, displays scheduled work overtime based on the value stream's pitch. But instead of placing the production Kanban folders in slots within a box, the value stream manager manually distributes the Cards and folders to the operators.

As a quick aside, the IT department may be asked to implement electronic equivalents of the Kanban Boards, Heijunka box, and Visual Pitch Boards. In Part Two of this book, we will learn how VSM tools provide these capabilities.

Finally, we need to update the VSM Storyboard with the future state map – leveling phase improvements. The VSM team needs to decide what icons they plan to use to indicate Kanban Boards, paced withdrawals, Heijunka boxes, Kanban folders or Cards, and Visual Pitch Boards.

This section completes our introduction to future state mapping, the sixth step in our VSM methodology. In the next chapter, you will learn how to implement Kaizen plans to guide your continuous improvement initiatives.

Summary

In this chapter, you learned about the three phases of future state value stream mapping. These phases include assessing the value stream's ability to manage customer demands, implement continuous flows, and level customer orders to optimize production capacities. In addition, you learned how to develop and evolve the future state map across these three phases.

As part of your learning, this chapter continued with the original IT-oriented value stream example, to show you how the VSM team moves from the continuous state assessment of work and information flows to analyzing a preferred future state. You completed the exercise by noting that the Sprint-based practices of Agile and Scrum implement batch processes inherently, which is a form of waste in Lean. However, you now know that batch processing can be eliminated by moving to Kanban-based production scheduling, as well as by implementing integrated and automated CI/CD and DevOps pipeline flows.

Having read this chapter, you now have the knowledge to evaluate and implement Lean improvements across value streams to address issues associated with aligning production with customer demand, improving continuous flows, and leveling production to meet variations in customer demand. With this information, you have developed improvement strategies in the form of discrete Kaizen Bursts.

In the next chapter, you will learn how to create and implement Kaizen plans to execute your future state improvement strategies.

Questions

Please take a moment to answer the following questions to ensure you have a solid grasp of future state mapping:

1. What are the three phases of future state value stream mapping?
2. What is the goal of the customer demand phase?
3. What is the goal of the continuous flow phase?
4. What is the goal of the leveling phase?
5. How is Takt time calculated, and what is its purpose?
6. How is pitch calculated, and what is its purpose?
7. What is a critical issue when you're managing customer demands across a value stream?
8. What is the primary objective of phase 2 – continuous flow?
9. In an ideal state, what is the objective of production leveling?
10. Why do the iterative Agile and Scrum-based Sprints inherently implement batch-oriented processes, and how can those strategies be improved?

Further reading

Tapping, D., Luyster, T., Shuker, T. (2002) *Value Stream Management. Eight Steps to Planning, Mapping, and Sustaining Lean Improvements*. Productivity Press. New York, NY.

Tapping, D., Luyster, T., Shuker, T. (2003) *Value Stream Management for the Lean Office. Eight Steps to Planning, Mapping, and Sustaining Lean Improvements*. Productivity Press. New York, NY.

Tapping, D., Kozlowski, S., Archbold, L., Sperl, T. (2009) *Value Stream Management for Lean Healthcare. Four Steps to Planning, Mapping, Implementing, and Controlling Improvements in All Types of Healthcare Environments*. MCS Media, Inc. Chelsea, MI.

10
Improving the Lean-Agile Value Delivery Cycle (VSM Steps 7 and 8)

In the previous chapters, you learned how to conduct a VSM initiative, map the current state, and then map three phases of desired future states. At this point, the VSM team is ready to begin the improvement activities. VSM implements the Lean concepts of Kaizen to make continuous improvements. The VSM team now knows how to apply the VSM tools to make Lean improvements in their IT value streams and other organizational value streams.

Lean improvements are distinctively different from Agile-based improvements in terms of scope of work, timeframes, costs, and authorities. In this chapter, you will learn that Lean improvements tend to address issues at a strategic level that require portfolio investments and executive-level decision making, at least initially. In contrast, Agile-based improvements tend to operate at a tactical level and within the Agile team's scope, and within shorter timeframes measured in individual Sprints.

Both Lean and Agile practices are necessary and should be integrated within the organization. However, since this book is about value stream management, our focus is on making Lean-oriented value stream improvements, specifically across IT-oriented value streams.

In our generic VSM methodology, there are three steps related to Kaizen: first, identifying the Kaizen bursts – as improvement opportunities – and then planning and implementing your Kaizen plans. You learned how to identify Kaizen opportunities in the previous chapters. This chapter provides instructions on constructing a Kaizen plan and how to implement it.

Lean improvements are, at their root, business transformations. VSM initiatives help reengineer business processes to create value streams as Lean production flows. The word production flow does not always imply that products are developed for external customers. For example, some software-oriented value streams develop and deliver software products to support other internal business operations or operations-oriented value streams.

We will cover all these topics in this chapter. Specifically, by the end of this chapter, you will be able to create and implement Kaizen plans as part of your Lean business transformation.

In this chapter, we will cover the following topics:

- Combining Lean and Agile practices
- Making continuous Lean-Agile improvements
- Creating Kaizen plans – VSM step seven
- Implementing Kaizen plans – VSM step eight
- Summarizing the VSM methodology

Combining Lean and Agile practices

The current trend among Agile methodologists is to combine the software development concepts behind Agile with those associated with Lean production processes. The integration of Lean and Agile practices became mainstream only after Mary and Tom Poppendieck promoted Lean as a component of Agile practices in their book, *Lean Software Development: An Agile Toolkit* (Poppendieck, 2003). The impact of their book was significant, and most modern Agile methodologies, such as **Scrum**, **Large Scale Scrum (LeSS)**, **Discipline Agile (DA)**, and the **Scale-Agile Framework® (SAFe®)**, now claim to have Lean underpinnings.

Still, the concept of Lean-Agile practices is relatively new as an IT discipline. Most of the so-called Lean-Agile methodologies do not promote nor teach comprehensive methods to make Lean-oriented production improvements. Instead, most Lean-Agile methodologies state that Lean or Lean thinking principles are built into their methodologies.

In other words, the methodologists who make such claims believe that merely following their practices can make organizations Lean. But, true or not, Lean practices are pretty evolved, and embedding Lean's concepts in other methodologies, without also implementing the discipline of value stream management, takes away from the rigor of its proven production and value delivery improvement methods.

While both Agile and Lean practitioners promote the concepts of continuous improvements, there are fundamental differences in philosophies about the improvement process, timeframes, and the scope of work involved. We'll take a look at these differences in the next section.

Making continuous Lean-Agile improvements

By now, it must be apparent to you that the organization's value stream management initiatives are not one-time events. Instead, they are ongoing and cyclical over the lifetime of the product line. However, in this chapter, you will discover that many of the initial Lean improvement initiatives tend to have a larger scale than Agile-based continuous improvements associated with team-based retrospectives.

That's not to say that Lean improvements can't be made on a small scale. Fundamentally, everyone in a Lean organization is encouraged to uncover problems that impede their ability to work, find solutions, and implement them. Still, agile teams and individuals typically cannot make wholesale changes to equipment and tools, nor can they procure new equipment and tools to improve continuous flows across the value stream, without formal approvals from their executives. Implementing large-scale improvements and business transformations are where the disciplines of Lean and VSM shine.

Large-scale IT value stream improvement issues manifest when an IT organization wants to implement a **continuous integration/continuous delivery** (**CI/CD**) or DevOps pipeline. These investments are typically larger than an agile software development team, or even a software product team, has the authority to approve. For these reasons, the scope of change tends to be larger in Lean-oriented improvements than in Agile – at least in the early stages – so the timescales and investments tend to be larger.

The goal of Lean-Agile is to combine the best of both worlds of doing business. Both concepts have more in common than not. For example, both the Agile and Lean concepts have a focus on delivering customer-centric value. Both concepts seek greater production efficiencies, improved quality, and rapid delivery. And, both concepts encourage continuous improvements.

Agile, Scrum, and Lean all share the notion of continuously improving our operations. However, Lean practitioners employ value stream management practices to guide improvements, while Agile practitioners tend to use retrospectives.

VSM implements a much more rigorous process for continuous improvements, called **Kaizen**, compared to Agile-based Retrospectives. Lean's Kaizen-based improvements tend to look at the value stream holistically, from front to end, to make improvements across product and information flows. As a result, the scope of Kaizen-based improvements may span timeframes and investments beyond those that can be made at the small agile-team level.

Put another way, sometimes, we need to tear complex things apart before figuring out how to put them back together as a better operating system. And because the investments are so significant, we need to prioritize each proposed change in terms of their contributions to delivering the most value in the shortest possible time.

As we've worked through the continuous and future state mapping exercises for our IT value stream, we've identified many improvement opportunities. Specifically, the Kaizen Burst icons highlight the improvement opportunities that were identified in our future state maps. Agile and Scrum practices seek incremental improvements based on assessments of real-time issues that need immediate attention. In contrast, value stream management takes a longer-term view to assess structural changes to organizations and work and information flows.

The VSM team will work with the value stream operators and stakeholders to incrementally implement the recommended Kaizen improvements. Still, the planning horizon is much longer than those recommended in Agile and Scrum, at least during the initial VSM team engagement. Moreover, VSM improvements tend to be strategic, with investment decisions being made at the portfolio level.

Both types of continuous improvement concepts, Agile and Lean, are essential. But as you discovered in *Chapter 5, Driving Business Value through a DevOps Pipeline*, significant investments are required to achieve a Lean IT value stream across the development and operations departments. Such expensive improvements require executive-level buy-in and approvals, and it takes time and effort for the IT department to implement a mature DevOps capability.

Now that you understand the different objectives in Lean versus Agile-based continuous improvements, we can move on and understand how to develop a VSM-based Kaizen plan.

Creating Kaizen plans – VSM step seven

There is a real danger of failure when incrementally implementing a CI/CD or DevOps toolchain and pipeline on an ad hoc basis. To start, executive managers may not fully understand the time and costs involved, and may resist when they see unexpected and unplanned **Capital expenditure** (**CAPEX**) requests that have been sent to them for approval. The development and operations teams will become frustrated if their toolchain and platform requests are not approved. There are tools, as well as process integration and security issues, that must be addressed when developing the DevOps pipeline, and internal customers and stakeholders may have false expectations of how long the improvements may take.

DevOps is a business transformation activity. It's much more of a business process reengineering program than an incremental business process improvement initiative, and the DevOps initiative needs to be treated accordingly. In other words, DevOps is a strategic investment that must be planned and executed at the portfolio level. This means the VSM team must conduct rigorous planning, provide detailed budgets and schedules, and lay out a roadmap for its rollout to support the organization's other Lean value stream initiatives.

In this section, you will learn how to build a Kaizen plan for your VSM initiative. So, let's get started.

Connecting to a business strategy

With the completion of the three-phase future state mapping exercise, the VSM team has a broad understanding of the improvements that need to be made. Now, the VSM team must learn how to implement the improvements, which requires a plan.

It's not necessary to try to get the plan right and complete it at the start. It's better to start with what we know, find out what we don't know, and make informed improvements to the plan as the team goes along. Such an approach is consistent with Agile views on improving software. First, we must implement what we think our customers need and want. Then, we must show them what we have, and then take their feedback to make it better incrementally. The same strategy holds for Kaizen planning and implementation.

At every phase of the VSM initiative, the team begins by asking a series of questions. The same strategy is valid for Kaizen planning. But this time, the VSM team's focus is on aligning improvement activities in the context of strategic intent. In other words, what are the goals and objectives that have been set out by the organization's executives who approved the VSM initiative? Some such questions are as follows:

- Who are the value stream's customers, and how will they benefit from the VSM improvements?

- How does this VSM initiative support the strategic goals of the organization?

- How was the VSM initiative cost justified as a high-priority portfolio investment? That is, what are the executive-level expectations that justified the investments?

- The VSM initiative supports which internal or external products?

- The VSM initiative impacts which internal and external organizations?

- What are the expected quality improvements for this initiative?

- How will the Lean IT value stream support the organization's other Lean value streams?

- Are there sections of the value stream where improvements have a bigger impact on the overall productivity of the system?

  a. In other words, are there segments of the value stream that negatively impact the flow and throughput of the value stream as a whole?

  b. Are there segments of linked activities across the value stream that can be combined into simpler, more efficient activities?

- How should we prioritize the stream improvement activities that were identified in the future state mapping exercise?

- What types of investments are required to implement each of the Kaizen improvement plans?

- What kind of training or skills are required to support each of the identified improvement recommendations?

- What is the optimal schedule for rolling out the identified Kaizen improvements?

It's essential that the VSM team clearly defines the qualitative and quantitative metrics for all the preceding questions. Ultimately, these metrics define the effectiveness of each improvement action.

Planning Lean improvements across phases

Just as the VSM team identified **future state improvements** across three phases, the improvement plan's rollout should follow the same three phases. These phases are as follows:

- Sub-plans to meet **customer demand**
- Sub-plans to improve the **process flow**
- Sub-plans to **level the work**

These three sub-plans map directly back to the future state Kaizen plans that were identified in the previous chapter (*Chapter 9, Mapping the Future State (VSM Step 6)*). As a quick recap, future state mapping guides improvements across the following three phases:

- **Customer demand phase**: Evaluates customer demands for products, work items, and services, including customer-driven variations in quality, features, or functions, and lead times.
- **Continuous flow phase**: Seeks to improve production flows to match customer demands.
- **Leveling phase**: Implements strategies to distribute work, both by volume and variety, to reduce bottlenecks and waiting, and to minimize lot sizes. Recalling that the ideal is a lot size of one.

Don't forget that the VSM team identified multiple improvement opportunities for each phase. Therefore, the Kaizen plan should address all the recommended improvement initiatives across each phase.

Developing Kaizen plans

Again, unlike the Agile concepts of identifying and implementing improvements across every **Sprint**, the Lean improvements will likely take months to roll out. A primary reason for this is the need to identify the investments needed to make the necessary tools, equipment, and layout changes, gain executive approvals, and fit them within a portfolio budget cycle.

The proposed changes will likewise require time to design and then procure, deploy, and test the necessary tools, platforms, and equipment. The VSM team cannot forget the need to bring the organization's human talent up to speed on the changes. The Kaizen plan should include **time** and **resources** for mentoring, coaching, and training. In this section, you will learn how to develop a Kaizen plan using three primary tools; namely, the Monthly Kaizen Schedule Plan, the Chart of VSM Objectives and Measurables, and the Detailed Monthly Kaizen Schedule Plan.

If the VSM team prefers, they can use a project management scheduling tool, such as MS Project, to develop a **Gannt chart** of the Kaizen schedule. But a simple worksheet or large whiteboard is more than sufficient to create a **Monthly Kaizen Schedule Plan**.

The following figure shows an example of a Monthly Kaizen Schedule Plan as an Excel worksheet. This worksheet visually displays the planned improvement initiatives for each of the Kaizen Bursts across each of the three phases of future state improvements. In addition, the VSM team updates the Monthly Kaizen Plan Worksheet with new proposed improvement initiatives that have been identified over time:

Monthly Kaizen Schedule Plan														
	Value Stream:								Date					
Phase	Kaizen Burst	Planed Improvement Change	Jan	Feb	Mar	Apr	May	Jun	Jul	Aug	Sep	Oct	Nov	Dec
Demand														
FLOW														
LEVEL														
	Δ = Start Date	➡ = Ongoing Work	▲ = Planned Finish Date											

Figure 10.1 – Monthly Kaizen Schedule Plan

The Monthly Kaizen Plan Worksheet is an overview of planned Lean improvement initiatives; therefore, they it does not provide much detail on the tasks associated with each Lean improvement initiative. As planning progresses, more details are exposed, and the VSM team uses a different visual display to track those details and inform others of their progress. The detailed plan may be called a **Kaizen Milestone Chart** or **Monthly Kaizen Schedule**.

On an ongoing basis, the VSM team uses the symbols depicted at the bottom of the Monthly Kaizen Schedule Plan (*Figure 10.1*) to update the status of each Kaizen Burst within its calendar fields.

Another essential visual display is a chart showing **Lean measurables**, including baselines and target values, objectives, goals, the state of the proposed change, and identified risks and issues. It is called the **Chart of VSM Objectives and Measurables**, and the purpose of this chart is to provide a highly visible display of improvement objectives, goals, and metrics for the VSM initiative. It also identifies risks and issues associated with each recommended improvement objective.

The following figure shows an example of a Chart of VSM Objectives and Measurables.

Date:						
VSM Team Lead:						
VS Manager:						
Change Objectives	Measurable Goals	Baseline Metrics	Target Metrics	State of change	Risks	Issues
☑ - Completed	☐ - Still Open	☒ - Unsuccessful				

Figure 10.2 – Chart of VSM Objectives and Measurables

Note that risks and issues are broken out separately. The reason for this is that, by definition, *Risks* are events that might happen, while *Issues* are problems that have already impacted our project. The difference is vital because the VSM teams should identify potential risks before they happen and decide what steps become necessary to avoid or mitigate the risks' negative impacts. Also, the VSM team should define contingency plans for the worst potential risks so that they already have a plan in place to minimize the impacts if they happen.

For example, let's say the VSM team recommends adopting a new **source code management** (**SCM**) repository and continuous integration tools. If something happens with the install, we want to have a backup and restore capability as a contingency plan, to roll back our original environments and data until we figure out what caused our new system changeover to fail.

The detailed monthly Kaizen plan includes the same elements as the Monthly Kaizen Schedule Plan, such as phase, planned tasks, and months. But the detailed Schedule Plan should include additional information, such as ownership assignments, estimated time to completion, and whether the task is past due. It also provides a more granular display of time over units of weeks, not months. The *State of Change* fields are updated with the symbols that were identified at the bottom of the Chart of VSM Objectives and Measurables (*Figure 10.2*).

The following figure provides an example display of a **Detailed Monthly Kaizen Schedule Plan**. As the name implies, this plan aims to learn about the proposed VSM improvement activities. Specifically, the plan provides space for identifying all the improvement initiatives, down to the task level:

Kaizen Detailed Schedule Plan

Value Stream: | VSM Team Members: | Date:

Task No	Task Names	Assigned To:	04-Jan	11-Jan	18-Jan	25-Jan	01-Feb	08-Feb	15-Feb	22-Feb	01-Mar	08-Mar	15-Mar	22-Mar	29-Mar	05-Apr	12-Apr	19-Apr	26-Apr	03-May	10-May	17-May	24-May	31-May
	Demand Phase:																									
	5S																									
	CI/CD																									
	Problem Solving																									
	Flow Phase:																									
	Kanban																									
	Facility Layout																									
	FIFO																									
	Test Automation																									
	Leveling Phase:																									
	Kanban Board																									
	Δ = Start Date																									
	➡ = Ongoing Work																									
	▲ = Completed																									
	: = Past Due																									
	--------------- One Month Out																									

Figure 10.3 – Detailed Monthly Kaizen Schedule Plan

The Detailed Monthly Kaizen Schedule Plan includes a **Task No** for each recommended improvement objective, again down to the task level. Descriptive Task**Names** highlight the work involved, and the plan should identify who is responsible for completing work and whether goals have been achieved. A timeline provides a visual display of **Start Date, Ongoing work, and Completed dates**. The VSM team should also make annotations to indicate when planned tasks are **Past Due**.

Milestones mark the start or completion of major events, using the symbols identified at the bottom of the Detailed Monthly Kaizen Schedule Plan (*Figure 10.3*). So, for each improvement activity, the VSM team identifies important events to measure the start, progress, and completion of their change initiatives. All milestones must be quantifiable in terms of the change objectives and measurable in terms of the extent of the activity's completion of stated objectives.

It's important to understand that VSM initiatives are project-based work and not based on Agile-based development strategies. That's not to say that VSM initiatives are incompatible with Lean practices. Still, Agile-based Retrospectives tend to be limited in time and scope of the authorities of the small agile team and within the duration of a Sprint.

In contrast, Lean initiatives tend to take a longer-term planning horizon, involve much larger investments that require executive-level buy-in and sponsorship, and tend to be more aligned with supporting corporate strategies.

VSM initiatives are tasked with identifying critical changes that are necessary to implement and improve lean practices across a value stream. The scope of work and investments are approved at an executive level and directly impact the organization's ability to meet its strategic goals.

In this context, VSM initiatives have the characteristics of a project. In other words, they have a defined scope of work, a defined set of deliverable tasks, a defined budget, and a defined schedule. However, the continuous improvement efforts will move to the Agile teams as part of their normal Sprint Retrospectives in the long run. With these initial Lean transformations completed and installed on an Agile-based framework, the **IT-oriented** value streams reform as Lean-Agile practices.

Now that the VSM team has created their Kaizen plans, they need to obtain approvals to proceed. This approval requirement is the topic of the following subsection.

Obtaining approvals to proceed

As noted previously, Lean improvement initiatives often involve significant investments. But they also have the potential for disrupting the value stream's day-to-day activities. Therefore, the VSM team must seek and obtain appropriate approvals before starting a new change initiative.

Note that this level of approval does not generally apply to Agile-based continuous improvement activities as they tend to focus on procedural changes at a local level. But given the time, resources, and investments associated with the larger VSM initiative, executive-level approvals are necessary.

The VSM team can use its **VSM storyboard** and **Kaizen plans** to summarize its lean transformation concepts. During the executive-level review, the VSM team should be prepared to answer the following questions:

- How does this project relate to the organization's strategic objectives?
- Why did the VSM team select this value stream, linked value streams, or aportion of a value stream for this Lean improvement initiative?
- What impact will the lean methods have on our internal and external customers?
- What throughput changes are expected?
- What product quality improvements are expected?
- What cost savings are expected, and over what timeframe?

Hopefully, the executive team was involved in the early planning sessions and formally sponsored the VSM team, complete with a defined **charter** to authorize their time and resources. However, it never hurts to remind the executives about the purpose and goals of the VSM initiative, and how the team's work maps back to supporting the organization's strategic goals and mission.

The VSM team's recommendations may sound overly aggressive and costly at first glance. The team must be prepared to back up their recommendations with sound logic, accurate data, and a risk-averse Kaizen strategy. As the VSM team prepares their presentation, they should keep the following in mind:

- Set realistic goals and estimated completion dates.
- Engage in open dialogue with executives, value stream managers, operators, and other critical stakeholders to obtain their buy-in before giving the formal presentation.
- Show draft VSM presentations and maps to everyone connected to the value stream and get their input.
- Keep the main presentation minimal, with bullets outlining key points, but have detailed slides available to get into the necessary details.
- Make the presentation visual with graphical and large- font presentation slides, plus a large display of the VSM storyboard.
- Ensure excellent work is recognized, including VSM team members', VA operators', and other vital stakeholders' work.
- Take the time to celebrate after getting approval, and then celebrate again after each successful Lean improvement initiative.

This is all you need to know about Kaizen planning. If you are already familiar with Agile concepts, you know that detailed project and schedule plans in IT don't make sense. Until we start working with our value stream customers, we can't know what solutions are best or optimal. Moreover, needs and priorities change over time, making detailed plans obsolete even before we begin our work. The better option is to get your basic VSM plan together, move forward with it, and then iteratively and incrementally improve it over time as you work to improve the value stream.

This section concludes our discussion on Kaizen planning. In the next section, you will learn how to implement Kaizen plans.

Implementing Kaizen plans – VSM step eight

In this section, you will learn how to implement your Kaizen plans. This last step is also the shortest VSM method to describe but arguably the most critical step and the lengthiest activity – it lasts the value stream's lifetime. As with Agile, in Lean practices, we never stop our efforts to improve.

This VSM step is also the most difficult to implement. The reason for this is that many, if not most, people are naturally resistant to change. The success of the VSM team's Lean improvement recommendations depends on their ability to get folks to buy in across the organization. You must begin this step by addressing the issue of change.

Addressing the issue of change

Obtaining organizational buy-in to implement the VSM team's recommendations won't happen overnight. It's best to work with a highly motivated value stream team who willingly serve as **innovators** and **early adopters** in the organization's Lean enterprise initiatives.

Unlike the original goals of business process reengineering, the VSM team should not implement its recommendations all at once. The only justification for doing so is if the organization is in a **burning platform** situation, where delays lead to the organization's bankruptcy or failure. Instead, the VSM team needs to work through its identified Kaizen Bursts, implementing changes iteratively and incrementally. This does not mean that the process should be unduly extended over time. The goal is to have rapid successes and use those early, and then use rapid-following successes to communicate the overall VSM initiative's value.

Following the *technology adoption life cycle* principles, initially outlined by Joe Bohlen and George Beal in their paper titled *The Diffusion Process*, the remainder of the organization's members will follow the new practices once they are convinced of the benefits of the change. The following figure provides a graphical depiction of the typical technology or product adoption curve:

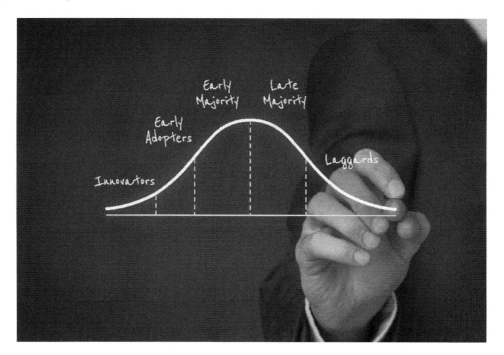

Figure 10.4 – Technology adoption curve

The technology adoption life cycle is a sociological model that describes the adoption or acceptance of a new product or innovation. When you look at the Bell Curve shown in the preceding figure, you will notice that labels have been placed across the curve: **Innovators, Ealy Adopters, Early Majority, Late Majority, and Laggards**. Let's take a moment to understand what these labels imply:

- **Innovators**: They are the first within an industry or an organization to implement new methods, tools, and operating models. They tend to like change and are less risk averse. In some situations, they may be in crisis mode (that is, burning platform) and have no choice but to change the way they do things.

- **Early Adopters**: They are the first to see the benefits derived by the innovators and quickly adopt the new ways of working. They also tend to be open to change and take on some risk, but they won't be the first to move.

- **Early Majority**: At this phase of a technology or business transformation life cycle change, things begin to take off. Enough people have paved the way to prove the benefits of the new technology or approach to work, and more people feel comfortable with the risks of adopting the new approach.

- **Late Majority**: These are among the most risk-averse and conservative people, who wait until the momentum for change is so great that the new approach is the way of doing things.

- **Laggards**: These people don't like change at all, may not be well informed, or may simply lack the resources to make the change. Therefore, they are the last to make changes.

While the innovators and early adopters lead the change, the change sticks within the organization when the early majority, late majority, and laggards see that the benefits outweigh the risks and accept the new way of doing business.

So, by now, you are probably wondering how to kick off a new Lean change initiative. The answer is that it's not so much a process as it is a checklist of potential change support actions, as described in the following list:

- Communicate reasons and intent every step of the way.

- Understand that those closest to the work often have good ideas of what needs to be fixed, why, and how.

- Address any personnel issues or inappropriate behaviors immediately.

- Reward and recognize the people supporting the VSM initiative.

- Resolve impediments and issues – and don't let them stop you.

- Don't be afraid to experiment to discover improved operating models.

- Executive sponsors and the VSM team need to be accessible, flexible, and willing to listen to input from value stream operators and stakeholders, while also staying focused on the Lean improvement goals.

- When making incremental changes, the positive effects are accumulative.

- Remember, we are in this for the long haul.

Now that you have a strategy to deal with the human aspects of change, let's break down the implementation strategy.

Guiding Lean business transformations

As noted in the introduction to this chapter, Lean is about making large-scale business transformations to improve value delivery, and then continuing to make improvements across entire value streams across the organization's lifetime. Technically, there are three phases for coordinating the work when making Lean business transformations: **preparation**, **implementation**, and **follow-up**.

We addressed the issues of preparation in the previous section on Kaizen planning. Implementation is *where the rubber meets the road,* and it's time to make changes. Following this, it should make sense that the VSM team needs to follow up to ensure that the changes stick. Moreover, the VSM team also needs to ensure that the value stream achieves the goals and metrics that justify Lean improvement investments.

Remember that Lean continuous improvement efforts are distinctive from Agile-based continuous improvement activities. Lean focuses on long-term planning and investments that make the organization tough to beat in competitive markets. On the other hand, Agile-based Retrospectives tend to be localized, relatively small, typically don't involve investments, and are implemented across very short iterations.

With its Lean improvement orientation, the objective of VSM is to eliminate all forms of waste. The goal is to help the VSM team build value streams that are efficient, responsive, and value-added from the customer's perspective. However, leveraging Pareto's principle, we know that each improvement simply elevates other issues to the top of the list. Each new Lean improvement moves the value stream in the direction of providing exceptional service to its customers.

VSM initiatives are big-picture improvement activities that are implemented incrementally and continuously. The VSM team uses their storyboard to guide their activities and explain to other stakeholders how the structured value stream management process improves value delivery.

Decomposing Lean improvement work

Through each of the three future state phases of demand, continuous flow, and leveling improvements, the VSM team focuses on making the improvements that were identified in the Kaizen Bursts. The improvement activities within each Kaizen Burst can be relatively small or very large initiatives, with multiple tasks and potentially involving significant investments.

The purpose of breaking down the work involved in each Kaizen improvement activity as events is to fully expose the necessary work and get all relevant stakeholders involved in the assessment. The VSM team may choose to employ the *User Story* format, as described in the Kanban Board section in the Leveling Phase, to express each Kaizen event's goals and objectives. These Kaizen events can be likened to work items in a Product backlog.

In fact, in an IT value stream, the Kaizen events can be included in a product backlog as the improvement work likely involves the value stream's operators' efforts. It's also possible to use a Kanban Board to manage and display the flow of work on the larger VSM initiatives across Kaizen Bursts and events.

Whichever method you choose for managing Kaizen events, there is additional information that the VSM team must gather and communicate. To do so, apply the following steps:

1. Identify the objectives of the Kaizen event and communicate them.
2. Identify the roles and responsibilities of the people who have been assigned to support the Kaizen events.
3. Define the scope of the team's efforts; that is, perhaps via a story or in Epic format.
4. Identify any training or information needs to support the Kaizen event.
5. Display the Kaizen event's projected start and completion dates on the Detailed Monthly Kaizen Schedule Plan as Milestones.
6. Identify potential risks and issues, and form mitigation strategies and contingency plans as appropriate.
7. Plan and coordinate the work necessary to complete the Kaizen event.
8. Seek executive-level support and approvals if additional investments or resources are required than what was initially conceived.
9. Update the VSM team charter if any new team members are required to support the effort.

Again, some Kaizen events are simpler to plan and execute than others. So, do just enough preparation and planning work to get things moving in the right direction. But also know that your understanding of what needs to be done improves over time through trial and error.

In the longer run, the VSM team needs to be prepared to revisit their value stream maps' currency and update them accordingly. The Gemba walks never stop. Value stream improvements never stop. Each Kaizen event requires a total VSM team and executive-level commitment to the initiative from start to finish. Otherwise, the work will lag and may not be completed.

This section completes our discussion on implementing our Kaizen plans to install Lean improvements across a value stream. But before we leave the topic of Kaizen, let's spend a few moments discussing why VSM initiatives require executive approvals as portfolio-level investments.

Managing VSM initiatives as portfolio-level investments

The VSM team and its sponsoring executives need to be patient in their efforts. VSM initiatives involve large-scale business transformations to implement Lean product and information flows. The business transformation to Lean may require months or even years to complete. The objective is to give the VSM team the time and resources to work their way through at least one VSM iteration across all three phases of the future state improvement activities (that is, demand, continuous flow, and leveling).

Once a VSM future-state value delivery improvement cycle completes, it may make sense for the VSM team to move on and support Lean improvement efforts in another value stream. The organization's executives must continuously support efforts to evaluate Lean improvement opportunities across the enterprise and align investment priorities as part of their portfolio planning activities. Larger organizations may have multiple VSM initiatives ongoing at any given time.

All VSM initiatives cost money, take time and resources, and require investments. Without sufficient frontend analysis, the organization's executives can't know how best to deploy their scarce resources for maximum gain. This issue is why modern Lean-Agile practices, such as **Disciplined Agile** and the **Scaled-Agile Framework®** (**SAFe®**), implement rigorous portfolio analysis techniques in their toolkits and methodologies.

Since they lack a Lean-Agile framework, the VSM team must align their activities with the organization's Portfolio Management priorities and seek investments through the Portfolio management process. Lacking a formalized portfolio management process, the VSM team must work with their executives to establish a formal mechanism to review the team's Lean investment strategies and priorities. Without such approvals, there is no practical way forward to implement the identified Lean improvements.

As with the other sections related to the eight VSM steps, we'll conclude our discussion of Kaizen with a subsection that summarizes the tools used to support the Kaizen implementation activities.

Leveraging the tools of Kaizen

If your VSM team is sticking with a manual system, the Kaizen implementation tools are the same as those used in the Kaizen planning and value stream mapping phases. The difference is that now, the tools serve as aids to implement the change processes. The VS methods and tools you've learned about can be used to improve Lean practices across development- and operations-oriented value streams.

The tools that support your Kaizen planning and implementation activities include the following:

- VSM Storyboard
- Current and future state value stream maps
- Monthly Kaizen Schedule Plan
- Chart of VSM Objectives and Measurables
- Detailed Monthly Kaizen Schedule Plan

With what you have learned in *Chapter 6, Launching the VSM Initiative (VSM Steps 1-3)*, through *Chapter 10, Improving the Lean-Agile Value Delivery Cycle(VSM Steps 7 and 8)*, you have the practical knowledge to initiate and conduct a VSM initiative to implement Lean improvements across a value stream. In the remainder of *Section 2* of this book, on *Implementing Value Stream Management (VSM) Methods and Tools*, we will turn our attention to understanding how modern VSM tools support CI/CD and DevOps pipeline development and improvement activities. Before we get to the remaining chapters, let's quickly review the VSM methodology.

Reviewing the VSM methodology

Throughout *Chapter 4, Defining Value Stream Management*, and *Chapter 6, Launching the VSM Initiative (VSM Steps 1-3)*, this book introduced value stream management by applying an eight-step process that collectively defines a proven VSM through a generic methodology. For example, this eight-step VSM methodology has proven to work in manufacturing, office administration, supply chains, and health care applications and industries.

The eight steps are as follows:

1. Commit to Lean

2. Choose the value stream

3. Learn about Lean

4. Map the current state

5. Identify Lean metrics

6. Map the future state

7. Create Kaizen plans

8. Implement Kaizen plans

This eight-step VSM methodology works in IT-oriented value streams too, as shown in the CI/CD pipeline use case provided throughout this part of this book. The IT-oriented VSM use case is purposely limited in complexity to focus on learning the VSM methodology. But the choice to use an IT-oriented use case was not by accident, as modern value stream management tools support implementing Lean practices across IT-oriented value streams.

Still, it does not make sense to employ multiple VSM methodologies across an organization when one will do. Each VSM team should feel free to modify the baseline VSM/Lean improvement strategy to improve its effectiveness in their unique environments. Moreover, in a digital economy, every VSM initiative across an enterprise likely requires support from the organization's IT department somehow.

In the previous chapters, a comment was made that DevOps capabilities are the "table stakes" necessary to compete in our modern digital economy. As a result, most modern VSM tools support the implementation, integration, and improvement of DevOps capabilities. But those same tool vendors note that VSM with DevOps also supports the organization's Lean improvement objectives. Thus, DevOps is a crucial enabler for adding value to whatever products and services the organization produces.

Summary

This chapter discussed the importance of continuously improving our value stream work and information flow capabilities. You learned that VSM and Agile share this principle, but their timelines and scope of effort are different. For example, Agile teams use Retrospectives to evaluate relatively small-scale improvements they can make over the next Sprint.

In contrast, VSM teams focus their efforts on more significant and Lean-oriented improvement initiatives that span lengthier timeframes and require larger investments. In addition, Agile teams' continuous improvements typically do not require executive management-level approval; VSM team improvement recommendations nearly always do.

Continuing with our eight-step VSM methodology, you learned how to create a Kaizen plan (VSM step seven) and implement the Kaizen plan (VSM step eight). You also learned how to develop and use several tools to plan and implement your Kaizen plans, such as the Monthly Kaizen Schedule Plan, the Chart of VSM Objectives and Measurables, and the Detailed Monthly Kaizen Schedule Plan.

In the next chapter, you will learn how VSM tools support Lean improvements being made across DevOps pipelines by providing real-time access to critical IT value stream data, dashboard-based visualizations, and metrics. VSM tools help DevOps team members and other stakeholders monitor and improve the flow of information and work across IT value streams and focus on customers.

Questions

1. What does the Japanese term Kaizen translate into in English?
2. What makes implementing DevOps capabilities an ideal project for authorizing an executive-level sponsored and authorized VSM initiative?
3. What is the purpose of the Monthly Kaizen Schedule Plan?
4. What is the purpose of the Chart of VSM Objectives and Measurables?
5. What is the purpose of the Detailed Monthly Kaizen Schedule Plan?
6. Future state improvement plans and activities involve what three phases?
7. What happens when the project-based work of a VSM initiative transfers to the Agile team?
8. Given the scope of change involved in a VSM initiative, what life cycle model best represents how the organization will evolve to adopt the new Lean principles?
9. Why are VSM initiatives treated as portfolio-level investment decisions?
10. What two scheduling and visualization methods are appropriate for managing work associated with Kaizen Bursts?

Further reading

- Poppendieck, M, Poppendieck, T. (May 2003) *Lean Software Development: An Agile Toolkit*. Addison-Wesley. Boston, MA.

- Tapping, D., Luyster, T., Shuker, T. (2002) *Value Stream Management. Eight Steps to Planning, Mapping, and Sustaining Lean Improvements*. Productivity Press. New York, NY

- Tapping, D., Luyster, T., Shuker, T. (2003) *Value Stream Management for the Lean Office. Eight Steps to Planning, Mapping, and Sustaining Lean Improvements*. Productivity Press. New York, NY

- Tapping, D., Kozlowski, S., Archbold, L., Sperl, T. (2009) *Value Stream Management for Lean Healthcare. Four steps to Planning, Mapping, Implementing, and Controlling Improvements in all Types of Healthcare Environments*. MCS Media, Inc. Chelsea, MI.

Section 3: VSM Tool Vendors and Frameworks

This section introduces you to modern VSM tool capabilities, VSM tool vendors, and the leading VSM methodologists or thought leaders. Starting with *Chapter 11, Identifying VSM Tool Types and Capabilities*, you will learn about the capabilities of modern VSM tools. Specifically, you will learn about the three primary categories of VSM tools, as defined by Gartner, including DevOps value stream management platforms (VSMPs), value stream delivery platforms (VSDPs), and continuous compliance automation (CCA) tools.

Then, in *Chapter 12, Introducing the Leading VSM Tool Vendors*, you will learn about the offerings from 15 VSM tool vendors spanning all three categories. Rather than regurgitating information available from other industry analysts, I invited a total of 24 vendors to tell me how they have positioned their products in the VSM tools industry and what they believe are their competitive strengths. The 15 VSM tool vendors identified in this chapter agreed to interviews and to showcase their capabilities.

Chapter 13, Introducing the VSM-DevOps Practice Leaders, introduces you to the VSM Consortium, The Project Management Institute's Disciplined Agile (DA), and Scaled Agile, Inc.'s Scaled Agile Framework® as the biggest thought leaders and providers of VSM methodologies applied to modern IT practices to improve CI/CD and DevOps pipeline flows. They are also the leaders in modern thought on the application of Lean-Agile practices to digital business transformation. Similar to the approach taken with the VSM tool vendors, each of these organizations worked with me directly to showcase their methodologies and activities related to value stream management.

Finally, *Chapter 14, Introducing the Enterprise Lean-VSM Practice Leaders*, introduces the original thought leaders behind value streams – the Lean Enterprise Institute (LEI) and LeanFITT™. Along with the Lean Enterprise Academy, these two organizations have been some of the leading researchers and thought leaders behind modern Lean and VSM practices.

For example, in 1994, in a Harvard Business Review (HBR) article titled *From Lean Production to the Lean Enterprise*, the founder of the LEI, James Womack, along with his collaborator Daniel T. Jones (founder and chairman of the *Lean Enterprise Academy*), coined the term *value streams*. In addition, Don Tapping, Todd Sperl, and their collaborators at LeanFITT have co-written more than 50 books on Lean practices, including some of the original works on the concepts behind VSM as a general methodology for implementing Lean production improvements.

This section includes the following four chapters:

- *Chapter 11, Identifying VSM Tool Types and Capabilities*
- *Chapter 12, Introducing the Leading VSM Tool Vendors*
- *Chapter 13, Introducing the VSM-DevOps Practice Leaders*
- *Chapter 14, Introducing the Enterprise Lean-VSM Practice Leaders*

11
Identifying VSM Tool Types and Capabilities

In *Predicts 2021: Value Streams Will Define the Future of DevOps Report* (published October 5, 2020), Gartner states that "By 2023, 70% of organizations will use value stream management to improve flow in the DevOps pipeline, leading to faster delivery of customer value." (`https://www.gartner.com/`) Clearly, Gartner believes that VSM, as an IT improvement strategy, is rapidly becoming mainstream.

As you can see from the preceding Gartner quote, VSM tools are rapidly gaining traction in the IT industry. But it would be a mistake to start implementing the tools before understanding the larger objectives of VSM, as well as how to implement a VSM activity across a value stream. The problem is that the data and metrics that VSM tools provide have little practical use unless we first understand Lean value stream improvements' goals and principles. That is why you spent the first four chapters learning how to apply a generic VSM methodology.

Now that you understand the goals, metrics, and activities associated with value stream management, we must look at the tools that support our ongoing VSM activities. This chapter will provide instructions on how to use the primary types of VSM tools in the market today. You will also learn about the different capabilities available in modern VSM tools.

In this chapter, we're going to cover the following topics:

- Leveraging VSM tools and platforms
- Enabling VSM tool capabilities
- Highlighting important VSMP/VSM tool capabilities
- Key issues addressed by VSM tools
- VSM tool implementation issues
- Enabling business transformations
- VSM tool benefits

Leveraging VSM tools and platforms

This section will introduce the types of tools and capabilities available in modern VSM tools. You will also find that the VSM tool industry promotes its ability to help implement Lean improvements to IT value streams. But the information that's available via these VSM tools can also support Lean improvement activities across all organizational value streams via their digital touchpoints.

VSM tools help implement and improve Lean practices across DevOps pipelines by providing real-time access to critical IT value stream data, dashboard-based visualizations, and metrics. This information helps DevOps team members and other stakeholders monitor and improve information flow and work across the IT value streams. Moreover, VSM tools provide information and analytics that help keep the IT value streams' focus on adding value to their customers.

In this chapter, you are going to learn the capabilities provided by VSM tools. But before that, we will start with an introductory discussion about the types of DevOps tools and processes that support the IT value stream's customer delivery capabilities.

In the same article mentioned in this chapter's introduction, Gartner outlines three types of supporting DevOps tools that transform the IT value stream's ability to deliver customer value rapidly and reliably. These tools and processes include the following:

- **DevOps value stream management platforms** (**VSMPs**): provide out-of-the-box connectors to integrate disparate DevOps toolchains and facilitate the orchestration of IT activities across the planning, releasing, building, and monitoring activities. VSMPs help to improve velocity, quality, and customer value by providing visibility and analytics across the IT value stream. When you look up **value stream management** (**VSM**) tools in a modern context, these are the types of tools you will typically find.

- **Value stream delivery platforms** (**VSDPs**): Provides integrated toolchains as out-of-the-box solutions, usually available as cloud-based CI/CD or DevOps platforms. VSDPs also include tools to support the visibility, traceability, auditability, and observability of activities across the software delivery value stream. These capabilities extend well beyond the traditional DevOps platform capabilities. In this sense, VSDPs combine the capabilities of the DevOps platforms with VSM tool capabilities. And you will find both DevOps platform vendors and VSM tool vendors merging into this shared space.

- **Continuous compliance automation** (**CCA**) **tools**: These help automate and expedite compliance and security-related tasks, replacing manual checklists, policies, and worksheets. Moreover, these tools provide visibility to potential issues early in the SDLC cycle, when corrections are easier to make and less costly. CCA tools should not operate in a vacuum, apart from the organization's CI/CD, DevOps, and VSM platforms and tools. It's better to have them integrated as part of the automated test capabilities with integrated VSM tools, as this helps support real-time monitoring, visibility of compliance, and security test results.

Gartner also identifies two critical processes, **Chaos engineering** and **IT resiliency roles**, that can help optimize IT value stream flows. Later in this book, we'll discuss the importance of incident management and service restoration. These are after-the-fact problem resolution tactics. Chaos engineering further identifies preventative measures the IT department can take to deliver high reliability in complex environments.

Similar to the preceding discussion, **disaster recovery** (**DR**) is also an after-the-fact problem resolution effort to bring a failed system back online. *IT resiliency roles* is an approach to linking DR teams and product teams as a preventative measure to deliver better resilience across the DevOps value stream.

Enabling VSM tool capabilities

A good strategy for any product owner is to assess customer requirements regarding their customers' capabilities. In other words, what do our customers expect our products to deliver to them in the way of capabilities that solve some issue or need they may have? Providing capabilities that address customer issues or needs is how we provide value. In this context, product features and functions deliver value through the capabilities they offer.

By definition, the word **capability** connotes an ability or the authority to do something. In software development, requirements analysis defines areas where our customers can't do or achieve something desirable. The objective is to create software products that deliver those capabilities.

But it's a mistake to think the word *capabilities* only refers to delivering some set of features or functionality. Instead, customers purchase things, such as software, to fulfill basic human needs, such as improving the following:

- Performance or productivity
- Health and wellbeing
- Economics or finances
- Personal image

VSM tools are no different. VSM tools need to add value to users to support their organization's IT value stream improvement initiatives. Yes, productivity and performance improvements are at the heart of making Lean production improvements. But those improvements also improve the health and wellbeing of the organization and potentially its customers. And a successful VSM initiative can improve the organization's economics.

But don't belittle the last area of concern: *image*. Large purchases and investments in VSM and DevOps tools and platforms can have an enormous emotional impact on executive and stakeholder decision making and buy-in. The same concerns are valid for employees when executives make wholesale changes to organizational structures and work activities. In the end, the most powerful motivator to make the investments and structural changes might just come down to improving the organization's image as an industry leader.

But I've digressed. So, let's move on and understand the capabilities that are delivered by modern VSM tools and why those capabilities matter.

Having read through the first four chapters of this book on applying a generic VSM methodology, you may have already guessed that a VSM tool should support VSM processes, including mapping, metrics, and analytics. If you added integration, automation, and orchestration to your guess, then you are even closer to understanding the expanded value of modern VSM tools.

In the *Identifying VSM tool capabilities* section we will introduce many of the leading VSM vendors. One of the vendors we will introduce, **ConnectAll**, promotes a view that a tool-agnostic VSM solution must implement the following six critical features:

- IT and business alignment
- Actionable and relevant data
- Data-driven, outcome-focused analytics
- Dynamic value stream visualization
- Workflow orchestration
- IT governance

This list is good to start with, so let's take a few minutes to understand what capabilities these features provide. In other words, before you read on, it will help if you replace the word *features* with the word *capabilities* as you read through each item.

IT and business alignment

In our modern digital economy, the IT function supports nearly every aspect of the business. For example, organizations may offer IT solutions as standalone products or integrated with physical products to provide enhanced features and functionality. But IT solutions also improve the productivity of other development- and operations-oriented value streams.

For these reasons, VSM must serve a greater purpose than simply improving CI/CD and DevOps pipeline flows. These improvements must also support the strategies, goals, and mission of the business as a whole. What this means is that your value streams are not limited to software development. Instead, software value streams extend into the business, supporting all organizational value streams.

In this context, a VSM solution must help the organization align its IT functions with the business by providing the following capabilities:

- Implementing real-time metrics to support Lean value stream improvements

- Implementing and visualizing **key performance indicators** (**KPIs**) across development- and operations-oriented value streams to improve speed and quality of delivery

- Providing end-to-end visibility of key metrics and outcomes across all portfolio investments

Having access to real-time data is a game-changer in VSM. However, it's of little value if it's not actionable and relevant to improving your ability to deliver value.

Actionable and relevant data

VSM is a continuous improvement activity from the perspective of Lean across our value delivery streams. VSM tools should provide metrics for measuring the performance of your value stream activities in terms of desired outcomes.

CI/CD and DevOps pipelines involve integrating, automating, and orchestrating work item flows across complex toolchains. Equally as important is the real-time flow of data across the tools that support work being orchestrated across your system's development and life cycle support processes.

As with the manual VSM processes defined in *Chapter 6, Launching the VSM initiative (VSM Steps 1–3)* through *Chapter 10, Improving the Lean-Agile Value Delivery Cycle (VSM Steps 7 and 8),* VSM tools help the organization identify waste in the form of bottlenecks and waiting caused by inefficient and unmatched flows. But software development also has much more variability in terms of product requirements than typical mass-production lines. For that reason, we also need information that helps us identify delays caused by orphaned software (*abandonware*), inaccurately defined configurations, ill-defined requirements, and unnecessary testing that is not value-added.

Moreover, as part of future state modeling, it's essential to have the ability to replace current state metrics with desired variables for *what if* testing. In effect, we can use VSM tools to simulate future state operations using the current state maps, metrics, and flows as a baseline for experimentation.

Data-driven, outcome-focused analytics

A VSM team's assessment of value stream performance is only as good as the metrics that drive it. In *Chapter 8, Identifying Lean Metrics (VSM Step 5)*, you learned which metrics help support Lean-oriented production improvements. You also learned that an excellent way to get these metrics is through Gemba Walks and meeting with value stream operators.

But what if you had access to real-time data that directly maps to the value stream metrics your VSM team defines as being critical to monitoring, as well as improving value delivery and production performance? That is the promise of modern VSM tools.

Of course, we need to do our homework first to define our current state flows, waste, and metrics. That's a human activity that VSM tools cannot eliminate.

Recall from our discussions on value stream mapping that we always start our assessments downstream with deliveries to our customers; then, we work our way upstream to assess how we deliver value. In other words, we start our analysis with customer requirements describing the desired value delivery outcomes and then work our way backward through the value stream activities – this helps us see for ourselves how or whether they contribute value from our customers' perspectives.

Therefore, before we can leverage data delivered by VSM tools, we need to visualize the value stream work and information flows, and areas of waste. As a quick review of *Chapter 7, Mapping the Current State (VSM Step 4)*, let's summarize the current state mapping process, as that effort forms the baseline for our future state improvement analysis:

1. Identify the customer (internal or external requirements; do the same for any partner relationships).
2. Draw the entry and exit points for the value stream.
3. Draw all processes between the entry and exit points, starting with the most downstream activities and working your way upstream to the initial order/backlog entry points.
4. Identify and define all activity attributes (information, materials, and constraints associated with each activity).
5. Draw queues between the activities and include wait time metrics.
6. Draw all communications links as information flows occurring within the value stream.
7. Draw the production control strategies in place at each value stream activity – primarily documenting push versus pull-oriented work and information flows.
8. Complete the map with any other data that helps refine our understanding of the work and exceptions to the standard processes.

It should be apparent that the entire VS mapping exercise requires human actions to complete the map until step eight. But it's not the map that's the most important – it's the exercise of going out to see how things work that drives the real insights for improvements. The integration and analytical capabilities of modern VSM tools give us access to real-time data on demand, which we need to ensure our findings and analysis are accurate.

The integration and automation capabilities of CI/CD and DevOps toolchains hide a lot of the activity details and metrics. VSM tools help make those activities and metrics visible and immediately available whenever needed. In addition, monitors and triggers can immediately point out anomalies (metrics outside the desired performance metrics) that need to be addressed.

That's not to say the Gemba walks of traditional VSMs are not a helpful concept. In a modern, agile-based software shop, team members frequently meet to assess opportunities for improvement. More importantly, all software requirements and production data are made readily and visibly available to managers, executives, and other stakeholders at any time. Modern VSM tools make the visibility of product production and delivery data more accurate, accessible, and readily available.

As organizations make their way through a digital transformation, value streams become data-driven, and VSM tools hold the key to unlocking that data. For example, once connected, the VSM tools provide accurate data on key performance metrics, such as process times, cycle times, lead times, flow times, wait times, value-added times, **mean time to repair** (**MTTR**), escaped defect ratios, WIP, blocker data, queues, throughput, and production impacts.

VSM tools can provide the data and analytical tools to help teams assess product issues and risks, including missed release dates, substandard NPS scores, untapped capacity, and inadequate test coverage. These analytics help decision makers evaluate alternatives for cost reduction, competitive positioning, and product fit in the marketplace.

In short, VSMs capture data, while analytical tools help the organization assess value stream performance and make better decisions to achieve their desired outcomes. Those outcomes must map back to the business's goals and objectives and the desired outcomes of the organization's customers. After all, revenues and profitability depend on our ability to deliver value to our customers.

VSM provides capabilities to access real-time data on-demand, plus analytical tools, and they also help make the data and analytics visible.

Dynamic value stream visualization

Having access to real-time data with powerful analytical tools is a critical capability provided by modern VSM tools. But, consistent with Agile practices, we also need to make sure the data is highly visible, assessable, and consumable by those who need it. VSM tools provide dashboards with distributed access via a secure network or internet-based connections to support visibility needs.

The VSM tools and platforms provide visualizations across all connected product value streams, with metrics and visual aids showing cross-stream integrations, relationships, and orchestrations. In large product development environments with multiple teams, the VSM tools provide end-to-end visibility of every work item and how they flow across value streams. The VSM tools provide information that the independent feature teams or larger requirement areas need to discover and help address dependency, integration, and synchronization issues.

While VSM tools provide access dynamically to real-time data, they also provide access to historical data across your value streams. The importance of this is that historical data allows us to diagnose issues to determine how, when, and why they evolved. And, of course, their *what if* capabilities allow us to explore alternative solutions before making investments in time, resources, and money.

Many VSM tools started as toolchain integration and automation platforms. In other words, CI/CD and DevOps pipelines evolved to integrate toolchains and automate activities across the traditional **software development life cycle** (**SDLC**) processes. But it wasn't long before the software industry understood that toolchain integration and automation are only one part of Lean-oriented IT value stream improvement activity. We also need orchestration.

Workflow orchestration

CI/CD and DevOps pipelines operate most efficiently by integrating toolchains, automating SDLC and potentially ITSM processes, and orchestrating work and information flows. Larger software products with work distribution across multiple product teams create a more complex environment. The teams must deal with integration, coordination, and synchronization issues to ensure the component work items function correctly within the more extensive integrated system.

Many VSM platforms support the collaboration of multiple development teams who must orchestrate and coordinate their work. The extension of VSM capabilities came about due to their historical underpinnings as integration platforms and their support for CI/CD requirements. Examples of orchestration capabilities include automatic triggers for builds, automated tests, and deployments.

Automating triggers assumes the development teams have employed their configurations as code. There are two types of generally accepted code-based configurations: **Configuration as Code (CaC)** and **Infrastructure as Code (IaC)**.

CaC involves developing configuration files, managed within a source code repository, to specify how your software applications need to be configured to work on different platforms or computing environments. CaC supports the versioning of application configurations, traceability of each software configuration version deployed across various environments, and the capability to deploy new software configurations without redeploying the application.

IaC supports automatically provisioning resources in computer data centers via machine-readable definition files, thus eliminating manual processes and interventions to reconfigure computing equipment. Data center operators must manually configure servers, networks, security systems, and backup systems in a traditional environment before each software deployment. This approach is a tedious, expensive, and labor-intensive process, spanning multiple skills. The configurations must be exact and consistent to ensure proper monitoring and visibility of their performance. As a result, many things can go wrong, adding more delays and costs of deployment. IaC helps avoid all those issues.

As an orchestration platform, VSM tools can centralize builds, CI/CD tests, and releases/deployments. The cross-functional nature of DevOps and its supporting VSM platforms improves collaboration between Development, Quality, and Operations teams. Finally, VSM dashboards provide data and analytical tools to provide insights into how configuration and process changes can impact future releases.

Another critical issue in IT is implementing effective controls over IT governance policies and compliance requirements, which we'll discuss in the following subsection.

IT governance

CIOs and other IT executives have fiduciary responsibilities to manage and protect the organization's IT assets and investments. There are also financial, regulatory, and legal requirements that must be followed to help us avoid legal and financial risks. As a direct result, IT organizations require some control over the teams that develop and support the organization's computing systems, networks, security systems, and software applications.

To support compliance requirements, IT organizations often implement IT frameworks such as ITIL, CMMI, COBIT, HIPAA, INFOSEC, and ISO 27001. There are many other IT frameworks available. Most of these frameworks are rich in policies and procedures but lacking in enforcement capabilities and details.

While it's easy enough to write documentation to specify standards, policies, and procedural requirements, it's much more challenging to provide oversight to ensure everyone is following the guidance. Fortunately, IT governance is another area where VSM vendors have stepped in to provide automation support for governing the organization's IT policies, compliance requirements, and standards.

Modern VSM tools can orchestrate the processes associated with governing IT capabilities by supporting the aforementioned IT frameworks. In this capacity, the VSM tools offer centralized governance over the flow of work across an entire product value stream. The data and metrics offered by VSM platforms help provide visibility to the IT value stream pipeline, as well as product quality objectives and compliance requirements. The information that's available also provides evidence-based data to support tool investment decisions, staffing requirements, and productivity goals.

This subsection completes our discussion of general VSM tool capabilities. In the next section, we will learn about the common types of VSM tools available and how they support IT value stream production and delivery improvement capabilities.

Highlighting important VSMP/VSM tool capabilities

This section will introduce the fundamental capabilities provided by modern VSMP/VSM tools. This is a class of tools that focus on supporting VSM activities in a DevOps environment. More precisely, VSMP/VSM tools gather information across the DevOps-oriented Value stream and offer visualizations as a VSM dashboard for supporting digital transformations to Lean-oriented practices.

VSMP/VSM tools typically include the following types of VSM support capabilities in a DevOps environment:

- **DevOps value stream mapping**: End-to-end mapping of the current and future state IT value stream work and information flow.

- **DevOps workflow metrics**: This helps measure the rate of value delivery, including the four critical DevOps measures of *deployment frequency*, *mean lead time for changes*, *mean time to restore*, and *change failure rates*.

- **DevOps analytics**: This includes tools for evaluating the current state of the DevOps toolchain and processing its capabilities against future state recommendations. Analytics can include recording and analyzing lead time and cycle time measurements spanning the following DevOps value stream activities:

  i. Issue resolution

  ii. From planning new features to the first code commits

  iii. Feature branch creation to merge requests

  iv. Executing automated tests

  v. Performing code reviews

  vi. Configuring, provisioning, and orchestrating dev, test, and staging environments

  vii. Deploying to production

  viii. Enabling application and feature rollbacks and service restorations

- **DevOps orchestration**: This helps eliminate waste in DevOps value streams by coordinating and synchronizing work items and data flows across the DevOps toolchain.

- **DevOps workflow optimization**: This supports leveling work flowing across integrated and automated DevOps toolchains and pipelines.

- **DevOps information flow visualization**: This offers data and information outputs in the form of reports and dashboard visualizations with near real-time relevancy.

- **DevOps flow metrics**: This helps teams analyze the performance of the DevOps pipeline in terms of cycle times, lead times, and wait times.

Analytic tools help the IT organization assess the speed of developing a "*Done*" feature or function from ideation through deployment, the throughput of new features and functions over time (also known as *velocity*), the time spent on improving business value across categories of work (that is, *features*, *defects*, *risks*, and *technical debt*), the amount of **work in progress** (**WIP**), and time spent on value-added work versus waiting.

- **DevOps data cleaning**: This provides tools for discovering and correcting or removing corrupted, incorrect, or incomplete data records, tables, or databases that support the DevOps toolchain.

Many VSM tools offer a value stream data model and data store that normalizes data across activities, as well as data inputs from the disparate yet integrated CI/CD and DevOps toolchains. Normalization is the process of organizing data in a database to eliminate redundancy and inconsistent relationships and dependencies. A single VSM data source with normalization enables end-to-end data analysis across value streams and each product's life cycle.

- **What if analysis**: Available from analytical tools, this helps the DevOps or VSM team evaluate the impact of changing the DevOps value stream processes and metrics, without directly affecting the value stream pipeline processes and activities or their work and information flows. In effect, the current state metrics and activity flows captured by the VSM tools form a baseline to conduct *what if* analysis on future state improvement concepts.

- **DevOps tool integration**: This includes **application programming interfaces (APIs)**, adapters, and the connectors necessary to integrate DevOps toolchains with the VSM tools to integrate CI/CD and DevOps toolchains, automate activities, and orchestrate work and information flows.

Let's now take a quick look at the vendor offerings that have currently been identified in each of these three categories of tools.

Classifying VSMP/VSM tool vendors

DevOps VSMPs provide data and tools to monitor and assess strategic metrics such as release velocity and DevOps operational efficiencies. While **Gartner** refers to these tools as VSMPs, **Forester** refers to them as **value stream management (VSM)** tools.

VSMP and VSM tools serve as an integration, automation, and orchestration platform for third-party DevOps tools, of which there are many to choose. For example, **Digital.ai** provides a comprehensive list of DevOps tools within its **2020 Periodic Table of DevOps Tools**, which contains a subset of 400 products across 17 categories.

Current tool offerings that fit into the VSMP/VSM category include **ConnectAll**, **Digital.ai**, **Plutora**, **CloudBees Value Stream Management**, and **Tasktop Viz**.

Classifying VSDP tool vendors

The critical differentiator between VSDPs, compared to the previously identified VSMP and VSM tools, is whether they provision DevOps tools directly within their VSDP platforms. In some cases, the VSDP vendors may provide many DevOps tools as *out-of-the-box* solutions to eliminate pipeline integration tasks. In other cases, the integrated DevOps tools may come from third-party vendors, but the integration and automation work has already been done.

DevOps **value stream delivery platforms** (**VSDPs**) help orchestrate DevOps toolchains to integrate and automate SDLC processes associated with building, delivering, and deploying software. Since the VSDP platforms control the tools, they can create a central data store with normalized data that provides visibility and analytical capabilities across all pipeline activities from end to end.

We will look at the capabilities of modern VSDP tools in more detail in the next chapter. But for now, as a quick introduction, we will state that VSDPs support a myriad of SDLC and ITSM processes, including the following:

• Product planning	• Continuous deployment
• Build automation	• Application or feature rollback
• Continuous integration	• Release orchestration
• Test automation	• Automated security policy enforcement
• Continuous delivery	• Value stream metrics

Current VSM offerings that fit into the VSDP category include **ServiceNow**, **GitLab**, **HCL Accelerate**, **IBM UrbanCode Velocity**, **Jira Align**, and **ZenHub**.

VSMP, VSM, and VSDP have similar purposes and functionality. The critical difference is the degree to which the vendor provides a complete DevOps/VSM solution or provides a platform to integrate DevOps tools of your choosing. But for now, we will take a quick look at CCA tools that have a different but equally important role in improving business performance.

Classifying CCA tool vendors

CCA tools are also known as **governance, risk, and compliance** (**GRC**) platforms. These tools implement a capability to manage an organization's overall governance policies, enterprise risk management assessments, and compliance with laws and regulations. The objective of GRC is to align IT with the organization's business objectives while managing risks and meeting compliance requirements.

CCA tools/GRC platforms help improve decision making regarding IT alignment with business strategies and product line objectives. They help improve IT investments' prioritization by ensuring sufficient attention is paid to corporate compliance, risk management, and compliance issues. CCA tools/GRC platforms also help the IT department take an enterprise view to support corporate policies, managing risks, and regulatory compliance.

Finally, a critical element of CCA tools/GRC platform capabilities is to make IT systems and data secure. They do not replace the security software in use to protect applications and web-based services. Instead, they help ensure continued enforcement of policies, regulatory compliance, and the risk management assessments that are necessary to keep IT systems and data secure.

Rather than reinvent good practices, GRC platforms and tools often implement an underlying foundation of processes and policies from an industry-specified framework. Therefore, the CCA tools/GRC platform may implement a specific compliance framework such as **COBIT**, a risk management framework such as **COSO**, or an ITSM framework such as **ITIL**.

TrustRadius, a trusted review site for business technology, cites the following as examples of current GRC platforms (https://www.trustradius.com/):

• BusinessObjects GRC	• SAS Governance and Compliance Manager (Enterprise GRC)
• HighBond by Galvanize	• SAP Risk Management
• Invantive Control for Excel	• SAP Process Control
• Mitratech PolicyHub	• ServiceNow Governance, Risk, and Compliance
• RSA Archer	• Wdesk

So far, we have evaluated the types and capabilities of VSM tools and platforms. You learned about three basic categories of tools or platforms that support transforming IT value streams into Lean DevOps pipeline environments. Then, we took a deeper dive into the capabilities offered by modern VSM tools that support digital transformations via DevOps-oriented IT value streams. We will hold off on assessing the capabilities of VSDPs and CCA tools until the next chapter, where we will look at driving business value through a DevOps pipeline. Now, let's look at some of the critical issues addressed by implementing VSM tools and platforms.

Key issues addressed by VSM tools

In our digital economy, software products enable value delivery in three forms. First, the software is often sold as a standalone product. Second, the software supports other organizational value streams such as those discussed in *Chapter 4, Defining Value Stream Management*, including those discussed in the *Identifying value streams* section. Third, VSMs can help improve software delivery velocity across CI/CD and DevOps pipeline flows, from concept ideations through to delivery and support.

Throughout this book, you have learned that the enablers of software delivery include *collaboration, integration, automation*, and *orchestration*. But you've also learned that the velocity of software deliveries must support the flows and delivery of other organizational value streams. Therefore, the velocity of software development must be synched with the demands driven by the other organizational value streams that rely upon it.

True, software delivery value streams are complex in their own right. But they are exceedingly more complex when considering the critical impact software deliveries have on other organizational value streams. In short, our emergent digital economy drives the need to deliver value through software, as well as IT networks and infrastructures, in support of value deliveries across all organizational value streams.

Few worthwhile things in life are free, or easy to obtain, or even without issues. So, let's set our expectations correctly by identifying the issues any VSM team or initiative is likely to face.

VSM tool implementation issues

As with any set of software delivery tools, there are implementation issues the organization must address before committing to procuring a VSM platform. The issues highlighted in this section apply to both installing DevOps and VSM capabilities at an enterprise scale. We will address the subject of DevOps platform and tool implementation issues in much greater detail later in *Chapter 15, Defining the Appropriate DevOps Platform Strategy*. So, for now, we'll limit the conversation to VSM tool implementation issues, which includes the following:

- Breaking down organizational silos
- Developing knowledge, skills, and resources
- Getting executive buy-in
- Knowing how to get started
- Lacking process maturity

- Overcoming budget constraints
- Maintaining governance and compliance

Let's get into the details of this list to understand what the issues are and the approaches we can take to address them head-on.

Breaking down organizational silos

Turf protection is not a new problem, but it is one of the most critical issues any organization faces. Successful organizations evolve to build an economy of scale that makes them efficient and profitable. The problem is that the increased organizational size often leads to bloat, over-processing, inefficient layers of management, and functional-oriented departments that move decision making increasingly further away from the product line. The result is less efficiency and much less flexibility and agility.

Modern-scale Scrum and Lean-Agile practices offer methods to break down organizational silos. An example of a method that helps break down silos is DevOps, where development teams and operations teams collaborate to ensure information flows both ways across the IT organization.

Developers need to work with Operations teams to ensure the products they develop are adequately tested and supported once they go into production. Similarly, the Operations teams need to provide feedback to the Development teams on issues they face in supporting, operating, securing, and maintaining business applications.

Lean processes implement continuous flows but are based on a pull-oriented paradigm. In effect, communications across the pipeline activities are both supported and constrained by Lean's pull-oriented product control systems.

Still, organizations may retain some of their functional orientations to build domain skills and capacity across value streams. In such cases, everyone in the organization must understand that decision making and authorities must be pushed down to the value streams as much as possible. And, for those issues that exceed the ability of local authorities to resolve, the executives must establish open communications channels and have access to informative data and metrics, via charts and dashboards, in near real time.

As you learned in *Chapter 7, Mapping the Current State (VSM Step 4)*, executives, managers, and VSM team members must practice **Gemba**. In other words, they must go to *the actual place* where work is performed to see what's going on and learn about the impediments and issues directly from the value stream operators. Through collaboration with the operators, the executives, managers, and value stream team members can work through the issues to gain the information they require to make effective decisions and plans.

Developing knowledge, skills, and resources

Building the proper skills to conduct software development in a CI/CD or DevOps pipeline environment is not a straightforward issue for IT shops. But, in smaller shops, the teams tend to evolve those skills over time. However, building the knowledge, skills, and resources to implement DevOps pipelines at an enterprise scale is a considerable challenge that cannot be taken lightly.

In the following subsection, we'll deal with the issues of platform and toolchain investment costs. But there is also the issue that many of the software development teams are likely working on legacy applications and enterprise-class **commercial off-the-shelf** (**COTS**) software applications. The longer they have worked on those applications, the further their skills may have lagged behind modern methods and tools.

While these are not insurmountable issues, executives who wish to transition to a DevOps-centric approach to software delivery must make investments in their people. The development costs of our people are as much a part of the business transformation expense and ROI as the investments the organization makes in terms of platforms, infrastructures, and tools.

Getting executive buy-in

Few things in life are free. I'm in a situation where organizational executives wanted to reduce costs in one vendors' application life cycle management platform and used a DevOps transformation initiative to justify the move. Unfortunately, the decision makers did not fully appreciate the investment costs in both people and tools to transition.

While executives can mandate a transition to DevOps, there's probably a much more significant investment in people and tooling than they have imagined. Adding in VSM to improve pipeline flows is an intelligent move. But that work also adds to the investment costs in developing skills, platforms, and tooling.

This issue was discussed in *Chapter 6*, *Launching the VSM Initiative (VSM Steps 1-3)* It's hard to get executive attention and buy-in to set aside people to perform work that does not directly contribute to building and delivering value to customers. Nevertheless, making Lean improvements is critical to ensuring the organization, as a whole, is delivering value optimally. This requires investments in people, processes, and tools to improve value stream pipeline flows.

The same issue is true with investing in the development of IT value stream pipelines via DevOps and VSM platforms and tools. Someone within the organization with the proper authority will have to build the business case to make these in people, processes, and tools. Ideally, the person leading the effort is a CTO, CIO, or CEO, or at least a line of business executive. If not, someone in the organization will need to take the bull by the horns and build the business case.

In the next section, you will learn how applications can be evaluated on a **return on investment** (**ROI**) basis to justify the investments in installing DevOps and VSM capabilities.

Overcoming budget constraints

Let's face it: organizational budgets are constantly stressed. There are always more things to invest in than the organization can afford. That's a given. DevOps- and VSM-related investments are portfolio-level decisions. In other words, they impact the mission and strategies of the business, and they need to be evaluated as such.

The **Scaled Agile Framework**® (**SAFe**®), as an example, addresses portfolio-level investments in two forms. One is product-related, while the other is something they refer to as an **Architectural Runway**. The product investments are easy to understand, as they directly relate to the value the organization delivers.

The term *Architectural Runway* probably seems a bit odd, and no – we're not talking about designing and building airports. Instead, Architectural Runway refers to investments made to create the future state technical foundation for developing business initiatives and implementing new features and capabilities. DevOps and VSM are the primary investments organizations make in their Architectural Runway to improve their value delivery capabilities in a digital economy.

Knowing how to get started

This topic is the reason you bought this book, I hope. In *Chapter 6, Launching the VSM Initiative (VSM Steps 1-3)* through *Chapter 10, Improving the Lean-Agile Value Delivery Cycle (VSM Steps 7 and 8)* you learned how to apply a generic eight-step VSM methodology. You know to conduct a VSM initiative across any type of value stream. Over time, you can modify the approach taught in this book and make it your own.

But one point I want to make is that modern VSM tools help orchestrate your flows, and they provide you with the metrics and visibility to make Lean-oriented improvements across your IT value streams. But the tools should not replace the human aspects of collaborating to understand and improve your pipeline flows. Metaphorically speaking, don't be afraid to work as a group and get your hands dirty in the data and analytical aspects of VSM.

Lacking process maturity

This subsection's heading is not meant to imply the implementation of a formal process maturity program. However, as the saying goes, *practice makes perfect*. OK, agreed, that's not an Agile nor Lean-oriented concept. In our Lean-Agile orientation, we constantly seek improvements to our processes and activities. But Lean doesn't work unless we also have mature standard practices.

The issue of having standards was addressed in *Chapter 4*, *Defining Value Stream Management*, on the need for standardized work, and specifically in the section on the 5S system. Recall that the fourth item in the 5S system is **Seiketsu** (standardization) – incorporate 5S into standard operating procedures. Create guidelines to keep them organized, orderly, and clean, and make the standards visual and obvious.

The reason for having standardized processes is that we can't have optimal flows if we have done the work to reduce waste and then ensure waste is not allowed to creep back in. Yes, we can and should continue to seek improvements for our value stream flows, but we should always build from our base of proven, standardized processes.

Maintaining governance and compliance

The last item in our list of VSM tool implementation issues deals with governance. Recall from the first section of this chapter, *Leveraging VSM tools and platforms*, that Gartner includes CCA tools as an essential DevOps tools category that help transform the IT value stream's ability to deliver customer value rapidly and reliably.

In the *IT governance* subsection, you also learned that CIOs and other IT executives have fiduciary responsibilities to manage and protect the organization's IT assets and investments. In that subsection, we primarily discussed IT governance as a critical element to ensure fiscal responsibility and minimize legal liabilities. However, there are other governance issues related to health (such as HIPAA in health-related privacy and security), safety (such as compliance with OSHA), and user accessibility issues (governed by 508 compliance). There are many more compliance requirements, many of which are regulated by government agencies.

This is the end of this section on VSM tool implementation issues. In this section, you learned that budgeting and executive buy-in are critical issues. Without executive buy-in, budgets will not be made available to implement DevOps and VSM platforms. Executives need to see value in supporting the business's mission and strategies to justify their investments. With that objective in mind, we will now explore how VSM and DevOps support business transformations that help the organization compete in our digital economy effectively.

Enabling business transformations

Throughout this book, you have been told that VSM is an approach to making Lean improvements. Moreover, you have learned that Lean improvements often require more significant investments than those that can be approved and authorized at the small Agile team level. But the outcomes and benefits of Lean transformations are much greater too.

VSM is the transformative process of delivering business value across the organization. And it is in that context that organizations need to evaluate their investments in VSM initiatives and tools. This section will explore some of the applications that help executives justify the strategic investments in VSM tools and processes.

Providing metrics to show business value

If you did not skip *Chapter 4*, *Defining Value Stream Management*, you should already understand the importance of capturing relevant metrics to improve value delivery. Modern VSM tools make it much easier to capture snapshots of data in real time.

Moreover, in modern CI/CD pipelines, activity flows are measured in microseconds. A human can't capture meaningful metrics in those time frames with a clock or stopwatch. But the VSM tools can. That frees up humans to perform analysis. The metrics tell us where there are inefficient flows, waiting, and bottlenecks. They can even tell us where in the pipeline those areas of waste occur. But it's human beings who need to go in to do the work to figure out how to resolve any identified issues.

Understanding costs across organizational value streams

The ability to identify costs goes hand in hand with metrics. In Lean, all forms of waste hinder our ability to deliver value, and therefore all forms of waste create non-value-adding costs.

Recall from *Chapter 4*, *Defining Value Stream Management*, how James Martin chronicled 17 common organizational value streams, reshown in the following table. The more value streams we have interconnected, the more rapidly non-value-added costs can accrue:

Customer engagement	Procurement services	Marketing	Legal Department
Order fulfillment	Product-design engineering	Market–information capture	IT–application development
Customer services	Research	Product maintenance	IT infrastructure
Human resources	Leased and capital asset management	Financial management	Enterprise engineering
Manufacturing			

Figure 11.1 – James Martin's list of 17 conventional business value streams

We've discussed how software development value streams support other operational value streams throughout this book, such as those listed in the preceding table. For example, software development teams may implement software products, be it COTS or custom, to improve order fulfillment or customer service delivery. Delays in software delivery to those two *operations-oriented* value streams may cost the organization customer orders or future business.

The same principles apply to marketing and market information capture. We discussed these issues in *Chapter 6*, *Launching the VSM Initiative (VSM Steps 1-3)*, in the *Integrating value streams* section. Here, we implemented the **Adaptive Productizing Process**. In a modern Agile context, we have product owners making development decisions based on market intelligence created by the marketing and product management value streams. However, the speed, accuracy, and actionability of market-driven intelligence are severely handicapped by manual processes.

Moreover, the software may drive many of the process improvements associated with building physical products in modern manufacturing facilities. For example, manufacturing equipment often has control systems that monitor processes and the flow of materials, information, and work.

Additionally, countries with higher labor rates have found it necessary to implement modern factory automation and robotics capabilities to improve quality and productivity with lower labor costs. But factory automation and robotic systems must be programmed.

With these examples, it should be apparent that IT value streams have linkages to the organization's other value streams. And, just as we are using VSM and DevOps platforms to integrate, automate, and orchestrate IT value streams, we must apply the same capabilities across all linked value streams to ensure optimized flows across the entire value delivery chain.

Understanding value stream lead and cycle times

Improving our delivery time to market is an essential requirement of virtually any business transformation activity. And the key to improving value delivery is by making improvements to value stream lead and cycle times. We covered this subject at length in the previous chapters, so there's no reason to explain why again here.

The critical point to be made here is that VSM platforms provide the means to have an accurate view of value stream lead and cycle times across the DevOps pipeline, from front to end. Additionally, as part of the VSM tools solution, having "what if" analytical capabilities allows the organization to try out alternative improvement scenarios.

It's important to remember that making local optimizations at the activity level may or may not have any real impact on improving overall productivity and throughput. In other words, cycle time improvements may not create lead time improvements. That's because we need to address those activities that most hinder flow, and we need to know which activities have the lengthiest cycle times that impede our pipeline flows.

Another thing to consider is that customers won't see nor value cycle time improvements at the activity level. What they care about is time to delivery, and that's measured as lead time.

Managing risks across value streams

VSM and DevOps tools and platforms improve risks across IT value streams by significantly reducing the possibilities of having unexpected issues crop up. Modern VSM tools integrate tools to enable the continuous flow of information and work. DevOps platforms' CI/CD capabilities help automate SDLC activities within the pipeline, thus minimizing the potential for human errors and delays. These VSM tools provide orchestration capabilities that affect continuous and optimized flows.

Moreover, when things change in our pipeline, be it changes in customer demand or suboptimal flows, the metrics and analytic capabilities of the VSM tools provide the information you need to assess alternatives and make decisions before the risks become issues.

Analyzing patterns and trends

In traditional Lean product processes, product development teams use Six Sigma techniques to monitor performance parameters, which indicate trends toward the upper and lower boundary points of our production processes and quality goals.

The metrics we identified in *Chapter 8, Identifying Lean Metrics (VSM Step 5)*, establish the goals of our value stream activities. The current and future state mapping activities help us establish the upper and lower boundaries we need to operate within to optimize our pipeline's materials, information, and workflow. And, as you might surmise, modern VSM tools provide monitoring and visualization capabilities to see how our value stream activities are trending against those goals and boundaries.

VSM tools also provide visibility into the product backlogs. This helps us monitor how work is queued at the frontend of the pipeline and how it progresses through the pipeline. We can see how well refining and scoping the requirements match reality once the work is introduced to the development pipeline. We can also use the data monitoring and visualization capabilities of the VSM tools to see whether something is breaking in our DevOps pipeline, including the production environments. For example, it's helpful to know when and if we have applications, data stores, networks, servers, or security components that are failing. In traditional IT shops, these functions are siloed. Before the advent of modern VSM tools, bringing all the data together into one monitoring and visualization platform was challenging.

Accelerating improvements with AI

The use of **artificial intelligence** (**AI**) in VSM tools is another capability that is emerging in modern VSM platforms. Definitionally, AI-based tools and platforms mimic a human's ability to think, referred to as cognitive functions, which can include human-like activities such as learning, perceiving, problem solving, and reasoning. However, cognitive AI is only a subset of the larger field of AI. So, let's look at the distinctions between the two before getting into the details of AI:

- **Cognitive computing**: This is a narrow subset of AI that seeks to create systems that understand and simulate human reasoning and behavior.
- **AI**: These are systems that apply pattern recognition capabilities across large datasets to augment human thinking for solving complex problems.

Machine learning takes AI another step further by implementing capabilities to learn and improve from experience without an explicit programming approach. This branch of AI creates applications that are programmed to find patterns and trends in massive volumes of data and then use that data to discover, through trial and error, optimal approaches to achieving goals they are programmed to accomplish.

In other words, AI systems with machine learning capabilities evaluate data in terms of their goals, and then apply different strategies to accomplish those goals without the programmers telling them how to do it.

In effect, machine learning systems apply the same types of iterative and incremental development processes that Agile programmers use to accomplish their goals – except the computers can process much more information and do so much more quickly than humans. Nevertheless, the patterns and strategies quickly identified by the AI systems do not remove the need for humans to analyze the findings, make decisions, and perform the necessary work to resolve the negative trends.

AI researchers branch the discipline of AI into four types and seven patterns. The four types of AI form increasingly higher-level tiers of capabilities and include the following:

- **Reactive machines**: These are the oldest and simplest form of AI. In this case, an AI application is programmed for a single purpose and reacts to inputs according to their instructions, without saving any findings. In other words, these AI systems only "react" to current inputs, potentially applying millions of calculations before selecting an optimal result for each situation that's encountered.

  An example of this type of AI system is applications that compete against humans in playing games, such as chess.

- **Limited memory**: This is one step beyond reactive machines, where AI systems incorporate limited memory to maintain knowledge gained from previously learned information, stored data, or observed events. The goal of such systems is to build experiential knowledge that is immediately useful but fleeting in terms of time and purpose.

  For example, autonomous vehicles monitor their surroundings to identify threats and obstacles, make predictions of trajectories, respond accordingly, and then move on to reassess their surroundings and continue to react accordingly. Such systems need to retain sufficient information about their immediate environment, but then forget and rapidly move on to evaluating incoming data and responding appropriately to the next set of environmental conditions.

- **Theory of mind**: These types of AI systems attempt to mimic human decision making and communications with the same contextual thoughts and emotions that affect human behavior. This type of AI system must learn rapidly and react to facial expressions, body language, and emotional responses from human beings they are interacting with.

  The Theory of Mind AI systems application includes establishing human-like, responsive, and empathetic communications with human beings. As these capabilities mature, the application for Theory of Mind-based AI systems improves human-like communications in call center and customer service environments.

- **Self-aware**: AI systems attempt to achieve human levels of consciousness. Here, we can think of robots and computing systems that understand their existence, think for themselves, have desires, and have emotive feelings and experiences.

  Self-aware AI systems do not exist. Such potential applications could assist humans with various life or work tasks, where empathy and self-awareness can help ensure safe conditions during interactions with humans. In the old Jetson cartoon, you can imagine the cleaning robot, Rosey, as a potential future application.

  Of course, a well-known negative example of this type of capability comes from the novel and movie *2001: A Space Odyssey*, by Author C. Clarke and the fictional AI computer, **Hal**. Hal is an onboard computer in the Discovery space shuttle who becomes self-aware. When Hal makes an unintentional error, he becomes fearful that he will be shut down and thus terminated. So, he begins to kill the Shuttle astronauts, fearing they will learn of his mistake.

OK, with that negative concern expressed – not to belittle it – let's move on and discuss the current realities, limitations, and capabilities of AI-based technologies. According to *Cognilytica*, a leading market research firm on the state of AI adoption, the seven patterns of AI are as follows:

- **Autonomous systems**: These are the AI systems that focus on specific tasks to achieve a directed goal or interact with their surroundings with minimal to no human involvement. There are two types of autonomous systems. The first is a physical and hardware-oriented product such as autonomous vehicles. The second type of autonomous system includes software systems or virtualized autonomous systems such as software bots.

- **Conversation and human interaction**: These directly interact with humans via a natural conversation, with interactions spanning voice, text, images, and other written formats. The goal is to enable computer-to-human communications in plain-spoken languages or even human-to-human communications, where language differences or disabilities interfere. Such systems can also generate information in text, images, video, audio, and other media formats meant for human consumption.

  Another goal is to implement *Theory of Mind* capabilities to improve understanding between participants. Such applications provide situations where the accurate two-way conveyance of information is critical to supporting a business or social interaction.

- **Goal-driven systems**: This applies machine learning and other cognitive approaches to learning through trial and error to find an optimal solution. Some people believe that it may be possible to apply trial and error processes to learn anything theoretically.

  Goal-driven AI systems are most valuable when we know what our desired outcome is, but we're not sure how to get there, and there are many alternative approaches to work our way through. Recall the issues we discussed regarding the exponentially expanding inter-relationships between nodes in large, complex systems in *Chapter 3*, *Analyzing Complex System Interactions*. Goal-driven systems apply a brute-force approach to discover optimal outcomes by evaluating all potential scenarios.

- **Hyper-personalization**: This is an application of machine learning that's used to develop unique profiles of individuals, with continued learning and adaption over time to support various purposes. For example, the AI system may, based on individual preferences, display relevant content, recommend relevant products, and provide personalized recommendations and guidance. Hyper-personalization systems evaluate each person as a unique individual.

  The applications of hyper-personalization include provisioning personalized health care, financial services, directed insights, product information, general advice, and feedback.

- **Patterns and anomalies**: These can be detected by applying machine learning and other cognitive approaches. The objective is to identify patterns in the data and discover higher-order connections between information. More precisely, the goal is to gain insights on whether any given piece of data within a more extensive dataset fits an existing pattern. If it does, the data fits within and strengthens the pattern; if not, it's an outlier. In other words, the primary objective of this pattern is to find which one of the things is like the other and which is not.

This AI strategy is applied within VSM tools and platforms to discover patterns and trends.

- **Predictive analytics and decisions**: This strategy employs machine learning and other cognitive approaches to understand how learned patterns can help predict future outcomes by leveraging insight gained by analyzing system behaviors, interactions, and data.

    Predictive analytics is another AI application within modern VSM tools and platforms, as the predicted outcomes can help guide humans in decision making. The most important aspect of this pattern is that humans are still making decisions, but the tools are helping humans make better and more informed ones.

- **Recognition**: Recognition-based AI systems use machine learning and other cognitive approaches to identify and determine objects or other desired things to be identified within some form of unstructured content.

    Structured data is highly organized and formatted to be stored, managed, and searched for within relational databases. In contrast, unstructured data has no predefined format or organization, making it much more challenging to collect, process, and analyze.

    Examples of unstructured content include information available in images, video, audio, or text file formats. The objective of AI-based recognition systems is to identify, recognize, segment, or otherwise separate some part of the content so that it can be labeled and tagged for future use. By tagging and labeling unstructured data, the files and metadata can be managed within a relational database and other structured data.

    The value of using recognition systems is that they are much quicker and potentially more accurate than humans performing the exact same identification and cataloging tasks. Such applications include image and object recognition, facial recognition, sound and audio recognition, item detection, handwriting and text recognition, gesture detection, and identifying patterns within a piece of content.

By now, you should have the idea that AI systems are not quite the black boxes they may seem to be, nor are all the AI patterns applicable to use in VSM tools and platforms.

AI and machine learning systems do the heavy lifting in VSMs to search volumes of data to find relationships and patterns that would take humans hundreds of person-hours to find. AI systems aren't performing magic; instead, they follow a set of rules and tasks humans have directed.

Computing systems can faithfully follow their coded rules and algorithms, precisely apply mathematical and logical expressions innumerable times, all the while searching through volumes of data – with no errors. Comparatively, humans don't do those kinds of tasks very well. Moreover, assuming anyone wanted such a task in a DevOps environment, the work pace is measured in microseconds, and no human would be able to keep up.

Finally, just like humans, some AI systems learn from their experiences and reapply what they've learned to gain new insights and evaluate potential solutions to complex problems.

Humans have always created tools to make their lives easier and more comfortable. This situation is no different when those tools are AI-based VSM tools. They make our jobs easier and our work more productive. But, as with any tool, humans must control AI tools for productive and humane purposes.

Governing the software delivery process

We addressed the subject of IT governance in the previous subsection, titled *Maintaining governance and compliance*. The context here was maintaining governance policies and standards that IT must support. Here, the issue is using VSM and DevOps tools to improve the governance of the overall software delivery process.

In DevOps pipeline flows, the system's development life cycle follows the same patterns as the traditional and agile models but at a greatly accelerated rate. In other words, we still follow a process that includes identifying a business or user problem, gathering requirements, and then architecting, designing, building, testing, and deploying a solution to deliver customer-centric value. But the speed is so great in DevOps pipelines that we need to ensure proper governance of the process through its execution.

There are definitely business, industry, and regulatory compliance aspects to implementing governance as part of the software delivery process, and those compliance requirements also operate at an accelerated rate.

The critical capability here is that VSM tools operate at the same speeds as integrated and automated DevOps pipelines. Modern VSM tools implement and enforce governance policies without human intervention, and thereby minimize risks that humans will miss critical process and compliance requirements at the accelerated pace of software development and delivery.

Managing value streams as continuous flows

The critical issue with the traditional Waterfall software development model was that it did not enforce a Lean-oriented production process. The entire system development life cycle was segmented and extended beyond reasonability. The traditional waterfall model was entirely out of step with the Lean production processes that organizations implemented across their other value streams.

Agile practices helped a bit by implementing iterative and incremental development patterns. But the early agile methodologies, such as Scrum, still enforced batch processing in the form of Sprints. Kanban Boards helped improve flows within the Sprint but did not improve overall system development pipeline flows.

CI/CD and DevOps pipelines implemented integrated toolchains and automation strategies to improve work and information flow from end to end, including extending into operations-oriented support activities. But that still leaves the matter of orchestration to ensure proper and efficient pipeline flows, as well as to manage governance and compliance requirements throughout the software delivery process.

Modern VSM tools implement orchestration capabilities from end to end across the software development and operations-oriented value streams. With DevOps VSM tools, the organization can achieve continuous and optimized software delivery and support flows.

Visualizing value streams

In a modern DevOps pipeline, most activities occur in an automated and orchestrated fashion, without human intervention. Without visualization capabilities, we would have to take things as a matter of faith that the pipeline is operating as intended. Unfortunately, this means that if there are issues, we generally won't find out until after the fact, when we have a more significant problem to deal with due to missed deliveries or missed requirements.

Modern VSM tools provide visualization capabilities that demonstrate key metrics and pipeline flows. These tools also provide graphical visualizations to help depict queuing and waiting for work items. In short, modern VSM tools help identify areas of waste that need improvement and provide visualization capabilities to see where that waste lies.

Improving cross-functional and cross-team collaborations

This area is the original purpose of DevOps: to enable collaborations between development- and operations-oriented teams. But communication and collaboration must occur across the entire value delivery chain and all the value streams – not just development and operations teams.

In our modern digital world, it's not unusual to have collaborating teams spread out across large worksite locations, geographic regions, and even international boundaries. The tools that are used for communicating, collaborating, and orchestrating work include project management software, video conferencing, office chat or instant messaging systems, file sharing, online and real-time collaborative document revision tools, document management and synchronization tools, online whiteboards, and version control tools.

The value of these capabilities is that it's nearly impossible to maintain continuous flows and orchestration of work without constant and appropriate communication and collaboration. The more geographically dispersed the organization and its customers and supply chain partners are, the more these tools become necessary.

Improving value stream efficiencies and handoffs

This entire book is about improving production flows across value streams of all types, but IT-oriented value streams in particular. The IT industry has transitioned through a paradigm shift that moved production from the traditional project-based flows to Agile's batch-oriented workflows, and then to modern CI/CD and DevOps pipeline flows. Those organizations that effectively implement DevOps capabilities have a distinct competitive advantage over those that do not.

While some of the concepts behind DevOps can be made possible without integrated toolchains and automated processes, those environments will not be competitive with other organizations that have fully invested in the DevOps and VSM tools. Quite simply, DevOps and VSM platforms offer accelerated software deliveries with higher quality than the traditional and Agile-based practices.

That's not to imply that DevOps or even VSM is something different to Agile. By analogy, turtles and rabbits are both types of animals, but rabbits are much faster than turtles. The same is true in IT. DevOps pipelines are much faster at delivering software value than traditional or Agile-based workflows. They are also more efficient and tend to deliver higher quality products.

Improved quality

The previous subsection mentioned that IT shops that have implemented DevOps and VSM platforms tend to deliver higher quality products. Let's take a moment to examine why.

In the traditional Waterfall model, testing is the last activity that's performed before deployment. The problem with this approach is that the code base is entirely built by that time and likely hiding a million and one bugs. That's perhaps a slight exaggeration, but there will be many bugs – guaranteed. Worse, they will be hard to isolate and fix at that late stage.

Agile practices are much better in that the development teams are building smaller increments of code iteratively and testing each new increment of functionality along the way. So, even if the software is delayed across several sprints to go out as a formal release, the software code is generally better tested than in the traditional model.

But CI/CD and DevOps pipelines take things to a whole other level but automating testing and provisioning the test environments on demand. For example, I worked in a shop where each day's code was run through a series of tests, often tens of thousands of tests, every night. As a result, it was extremely rare to see a bug make it into production.

This type of capability can be installed in an Agile team. But the next step is to deliver tiny increments of functionality – often referred to as microservices – often many times a day or even many times over an hour, and dynamically spin up production-like test environments on demand to test each new micro-release of the software. That is what continuous delivery is all about.

But some organizations take the CD concept even further and allow each new code release that passes all functional, non-functional, and performance tests to go directly into production. The development team may release new features and functions to select groups of users, by roles, within the production environments. This helps minimize risks by having a small group of users validate the feature or function's functionality before making a full-scale deployment to all users.

Performing what if analysis

We have touched on this subject serval times in this book. Organizational investments, DevOps skills, and toolchains are not inexpensive, nor are they quick to implement across larger organizations. Such organizations need to make changes incrementally to afford these investments and minimize potential disruptions as the development teams come up to speed.

As you now know from reading the VSM methodology chapters (*Chapter 6, Launching the VSM initiative* (*VSM Steps 1-3*) through *Chapter 10, Improving the Lean-Agile Value Delivery Cycle* (*VSM Steps 7 and 8*)), VSM achieves desired future state operations incrementally over time. The basic idea is to evaluate all activities across your value stream flows and prioritize them based on eliminating the most waste for the least cost. This strategy will incrementally improve value stream flows quickly and cost-effectively. Most importantly, the Lean-Agile process improvement activities never stop. We can always do better.

But then the question is, how do we know which alternative approaches are best to take us from the current state to a better future state of operations? That is where the *what if* capabilities of VSM tools and platforms come into play. In effect, we can simulate making changes to products, equipment, processes, and activities before making the investments to see the effect on the overall productivity of the value stream.

Reusing templates for better standard work items

DevOps VSMP, VSDPs, and CCA tools may include tools that help simplify tedious though relatively common work. For example, VSMP tools may include Adaptor forms and templates to input parameters to connect databases and applications. Both VSMP and VSDPs may include value stream mapping tools and templates to expedite the development of current state and future state maps. On the other hand, CCA tools may include templates that their systems populate as audit trails to demonstrate compliance with regulatory requirements.

Unifying data and artifacts

Large enterprises with multiple product lines must assess value stream productivity when the functional departments and values streams all use different data sources and artifacts to monitor, govern, and document their activities. The situation worsens when the organizations rely on manual labor to capture and reformat the information for management, customer, and stakeholder consumption.

Lean and VSM practices give us common semantics to describe how to improve value delivery. That's half the problem solved. The other half is to eliminate the manual labor of collecting, transforming, and delivering information. Though the information may be valuable for decision making, it's probably late, and the work is non-value-added from our customers' perspectives. Modern VSM platforms address these issues by automating data capture in real time, as well as providing tools that allow the data consumers to visualize and analyze the value stream data at any time and with multiple tools and formats.

Integrating, automating, and orchestrating value stream activities

Lean product improvements encompass the integration, automation, and orchestration of value-adding activities, no matter the value stream. The objectives are to deliver customer-centric value more rapidly and with higher quality by eliminating waste. Modern DevOps and VSM platforms eliminate waste and improve productivity across software development, delivery, operations, and support processes.

However, software potentially touches all organizational value streams. Therefore, we must use DevOps and VSM methods and tools to integrate, automate, and orchestrate all value stream activities via software solutions.

Providing a common data architecture

Many IT organizations allow their development teams to select different tools for their integrated CI/CD and DevOps toolchains. Providing this flexibility is the predicate upon which DevOps VSMPs operate. While the VSMP strategy provides a great deal of flexibility and use of best-in-class tools, the downside is that each tool potentially has a different datastore and data model, making it more difficult to retrieve, normalize, and use data across the toolchain.

VSDP vendors solve this problem by minimizing the tool options and integrating them in a single data store with normalized data across all value stream activities. With VSMP tools, each data source must be mapped to a central repository. In either case, the value of having a single data store that contains normalized data is that queries operate end to end on all the data items that have been managed for the value streams, as well as their activities. In short, single-source data stores with data normalization makes it easier to generate reports, conduct analysis, and create graphical visualizations of pipeline flows.

Developing and populating key performance indicators

Definitionally, **key performance indicators** (**KPIs**) are the organization's defined *key* indicators of progress toward an intended result. Organizations may define KPIs to support strategic and tactical objectives. KPIs are metrics-based, as the results must be measurable to determine progress against our goals and objectives.

Modern VSM tools provide up-to-date and accurate metrics that are mapped to the organization's KPIs, giving the executive better confidence in their decision-making processes. For example, as part of portfolio management, key executives and product managers make investment decisions based on customer demands, competitive price points, and historical and planned cost factors. In addition, as product development proceeds, it's vital to access real-time metrics to evaluate actual against planned performance, as this helps enable timely course corrections.

We've come to the end of the *Enabling business transformation* section. In the next and final section, we'll explore the benefits of investing in VSM skills, tools, and platforms.

VSM tool benefits

In the previous section, you learned about the capabilities provided by modern VSM tools and platforms. Now, you are going to learn how to explain their benefits.

Some of the key benefits offered by implementing VSM tools are discussed next. Many of these benefits were discussed in the previous section. So, let's recap here in summary form:

- **Improved quality of releases**: VSM tools and platforms monitor DevOps performance parameters, enforce standard production processes and compliance requirements, and ensure value stream activities stay within upper and lower boundary points to achieve optimal workflows and meet quality goals.

- **Quicker time to release**: VSM tools and platforms help integrate, automate, and orchestrate DevOps pipeline flows. They also help embody Lean concepts of eliminating waste to achieve the fastest and most efficient software value delivery system.

- **Measurable outcomes of business value**: VSM tools provide the metrics your organization needs to measure current state performance, predict future state production and delivery capabilities, and ensure transitions meet expectations.

- **Reduced risks and waste**: VSM tools and platforms faithfully implement standard processes and compliance requirements without error, minimizing the potential to introduce risks and non-value-added waste.

- **Cost reductions**: With VSM tools guiding DevOps production, the organization can be assured it is operating optimally with minimal waste. Real-time metrics and analytical tools help the organization discover and eliminate sub-optimized activities and evaluate alternative approaches to improve productivity and value delivery.

- **Better orchestration of toolchains**: The orchestration capabilities of VSM tools help detect bottlenecks in the DevOps pipeline, implement standardized processes, integrate and enforce security and compliance requirements, and synchronize and coordinate the steps required to develop and release applications – including manual activities.

- **Improved compliance and auditability**: CCA tools help automate and expedite compliance and security-related tasks, replacing manual checklists, policies, and worksheets. Most of all, CCA tools help eliminate risks and legal liabilities associated with compliance failures.

This section completes our discussion on leveraging VSM tools and platform capabilities, as well as this chapter on improving the Lean-Agile value delivery cycle. Let's summarize this chapter and then look at a set of questions that will help you retain what you have learned in this chapter.

Summary

In this chapter, you learned how VSM tools support the Lean improvements across DevOps pipelines by providing real-time access to critical IT value stream data, dashboard-based visualizations, and metrics. VSM tools help DevOps team members and other stakeholders monitor and improve the flow of information and work across the IT value streams and focus on the customers.

You also learned about the three primary types of VSM tools – VSMP/VSM, VSDP, and CCA, and the capabilities they should provide. Next, we covered the kinds of implementation issues you can expect when promoting these tools in an organization. Then, you learned about numerous potential applications for VSM tools and platforms and the benefits that justify the investments.

The next chapter will introduce the current industry-leading tools. We explore each tool's strengths and discuss real-life use cases while highlighting their strengths for that particular scenario.

Questions

1. Why did this book present a proven eight-step VSM methodology before getting into the topic of VSM tools?

2. What are the three types of DevOps tools that can help transform your IT value stream's ability to deliver customer value rapidly and reliably?

3. What is the primary feature available in DevOps value stream management platforms (VSMPs).

4. What are the key benefits of DevOps VSMPs/VSM tools?

5. What is the purpose of GRC tools and platforms?

6. What are the primary features available within value stream delivery platforms (VSDPs)?

7. What are the primary benefits of VSDPs?

8. What is the purpose of DevOps workflow metrics?

9. What is the purpose of DevOps orchestration?

10. What is the primary benefit of what if analysis tools?

Further reading

*   Betts, D., Saunderson, C., Blair, R., Bhat, M., Scheibmeir, J. Ennaciri, H. (Oct 2021), *Gartner Research Predicts 2021: Value Streams Will Define the Future of DevOps Report* (published October 5, 2020), ID: G00734377. https://www.gartner.com/en/documents/3991376/predicts-2021-value-streams-will-define-the-future-of-de. Accessed March 1, 2021.

*   Condo, C., Mines, C., Giudice, D.L., Dobak, A., Hartig, K. (July 2020) *The Forrester Wave™: Value Stream Management Solutions, Q3 2020 Report.* https://www.forrester.com/report/The+Forrester+Wave+Value+Stream+Management+Solutions+Q3+2020/-/E-RES159825. Accessed March 1, 2021.

*   Corporate, April 4, 2019. *AI FUNDAMENTALS, The Seven Patterns of AI.* https://www.cognilytica.com/2019/04/04/the-seven-patterns-of-ai/#:~:text=The%20Seven%20Patterns%20of%20AI%201%20The%20Seven,9%20Combining%20multiple%20patterns%20in%20a%20project.%20. Accessed April 30, 2021.

12
Introducing the Leading VSM Tool Vendors

In the previous chapter, you learned some of the essential capabilities of modern VSM tools. You also learned how to identify the three types of VSM tool classifications.

We also delved into the subject of common VSM tool implementation issues, the role VSM tools play in supporting digital business transformations, and their key benefits. Now we are going to move on to introduce the leading software tool vendors with industry-acknowledged VSM capabilities.

Rather than regurgitating what other industry analysts have written, I reached out to leading VSM tool, methodology, and service providers and asked them to tell us why their customers choose their products. Those vendors who chose to be interviewed for this book are listed in this chapter. In my interviews, I asked their designated representatives to explain what they believe their particular strengths are and why. They also had the opportunity to present one or two customer use cases they believed help showcase the strengths of their VSM tools and services.

In this chapter, we're going to cover the following topics:

- Putting modern VSM tools in perspective

- Improving value delivery

- Using VSM beyond CI/CD and DevOps

- Listing the leading VSM Tool Providers

We'll begin our journey through the leading VSM methods and tools with a word of caution.

Putting modern VSM tools in perspective

From the previous chapters, you now know that the concepts behind VSM are not new and have been applied to many industries and innumerable value streams. You also now know that VSM emerged from the discipline of Lean production improvements. Unlike traditional hierarchical and functional-centric views of making process improvements, Lean improvement structures organizational activities as orchestrated flows to deliver value optimally to internal and external customers.

Since VSM is fundamentally a strategy to help organizations marshal their resources to make Lean improvements, we spent some time in this book learning about Lean. And from that training, you now know that Lean is a system for planning and implementing continuous process improvements. The focus is on developing efficient production and information flows by eliminating all forms of waste from the customer's perspective. As a quick reminder, the common types of waste include **defects**, **inventory**, **motion**, **overprocessing**, **overproduction**, **transportation**, and **waiting**.

Improving value delivery

In *Chapter 4, Defining Value Stream Management*, you learned that James Martin articulated 17 common values streams. In his book *The Great Transitions*, Martin writes about the importance of defining and improving **value stream flows** as part of any business process redesign effort.

Martin built his concepts on Thomas Davenport's paper *Process Innovation: Reengineering Work through Information Technology*. In his paper, Davenport breaks down organizational value-adding processes into three categories:

- Product design, development, and manufacturing processes
- Customer-facing processes, including marketing and sales management, order management, and customer service
- Management and administrative processes

The important takeaway is that both Martin and Davenport evaluated process reengineering and process improvement initiatives through the lens of making value-based or value-delivery improvements, and with IT as a critical enabler of installing business process innovations. Furthermore, their writing explains why organizations cannot find real business process improvements by building processes and systems that maintain the status quo across hierarchical, bureaucratic, and functional domains. Put another way, Martin and Davenport advocated using IT to redesign business processes, but doing so from the perspective of adding value.

Based on what you've learned in this book, it should be apparent that VSM as a discipline has little to do with software tools, or even with making improvements to your organization's CI/CD and DevOps pipeline flows. VSM is much bigger and more important than that.

Using VSM beyond CI/CD and DevOps

Commercial companies, government agencies, and non-profits exist to deliver value in products, services, or other forms of desired results and outcomes. In our modern digital economy, Martin and Davenport's insights are more critical than ever. Improvements to our CI/CD and DevOps pipelines can improve our ability to deliver value across all organizational value streams.

But, of course, none of your CI/CD, DevOps, and VSM toolchain investments will amount to much if your IT organization is not synced up to support the organization's other value streams. Thus, it's essential to understand that your organization can expend much time, money, and effort on purchasing CI/CD, DevOps, and VSM tools and still fail to improve your value delivery capabilities.

CI/CD, DevOps, and VSM toolchain investments are examples of potential Kaizen Burst activities to enable other critical value stream improvements. Therefore, such investments are not inexpensive and become portfolio-level investment decisions supporting the organization's core business mission and strategy. However, CI/CD, DevOps, and VSM toolchain investments are foundational as they support any other VSM initiatives and must be evaluated in that light.

This concern is why so much space is devoted in this book to implementing a VSM initiative beyond the IT function. However, the primary driver for improving IT is to improve the other development and operations-oriented value streams they support. In other words, your IT-oriented Kaizen Bursts will be driven by other value stream improvement requirements. With this understanding, let's introduce the current tools and thought leaders in VSM.

Listing the leading VSM tool providers

This chapter introduces you to the leading VSM vendors, as identified by various industry analysts, such as **Forrester Research**, **Gartner Inc.**, **GIGAOM**, **SD Times**, and others. However, I have purposely steered away from repeating the views of these other industry reports regarding specific product offerings.

Instead, my goal in this book was to identify the leaders and then let each VSM vendor tell their own story if they chose to do so. Their stories are found in the sections that follow. But, before we get to that section, we need first to learn who the perceived leaders are. So, *Figure 12.1* shows the current list of VSM tool and methodology vendors, placed in alphabetical order:

- Atlassian
- Blueprint
- CloudBees
- ConnectALL
- Digital.ai
- Disciplined Agile (DA)
- Gitlab
- HCL Software

- IBM
- JAMA Software
- Kovair
- Micro Focus
- Panaya
- Plandek
- Planview
- Plutora

- Quali
- Scaled-Agile Framework® (SAFe®)
- ServiceNow
- TaskTop
- Targetprocess
- Tasktop
- Zenhub
- VSM Consortium

Figure 12.1 – List of LEADING VSM METHODS AND TOOLS VENDORS

I have added three VSM methodology companies, **Disciplined Agile**, **SAFe**, and the **Value Stream Management Consortium** (**VSMC**), which provide guidance on VSM applied to scaling Lean and Agile practices. However, the descriptions of their offerings are included in the next chapter, *Chapter 13, Introducing the VSM-DevOps Practice Leaders.*

As you read through the information on each listed VSM vendor, bear in mind how they support the improvements of CI/CD and DevOps pipelines from a Lean-oriented perspective. Also, recall that the three essential elements of a mature CI/CD or DevOps pipeline are *integration*, *automation*, and *orchestration* capabilities.

Finally, recall that VSM is a proven, effective, and disciplined step-by-step methodology for understanding and applying the principles and practices of Lean thinking. VSM as a discipline has been practiced for decades, applies across all organizational value streams, and has its roots in the Lean production concepts employed in the **Toyota Production System (TPS)**.

The remainder of this section introduces the industry's current leading VSM tool vendors to summarize their capabilities. It's important to note that not all of these tools claim to have VSM support as a focus. For example, some DevOps and CI/CD tools vendors, such as **Atlassian**, have a vital role in software projects and product management. But we need to explore how their products might be employed in a VSM initiative.

Atlassian

Atlassian is an Australian team collaboration software tool company. Although Forrester Research includes Atlassian in their *Forrester Wave™: Value Stream Management Solutions Scorecard (Q3 2020)*, Atlassian does not have a stated value stream management strategy. Nevertheless, Forrester gives the company high marks for its product vision, performance, partner ecosystem, and market presence.

When I asked Atlassian for a quote on their position relative to value stream management, I was told the following:

"While we don't sell a VSM solution specifically, our products are decisively used to span the development and operational value streams from concept to customer and back (learning loops). We believe in an open approach, so we integrate with just about everything, and we believe in being somewhat unopinionated so that our customers can design their optimal way of working."

With this information in mind, let's see how Atlassian fits into the VSM picture.

Two college friends, Mike Cannon-Brookes and Scott Farquhar, developed in 2002 what is arguably the number one project management software, **Jira**. Jira started as an issue tracking platform for software developers. However, in its current form, Jira Software helps Agile software development and support teams *plan*, *track*, and *release* their software.

Jira's capabilities to plan, track, and support project management are not limited to software development and IT operations activities. Organizations also use Jira to support collaborations across other value stream flows, such as product management, marketing, and sales. The objective is to support cross-team collaboration across all organizational value streams to coordinate product strategies, evolution, development, support, and sustainment activities.

Atlassian has grown in size and products over its nearly two decades of existence and currently offers 13 product offerings, spanning the following 4 solution areas:

- Plan, track, and support

- Collaboration

- Code, build, and ship products

- Security and identity

Atlassian's tools collectively provide real-time visibility at an enterprise scale and help the enterprises aggregate team-level data to make all work visible across the organization in real time.

The company mentions the use and benefits of value stream mapping as an analytical technique to optimize your CD pipeline in an article titled *What is value stream mapping?* *at* https://www.atlassian.com/continuous-delivery/principles/value-stream-mapping. But Atlassian does not offer an integrated value stream mapping tool as an out-of-the-box solution.

Organizations often integrate Jira as a collaboration solution supporting their CI/CD and DevOps toolchains and VSM platforms. For example, a commonly promoted Jira integration is with ServiceNow to support bi-directional collaborations spanning issues and project management across CI/CD and DevOps pipeline and ITSM processes.

Atlassian's website: https://www.atlassian.com/

CloudBees

CloudBees is another VSM solution provider with its roots in connecting the DevOps toolchain to automate and improve the software delivery process. Forrester Research ranks CloudBees as a Strong Performer, while GigaOm ranks CloudBees as a *Fast-Mover* entering the inner circle of its GigaOm Radar for VSM.

CloudBees combines both software delivery and VSM into one platform by providing core capabilities: **continuous integration (CI), continuous delivery (CD)**, release orchestration, analytics, and feature flagging. In doing so, organizations can exponentially increase visibility, consistency, and collaboration throughout the development life cycle—the essence of VSM. Keeping these core tools together also expands audit readiness because teams and processes are more easily measured and managed, plus it eliminates the need for separate products for the execution plane and the control plane.

Figure 12.2 provides a quick list of the core capabilities provided by the CloudBees platform:

The CloudBees Platform Connected, automated, end-to-end software delivery
Continuous Integration Build and test at scale
Continuous Delivery Eliminate scripts and automate deployment pipelines
Release Orchestration Adaptable model-driven release orchestration
Analytics A single source of truth for real-time visibility
Feature Flagging Manage feature flags at scale

Figure 12.2 – CloudBees platform capabilities

CloudBees' platform supports what the company states are the five pillars of software delivery automation and management:

- **Connected processes**: Orchestrate software delivery and connect functions efficiently to bring ideas to market with maximum value and adoption.

- **Compliance as Code**: Centrally enforce policy, access, and standards across all pipelines and ensure the use of only approved, immutable components, automation, and environments.

- **Common data model:** Make data available from end to end and captured and stored in a standardized data model to facilitate collaboration, connected processes, and shared insights.

- **Universal insights**: Enable understanding and continuous learning from data across all functions throughout the organization.

- **Continuous COLLABORATION AND IMPROVEMENT**: Allow collaboration across functions and teams surrounding the software delivery organization to amplify their value creation and delivery efforts.

The CloudBees customer base has deep roots in the open source Jenkins development community; Jenkins is used to build, test, and deploy software in CI and CD environments. As a result, their tools place emphasis on improving development and deployment process efficiencies.

The CloudBees platform maps the value stream by modeling the software delivery pipeline from code commit into production. The pipeline model includes the path to production, approved components, gates and thresholds, testing orchestration, deployment automation, and toolchain integration (and data) in a graphical view. Built-in analytics include configurable dashboards for the DORA metrics and wait times, execution times, and durations for each stage. An AI/ML component produces risk scoring for each release based on developer, code base, and CI influences.

In their reports, industry analysts said they wanted to see CloudBees evolve their VSM capabilities to support improved business outcomes with better linkages to business metrics and dashboards. CloudBees has responded with additional metrics under development, including a range of flow metrics and business metrics such as value, cost, quality, and happiness.

In sum, on top of its strengths in CI/CD, release orchestration, and feature flag capabilities, the CloudBees platform offers the ability to map, manage, and govern a value stream end to end—from ideation to production—and provides superior support for integrating third-party tools.

Additional information is available on CloudBees and its offerings can be found at `https://www.cloudbees.com/`.

ConnectALL

ConnectALL's roots lie in developing adaptors and connectors for **application lifecycle management** (**ALM**) tools such as Sarena (now Micro Focus ALM) to other software tools for development, configuration management, and project management, including Perforce, ClearCase, and Jira, respectively. In addition, the company has continued to evolve its connectors to support integrations with IBM Rational, HEAT Software, Git, and Rally.

ConnectALL LLC was officially formed in 2018, created initially as a joint venture between Orasi and Go2Group. Discussions between Lance Knight and Brett Taylor (now a board member) began in December 2016 on the need for a new approach to value stream management. Lance Knight joined the company in 2017 as its President and COO, and he and Brett began to position ConnectALL for this move strategically. Also, Tom Stiling (Now the Chairman of ConnectALL's Board) joined the effort. As a result, the three partners began to establish ConnectALL as a separate entity in 2018, focused on VSM.

Andrew Fuqua, SVP of Products, joined the company in 2018 to help drive the company's product strategy. Also, Eric Robertson, SVP Strategic Advisor, was recently hired to guide the company's future as a leader within the VSM industry. The team's collaboration and resulting products have received favorable reviews from **Forrester Research**, **Gartner**, and **SD Times**.

The ConnectALL strategy has the goal "*to deliver to 'the human side*" of software. Thus, while ConnectALL's integration tools are top-notch, they do not view VSM as limited to supplying integration tools and flow orchestration capabilities. Instead, they see much greater value from their VSM tools coming from human-driven assessments. The assessments help ConnectALL's customers discover areas to improve *agility*, *traceability*, *predictability*, and *velocity*. The VSM assessments, in effect, implement human-directed Lean improvement initiatives, as discussed in chapters 6 through 10 of this book.

ConnectALL's VSM assessments start before their customers make a VSM tools procurement investment, and the assessments continue beyond tool purchases. Most importantly, ConnectAll's VSM vision takes its tools beyond improving CI/CD and DevOps pipeline flows to align digital initiatives across the organization to improve business outcomes and improve the speed at which its customers can deliver software.

ConnectALL's focus in VSM is to help their organizations *see*, *measure*, and *automate* their value streams. They do this by connecting tools. While integration is undoubtedly an essential piece of ConnectALL's VSM solution capabilities, their larger vision is to connect tools as their primary value proposition. The connection of tools allows companies to gather metrics, draw value stream flows, analyze alternatives, and orchestrate preferred value stream flows.

A key differentiator for Connect ALL's products is its patent-pending **Universal Adapter**. The Universal Adaptor enables their platform to connect with any other tool with a REST API, making it possible to quickly integrate other tools across CI/CD and DevOps pipelines.

ConnectALL uses their Value Stream Visualizer as an aid in their Value Stream Assessment workshops. *Figure 12.4* illustrates an example of a ConnectALL value stream map:

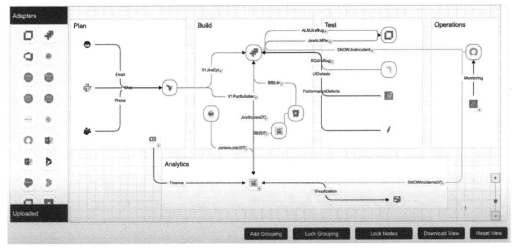

Figure 12.3 – ConnectALL's Value Stream Visualizer

ConnectALL's VSM platform offers four key capabilities: **integration**, **flow metrics**, **workflow orchestration**, and **governance**. Their VSM platform connects tools in your software delivery value stream by offering built-in vendor adapters for bi-directional or uni-directional synchronization of work and information flows across the entire value stream. The platform also offers workflow orchestration and governance capabilities out of the box.

ConnectALL's **Insights Analytics** product uses ConnectALL's Adapter to pull raw data from the disparate tools supporting your value stream into their standardized data model. In addition, the visualization capabilities of Insights make data for metrics such as flow, Lean, DevOps, and IT performance visible, transparent, and available.

You may be interested in this landing page, which includes some case studies: https://www.connectall.com/resources/case-studies/.

ConnectALL's website: https://www.connectall.com/

Digital.ai

Digital.ai has a unique VSM platform that addresses a common problem that most large enterprises face: *keeping developers happy and productive by "allowing teams to select" and continue using their chosen tools.* Doing so requires offering pre-built, intelligent integrations for hundreds of diverse DevOps solutions.

Digital.ai publishes the annual **Periodic Table of DevOps Tools**, consisting of practitioner-rated DevOps applications to make their point about disparate toolchains. The current 2020 version of their periodic table has more than 400 products across 17 unique categories. You can download it here: `https://digital.ai/periodic-table-of-devops-tools`.

The Digital.ai VSM platform connects the entire software delivery lifecycle, no matter your chosen tools and vendors. Compare Digital.ai's developer-friendly platform to the costly alternative of starting from scratch using a new set of technologies from a single vendor.

Initially, there are many perceived benefits to this approach, including access to cutting-edge technologies and new ways of thinking and solving problems, which is why it often tends to be an attractive initial consideration. But once the theory confronts reality, most enterprises find that a *rip-and-replace* of tools adds risk and complexity, increases downtime and costs, and often requires learning new tools and processes.

Even worse, hundreds of supporting processes and automation built around these existing tools may need to be changed. Applying this big-bang approach drains the team's energy and available capacity, moving the focus away from the goal of the digital transformation. Instead, the organization must become digitized to improve operational efficiency and become a digital business that can rapidly innovate.

Digital.ai's unified VSM platform connects your business and development value streams. It offers end-to-end oversight and governance of the DevOps pipeline and other supporting tools and organizations (portfolio planning, customer support, operations, and sales, among others) that help improve business outcomes.

While most value stream tools simply help improve software development and DevOps efficiency, *Digital.ai's solution connects Agile planning and portfolio management, continuous testing, application protection, software development lifecycle management, release and deploy orchestration, and end-to-end AI-powered intelligence.* Its platform enables large, complex enterprises to optimize the CD pipeline for maximum value delivery and quality instead of compliance with fixed delivery plans.

Digital.ai believes a VSM platform must provide end-to-end oversight and governance of the DevOps pipeline. It does this by integrating data across the entire software lifecycle toolchain, applying business analytics and AI/ML techniques to offer real-time visibility into business and development value streams metrics and KPIs, providing actionable insights (*Figure 12.5*):

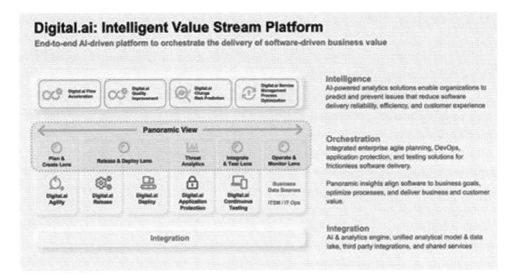

Figure 12.4 – Digital.ai: Intelligent Value Stream Platform

Digital.ai is one of the few (if not the only) VSM platform solution providers that has understood the need to apply AI/ML and connect business and development stream metrics and KPIs. Their VSM platform helps accomplish this goal by providing a unified data model and the pre-built metrics and dashboards necessary to assess the flow of value to customers.

As an example of these capabilities, Digital.ai employs AI/ML to look inside and across organizational silos to aggregate data, forming a holistic view of information. It then offers actionable insights across sales, marketing, finance, development, operations, and technology teams.

Digital.ai offers several solutions that support value *stream intelligence and managing the risk of change*. These include the following:

- Analytical lenses for the Plan and Create, Integrate and Test, Release and Deploy, and Operate and Monitor lifecycle segments, as well as a panoramic lens for total lifecycle views that combine business and technology data

- AI and ML to optimize service management, change risk prediction, flow acceleration, and quality improvement

Value stream *orchestration* solutions from Digital.ai include the following:

- Agility for agile planning and portfolio management (formerly **Collabnet | VersionOne**)

- Release and Deploy DevOps solutions for release and deployment orchestration (previously **XebiaLabs**)

- Continuous testing (formerly **Experitest**)

- Application protection (previously **Arxan**)

More information on Digital.ai's solution is provided in Section Two of the book, *Identifying VSM Methodology Providers*.

The essential elements of Digital.ai's Value Stream Platform are as follows:

- **Applied Intelligence**: The Digital.ai platform automatically and intelligently guides software delivery orchestration to accelerate the flow of value and predict change failures and schedule risk.

- **Common Data Model** (**CDM**): Digital.ai's CDM facilitates aggregating and harmonizing data and applying AI and ML. Digital.ai's robust AI platform capabilities analyze data across all value streams, creating a 360-degree digital view of business outcomes and technical outputs.

- **Normalized View**: The CDM supports an intelligence layer, which provides a holistic view, or lens, of a customers' digital world appropriate for consumption by technical executives and business leaders.

- **Panoramic 360° digital view**: A 360-degree view enables value delivery improvement from concept to cash, aligning technology improvements with the organization's broader business goals and objectives.

The key highlights of the Digital.ai value stream platform are as follows:

- Multi-tenant, purpose-built-for-cloud hosting or on-premises deployments.

- Shared services (for example, user management, single sign-on, licensing) enables seamless collaboration and alignment of users, tools, methodologies, and teams.

- The CDM and platform integrate data across various tools and business systems.

- Analytic lenses offer a panoramic, 360-degree view that allows business and technology groups to finally align and measure the impact of technology investments on business outcomes.

- Intelligent software lifecycle orchestration applies AI and ML to visualize all the work necessary to produce solutions and identify delays, bottlenecks, handoffs, and excess work-in-progress.

- Built-in AI/ML identifies potential change failure and reduces associated incident **mean time to resolution (MTTR)**. In addition, it can look back and investigate systemic root causes of technology change issues that span people, processes, and technology.

- Apply AI/ML models that find, predict, and address issues across the value stream, supporting data-driven decisions.

- Connect development outputs to business outcomes to understand the impact of technology investments to develop new features and products.

The Digital.ai value stream platform offers visibility across teams, tools, and processes. As a result, organizations can effectively measure value and quality, such as customer satisfaction and retention, application usage and security, execution efficiency, revenue, and growth.

Besides supporting all major Agile (**Scrum**, **Kanban**) and scaling frameworks (**SAFe**, **DA**, **LeSS**), Digital.ai promotes a VSM methodology, which optimizes *people*, *processes*, and *technology* to continuously improve business value flow, from ideation to customer delivery.

In Digital.ai's view, measuring output metrics (such as the number of features created, cycle time, velocity, and the number of deployments) is only part of the VSM story.

> *"We also must capture and measure data that supports better business outcomes and user experience. Consequently, one must understand where friction exists within the customer journey, eliminate waste and delays, and increase customer delight. It's absolutely vital to connect outputs from your customer-facing systems to understand how people react to your brand's user experience and products. Knowing this allows your organizations to quickly adapt and positively improve your bottom line (cost, revenue, customer lifetime value, end-user satisfaction, and more."*

> *Mike O'Rourke, VP and Chief R&D Officer, Digital.ai*

Digital.ai offers a complete set of *DevOps* offerings that help organizations dramatically improve their IT organization's Lean outputs and connect them to customer experiences and business outcomes. This approach creates an unparalleled view of potential improvements that can move the needle toward better business results.

Digital.ai provided two cases for this book. The first use case is from a large U.S. insurance company that uses Digital.ai's software tools to support their digital transformation activities:

Large U.S. Insurance Company

Business Application

- A digital transformation with buy-in from teams to the CEO to apply value stream management with SAFe

Business Issues/ Objectives:

- Lacked visibility to progress across strategic initiatives, product roadmaps, divisions, and teams.
- Release Train Engineers (RTEs) had no time to measure and improve value flow.
- Scrum Masters did not have the time to continuously improve their SAFe events and eliminate handoffs, delays, and other bottlenecks.
- Portfolio Managers were always firefighting and could not focus because actionable insights from their data were not available.
- The company employed multiple tools from different vendors for each development process step, making end-to-end visibility extremely difficult.

Digital.AI Solution

- The company integrated its business processes with Digital.ai's enterprise agile planning and release orchestration products.

Results to date:

- Enabled alignment of strategy with DevOps work and software investments, creating end-to-end orchestration and a comprehensive view of their development processes.
- More than 10,000 IT professionals fully view their development flow from idea to customer value delivery.

Figure 12.5 – First use case

The following Digital.ai use cases highlight a global retailer's experience of using Digital. ai's software products to provide end-to-end visibility across the disparate tools used in their DevOps pipelines and evaluate the effectiveness of their value streams:

Global Clothing Retailer

Business Application

- Suffering from multi-billion-dollar losses, mainly attributed to a sharp decline of brick-and-mortar retail sales resulting from COVID-19.

Business Objectives:

- Increase their digital footprint by 50%, improving their ability to sell more goods and services to consumers online.
- Their digital transformation plan included three primary focus areas: unification of internal and external data, continuous lean improvement, and "instant" visibility.

Digital.AI Solution

- They integrated agile planning, release, and deployment data by using Digital.ai Agility and Release products.

Results to date:

- The company now has end-to-end visibility across the development life cycle, including data from over 15 third-party tools.
- Adopted agile, lean, and DevOps practices and measured progress immediately with out-of-the-box dashboards and industry-standard metrics.
- They now generate value stream reports to identify and eliminate bottlenecks and release delays, significantly improving time-to-market and downtime.
- To date, they have achieved a 50% growth in digital sales and a 40% improvement in direct-to-consumer sales.

Figure 12.6 – Digital.ai use cases

Digital.ai's website: `https://digital.ai/`

GitLab

GitLab is acknowledged as a VSM leader by several industry analysts, such as **Forrester Research** and **GigaOM**. GitLab is fundamentally a DevOps platform provider. The GitLab DevOps platform integrates planning, development, operations, and security teams via a single application. GitLab also promotes their platform's ability to help "*teams accelerate software delivery from weeks to minutes while reducing development costs and security risks.*"

With its end-to-end DevOps platform, GitLab enables end-to-end visibility throughout the entire software delivery lifecycle. But since GitLab provides the necessary tools in one application, the software development teams avoid the so-called **DevOps toolchain tax** that occurs when the teams must also support the development and sustainment of the DevOps toolchain integration and automation capabilities.

Put another way, the DevOps toolchain tax is the added cost of the development team having to support two simultaneous software delivery activities. One activity supports the development of their customers' products – value-added work from our customer's perspective. The other set of activities supports developing their DevOps pipeline environments – which is not value-added work.

GitLab's Value Streams Analytics is an out-of-the-box feature that helps teams visualize and manage the overall DevOps flow cycle time from ideation to customer delivery. GitLab's Value Streams Analytics provides reporting on common workflows and metrics from a single data model.

Though customizable, GitLab's Value Streams Analytics provides default stages to represent the GitLab flow, including the following:

- **Issue** (*Tracker*): Time to schedule an issue (by milestone or by adding it to an issue board)
- **Plan** (*Board*): Time to first commit
- **Code** (*IDE*): Time to create a merge request
- **Test** (*CI*): Time it takes GitLab CI/CD to test your code
- **Review** (*Merge Request/MR*): Time spent on code review
- **Staging** (*Continuous Deployment*): Time between merging and deploying to production

GitLab also provides default labels for eight types of Issues: **bug**, **confirmed**, **critical**, **discussion**, **documentation**, **enhancement**, **suggestion**, and **support**. In addition, GitLab promotes their single-click drill-down capabilities to the level of work items, allowing the teams to remove blockages immediately upon discovery. GitLab also provides **Scoped Labels** and **mutually exclusive labels** (such as workflow::edit and workflow::design) that can be used to model custom workflows, which can then be visualized using Kanban-style boards or the **Insights dashboard**: `https://docs.gitlab.com/ee/user/project/insights/#insights`.

From the perspective of the software delivery teams, GitLab provides a single tool, eliminating the toolchain integration and automation headaches of managing disparate tools otherwise required to sustain a mature DevOps pipeline. Most importantly, GitLab's DevOps/VSM platform strategy gives the developers time to deliver value and means they do not have to spend time resolving technical debt issues associated with managing their DevOps environments.

GitLab's VSM page can be found at `https://about.gitlab.com/solutions/value-stream-management/`.

HCL Software

HCL Software is a division of **HCL Technologies** that develops and delivers more than 50 software products innovative software products built around DevOps, digital, IoT, cloud, automation, cybersecurity, and infrastructure management. It is one of the largest software providers in this review, with over $1 billion in annual revenue and 4,200 employees operating in more than 50 countries, counting more than 20,000 enterprise customers.

HCL Software DevOps, shown in *Figure 12.5*, is a key pillar of the portfolio, offering a complete and intelligent enterprise software value stream platform from planning to production and from mainframe to microservices:

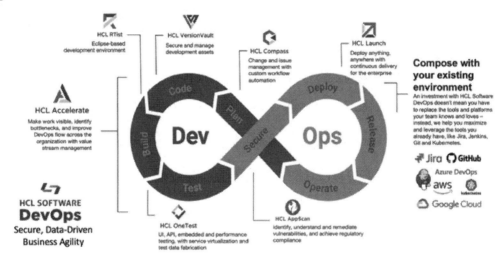

Figure 12.7 – HCL Software DevOps

HCL Software DevOps is a suite of best-of-breed product offerings that are loosely coupled yet highly integrated across the portfolio and the ecosystem of DevOps tools. Additionally, an open plugin framework allows enterprise customers to quickly connect one or more of the solutions into their existing environment. Customers looking for a comprehensive DevOps solution may adopt the entire platform. *Figure 12.5* shows the set of products, which includes the following:

- **HCL Accelerate**: An intelligent **VSM platform** that enables continuous improvement by integrating with many tools across DevOps environments to visualize value stream flow, capture actionable insights, and automate release processes.

- **HCL OneTest**: An integrated suite of **software automated testing** tools including UI, performance, and API testing throughout project lifecycles. It features a scriptless, wizard-driven, test authoring environment and supports more than 100 technologies and protocols.

- **HCL AppScan**: A suite of comprehensive **application security testing** and management offerings including SAST, DAST, IAST, and SCA on web, mobile, and desktop apps that integrate directly into your software development lifecycle tools and processes.

- **HCL Launch**: A CD engine that automates application deployments, middleware configurations, and database changes to on-premises and cloud-based development, test, and production environments.

- **HCL Compass**: HCL Compass is a powerful low-code **DevOps workflow engine** that enables enterprises to quickly stand up custom processes for Agile management, quality management, IT service management, and more.

- **HCL VersionVault**: HCL VersionVault is a secure, enterprise solution for **version control and configuration management**. It provides controlled access to soft assets, including code, requirements, design documents, models, schematics, test plans, and test results.

- **HCL RTist**: HCL RTist is an **Eclipse-based modeling and development environment** for creating complex, event-driven, and real-time applications. It is specifically designed to help software engineers with feature-rich tooling for design, analysis, building, and deploying embedded, real-time systems and IoT applications.

HCL Software DevOps offerings have been designed to help the most complex organizations, often in regulated industries, that require advanced approaches to minimizing risk, managing cost, and driving revenue. Many improvements can be achieved through DevOps *Day 1* solutions that are primarily focused on automation in a CD pipeline. These solutions include establishing an automated, controlled path to production typically enabled through CI, CD, test, and security tooling. The ROI of these practices using HCL Software DevOps solutions has been well documented and summarized as better quality, faster time to market, lower costs, and higher employee morale.

As DevOps has entered its second decade, HCL has found their forward-thinking customers often are focused on addressing DevOps *Day 2* challenges, which include the following:

- Connecting IT value to business value

- Adapting organizational culture and alignment

- Scaling best practices across the enterprise

- Optimizing flow across the end-to-end value stream

- Managing across many tools and decades of technology platforms

- Minimizing risk from security and quality exposure

- Shifting security, quality and governance left

- Increasing the frequency of production releases

With HCL Accelerate unifying the value stream, enterprises are enabled to address these *Day 2* challenges. Software delivery can be established as a core enterprise competency that aligns IT activity to business outcomes for success in this digital age. The ability for organizations to proactively and effectively create business agility, secure products, and resilient operations using HCL Software DevOps is showcased in *Figure 12.6*:

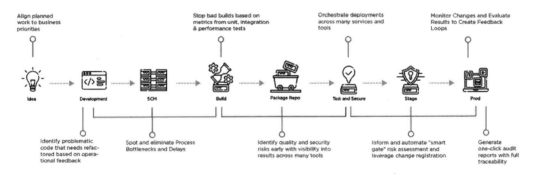

Figure 12.8 – HCL Software DevOps intelligent value streams

Beyond product capabilities, HCL enables customers to succeed by providing a white-glove service and support experience atypical of large enterprise software providers. This approach is derived from HCL's roots in the IT service business and is tangible from first engagement to pilot to enterprise-scale operations. Early in the process, technical advisors will host no-fee value stream workshops to identify improvement opportunities and define a path to achieving business objectives. Then, utilizing the HCL SoFy (`hclsofy.com`) cloud-native environment, customers can spin up instances of the HCL Software DevOps products for hands-on demos and trials. Finally, as customers move forward with implementation, HCL assigns customer advocates to accounts for regular collaboration to ensure maximum business results are achieved. This approach has led to some of the highest **Net Promotor Scores (NPS)** in the industry (NPS 60+) and deep customer success.

To learn more about HCL Software and its VSM platform, visit `https://www.hcltechsw.com/DevOps/`.

Kovair

Kovair Software is a Silicon Valley software product company that provides integrated software tools supporting global product development and management. Historically, Kovair is known for its *Omnibus Integration Platform* – an **Enterprise Service Bus (ESB)** platform that integrates 110+ third-party (best-of-breed) software tools and other applications via their off-the-shelf integration adapters and plugins. In addition, Kovair's integration platform supports DevOps, **application lifecycle management (ALM)**, and **project portfolio management (PPM)** requirements.

However, Kovair also promotes their platform's support for digital transformations and installing VSM solutions that provide visibility across the organization's business. In this context, Kovair is rebranding the company's products along the lines of **Kovair VSMP (Value Stream Management Platform)**, **Kovair VSDP (Value Stream Delivery Platform)**, **Kovair PPM (Project and Portfolio Management)** for DevSecOps, and **Omnibus** as its **integration Platform as a Service (iPaaS)**-based integration platform.

Kovair VSMP/VSDP solutions are already capable of merging organizational data, processes, and applications from legacy ALM into the cloud with DevSecOps. For example, Kovair's Project Portfolio Management and its iPaaS-based Omnibus serve a VSMP framework. And Kovair promotes its ALM and DevOps platforms as VSDP solutions.

Kovair automates toolchains with **workflow** and **policy engines** to help create a system of automated governance and visibility across all business communications and best-of-breed third-party solutions, including new solutions such as **Smart City 5G Enablement of Services** and Digital Transformation. Finally, Kovair can also help IT transform itself from a cost center to a value center, with business outcomes integrated and managed.

Though not currently recognized by Forrester Research or GigaOM, Kovair Software was recognized in Gartner's *2020 Market Guide for DevOps Value Stream Management Platforms*, and SD Times also reported on Kovair's VSM capabilities in their article titled *A guide to value stream management solutions* (SD Times, January 6, 2021).

Kovair's VSMP solution serves as a *Sales Pipeline CRM for Capturing Revenue Opportunities*, with dashboards of KPIs related to business outcomes, which is unique. In other words, Kovair metrics track lifecycle costs for all organizational value streams and products, not just software. And they tie their value stream metrics to projected and realized revenues, not just cost savings.

Kovair also promotes its VSMP as offering unique capabilities in the following areas:

- **Targeted and systematic waste reduction**: Kovair provides a unified view to senior management, through middle management to the operations, administration, sales, and logistics teams. This capability enables early detection of bottlenecks and the elimination of waste at every step of delivery.

- **Ensure Process Governance**: Kovair offers a task-based workflow both at the macro and micro levels to ensure governance across and within every team involved in delivery.

- **Improve cross-functional collaboration**: Kovair enables collaboration between tools, processes, and teams over a hybrid infrastructure environment.

- **Gain improved productivity**: Kovair provides complete visibility across the triple constraints of time, resources, and costs, enabling better productivity through efficient use of resources.

- **Increase Process Efficiency**: Kovair offers secure and efficient integration seamlessly with best-of-breed applications via Kovair's award-winning Omnibus multi-cloud iPaaS solution.

- **Continuous Product Lifecycle Management**: Kovair offers complete project and portfolio management capabilities.

- **Seamless iPaaS Integration**: Kovair offers third-party integration with best-of-breed solutions.

- **Concurrent Multi-Modal IT**: Kovair offers multiple IT methodologies, Waterfall, Iterative, V-Model, and Agile (Scrum and Kanban), all from a process-driven platform.

Kovair's software products offer task-based workflow implementation and visualization capabilities of crucial software development activities with associated data that help product teams discover areas for improvement to optimize value stream flows.

Kovair does not enforce or promote a specific VSM methodology. Instead, Kovair allows existing or newer project management processes and methods to be ideated and deployed with Kovair's Workflow Engine, with process automation, governance, and project and portfolio management.

Readers can find more information on Kovair's platforms at the **Kovair Software website**: https://www.kovair.com/.

Micro Focus

Micro Focus is one of the world's largest enterprise software providers. Their products deliver trusted and proven mission-critical software that keeps the digital world running. With a pragmatic, disciplined, customer-centric approach, enterprises can run and transform to succeed in today's rapidly evolving marketplace. Micro Focus' portfolios span a diverse set of capabilities across IT operations, cybersecurity, information governance, mainframe, big data, and application delivery.

Micro Focus needed to transform its company through DevOps to empower their customers with their own digital transformations and grow its business. To drive this change, Micro Focus created a software factory that aligned its strategic planning with an integrated set of tooling, services, data, and processes that enables the company to plan, build, test, release, operate, and manage the software delivered to their customers.

The company's journey started with a gap analysis into how they deliver and enable end-to-end value streams. They categorized these into four initial components: **Plan** (strategy-to-portfolio), **Build** (requirement-to-deploy lifecycle), **Request-to-Fulfill** (**R2F**), and **Detect-to-Correct Lifecycle** (**D2C**). As products pass through the activities of a chain, they gain value at each step along the way. A value chain framework allowed Micro Focus to identify the activities that are especially important for the advancement of strategy and attainment of goals.

Micro Focus's application delivery solutions are a critical component of the software factory. They allow teams the freedom and autonomy to move quickly coupled with a central point of visibility and a layer of governance that aligns to business objectives. With an open framework, teams can integrate the vast ecosystem of tools to optimize the flow of work, reduce the overhead in managing complex toolchains, and provide insights to improve continuously.

Micro Focus' integrated solution approach allows value stream participants to visualize and contextualize the activities in a product value stream and track flow and value through multiple phases. Embedded across these solutions is the ability to ingest and intelligently analyze data across multiple sources to observe trends, identify bottlenecks, find correlations, and detect anomalies to foster continuous improvement.

The approach solves common challenges faced by enterprise organizations, such as lack of prioritization of high-value customer demand, inability to track flow across a product value stream, and poor understanding of process friction and execution constraints. Key products include the following:

- Project and Portfolio Management acts as the business backbone to establish strategic vision and goals and align to epics, features, product backlog items, and user stories.

- ALM Octane serves as the central nervous system where work, risk, and quality are managed from planning to release.

- PulseUno provides a single unified, secure, Git-based developer platform to track the value of change across code, build, review, and artifact capture.

- Continuous testing solutions for functional (UFT), performance (LoadRunner), and application security (Fortify) scales automated testing as part of the software delivery pipeline at every commit, every step or gate, and through to production.

- Deployment Automation seamlessly enables deployment pipeline automation, reducing cycle times and providing rapid feedback on deployments and releases across all your environments.

Micro Focus takes a software factory view to install DevOps capabilities. Additional background on this topic can be found here:

- **DevOps at scale: How to build your software factory:** `https://techbeacon. com/devops/devops-scale-how-build-your-software-factory`

- **Create a software factory to evolve DevOps and speed transformation:** `https://www.microfocus.com/en-us/digital-transformation/ our-perspective/software-factory`

For more information on the company and its products, visit the **Micro Focus website** at: `https://www.microfocus.com/en-us/solutions/accelerate-application-delivery`.

Plandek

Plandek provides a complete Agile and delivery metrics **business intelligence (BI)** platform that provides an end-to-end view of their clients' software delivery cycles. While it is not a complete VSM platform solution, Gartner recognized its platform as a global top 10 vendor in Gartner's new *DevOps Value Stream Management Platforms Market Guide*.

Their vision is to apply data science to the software delivery process, offering intelligent insights to deliver software products better. Teams use Plandek's *predictive data analytics* capabilities to reveal hidden risks, improve end-to-end delivery performance, and address their thorniest software delivery questions, such as the following:

- Are we achieving the goals of our Agile, DevOps, and business transformations?
- How can we help our Agile teams deliver value more quickly and predictably?
- How can we objectively compare the performance of our software delivery teams?
- How can we shorten the time to market and increase velocity?
- How are we performing compared to other companies in our industry?
- How can we give our teams the metrics they need to improve as a continuing process?

SD Times claims Plandek has unique integration and data mining capabilities that enable it to integrate with multiple value stream delivery toolsets (for example, **Jira**, **Git**, **Jenkins**, **Azure**, and **DevOps**) to obtain pipeline metrics. In addition, Plandek's data mining capabilities provide access to delivery metrics from end to end across the pipeline, exposing patterns so that their customers can make informed decisions to improve software delivery efficiencies, quality, velocity, and predictability.

Plandek also provides customizable dashboards that provide visibility to critical metrics and KPIs allowing product delivery teams to do the following:

- Empower teams to deliver valuable software faster, more predictably, and more frequently.
- Reduce delivery and infosec risk and improve governance at scale.
- Put value stream metrics and analytics at the heart of VSM initiatives.

Plandek gets high marks in the following areas:

- Stack and process agnostic

- An analytics solution that does not require an orchestration layer

- Enterprise scalability and security

- Offers a complete end-to-end view of software delivery pipelines

- Supports team collaboration, continuous improvement, and product visibility and reporting

Plandek offered two case studies for inclusion to demonstrate the effectiveness of their metrics and analytics platform as a DevOps VSM point solution.

Figure 12.7 summarizes the first case study offered by Plandek:

FTSE 50 Multi-national data and publishing business
• Uses Plandek as a key element to support their value stream management initiatives spanning their global software delivery teams involving more than 2500 engineers. • Cycle time reductions were identified using Plandek's software as a key opportunity area for improvement. • An OKR to reduce cycle time by 25% in six months during 2020. **The results to date:** • Using the delivery and engineering metrics available within the plan deck platform, the targets were both achieved, plus they gained a 25% increase in velocity of delivery.

Figure 12.9 – Plandek customer use case #1

And *Figure 12.9* summarizes the use and results of a second Plandek customer use case:

Large multinational conglomerate operating in 12 countries plus Europe in the US
• Client uses Plandek's customizes dashboards across the delivery organization to provide metrics, analytics, and reporting. • Their specific application is to support their continuous improvement process. **The results to date:** • Reduce cycle time by 75%. • Reduced hot- fixes in production by 54%. • Doubled commit frequency by engineers. • 15% increase in deployments per day.

Figure 12.10 – Plandek customer use case #2

Plandek provides a robust BI capability to support decision-making gathered from the toolchains that support end-to-end CI/CD and DevOps pipeline activities.

Plandek's website: `https://plandek.com/`

Plutora

Plutora offers a highly rated VSM platform recognized as a leader by the **Enterprise Management Associates (EMA)**, **Forrester Research**, and **GigaOM**. They are also a founding member of the **VSM Consortium**.

Plutora promotes their VSM platform as providing a complete software delivery management solution engineered to improve time-to-value. In this context, the Plutora platform offers the following capabilities for software delivery management support:

- **Value Stream Management**: Seamlessly brings together product owners, release and development managers, risk and compliance teams, and engineering and deployment teams to deliver value and support continuous end-to-end improvements across the SDLC.

- **Release Management**: Define and schedule hierarchical releases, track dependencies, manage approvals, and maintain compliance while accelerating change across the entire enterprise portfolio.

- **Test Environment Management**: Centralize bookings, resolve conflicts, and track system dependencies. Eliminate error-prone manual configuration management and change control processes.

- **Deployment Management**: Helps streamline deployment processes across teams to minimize risk and accelerate cut-over events. Manage the planning, approval, coordination, and execution of production cut-over activities across multiple teams. Use analytic capabilities to streamline audits and inform post-implementation reviews.

- **Predictive Analytics**: With integrated and normalized data from end to end, made visible through customizable dashboards, users have a single source of truth for software delivery from idea to production on an enterprise scale.

It's essential to note that Plutora positions its VSM platform as a software development data platform, providing the infrastructure necessary to integrate, automate, and orchestrate software delivery pipelines. Most importantly, its data-centric VSM platform, robust analytics engine, and common data model provide real-time access to critical data for decision making. In their words, *"it all comes together in the analysis and display of our rich set of metrics and dashboards that provide organizations with the insight they need to deliver the most value to their customers through their development efforts."*

Plutora recognizes that many project management and tools embed useful VSM data and analytical capabilities. However, the challenge for decision-makers is to navigate multiple value stream dashboards, then make sense of end-to-end pipeline flows. For these reasons, Plutora promotes the need for a dedicated analytics platform that pulls data from multiple platforms.

Overseeing your software delivery process

The Plutora VSM platform provides a comprehensive set of tools to oversee the entirety of your software delivery people, processes, and tools. Plutora's VSM platform works regardless of management methodology, automation support, or the third-party tools employed by the organization. Its purpose is to help scale Agile and DevOps strategies across the enterprise.

Figure 12.9 graphically portrays the three categories of tools within Plutora's VSM Platform, *Decision Making & Analytics, Management & Orchestration, and Integration & Common Data Model*:

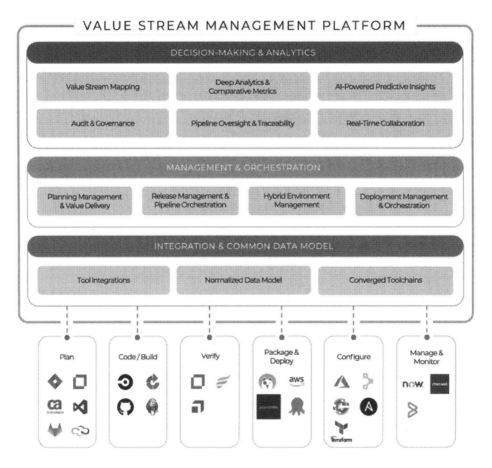

Figure 12.11– Plutora's VSM platform

Plutora's platform implements a **Decision-making and Analytics** layer at the top-most layer that captures, manages, and provides access to SDLC data related to your KPIs. This layer also provides access to pipeline metrics and predictive analytics capabilities to support software deliveries across your digital business.

Plutora's out-of-the-box metrics and reporting capabilities (including monitoring the **DORA Four** metrics) provide accurate and near real-time information on pipeline flows. In addition, Plutora's dashboards display metrics encompassing measuring performance against the release planning process against business-facing outcomes and priorities.

Plutora recently released an expanded data-centric VSM platform that offers enhanced VSM flow metrics. The flow metrics help organizations monitor and manage value stream flows to measure efficiency and identify bottlenecks more precisely across software delivery pipelines continuously. With its data-centric platform and common data model, Plutora's customers can manage the metrics for any pipeline, development style, or tooling to achieve greater business outcomes through enhanced data-driven decisions.

Plutora's **Management and Orchestration** layer provides control, visibility, and automation of DevOps pipeline flows at the mid-tier layer. A significant and recent improvement in this layer is Plutora's *Planning Management and Value Delivery* capabilities supported by deeper integration with planning tools and a common data model across disparate tools. Plutora's common data model was always there. But the new release enhanced it with its planning management integration; plus the company has built additional scale into the platform to reflect its changing utilization as a mature data platform.

The enriched data offers a complete time series and change history across product lifecycles and software delivery flows. Product leaders can utilize enterprise-class analytics and reporting tools to achieve complete visibility across the entire portfolio and produce data that can identify trends and patterns in the software development process with time-based analytics.

Plutora's VSM platform provides the means to orchestrate work across your disparate CI/CD and DevOps toolchains. Release and deployment management are obvious orchestration applications. However, an equally important need is to orchestrate pipeline work in a hybrid environment. For example, it may be necessary to integrate applications on-premises that need to persist alongside other applications within a cloud environment.

The **Integration and Common Data Model** layer provides connectivity to the organization's CI/CD and DevOps tools, Agile planning tools, **project portfolio management** (**PPM**) tools, and production and post-production tools, eliminating the need to use integration brokers to code point-to-point toolchain integrations. Instead, the platform's connectors integrate data from disparate tools and prove a standard and normalized data model to support end-to-end analytics across IT value streams. This integration and analytics spans the entire value stream, from idea to cash, including Agile and DevOps-oriented people, processes, and tools.

As a value stream improvement and portfolio management tool, teams can model their value streams, store and manage metrics data, and reference the metrics individually across pipeline activities or rolled up into portfolio views. Product teams can implement controls, such as automated or manual review gates, governing build, release, and deployment activities. The provisioning of a standard data model with integrated analytic tools enables visualization of bottlenecks and areas of waiting, supports decision-making, and provides input into planning and resourcing activities.

Aligning software development with business goals

Plutora promotes their VSM platform as a tool to help fill the gap between business goals and software development, thereby reducing time-to-value. They further view this as a five-step activity:

1. **Managing your remote software factory**, making work visible with smart dashboards and automating governance to improve organizational performance.

2. **Creating a single source of truth** by integrating disparate data sources into a common and normalized data model that provides end-to-end and real-time views of your software development lifecycle activities.

3. **Giving full control, visibility, and automation** across testing, deployment planning, and release management activities, orchestrating multiple pipelines from ideations to production, improving productivity, eliminating waste, and managing risks.

4. **Enabling a smart digital business** by employing advanced KPIs, metrics, and predictive analytics across your entire software delivery process empowers your digital business. The idea here is that you cannot continuously improve the activities you do not continuously measure and analyze. Also, manage risks by automating governance and compliance requirements utilizing criteria gates and audit history.

5. **Reducing time-to-value** by identifying choke points, eliminating waste, increasing efficiency, and reducing time-to-value to achieve a competitive advantage.

Improving the software delivery process

Plutora identifies many potential applications for VSM to improve the software delivery process:

* Optimize CI/CD Pipelines
* Applying Analytics for Digital Transformation
* Enabling Enterprise Release Management
* Test Management Automation

* Supporting Remote Work Environments
* Scaling Autonomous Teams
* Implementing the Scaled Agile Framework (SAFe)
* Informed decision making

Figure 12.12 – Potential applications for VSM

As a VSM solution, Plutora provides a robust integration, automation, and orchestration platform. The objective is to use Plutora's VSM platform capabilities to achieve a competitive advantage by identifying bottlenecks, eliminating waste, increasing efficiency, and reducing the time-to-value.

Plutora website: `https://www.plutora.com/`

Quali

Quali is another software company that does not explicitly address full-scale VSM platform requirements but provides necessary components within any CI/CD or DevOps pipeline. Quali's *CloudShell Colony* is an SaaS platform for delivering **Infrastructure Automation at Scale**. More precisely, CloudShell Colony offers self-service automation and governance capabilities to streamline application development, testing, and release into production. In addition, its software supports the deployment and governance of complex software applications on cloud technologies, including AWS, Azure, and Kubernetes.

Quali's inclusion in this list is due to its support of automating governance policies, one of Gartner's three categories in its definition of VSM tools: **continuous compliance automation (CCA)** tools. However, it would have to be purchased as an add-on to support broader VSM platform requirements within an enterprise.

The primary product Quali promotes to support VSM initiatives is **CloudShell Colony**, which was formally renamed **Torque** on June 22, 2021. Our primary strength comes from a consistent focus on making it practical, even easy, to leverage the **application-centric environment** as a primary organizing construct.

Quali's application-centric environment combines application, infrastructure, and data resources. Taken together, with all of its systemic dependencies and intricacies, as a whole logical unit, it provides a better way to continuously design, deliver, operate, optimize, and govern the cloud infrastructure resources needed to power development and DevOps value streams.

On the surface, this may not seem like a big deal because you can certainly use any number of tools and methods to discretely, or even in some combinations, automate the provisioning and configuration of these individual resources. Unfortunately, however, most have been designed around executing individual actions, leaving the larger context, the systemic logic, and dependencies to be defined manually, individually, and often inconsistently, if at all.

Torque by Quali takes the opposite approach, starting from an expectation that whole systems comprising multiple resource types and configurations are what developers and DevOps product teams need to develop and deploy. Ultimately, the IT operations teams are responsible for delivering, running, and governing the value prioritized by the product owners.

The previous statement does not mean to imply that only whole environments can be designed and delivered on demand by Torque; quite the contrary. Defining individual resource types does not constrain future abilities to automate the on-demand composure, the stitching together, of the different resource types to work together as desired. Users can also change cloud providers after the initial deployment without affecting the application-centric environment.

Another core strength comes from another combination of assumptions that Quali's product Torque was designed around:

- Managing cloud costs and policy compliance is essential for being good stewards of the business and representing a vital data source to identify inefficiencies and drive optimization efforts.

- Getting cost and policy compliance data that is accurate, timely, and useful is hard to do, and it's even harder to do without introducing speed-killing friction into the workflow.

- Environments and their supporting resources are rarely deployed from a lifecycle perspective, much less with an easy way to manage them from a lifecycle perspective. Products themselves and the products and value streams they support have a useful lifespan, after which they should be either refactored or retired.

Torque helps meet cost and governance needs by automatically tagging resources used with cost, policy, and role information in addition to the technical attributes that are, in turn, analyzed via Torque's reporting and dashboards or available for analysis in other tools.

Torque is also built from a product lifecycle perspective. Application-centric environments have an expected lifespan that, by definition, is used to help drive product (environments in this case) improvement and reduce cloud resource waste by automatically decommissioning unused resources.

Another critical capability of Torque is its utilization of and integration with DevOps toolchains, making it easier for developers, DevOps product teams, and IT operations teams to take advantage of its automation and orchestration capabilities. In this context, Torque becomes a natural part of their customers' workflows. For example, environments can be requested and delivered based on a code commit (triggering a CI/CD pipeline run) via the command line, API calls, or GUI.

Quali believes the totality of these capabilities positively impacts and provides additional insight into lead time, cycle time, throughput, WIP, flow efficiency, and work profiling.

Quali does not currently promote or employ a specific VSM methodology at this point. That said, they note that the two frameworks or value stream concepts they encounter most frequently in their customer engagements are SAFe and Gartner's DevOps Value Streams.

Quali provided a relevant customer case study from Resident (*Figure 12.10*) that they believe illustrates their products' positive impact even within ostensibly modern, digital businesses:

Resident, a direct-to-consumer home furnishing brands

Business Application
- Support fast-growing luxury hybrid mattress business, DreamCloud.
- needed a way to innovate faster while continuously providing an exceptional experience for their customers through a modern online eCommerce platform.

Business Issues/ Objectives:
- Globally distributed teams of developers were sharing static integration and staging environments.
- DevOps teams backlogged by ongoing environment maintenance and troubleshooting created friction and delayed innovation.

Quali Solution
- Quali CloudShell Colony (now Torque)
- Amazon Web Services Public Cloud

Results to date:
- Provide environments to global teams in under 5 minutes.
- Consume native AWS services.
- Increase development speed with dynamic environments.

Figure 12.13 – Quali customer use case

Quali's primary value to improvement initiatives beyond IT/CI/CD or DevOps lies in their ability to facilitate faster and more specific experimentation with application releases and updates via their automation of blue/green deployments. For example, the marketing department wants to try a new set of messages targeted over a certain period, while business operations would like to offer new payment processing options before further rolling out a new release. Quali's Torque product helps simplify and expedite the feedback loop.

You can find more about Quali and its products at their website: `https://www.quali.com/`.

ServiceNow

ServiceNow offers a single platform, the **Now Platform**®, that integrates, automates, orchestrates software delivery pipeline flows. ServiceNow promotes its Now Platform as providing capabilities to "*deliver cross-enterprise digital workflows that connect people, functions, and systems to accelerate innovation, increase agility, and enhance productivity.*"

The platform incorporates a single, unified data architecture that supports end-to-end pipeline visibility and analytics. As a result, ServiceNow users can trace pipeline activity flows from the customer to the developer through their data model.

ServiceNow recognizes that organizations need to deliver business value and that VSM offers the best approach to manage and improve the flow of value across the enterprise. It is in this context that ServiceNow employs VSM.

Many of ServiceNow's customers are still making the transition from projects to product-oriented management strategies. Therefore, DevOps platforms must support these transitions as hybrid software development and delivery environments in the short run.

ServiceNow delivers a wide range of capabilities beyond VSM through one of the most tool-intensive platforms in the software industry, with a comprehensive scope of products offered. Conceptually, ServiceNow promotes its products as supporting digital workflows to optimize how things get done for any business:

- **IT workflows** to optimize IT service operations, align investments with priorities, and manage risk, security, and costs.

- **Employee workflows** make it easier for employees to get the information they need when they need it, break down silos by supporting value-based delivery streams, and improve productivity.

- **Customer workflows** create a seamless customer experience and improve retention with the efficient delivery of services through customized self-service models.

- **Creator workflows** to help citizen and professional developers quickly and safely build cross-enterprise applications via low-code software capabilities and connected digital workflows.

ServiceNow offers one of the most comprehensive product lines in the software industry, with 47 products listed in their product directory. However, all of these products would only serve as point solutions if not for implementing workflow capabilities – used in context with VSM as the approach to affect Lean-oriented improvements across the enterprise.

VSM solution offerings

The point of ServiceNow's workflow strategies is to use information technology to support the implementation, visibility, and improvements of value stream delivery flows, no matter what the organizational structures might look like. Or, from the perspective of implementing Lean improvements, ServiceNow tools help organizations integrate, automate, and orchestrate their value stream flows. This approach is the only way organizations can break down the organizational silos that work against streamlined value deliveries.

VSM is an approach that customers can take utilizing the ServiceNow platform. Individual ServiceNow products that run on the Now Platform come into play depending on the use cases and methodologies that the customers wish to adopt.

The Now Platform provides the basics such as integration technologies, a standard data model that is called Service Graph, advanced analytics and reporting, action workflows, artificial intelligence, and machine learning. *Figure 12.11* provides an example of how data from Service Graph helps organizations visualize interactions and results across a pipeline execution:

Figure 12.14 – Visualize interactions and results across a pipeline execution

An example of a use case might be a software product value stream where the Now Platform provides connectivity and insights into the plan-build-operate-service lifecycle. The essential ServiceNow products in the software product value streams are IT Business Management, DevOps, and IT Service Management.

Key differentiators and strengths

ServiceNow's key differentiator is the breadth and scope of the workflow and connectivity that is supported. For example, in the software value stream, many vendors in this space focus on the areas of delivery between code commit and deployment The ServiceNow approach covers the entire value stream from customer demand to product usage.

The Now Platform also connects to other management areas within an organization with the same single data model. Examples include their employee (HR) and customer service workflows.

1. Pipeline integration platform:

   a. Abstracted and correlated data model (across many types of sources).

   b. Central platform tool for connectivity called the integration hub, alongside APIs and toolkits that provide out-of-the-box integrations to a wide range of targets (including and going beyond the DevOps tools and platforms), as well as the ability for partners and customers to easily add their integrations that use ServiceNow's workflows and data model.

2. Metrics and analytics:

   a. One connected data model from ideation to what is happening in production, especially if you are already managing production in ServiceNow IT Operations Management (availability and performance) and IT Service Management (management and governance). For example, showing the change failure rate (a commonly used accelerate metric) is easy as ServiceNow runs the systems that know when changes occur and when they fail.

   b. Out-of-the-box insight dashboards with data normalized from all the sources make reporting across teams using different DevOps tools simpler.

   c. Complete BI platform that supports deep analytics, real-time metrics, time series analysis, ease of customization, and personalization. A low-code/no-code approach to metrics creation.

3. Linkages or strategies support other organizational value stream improvements:

   a. Works with any data that can be brought into ServiceNow and connected to many other business systems and infrastructure monitors across organizations.

4. Tools support integration, collaboration, and orchestration across Dev and Ops:

   a. An information and management layer supports collaboration via tailored dashboards for each persona or role, delivering flow metrics and out-of-the-box DevOps metrics based on those promoted by Dora/Accelerate.

So far, we have discussed the Now Platform in the context of its many tools and capabilities. But equally important is how we apply their tools to support the organization's VSM initiatives.

VSM methodology

Customers can leverage the platform and products to implement the methodologies and use cases that best meet their needs. In addition, ServiceNow expects to focus on business outcomes (including capturing and managing financial data, collecting efficiency metrics, and identifying areas for improvement).

Many ServiceNow customers are taking a project-to-product shift facilitated by maintaining a hybrid approach while they make the transition, meaning that the project and program management functions can operate at a corporate or program level while working seamlessly with scaled Agile and team-based approaches.

Supporting Lean improvements beyond the IT organization

ServiceNow customers can use the platform from idea to production, get feedback from their end users, capture product ideas and demands, and provide strategic input into the product backlog with IT Business Management. They can also track the delivery process with ServiceNow DevOps and service their end users with IT Service Management or Customer Service Management.

Visibility in ServiceNow applications is not limited to measurements of pipeline flow and other Lean improvement metrics. For example, users apply the **DevOps Pipeline UI** view to show pipeline stage progression and details for each app, as shown in *Figure 12.15*:

Figure 12.15 – Set up user-created integrations for additional planning, coding, and test tools

This end-to-end workflow on a single platform with a single data model provides customers with excellent visibility into the process and opportunities for optimizing the value string beyond the technical teams. In addition to tracking the value being delivered, our platform also helps capture the cost of the value stream so that customers can make informed investment decisions.

Customer use cases

ServiceNow provided the following customer use case as an example of the employment of their platform to implement an end-to-end DevOps pipeline solution:

DNB (Bank in Norway)

Business Application
- To remain main competitive by reducing time to market with innovative and relevant products.

Business Issues/ Objectives:
- The IT organization needed to implement an end-to-end and value-based delivery perspective that required a change in developer behaviors.
- There was tension between Agile developers, who wanted to speed up time to market and Change Managers, who had to adhere to strict processes.
- DNB had unstable IT systems and wanted to improve the speed of their development.
- Auditable DevOps became necessary as a way to balance control against the go-to-market needs of the developers.

ServiceNow Solution
- DNB recognized Value stream management offered by ServiceNow DevOps would be the success factor for implementing DevOps Change Automation.
- DNB has implemented DevOps methodology using ServiceNow automation.

Results to date:
- Employed ServiceNow to automate all change tickets, eliminating all manual steps.
- 20 hours per week saved on change tickets for the two teams processing change tickets.
- The end-to-end value stream approach reduces administrative efforts for developers, eliminating bottlenecks that save an average of 15 minutes per developer every day.
- The implementation of auditable DevOps improved their development teams' work satisfaction.

Figure 12.16 – Customer use case

A detailed description of the DNB use case is available at the following URL: `https://www.servicenow.com/customers/dnb.html`.

DNB notes the importance of managing and leveraging their product delivery value streams to improve performance and efficiency and encourage certain desired behaviors. Therefore, they encouraged developer behavior by providing fully automated change governance when the following conditions existed:

- You implement an approved CI/CD pipeline toolchain, and the deployment process is at least partially automated.

- You have a minimum set of mandatory data in your pipeline tools needed for the change ticket to be automatically approved.

- You have a set pipeline that separates environments used for production, **user acceptance testing** (**UAT**), systems testing, and development.

- You always run the different tests in dedicated environments.

- All tests run successfully.

- You have to find the schedule stating when you are allowed to deploy to production.

- You have no critical or significant incidents on your service.

DNB's use case highlights a critical point discussed throughout this book on the need to implement **infrastructure as code** (**IaC**) to support automated testing and provisioning of testing environments on demand. We will revisit this subject in *Chapter 15, Defining the Appropriate DevOps Platform Strategy*, and *Chapter 16, Transforming Businesses with VSM and DevOps*.

Readers can find out more about ServiceNow, the Now Platform, and the approach to VSM by visiting their DevOps website at `https://www.servicenow.com/products/devops.html`.

Tasktop

Tasktop is another industry-leading VSM platform vendor with high ratings from industry analysts, such as **Forrester Research** and **GigaOM**. The company's key message is *Transforming businesses into high-performing tech companies*.

In addition, its CEO and founder, Dr. Mik Kersten, wrote the Amazon best-selling book *Project to Product*, which helped explain to the software industry why we had to move away from the traditional project-based management philosophies to product-based management structures and strategies. Dr. Kersten's book also introduced the **Flow Framework®**, which provides a management framework and infrastructure model to help bridge the gap between business and technology. Moreover, it provides a guide on making the transition from focusing on projects to products.

The Flow Framework helps organizations align technology investments with business value by visualizing and measuring the value streams encompassing the complete set of activities that bring software or SaaS to the market. It also provides a common language to help guide business and technology stakeholders in setting priorities and measuring outcomes.

The Tasktop VSM platform, which implements the Flow Framework, is designed to provide the language, metrics, and models to practice VSM over any toolchain and any organizational structure. It has two primary applications, namely **Tasktop Viz™** and **Tasktop Hub**, as depicted in *Figure 12.13*:

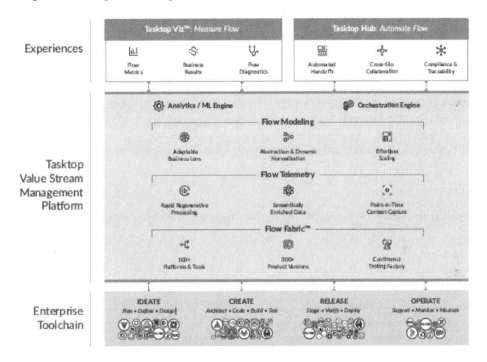

Figure 12.17 – The Tasktop VSM platform

Tasktop's VSM platform implements three critical capabilities for VSM that do not typically exist in-house:

- A blueprint for mastering software at scale
- A robust data capture and storage layer
- A scalable and adaptive business lens over raw factual data

While the platform provides extensive and sophisticated bi-directional integration capabilities, the connections also provide visibility to data and analytics. Connectors to 60+ Agile and DevOps tools provide pipeline data for visualization, decision-making, and triggering events based on user-defined rules.

The Flow Framework builds on an **integration model** that provides connectivity across **Ideate**, **Create**, **Release** and **Operate** lifecycle tasks. Building on the integration model is an **Activity Model** that provides traceability of artifacts produced by the organization's value streams. Finally, a **Product Model** aligns value stream activities with customer-centered deliveries.

Given its foundations in Lean, the Flow Framework seeks to improve flow in service of business results. But instead of the standard work and information flows of traditional Lean improvement practices, the Flow Framework evaluates the flow of four Flow Items in software delivery (*Figure 12.14*) and their relative distribution:

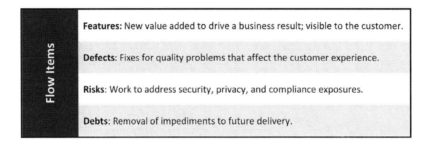

Figure 12.18 – Flow Items

The Flow Distribution model represents potential adjustments in the flow of features, defects, debt, and risk. These adjustments occur situationally and are commensurate with the product's lifecycle stage to maximize business value.

Flow Distribution is essential in helping businesses (product/line-of-business owners), and technologists evaluate cause and effects when adjusting flows. For example, optimizing for higher flow velocity for features to capture new market opportunities may come at the expense of working on other critical items, such as fixing bugs and reducing technical debt. The bugs cause negative reviews with customers, impacting future deliveries and sales, while the accumulating technical debt makes delivery of future enhancements increasingly difficult and expensive. Finding the right balance is crucial for the product's long-term success.

As with any Lean initiative, metrics and business outcomes are critical in Tasktop's Flow Framework, as shown in *Figure 12.15*:

Flow Metrics	Business Results
• Flow Velocity	• Value ($)
• Flow Efficiency	• Cost ($)
• Flow Time	• Quality
• Flow Load	• Happiness

Figure 12.19 – The Flow Framework: flow metrics and business results

Tasktop recognizes that many large-scale organizations, driven by their immediate needs for visibility and cost-efficiency, consolidate their DevOps toolchains around 2–3 core work management tools for Agile execution and IT service management.

Unfortunately, those are execution-focused tools, designed to support small Agile-oriented teams employing Scrum, Kanban, or Squad methodologies. Team-oriented tools are too siloed to support effective decision-making when executive leadership oversees budgets in the tens or hundreds of millions of dollars with thousands of technology practitioners.

Moreover, those tools' end-to-end pipeline support capabilities are minimal, not supporting PPM, UX design, compliance, InfoSec, testing, and other IT practitioners involved in the software value delivery chain. Eventually, the need for those purpose-built tools and systems of record becomes apparent, leading to an increasing number of siloed tools and pipeline data.

Organizations cannot overlay and abstract the end-to-end value stream data in such an environment, including all its constituent but siloed tool domains. As a result, their executives are bound to make misinformed decisions based on partial information.

Tasktop points to data from a Forrester Report that notes that line-of-business executives make 65% of tech-buying decisions. Therefore, it's imperative that IT becomes much more focused on generating business value and ROI (Craig Galbraith, Forrester, 2020).

Tasktop promotes its ability to deliver precisely that business-focused visibility in support of data-driven IT investments, helping technology and product leaders implement a managerial framework fit for the Age of Software.

Moreover, Tasktop's products replace pen-and-paper value stream mapping exercises and thereby take the practice of VSM into our digital economy. The end-to-end views supported by Tasktop's tools generate a live, shared, and actionable view of how to accelerate value creation in software portfolios.

Tasktop promotes the following benefits experienced by their customers:

- Shorten time-to-market by an average of 75%

- Can identify where to spend their next dollar

- Have visibility to see live value stream maps, lit up with their bottlenecks

- Can make the shift from projects to transparent and measurable product value streams

Tasktop's VSM platform offers visibility across individual products and within portfolios. Decision-makers can use the information to determine priorities and address issues causing delays and bottlenecks. In addition, what-if analytics provide visibility into the benefits and cost savings from proposed flow improvements. Tasktop lists many customer references on their website, which can be found at `https://www.tasktop.com/customers`. Some of Tasktop's client references include the following:

More information is available on **Tasktop's website**: `https://www.tasktop.com/`.

Figure 12.20 – Tasktop customers

Apptio/Targetprocess

Targetprocess, acquired by Apptio in February of 2021, is fundamentally a software platform that aid in the adoption and scaling of Agile in all its forms. Specifically, the platform offers a visual platform to help IT organizations adopt and scale Agile across their enterprise. In addition, it is also a comprehensive toolchain integration platform.

In this context, Targetprocess supports scaled Agile approaches such as **Disciplined Agile**, **Large Scale Scrum (LeSS)**, **Nexus**, **SAFe**, **Scrum**, **XP**, or a custom-built or hybrid Agile framework to achieve business agility and improve value flows throughout the organization. In addition, Targetprocess supports the implementation of Agile practices at the program, product, and team levels.

Targetprocess supports continuous software deliveries with native integrations to CI/CD and DevOps pipeline tools, such as **Jira**, **Azure DevOps**, **BitBucket**, **GitLab**, **GitHub**, **Jenkins**, and **Phabricator**. Targetprocess also helps align the activities and goals of product management, ITSM, sales, and marketing functions with integrations to the tools they use, such as **MIRO**, **SalesForce**, **Zendesk**, and **ServiceNow**.

Forrester Research ranks Targetprocess as a Strong Performer in their *Forrester Wave™: Value Stream Management Solutions Report* (Q3 2020) and as a Leader in the *Gartner* 2021 and *2020 Magic Quadrant for Enterprise Agile Planning Tools*.

Targetprocess helps align business interests with its implementation of **objectives and key results (OKRs)**, financial controls, and an integrated analytical engine. The support of OKRs helps organizations observe disconnects between business goals and related development efforts. The ability to connect business functions with development is one of Targetprocess's strengths.

Targetprocess supports human resource management within its standardized data model across pipeline activities, enabling planners to factor in resource costs, schedules, and allocations. Targetprocess also provides an extensive list of out-of-the-box metrics, and the metrics are extendable, customizable, and available across the toolchains through its tool integrations.

Targetprocess website: https://www.apptio.com/products/targetprocess/

ZenHub

ZenHub is another tool that is not a VSM platform, but it does provide project management and project data display functions, much like Atlassian's Jira software products. However, ZenHub's approach is different in that their suite of team collaboration and project management tools directly expand the functionality of GitHub's cloud-based version control capabilities.

ZenHub's software products provide a layer of abstraction on top of the GitHub source control management repository, delivering project management, planning, workflow automation, and reporting capabilities. In addition, the ZenHub tools use data that's already available within GitHub to provide visibility, reporting, and automation capabilities across the software development pipeline of activities.

The benefit of ZenHub's approach is that software developers and other stakeholders do not need to maintain records in an external system, such as Jira or Asana's products. Instead, ZenHub's products pull information directly and automatically from GitHub based on its commit records. Thus, while other project management software vendors integrate GitHub into their products, ZenHub's approach extends GitHub directly.

The ZenHub approach reduces manual re-entry of data across multiple disparate tools otherwise required to manage source code and artifacts and plan and manage software development activities. Instead of working across multiple third-party applications, ZenHub users move between tabs within the GitHub UI, working with project data that is already shared and available.

ZenHub supports Sprint planning and estimating by connecting, rolling up, and distributing work item information across epics, stories, features, change requests, bug lists, and technical debt work requirements. Additionally, ZenHub supports VSM requirements, providing visualization and reporting capabilities that show work progress and pipeline efficiencies, and help identify bottlenecks via its cumulative flow charts.

At the time of this writing, ZenHub offers seven tools, as shown in *Figure 12.17*:

ZenHub Software Products	
Boards	A visualization tool that aggregates and displays information from multiple GitHub repositories to track and manage work.
Reporting	Generates product development reports in real time from data retained within GitHub to track and predict progress and identify bottlenecks.
Roadmap	Provides a visual timeline display of project progress so that executives, team members and other stakeholders can see how their work contributes to a project's success.
ZenHub Browser Extension	Since GitHub is a cloud-based tool, accessed via a web browser, the ZenHub browser extension eliminates the need to install software apps and tools.
Workflow Automation	Automatically syncs your project whenever GitHub issues are updated and completed. Automates handoffs, and tedious and repetitive tasks.
Sprint Planning	Automates your sprint planning process by setting team sprint schedules, automatically populates issues, and moves unfinished work into upcoming sprints.
Planning Poker	A tool that simplifies and expedites the consensus-based, gamified technique for estimating work and generating story points.

Figure 12.21 – ZenHub software products

ZenHub products are a good fit for those organizations that have already committed to using GitHub for distributed version control and **source code management** (SCM).

This section ends the introduction to the leading VSM vendors. As you continue to explore this topic on your own, you will find other VSM vendors with solid credentials who were not listed in this book. The primary issue is that some vendors either did not respond to my queries or decided they did not want to participate in the interviews.

Summary

This chapter briefly introduced 19 industry-leading VSM tool vendors and their software offerings. These vendors made our list because one or more IT industry analysts, such as Forrester Research, Gartner, GigaOM, and SD Times, have reviewed and designated the vendors as having relevant offerings in the VSM tool and platform category of software tools. The focus of our reviews is on each vendor's applications and strengths. You also read several use cases highlighting how some of the products were used to improve CI/CD or DevOps pipeline flows.

In the next chapter, you will learn about four leading VSM methodology providers, **Disciplined Agile (DA)**, Scaled-Agile, **the Lean Enterprise Institute (LEI)**, and LeanFITT™. Each provides an approach to implementing VSM practices.

Questions

1. True or false: VSM is strictly a tools-based approach to implementing improvements across your CI/CD and DevOps pipelines.

2. True or false: VSM is a Lean-oriented approach to making value stream improvements.

3. As a quick reminder, what are the common types of waste in Lean production?

4. Who were two of the original contributors to the ideas behind applying Lean concepts and value streams within software development?

5. Through what aspect or lens did Davenport and Martin view the role IT plays in value stream improvements?

6. What are the potential applications for AI and ML in VSM?

7. What are the three essential capabilities employed within a CI/CD or DevOps pipeline?

8. Fundamentally, what is VSM?

9. What are the roots of VSM?

10. Trick question: Are the four DORA metrics the only useful metrics in VSM?

Suggested reading

1. Martin, James. (1995) *The Great Transition. Using the Seven Disciplines of Enterprise Engineering to Align People, Technology, And Strategy. Amacon.* New York, New York

2. Davenport, Thomas. (1992). *Process Innovation: Reengineering Work Through Information Technology. Ernst & Young – Center for Information Technology and Strategy. Harvard Business School Press, Boston, Massachusetts.* `https://www.researchgate.net/publication/216300521_Process_Innovation_Reengineering_Work_through_Information_Technology`

3. Kersten, Mik. (July 15, 2020) *The Rise of Value Stream Management (VSM). Founder & CEO of Tasktop.* Originally published on the Tasktop blog on July 15, 2020. Also posted on LinkedIn. `https://www.linkedin.com/pulse/rise-value-stream-management-vsm-mik-kersten/`

13
Introducing the VSM-DevOps Practice Leaders

In this chapter, you will learn about the current leading VSM practice leaders. We will start with an introduction to the VSM Consortium, a not-for-profit trade association funded by members (vendors and enterprises) and open to all to support the emergence of the value stream management market through research, learning, networking, and open source projects.

Next, you will learn about the Project Management Institute (PMI) approach to implement VSM strategies and methods via their DA-FLEX offerings. PMI acquired **Disciplined Agile (DA)** and **FLow for Enterprise Transformation (FLEX)**, both well-established and recognized leaders in their respective fields, to build their Lean-Agile practices, training, and certification programs. DA provides PMI's Agile practices in software development. In contrast, but complementary, you will learn how FLEX is a framework based on Systems Thinking that provides a comprehensive set of portfolio, Agile product management, executive/management, and program and team patterns for success based on Lean-Agile principles and practices.

Next, we'll move on to learn about Scaled Agile's approach to value stream management as part of their **Scaled Agile Framework™ (SAFe™)**. Specifically, Scaled Agile implements value stream management as part of its SAFe DevOps curriculum and training.

In this chapter, we're going to cover the following topics:

- The VSM Consortium
- PMI's DA FLEX
- The **Scaled Agile Framework (SAFe)**

By the end of the chapter, you will have foundational knowledge about the approaches taken by the three leading Digital VSM practice leaders to implement effective value stream management practices.

The VSM Consortium

The **Value Stream Management Consortium (VSMC)** is a new organization established on March 3, 2021, to help organizations worldwide deliver customer value by adopting and advancing value stream management tools and practices. The objective of the VSMC is to serve the whole VSM community by helping drive value stream management standards and innovation through leadership and community.

Defining VSMC's purpose, mission, and goals

The VSMC aims to advance value stream-centric ways of working in technology teams to lead higher-performing organizations. The VSMC operates as a not-for-profit trade association. Its mission is to cultivate and nurture the emerging market for digital value stream management and help the community learn, devise practices and standards, and grow through its use.

The VSM Consortium is open to all people and organizations interested in applying value stream management as a business transformation and customer value delivery improvement strategy. Funds for the VSMC are primarily raised through its membership fees, but plans are underway to also include the resale of VSM-related learning products.

Structurally, the VSMC implements Lean practices and value streams as its operating model, while its funding supports VSMC *Research*, *Learning*, and *Outreach* value streams.

Though founded by several of the leading VSM tool providers, the objective is to let VSMC members drive the direction of future enhancements to VSM methods and tools. The VSMC members will also play a critical role in building a knowledge base of VSM practices.

Building the VSM industry through collaboration

The VSMC was founded by five technology leaders, **Digital.ai**, **HCL Software**, **Plutora**, **ServiceNow**, and **Tasktop**. The charter established for the VSMC by its founders is to *help organizations worldwide improve performance and improve customer value deliveries through the adoption of value stream management (VSM).*

Though competitors on the open market, these founding companies recognized that real and sustainable growth to the VSM industry required worldwide and industry-wide collaborative research to guide the VSM tool, platform, and services developed through the early adopter stage. No single company could take on the scope of this work by themselves. Moreover, the research had to be unbiased and vendor-agnostic.

The founders recognized the importance of extending their collaborations to organizational and individual practitioners worldwide from the start. As a result, the founders established the VSMC as a member association for both enterprises and individuals working with value stream management practices and platforms to meet this objective.

Helen Beal, Chair of the VSMC, offers the following value proposition for establishing the VSMC as a professional community of technologists and practitioners:

> *"By creating this community, we will increase and accelerate the use of VSM, while developing and instilling best practices and standards. And, ultimately, just like the practice of VSM itself, we will help deliver the utmost value to industry practitioners."*

Delivering customer value through software

The VSMC is still in its infancy, but aims to become the foremost professional organization to drive VSM practices, innovation, and adoption. The purpose of the VSMC is to help the software industry deliver VSM products and services that help organizations achieve business transformations that deliver value in our digital economy.

VSM achieves this goal through a comprehensive software life cycle orchestration process that provides value stream managers, release managers, DevOps managers, product managers, and leadership with the data, visibility, and analytical tools necessary to improve software delivery pipelines.

Shepherding the VSM industry

The VSMC will serve as a central hub of information and education on the practice and adoption of value stream management. Ongoing research will help inform organizations on how to measure value and become higher-performing as a result. In addition, training and certifications programs will support member collaboration worldwide and help make VSM the industry-standard way of working.

The VSMC works with leading analysts to apply scientifically sound principles to its information gathering and analytical activities. The objective is to discover insights that offer solid guidance to teams and organizations adopting value stream management principles to improve their value delivery performance.

Offerings in progress

The Consortium's initial research offering will be *The State of Value Stream Management Report*, which will measure how teams apply value stream management principles, practices, and metrics to influence their value stream management outcomes. The VSMC Board has launched its first survey, and its initial findings will be available in June 2021.

Later in 2021, the VSMC will investigate value stream mapping principles and practices and work with their membership community to address their specific needs and priorities. The first VSMC online learning is the *Value Stream Management Foundation* course due for release in August 2021.

Though the VSMC is in its early days, *The State of Value Stream Management Report* alone will be a powerful tool to help organizations worldwide see how other organizations benefit from VSM methods, tools, and services and which approaches are working best with context-based guidance. The Value Stream Management Foundation course will help practitioners build the necessary skills to help their organizations employ VSM effectively. As practices evolve, the VSMC will create new guidance to inform its membership.

Findings from the initial VSMC report

As of the date of this writing, the first VSMC report has not been released. However, I have seen the initial draft and the summary findings are very interesting. The Chair of the VSMC, Helen Beal, was kind enough to allow me to share these summary findings in this book.

"While there are still significant challenges around the adoption of VSM, the following three key practices are evidence of a shift toward broader adoption:

- *Organizations are identifying value streams and organizing around them:*

  As organizations need to continuously innovate, it is essential to understand the key value streams, gain visibility into them, and organize around them to then improve value delivery.

- *Product-oriented teams are more popular than project-oriented teams:*

  Product focus binds the team more closely to the producer-consumer relationship. Value is determined by the products' consumer utilization, rather than abstract outputs defined by the project, or program.

- *People have roles specifically focused on value stream-centric ways of working:*

  By defining organizational roles in terms of the value stream, individuals know their spheres of responsibility. Having specifically defined roles that own the adoption, thinking about and changing how value is managed is a significant step toward the adoption of this concept."

Full disclosure

The VSMC Board elected me to an advisory role in April 2021 to help them in the following three areas:

– Guidance around value stream roles and learning paths

– Connecting VSM to other digital delivery frameworks

– Networking through the enterprise and consulting community

These initial findings are exciting, and I look forward to helping the VSMC meet its learning objectives and participating in the journey of discovery.

PMI's DA FLEX

The **Project Management Institute** (**PMI**) is best known for its training and certifications programs around traditional project management practices. However, PMI acquired two companies, **Disciplined Agile** (**DA**) and Net Objectives, in 2019 to establish a professional training and certification path for their members desiring to learn and apply **Lean-Agile** practices. DA has a focus on implementing Lean and Agile practices in software development. At the same time, Net Objectives developed **FLow for Enterprise Transformation** (**FLEX**), a framework based on systems-thinking, offering a comprehensive portfolio, Agile product management, executive/management, program, and team patterns for success based on Lean-Agile principles and practices.

Rather than building these methodologies from scratch, the PMI wisely chose to acquire established companies and methodologies to accelerate the development of their Lean-Agile certification programs and offerings. The work ahead of the PMI involves integrating the two practices as a seamless offering. PMI refers to their combined Lean-Agile approach as *DA*, with their enterprise offering being the DA Value Stream Consultant based on FLEX.

PMI offers *five* training and certification programs in support of its DA FLEX acquisitions, which are as follows:

- **Disciplined Agile Scrum Master (DASM) Certification**
- **PMI Agile Certified Practitioner (PMI-ACP)° Certification**
- **Disciplined Agile Senior Scrum Master (DASSM) Certification**
- **Disciplined Agile Value Stream Consultant (DAVSC) Certification**
- **Disciplined Agile Coach (DAC) Certification**

DASM operates at the single and small team levels, while DASSM guides how to get multiple teams to collaborate. Additionally, PMI will soon release a multi-team coach certification. Finally, **Disciplined Agile Value Stream Consultant (DAVSC)** is an enterprise-scale implementation of DA FLEX.

Many of the DA FLEX certifications, though useful for learning Agile-based roles and practices, are not relevant to the topics of DevOps and VSM. As a result, the bulk of the information covered in this section centers around the DAVSC training and certification programs. DAVSC provides a combination of Lean, Flow, Theory of Constraints, and Organizational Development theories and practices and serves as the foundational learning behind PMI's approach to value stream management.

The relationship between DAVSC and FLEX is as follows:

- DAVSC is based on the job task analysis for a person attempting to improve an organization's ability to create value.
- The system that supports this is FLEX.
- The DAVSC workshop teaches these responsibilities and how to achieve them.

Now that you understand the scope of the Lean-Agile offerings in DA FLEX, we can start to drill down into the DA toolkit to see how the framework is put together and how it supports Lean-Agile practices. Let's get started with an introduction to Disciplined Agile's core philosophy, *Choose your way of working (WoW)!*

Fitting Lean-Agile practices to support your way of working

PMI does not promote DA FLEX as a framework. Instead, the organization promotes DA FLEX as a toolkit that includes practices that work together. The distinction between frameworks and toolkits is subtle, so let's take a few minutes to understand the differences.

Definitionally, **frameworks** provide a basic structure that underlies a system, such as software development and delivery. At a conceptual level, software development frameworks provide a structured approach to applying Lean and Agile practices. For example, SAFe™ and scaled Scrum-based frameworks provide a set of organizational structures, events, and processes to implement their Lean-Agile practices. They are both very prescriptive in their approach to implementing Lean and Agile practices by implementing small team roles, structures, events, and time-boxed development cycles. Scrum and SAFe practitioners apply various processes, techniques, and methods within their frameworks. However, the basic structures and events remain intact.

In contrast, DA FLEX takes issue with the idea that one approach to implementing Lean-Agile practices works equally well for all organizations. Instead, they promote the view that organizations must review alternative strategies and tools to evaluate which fits better with their needs and cultures. Hence, PMI promotes DA FLEX as a toolkit. The basic idea is that value stream teams choose the right tool for the right job. Also, as a toolkit, the PMI implements its DA FLEX toolkit as a standalone Lean-Agile approach to improve value streams and extend this to other frameworks.

Philosophically, DA FLEX incorporates the concepts behind value stream-based continuous flows, Lean improvements, Theory of Constraints, Organizational Development, and human behavior. At issue is the concern that hierarchical organization structures, based around business functions, are antithetical to supporting Lean flows around value delivery.

Before we discuss how DA FLEX supports value stream management, we need to spend some time reviewing each offering independently, **Discipline Agile** and **FLEX**, to understand their respective contributions to modern Lean-Agile practices.

Choosing your way of working with DA

Co-created in 2012 by Scott Ambler and Mark Lines, DA is a process decision toolkit that helps individuals, teams, and enterprises optimize their **Way of Working** (**WoW**) in a context-specific approach. Scott Ambler and Mark Lines are well known in the software development industry because there is no single software development strategy that works well in all customer situations. So instead, users of the DA toolkit can choose between six different software development life cycle approaches and between hundreds of methods and tools with context-based guidance on their potential applications.

The **DA toolkit** incorporates the concept of **process blades** to help teams and organizations guide their selection based on their unique software development needs. In turn, the process blades guide users on how to apply selected techniques to enhance critical organizational capabilities.

Each process blade provides information on its philosophical underpinnings or **Mindsets**, the roles and responsibilities of **People** applying the techniques, descriptions of streamlined business processes as **Flows** to improve business agility, and employment **Options** to address situational needs. Collectively, *Mindsets*, *People*, *Flows*, and *Options* represent four views into the DA toolkit.

Besides its four views, the DA toolkit also offers four levels of process blades, spanning **Foundations**, **Disciplined DevOps**, **Value Streams**, and its **DA Enterprise**. As shown in *Figure 13.1*, the DA toolkit currently provides context-specific guidance on 24 well-defined process blades:

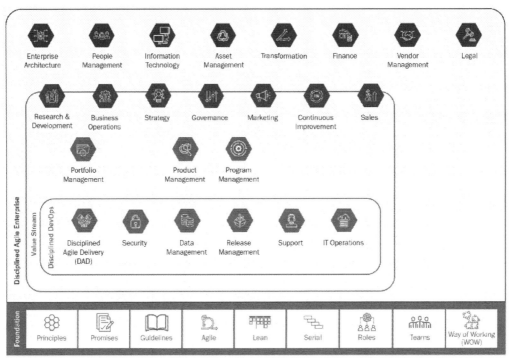

Figure 13.1 – The DA toolkit

As you can see in *Figure 13.1*, the DA toolkit includes four layers: Foundations, Disciplined DevOps, Value Streams, and Disciplined Agile Enterprise. We'll look at these four layers in more detail in the following subsection.

Installing Lean-Agile practices on an enterprise scale

The **Foundations** layer of the DA toolkit guides the underlying principles and concepts that form the DA mindset. The layer also introduces the fundamental concepts and differences between Agile, Lean, and Serial (traditional) software development approaches, roles, and team structures, as well as the concepts behind choosing your WoW.

The **Disciplined DevOps** layer provides guidance and techniques for streamlining software development and IT operations activities. An important differentiator is DA's systems-thinking approach to visualizing and understanding the complexities behind DevOps workflows, as shown in *Figure 13.2*:

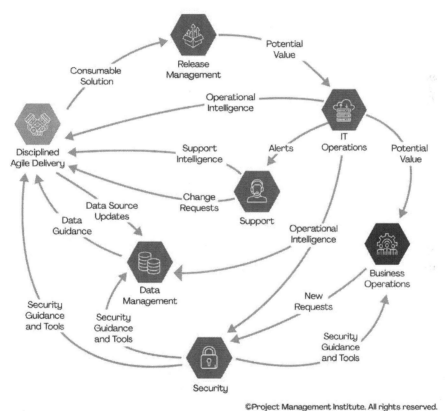

Figure 13.2 – The workflow of disciplined DevOps

A systems-oriented diagram, such as shown in *Figure 13.2*, is a bit more complex than a value stream map or workflow diagram. But you can use the knowledge you gained in *Chapter 3*, *Analyzing Complex Systems Interactions*, to work your way through it.

The **Value Stream** layer incorporates Lean-Agile principles acquired from FLEX, which you'll learn about in the next section. For now, understand that FLEX is a Lean-oriented approach to increase value realization. The process blades within this layer provide both a visual map and a guide to making value-based improvements across the organization's interconnected value streams.

The **Disciplined Agile Enterprise** (**DAE**) layer provides business management guidance to support the construction and sustainment of a Lean-Agile enterprise. DAE's process blades help the organization develop the ability to sense and respond quickly to changes in the marketplace.

> **Note**
> Readers who want to learn more about Disciplined Agile can read my previous book, *Scaling Scrum across Modern Enterprises*.

Now that you have a basic understanding of Disciplined Agile, let's understand how FLEX brings a life cycle approach to implementing Lean-oriented value delivery improvements within the DA toolkit.

Before we discuss the application of FLEX as a value stream management tool, we first need to visit the DevOps layer of the DA toolkit.

Implementing DevOps with DA FLEX

The DA toolkit devotes an entire layer of process blades to DevOps. The DevOps process blades include the following:

- **Disciplined Agile Delivery** (**DAD**): A people-first, learning-oriented hybrid agile approach to IT solution delivery

- **Security**: Describes approaches to protect your organization from information, cyber, virtual, and physical threats

- **Data management**: Promotes a pragmatic, streamlined approach to managing data as a critical asset that must support the rest of your organizational processes

- **Release management**: Encompasses planning, coordinating, and verifying the deployment of IT solutions into production

- **Support**: Outcome-based techniques to implement Help Desk or End User Support to help customers work with the solutions produced by your delivery teams

- **IT operations**: Outcome-based techniques to manage and govern your IT ecosystem

Scott Ambler and Mark Lines appropriately concluded that DevOps is now the minimum table stake that allow an organization to compete in our digital economy effectively. The competitive advantage of streamlining your organization's CI/CD and DevOps pipeline flows is impossible to duplicate via traditional, or even agile-based software delivery approaches.

PMI's contributions to DevOps do not lie in toolchain integration, automation, or orchestration capabilities. Instead, its DA toolkit provides comprehensive guidance on implementing and maintaining end-to-end DevOps infrastructures and pipeline flows.

Since this part of the book has a central focus on value stream management, let's move on to look at how DA FLEX, via the Value Stream layer within the DA toolkit, helps organizations work their way through Lean-oriented business transformations and improvements.

Achieving business agility with FLEX

FLEX gives the PMI an industry-leading approach to achieving business agility based on Lean-thinking and systems-thinking patterns. Al Shalloway, who developed FLEX, defines organizational business agility as the *quick realization of value predictably, sustainably, and with high quality.*

With FLEX, organizations use Lean principles to discover what's not working at a system level and why. But it's also important to note that *FLEX is PMI's new approach to implementing value stream flows intending to improve value deliveries using value stream management techniques.*

Enterprise transformation is such an essential objective of FLEX that it forms the basis of the acronym **FLEX (FLow for Enterprise Transformation)**. In other words, FLEX enables enterprise transformation through the effective implementation of value stream flows.

DA FLEX connects an organization's strategies to the execution of activities at the level of value delivery. The DA FLEX approach helps organizations to streamline their complex business systems to expose more effective value stream flows, enabling you to make decisions for improving each part of the organization within the context of the whole business system.

While businesses need innovation to improve their competitiveness, they also need to improve value delivery. In this context, the process blades within the Value Stream layer of the DA toolkit establish end-to-end value realization activities supporting the organization's products and services.

As was I in my early career, Al Shalloway was greatly influenced by Eliyahu M. Goldratt's book, *The Goal, A Process of Ongoing Improvement*, which introduced us to the *Theory of Constraints* (Goldratt, 1984, 2014). While Lean improvement initiatives, like VSM, emphasize the identification of bottlenecks as choke points that introduce delays, Goldratt's work helps us look closer to evaluate the constraints that cause our production delays.

For example, maybe we have a slow process, or multiple work item flows through our pipelines. We might have too much work for the system's design or lack of visibility to see issues when and as they arise. Or perhaps we have overly bureaucratic processes and approvals that restrict flows.

The FLEX approach helps the value stream team identify bottlenecks, the wastes that cause them, and evaluate methods to eliminate or reduce those wastes and improve workflows. The FLEX approach is a form of VSM methodology that has the following steps:

1. Define value-based workflows and organizational structures.

2. Identify the impediments to achieving the desired flows and structures.

3. Identify potential solutions to remove the impediments.

4. Apply systems and Lean Thinking to define improvement priorities working within the organization's culture.

5. Implement the proposed solutions in order of priorities and evaluate their effectiveness against the predefined goals and metrics.

6. Continuously analyze, replan, and repeat the FLEX process.

As you read through this section, it's important to note that FLEX is explicitly designed to support knowledge-oriented work. Also, Al's current thinking on the role of value stream management encompasses a holistic view of the organization built on insights gained from his years of Lean-Agile consulting experience. The following section details those insights.

Defining values streams in DA FLEX

DA FLEX defines a value stream in a manner that is consistent with other Lean disciplines, such as that found in Wikipedia: `https://en.wikipedia.org/wiki?curid=55610257`.

> **Value streams**
>
> A set of actions that take place to add value to a customer from the initial request through the realization of value to the customer. The value stream begins with the initial concept, moves through various stages of development, and on through delivery and support.

As you learned in the mapping value stream exercises in *Chapter 7, Mapping the Current State (VSM Step 4)*, and *Chapter 9, Mapping the Future State (VSM Step 6)*, DA FLEX makes the point that a value stream always begins and ends with the customer. They also make the distinction between the work within a value stream and the people doing the work. Their concern is that conflating the two works against the organization as value streams have a singular focus while people may support work in multiple value streams.

Another critical point is that organizations must shift from focusing on keeping people utilized to the throughput of value. While functional organizational structures can improve local efficiencies around developing critical skills and competencies, at the same time, they create waiting, bottlenecks, and other forms of waste from the perspective of executing lean value streams.

Figure 13.3 shows a graphical display of work flowing across the value stream (*green arrows*) with a traditional hierarchical management overlay (*red arrows*):

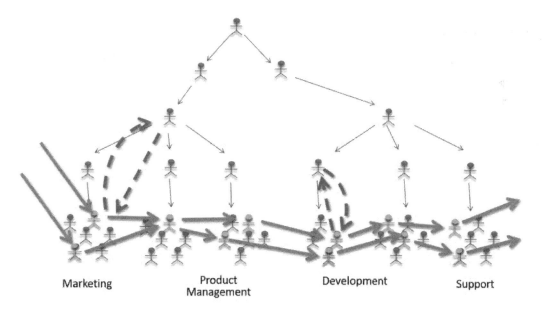

Figure 13.3 – Work flowing across the value stream with hierarchical management overlay

So, in the traditional management structures, we have work flowing in one direction, horizontally, as cross-functional flows, while decision making and approvals flow vertically within functional hierarchies. So, the question DA FLEX first asks is who is managing the end-to-end flow of value delivery?

It's a great question to ask because no single person is assigned to manage product flows in the traditional model. Instead, it is management by committees, with conflicting agendas and objectives. So, first and foremost, we have to fix that problem – an organizational structural alignment problem. And then, we need to make sure that we have defined efficient and streamlined flows with minimal waste.

Ultimately, the objective of improving organizational value streams is to improve business agility. Since FLEX implements the Value Stream layer within the DA toolkit, let's review how FLEX helps organizations evolve their value streams to improve business agility.

Improving business agility with DA FLEX

DA FLEX defines business agility as having the ability to realize the highest business value in the shortest amount of time, consistently, sustainably, and with high quality. By delivering incremental value across all value streams, the organization can adjust when and as needed, changing direction at the lowest cost.

This level of flexibility leads to lower risks and stress to those who work to deliver value across the organization's value streams. In this context, DA FLEX teaches that the primary objective of improving value streams is to establish business agility.

Applying systems thinking with DA FLEX

DA FLEX takes a holistic view of improving an organization, using the same systems-thinking concepts you learned in *Chapter 3, Analyzing Complex Systems Interactions*. Recall from the previous chapter that system thinking evaluates complexity through the lens of interactions across all the elements that participate in a system. With more elements, the system's complexity goes up due to an exponentially increasing number of potential relationships and consequential impacts.

The FLEX approach with the DA toolkit's value stream applies the same principles of systems thinking. We need to optimize the whole across our business systems. **Local optimizations** almost always fail to meet expectations if we haven't done the work upfront to ensure the change addresses an area of waste that affects the system's performance as a whole.

In his discussions, Al Shalloway points out that we cannot apply **Reductionist Thinking** to address complex issues in systems. For example, Al notes that if we try to construct a car with all the best parts available and try to assemble them, we will fail to build a car that works. You won't even have an automobile because the parts simply won't work together.

The scenario Al uses comes from a presentation that Professor Russ Lincoln Ackoff gave in 1994 at an event hosted by Clare Crawford-Mason and Lloyd Dobyns to capture the learning and legacy of Dr. W. Edwards Deming. At the time, Dr. Ackoff was the Anheuser-Busch Professor Emeritus of Management Science at the Wharton School, University of Pennsylvania.

The presentation is entitled *If Russ Ackoff had given a TED Talk*: `https://www.youtube.com/watch?v=OqEeIG8aPPk`. It's worth spending a few minutes watching this presentation as he makes the case on why local optimizations can never work.

There is so much to unpack in Dr. Ackoff's discussion. For example, he speaks about the difference between *continuous improvement* and *discontinuous improvement*. The point he makes is that continuous improvements are for followers, and those followers can never lead. Instead, the leaders leapfrog the competition through discontinuous improvements. In other words, leadership positions come through innovations.

Another critical comment that Dr. Ackoff makes is that he agrees that the positive Japanese impact on the overall quality improvements across the automobile industry is undeniable. Still, he also points out that while *the Japanese are doing things right, they are doing the wrong thing*. He made this statement in 1991, taking issue with the amount of pollution and congestion in our urban cities. Ackoff's discussion occurred well before the issue of climate change became a foreground concern.

Dr. Ackoff notes that there is a difference between **efficiency** and **effectiveness** and that quality needs to be addressed in terms of the latter. He likens efficiency to *knowledge*, but effectiveness to *wisdom*. Therefore, from a system perspective, quality must address both efficiency and effectiveness in delivering value. That is to say, we need to apply wisdom along with our knowledge.

In short, what good is it to have higher quality automobiles to drive if, at the same time, they are destroying our environment and our overall quality of life? So, we need to take a holistic view of quality and its contributions to deliver the most valuable product from our customers' perspectives.

Building people into our frameworks

Across Lean and Agile practices, frameworks provide a system or pattern to accomplish work. However, DA FLEX takes issue with the concepts behind frameworks because they don't account for the people who use them. For example, frameworks that seem overly restrictive or work against an organization's culture and operating system inevitably lead to friction and resistance.

The DA FLEX approach implements its WoW concepts precisely to address the issue that overly prescriptive frameworks do not address the complex interrelationships between the people operating within them from a system-thinking perspective. In other words, regardless of the Lean or Agile approach employed, we need to address the interactions between people, processes, and events systemically. Thus, the DA FLEX approach implements their toolkit as organized process blades, each of which includes related sets of methods and tools that organizations employ situationally to fit their needs in the value delivery systems they operate.

Orchestrating value stream flows

Lean Thinking provides an approach to managing the complexity of systems by orchestrating the flow of information, people, and materials around value delivery goals. In other words, to the greatest extent possible, we eliminate the ability to have our system components participate in interactions that do not support our value delivery goals.

DA FLEX implements its Value Stream layer within the DA toolkit to help organizations recognize the flow of value, in multiple streams, across the organization. All of those value streams support product deliveries and must do so in an efficient and organized manner.

This means we cannot simply look at the components that make up our organization in isolation. Our value streams are systems, and we need to manage the relationships between the participating components. On the positive side, value streams bring visibility to our value delivery flows. They also uncomplicate the process of value delivery.

On this latter subject, Al Shalloway makes the following observation:

> *"Although there are many reasons for resistance to change, they all tend to show up as local optimizations. Not a surprise given fear is in many organizations, and few approaches truly attend to the value stream."*

In other words, organizations develop cultures around the way they conduct business, which is highly influenced by their traditional hierarchical and functional organizational structures. As a result, business processes tend to support the localized goals and objectives of the people within the functional domains. While the processes may be optimized for the needs of the department, they probably aren't in terms of supporting value-based horizontal business flows.

But we also need to understand that the furthest upstream activities have the most significant impact on downstream activities. This means that problems at the start of a value stream, if not quickly caught, can disrupt the entire value stream delivery system, and it may be challenging to isolate the root cause of the problem.

Organizations typically have multiple value streams that support their overall product development and delivery capabilities, and these value streams are interconnected. For example, product management informs the intake process for the product backlog, which lies in a development-oriented value stream.

While it's reasonably simple to add, modify, or delete activities within a value stream, it's much more disruptive to the organization to add new value streams due to the number of potential cross-value stream impacts. In addition, the interconnected value streams create an even larger and more complex system of interrelated activities. Therefore, we want to start thinking about end-to-end flows at the start of our VSM initiatives.

Engaging executives and managers

Recall from our introduction to FLEX that it is fundamentally a business transformation activity to improve value delivery via Lean-Agile organizational structures and practices. It should be apparent then that DA FLEX operates at a strategic level and therefore requires buy-in and sponsorship from its senior executives.

On this subject, Al Shalloway offers the following observation:

> "Executives often misplace where the challenges in a value stream are – they often think it's in the dev area. Proper value stream management – in particular, visibility of work and delay – can be used to make the true constraint of the system visible to executives who otherwise just see the effects of what they are doing and not the cause – which is often the result of decisions they've made."

DA-VSC graduates learn how to implement workshops for executives and managers to talk about their customers to support an organization's strategic business transformation objectives. Ideally, everyone meets in a room with at least one large whiteboard as the meetings sometimes involve 30 to 40 people.

The assembled team divides the whiteboard into two sections: one side for business-oriented value streams and the other for **Implementation and Support**-oriented value streams. In between is an **Intake queue** containing a list of business improvement work items that the organization needs to focus on to effect the desired business transformation.

Al Shalloway refers to the intake queue as a list of **Minimum Business Increments (MBIs)**. An MBI represents the smallest increment of deliverable value in the form of a product, service, or result. The team assesses each MBI from a business perspective, wherein each deliverable meets the needs of targeted customers and fits within the approved strategy of the business.

As you see in *Figure 13.4*, the Business section is further divided into Portfolio and Product management functions. At the same time, the Implementation and Support side of the board has sections to display information on Development Intake, Development, Integration, and Deploy and Support activities.

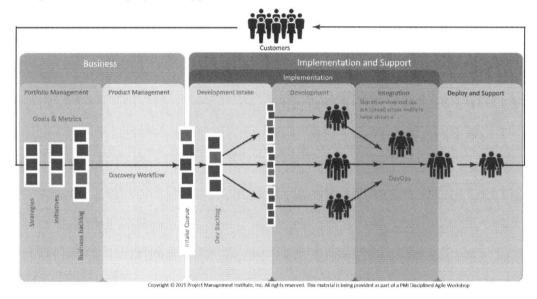

Figure 13.4 – Disciplined Agile process goals by phase

The **portfolio management** value stream guides investments in support of the mission and strategies of the entity. **Goals and metrics** describe what the executives expect to accomplish with the strategies and the quantifiable measurements that indicate the achievement of the goals. Each investment spawns an **initiative** tracked across its life cycle in respect to its defined goals and metrics. The initiatives are managed in a **Business Backlog**.

The **Product Management** value stream involves a **Discovery Workflow** to assess value stream delivery needs to meet the organization's strategies, goals, and metrics. These discovered business needs define the necessary deliverable items at a more granular level to achieve the business transformation. These business improvement work items are evaluated and prioritized before managing them as tasks within the intake queue.

The intake queue forms a boundary line between the Business and Implementation and Support functions. From this point forward, the work items follow a Lean-Agile-based development and delivery pipeline flow.

Almost every value stream in our digital economy relies on software, hardware, security, and other infrastructure components to improve business agility. Therefore, DevOps is the preferred development and delivery pipeline strategy when digital enhancements can aid value stream flows as it is the most efficient IT value delivery system.

Still, regardless of the extent of involvement of the IT organization, value stream implementation and improvement activities follow a Lean-Agile process that involves pipeline flows across **Development Intake**, **Development**, **Integration**, and **Deploy and Support** value streams.

Focusing Solution Teams

The FLEX approach to implementing MBIs is to organize people around the Focused Solution Team structure. Solution teams are product-focused, operating in an agile manner. In other words, a Focused Solution Team is limited to defining the solution needed to fulfill the requirements of the MBI.

Frequently, an MBI is too large to be developed by a single small Agile team. When this is the case, FLEX breaks the solution team into **Feature Teams** and **Core Teams**. Feature teams are fully functional with all the technical skills and resources needed to develop the product features identified. In contrast, the core teams tend to contain specialists needed to augment the feature teams. For example, the core teams may work on platform configurations, integration, and the automation of toolchains and augment the Feature teams when necessary.

In some cases, it may be necessary to borrow resources or even contract resources temporarily. In such cases, the borrowed members remain with the feature or core team within the solution team, as assigned, and they participate in their borrowing team's daily standup meetings. However, unlike the core teams, borrowed members may also continue to support their customarily assigned duties and participate in the daily standup meetings of their home team.

Both feature and core teams use Kanban-based production control systems to pull work items from the product backlog. They also operate in collaboration to deliver the product of the MBI.

People operating within a solution team are 100% dedicated to the work of the solution team. Recall that task switching/multi-tasking are forms of waste that hinder productivity as people must take non-value-added time coming back up to speed from where they left off as they move from one task to another.

Now that we understand how Disciplined Agile and FLEX operate within the DA toolkit, let's move on to understand how DA supports the collaborative work of multiple product teams.

Aligning multiple teams with Lean-Agile thinking

This section explains how DA FLEX supports three critical principles of Lean Thinking — *Systems Thinking, management creating the context for the teams, and removing delays* – for software development. As you read through this section, recall that Lean value streams are the organization's value-added workflows from *concept* to *consumption*. Also, let's quickly look at the three principles behind Lean in DA FLEX:

- **Systems thinking**: Looking at the business as a complex and highly integrated system that requires the participating elements to work in an orchestrated manner to accomplish its purpose.

- **Management oversight**: Management must create and communicate the context guiding the teams' work to self-organize in ways that support the strategies and goals of the business.

- **Removing delays**: To eliminate the waste of waiting. In software development, this means we don't create requirements until we are ready to work on them, nor do we write code until we have defined the requirements, established its acceptance criteria, and have the infrastructure in place to integrate and test it with the mainline code base rapidly. We must also remove the delays from making an error until detecting and fixing it.

DA implements its principles as guidance, not mandates. In fact, DA is fundamentally about giving people and organizations more choice when it comes to supporting their specific situations. We'll explore how DA encourages choice in the following subsection.

Establishing a new kind of discipline

It's important to understand that the term **Disciplined Agile** does not at all imply a desire to install a *heavy-handed* approach to improving agility. On the contrary, DA FLEX acknowledges that too much management, over-planning, over-design, and overly large projects are ineffective, dooming software projects to failure. However, Al Shalloway also notes that *undisciplined teams that use Agile as a justification to avoid doing what is necessary are also not effective … and, by the way, are not Agile.*

The origins of Agile have their roots in so-called lightweight software development methodologies and evolved to coordinate the work of small teams to improve software delivery performance. But we also need methods to improve agility on an enterprise scale to improve our end-to-end value delivery capabilities, usually involving multiple value streams.

Cross-team dependencies require greater discipline to resolve enterprise-wide integration, automation, and orchestration concerns across value streams. Unfortunately, the *team-of-teams model* for scaling Agile has issues because it forms a new functional model. As a result, every team is disconnected from understanding their contributions to the flow of value. In other words, the teams tend to focus on resolving cross-team issues in isolation instead of looking at their participation in the value delivery system as a whole.

Along these lines, it may make sense that we can simply extrapolate the small team concepts of Agile and make them work in large or multiteam environments. But that view ignores the fact that the dynamics between team members are quite different from the dynamics between teams.

Therefore, we need to extend Agile's small-team models to address development and operations-oriented issues at a local level but implement Lean-oriented flows to coordinate and improve the speed of deliveries across all the organization's value streams. This strategy is the essence of the Lean-Agile disciplines.

The Lean-Agile approach improves *organizational workflows to remove delays in receiving feedback, detecting errors, using information, and ultimately, delivering value.* In this context, software development efforts must be directed to support the integration, automation, and orchestration needs of the more extensive business system and its value streams.

Focusing on value stream flows

DA FLEX is a scaled approach to enterprise-wide agility that applies Lean-Agile concepts to improve value delivery across multiple teams. DA FLEX implements Lean-Agile flows across teams. Multi-product, multi-team agility can be achieved by focusing on work and information flows and ensuring that everyone agrees to make certain decisions at certain places in the value stream.

While we may still manage people vertically, we need to manage value delivery flows horizontally. Recall our discussions around *Figure 13.3.*

The flow of value is always horizontal. Measuring the utilization of resources vertically, within functional departments, or even disparate teams, creates disconnects from the flow of value, leading to local optimizations with little chance to improve the organization's overall productivity. Therefore, our most essential measurements evaluate time to markets to discern the constraints responsible for delays and adding costs across our value streams.

Understanding the discipline behind DA FLEX

Two sections back, *Establishing a new kind of discipline*, we noted that DA FLEX establishes a new kind of discipline that enables multiple teams to collaborate effectively to improve flows. We didn't say what those disciplines are but will now. DA FLEX promotes three disciplines to improve multi-team performance, and they should look very familiar to you if you've read this book carefully:

- **Discipline #1**: *Stakeholders cannot start more projects than the development organization can take on.* And the best approach to ensure this happens is by employing pull-oriented production control systems, such as Kanban.

- **Discipline #2**: *Teams required to deliver the selected value must work in unison.* Large software organizations with multiple teams may split work across products, components, features, or large requirements. Split teams always have dependency issues.

  Those dependencies become more challenging to address if each team maintains its product backlog and work pulls items in a manner that is efficient to them, which essentially is a form of local optimization. We need one product backlog and to have all the teams assigned to a product pulling from that one product backlog based on its priorities.

  Moreover, each team's work must be integrated into a shared source control repository with new unit-level code tested regularly, usually multiple times a day, against the mainline code to ensure the new code does not introduce bugs. Those bugs become increasingly challenging to find and fix as the code grows around them.

  Finally, we need the frequent release of increments to customers for review and testing. If we wait and customers don't like something we've done, the changes become much more challenging to make.

  A Lean Thinking approach implements the shortest viable cycle times (from conception to consumption) and has the fewest delays along our value stream pipelines. Ideally, we want the rapid customer and product testing feedback loops built-in throughout our entire value stream systems.

- **Discipline #3**: *Teams must let someone who sees the bigger picture decide what they should be working on.* This sentence may seem a bit like a *Duh* comment. But it's easier to go wrong here than many might believe. Executives must communicate the business's strategies, priorities, and goals up and down the value delivery chain. They must practice Gemba to see for themselves what is going on at a tactical level. And they must seek input from those performing the work.

At the same time, the value stream operators cannot decide what work they should focus on or what their product backlog priorities should be. Only the product owner has that authority, and they will wisely seek counsel from the teams and their members before making product backlog priority decisions. Specifically, they must seek advice from the value stream teams to obtain real-time information regarding identified bugs and other issues of technical debt that can cause future state or downstream problems.

Allowing choice is a good thing

In this section, we address another issue regarding the use of a disciplined multi-team approach to improving agility. As it turns out, allowing choice is an integral part of a disciplined approach to build and maintain Lean-Agile business systems.

Enabling choice is not the free for all it may at first appear. Discipline is required to achieve an organization's whats consistently so teams can work together. But the *hows* of mandating predefined processes and tasks are left to those doing the work. Unfortunately, the traditional Waterfall-based project management practices approach was to mandate both the *what* and the *how*.

Too often, planners employed virtually all the practices defined within their corporate SDLCs – perhaps believing more is better. But it never is. The organization's SDLC processes and taxonomy and recommended activity dependencies often bloated project schedule plans with unnecessary and non-value-added tasks.

DA FLEX offers hundreds of techniques, but it would be rare that more than a couple apply to any specific software iteration. Therefore, teams choose only those patterns and techniques that best support their current needs. And only the teams evaluating the techniques have the information to know which techniques are helpful and apply to their specific needs. But it's also helpful to have a repository of predefined and contextually valuable practices that can be reused and situationally refined to suit each new application.

This section completes our discussion on the alignment of multiple teams with the DA FLEX approach to Lean Thinking. Now let's move on to review a proven approach to the successful enterprise-wide adoption of DA FLEX.

Adopting the DA FLEX model

The successful adoption of DA FLEX tends to revolve around a few core concepts, as follows:

- Focus on defining and establishing value streams from the start:

  – You must move away from project-based or other push-oriented production control methodologies.

  – Instead, adopt a product-oriented focus, use pull-oriented production flows, and improve value deliveries organization-wide.

  – Suppose you've skipped a few chapters in this book. In that case, that means we seek more efficient flows of materials and information by eliminating waste, streamlining workflows around a steady cadence, and pulling products on-demand only when downstream capacity is available.

- Evaluate the proper pace of adoption in terms of the organization's culture and reasons for the adoption:

  – For example, applying DA FLEX as a potential competitive advantage is one level of motivation, but quite different from those who are already facing a burning platform situation.

  The former is a *like-to-have* situation, while the latter situation is a *must-have*.

- Create a tailored approach to your adoption:

  – Remember, DA FLEX is a toolkit with guidance on using the information situationally; it is not a framework.

  Use the tools that make sense to improve the success of your adoption.

- Guided continuous improvement starts from the beginning of the MBI initiative and continues throughout the life of a value stream without changing the improvement process.

- Focus on the workflow itself and not on DA FLEX:

  – Again, the DA toolkit provides tools for situational needs you apply to address your unique situations.

Now that you understand the essential elements behind the adoption of DA FLEX, we'll take a look at the playbook that guides the adoption.

Implementing the DA FLEX playbook

From a conceptual point of view, DA FLEX promotes the view that value streams from different companies – even in different industries – are surprisingly similar. This is similar to the view espoused by James Martin in his book *The Great Transition* (Martin, 1995). But, on the other hand, the differences are what deliver value and competitive advantage. So, determine what's needed for your organization and recognize that there are no universal solutions.

Companies have products or services that they need to develop, improve, or change, and so they undertake work, expecting value in return. Organizations with additional constraints, such as the regulation of specialized hardware, have similar idealized value streams but with added factors to which to attend.

With these concepts in mind, DA FLEX starts with a description of fit for purpose and a way to continuously improve. The objective is to avoid being overly simplistic while not being complicated. Thus, its starting analysis method provides the basis for an organization to keep improving.

The DA FLEX playbook has the following steps:

1. **Understand the idealized value stream**: To move from the current state to a desired future state. Understand what the idealized value stream looks like.

2. **See the challenges**: What must be overcome, such as budgets, executive approvals, new improvements to processes and equipment, new skills, and other potential change items. Assess to understand your challenges.

3. **Identify actions**: To solve your problems based on priorities that offer the most customer value for the financial resources, time, and people available to work on the change.

4. **Improvement backlog**: To track identified and prioritized improvement objectives. Keep in mind your organization's culture, assign someone responsible for leading the change, and identify the opportunities for change.

    Delay or avoid prioritizing proposed change items that are not in scope or that stakeholders will not support, and work items that create a cognitive overload.

5. **Keep improving**: Continuously add to the improvements backlog, refine the work items, and re-prioritize to align with customer demands and market opportunities.

As your organization works through this iterative and incremental improvement process, constantly visualize what your idealized value stream looks like. Now let's look at how we go about planning a DA FLEX engagement.

Planning the DA FLEX initiative

At this point, the organization has decided to adopt DA FLEX. They have expective management buy-in and sponsorship. The adoption team and other involved stakeholders understand the DA FLEX playbook. So now it's time to plan the initiative.

Just as agile-based disciplines have product backlogs, the DA FLEX adoption team creates an improvement backlog that guides the activities of improving value realization for our customers. But, again, DA FLEX views prescriptive approaches as ineffective and therefore recognizes that customization is necessary. The customization is achieved by following the **DA FLEX Engagement Pre-Planning Process** shown in *Figure 13.5*:

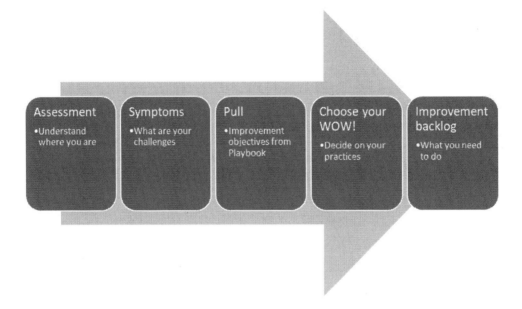

Figure 13.5 – DA FLEX engagement pre-planning

The DA FLEX engagement pre-planning process is pretty straightforward, as you can see from *Figure 13.5*. First, the team performs an **Assessment** to determine the current state of product flows. Next, they assess **Symptoms** regarding challenges they face to transition from the current state to a desired future state with much less waste and better flows.

Since DA FLEX is essentially a lean-oriented improvement toolkit; the engagement pre-planning process also uses **Pull**-oriented control strategies to work on desired objectives from the playbook in order of priorities. Priorities are always established to ensure that the engagement team is always focused on improving those values stream activities that have the most significant positive impact on end-to-end flows. Then, as the team engages in the DA FLEX adoption, they choose their **WOW** from the options available in the DA toolkit.

With the DA FLEX playbook objectives chosen and desired WOW options selected from the DA toolkit, the team now identifies work tasks to move from the current state to the desired future state. Next, those work items are managed in an **Improvement Backlog**, with priorities again based on the most impact in terms of improving end-to-end flows.

Managing change through phases

DA FLEX implements a three-phased approach to facilitate change, including business transformations across an enterprise. The three DA phases are as follows:

- **Inception**: A project initiation phase, start up phase, or iteration/sprint zero.

- **Construction**: Build or configure consumable solutions with sufficient functionality to meet the current needs of your stakeholders.

- **Transition**: Execution of a plan to transition to the desired future state.

Each phase includes DA process goals that help to guide users through the process-related decisions necessary to tailor and scale agile strategies. In addition, the process guides provide options to support each organization's unique operating environments, situations, and desired outcomes.

We won't dive any further into a discussion on the process goals, outcomes, and techniques available within the DA toolkit as there are too many to list here. However, those readers who wish to learn more can find additional details on the PMI's website at `https://www.pmi.org/disciplined-agile/start-here`.

Spanning all value streams

The roots of FLEX lie in the applications of Lean, Kanban, product portfolio management, and agile design to information technology. However, as a generic Lean-Agile approach to business transformations, FLEX also helps companies transition to Lean and Agile methods enterprise-wide.

In our digital economy, we cannot get away from the need to use IT as a business enabler. Still, lean-oriented value streams cut across all functional hierarchies, including the IT department. All of the methods employed by FLEX are based on the abstractions underneath – IT foundations of Flow, Lean, and Theory of Constraints. As a result, the practices of FLEX can be applied to all value streams.

Now that we've addressed the application of DA FLEX to value streams, we need to take a quick look at how DA FLEX categorizes its value streams.

Categorizing value streams

Many Lean practitioners talk about two basic categories of value streams – **development**-
and **operations**-oriented. For example, both Scaled Agile and the Lean Enterprise
Institute identify these two categories. But recall that James Martin was much more
granular in his descriptions, identifying 17 common types of value streams. So, the
difference is one of granularity. In the end, all organizations have more than 2 types
of value streams, and most will have fewer or greater than 17 value streams.

DA FLEX introduces their Lean-oriented concepts around four types of generalized value
streams – development, operational, enabling, and support. They define these four value
stream types as follows:

- **Development**: Creating a product/service that provides value to the customer.

- **Operational**: How a customer goes about adding value.

- **Enabling**: A value stream that enables the output of a development value stream
  to be used within an operational value stream; for example, the internal IT shop
  building a software application or web-based system to implement product catalogs
  and product order taking.

- **Support**: A value stream to support an operational value stream. Here, we can use
  as an example a reseller or partner program that augments the sales and delivery
  capabilities of the organization.

DA FLEX is an approach geared to implementing Lean-Agile practices to effect business
transformations that improve business agility. In this context, DA FLEX leverages software
delivery value streams as critical enablers. But it should also be clear that DA FLEX looks
well beyond the IT function to improve business agility across all organizational value
streams. We'll now take a look at DA FLEX in this light.

Taking a holistic view of VSM

A central premise of this book is that VSM cannot simply be about the application of
modern VSM tools to improve CI/CD and DevOps pipeline flows and software value
delivery. In our modern digital economy, we use computing systems, highspeed networks,
and software to improve everything – people's lifestyles, business processes, information
access and analytics, product functionality, and control systems. Therefore, our modern
VSM tools must help IT organizations improve value delivery across all these types of
use cases.

As Al Shalloway worked with his clients, he realized that organizations must employ Lean-Agile practices across the enterprise and not just in software delivery. In short, Al realized organizations must take a holistic view of the organization as a complex and interacting system to successfully implement Lean-Agile practices that deliver value in our digital economy.

The following seven subsections document his insights on applying Lean-Agile practices supporting business agility in a digital economy. In addition, I've taken the liberty, with Al's permission and review, to expound on his initial observations.

Before we get started, let's understand the intent of the content in this section. In Al's words, the following list of activities and strategies *represent 80% of what most companies need to learn how to do.*

Portfolio management

This subsection highlights the activities and objectives within portfolio management that have the most impact on supporting the Lean-Agile enterprise.

- **Implement Agile budgeting and Lean funding**: Lean-Agile budgeting supports innovation strategies that are reviewable on at least a quarterly basis. Product funding is continuous, spanning a product line's entire life cycle, and allocated on a just-in-time basis.

  In other words, Lean-based improvements require the funding of continuous value stream activities, the opposite of how funding is allocated on time and scope-limited projects. The primary issue is that project-based accounting hinders innovations due to the risks of missing planned scope, schedule, and delivery constraints. But, of course, project plans are invariably out of date – even before the ink dries.

  In contrast, value streams live on to develop and deliver products. Both the products and the value stream activities improve over time through constant innovations. Therefore, Lean-Agile budgets are longer-term investments that require frequent assessments, adjustments, and fine-tuning.

- **Fund the entire endeavor**: All too often, companies focus on the value proposition without regard to the supplemental or ancillary factors required for the value proposition to be consumed by its intended customers.

- **Coordinate CAPEX and OPEX expenditure**: Develop **CAPEX** (depreciable assets) and **OPEX** (operating expenses) funding plans at the same time to avoid building something that is not financially viable. CAPEX also facilitates the coordination of development and operations that is often needed.

- **Define strategies with measures**: Metrics create clarity on planned investment areas and how to quantify them. The metrics, in effect, are the acceptance criteria that ensure the achievement of the business value propositions that justified the investments.

- **Implement portfolio management to drive business strategies**: Portfolio management is a discipline that looks across products and services to provide clarity on which investments provide the greatest value in supporting the mission and strategies of the business.

Portfolio management activities determine the investments and priorities necessary to achieve corporate mission, strategy, and goals, with many of those investments related directly to products. In the following subsection, you learn how product development and delivery activities are managed.

Product management

This subsection highlights the activities and objectives within product management that have the most impact on supporting the Lean-Agile enterprise.

- **Implement discovery intake workflows**: It's essential to implement a strategy to take high-level product requirements from initiatives to backlog items to a **minimum viable product (MVP)** and **minimum business increments (MBIs)**.

- **Improve the quality of the customer's experience**: The quality of our customer's experience is directly proportional to the degree to which you attend to the customer's operational value streams and the value they provide. Again, user stories and acceptance criteria metrics define quality from our customers' perspectives or customer personas. A customer persona, or buyer persona, is a fictional archetype representing the critical traits of a large segment of our customers.

- **Employ the use of MBIs and MVPs**: MVPs are investments in new products where a return is not guaranteed. In contrast, MBIs are investments in existing products where returns are expected. All development and expansion of services should be done in small increments using MBI or MVP.

    In other words, in each build iteration, construct just enough features to be usable by customers and then use their feedback to drive requirements for future product development enhancements.

The distinction between MVPs and MBIs is essential. MVPs guide the creation of new products where a marketing infrastructure is likely not in place. In contrast, MBIs guide enhancements to a product for an existing customer base, and the work may span multiple development teams and other value streams. Funding needs to be made available for both endeavors across the life cycle of the product.

- **Define the 'definition of ready' for classes of service**: Agree to **Kanban classes of service (CoS)** and then define a definition of ready for each. For example, define acceptance criteria or definitions of done.

  Kanban employs the concept of CoS to help teams optimize the execution of their backlog items. Effectively, CoS implements policies governing development intake rules and always in consideration of the interests of customers.

- **Sequence MBIs and MVPs**: MBIs or MVPs are sequenced based on priorities within the intake queue. The highest feature-oriented priority work items deliver the customer's highest value from the customers' perspective, which always involves analyzing the development and delivery costs against the overall profitability or affordability of product deliveries.

Now that we know what's involved in managing product development and delivery activities, we need to understand how to inject new orders into our development and delivery systems.

Development intake

This subsection highlights the activities and objectives within development intake that have the most impact on supporting the Lean-Agile enterprise:

- **Define the development intake process**: The development intake process is a well-defined agreement on how to initiate work to be planned. The development intake process follows formalized governance policies that can be automated via machine-readable formats. Without well-defined intake workflows, organizations can't see what work is actually taking place. As a result, they tend to work on too many things.

- **Plan value flow**: Achieve an agreement on both the order of the work items and how to manage the identified dependencies. In a lean-oriented workflow, VSM initiatives seek to minimize dependencies, integrate and automate value stream activities, as well as orchestrate work and information flows across dependencies.

- **Implement a program-level backlog**: The program backlog includes MBIs, MVPs, features, bug fixes, and technical debt releases for development in the following value delivery flow or portfolio planning horizon.

New products introduced into our system follow specific product development flows. Therefore, we need to build our pipeline flows to support these products, as discussed in the following subsection.

Product development

This subsection highlights the activities and objectives within product development that have the most impact on supporting the Lean-Agile enterprise:

- **Define MBI/MVP acceptance criteria**. Anything we build must have quantifiable measures that indicate both the capabilities and level of performance desired by the product's customers. Through its VSM initiatives, the organization must evaluate the effectiveness of the acceptance criteria for every type of deliverable artifact.

- **Implement small teams to improve work**: The implementation of small teams supports collaborative work environments to minimize handoffs and hand-backs between value stream participants. People who work in teams have a shared goal and shared mission. With Lean-based flow and production control strategies, such as Kanban, they achieve higher throughput at the MBI, feature, and story levels.

> **Note**
> Disciplined Agile provides numerous Lean-Agile models to deploy and manage small teams. Additionally, my previous book, *Scaling Scrum across Modern Enterprises*, is all about scaling Scrum and Lean-Agile practices across multiple product teams and on an enterprise scale.

- **Self-contained domain skills**: The best team has members with overlapping and all-encompassing domain skills to ensure they have all the resources and skills necessary to build high-quality and maintainable products and services.

- **Organize around value creation**: Organize the development group to create an effective value stream. Large value streams that span multiple activities, distributed workstations, or geographic locations, as well as multiple knowledge domains, must employ team-of-team integration, dependency, and synchronization strategies.

- **Create cross-functional teams**: Cross-functional teams have all the skills, capacity, and resources to do the work assigned to them. It's also essential to build your teams with diverse work experiences and cultural backgrounds to bring a broader level of experiences and knowledge to problem solving. While small teams are ideal, they are often not practical or don't provide the capacity for larger and more complex product deliveries. FLEX introduces additional team structures to accommodate these realities.

- **Shift-left with continuous quality verification**: Development teams must verify quality after each step and automate the process wherever possible. In the traditional Waterfall model, testing is a late-stage activity that created all kinds of issues with defect and bug identification and resolutions, which often led to product release delays. Modern iterative and incremental development practices allow defects and bugs to be discovered and resolved earlier and easier, with minimal impacts on planned production releases.

- **Design in product maintainability, resilience, and robustness**: The architecture and design of the product or service must support its maintenance and enhancement at a low cost. The key to leveraging architecture and designs in Lean-Agile development environments is to maintain options in the face of uncertainty. Two terms are often employed to describe strategies for Agile-based architecture and designs. One is **evolutionary architectures**, and the other is **emergent design**:

    – *Evolutionary architecture* concepts seek to incorporate changeability in a product's architecture to make it easier to change later to support previously unidentified functional and non-functional requirements. Nel Ford, Rebecca Parsons, and Patrick Kua outline evolutionary architecture concepts in their book *Building Evolutionary Architecture: Support Constant Change* (Ford et al., 2017).

    – *Emergent design* is a concept that promotes a strategy to allow development teams to build functionality driven by requirements and lets the design emerge as an outcome. The emergent design strategy requires constant refactoring of software to merge redundant capabilities across released increments with a streamlined, simpler, and higher-performing code base. Emergent design should be guided by patterns-thinking.

    Scott Bain of the PMI integrates design patterns, patterns-thinking, and the discipline required for quality design, as described in his book *Emergent Design: The Evolutionary Nature of Professional Software Development* (Bain, 2008).

- **Change Vector Tracking** is an iterative and reflective software engineering practice that supports emergent design. First, developers evaluate different design options in terms of a functional requirement defined as *modifiability*. Then, as business requirements change, they are tracked as a potential *vector* that may require software refactoring.

Product development activities work best when the people, skills, processes, and activities are integrated to create the efficient and streamlined use of organizational resources as Lean-oriented production flows.

Integration

This subsection highlights the activities and objectives supported by integrating people, skills, processes, and activities that impact the Lean-Agile enterprise:

- **Leverage DevOps**: The critical concept here is to have IT development and support teams working together. First and foremost, DevOps is a collaboration strategy to align the work of both IT functions. The benefit of having such collaborations is to minimize the potential for failed releases by getting the two sides of IT to work together and to identify potential problems and opportunities for improvements before a release goes out.

  Of course, in its modern form, DevOps is also a software tools-based integration, automation, and orchestration strategy that effectively brings Lean production practices to the software development and delivery pipeline.

  It is helpful to note that for all the well-deserved attention given to DevOps, it is merely applying lean-based value stream management principles to IT-oriented value streams at the end of the day. The same concepts are valid for CI/CD pipelines. Both are examples of lean production flows applied to a stream of IT activities.

- **Implement continuous integration capabilities**: In software engineering, CI is the practice of merging all developers' working copies of their code to a shared mainline repository, such as Git or GitHub, multiple times per day.

  However, the CI concept is equally valid when implementing Lean practices generally. In such cases, multiple teams integrate their work into the whole product or service frequently. For example, the teams' work might involve integrating work items within a single value stream or orchestrating work items across multiple, but interconnected, value streams.

- **Shared services pool**: Most agile-based methodologies promote the concept of creating autonomous and fully self-contained teams to create products or deliver services. By self-contained, we mean they have all the skills and resources required to develop the product or service.

  Still, sometimes new requirements may require skills beyond those available within the team. In such cases, the organization must have sources to provide specialized services on-demand to augment the teams' skills. In addition, if the new requirement is a long-term need, the team is expected to have one or more of its members develop the new skills.

- **Provide system demos**: In both the iterative and incremental development strategies of Agile and the continuous flows of Lean, the common goal is to deliver customer value. However, the definition of requirements and acceptance criteria is not an infallible process. If nothing else, many times, customers cannot envision what they need until they have a working prototype in hand.

  As with all Agile practices, DA FLEX implements the practice of demonstrating end-to-end product functionality frequently, usually with every development iteration and release of incremental value. Even in a fully automated DevOps environment with frequent releases of business services directly into production environments, it's still a good practice to release each new increment of functionality to a subset of users who can evaluate its functionality in terms of their acceptance criteria. Those released services will have a limited impact if something is wrong, and they can be pulled back and fixed before allowing a full-scale release.

- **Development coordinates with customer support**: This concept is the premise behind DevOps. Development attends to their impact on customer support to provide visibility of what is coming down the pipeline. Developers also work with customer support staff (when and as needed) after release.

  The objectives are to resolve potential problems before making their way into production and quickly resolve problems that make it into production. The joint teams should review the lessons learned to prevent future problems. The two teams discuss and resolve software defects, maintainability, sustainability, performance, failover, security, and potential enhancements identified by the support staff.

- **Coordinate development with marketing**: In several Lean-Agile practices, such as Scrum, SAFe, and Disciplined Agile, a product owner manages the product backlog activity to identify requirements, work item refinement, and set development priorities. While the product owners are ultimately responsible for all product deliveries, they must work directly with the development team, customers, and other stakeholders to make informed decisions.

  Still, descriptions of the product owner function are highly simplified in virtually all Lean-Agile methodologies. Their role is tied directly to the much broader responsibilities of the product management and marketing organizations. Recall our discussions on **Adaptive Marketing** processes and activities in the *Integrating value streams* section of *Chapter 6, Launching the VSM Initiative (VSM Steps 1-3).*

- **Bottom line**: The development teams must inform the marketing and product management function on what is being released and ensure they have sufficient knowledge to build the products, capabilities, and features that customers want at a price point their customers can afford, or are willing, to pay.

Note how this coordination of different parts of the value stream is facilitated by using MBIs, which include the necessary players involved in creating them and ensuring they can be readily consumed. Finally, those organizations that employ Lean-Agile practices will always have a distinct competitive advantage over those that do not. So, let's now look at how we manage activities and objectives across value streams.

Across value streams

This subsection highlights the activities and objectives across value streams that have the most impact on supporting the Lean-Agile enterprise:

- **Ensure visibility of all work across all workflows**: The entire point of organizing around value streams is coordinating work around value delivery to improve flows and eliminate waste by eliminating delays in the workflow and obtaining quick feedback. That's hard to accomplish if we can't see the work or how it's performed. We need value stream maps, process guides, and metrics to get started. But, with modern VSM tools, we can also have real-time access and visibility to the flow of work and how well we are performing against our delivery goals.

- **Establish safe work environments**: This human element is critical to building sustainable work environments in both Agile and Lean practices. People must feel safe to 1) openly communicate their work-related issues and concerns, 2) showcase what they do visibly, and 3) not get crucified for work results or outcomes they have no control over.

  Agile and Lean practitioners understand that we live in a stochastic world full of variables beyond our control that can, and will, impact our work. Therefore, both Lean and Agile practices implement techniques to identify variances to our plans, evaluate new opportunities, and explore methods to improve our work results.

  When safety is missing, people tend to focus on local optimizations around their tasks. Unfortunately, this only strengthens the barriers that value stream management is trying to break down. By focusing on the end-to-end relationships across our value streams, we can avoid focusing on ineffectual local optimizations.

- **HR and education departments must evolve to support business agility**: HR and education policies need to enhance agility, not work against it. Those departments must encourage the development of a learning enterprise and make sure people have time built into their schedules for learning. Our employees also need access to resources for continued learning in the fields that support their work within the enterprise.

Organize people to work as teams around value delivery and do not pigeonhole them into functional departments. Similarly, management structures need to align with value delivery. Finally, we must create collaborative work environments that drive continuous improvements.

We need our people to feel safe when highlighting their concerns or when identifying opportunities for improvements. Therefore, we need to create cultures of respect and tolerance for diversity (race, genders, skills, experiences), even as we require excellence within and across our teams.

Compensation plans need to support growth in related skills and experiences, not just years in services. Compensation related to years in services is better tied to minimizing the adverse effects of inflation. At the same time, it's better to tie promotional pay raises to growth in skills and certifications that support the business needs of the enterprise.

Finally, organizations also need to use their bonus plans to drive team performance, not individual performance. Lean-Agile teams, not individuals, provide a competitive advantage in our modern digital economy.

As with any Agile or Lean-Agile methodology, roles must be clearly defined to understand responsibilities. Therefore, we discuss the roles involved in DA FLEX in the following subsection.

Roles

This subsection highlights the necessary roles and responsibilities required to support the Lean-Agile enterprise:

- **Lean-Agile leadership and management**: Lean-Agile leaders and managers focus on improving the environment people work in, providing adequate guidance, and avoiding micro-management.

  The people performing the work often best understand the issues that hinder their work. Managers practicing GEMBA see the problems for themselves, and they can speak with the people who are dealing with those issues day-in and day-out and work in collaboration to define working solutions. Moreover, managers and leaders are in a better position to make informed decisions on required investments.

- **Value stream manager**: Each value stream must have a person who is responsible for the end-to-end delivery of customer value. The dedicated value stream managers help the Lean-Agile organization move away from local optimizations at a functional or local level to implement effective and efficient end-to-end production flows that deliver customer value.

- **Business architect**: Organizations must have a competent and influential business architect. The business architect has a focus on defining business structures that align implementation tactics with business strategies. Business architecture has its roots in business process reengineering.

  The object management group defines business architecture as follows: *Business architecture is a blueprint of the enterprise that provides a common understanding of the organization and is used to align strategic objectives and tactical demands.* Business architects oversee the organization's structure in the areas of business governance, processes, and information. In addition, they evaluate the organization's current capabilities to implement its strategies, determine a preferred future state, and define the roadmap to implement the future operating model.

- **Enterprise architect**: In contrast to business architects, who focus on process-centric alignments of business with strategy, the enterprise architect takes an information-centric view of the enterprise.

  Enterprise Architecture (**EA**) evolved from a paper written by John Zachman in 1987 entitled *A Framework for Information Systems Architecture*. More recent EA frameworks include **The Open Group Architectural Framework** (**TOGAF**), the **Federal Enterprise Architecture Framework** (**FEAF**), and **Gartner's Enterprise Architecture Framework**.

  > Note
  >
  > In the article entitled *Business Architects versus Enterprise Architects: The Battle Must End*, John Maynen makes the following statements:
  >
  > *"Simplistically, business architecture is about what a business does, while enterprise architecture is about what a business knows. And both disciplines are concerned about "why?" so that a business does what it needs to do and knows what it needs to know"* (`https://www.linkedin.com/pulse/business-architects-vs-enterprise-battle-must-end-john-maynen/`).

- **Product manager**: For each product or service, there is someone who fills the role of product manager. Their role is different from the value stream manager in that the product manager has sole responsibility for discovering, articulating, and realizing the products customer's value.

  Product managers establish the product's vision and create the development roadmap. They capture, analyze, and document customer needs, product capabilities requirements, and niche market opportunities. Critically, they must have the ability to see new or emergent product needs even before customers become aware that they have those needs.

Product managers analyze and consider the competition within their industry and product lines. Their assessments help build the business case for investments for a new product line or enhancements to an existing product. Finally, they present their business cases and ROIs to the organization's executives and portfolio management team.

Finally, they serve as product advocates across the company and promotions to customers, the media, and industry analysts.

- **Program manager**: A product manager attends to bringing all of the required pieces together for each product or service line, usually guiding activities funded as a strategic portfolio-level investment.

  Product delivery seldom involves only one value stream, and many of those value streams have points of interaction. Just as we need to integrate, automate, and orchestrate work within a value stream, program management applies the exact strategies to cross-value stream operations.

- **Product owner**: Product managers must ensure that there are sufficient product owners to implement their product strategies effectively. In agile-based disciplines, product owners have sole responsibility for development outcomes and priorities.

  That is not to say they do not obtain input from the development team, customers, and other stakeholders. They absolutely must have a clear understanding of what customers want, and they need to understand the development trade-offs in work related to functional versus non-functional requirements, fixing bugs, and working to reduce technical debt. And they must evaluate the cost-benefit relationships across work items within their product backlogs. But, in the end, only one person can be the ultimate decision maker on development priorities, and that person is the product owner.

You now understand all the roles involved in supporting Lean-Agile practices in DA FLEX. DA FLEX is not a one-time activity. As with any Lean or Agile approach, DA FLEX implements a continuous improvement strategy. We'll explore how that works in the next section.

Implementing a life cycle change strategy

Back in the section entitled *Choosing your way of working with DA*, you saw how the DA toolkit positions FLEX as the level that supports the implementation of value streams. The Value Stream level was depicted graphically in *Figure 13.1* as a set of process blades that guide the 10 value streams identified by the purple hexagons.

Figure 13.6 offers a different view of eight of these value streams working in concert with six areas of focus from the DA FLEX **DevOps layer**. This section might be the most important in showcasing how DA FLEX integrates lean value streams with DevOps as a value stream management cycle of improvement:

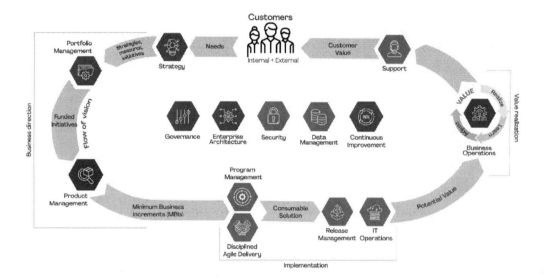

Figure 13.6 – The DA FLEX life cycle

As you can see from *Figure 13.6*, the DA FLEX life cycle is a continuous improvement process that also operates as a flow. In Lean, we always start and end with the customer in mind, which is equally valid with the DA FLEX approach.

Starting with our customers, we work our way around counter-clockwise following this outline:

- **Strategy**: To develop a business strategy that supports our targeting customers' needs while also supporting the business's mission

- **Portfolio Management**: To evaluate investment strategies in support of the strategy

- **Product Management**: To define MBIs necessary to sustain the business

- **Program Management and Disciplined Agile**: To define a set of viable product offerings that deliver value by offering solutions to their needs

- **Release Management and IT Operations**: To properly sustain our developed products

- **Business Operations**: To realize value, learn from our experiences, and adjust to improve our way of working

- **Support**: To ensure our customers receive maximum value during the use across the life of our products

Using the five whys to get to the root cause

DA FLEX cites a use case where the 5 Whys of Lean are used to get to the root cause of a seemingly IT-related problem that turned out to have its roots in a process failure in an entirely different value stream. Let see how using the 5 Why questions technique helps the team get to the root cause.

As you read through this use case, bear in mind that the 5 Why strategy involves asking why something happened and then continuing to ask why, iteratively exploring the cause-and-effect relationships underlying a particular problem until we get down to the root cause of our issue:

Question 1:	"Why do we have to rework the system?"
Answer:	"Because the programs do not function properly on our customers' servers."
Question 2:	"Why do the programs not function properly on our customers' servers?"
Answer:	"Because the code was designed one way, but the servers are configured for another way."
Question 3:	"Why are our customers' servers being configured differently from how it was expected?"
Answer:	"Because our customers are not following our guidelines for server configuration."
Question 4:	"Why are our customers not following our guidelines for server configuration?"
Answer:	"Because they aren't aware of the guidelines."
Question 5:	"Why aren't these customers aware of them?"
Answer:	"Because sales, who is supposed to make sure they know of this configuration requirement, isn't telling them."
Question 6:	"Why aren't our salespeople telling our customers they need to do this?"
Answer:	"Because when a customer is ready to buy, sales tend to shut up and just get the contract signed. Closing the deal seems to be the most important thing to sales."

Figure 13.7 – Five Whys use case

This process takes more time to execute than it takes to explain. But did you see how the questions started to address a concern that impacted the IT department and precisely why they needed to rework one of their software products? But, when all was said and done, the real issues turned out to be a value stream process failure in sales that prematurely ended their responsibilities without a proper handoff of server configuration requirements.

This section concludes our introduction to PMI's DA FLEX acquisitions and its applications to implementing DevOps and value stream management capabilities. It is one of two modern Lean-Agile methodologies presented in this book. The other is SAFe, which is covered in the next section.

Scaled Agile Framework (SAFe)

SAFe is the leading framework for scaling Agile across the enterprise. It provides four configurations to implement Lean-Agile practices in a large enterprise where the small team structures of traditional Agile approaches are insufficient to manage work in large economies of scale. With more than 20,000 enterprises worldwide practicing SAFe and more than 800,000 individuals trained to date, **SAFe** is the world's leading framework for scaling Lean-Agile practices across the enterprise.

Relevant to the topic of this book, value streams are a core construct of a SAFe portfolio and are woven into the fabric of the framework and provide execution guidance for all people and levels within the organization. In this section, you will learn how SAFe employs Lean-Agile concepts, including the alignment of human talent and business resources around delivering value as horizontal flows. You will also learn how SAFe implements value stream management as part of its SAFe DevOps strategies. Let's start this section with an introduction to SAFe's implementation of value streams.

Organizing around value streams

A value stream is the primary construct for understanding, organizing, and delivering value in SAFe. SAFe introduced value streams into the framework in 2013, which introduced operational and development value streams, along with value stream mapping to their enterprise community of users. Understanding and continually optimizing value streams is key to practicing SAFe effectively.

The development value stream is a long-lived series of steps used to create value—from concept to the delivery of a tangible result for the customer—and is the focal point of value stream management in SAFe. The development value stream identifies a chronological flow of activities, as shown in *Figure 13.8*:

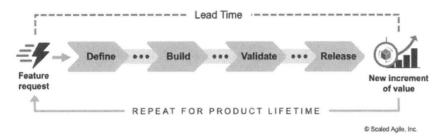

© Scaled Agile, Inc.

Figure 13.8 shows that there is an initial request followed by a pipeline flow that delivers incremental value and that there is a lead time associated with meeting delivery expectations. The delivery flow as a process repeats for the life cycle of the product. The key elements defined in *Figure 13.1* are defined in the list that follows:

- **Trigger**: An important event initiates the flow of value, such as a feature request or new solution idea. It ends when some unit of value—a product, service, or specification—has been delivered.

- **Steps**: The chevrons in the middle are the cross-functional activities required to define, build, validate, and release that unit of value.

- **Value**: The customer receives value when all the steps have been completed and the delivered solution meets their expectations. The organization may realize revenue, cost savings, customer satisfaction, or a combination of these in compensation.

- **People and systems**: Development value streams also include the people who do the work, the systems or equipment they operate, and the information and materials that flow from step to step.

- **Lead time**: The time from the trigger to the delivery of value is the lead time. Shortening the lead time accelerates the time to market. The easiest way to shorten the lead time is to identify and reduce (or remove) non-value-added activities and wasteful delays. That's the primary focus of Lean Thinking.

The flow of value in Lean moves horizontally across functional departments. As we've learned throughout this book, true customer value comes from aligning activities as efficient and streamlined flows from concept to delivery, which means we need to break down functional silos that generate waste, create waiting, delay deliveries, and increase costs. SAFe supports the horizontal flows of Lean production processes via its **Agile Release Trains (ARTs)**.

This concept is shown in *Figure 13.9* as a long-lived ART. Note that the larger arrow below the train depicts the flow of value horizontally, typically crossing such functions as software development, product management, information security, compliance, and operations. Also note, however, that the smaller return arrow indicates the process is iteratively applied to continuously provide incremental value deliveries:

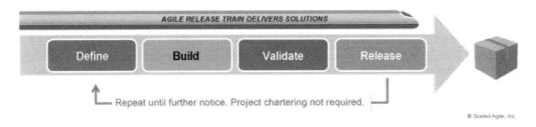

Figure 13.9 – The cross-functional Agile Release Train

Figure 13.9 shows graphically that the ARTs implement product delivery flows; in this case, Define, Build, Validate, and Release activities. In other words, the ART is supporting value stream deliveries and is aligned around adding value. We'll look at the value-based deliveries of ARTs in more detail in the following subsection.

Aligning ARTs around value

SAFe recognizes fundamental team topologies (as defined by Skelton, Pais, 2019) to help with the job of team and ART design, which are defined as follows:

- **Stream-aligned team**: Organized around the flow of work and with the ability to deliver value directly to the customer or end user

- **Complicated subsystem team**: Organized around specific subsystems that require specialist skills and expertise

- **Platform team**: Organized around the development and support of platforms that provide services to other teams

- **Enabling team**: Organized to assist other teams with specialized capabilities and help them become proficient in new technologies

ARTs (`https://www.scaledagileframework.com/identify-value-streams-and-arts/`) guide the flow of value but are limited in size, typically consisting of 50–125 people. Limiting the size of an ART helps to minimize the complexities that come with expanding networks of people in large organizations. *Figure 13.10* shows three possible scenarios for ART design:

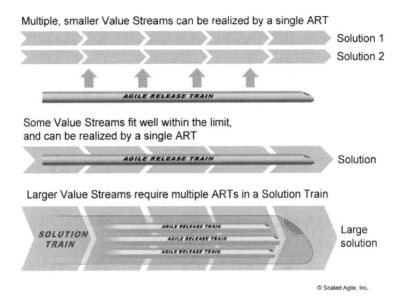

Figure 13.10 – Three possible scenarios for ART design

Figure 13.10 graphically displays three value stream delivery scenarios supported by SAFe, as described next:

- A single ART supporting multiple value streams

- A single ART supporting one value stream

- Multiple ARTs participating in the development and delivery of large solutions

The ARTs support value stream deliveries in the form of a holistic solution or related set of products or services. The ART is a long-lived, cross-functional team of Agile teams that delivers value continuously. A goal of SAFe is to minimize dependencies between ARTs in order to minimize systemic communication, integration, and delivery issues. Thus, any given ART can release its solutions independently of other ARTs, maintaining a continuous flow of value to its customers.

In some cases, solutions require multiple ARTs working in tight synchronization. For example, delivering a new satellite system, complex medical device, or aircraft may involve thousands of individuals across many enterprise and supplier functions. SAFe implements its **Solution Trains** and the **Large Solution** configurations as shown at the bottom of *Figure 13.10* to manage this level of complexity.

SAFe also implements a Lean-Agile model to improve business agility on an enterprise scale to compete effectively in a digital economy, which we'll look at more closely in the next subsection.

Competing in a digital economy with SAFe

Scaled Agile promotes its strengths as providing enterprises and partners with the value stream guidance, tools, and resources they need to succeed in the digital age. This includes identifying and mapping value stream activities, to managing and optimizing them. SAFe incorporates Lean, Agile, and DevOps practices that enable value streams. Along with their global community of 450+ partners and 12,000+ SAFe Program Consultants (SPCs), Scaled Agile has developed significant expertise at applying all these concepts in concert to support digital transformation initiatives.

However, unlike James Martin, with his 17 common value streams, SAFe aggregates value streams into just two types, **Operational** and **Development** value streams, although it does provide examples of each type of value stream, as defined and identified here:

- **Operational value streams**: The sequence of activities needed to deliver a product or service to a customer. Examples include manufacturing a product, fulfilling an eCommerce order, admitting and treating a patient, providing a loan, and delivering a professional service.

- **Development value streams**: The sequence of activities needed to convert a business hypothesis into a technology-enabled solution that delivers customer value. Examples include designing and developing a medical device, developing and deploying a CRM system, and an eCommerce website.

SAFe is another organization that realized that DevOps capabilities are key to competing in our digital age. As a result, they were quick to include DevOps within their framework.

Leveraging DevOps to support the digital enterprise

In 2018, Scaled Agile released its SAFe DevOps course with the aim of providing DevOps education and value stream thinking for the entire organization, not just CI/CD guidance for technical practitioners. The SAFe DevOps course involves technical and non-technical practitioners and leaders across functions in value stream mapping, bottleneck analysis, and value stream optimization. Consistent with the software industry's current VSM tool concepts, SAFe includes value stream management as a core DevOps practice, defined as follows:

Value stream management

VSM is a business practice that focuses on increasing the flow of business value from customer requests to customer delivery (Kirsten, 2020). VSM provides lightweight, end-to-end governance of the continuous delivery pipeline and optimizes it for maximum value delivery, as opposed to maximum adherence to fixed delivery plans.

VSM includes specific practices such as value stream mapping, analyzing flow efficiency through the end-to-end delivery pipeline, and setting targets for delivery speed, quality, and value. VSM also involves specialized software platforms that integrate with other tools throughout the pipeline to collect and reveal real-time data regarding the health of the value stream: `https://www.scaledagileframework.com/devops-practice-domains/`.

SAFe employs a specific VSM methodology, in the context of both mapping and management of value streams. The SAFe VSM approach covers the entire value stream – from customer request through the delivery of valuable, digitally enabled technology solutions that goes beyond *CI/CD* or *DevOps* pipeline applications. In other words, the SAFe VSM methodology supports Lean-oriented improvements across all organizational teams and functions, not just development and operations.

In this broader, enterprise context, Scaled Agile defines VSM as follows:

"Value Stream Management (VSM) is a leadership and technical discipline aimed at maximizing business value flow through the end-to-end solution delivery life cycle. VSM implements Lean, Agile, and DevOps values, principles, and practices across functions in the continuous operation, measurement, and optimization of value streams, from customer requests to solution delivery."

As you know from reading this book, value stream management is fundamentally a mechanism to make Lean-oriented improvements across an organization. So, let's take a look at how Scaled Agile employs Lean practices within their framework, while also accruing the benefits of dividing work among numerous small Agile teams.

Making Lean-Agile improvements with SAFe

Recall that Agile, as expressed in the *Manifesto for Agile Software Development*, is fundamentally a set of values and principles to guide small teams in their quest to deliver customer-centric value. The values behind the Agile manifesto place a premium on individuals and interactions, working software, customer collaborations, and responsiveness to change. The 12 Principles of the Agile Manifesto lay out objectively how an Agile organization operates: `http://agilemanifesto.org/`.

Still, the authors behind the Agile Manifesto were solving problems related to the traditional Waterfall model, which was not responsive to meeting customer needs or building software efficiently. So, the focus of the authors was primarily limited to the scope of authority given to relatively small software development teams. Therefore, appropriately, SAFe implements Agile practices at the small team level.

However, organizations must also deliver value across all organizational value streams as cross-cutting processes that operate horizontally and efficiently across all the departments and functions of the business. That is the focus of Lean production concepts, which SAFe also implements.

To achieve business agility, SAFe value streams require the employment of all the skills necessary to deliver products and solutions. This necessarily includes other business functions such as finance, contracts, quality, HR, security, product management, and marketing, to name a few. And for SAFe's cyber-physical systems builder customers, that extends to hardware teams, parts suppliers, and logistics partners.

In other words, value stream management supports Lean improvements across the organization, not just IT. But information technology, and particularly DevOps, is a critical enabler of value stream improvements. The trick is to align the efforts of DevOps teams to support value stream improvement across the enterprise in a coordinated and effectively prioritized manner.

> **Note**
>
> Scaled Agile is in the process of expanding their *beyond IT* guidance in this area. It currently includes workshops and articles for hardware, marketing, HR, and compliance (quality, security, and so on), each explaining their role in a Lean-Agile, value stream-focused organization.

The SAFe approach to VSM balances the thoughtful application of Agile and DevOps practices, supporting tools, and metrics, while also supporting Womack and Jones' five principles of Lean Thinking across the enterprise. This book introduces the **Five Lean Principles** in the next chapter, *Chapter 14, Introducing the Enterprise Lean-VSM Practice Leaders*, in the section on the **Lean Enterprise Institute (LEI)**.

Given SAFe's focus on the implementation of Lean practices, value stream identification is integral to implementing SAFe and it is an early activity on the SAFe implementation roadmap. Additionally, Scaled Agile embraces Karen Martin and Mike Osterling's method of value stream mapping.

So far in this section on SAFe, we have learned that Scaled Agile promotes Lean-Agile concepts to compete in our modern digital economy. We've learned that SAFe guides businesses to organize around development and operational value streams. And we've learned that SAFe embeds value stream management concepts throughout the framework, both in its DevOps guidance and beyond. There is a lot more to SAFe than this, but before we go any further, we need to understand the four configurations of SAFe.

Selecting the right SAFe configuration

For this section, refer to *Figure 13.4*. At first glance, the SAFe for Lean Enterprises diagram appears to be fairly complex, but we can simplify the information contained in the diagram by breaking it down into SAFe's four constituent configurations:

- **Essential SAFe**: The basic configuration that implements iterative cadence with incremental releases leveraging a long-lived team of Agile teams (Scrum, XP, and Kanban) organized around **Agile Release Trains (ARTs)**.

- **Large Solution SAFe**: Multiple ARTs can work in concert as a solution train for very large product development efforts.

- **Portfolio SAFe**: Established the **Lean Portfolio Management** discipline to align product and infrastructure investments over multiple planning horizons, and consistent with Lean accounting practices.

6. **Full SAFe**: Installs all four configurations to enable business agility on an enterprise scale:

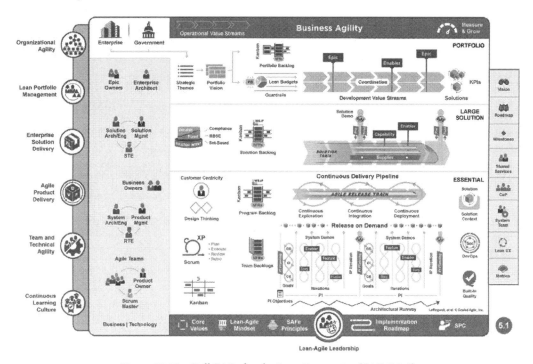

Figure 13.11 – Full SAFe for the Lean Enterprise (SAFe™ 5.1)

Looking at the left column of the Full SAFe diagram (*Figure 13.11*), you can see that SAFe implements more roles than those commonly found in other Agile frameworks. But there is also some consistency with roles found in Scrum in that Agile teams, ARTs, and solution trains all have three key roles:

- **Scrum Master / RTE / STE**: Servant leaders for Agile, ARTs, and solution trains, respectively

- **Product Owners / Product Managers / Solution Management**: Responsible for product backlog priorities for Agile teams, ARTs, and solution trains, respectively

- **Development Teams / System Architect/Engineer / Solution Architect / Engineer**: Develop products at the Agile team level, and design or engineer products and solutions at the ART and Large Solution level.

SAFe also makes sure that business owners remain involved in guiding product development and delivery activities. Business owners typically have **Return on Investment** (**ROI**) responsibilities in their value streams.

At the Portfolio Configuration Level, SAFe implements Epic Owners and Enterprise Architects to guide strategic investments in products and infrastructure and resolve technical debt at an enterprise level. Where the other roles operate on relatively short program increments, typically 8–12 weeks long, the Portfolio level executives plan over 1 to 3+ year planning horizons.

There's still a lot more to learn about SAFe, but more than we can cover in this book. Readers who want to learn more about SAFe can read my previous book, *Scaling Scrum Across Modern Enterprises* (Rupp, 2020). But let's get back to the subject of improving value via SAFe's DevOps concepts.

Achieving continuous value delivery

We're now going to dive more deeply into SAFe's approach to DevOps in support of an organization's continuous delivery pipeline. As depicted in *Figure 13.12*, Scaled Agile breaks out pipeline flows into four parts – **Continuous Exploration (CE)**, **Continuous Integration (CI)**, **Continuous Deployment (CD)**, and **Release on Demand (RoD)**:

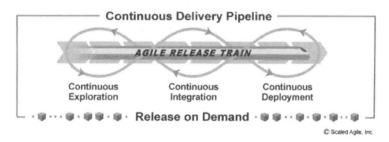

Figure 13.12 – The Continuous Delivery Pipeline (CDP)

There's a lot going on in this diagram, so I'll break it down in the following bullet list:

- **Continuous Exploration (CE)** focuses on creating alignment on what needs to be built. Here, the focus is on understanding market opportunities and customer demands. The objective is to identify the requirements for a **Minimum Viable Product (MVP)** and **Minimum Marketable Features (MMF)**. This work also includes architectural and existing product modification assessments leading to a refined understanding of the capabilities and features required to meet customer and market needs, which are then prioritized and managed within the Portfolio, Program, and Team backlogs.

- **Continuous Integration** (**CI**) focuses on taking features from the Program backlog and implementing them. Here, the work has a focus on product designs (for example, designing a user story map), and may include development of prototypes for user feedback. As specific features are clearly understood and refined, the Agile Teams implement them according to a typical Agile approach, such as XP, Scrum, or Kanban. All products and associated artifacts must be maintained under version control, built, and integrated into a full system or solution, and tested end to end before user and performance validations in a production-like staging environment.

- **Continuous Deployment** (**CD**) takes the changes from the staging environment and deploys them into production. Even though the products have undergone continuous testing, production deployments must be monitored and verified to meet all acceptance criteria. This step migrates new functionality to production, but the business determines the appropriate time to release it to customers. Controlling rollouts also allows the organization to respond to issues and rollback or fix forward when necessary. All artifacts associated with a specific release must be maintained under configuration management controls to ensure maintainability of the products and solutions over time.

- **Release on Demand** (**RoD**) is the ability to make value available to customers all at once, or in a staggered fashion based on market and business needs. This strategy allows the business to release new products when market timing is optimal and minimize the amount of risk associated with each release. For example, changes to enterprise software applications usually affect business processes, and we need to make sure that we communicate with and train affected employees and other stakeholders on the upcoming changes. RoD also encompasses critical pipeline activities that preserve the stability and ongoing value of solutions long after release, for example, **IT Service Management** (**ITSM**) and **IT Operations Management** (**ITOPs**) processes. Finally, RoD contains critical *measure* and *learn* activities, which close the loop on hypothesis-driven development and fuel continuous learning and experimentation.

The CDP represents the workflows, activities, and automation needed to guide a new piece of capability or functionality from ideation to an on-demand release of value to the end user. The objective of CDP is to optimize pipeline flows. So, let's take a closer look at how the CDP process works.

Improving pipeline flows in SAFe

SAFe implements processes for pipeline flow improvements that will look very familiar after reading *Chapter 6, Launching the VSM initiative (VSM Steps 1 - 3)* through *Chapter 10, Improving the Lean-Agile Value Delivery Cycle (VSM Steps 7 and 8)* of this book, where we applied the generic VSM methodology to improve a CI/CD pipeline flow. The improvement steps in SAFe include the following:

- Map the current flow.

- Capture relevant metrics:

  - Process time, lead time, delay time, and **percent complete and accurate** (%C&A)

- Align current workflow to the continuous delivery pipeline:

  - Exploration-related activities

  - Integration-related activities

  - Deployment-related activities

  - Release and post-release-related activities

- Identify opportunities for improvements.

- Build continuous delivery capabilities via **Portfolio**, **Solution**, and **Program Kanbans**. The work item types flowing through them are *Epic*, *Capability*, and *Features*, respectively.

> **Note**
>
> Note that SAFe employs the same general pipeline flow improvement and continuous delivery strategies at the Portfolio, Solution, and Program levels.
>
> Also, SAFe implements the concept of **Architectural Runway** to identify and manage technology investments that improve delivery capabilities, for example, making investments in DevOps toolchains.

- Relentlessly improve through continuous measurement, reflection, and learning.

The online SAFe guidance on value stream mapping does not explicitly address future state mapping. However, Scaled Agile promotes future state mapping as a critical exercise and includes it in the value stream mapping exercises within the SAFe DevOps class. Scaled Agile is also developing a broadly consumable (not just for DevOps customers) value stream mapping workshop, which will include detailed guidance on future state mapping.

Scaled Agile understands that there are several reasons why we cannot ignore mapping the desired future state. So, let's take a look at some of the issues that arise when we fail to map the future state when identifying opportunities for improvement.

Mapping the current and future states

Though we will often start with high-level current and future state maps, ultimately, we must get down to more granular levels of detail and identify lower-level activities involving work and information flows, tools and tool configurations, decision making, and manual interventions.

With detailed and accurate current state maps, we can identify unnecessary activities that can be aggregated and improved through new tools and configurations. We can identify activities that can be improved through automation, and we can explore better methods and tools to orchestrate work and information flows. In short, the future state maps can look very different from the current state maps, and there can be more than one future state map as the VSM team evaluates their options.

Future state maps provide visibility to an idealized state so that all value stream members, executives, and other stakeholders have a shared vision of their target objectives. Some changes can occur with little cost and effort, but others may require investments that span multiple planning horizons. We don't want to lose that vision, which the current state maps won't show.

Finally, the metrics that indicate our areas of waste and unbalanced flows that cause queuing, waiting and additional costs don't tell us a thing about how to fix our problems. We have to do the work, evaluate alternatives, and create future state maps showing our improvement options, including time, resource, and cost estimates to implement each proposed alternative. In this context, future state maps are very much part of the improvement identification and assessments process.

You should now have a general understanding of how SAFe implements continuous delivery pipelines across all SAFe configurations. Now let's move on to understand how SAFe DevOps improves continuous delivery pipelines.

Enabling the CDP with DevOps

This is the point where SAFe diverges from traditional VSM concepts by positioning DevOps as a critical enabler of success, as well as extending its application of DevOps to the entire value stream. Of course, you now know that DevOps is the critical enabler to compete in our digital economy; and that is the position that Scaled Agile adopts, too. In this context, SAFe DevOps follows the VSM tool initiatives we discussed in *Chapter 11, Identifying VSM Tool Types and Capabilities*.

In this subsection, we're going to get into the details of how **SAFe DevOps** supports improvements to continuous deliveries. This topic will also take us back to the discussion of value stream management as it's applied within SAFe. As you will find, SAFe DevOps encompasses a number of concepts that we will only briefly cover.

For this section, please refer to the following figure:

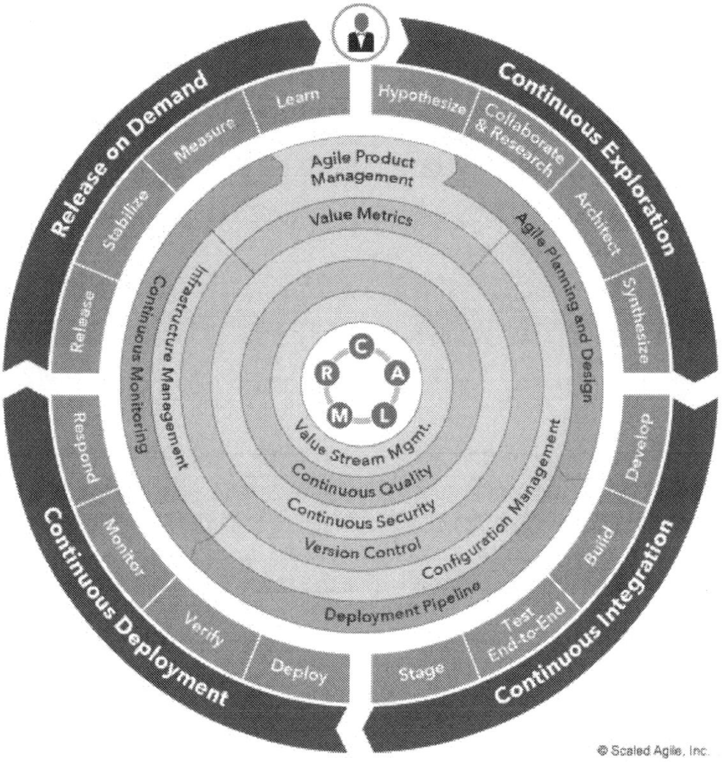

Figure 13.13 – DevOps enables the CDP

The first thing you should notice in *Figure 13.13* is the outer rings depicting the four components of the previously identified CDP, to include **continuous exploration**, **continuous integration**, **continuous deployment**, and **release on demand**. But now we see that SAFe DevOps includes pipeline activities for each CDP stage.

At the center of SAFe's DevOps meta-model is SAFe's CALMR approach to DevOps, which is a continuous delivery mindset that guides all decisions and actions throughout the CDP. The **CALMR** acronym stands for **Culture**, **Automation**, **Lean** flow, **Measurement**, and **Recovery**. Let's look at each of the elements of CALMR in a bit more detail:

- **Culture** of shared responsibility
- **Automation** of the CDP
- **Lean flow** accelerates delivery
- **Measurement** of flow, quality, and value
- **Recovery** reduces risks and preserves value

The focus of SAFe DevOps and its CALMR approach is to center the ARTs on achieving extraordinary business outcomes. Those outcomes don't arise from simply automating tasks in the pipeline. The real benefits come from applying automation, Lean, measurement, and recovery techniques in a way that builds a thriving continuous delivery culture.

The internal rings of the SAFe DevOps diagram highlight the component capabilities required to establish a mature DevOps environment. These include, from the center outward:

- **Value stream management**: The approach used to make lean-oriented improvements across value stream flows. In SAFe DevOps, the goal is to increase the flow of business value from customer requests to solution delivery.

- **Continuous quality**: Ensuring we deliver products and services and conformance with requirements and their defined acceptance criteria. Under SAFe, quality is built in early in the pipeline and continually managed throughout a solution's life cycle. Quality practices include specific practices such as hypothesis-driven development, **behavior-driven development (BDD)**, **test-driven development (TDD)**, A/B testing, and exploratory testing. Automation is used to enhance the speed and accuracy of testing throughout the value stream.

- **Continuous security**: Helps ensure the safety of our information, products, and services not only for our own organization, but for our partners, stakeholders, and customers. Security practices include security by design, threat modeling, security-as-code, and automation in vulnerability scanning, penetration testing, and intrusion detection.

- **Version control**: Ensuring proper processes are in place to rigorously identify all the artifacts created in our value stream flows. Artifacts include application code, server, network, and firewall configurations, database scripts, requirements, and test scripts. All versions need to be stored in a common repository to ensure solutions and environments can be built, deployed, repaired, and decommissioned on demand.

- **Configuration management**: Ensuring proper processes are in place to rigorously identify all the artifacts associated with each and every product release. Where version control emphasizes *how* to manage different versions of artifacts, configuration management emphasizes *what* to manage for each release. In a modern DevOps context, configurations tend to be managed as *as-code* – infrastructure-as-code, security-as-code, and compliance-as-code.

- **Infrastructure management**: Ensuring we have a robust, sustainable, secure, and supportable infrastructure in which to develop and deliver our products and services. The objective of infrastructure management is to ensure the stability and resiliency of deployed solutions so that maximum value can be realized. Where configuration management installs a set of design-time practices, infrastructure management installs a set of runtime practices.

- **Agile product management**: Places a focus on continuous learning, but also encompasses customer centricity, hypothesis-driven development, design thinking, Lean Startup, and market research practices. The goal of this domain is to ensure that the CDP is always calibrated to deliver specific, measurable business outcomes.

The outer rings within the inner concentric circles indicate four critical practice domains that represent a solution's path through the system. The three practice domains include the following:

- **Agile planning and design**: Provide inputs to development, including desired business outcomes, solution scope, architecture, and design, to improve continuous deliveries.

- **Deployment pipeline**: This is the CI/CD portion of the software pipeline delivery model.

- **Continuous monitoring**: Includes full stack telemetry, observability, proactive issue detection, visualization, AIOps, and analytics to measure and maintain business value with a high degree of precision.

SAFe customer use cases

Scaled Agile makes the point that you can't really do SAFe without value streams, and they believe that many of their case studies speak directly to this. All of the SAFe customer stories can be found at the following URL: `https://www.scaledagile.com/customer-stories/`.

And more specifically, the use case located at this URL, `https://youtu.be/02IPXgYlNkY?t=2331` (minute 39), speaks directly to the power of value streams.

Scaled Agile presented the following use case describing how PCCW Global/Hong Kong Telecomm implemented ARTs to support the launch of several newly implemented value streams:

PCCW Global/Hong Kong Telecomm
Business application: • Since 2018, PCCW Global has been on a continuous journey of launching value streams and ARTs • The need to break down silos and adopt an Agile way of working to resolve disconnects between business and IT functions
Business issues/objectives: • During their SAFe business transformation, they concluded that the company needed to completely change its value streams. • Specifically, they needed to be a technology company operating under a platform economic model, where they can be both a supplier and a consumer, allowing infrastructure and applications to come together.
Solution: • They redefined their value streams to deliver value in a new way, to support the new economic model. • Had to repurpose their systems and create new ARTs to support the new value streams.
Results to date: • Started out as a managed services global carrier and evolved to become a meeting place for applications and infrastructure

Figure 13.14 – PCCW Global/ Hong Kong Telecomm use case

This section ends our discussion on the Scaled Agile Framework and the chapter as a whole. In this section, you learned how SAFe supports implementing value streams through their agile and solutions-oriented release trains. SAFe provides direct guidance on leveraging the resources of a large enterprise, taking advantage of their economies of scale while supporting their digital transformations through Lean-Agile improvements. Like Disciplined Agile, SAFe includes DevOps as a critical enabler to improve software value deliveries in support of the organization's digital improvement objectives.

We'll now end this chapter with a summary, followed, as always, by questions.

Summary

In this chapter, you learned about three organizations supporting the implementation of the VSM concept in a modern Lean environment, specifically leveraging improvements to DevOps pipeline flows to streamline an organization's software value delivery capabilities. First, you learned about the VSMC, a not-for-profit trade association funded by members (vendors and enterprises) to conduct research, learning, networking, and open source projects related to value stream management methods and tools applied to software delivery improvements.

Next, you learned about PMI's new DA FLEX acquisitions as its approach to helping organizations install Lean-Agile practices on an enterprise scale. In this section, you've learned that the DA toolkit helps you, your teams and your organizations choose their WOW best supporting their unique circumstances. You've also learned how FLEX is PMI's approach to implementing value stream flows and improve value deliveries using value stream management techniques.

The third Lean-Agile/VSM implementation approach you learned about is SAFe™ – the current leading framework for scaling agile practices on an enterprise scale. You've learned that SAFe DevOps is Scaled Agile's approach to implementing VSM concepts as part of DevOps to maximize business value flow through the end-to-end solution delivery life cycle. You've also learned how SAFe DevOps implements VSM, Lean, Agile, and DevOps values, principles, and practices across functions in the continuous operation, measurement, and optimization of value streams from customer requests to solution delivery.

Now that we have covered the leading VSM methodology providers supporting DevOps-based improvements, we will move on to *Chapter 14*, *Introducing the Enterprise Lean-VSM Practice Leaders*. In that chapter, you will learn about two of the leading Lean methodology and training organizations, **Lean Enterprise Institute** and **LeanFITT**. These two organizations defined the original concepts behind value streams and value stream management, respectively.

Questions

1. What is the purpose and objective of the VSMC?
2. Structurally, the VSMC practices what it preaches by aligning its work around three value streams. What are they?
3. What is the initial research offering provided by the VSMC?
4. PMI acquired two companies to jump-start its Lean-Agile practices. What were those two companies, and what were their offerings?

5.   What is Disciplined Agile's approach to assisting Lean-Agile teams?

6.   What is the purpose of process blades within the DA toolkit?

7.   What are the four layers of the DA toolkit?

8.   What role does FLEX play within the DA toolkit?

9.   State the importance of value streams within the **Scaled Agile Framework**® (**SAFe**®).

10. What are the key elements of Lean value streams within SAFe?

11. In a broader, enterprise context, how does SAFe define value stream management?

12. What are the flows that contribute to SAFe's **Continuous Delivery Pipeline** (**CDP**)?

13. What is the relevance of DevOps to SAFe's CDP?

14. What does the acronym CALMR stand for, and what is its purpose?

15. What role does value stream management play in SAFe DevOps?

Further reading

- Ward, Allen (2004), *Lean Product and Process Development* (video). Lean Enterprise Institute, 2004.

- Kirsten, M. (July 2020), *The Rise of Value Stream Management (VSM)*: `https://www.linkedin.com/pulse/rise-value-stream-management-vsm-mik-kersten/`.

- Skelton, Matthew, and Manuel Pais, *Team Topologies: Organizing Business and Technology Teams for Fast Flow*. IT Revolution Press, 2019.

14

Introducing the Enterprise Lean-VSM Practice Leaders

This chapter provides instructions on the leading Lean-oriented practice and methodology leaders, including the **Lean Enterprise Institute** (**LEI**) and **LeanFITT™**. These two organizations are included because Lean practices evolved separately from Agile, and these are two of the longest operating thought leaders behind the Lean movement.

LEI was founded in 1997 by management expert James P. Womack, Ph.D. and his colleague, Daniel T. Jones. Womack and Jones coined the term *value stream* in an article published in the *Harvard Business Review* magazine, *From Lean Production to the Lean Enterprise* (Womack and Jones, March-April 1994; `https://hbr.org/1994/03/from-lean-production-to-the-lean-enterprise`). LEI promotes on its website that the organization "*conducts research, teaches educational workshops, publishes books and eBooks, runs conferences, and shares practical information about lean thinking and practices.*"

The second organization, LeanFITT™, developed the **value stream management** (**VSM**) methodology used in this book (*Chapter 6, Launching the VSM Initiative (VSM Steps 1 - 3)* through *Chapter 10, Improving the Lean-Agile Value Delivery Cycle (VSM Steps 7 and 8)*), as a reference model to make Lean-oriented improvements across a **continuous integration/continuous delivery** (**CI/CD**) pipeline flow. LeanFITT has a broader focus on VSM, improving all organizational value streams, not just those in **Information Technology** (**IT**). The LeanFITT™ team has collaborated, since 2001, in authoring more than 50 books and learning tools and materials on VSM as a practical approach to making Lean improvements enterprise-wide and across any type of value stream. LeanFITT's founders were the original thought leaders in the early development of VSM concepts and methodologies.

In this chapter, we're going to introduce the relevance of these two companies to VSM in the following sections:

- Going all-in on Lean

- Introducing LEI

- Getting started with Lean

- Implementing a phase-based approach to Lean improvements

Going all-in on Lean

By now, you should fully understand the premise behind this book:

> **Understanding the bigger VSM picture**
>
> *Our modern VSM tools-oriented industry will have a very short life if organizations do not fundamentally understand that VSM is not limited to making flow improvements to CI/CD and DevOps pipeline flows. Those are critical objectives. However, the much larger opportunity is to deploy our improved IT pipeline flows and resources to improve the products and value streams across the organization. Otherwise, companies will spend much money, time, and effort installing integrated, automated, and orchestrated toolchains only to find they have little impact on the organization's bottom line and its value delivery capabilities.*

At issue is the fact that improving one of the organization's value streams, from a systems-thinking perspective, is a form of local optimization if we don't look at its contribution to the system as a whole. Thus, we need to use our improved IT value stream delivery capabilities to drive improvements across the organization's other value streams. We do that by using the same VSM methods taught in this book but applied across all organizational value streams.

In the process, we will find that many potential value stream improvements have an information, integration, automation, and orchestration component that IT can address. So, the justifications to our investments in improving IT CI/CD and **development-operations** (**DevOps**) pipelines are not derived from the accelerated delivery of software, at least not in a vacuum. Instead, the larger justifications come from using software to accelerate Lean-oriented improvements across all organizational value streams.

In *Chapter 7, Mapping the Current State (VSM Step 4)*, the VSM team selected improvements to a CI/CD pipeline as its high-priority Lean improvement initiative. The purpose of that selection was to highlight that IT can be the exclusive subject of a VSM improvement initiative. However, the VSM team could have easily selected another organizational value stream, where improvements to the CI/CD pipeline were one of the identified Kaizen Bursts (improvements) necessary to improve work and information flows within the targeted value stream.

Therefore, we need to employ a generic VSM methodology and let the organization's strategic goals, portfolio investment priorities, and current state-future state analysis lead to identify and select our Lean improvement objectives. Since Lean production improvements are the operative concepts behind VSM, we shouldn't have different VSM approaches for different value streams.

So, it should be apparent that the importance of LEI and LeanFITT organizations is not related to leveraging the power of modern VSM tools. Instead, they have laid the groundwork on using VSM as an approach to improve all organizational value streams, including those in IT, to efficiently deliver value in support of the mission and priorities of the business.

With this foundation laid, let's move on to learn about LEI and LeanFITT. First, we'll start with an introduction to LEI.

Introducing LEI

In this section, you will learn about LEI, perhaps the best-known Lean training organization due to its founder's deep studies into the principles of Lean practices developed initially at Toyota and then widely adopted across the world.

Training and certification programs

LEI is a 501(c)(3) nonprofit based in Boston, **Massachusetts** (**MA**). Its stated mission is to make things better through Lean thinking and practice.

LEI was founded in 1997 by management expert James P. Womack, Ph.D., who wrote the seminal book on Lean, *The Machine that Changed the World*. Today, LEI promotes its efforts to conduct research, teach educational workshops, publish books and e-books, run conferences, and share practical information about lean thinking and practice.

Compared with traditional "*think*" tanks, LEI views its organization as a *do* tank. As you will find in later sections, LEI applies the same Lean principle to guide its research activities. Specifically, it develops hypotheses about lean thinking and experiment to see which approaches work best in the real world. It then writes up and teaches what it has discovered to offer new methods for organizational transformation.

LEI strives to answer the simple question every manager should ask: *What can I do on Monday morning to make a difference in my organization?* By creating a robust lean community through its website and public events, the goal of LEI is to give managers the courage to become lean change agents.

> **LEI's mission statement**
> "*Make things better, through lean thinking and practice.*"

LEI carries out its mission through the following value streams:

- Lean education
- Lean learning materials
- Co-learning partnerships
- Lean Summit conferences
- LEI's website: `https://www.lean.org/`

In addition, LEI's practitioners exchange information across the world through the Lean Global Network (`http://leanglobal.org/`), consisting of more than a dozen nonprofit organizations similar to LEI, all sharing a joint mission in different countries.

LEI is a professional resource to companies, executives, managers, team leaders, and team members. Anyone wishing to join the transformation to a lean way of creating value is welcome to join LEI's Lean community (`https://www.lean.org/WhoWeAre/why_join.cfm`). The LEI organization exists to support everyone who is starting or continuing the lean journey.

Articulating VSM concepts

LEI does not explicitly define VSM. However, readers can find several articles linked to the topic on LEI's website.

For example, James Womack wrote an article in 2002 titled *Substituting Money for Value Stream Management*. The premise behind that article is that he often found company line managers and executives are *"given a set of key metrics -- each with a stretch goal for this year -- and motivated by a bonus to reach the goals."*

The issue is that those managers and executives have multiple value streams running through their functional departments, but the metrics and financial incentives drive department or facility-level improvements. As Womack states: *"natural conflicts have emerged between what's best for the department or facility and what's best for the product as its value stream flows from start to finish through many departments and facilities."*

Womack notes that other problems arise that create **exhaustion** among those responsible for resolving them. He boils the issues down to the following three root causes:

- **Lack of a policy deployment process** to prioritize improvement initiatives and to down-select to a shortlist that can reasonably be accomplished and stabilized each year.

- **No assigned value stream managers** with the responsibility to look at the entire value stream for each product family, to optimize the whole rather than the parts.

- **Multiple and conflicting metrics**, without prioritization or training, can lead to exhaustion and a constant sense of failure.

In 2009, Dan Jones, then the Chairman of the Lean Enterprise Academy, wrote an article titled *Value Stream Management*. In this article, which coincided with the ending of the so-called "Great Recession", Jones discusses the *"growing impact of the web in opening up the possibility of turning customers from strangers to partners."* The premise of his article is that the web establishes a closer connection to our customers, turning them into demanding partners. Specifically, these customers demand that we *"deliver exactly what they want, when, where and how they want it and to significantly improve the experience of using these products and services while minimizing the impact on the environment"*.

Still, when he wrote the article, many companies had 200- to 300-day supply chains, and retailers could respond to their customers' demands. Jones found that suppliers highlighted 98% service delivery levels, but in reality, they were only accepting ~70% of their retailers' orders. The only way to close this gap is to apply VSM concepts to decrease supply chain lead times from months to days.

However, Jones notes the greatest obstacle to the successful application to VSM is because "*functions, departments and business units have become too powerful and act in their own interests.*" In other words, organizations ignore the voice of the customer to support functional, bureaucratic, and self-serving interests.

Jones' observations are not much different from those made by Womack in his article 7 years earlier. Putting the control of value delivery into the hands of hierarchical and functional departments takes the focus away from the flow of value from the perspective of the organization's customers. Jones notes that the best way forward requires rebalancing the power of functional organizations by introducing value stream analysis and VSM. We also need to apply scientific methods of experimentation to resolve problems and find better ways to design the management systems necessary to create and sustain new systemic solutions to our development, operations, and supply chain delivery problems.

Implementing the core concepts behind Lean

The central idea behind Lean is to maximize customer value while minimizing waste. More simply put, lean means creating more value for customers with fewer resources.

A lean organization understands customer value and focuses its key processes on increasing it continuously. The ultimate goal is to provide perfect value to the customer through a perfect value creation process with zero waste.

Lean thinking changes the focus of management from optimizing separate technologies, assets, and vertical departments to optimizing the flow of products and services through entire value streams that flow horizontally across technologies, assets, and departments to customers. Eliminating waste along entire value streams creates processes that need less human effort, less space, less capital, and less time to make products and services at far lower cost and with much fewer defects than traditional business systems. Companies can also respond to changing customer desires with high variety, high quality, low cost, and decreased throughput times. Also, information management becomes much simpler and more accurate.

More details on this subject are available on LEI's website at `https://www.lean.org/WhatsLean/`.

Getting started with Lean

LEI does not promote Lean as a **grand theory** where one size fits all. Instead, LEI views Lean as an approach to develop a set of standard practices for your organization based on experiments. The Lean process starts by defining a value-creating process in the form of a **value stream** or **model lines**. Next, organizations identify their value streams and use value stream mapping techniques to describe current and future state flows.

LEI's definition of value streams is contained in the call-out box that follows.

> **Value streams**
>
> All of the actions, both value-creating and non-value-creating, are required to bring a product from concept to launch (also known as a **development value stream**) and from order to delivery (also known as an **operational value stream**). These include actions to process information from the customer and actions to transform the product on its way to the customer.

Invariably, the lean transformation efforts will identify problems, issues, and areas of waste that prevent efficient flows of information and products. Lean transformation teams address each issue as a unique problem-solving activity.

LEI proposes using the **A3 technique** as the best way to form a hypothesis about how to make things better. Specifically, A3 is a technique to solve both large and small problems that inevitably show up every day.

As with the process behind **risk analysis and improvements**, A3 looks beyond the symptoms that we can easily see to discover and address the root causes. Only by addressing the root causes can we hope to resolve problems and keep them at bay.

A3 was developed as part of the **Toyota Production System** (**TPS**). The A3 content is always published as a one-page report. In fact, the acronym A3 comes from the European standard A3 paper size (11 inches by 17 inches or 29.7 cm x 42 cm).

A3 incorporates three roles, as shown here:

- **Problem owner**: They are responsible for managing the A3 process and creating and maintaining documents.

- **Responders/stakeholders**: These are the people up and down the value stream, plus executive managers who are most interested and impacted by the outcomes of the A3 project.

- **Mentor/coach**: This is an expert Lean practitioner who gives guidance and prompts the problem owner to find the solution, but not to give answers or offer solutions.

The A3 reports contain information related to the problem-solving effort, as shown in the following screenshot:

A3 Report	

1) **Background**
   - Importance
   - Context
	5) **Countermeasures**
	   - Possible Solutions
	   - Go back to Goals
	   - Add details as necessary

2) **Current Situation**
   - Problem Statement
   - Process Mapping
	6) **Implementation**
	   - List of Action Items
	   - Assign task responsibilities

3) **Set Targets/ Goals**
   - Desired Outcome
   - Success Metrics
	7) **Follow-up**
	   - Report results
	   - Standardize or modify

4) **Root Cause Analysis**
   - 5 Whys
   - Dig Deeper
   - Find Initial Problem
	Report Team:
	Leader:
	Team Members:
	Department:
	Date:

Figure 14.1 – Typical A3 report content and format

Now that you've seen a brief example of the A3 format, let's get more into the details of how the report is used.

Improving through experimentation

You should be aware that there are many variations of the A3 report in content and format. None of these are wrong, so long as they help your team get to the root cause of your problem.

The basic strategy is to identify where you are, then identify the business problem or opportunity and its root cause. Use metrics to measure performance gaps and determine the potential countermeasures. The problem-solving team uses the traditional **plan-do-check-act** or **plan-do-check-adjust** (**PDCA**) cycle to experiment against the available options to identify and select the best approach.

Through countless engagements, LEI has learned that Lean transformation efforts must be led by line managers, and not by a community of practice or a CI team. Line managers include the **Chief Executive Officer** (**CEO**), **Chief Operations Officer** (**COO**), **Chief Financial Officer** (**CFO**), Executive/**Business Unit** (**BU**) Head, Department Head, Facility Manager, Area Leader, or Line Manager. So, in other words, problem-solving efforts occur at all levels of the organization but are always led by the most in-line executive or manager.

In contrast, the **Communities of Practice (CoPs)**, CI teams, or VSM teams serve in the role of mentors and coaches.

Reflecting, sharing, and improving

LEI's approach to lean improvements is not a one-off problem-solving activity. Instead, with each problem-solving effort, the team reflects on what they've learned. But if the learnings stay within the assessment team, the organization as a whole cannot evolve.

Therefore, lean transformations depend upon sharing lessons learned vertically and horizontally across the organization and its value streams. The Japanese term for this is **Yokoten**, which is essentially the spreading of good ideas. Finally, we need to keep on experimenting to find new ways to improve. That is the essence behind achieving CI—identifying and resolving problems as a never-ending work cycle.

Let's take a moment to summarize what we've learned so far.

In summary, LEI's approach to Lean transformations involves the following:

- Identifying and mapping your value streams
- Solving problems via the A3 problem-solving model
- Using experimentation to improve continuously
- Reflecting on what was learned
- Sharing our findings with others throughout the organization
- Maintaining CI

Now that we understand LEI's approach to Lean transformation, let's take a quick look at LEI's principles guiding its Lean practices.

Defining the principles of Lean

LEI defined five principles behind its Lean practices, as noted on the Lean.org website: `https://www.lean.org/WhatsLean/Principles.cfm`. The principles define a flow for guiding Lean implementations.

"The five-step thought process for guiding the implementation of lean techniques is easy to remember, but not always easy to achieve:

1. Specify value from the standpoint of the end customer by product family.
2. Identify all the steps in the value stream for each product family, eliminating whenever possible those steps that do not create value.

3. Make the value-creating steps occur in tight sequence so the product will flow smoothly toward the customer.

4. As flow is introduced, let customers pull value from the next upstream activity.

5. As value is specified, value streams are identified, wasted steps are removed, and flow and pull are introduced, begin the process again and continue it until a state of perfection is reached in which perfect value is created with no waste."

LEI portrays its five Lean principles as a cyclical process, shown in the following screenshot:

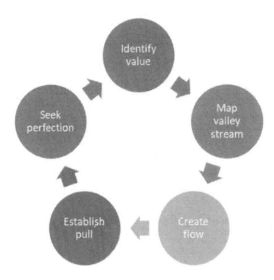

Figure 14.2 – LEI's principles of Lean

Now that we understand LEI's Lean principles, let's take a quick look at the breadth of potential applications in which Lean applies.

Applying Lean across the organization

LEI makes it clear that Lean is not simply used to improve manufacturing production processes. Lean-oriented approaches improve every business and every process within the business. Lean also operates as a strategic initiative and not as a singular-use or tactical program. Nor is Lean a cost-reduction program; instead, Lean is a way of thinking and acting to improve value delivery across the entire enterprise.

LEI provides more information on this topic at the following web page: `https://www.lean.org/WhatsLean/`

LEI notes that **transformation** or **lean transformation** is often used to characterize a company moving from an old way of thinking to lean thinking. Lean requires a complete transformation of how a company conducts its business.

Lean does not happen overnight. Instead, organizations must take a long-term perspective and persevere. So, let's take a moment to understand the business issues that justify a Lean transformation.

Implementing Lean to drive business transformations

LEI founders Womack and Jones outlined three fundamental business issues that should guide the transformation of the entire organization (`https://www.lean.org/WhatsLean/`). These are listed here:

- **Purpose**: Which customer problems will the enterprise solve to achieve its own purpose of prospering?

- **Process**: How will the organization assess each major value stream to make sure each step is valuable, capable, available, adequate, and flexible, and that all the steps are linked by flow, pull, and leveling?

- **People**: How can the organization ensure that every important process has someone responsible for continually evaluating that value stream in terms of business purpose and lean process? How can everyone touching the value stream be actively engaged in operating it correctly and continually improving it?

Now that we know what drives an organization to adopt Lean practices, let's look at methods to develop Lean action plans.

Creating a Lean action plan

While every individual or company embarking on a lean journey will have different challenges based on their particular set of circumstances, several crucial steps can help reduce resistance, spread the right learning objectives, and engender the type of commitment necessary for a lean enterprise. LEI provides more details on this topic at the following web page: `https://www.lean.org/WhatsLean/GettingStarted.cfm`.

Getting started

LEI promotes the following action-oriented steps to start the organization and adopt Lean as the new operating model:

- **Find a change agent**, a leader who will take personal responsibility for the lean transformation.

- **Get lean knowledge** via a sensei or consultant who can teach lean techniques and implement them as part of a system, not as isolated programs.

- Find a lever by **seizing a crisis** or by creating one to begin the transformation. If your company isn't in crisis, focus attention on a lean competitor or find a lean customer or supplier who will make demands for dramatically better performance.

- **Forget grand strategy** for the moment.

- **Map the value streams**, beginning with the current state of how material and information flow, then draw a leaner future state of how they should flow, and create an implementation plan with a timetable.

- **Begin as soon as possible** with an essential and visible activity.

- **Demand immediate results** and don't let things get bogged down through a lack of leadership, support, or sufficient priorities.

- **Expand your scope** to link improvements in the value streams and move beyond the shop floor to office processes as soon as you've got momentum.

Now that we know how to get started, we also need to understand the organizational structures supporting Lean transformations.

Creating an organization to channel your value streams

Lean production processes will change the way your organization operates. While organizations may choose to maintain hierarchical and functional departments to build and maintain skills, value delivery leadership must move to support cross-functional value stream deliveries, if it existed at all. In other words, value flows horizontally even when your management structure operates vertically.

LEI provides the following guidance to organizations implementing Lean transformation strategies:

- Reorganize your firm by product family and value stream.

- Create a lean promotion function.

- Deal with excess people at the outset, and then promise that no one will lose their job in the future due to the introduction of lean techniques.

- Devise a growth strategy.

- Remove the anchor-draggers.

- Once you've fixed something, fix it again.

- Two steps forward and one step backward is OK; no steps forward is not OK

Organizations adopting Lean as a new operating model must also install business systems to encourage and support lean practices, which is discussed in the following subsection.

Installing business systems to encourage Lean thinking

Creating an action plan and realigning resources are critical endeavors to support a Lean transformation. However, the practices won't stick unless the organization's executives install the necessary business systems to support and encourage lean-oriented transformations. With this objective in mind, LEI recommends the installation of the following business systems:

- Utilize policy deployment.

- Create a lean accounting system.

- Pay your people in relation to the performance of your firm.

- Make performance measures transparent.

- Teach lean thinking and skills to everyone.

- Right-size your tools, such as production equipment and information systems.

At this point, we have action plans in place, an organizational structure that supports the goals of the Lean transformation, and business systems to encourage long-term adoption of Lean thinking. We now need to take steps to complete the Lean transformation.

Completing the transformation

The final activities within the organization's Lean action plan help resolve the issues identified by Womack and Jones in their articles on VSM. These actions focus on aligning your supply chain partners to value delivery and doing so on a global basis. We also need to make sure the leadership and decision-making processes align to support our Lean adoptions.

LEI recommends the following activities to complete or round out your Lean transformation action plans:

- Convince your suppliers and customers to take the steps just described.
- Develop a lean global strategy.
- Convert from top-down leadership to leadership based on questioning, coaching, and teaching and rooted in the scientific method of PDCA.

LEI provides a framework to support Lean transformations, which is the topic of the next section.

Applying LEI's Lean transformation framework

LEI has found that effective enterprise transformations involve change across five dimensions. LEI uses the metaphor of a house to explain the five dimensions of change. The components of the *House of Lean* include the following:

- **The roof**—Objectives, goals, and aspirations to protect us from the surrounding environments, such as these:

  a. What is our value-driven purpose?

  b. Every situation is different, as are our countermeasures, so our approach must be different.

- **The walls**—The pillars that hold up our roof, which include the following:

  a. **Process**—What is the work to be done?

  b. **Capability**—What capabilities do we need to do the work, to solve our problem, to fulfill our purpose?

- **The foundation**—This includes our fundamental way of thinking, our mindset, and our underlying assumptions:

  a. **Explicit assumptions** that we are aware of and that inform all our activities

  b. **Hidden assumptions** that we don't know about

  c. **Lean transformations gap** to move from our current culture to an ideal culture

The House of Lean helps us improve our fundamental thinking about cause and effects by asking the following questions:

- Which **problems** do we need to solve?
- What is the **purpose** or goal we are trying to achieve?

- What is the **work** that needs to be done?

- What is the process or **flow** of work needed to improve our situation?

- What **capabilities** are required, and how will I grow them?

- Which **management systems** do we need to define?

- What **behaviors** are required to build the capabilities necessary to perform the work that will help us solve our problems?

The following screenshot provides a graphical display of LEI's House of Lean:

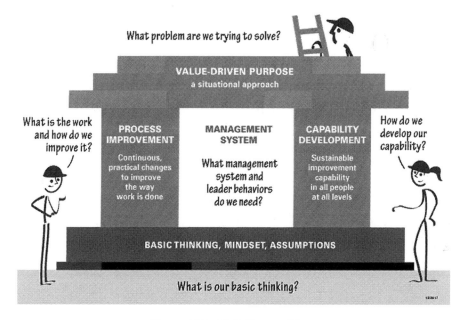

Figure 14.3 – LEI's House of Lean

LEI partners with other companies to apply its scientific method to seek CI to Lean transformation processes. The partnerships are formed under LEI's **Co-Learning Partners program**, introduced in the following subsection.

Co-learning partnerships

For several years now, LEI has partnered with a select group of companies to help them on their lean journeys and jointly conduct experiments on the best approaches to lean transformations. Qualified partner companies get access to LEI thought leaders, such as John Shook, Jim Womack, and Mark Reich, as well as LEI coaches and **subject matter experts** (**SMEs**).

Partners include traditional manufacturers applying lean methods across the entire enterprise. Still, LEI also partners with companies pioneering lean applications in a range of service industries, including retail, healthcare, and financial services.

Through these partnerships, LEI maintains up-to-date and real-world knowledge from these activities, providing the basis for future LEI publications, training, and research.

Co-learning partners are making investments in their time and resources, and there has to be something in it for them. LEI cites the following benefits gained by its partner companies:

- Coaching and mentoring of senior leaders
- Lean transformation project support
- Strategy planning and deployment (a.k.a. Hoshin)
- Customized learning opportunities
- Gemba-based improvement activities
- Action research and co-learning experiments
- Documented learning shared partner-to-partner and with the broader lean community (with approval)
- Interaction with the partner community
- Exclusive partner-to-partner learning activities
- Seats at LEI's practical how-to public workshops
- Seats at the informative and inspiring Lean Summit conference
- Discounts on books and other products

You can find more information about the Co-Learning Partners program at the following web page: `https://www.lean.org/WhoWeAre/CoLearningPartners.cfm`

This section completes our introduction to LEI. In the next section, you will learn about LeanFITT™ and its contributions to VSM development.

Training and tools from LeanFITT™

LeanFITT™ was established by Don Tapping, Rob Ptacek, Todd Sperl, and Abhishek Paul. From your reading of *Chapter 6, Launching the VSM Initiative (VSM Steps 1 - 3)* through *Chapter 10, Improving the Lean-Agile Value Delivery Cycle (VSM Steps 7 and 8)*, you may recall that Don Tapping and his collaborators defined the eight-step VSM methodology used earlier in this book, which we employed as a use case to evaluate and improve CI/CD pipeline flows from a Lean-oriented perspective.

As a collective effort, the LeanFITT™ team has collaborated since 2001 to author over 50 books and learning tools and materials on Lean and VSM practices. Employing knowledge gained through their collaborations, the LeanFITT company provides a set of Lean tools to support your Lean improvement initiatives. The **FITT** part of LeanFITT stands for **Functional**, **Integrated**, **Technology**, and **Training**.

LeanFITT started as a consulting firm but evolved to develop and deliver both methods and tools to support Lean production processes. For example, under development since 2014, the LeanFITT tools consolidate the team learnings, with delivery made available using enhanced software tools. The tools facilitate Lean team collaborations with simpler approaches, compared to Lean's manual options. As a result, the LeanFITT system of tools helps organizations deploy Lean concepts more quickly and sustainably.

LeanFITT's tools offer knowledge-based guidance to VSM teams, Lean practitioners, executives, and other stakeholders participating in value stream improvements. Each LeanFITT tool provides the following features:

- Detailed content explaining their purpose and practical applications
- **Sensei tips** from industry Lean Sigma experts
- Leadership tips for leaders at all levels to better engage employees
- Action items that are tracked with notifications and allow for notes and pictures/photos

The objectives of the LeanFITT tools are to harness the power of CI, employee engagement, standardized knowledge, and tool usage to inspire process changes that make a big impact. With that understanding in mind, let's review their tools.

Offerings from LeanFITT™

The LeanFITT system offers methods, tools, and techniques to improve organizational processes, people, and profits. As a complete set, the LeanFITT system includes the following 12 tools to support their respective methods and techniques:

Lean Tools	Methods and Techniques Supported
5S	The means and methods to ensure areas, files, folders, and so on are systematically kept clean and organized.
A3 Project	The means and methods to "tell the CI story" logically and visually.
DMAIC	The means and methods to use a statistical-based five-step problem-solving methodology. The **DMAIC** acronym stands for **Define, Measure, Analyze, Improve,** and **Control.**
Gemba Walk	The means and methods to gain a thorough understanding of the process, ask questions, and provide support and insights.
Kaizen Project	The means and methods to determine, plan, and track a Kaizen event.
Leadership	The means and methods to eliminate team issues during a Kaizen event.
Lean Overview and Assessment	The means and methods to create a baseline that improvement activities will address.
Mistake Proofing	The means and methods to thoroughly analyze a process for potential errors.
PDCA	The means and methods to use an iterative four-step problem-solving methodology. PDCA is an iterative and cyclical continuous process and product improvement method.
Standard Work	The means and methods to establish and control the best way to complete a process without variation from the original intent.
Value Stream Mapping	The means and methods to create a visual representation of the material and information flow, both current and future states, as well as queue times between processes for specific customer demand.
Waste Walk	The means and methods to visit a process area being considered for improvement, ask questions, and then identify process waste.

Figure 14.4 – LeanFITT™ Lean tools

Customers can use LeanFITT tools to support their needs in an ad hoc manner. However, the company promotes a four-phased approach to implementation, which you'll learn about next.

Implementing a phase-based approach to Lean improvements

The LeanFITT system employs a four-phased approach to make Lean improvements to organizational processes. The objectives of their LeanFITT implementation methodology are to **achieve positive behavior changes** toward a **CI mindset**, making a high level of discipline and standardization simple and easy to follow, and creating **a positive shift in organizational culture and profitability**.

Let's take a quick look at LeanFITT's four-phase approach to creating a Lean enterprise.

Phase 1 – Getting people trained and engaged

As we discussed in *Chapter 6*, *Launching the VSM Initiative (VSM Steps 1-3)*, an organization needs to make sure that the participants in the VSM initiative understand the principles of Lean. We also need to make sure the value stream is identified and that executives and stakeholders support and engage in the Lean improvement's efforts. Finally, we use the value stream mapping activities you learned in *Chapter 7*, *Mapping the Current State (VSM Step 4)*, and *Chapter 9*, *Mapping the Future State (VSM Step 6)* to identify waste and eliminate this through **Kaizen bursts** (identified lean improvement initiatives).

The LeanFITT tools used in this phase include **waste walks**, **5S**, **PDCA**, **Kaizen projects**, **value stream mapping**, and other tools as appropriate. Primary activities include the following:

- Identifying the key users
- Developing and implementing individual and team or group development and training plans
- Understanding the business case and identifying waste and improvement opportunities
- Testing your knowledge, receiving feedback, and earning rewards

This phase has a focus on finding and evaluating approaches to eliminate waste. As this phase winds down, the organization moves on to standardize and improve its Lean implementation processes.

Phase 2 – Standardizing the improvement process

In this phase, the VSM team seeks to standardize its lean improvement process, leveraging the LeanFITT tools and adding in DMAIC. DMAIC is a **Six Sigma**-based improvement process.

A Six Sigma process is one in which 99.99966% of all instances of a process or product are free of defects. Six Sigma strategies set and monitor upper and lower boundaries on process and product defect metrics to discover trends before deviations have catastrophic consequences. As deviations from the statistical norms are observed, the team quickly analyzes and addresses the causes of the variances.

The LeanFITT tools used in this phase include **standard walks**, **A3**, **Gemba walks**, **5S**, **PDCA**, **DMAIC**, and other tools as appropriate. Primary activities include the following:

- Implementing targeted and results-focused improvement projects
- Applying LeanFITT™ tools for improvements
- Measuring and tracking improvement progress
- Sharing results with others

The activities of this phase have a focus on eliminating the waste identified in *Phase 1*. Successful elimination of waste will improve the organization's delivery of customer value.

Lean improvements operate at a strategic level and organization-wide. But, as with any business transformation initiative, change is hard. Change cannot be mandated—it has to be led and the reasons for the change must be communicated, else others within the organization will feel threatened and resist.

Moreover, people generally want to join efforts and organizations that have successful outcomes. So, the executives sponsoring LeanFITT need to promote their initial successes to gain further buy-in throughout the organization. The executives also need to make opportunities available throughout the organization to train people in other value streams to apply Lean practices, methods, and tools. These are the objectives of the next phase.

Phase 3 – Energizing the team with active involvement and transparency

In this third phase, the successes of previous Lean improvement efforts are socialized, and individuals both within and leading the initial efforts are recognized for their achievements. LeanFITT promotes the use of metrics and visibility of efforts to encourage organizational support and buy-in to the new way of working, as with any Lean initiative. These objectives are the focus of *Phase 3* activities.

The LeanFITT tools used in this phase include **standard walks**, **A3**, **Gemba walks**, **5S**, **PDCA**, **DMAIC**, and other tools as appropriate. Primary activities include the following:

- Promoting and making visible the results from LeanFITT™ tool applications and projects
- Tracking and sharing team improvement project progress and action items
- Standardizing and expanding training throughout the organization
- Sharing success stories

At this point, the teams leading the Lean improvements can take a bow for their successes. Celebrating success is a good thing. However, the organization cannot stop here. Lean is about making CI across product life cycles and across the life of the organization.

Phase 4 – Making Lean routine and sustainable

Organizations that stop improving become stale and put their business at risk. Other competitors will see opportunities to claim market share with new products, often driven by digital enhancements to products and the organization's value streams. This fourth phase seeks to sustain and even build upon your Lean-oriented competitive advantages.

The LeanFITT tools used in this phase include **standard walks**, **Gemba walks**, **PDCA**, **mistake-proofing**, and other tools as appropriate. Primary activities include the following:

- Continually monitoring and adjusting progress and activities to address current needs
- Implementing action items to drive continual improvements
- Measuring and sharing tangible dollar savings and intangible savings such as improved communications and teamwork
- Making continual improvements and LeanFITT™ your organization's culture!

Lean and Six Sigma often address issues of quality, of which there are a host of methods and tools that support quality improvement objectives. As you might imagine, LeanFITT provides quality improvement tools in its product offerings.

Improving quality with LeanFITT

LeanFITT includes nine methods and tools for improving quality, as shown in the following screenshot:

Quality Tools	Methods and Techniques Supported
5 Whys Analysis	The means and methods to use organized brainstorming to methodically determine the causes of a problem (that is, effect).
Brainstorming	The means and methods to generate a high volume of ideas that are free of criticism and judgment within a short time period.
Fishbone Diagram	The means and methods to graphically display and explore, in increasing detail, all the possible causes of a problem or issue.
Histogram	The means and methods to collect and utilize data to display shape and distribution.
Impact Map	The means and methods to identify solutions likely to have the greatest impact on the problem with the least amount of effort.
Pareto Chart	The means and methods to collect and display data in bar chart format representing the 80/20 Pareto principle.
Run Chart	The means and methods to collect and display several data points over time.
Scatter Plot	The means and methods to collect and display data to study the possible relationship between one variable and another.
Stakeholder Analysis	The means and methods to collect and help determine the key people who have influenced project success.

Figure 14.5 – LeanFITT™'s nine methods and tools for improving quality

This section ends our discussion on LeanFITT and also this chapter on leading practices in VSM. In the next chapter, which also begins *Section 3* of this book, we will dive into the subject of DevOps once again. Before we get there, we'll end this chapter with a summary and a list of questions to help you verify and improve your retention of the content discussed.

Summary

In this chapter, you were introduced to the two organizations that have played an instrumental role in the development of Lean practices and VSM. We began with an introduction to LEI. LEI conducts research, teaches educational workshops, publishes books and e-books, runs conferences, and shares practical information about lean thinking and practice.

You were also introduced to LeanFITT. The partners who founded LeanFITT have contributed to more than 50 books on Lean practices. They also wrote some of the earliest books on VSM and were very involved in the early development of VSM practices and methodologies.

We are now ready to move on to *Section 3* of this book, which describes the complexities and approaches to installing modern DevOps pipelines and toolchains. The first chapter, *Chapter 15*, *Defining the Appropriate DevOps Platform Strategy*, addresses two critical issues. The first issue is avoiding DevOps implementation pitfalls that all organizations face when attempting to implement a mature DevOps pipeline and toolchain strategy. The second issue is determining which DevOps platform implementation strategy is most appropriate for your organization. Specifically, you will learn about four approaches to implementing a DevOps pipeline.

Finally, the last chapter, *Chapter 16*, *Transforming Businesses with VSM and DevOps*, discusses a potential future state where modern VSM tools not only assist in improving IT-based value streams but all the organization's value streams.

Questions

1. Who coined the term *value streams*?
2. What is the relevance of LeanFITT on top of our discussions on VSM?
3. Which concerns did James Womack describe relating to organizational use of money as incentives for functional managers and executives?
4. How does LEI define value streams?
5. In LEI, what is the purpose of a Lean action plan?
6. What is the stated purpose of LeanFITT's offerings?
7. What are LeanFITT's four phases in their approach to creating a Lean enterprise?
8. What is an A3 project?
9. What is a Six Sigma process?
10. LeanFITT has two sets of tools—what are they?

Further reading

1. *Martin, James (1995). The Great Transition. Using the Seven Disciplines of Enterprise Engineering to Align People, Technology, And Strategy. Amazon. New York, New York.*

2. *Davenport, Thomas (1992). Process Innovation: Reengineering Work through Information Technology. Ernst & Young – Center for Information Technology and Strategy. Harvard Business School Press, Boston, Massachusetts.* Retrieved from `https://www.researchgate.net/publication/216300521_ Process_Innovation_Reengineering_Work_through_Information_ Technology`.

3. *Kirsten, M. (2018). Project to Product. How to Survive and Thrive in the Age of Digital Disruption with the Flow Framework. IT Revolution. Portland, OR.*

4. *Cardoza, C. (January 6, 2021). A guide to value stream management solutions. Buyers Guide.* Retrieved from `https://sdtimes.com/value-stream/a-guide- to-value-stream-management-solutions-2/`. Accessed May 20, 2021.

5. *Collins, J. (September 29, 2020). GigaOm Radar for Value Stream Management v1.0.* Retrieved from `https://gigaom.com/report/gigaom-radar-for- value-stream-management/`. Accessed May 20, 2021.

6. *Condo, C., Mines, C. (July 15, 2020). The Forrester Wave™: Value Stream Management Solutions, Q3 2020. The 11 Providers That Matter Most And How They Stack Up.* Retrieved from `https://www.forrester.com/report/The+Forrest er+Wave+Value+Stream+Management+Solutions+Q3+2020/-/E- RES159825`.

7. *Rupp, C. G. (2020). Scaling Scrum Across Modern Enterprises: Implement Scrum and Lean-Agile techniques across complex products, portfolios, and programs in large organizations. Packt Publishing. Birmingham, England.*

8. *Ford, N., Parsons, R., Kua, P. (2017). Building Evolutionary Architectures: Support Constant Change. O'Reilly Media, Inc. Sebastopol, CA.*

9. *Zachman, J. (February 1987). A Framework for Information Systems Architecture. IBM Systems Journal 26, 276-292.*

10. *Kersten, Mik (July 15, 2020). The Rise of Value Stream Management (VSM).* Founder and CEO of Tasktop. Originally published on the Tasktop blog on July 15, 2020. Also posted on LinkedIn. Retrieved from `https://www.linkedin.com/ pulse/rise-value-stream-management-vsm-mik-kersten/`.

11. *Ennaciri, H., Bhat, M., Betts, D., Saunderson, C., Herschman, J., Murphy, T. (September 29, 2020). Market Guide for DevOps Value Stream Management Platforms.* ID: G00730782. Retrieved from `https://www.gartner.com/en/documents/3991130/market-guide-for-devops-value-stream-management-platform`.

12. *Ackoff, R. L. (1994). If Russ Ackoff had given a TED Talk. YouTube.* Published by Steven Brant. Posted on Oct 23, 2010. Hosted by Clare Crawford-Mason and Lloyd Dobyns to capture the learning and legacy of Dr. W. Edwards Deming. (`https://www.youtube.com/watch?v=OqEeIG8aPPk`)

13. *Robinson, F. (2001). MVP: A Proven Methodology to Maximize Return on Risk.* Accessed May 29, 2001. Retrieved from `http://www.syncdev.com/minimum-viable-product/`.

14. *Ries, E. (2009). Minimum Viable Product: a guide. Startup Lessons Learned.* Accessed May 29, 2001. Retrieved from `http://www.startuplessonslearned.com/2009/08/minimum-viable-product-guide.html`.

15. *Womack, J. (November 2002). Substituting Money for Value Stream Management. Lean Enterprise Institute. Boston, MA.* Retrieved from `https://www.lean.org/womack/DisplayObject.cfm?o=686`. Accessed May 30, 2021.

16. *Jones, D. (December 2009). Value Stream Management. Lean Enterprise Institute. Boston, MA.* Retrieved from `https://www.lean.org/common/display/?o=1284`. Accessed May 30, 2021.

17. *Goldratt, E. M., Cox, J. (1984, 2014). The Goal: A Process of Ongoing Improvement. Fourth Edition. North River Press. Great Barrington, MA.*

18. *Bain, S. L. (2008). Emergent Design: The Evolutionary Nature of Professional Software Development. Addison-Wesley, A Pearson Education company. Upper Saddle River, NJ.*

19. *Ward, Allen (2004). Lean Product and Process Development* (video). *Lean Enterprise Institute, 2004.*

20. *Kirsten, M. (July 2020). The Rise of Value Stream Management (VSM).* (`https://www.linkedin.com/pulse/rise-value-stream-management-vsm-mik-kersten/`)

21. *Skelton, Matthew, and Manuel Pais. Team Topologies: Organizing Business and Technology Teams for Fast Flow. IT Revolution Press, 2019.*

Citing LEI use case studies

LEI cites four customer use cases to showcase the success of their co-learning program. The following list contains the names of the use cases, all of which are currently available on LEI's website (`https://www.lean.org/common/display/?o=3342`):

- `Thrustmaster Comes Around`

- `Fighting Cancer with Linear Accelerators and Accelerated Processes`

- `Lean + Circular Principals = a New True North for Manufacturer`

- `Using Plan-Do-Check-Act as a Strategy and Tactic for Helping Suppliers Improve`

Section 4:
Applying
VSM with DevOps

This final part of the book addresses three critical issues related to DevOps platform implementations:

- Avoiding DevOps implementation pitfalls
- Deciding on the appropriate DevOps platform strategy
- Using VSM and DevOps platforms to support digital business transformations

Geared toward non-technical readers and novice practitioners, *Chapter 15*, *Defining the Appropriate DevOps Platform Strategy*, discusses the complexity of implementing DevOps toolchains and pipelines. The chapter begins with discussions with five DevOps implementation experts who share their views on DevOps platform implementation issues and approaches to deal with those issues. Then, you will learn about four potential DevOps platform implementation strategies and the pros and cons of each. Finally, you will learn strategies to address 18 potential pitfalls when implementing DevOps platforms.

Finally, *Chapter 16, Transforming Businesses with VSM and DevOps*, summarizes what you have learned in this book while emphasizing the use of VSM to lead Lean business transformations in a digital economy. Specifically, you will learn how to integrate organizational VSM initiatives to make the best use of your improved software delivery pipelines.

In the second section of this book, you learned a generic VSM methodology that supports all value stream improvements. In the final chapter of this book, you will learn about the VSM Consortium's VSM Implementation Roadmap, which applies both Lean and Agile improvement concepts to implement VSM tools to improve software delivery capabilities in support of digital business transformations. We will wrap up the book with strategies to use OKRs with your VSM tools, align corporate strategies with portfolio investments in VSM and DevOps tools, identify potential failure points, and expand the vision for modern VSM tools.

This section includes the last two chapters of the book:

- *Chapter 15, Defining the Appropriate DevOps Platform Strategy*
- *Chapter 16, Transforming Businesses with VSM and DevOps*

15
Defining the Appropriate DevOps Platform Strategy

Congratulations! If you've made it this far, which is the start of *Section 4* of this book, you are about to enter the final set of topics that will be covered in this book. Specifically, we will now turn our attention to understanding the approaches we can use to implement DevOps capabilities, as well as how to use those capabilities to support digital business transformations.

There are four primary main topics that will be covered in this final section on applying DevOps to drive digital business transformations, as follows:

- Avoiding DevOps implementation pitfalls
- Deciding on an appropriate DevOps platform strategy
- Addressing the pitfalls of DevOps implementations
- Interviewing the experts
- Dealing with corporate implementation mandates
- Dealing with creative versus repeatable pipeline activities

We will cover the first three topics in this chapter before discussing how we can use VSM and DevOps tools to help affect digital business transformations in *Chapter 16, Transforming Businesses with VSM and DevOps*. In this chapter, you will learn about four basic DevOps implementation strategies, as well as the pros and cons of each. Then, we'll move on and discuss some of the pitfalls that can harm a DevOps implementation initiative. Finally, we'll review 18 strategies that can help improve your DevOps toolchain implementations.

Much of the information presented in this chapter comes from DevOps experts and the VSM and DevOps tools companies that were interviewed for this book. However, we've waited to recommend these strategies as they are relevant regardless of the DevOps tools and toolchains your organization may select for deployment.

We must address the implementation options and issues before we move on to the next chapter, because it won't matter how much benefit can be derived from VSM and DevOps tools if we fail to deploy them. Successfully deploying our VSM and DevOps methods and tools is necessary to support our digital transformations.

In the next chapter, you will discover that modern VSM tools and practices support aligning DevOps-based software deliveries to make other organization value stream improvements. In this sense, we will have come full circle to show how improved software delivery capabilities support the organization's value stream improvements, which are necessary to compete in our modern digital economy.

With these objectives in mind, let's begin by exploring the potential pitfalls of DevOps implementations.

Avoiding DevOps implementation pitfalls

While preparing to write this chapter, I interviewed several people whose opinions I value as expert practitioners in deploying DevOps tools and toolchains. They are **Scott Ambler** (Vice President and Chief Scientist for Disciplined Agile at the Project Management Institute), **Al Wagner** (HCL Software VSM and DevOps Evangelist), **Helen Beal** (Chief Ambassador at DevOps Institute and Chair of the VSMC), **Pramod Malhotra** (DevOps Services Executive), and **Joel Kruger** (Senior DevOps Engineer specialized in developing reusable software factories).

Helen Beal's credentials in the DevOps and DevOps communities are immense. She explains how DevOps implementations typically evolve to include multiple tools and the need for VSM tools to both improve and orchestrate software delivery workflows. Scott Ambler approaches DevOps from a Lean-Agile perspective and choosing your **Way of Working** (**WoW**) when implementing DevOps platforms.

Pramod Malhotra discusses his DevOps implementation experiences as a Federal Prime and commercial systems integration contractor. Al Wagner will represent the point of view of a VSM/DevOps platform vendor. Finally, Joel Kruger will discuss the benefits of creating downloadable CI/CD and DevOps configurations as reusable software factories.

With these initial introductions made, let's get going.

Interviewing the experts

In this section, we will understand the views of five industry experts and their take and ideas on DevOps.

Interview with Helen Beal

Helen Beal is a DevOps and Ways of Working coach, Chief Ambassador at **DevOps Institute**, Ambassador for the **Continuous Delivery Foundation**, and the Chair of the **Value Stream Management Consortium** (**VSMC**). She provides strategic advisory services to DevOps industry leaders and serves as an analyst at **Accelerated Strategies Group**.

I am privileged that Helen agreed to serve as a technical reviewer for this book and wanted to contribute her thoughts for this chapter. I've also had the opportunity to work with Helen as one of the advisors of the VSMC. So, with this introduction made, let's hear what Helen has to say.

Developing a DevOps mindset

Helen starts by stating that she does not believe that organizations should create DevOps teams. Instead, she views DevOps as a mindset and not so much an organizational structure. As she puts it, *"instill the mindset that DevOps is a cultural movement for the whole organization and design value stream teams that practice DevOps."*

Value streams are the fundamental organizational structure for delivering value in a Lean enterprise. DevOps is a collaboration and technical implementation strategy that supports value streams in IT. So, in this context, Helen's statement makes overwhelming sense.

DevOps began as a collaboration strategy to align the efforts of software development and operations teams to improve value-based software delivery capabilities. You also know now that mature DevOps pipelines collectively implement tool integrations, activity automation, and work and information orchestrations to improve value stream flows. DevOps requires a change in thinking and culture to align software delivery with value streams.

Empowering people

DevOps changes the way people work within and across the organization. For that reason, DevOps affects the organization's people and its culture. Helen goes on to note that we must empower people to participate – *"people don't like having change done to them – they have to be given autonomy to find their own way forward."* Helen also notes that it's hard to become empowered if you haven't been for a long time.

Leading the way

Helen makes the point that *leaders lead*. Therefore, they can't take a backseat role in overseeing the deployment of DevOps tools and toolchains, as well as the organizational changes that must come to utilize this new way of working effectively.

To be effective in their roles, the executives within the organization must learn the skills and principles of DevOps before they come out with any mandate for its use. Otherwise, they can't possibly make informed decisions on tools, related budgets, aligning resources, and training requirements.

Helen observes that many leaders think they are *above learning*. Instead, leaders need to retrain the organization, starting with themselves. DevOps moves the organization away from a traditional hierarchical and command and control structure. Therefore, its leaders – including the organization's executives, managers, and coaches – must have the skills and knowledge to encourage their teams to self-discover ways to improve and help remove the impediments identified by their teams.

Evolving over transforming

A trend among many analysts today is to speak about using Lean-Agile practices to support business transformations. In this book, you have heard me describe how we can use VSM and DevOps methods and tools to support business transformations to compete in our modern digital economy.

However, Helen is concerned that the notion of effecting business transformation is too *big bang* and that many people have change fatigue from previously failed transformations. Instead, Helen believes we are better served by aiming for evolution with continuous and incremental improvements. In this context, Helen believes it's better for the organization to steer its efforts toward achieving a culture of continuous evolution, and not a one-time and relatively short-term business transformation objective.

Making time to learn

Helen noted previously that the organization's leaders must gain knowledge to support an effective DevOps transformation. But that same learning requirement extends throughout the organization, and time and resources must be made available for their continued education.

These training requirements mean the organization's executives must make time for learning. In other words, continuing learning must be viewed as an ongoing job requirement and not a nice thing to have.

DevOps evolution requires all humans in an organization to unlearn long-held beliefs and practices (for example, PRINCE, project management, and so on) and learn new ways of thinking and working. Helen notes that humans have cognitive load limits, and it takes time to learn and practice new behaviors. Therefore, time must be allocated to learning outside of **business as usual** (**BAU**) and new feature development and resolution.

Resolving technical debt

Though not technically part of training, Helen made the same point about resolving technical debt. In other words, organizations need to build time into their busy schedules to refactor software code, as this helps address performance issues that accumulate when the teams are focused on conveniently delivering new features. Similarly, the development and support teams need to improve a product's architecture and design and implement new technology improvements from time to time.

Building the DevOps platform

Helen points out that new DevOps tools become available all the time and that their requirements change over time, too. Therefore, software delivery teams need to build an adaptable DevOps framework – think API first. Taking on a DevOps framework strategy helps ensure the platform remains extensible over time, allowing new capabilities and future technologies to be integrated to support the organization's evolving software delivery needs.

Another important consideration is to aim for traceability throughout the toolchain. Helen believes you should accept that your DevOps platform will become a heterogeneous toolchain, even if you start with a commercial **DevOps as a Service (DaaS) platform**. Supporting an evolutionary approach to make continuous improvements in your DevOps toolchains will drive that eventual outcome. On the positive side, your VSM platform will hook it all together for you.

Also, Helen believes you should aim to provision your DevOps toolchain/VSM platform as a service to your value stream teams. While teams can have different requirements and tools, you can separate the architecture or categories of your toolchain from the actual toolchain and switch tools out (for example, NUnit for .NET unit tests, JUnit for Java unit tests). We'll discuss this topic more in the *Adopting software factory strategies* and *Building reusable software factories* sections, both of which discuss how downloadable and self-service configurations can serve as reusable software factories.

Overcoming DevOps implementation challenges

Helen believes it's difficult to establish a common view of what DevOps is in an organization. Some people may think of it as just a piece of automation, such as implementing a CI/CD pipeline. Others recognize that the breadth of DevOps includes the entire value stream, connecting all parts of the business and incorporating Agile, Lean, **site reliability engineering** (**SRE**), DevSecOps, DataOps, or AIOps.

Regardless of how your organization elects to define DevOps, make sure you have evangelists and communities of practice define and socialize why and how DevOps supports your business.

Helen notes that the most common challenge when implementing DevOps is around culture. The tools and toolchains are the easiest things to see and implement. But it's changing people's thinking and ways of working that is much harder to accomplish in practice.

To affect cultural change toward positive outcomes, Helen believes the organization must actively build psychological safety, train leaders to distribute authority, invest heavily in continuous learning, and teach people to talk about their emotions, feelings, and behavior. In addition, she suggests organizations employ the latest findings in neuroscience in their efforts to help create real and lasting change.

Finally, Helen discussed the relevance of KPIs and OKRs to define the goals and objectives for your DevOps implementation activities. But she also notes that they should not be inflicted on teams. Instead, allow your DevOps teams to define and measure their objectives and metrics. And make sure your teams have the tools (that is, VSMPs) to monitor their results continually and in real time.

Interview with Scott Ambler

Scott is the co-creator, along with Mark Lines, of **Project Management Institute** (**PMI**)'s **Disciplined Agile** (**DA**) toolkit. Scott works also with Al Shalloway, the thought leader behind DA FLEX. **Disciplined DevOps** is one of the layers of the DA toolkit, and it is from this perspective that Scott discusses DevOps implementation pitfalls and platform strategies.

Scott has extensive IT experience and has shared his knowledge for years. He has authored or co-authored over 20 books in the IT and process space and has worked with organizations worldwide to help them improve their way of working. Scott is currently the Vice President and Chief Scientist for DA at PMI.

You can't buy DevOps

Scott believes that the greatest implementation pitfall, when it comes to DevOps, is when the decision-makers do not understand the scope of the challenge. Too many organizations want to *install DevOps*, thinking that they can buy their way out of their current mess. Or, they think they can *transform to DevOps* in a few short months. Nothing can be further from the truth.

Successful DevOps implementations require significant and long-term investment in people, processes, and technology. First, there is a significant people issue. Every firm Scott has worked with needed to develop new skills, implement training programs, and find or develop mentors and coaches to support the learning journey. DevOps also clearly requires new WoW, as you've seen throughout this book, plus investments in tools and technologies to support this new and evolving WoW.

DevOps is about more than Dev and Ops

The most important observation that Scott makes about DevOps, echoing what Pramod and Al share, is that it is about more than just merging *Development* and *Operations*. In disciplined DevOps, one of the four layers of the DA toolkit, PMI has melded together six key aspects of enterprise-class DevOps:

- **Solution delivery**: This is a fit-for-purpose, tactically scalable approach to software-based solution delivery. Called **Disciplined Agile Delivery** (**DAD**), it weaves all aspects of solution delivery to produce consumable solutions from beginning to end. Consumable means that something is functional (it works), usable (it works well), and desirable (people want to work with it). A solution potentially includes software, hardware, documentation, business process improvements, and organization structure improvements. Agile teams typically focus on producing working software, where DA teams focus on producing consumable solutions – a big difference.

- **DevSecOps**: Disciplined DevOps builds security, both information/cybersecurity and physical security, practices right into the toolkit for the reasons that Pramod and Al share. Security should never be an afterthought.

  In this chapter, we'll see the acronym DevSecOps used oftentimes in lieu of the more traditional DevOps acronym. Where DevOps evolved as a collaborative strategy to break down the silos between development and operations, DevSecOps brings security into the collaborations. In other words, security is involved in each phase of the software development cycle as a part of the team, and not a siloed function.

  The goal of DevSecOps is to avoid security issues cropping up in a deployed software solutions. To achieve this goal, the DevSecOps pipeline includes integrated, automated, and orchestrated threat modeling and security testing activities. The automation capabilities ensure each new code change is thoroughly tested with attending reports and alerts generated detailing any potential vulnerabilities.

  In a DevSecOps pipeline, security is not limited to software coding and testing activities. Once released, monitoring tools continuously scan for threats and vulnerabilities, generating incident reports when and as they are discovered.

- **Data DevOps**: Data is the lifeblood of your organization, yet it's often ignored or at least treated as a low priority in most DevOps implementations. What is the value of deploying changes to your software many times a day if you can't also deploy changes to your data at the same rate?

- **Multi-solution support**: The DevOps philosophy of *you build it, you run it, and you support it* is a valuable motivator for better collaboration and process improvement. But it doesn't scale. When your organization has hundreds, or even thousands, of systems in operations, your end users need a common and coherent strategy to get support.

- **Common IT operations**: Once again, if you have many solutions running in production or supporting many DevOps pipelines or both, you want to support some common operational infrastructure to streamline things. In several organizations, Scott helped them identify the common, shared infrastructure and what is unique to support the needs of individual teams. How you treat, support, and evolve shared infrastructure is different from how you treat application-specific functionality. Scott's goal is to help his clients learn how to work with and evolve the two types of infrastructures accordingly.

- **Business operations**: Time and again, Scott has found that you don't want to restrict Ops to IT operations. That's certainly important, but if your business operations aren't comparatively flexible, you're better off investing effort in improving that aspect of your value stream first.

Scott believes a critical danger in DevOps implementations comes from ignoring the fact that there is more to DevOps than merely telling Dev and Ops teams to start working together in collaboration. Disciplined DevOps shows how all these critical aspects fit together in a streamlined and evolvable manner. And it also shows how to improve in each of these areas in parallel, but still as a collaborative effort.

In the next six subsections, Scott will explain how DevOps is employed within the DA Toolkit.

We'll start with the first DevOps concept, *Start with a mindset*.

Starting with a mindset

Scott points out that the Agile Manifesto, which most people point to as a description of the Agile mindset, was written over 20 years ago to address the problems of that time. But times have changed, and we've learned a few things along the way. Scott stresses that the mindset that was captured in the Agile Manifesto is a great start, and that there are many great ideas around a DevOps mindset that you've learned in this book, but what we really need is a mindset for business agility. Although DevOps is an enabler of value streams and business agility in general, it doesn't exist in a vacuum. To be successful, you need to look at the bigger picture beyond DevOps.

This approach is what PMI has done with the DA toolkit, including its DA Mindset, which captures principles, promises, and guidelines for business agility. A common mindset for business agility provides a foundation from which people can collaborate and work together, supporting the creation of a shared culture among your disparate teams.

Unexpectedly, the DA community found that this still wasn't enough. People from different domains come to the table with their own unique experiences, skillsets, priorities, and ways of looking at things. For example, security professionals have their unique philosophies, as do data professionals, marketing professionals, product managers, and other critical stakeholders. So, not only do we need the foundational principles, promises, and guidelines of the DA mindset, but we must also extend them with unique philosophies for each of the groups, or tribes, within our organizations.

Each process blade within DA, what DA calls process areas – such as security, data management, enterprise architecture, IT operations, and many others – extend the DA mindset with several philosophies pertinent to that domain. This approach enables people to focus on those process areas to tackle the challenges they face with a fit-for-purpose mindset for their context, all while sharing a common culture with the rest of the organization.

To summarize, DA promotes the idea that we need a common mindset to interact well with others. And *we must also respect the differences that people bring to the table, including their outlooks*. Success in DevOps requires everyone to evolve their way of looking at the world and apply their unique strengths in new ways.

Your technical debt has come due

If Scott had to pick a single reason for the slow implementation of DevOps within organizations, it would have to be technical debt. Poor quality source code and a lack of automated regression tests have been the bane of anyone bringing DevOps into their organizations for years. But data-oriented technical debt and quality problems with your data sources have been a blind spot for many organizations for years. Although senior leadership often recognizes there's a problem, they've often given up on ever trying to address it. But unless your organization addresses all aspects of technical debt, you will struggle to implement DevOps successfully.

Belying the name, the primary causes of technical debt aren't technical in nature but rather people oriented. In fact, Scott's experience is that most technical debt stems from project management thinking and behavior. In particular, the desire to be *on time and on budget* tends to force teams to produce lower-quality solutions than they would prefer, thereby increasing technical debt. The *we'll fix it later* claim rarely materializes. And, of course, the poor levels of training in design and architecture concepts and techniques are also contributors to technical debt.

Over the years, every organization Scott has worked with – spanning software firms, financial organizations, manufacturers, and grocery chains – needed to invest in paying down technical debt. However, investing in software quality, automated tests, and improving data quality always proves to be the lion's share of your DevOps infrastructure investment, requiring years of hard work to resolve.

Evolving into a fit for purpose DevOps strategy

The DA toolkit takes a very different approach to providing process advice. Frameworks such as SAFe or LeSS provide a collection of *best practices* that prescribe what to do, which can be an excellent start. But it's only a start. Scott believes your organization is unique and facing a unique and evolving situation, so you need to go beyond Agile frameworks.

Instead, the DA toolkit tells you what to think about, provides options to address the challenges you face, and describes the trade-offs of those options. It puts you in a position to decide on what techniques to experiment with to develop your fit-for-purpose approach. It supercharges the "fail fast" improvement strategy by helping you make better decisions and thereby fail less often, leading to faster improvement.

Once again, Scott notes that a common implementation pitfall is thinking that you can install or quickly transform into a DevOps organization. You really can't. Instead, you need to do the hard work to evolve into DevOps. You want to have a fit-for-purpose DevOps strategy that reflects your organization, your people, and your goals, leading to your desired outcomes. You need to take responsibility for your WoW, and the DA toolkit helps you do exactly that.

You can buy some of your DevOps infrastructure

We've talked about DevOps platforms. Yes, you can buy DevOps tooling or adopt cloud-based **DevOps as a Service (DASS)** options and combinations thereof. So, the situation isn't entirely bleak, but you still need to install and configure the tooling. You still need to train people so that they know how to use. You still need to use the new infrastructure effectively. And as Scott pointed out earlier, you also need to invest in paying down technical debt. A vital aspect of that is infrastructural – such as developing automated tests. So, in short, you can buy some of your infrastructure, but you'll need to build a lot of it yourself.

Disciplined DevOps is table stakes for Agile enterprises

You can do the hard work of figuring out how development, operations, security, data, and support all fit together. And you can work through how it all supports your value streams and fits into your overall organization. Alternatively, you can look at the DA toolkit, which has already done all this heaving lifting, and use that as a starting point.

The DA toolkit shows how it all fits together, going far beyond DevOps to address how to effectively implement value streams and then support them at the enterprise level. Being choice-based, rather than prescriptive, teaches your teams how to evolve a fit-for-purpose *WoW* to be as effective as it can be, yet still fit into the overall value stream they're part of. And, of course, Lean governance strategies are woven through the toolkit; otherwise, chaos would ensue.

Evolving with the times

There are two critical and unfortunate observations that you must embrace if you're to be successful with DevOps:

- **Your organization is unique**: We've said this before; the implication is that you need to choose your WoW so that you have something that is fit for purpose.

- **Your environment is fluid**: Your WoW cannot be static; instead, it must evolve as your situation evolves. You must become a learning organization that knows how to improve continuously.

DA teaches you how to get better at getting better. It explicitly shows you that you have options and how to choose the best option for your current situation. It embeds improvement strategies at the team and organizational level, and also embraces a guided approach to experimentation beyond the *fail fast* mantra of mainstream Agile.

There isn't an easy answer

Scott couldn't say this enough – there are no shortcuts. You can't buy a DevOps solution, you can't install one, and you can't quickly transform it into DevOps. Instead, you need to do the hard work of evolving your culture, evolving your WoW, and improving your infrastructure. His experience is that DevOps is about people, processes, and technology. His final admonishment is *ignore these issues at your peril*.

Interview with Pramod Malhotra

Having direct and extensive operational experience, Pramod is an executive with Salient CRGT who serves as the company's DevSecOps and application modernization thought leader. In addition, he has overseen numerous DevOps implementations in large commercial businesses and federal government agencies. Having worked with Pramod directly over the past 5 years, it's been interesting to see how his views have evolved along with the industry. Here are some of his insights.

Getting executive support

First, Pramod believes that any efforts to implement DevOps tools and toolchains will fail without executive-level support. This concern has been a recurring theme throughout this book. But Pramod has observed firsthand how difficult it is to implement DevOps at scale without executive leadership.

First, DevOps requires a cultural change that cannot be driven as a bottoms-up strategy. It's natural for people to resist change and to continue what they have been doing. For that reason, DevOps cannot be mandated either. Instead, executives need to take a leadership role to establish relevant **Objectives and Key Results** (**OKRs**) and help drive the organization to obtain the desired results.

On the other hand, the benefits of DevOps as a software delivery improvement strategy are worth the effort. DevOps improves software development capabilities, and everyone throughout the enterprise is affected in terms of how they do their work. In other words, in the digital economy, the software delivers value as standalone products, enables digitally enhanced features in physical products, and supports value stream process improvements throughout the enterprise.

Bluntly, Pramod would suggest organizations should not waste their time attempting to implement DevOps tools and toolchains unless they have chief and line of business executives, support to fund the initiatives, can allocate sufficient resources, and can hold people responsible for achieving identifiable and measurable outcomes with timeframes, budgets, and ROIs that justify the efforts.

Implementing effective training programs

Next, training throughout the enterprise is critical. DevOps' tools and toolchains cannot be thrown over the wall with the expectation that the development and operations teams can effectively use them. Moreover, the value streams that can benefit from DevOps-based software delivery capabilities need to understand what's possible and how to engage effectively with the IT organization. This statement is also true for business owners who depend on competitive software delivery capabilities to achieve the enterprise's strategies, goals, and objectives.

This training can extend beyond the organization's employees to include third-party consultants and vendors. For example, most government agencies and large commercial enterprises leverage external software development organizations to build applications that support the business. If the executives choose to commit to DevOps, then their consultants must make similar commitments.

Finally, stakeholders also need training on DevOps. I personally define the term stakeholders so that it includes anyone and everyone who has an opinion that matters. Anyone who has managed software delivery projects over any period will have experienced situations where external stakeholders affected the outcomes of their projects.

Sometimes, it's because those external stakeholders are competing for the budgets and resources that have been allocated to your projects. But other times, the stakeholders may not see the value of the work the software delivery team is performing, and they may feel left out of decision making. While Agile practices help address some of those communication and collaboration issues, we can't forget that the concerns and needs of our stakeholders are every bit as important once the organization moves to DevOps-based software delivery.

Going all in

In this book, you have learned about the importance of using value stream mapping to assess the current state of operations and identify improvement opportunities that help achieve a desired future state. So, different from Agile retrospectives – which evaluate areas for immediate improvements on a limited scale – VSM initiatives tend to take a larger and longer-term view to make sure that the entire value stream, as a system, operates with greater efficiencies and less waste.

DevOps is very much a Lean-oriented strategy to streamlining software development, delivery, and support functions as an integrated, automated, and orchestrated value stream. Conceptually, DevOps toolchains operate as a streamlined software delivery pipeline.

VSM offers an approach to evaluating a series of improvement opportunities that increases the flow of value across our software delivery pipelines. For reasons of financial and resource constraints, we may need to prioritize our investments over an extended time. But this does not mean that we can afford to do the assessments and implementations in an ad hoc manner. It is a combination of such improvements that allows a DevOps pipeline to deliver software value efficiently and rapidly.

Therefore, the executives of an organization must not allow their IT organization to go about implementing DevOps tools and toolchains in a piecemeal fashion. Implementing DevOps tools and toolchains is a strategic initiative. The organization needs to plan and guide their DevOps investments, just as they would any other product and portfolio investments driven by OKRs.

We'll get into the subject of OKRs in more detail in *Chapter 16, Transforming Businesses with VSM and DevOps*. But for the time being, know that OKRs establish high-level expectations in terms of desired outcomes and measurable results. In other words, executives should establish OKRs as guidance for those involved in the DevOps implementation, in terms of what the expectations are and the metrics that indicate successful outcomes.

Establishing a DevSecOps Center of Excellence (COE)

So far, we have discussed the importance of having executive leadership, effective training programs, and an end-to-end DevOps implementation strategy. But the organization also needs a center of excellence to establish governance policies, ensure the construction of reusable toolchain configurations, and provide resources for training, mentoring, and coaching.

After overseeing multiple enterprise-scale DevOps implementations, Pramod has come to the opinion that organizations need to select one vendor or group of experts (COE) to establish the organization's overall DevSecOps and CI/CD platform solutions. That's not to say that multiple groups cannot participate in the DevOps platform and tool selections and governance policies. Still, it's unwise to have different teams or groups working independently. Otherwise, the organization will end up with a hodge-podge of tools to license, track, integrate, support, and sustain over the life cycle of their DevOps platforms.

The COE should help set up and guide the development of the initial DevSecOps platforms as a prototype. When the prototype platform is ready, the COE should help guide one or more product teams in their transition to the new platform. As the software product teams use the prototype DevSecOps platform, the COE and software teams should collaborate to improve and perfect the platform to support wider-scale use.

A series of rolled deployments will help prove and build out its capabilities for wider-scale deployments for larger organizations. The COE must be prepared to tweak the platform as necessary to support new needs that are identified with each new deployment. This tweaking will include integration, automation, and configurations that support additional DevSecOps activities, tools, and toolchains.

Continuous learning and enhancements keep improving the primary platform, taking it to the next level. However, suppose you don't get the fundamental platform right. In that case, the organization will get off to a bad start, which could reduce executive support and thereby reduce opportunities for future investments and deployments. In contrast, building the right basic DevSecOps platform allows the organization to use VSM to justify further investments. But, more importantly, the VSM initiatives guide the expanded use of the improved DevSecOps platform to support digitally enabled value stream improvements across the enterprise.

By having one vendor or a CoE leading the DevSecOps practice and applying VSM principles, we avoid every team or every vendor needing to be an expert at DevSecOps and VSM practices. Think of it this way: we hire software developers to build software products, not build their DevOps-based software factories.

In most cases, we would not redirect the employees building products in manufacturing firms to build the factories they work in – nor should we expect our software developers to create their software factories. Yes, many can learn the skills of a DevOps engineer – with enough time and practice. But that time and effort take away from their regular jobs to deliver value in the form of new and enhanced software products. So, don't do that – it's a non-value-added waste of their time!

It is appropriate to encourage a very open and collaborative culture of feedback, including the COE, software delivery team members, and your related vendors. It is those collaborations that raise visibility on issues and contribute to improving your DevSecOps platforms.

Defining the roles and responsibilities of the COE

The COE includes your experts on DevSecOps tools and platforms. But it must also include or be aligned with the organization's IT architecture group. The responsibilities of your DevSecOps platform COE and IT architecture group include the following:

- COE's don't make anything – they are responsible for governance and policies:

  a. Establish a list of *dos and don'ts* in the form of DevSecOps governance policies.

- Work with executives and portfolio management functions to establish DevSecOps platform improvement programs and budgets.

Evaluate **Software as a Service (SaaS)** and DevSecOps vendor offerings:

a. Single DevOps platforms such as AWS, Azure, GitLab, or HCL Software.

B. Multitool platforms such as ConnectALL, Digital.ai, Plutora, ServiceNow, or Tasktop.

c. Define the workflow to initiate VSM and DevSecOps tool and platform requests and approvals.

d. Conduct **Analysis of Alternatives (AoA)**.

e. Work with legal, IT, and finance departments to negotiate licenses, terms and conditions, and **service-level agreements (SLAs)**.

f Establish and maintain the list of approved DevSecOps tools for use within the organization.

- Guide the work of any related VSM team and VSM initiative requiring software deliveries:

a. Conduct IT Budget Review Boards or support portfolio management functions to establish software value stream/product development support priorities.

Deciding on the appropriate DevOps platform strategy

In Pramod's opinion, he believes the best strategy is to go with a **DevSecOps as a Service (DaaS)** vendor instead of an open source tools strategy. DaaS examples include **Azure DevOps Services**, **GitLab**, and **AWS CodeDeploy**. He cites several reasons for this view, as follows:

- It helps avoid FISMA and FedRamp compliance and approval issues associated with obtaining security approvals to use open source tools within federal government agencies.

- The organization does not need to implement, integrate, and maintain disparate tools.

- The IT organization does not need to write **Infrastructure as Code (IaC)** configurations.

   For example, developing custom DevSecOps platforms requires hiring experts in IaC tools such as Ansible, Terraform, and others.

- He's become a fan of Azure Kubernetes Service.

   Organizations don't need to install Kubernetes, maintain Kubernetes, and deal with the complexity of Kubernetes.

Pramod believes most organizations can do quite well with DaaS-based solutions. However, larger digital and high-tech organizations such as Netflix, Amazon, Google, Walmart, and perhaps very large federal agencies have exceptional needs for performance and large volume software deliveries that justify building custom DevSecOps and CI/CD pipelines.

But Pramod also recognizes that some IT folks feel they have better control over the operations when they can incorporate specific tools instead of a service. And, let's face it, DevSecOps tool selections are emotional issues for many developers who have developed their skills and competencies around a specific set of tools.

Interview with Yaniv Sayers

Yaniv Sayers is a Fellow and CTO in Micro Focus responsible for its Application Delivery Management and Software Factory program. With over 20 years in the IT and SW industry, Yaniv has experienced and led various transformations. He and I met virtually and discussed our experiences on DevOps and VSM. He contributes to this section in an interview I conducted with him. We started with a discussion of major pitfalls in DevOps implementations', such as ignoring the organization's DNA and challenges around Big Data and applying the Software Factory approach to overcome the pitfalls.

Acknowledging your Organization's DNA

Yaniv stresses that ignoring an organization's DNA is a common mistake that many organizations make. In the digital era, organizations that want to remain relevant look at how leading high-tech companies such as Facebook, Google, Amazon, Spotify, and Netflix leveraged DevOps to move at the speed of a bullet.

These success cases inspire executives and other critical stakeholders. They may feel pressure to become more like these other organizations and think they can find similar success by implementing the practices and tools used by these other organizations.

However, these popular references to DevOps transformations apply mainly to organizations born in the digital era. Their people are digital natives, their processes are agile from the get-go, and their technologies are cloud-native.

That is very different from IT organizations in financial services, pharmaceuticals, or government. Many enterprises still use traditional software development methodologies, such as Waterfall or Water-Scrum-Fall processes. They include a broad range of technologies that range from mainframe to client/server to cloud, plus they have people who learned their skills in a previous era. Many are not yet comfortable operating or competing in our modern digital economy.

For the traditional enterprise, the challenge and even the meaning of running "faster" can differ from the digital native experience. These organizations have a different DNA, and Yaniv believes that fact must be acknowledged. They can be inspired by what digital native organizations have achieved and how they operate, yet they cannot simply follow the digital native implementation, and they cannot ignore their past and current environment. Instead, they need to continue running their current environment while setting a transformation plan that fits their DNA.

Becoming outcome Oriented

Most organizations take a technology-centric approach. They start with the tools and equipment and work out to the users or consumers – yet most fail to achieve the desired outcome. For example, just implementing an agile planning tool does not make a project agile. The project may still operate with long delivery cycles, no fast feedback, or people finding it difficult to transition to an Agile mindset. It was Grady Booch who famously said, "*A fool with a tool is still a fool.*"

Instead, it would be best to start by taking an outside-in view and working with the customers and consumers to align on the outcomes that matter to them and the value streams that empower these outcomes. Then, based on the desired outcomes, you can identify and determine the people, process, and technology changes required. For example, it may require you to train your people on new ways of working, defining new roles and responsibilities, enhancing existing processes, and implementing new tools – all of which need to occur in concert as a collaborative effort to achieve the expected outcomes.

Discovering the Art of Balance

Speed, quality, cost, and happiness do not compete; they don't operate in a silo, nor should they be considered as tradeoffs - they are intertwined. For example, suppose you focus on speed and neglect quality. In that case, low quality ultimately leads to the user and employee dissatisfaction. Low quality also increases rework, which leads to higher costs and increased technical debt, which collectively leads to slower delivery.

On the other hand, higher-quality reduces failures and the need for rework. Thus, improving quality reduces costs, increases delivery speed, and promotes happiness [employee, customer, and end-user].

Stakeholders should be aware that perceived short-term tradeoffs eventually lead to the reverse outcome for the long term. Instead, be conscious that tradeoffs are interdependent and intertwined. In this context, IT organizations need to balance speed, quality, cost, and happiness continuously.

Making better decisions through Big-Data

Yaniv often encounters stakeholders making key decisions based on gut feel and guestimates, which end in sub-optimal outcomes for the lucky ones and big failures for others—for example, prioritizing investments based on their belief of what users and customers may need without obtaining customer input and feedback, deciding whether to move a release into production without a clear understanding of the release quality and security risks, changing interfaces and data models without realizing the impact on other services.

When decision-makers lack access to required data, this is typically due to a set of reasons, such as organizational and political barriers that prohibit data sharing, a variety of "languages" within the different domains that make it challenging to have a shared context, lack of integration between systems that equates to no access and no traceability between data points.

With DevOps, the data challenge becomes even more extreme. There are higher continuous delivery cycles and shift to automation, the amount of data increases by levels of magnitude, and decision-makers need to make conscious decisions faster and continuously. In practice, it becomes a big data challenge.

Organizations that want to be successful with DevOps at scale must address the big data challenge, and access to data traceable by decision-makers is the first step. In addition, having the objective to enable value-driven deliveries, conscious and continuous decision making, analytics, and machine learning should transform big data into actionable insights.

Taking a Software Factory Approach

Yaniv states that Enterprise organizations that need to transform by implementing DevOps should consider taking a software factory approach. A Software Factory aligns the organization's strategic planning with an integrated set of services, processes, tools, and data that enables the organization to plan, build, test, release, and operate and manage the software delivered to their customers.

Start by creating a baseline taking an outside-in view and working with stakeholders to align on the outcomes and value streams that empower these outcomes. Then, map the main activities, roles, systems, and data and their interaction.

Yaniv also notes that you can also leverage frameworks such as IT4IT that provide references for common value streams. For example, in IT, DevOps-oriented value streams include activities spanning the receipt of a requirement through its delivery to the user or a user experiencing a problem until resolution or paying down technical debt.

Next, analyze issues, such as missing information for stakeholder decision-making, duplicate systems, error-prone manual activities, wasted time. For each, map possible improvement areas such as consolidating to a standard agile planning service to enable dependency management and transparency, an integration service to provide data visibility, a performance testing service to enable shift left, and earlier problem detection.

After mapping the values streams and analyzing the issues, you have a common language and understanding of outcomes that matter, current problems, and opportunities – in other words, the valuable services. Then, aim for shared services wherever possible and differentiated when required due to a business need.

So what is the mechanics to deliver a service? Yaniv notes they are precisely the same as those you use to deliver digital products - by taking an agile-based development approach with continuous improvement.

Yaniv states that IT organizations should take an iterative, continuous improvement approach for the service delivery, start small, and evolve as they go. He briefly describes the lifecycle to make this practical:

- **Select your critical value streams**: After analyzing the value streams, identify 2-3 services to improve. A value stream can be a knowledge base service, a quality management service, a security testing service, or any other critical IT service.

- **Create a Minimal Viable Product (MVP)**: The purpose of the MVP is to validate the value of the service and reduce unknowns and incubate it with a few consuming teams to get quick feedback. Then, learn and improve the service based on the feedback in short cycles.

- **Create a standard model**: The model serves as a blueprint that depicts the technology, people (roles and responsibilities), and the process needed to create a standard service system. Then instantiate the technology and the automation around it to ensure you can make it consumable, fulfillable and operational at a good enough level.

- **Go live**: Make your improved services globally available by publishing them to your consumers and placing the required infrastructures to scale them to meet demands. Then, measure and monitor your critical performance metrics and optimize accordingly. Finally, harvest learnings for the next iteration.

- **Rinse and repeat**: After completing your first improvement cycle, identify the next 2-3 services and cycle through this iterative, continuous improvement process again and again. Each cycle improves people, processes, and technology.

For enterprise organizations that need to transform by implementing DevOps, the Software Factory approach helps set a transformation plan to fit their DNA by starting small without over-engineering and allowing continuous improvement.

You can learn more about the Software Factory Approach recommended by Micro Focus at the following link: `https://www.microfocus.com/en-us/digital-transformation/our-perspective/software-factory`.

Interview with Allan Wagner

Allan "Al" Wagner is the Transformation Advisor/DevOps enthusiast within HCL Software's DevOps Advisory and Adoption group. He and I met virtually on several occasions and found an immediate affinity in our views on VSM and DevOps. He was kind to contribute to this section in an interview I conducted with him. We started by discussing the major pitfalls in DevOps implementations, which center on spending money in IT without seeing a return in quantifiable business value. Let's see what he has to say.

Spending money without verifiable results

When I asked Al what he viewed as pitfalls to DevOps implementations, he immediately came up with a specific and common use case. Specifically, as HCL's VSM and DevOps evangelist, he often hears their prospective clients note how their IT managers and executives are tired of spending money on IT, without showing value across the rest of the organization.

I submit that the issue is one I've addressed several times in this book. Without proper alignment, organizations can spend a lot of money, resources, and time implementing mature software delivery pipelines. Moreover, as Pramod noted in his interview, DevOps is not easy to learn and not easy to implement. Left to their own devices, many, if not most, software development teams, lack the support, funding, or even the skills to integrate, automate, and orchestrate software development pipelines.

Frankly, such work is not even their responsibility. Software developers produce value by delivering software products, not building software delivery platforms and pipelines.

Failing safely

Al noted that a major pitfall of implementing DevOps capabilities is that significant cultural and organizational change is required. He advocates that organizations should make incremental changes so that they can fail safely. IT organizations, and those that depend on their services, must understand that not everything will work out as planned. But to improve our chances for success, we should also spend some time and effort planning!

Managing through mandates

Al and I spoke about how DevOps programs often come down as mandates. The problems with such mandates are multifold. First, executive-level expectations may be out of line with reality. As a result, there is too often no pre-planning and inadequate funding for tools, platforms, and training. It's hard to properly identify budgets if there is no planning to determine the needs and requirements of the organization.

Also, without planning and building prototype DevSecOps platforms, we leave the work to every software development team to figure out – regardless of whether they have the time and skills to work on the issues. In the meantime, their software delivery work suffers.

And, even if the software development teams get past the platform development issues, there is likely no budget available to execute the implementations – certainly not on a large enterprise scale. The desired tools may not even be approved for use within the organization, affecting all security and risk-conscious organizations where compliance and governance are critical issues. Unplanned costs are also a factor. A mandate without an execution plan, a forecast budget, and the means to connect investments to value deliveries are useless. Everyone involved is set up to fail, which leads to frustration, more work, missed expectations, and, ultimately, mistrust.

In my previous book, *Scaling Scrum Across Modern Enterprises*, I told the story about my track coach, Al Cantello, at the US Naval Academy. Every day for 4 years, I heard him make the same statement over and over again: "*All you young whippersnappers! All you want is instant gratification!*" His point was that nothing worthwhile comes easily or quickly. As a two-time all-American javelin student-athlete and a former Olympian – who once held every national and international record in the javelin – he had every right to call us out when we needed to refocus our efforts.

My point in relating this story is that the same instructions apply to business. We need to understand our objectives, define and set measurable goals, plan how we will achieve our goals, and then work hard every day to achieve them. Mandates are useless without planning, prototyping (experimentation), budgets, and resources linked to specific objectives and key results. Moreover, the OKRs come first to guide our plans, experiments, budgets, allocation of resources, and work.

Getting it wrong

Here is the common scenario that Al Wagner cites. Over the years, organizations have been building out and funding full year or multiyear software development plans, only to be disappointed when the development team fails to deliver under the constraints of the project. At the start of the fiscal year, engineering teams may submit a budget estimate for each quarter or perhaps their full-year development plan. Through negotiation, an amount of funding would be approved by the business. But an even worse scenario is when the executives and managers dictate schedule, budget, and resources constraints solely on ROI considerations not informed by the realities of the work.

Still, engineering departments may gladly accept the constraints and work to develop the requested new feature or functionality, perhaps delivering updates once a quarter – or perhaps once over the annualized project budget. Eventually, stakeholders would have an opportunity to review and check out what engineering had built, only to realize that they didn't get what they wanted. Or, the demands of the business changed, and these changes were not communicated to development. Regardless of the outcome, the situation was always the same – a lack of business value and return on investment.

Agile practices emerged to align development efforts to support the evolving needs and priorities of the business and its customers. Specifically, Agile addressed the problems associated with the traditional project-based development model. Later, CI/CD and DevOps pipeline strategies evolved to deliver software products more rapidly and efficiently.

Agile development corrected the project-based software delivery model by having teams deliver earlier and continuously, embrace change, and deliver more frequently with closer alignment to the business. And to this day, those things still matter. What has changed or improved is an increased focus on delivering business value, with teams working to become more efficient and basing decisions on data, from ideation to implementation and beyond. This is the promise of CI/CD and DevOps-based software delivery pipelines.

Early on, as organizations began their DevOps journey, they may have empowered individual software development teams to select automated solutions to build and deploy their individual delivery pipelines. And while the individual teams probably loved the autonomy – it's an Agile thing – this approach created a bit of a mess, for all the reasons noted previously.

But there's another problem also at work. It is challenging for business leaders to make business decisions based on data when the engineering and product data resides in several different repositories and different formats.

Al notes that it is probably unrealistic to mandate that each product or project team use the same toolset across their delivery pipelines, since there are many factors that will determine the best tool or solution for the job. And, as noted previously in this chapter, we can't discount the impact that software developers and operations staff have on promoting their preferred methods and tools.

But organizations may be able to find a compromise by allowing teams to choose the best solution for the task at hand – provided there is integration with a solution (or solutions) that provides a holistic view or dashboard. This is what modern VSM with DevOps platforms offer – integrating tools across DevOps toolchains with a common and normalized data model, thus providing end-to-end and real-time visibility of software delivery pipeline flows.

Finding your sources of truth

Whether an organization chooses to construct its own dashboard or purchase a COTS-based VSM solution, there are several **sources of truth** that we need to access when hosting the data needed to populate a dashboard and make accurate business decisions. Al lists these *sources of truth* as follows:

- **Enterprise planning**: A shared enterprise planning tool that provides a view of all development activity across the organization.

- **Version control**: This implements a single version control system across the organization for storing all assets used in developing, building, testing, and deploying software.

- **Artifact repository**: A single location for all deployable artifacts.

- **Release orchestration**: A single source of data that orchestrates the automated deployment of software releases. It also offers an inventory view of the released versions and locations of deployed software.

- **Quality management**: A single source of data that provides details on the level of quality. Moreover, this capability supports traceability to link requirements to test cases, the executed tests, and the related test results.

- **Event management**: A single repository to holistically manage and coordinate the resolution of incidents across the enterprise.

Al notes that this approach to integrating disparate sources of truth still provides individual software delivery teams with flexibility around tool choice. But this strategy only works when there is an integration platform to link the shared data repositories that business leaders depend on to make informed business decisions.

Creating an acceptance strategy

These issues of lack of trust did not emerge overnight – they have been long in the making. We can't trivialize or shorten the process of breaking down the organizational barriers that formed over time. Moreover, organizations managed software product deliveries for too long as projects were constrained by uninformed budgets, schedules, and resources. This, too, sets up the IT department for failure.

Lean production processes that create continuous and predictable flows offer the best way to improve our way of delivering software value. But Lean also dramatically changes the way we work. It changes how we make decisions and measure progress. It also changes our tools and requires skills.

As Pramod noted in the previous section, we need our executive leaders to provide the resources that will help guide the organization through these changes. For example, the organization's leaders must find the resources and budgets to install the following:

- COE
- Coaches and mentors
- Thought leaders
- Change advocates and innovators
- Prototype engagements
- VSM and DevOps toolchain procurements

Without these resources and a determined effort, any enterprise-scale VSM and DevOps platform implementation exercise is doomed to fail. And, as Al puts it, *"When bad things happen to good people, they will go back to what they know."*

Moving forward

Al presents some common-sense steps for moving forward to a more desirable future state that's possible through VSM and DevOps methods and tools, as shown in the following list:

- Build time into weekly schedules for learning.
- Crawl/walk/run to make incremental steps toward success.

  Al states: *"You may have to slow down to go faster."* For example, you must allocate time, effort, and resources to address issues associated with technical debt.

- Don't start a VSM or DevOps platform implementation initiative without executive support.

- Disconnect from project and program management-based release schedules:

  a. PM-based schedules are driven by monetary and ROI considerations that are disconnected from the day-to-day realities of supporting evolving market changes, customer needs, and customer priorities.

  b. The PMO cannot be expected to understand the dev teams' capacities and constraints.

  c. The team lead needs to be involved in advance while developing the schedule and negotiate with product management on how they should proceed; for example:

  A. Do we need more people?

  B. Is everything a priority?

  C. What WIP limits should we establish in our pipelines?

  D. Evaluate throughput as a flow to establish burndown rates.

  E. Establish mechanisms to collaborate better within the team and with our internal or external customers.

This list provides a starting point for moving forward to a successful VSM and DevOps tools implementation. But none of this matters if we don't also recognize that the investments must drive value.

Adding value

A basic reality in business is that there are almost always more things to work on than the organization has the time, money, and resources to take on. So, fundamentally, what's more important is to understand our priorities in terms of deciding what adds the most value in terms of our customers and the organization's OKRs. So, focus on what delivers the most value for the investments, and then use flow to deliver the value incrementally.

Al puts it this way: "*Focus on products and continuously delivering incremental change that delivers value to the business.*" He also notes that "*Happier people are delivering higher quality software more frequently to the end user.*" Al also stated that happier working environments eliminate retention issues as people tend to prefer to work in highly productive development organizations.

We'll come back to the topic of adding value in *Chapter 16, Transforming Businesses with VSM and DevOps*. In fact, using VSM to drive software delivery value across all organizational value streams is the central theme of this book. For now, let's move on and look at four potential DevOps platform implementation strategies.

Jumping onto the cloud-native bandwagon

As a final point, Al Wagner made an important observation that many organizations seem to be jumping onto the cloud-native bandwagon. Cloud-native environments offer tremendous flexibility for leveraging the resources of **Infrastructure as a Service (IaaS)** providers as a fee-based and pay-per-use service that offers continuous integration, container engines, and cloud orchestration capabilities.

However, Al also makes this critical point: "*The legacy systems being used by large enterprise corporations– built with years and years of unique capabilities – are not going away any time soon. The mainframe is not going away; it is not dying. The reason for this is because modernizing these legacy system and application capabilities has a considerable cost. [The organization must ask] is there an ROI to justify the rewrites and migrations?*"

We'll discuss this issue again later in the *Deciding on the appropriate DevOps platform strategy* Subsection. Specifically, it may make sense to operate a hybrid-cloud environment over an extended period.

Interview with Joel Kruger

Joel Kruger is a DevSecOps engineer and AWS solutions architect with 10 years of experience building CI/CD pipelines in commercial and federal sectors. He is also an expert in employing container orchestration systems for automating computer application deployments at scale. In his current role, he is constructing reusable CI/CD pipeline configurations for a large federal agency with hundreds of software product teams. Joel is a proponent of building CI/CD pipeline configurations as downloadable and self-serve software factories. It is from this perspective that he discusses potential DevSecOps implementation pitfalls and platform implementation strategies.

Leveraging reusable configurations

Joel notes that **configuration management (CM)** is not a new concept and is a necessary set of practices, policies, and repositories to maintain a product across releases over its life cycle.

Joel notes the idea of CM comes from other institutions, such as the military, and that the software community borrowed those ideas and retrofitted them to protect our organization's IT assets. Joel also points out that CM was traditionally a purely manual task, usually completed by a system administrator or junior developer. But, in smaller projects, the CM task can fall to more senior developers.

Regardless, the CM role involved a lot of manual work to document the system's state carefully. But those days are rapidly disappearing, as the industry is moving to implement Configuration as Code. It's not that CM is going away; instead, we can reduce the amount of non-value-adding work involved to capture, maintain, and use certain information. These changes came from the need to accelerate configuration tasks across CI/CD and DevOps pipelines, support cloud-based computing environments, and implement new API-based automation tooling.

However, sometimes, CM is confused with version control. There are some similarities in that both activities track versions of products, product components, and information artifacts as they evolve. The primary difference is that version control identifies individual components as they change, irrespective of whether they are included in a production release. In contrast, CM processes track the versions of all the software and infrastructure components, as well as other information artifacts related to each release of a product across its life cycle.

We've already discussed how IaC is the practice of ensuring all provisioned infrastructure is automated through code. But a supplementary purpose of IaC is to establish a written record of the services that exist, where they are located, and under what circumstance they are deployed.

CM may seem like an overly bureaucratic and non-value-added task. However, that's not true because the organization must protect its IT assets over their respective life cycles. So, it's not that its CM that is non-value-added; it's the manual processes we have to employ to record, save, and relate code and other artifacts to software releases that are burdensome. Therefore, organizations may find it easier to document the use of code and other artifacts via IaC, to maintain a full record of all the technology assets a company owns and has deployed.

Joel points out that as a software product matures, not all its components and information artifacts change with each release. However, things can get out of sync very quickly from a versioning perspective. Therefore, CM is necessary to maintain the product's performance, functionality, and physical attributes associated with the unique set of requirements, design, and operational information specified for each release.

While CM is not a new concept, what is relatively new is automating the deployment of new releases through configurations implemented as code, in the form of **Infrastructure as Code (IaC)** and **Configuration as Code (CaC)**. Both IaC and CaC fall under modern configuration management practices, and both use scripting languages to automate configurations across disparate environments. But the two terms have different contextual use meanings.

Let's take a look:

- **IaC**: This approach is used to define your IT infrastructure, such as networks, servers, load balancing, and security as a text file (script or definition file), that is checked into version control. The text files serve as the baseline source for creating or updating the specified environments. IaC provides an executable specification in machine-readable syntax and includes steps capable of producing virtualized infrastructure, can be versioned as a release, and tracked in SCM repositories.

- **CaC**: This defines how your software components interface with each other – by specifying parameters and settings for applications, server processing, and operating systems – that are also managed as configuration files in a repository. As a result, CaC makes it possible to build and test software code changes earlier in the pipeline, to discover and address issues sooner, and improve the quality of each release. As with IaC, CaC implements executable specifications in machine-readable syntax and includes steps to align application infrastructure configurations as a versioned release that's tracked in SCM repositories.

Now that you understand the basics behind IaC and CaC, let's learn what Joel has to say about how and why they are used.

Implementing IaC and CaC resources

Joel starts by noting that organizations should architect their business' IaC and CaC resources modularly via infrastructure functionality. For example, a classic web-based application includes a frontend user interface, backend business logic, and a database. Rather than placing all your configuration code in one file, it's best to break the code into separate files for each application layer. This modular structuring and decoupling strategy makes it easier to switch out components and systems over time.

This will help them better position their engineers to execute new software and infrastructure deployments swiftly, especially if any of the following events happen:

- Changing customer demands for specific tools and features.
- Needing to repurpose existing code snippets for other products or portfolios.
- Untenable increases in cost for previously implemented tools or third-party service providers.
- Rip and replace business mandates.

In practice, IT architectures are far more complex than the simple three-tier architectural model noted previously. Large organizations that contain hundreds of applications must support potentially hundreds or thousands of configuration options that can change over time.

At this point, Joel moved on to speak about using IaC and CaC concepts to improve interoperability.

Maintaining interoperability

Regarding IaC and CaC, Joel notes that you must construct your plans, playbooks, pipelines, and scripts with interoperability in mind. This strategy mitigates the amount of code refactoring and time that is needed to adopt new toolchains. It also minimizes the opportunity for significant disruptions to the rest of the operational infrastructure when those things occur.

Joel suggests the best approach is to encourage your developers to use input parameters, expressed as environment variables and boilerplate code configurations. This way, each component of your solution's portfolio can behave like a software function and be called on in any permutation of complimentary toolchain stacks.

Removing "secrets" from code

Application and systems security is a critical issue across all organizations, or at least it should be. However, Joel notes that he has seen too many developers take shortcuts in these issues by hardcoding passwords and system access inputs within their configuration files. His bottom-line admonishment is "*Don't hard code secrets in source control!*"

Instead, the much better option is to store them externally as encrypted data in a **Privileged Access Management** (**PAM**) tool such as HashiCorp Vault, Akeyless Vault, Thycotic Secret Server, BeyondTrust, or AWS Secrets Manager. Secrets Managers (or PAMs) typically inject sensitive information into container runtimes as environment variables or mount them as volumes. The bottom line is, developers must not make it easy for hackers to see an application's entry points, access codes, and other sensitive information.

Most Secrets Managers incorporate a client process that is intended to be run within microservice containers (Docker, Kubernetes) that can unlock secrets using an API key issued by the Secrets Manager server. In many cases, authorization can be configured at group or individual levels, per secret, or even dynamically for generating time-sensitive, single-use passwords. Joel notes that besides being more secure, parameterizing secrets is a critical step in ensuring that your software configurations are reusable, extensible, and scalable.

Items that IT organizations should specify as *secret* include usernames, passwords, tokens, API keys, SSH keys, PGP keys, TLS keys, TLS certificates, IP addresses, port numbers, domain names, secure strings, and sensitive files. Also, the IT organization should identify any other digital information that is considered secret or protected by your organization and include it in this list.

Avoiding configuration lockouts

Defining reusable configurations through code reduces the number of experts the organization must find and maintain to support its CI/CD and DevOps platforms. IaC and CaC also reduce the time and effort each software development team must expend to set up their environments, run their tests, and deploy their code. But all those benefits are lost if the configurations become unusable.

With this issue in mind, Joel strongly recommends that developers should not hard code key-value pairs that will prevent their IaC, CaC, or in-house code from becoming reusable. Instead, whenever possible, use inputs at the command line, API calls, or implement environment files that can be committed to source control and consumed by your automation flows.

Like parameterizing secrets, parameterizing crucial key/value pairs in your code is a critical step in ensuring that your software configurations are reusable, extensible, and scalable.

The following list contains key/value pairs items you should parameterize:

- **Resource Values**: CPU, memory, disk size, VM names
- **Cloud Provider Attributes**: Regions, availability zones, AMIs, VPCs
- **Network Configurations**: Subnets, IP addresses, domain names, DNS resolvers
- **Application Configurations**: App name, port numbers, versions, dependencies
- **Container Orchestration**: Container registries, image names, image tags

Now that we've covered how to hard code secrets while avoiding configuration lockouts, let's look at what Joel has to say about the need for frequent releases.

Encouraging frequent releases

Joel cited a frequently identified objective for CI/CD and DevOpsOps pipeline builds: *"If the master code branch of a product can't be successfully deployed to a production environment within 20 minutes notice, you aren't doing DevOps correctly. Only stable deployments that have been thoroughly tested to meet customer specifications count here."*

In other words, Joel encourages development teams to produce smaller units of improvement to the applications frequently. Joel recommends that product release processes be fully automated with push-button type implementations or as close to it as possible to accomplish this goal. He goes on to state that, with contemporary CI/CD tools, it is possible to build this capability, even in many legacy environments that still have mainframes *kicking around*.

Adhering to a rapid build and release philosophy ensures that your customers will experience a constant flow of desired improvements aligned with their needs. This strategy improves the customer experience, even when your products or services don't contain all the features that your customers desire yet.

The objective is to make sure each new release is incrementally *more* closely aligned with your customer's expectations, and never *less*. Just as importantly, this strategy takes tremendous pressure off your organization or business unit to deploy new features before they are ready. No IT organization wants to must roll back their releases because they weren't ready for production.

Instead, with fast build and deploy capabilities installed, customers are left with tangible evidence that their interests are constantly being considered before they lose interest in your products.

With frequent releases, often going out over different production environments, we need to make sure we build and deploy the right configurations with each release.

Configuring the right DevOps platform

Joel claims that there is no way around creating and maintaining scripts or configurations that utilize API-based infrastructure deployments. This statement is true regardless of whether your organization implements a SaaS or is operating on-premises or in the cloud DevOps platform.

Joel further notes that DevOps platform strategies fall into the following three broad categories:

- Declarative configurations
- Programmatic self-service SaaS/PaaS tools
- A combination of both

The benefit of using the declarative configurations strategy is that all IaC, CaC, and parameters can be stored and audited together in source control management. This strategy provides ease of change management and gives your organization a solid position in the event of a security audit.

Popular in the government and financial sectors, this strategy is often used when an enterprise forms a centralized BizDevOps team to author approved IaC, CaC, and automation templates that all development teams must standardize around. The benefit of this approach is that individual teams have more freedom to create and manage their operational infrastructure.

The downside is that automated pipelines won't scale as nicely as the self-service PaaS/SaaS approach. Many sprawling code repositories will likely be created, and each one will need to be tracked and maintained, along with their associated CI/CD pipelines and other artifacts.

On the other hand, Joel notes that the programmatic self-service SaaS/PaaS strategy is optimal if your organization prefers to standardize business processes around software kiosks, API-driven web services, ephemeral deployments, and third-party vendors. With this approach, infrastructure can be programmatically assembled, provisioned, and configured to suit various workloads on demand. Once each service's workload has been executed, any resulting artifacts and metadata get pushed to persistent storage, and the infrastructure that was previously utilized gets re-provisioned for use by others.

The benefit of this approach is that business processes can scale to demand and with less administrative overhead. The downside is that funneling activities into standardized processes can feel inflexible or restrictive to development teams. Another challenge with this strategy is tracing changes in governance and accountability.

Of course, Joel notes that it's never quite that cut and dry from a DevOps platform decision-making perspective. There are situations where governance and accountability take precedence over scalability. There may be other situations where transaction speed and velocity are more critical than maintaining extensive configurations for audit purposes in the same organization. So, large organizations should be prepared to maintain various DevOps platform solutions and configurations to support their disparate business needs.

Adopting software factory strategies

When federated effectively, an enterprise can decentralize to some extent by allowing individual CI/CD and DevOps pipeline development teams to build and maintain scalable services, that can then be consumed by other teams in the rest of the enterprise. This strategy is economical and leads to a culture of cross-functional collaboration, shared responsibility, and value stream productivity improvements. Joel notes that one very effective method for bringing these principles to life is developing software factories.

A **software factory** is a structured collection of related software assets that aid in producing computer software applications or software components according to specific, externally defined end user requirements through an assembly process. Leveraging IaC and CaC capabilities, the software factory concept enables rapid and automated infrastructure and application infrastructure deployments.

Joel's take is that organizations can extend these concepts to include business development and security operations applications. Essentially, a software factory applies traditional manufacturing techniques and principles to software development, infrastructure deployment, and business operations.

For those interested in exploring the technical details of implementing software factories and automation techniques, Joel provides more details on his website, `dynamicVSM.com`. This website serves as a convergence for DevOps and VSM technical tips and includes code snippets, cloneable demos, educational exercises, related information, and industry news.

Joel believes the adoption of software factories offers the most efficient solution to implementing Lean value stream fundamentals across your organization's DevOps platforms. The rapid software delivery capabilities of DevOps, when aligned to support business strategies and objectives, helps streamline all organizational value stream activities, which can significantly increase user productivity. Moreover, employing software factories with reusable configurations can help the IT development-oriented value streams establish standard and consistent user interfaces across all business applications, reducing the need for end user training.

Joel notes that businesses need to evolve to support emergent business, market, and customer needs. Likewise, the organization's business applications must evolve in lockstep to implement new process changes. The ease of deploying new and updated functionality, plus flexible user interfaces through reusable and extendable software factories, allows the organization's business applications to evolve to support emergent needs and assist end users in performing their tasks to implement the new business workflows.

We've reached the end of our interviews with DevOps implementation experts. In these interviews, you learned what the experts think regarding DevOps implementation pitfalls and platform deployment strategies. In the next section, you will learn about four common DevOps platform implementation strategies.

Deciding on an appropriate DevOps platform strategy

Now that you know some of the potential DevOps implementation pitfalls, we'll start learning about four optional DevOps implementation strategies. The platforms for deploying DevOps capabilities have evolved over time, and some are more common today than others.

In this section, you will learn about the four common DevOps implementation strategies, as well as their potential applications.

These four implementation strategies include the following:

- Building a custom DevOps toolchain

- Purchasing **DevOps as a Service/DevSecOps as a Service (DaaS)**

- VSM tools-based DevOps platform integration and orchestration solution

- Developing DevOps pipeline configurations as reusable software factories

Each option has its own set of pros and cons, which we'll explore in this chapter. We'll start our discussion by looking at building a custom DevOps platform solution option.

Building a custom DevOps platform

As this subsection's title implies, this approach involves internal DevOps engineering teams doing the work to integrate, automate, and orchestrate tools to form custom DevOps platforms. This was the only approach available in the early days of DevOps. You can liken this strategy, by analogy, to building a custom race car, plus the tooling to build it. Or, as another analogy, purchasing and building the equipment for your manufacturing facility and installing it. So, you end up owning both sets of problems – building the tools for your software delivery platform and building the platform.

There is no practical justification to do this today. There is no technical requirement that makes this an effective strategy. Instead, the sole motivations for going this route today are empire building and job security. Also, independent software development teams may go down this route on their own when they cannot secure corporate sponsorship and funding.

Al Wagner likes to refer to this strategy as *the gift that keeps on taking*. Organizations that go down this route fail to look at the downside of taking on the custom integrations, licensing, support, and maintenance issues. After a while, the DevOps engineering team spends more and more time maintaining the configurations and less time building software products. Moreover, if your DevOps engineering experts leave, the company is in a boatload of trouble!

Now, let's go to the other end of the spectrum to discuss the use of procuring a DevOps platform as a service, where all the tools to install a software delivery pipeline are made available and integrated.

Purchasing DaaS

This strategy involves purchasing an already integrated platform that includes an end-to-end toolchain to support software deliveries. Examples include **Amazon Web Services (AWS)**, **GitLab**, **Microsoft Azure DevOps**, and a host of independent companies that integrate third-party DevOps tools and offer them on the cloud as a DaaS product.

Vendor lock-in is the biggest downside to this approach, and their platforms may not support the tools your organization needs. On the other hand, virtually all DaaS vendors allow you to integrate other tools to create custom solutions. But what if your organization goes all in with customizations? In that case, they own the problems associated with integrating, automating, and orchestrating the disparate tools employed to develop the DevOps capabilities that run your business.

Moreover, your data is living inside someone else's environment. We all need to ask ourselves what happens if their or your systems go down. Software runs our digital world. Everything we do in business has a dependency on software. So, not having control over your data and application development pipelines has the potential for catastrophic consequences if they are hacked or go down.

Also, what happens if your DaaS vendor's tools and platform offerings become prohibitively expensive? Are you locked in and bound by an agreement that is financially painful to break? A journey to the cloud is very expensive and a multi-year project. Do you have the ROI to justify a DaaS rollout? And can you afford to lose or make up the DevOps implementation investments if you must make a change to another DaaS vendor?

Here's another concern. Let's assume you have an organization that's already made investments in DevOps tools and platforms. If your company is considering a mandate to move to a DaaS solution provider, the leaders and COE need to evaluate the company's ability to make it through the migration.

What if what you're doing isn't broke? The organization's executives need to take a deep look at what they are attempting to fix. Frequently, the executives are hoping to avoid DevOps tool investments and toolchain integration costs. And, they may have concerns about long-term maintenance costs and supportability issues. They are not wrong to have those concerns. But the organization must conduct a thorough investigation/analysis of alternatives before jumping into a major change of this magnitude. Also, don't force a mandate overnight. Take the time to plan the migration, including prototyping several rollouts before mass migration.

By the way, it's not that employing a cloud-based DaaS solution is a wrong decision. But, in many cases, a large-scale or enterprise migration to a platform-based tool suite may cost time and be resource prohibitive. We also need to consider the impact of a DevOps migration on our customers. Can we sustain our deliveries without loss of service through the migrations? How will we make sure we can quickly roll back any failed migrations?

DevOps is not usually about solving intractable technology problems – it's about solving a business problem. So, we need to approach migration to a DaaS-based solution as a business decision.

Al Wagner made an important observation that's relevant to this section: "*The mainframe is not dying; they are not going away. The legacy systems – built with years and years of unique capabilities – are not going away. Duplicating their capabilities is a huge cost. (The organization must ask) is there an ROI to justify the rewrites and migrations?*"

So, we've viewed the two extreme positions: one is to build your own DevOps platform solution, while the other is to purchase a fully enabled DaaS-based solution. Now, let's look at a couple of alternatives that lie in the middle: employing VSM tools and building reusable software delivery factories. First, we'll start with the VSM-based DevOps platform solution option.

Employing VSM tools

We can use VSM tools to assist with the Integrate, Automate, and Orchestrate capabilities of disparate tools. This comes back to the issues of integrating disparate toolchains and importing data as your sources of truth for decision-making; that is, business decisions should be made based on data in the six sources of truth: enterprise planning, version control, artifact repository, release orchestration, quality management, and event management. Whatever tools you have deployed, you need to integrate data into your data repository.

Use the end-to-end data to make decisions. We don't really care what DevOps tools you use for any given particular task, but you need to access the data that's maintained in that tool. So, it would help to have the tools communicate back to a source of truth with a common and normalized data model for analysis and decision making. It's the integrations back to the primary data source that are doing all the hard work. The downside is that the VSM tool may not have all the necessary integration adaptors and connectors. So, you may need to own the integration problem (via custom APIs) to address those issues or leverage a DevOps tools vendor's plugin framework.

Building reusable software factories

Create internal teams or use an external software integration team to develop software factories that build self-service CAC that can be downloaded via Git or other SCM tools. The definitions for each of these three categories are as follows:

- **Infrastructure as Code (IaC)**: Such as a terraform standup.

- **Pipeline as Code (PaC)**: The whole, seamless end-to-end integration, automation, and orchestration, which is done through a script upon a commit. This triggers a holistic set of API commands through Jenkins or Ansible. The whole thing is code.

- **Self Healing Pipeline**: Any errors in execution (Jenkins or other automation tools) would trigger a machine-readable error and use utilities and automated runbooks to correct and rerun the failed step.

In other words, if the DevOps team sees an automation failure occur and fixes it, then the team triages the problem to determine its root causes and to build a fix. Next, they code the fix as an automated runbook that operates within the Jenkins file to resolve that type of error, should it ever happen again in the future. (This is what we mean by self-healing).

This subsection completes our discussion on how to decide which DevOps platform implementation strategy is best suited for your organization's needs. You've learned about four basic strategies here. Now, we are going to discuss what you might do if your organization's chief executives mandate the adoption of DevOps capabilities without proper planning, preparation, and budgeting.

Dealing with corporate implementation mandates

DevOps is such a critical business enabler that chief and line of business executives may push the transition via a corporate mandate without taking sufficient time to plan, prepare, and budget the initiative to support an enterprise-scale deployment. When this occurs, the best DevOps implementation strategy is to go with **DevSecOps as a Service (DaaS)**. The IT department does not need to implement DevOps tools and maintain integrated toolchains to get started. And, when driven by corporate mandate, the decision-makers may not be aware of the technical implementation options, tools and toolchain alternatives, configuration and integration requirements, costs, and other issues.

DaaS is a multitenancy implementation concept. The term *software multitenancy* refers to a software architecture in which the software runs on at least one server, but more often on many virtualized servers and serves multiple tenants (customers). DaaS examples include **Azure DevOps Services**, **GitLab**, and **AWS CodeDeploy**. In addition, large organizations that need to deploy microservice-based applications across multiple environments might consider using **Azure Kubernetes Service**.

Critically, DaaS-based developers do not need to write IaC since the DaaS platforms already include an integrated toolchain. Most DaaS solutions are extensible, allowing software teams to add other tools as customizations to their essential platform services. If a delivery team wants to create a custom DevOps platform, they will need to have or hire experts in IaC tools such as Ansible and Terraform.

There are other considerations that can support rapidly deploying DevOps when mandated. For example, use a **user-centered design (UCD)** process to focus on the features and capabilities that will help the business. These tools allow customers and users to see what they want before you develop the code. As a result, the UCD process occurs before you write a single line of code!

Developers can use wireframe tools for UCD such as Adobe InDesign, AXURE, and Balsamic to create a visual display for business workflows. This is a great capability because it helps streamline the *Fuzzy Frontend* of development. UCD concepts also dramatically reduce design time and rework that results from defects in the code. Defects are misunderstood or previously unidentified requirements that your customers felt you should have known about and implemented.

Automated testing is a critical capability in CI/CD pipelines. Teams can use tools such as Leapwork (`https://www.leapwork.com/`) to implement a low code/no-code solution for automated testing.

VSM tools are even more vital to implement when executives mandate the implementation of DevOps capabilities. Everything tends to be rushed in such situations. After all, the mandate probably came down because the organization is failing to deliver sufficient value to its customers.

But how much worse will things be if the organization fails in its DevOps mandate? Modern VSM tools provide the metrics the software delivery teams need to improve their value-based deliveries and show the improvements they have made. In short, VSM tools help identify bottlenecks, orchestrate work, and improve pipeline efficiencies.

But there are still areas of the software delivery pipeline that are difficult to integrate, automate, and orchestrate. This is the topic of the next section.

Dealing with creative versus repeatable pipeline activities

One of the challenges with improving value stream deliveries is the challenges associated with automating or even estimating the scope of work involved in concept ideation, requirements definition, and analysis. In software development, we refer to this stage as the **Fuzzy Frontend**.

This term was originally coined by Peter Koen, a professor at the *Stevens Institute of Technology*. It refers to the value stream activities associated with creating new product ideas and concepts that need to be analyzed to determine customer fit and commercial viability.

Some of these activities are controlled by the product management or product owner function. This is because they alone have the responsibility of deciding what goes into a product and what does not. But the development teams are also involved as they must assess the difficulty and time required to implement each new requirement. In Agile, we refer to assessing requirements as **Product Backlog Refinement**.

The folks at HCL Software were kind enough to allow me to highlight their view of how the creative aspects of the Fuzzy Frontend fit in the overall software delivery pipeline, as shown in *Figure 15.1*.

An important feature of this software delivery pipeline diagram is highlighting the *creative versus repeatable* aspects of software development, which they break out as Agile versus DevOps practices.

Everything to the left of the vertical line is the fuzzy frontend, where creativity is a defining effort that is difficult to estimate. However, everything to the right is the commit and can be automated. So, everything to the left takes creativity, thought, design thinking, and so on, while everything to the right becomes part of an automated software delivery factory!

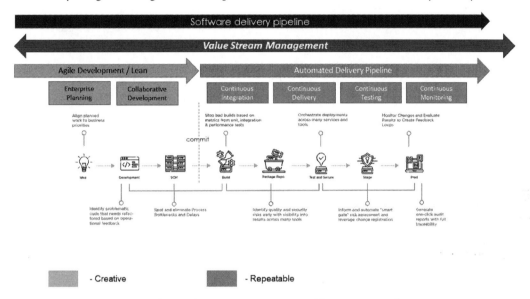

Figure 15.1 – Dealing with creative versus repeatable DevOps pipeline activities

Al Wagner articulates a DevOps implementation scenario as involving three phases, which he refers to as Day Zero, Day One, and Day Two. Let's understand each of them:

- **Day Zero** (to the left of code commit): Agile implementations of Agile practices governing Sprint planning, Sprint execution, releases, commits, and so on. This is the creative, Fuzzy Frontend side of development that is difficult to estimate and automate. Yet, these are the activities that keep our focus on the customer.

- **Day One** (to the right of code commit): This involves integrating, automating, and orchestrating DevOps pipeline activities. Here, the IID model is taken and made Lean through integration and automation toolchain capabilities.

- **Day Two**: This is the state we want to reach. That's the application of VSM – to focus on meeting business needs – which means we need to have a holistic view of both the fuzzy frontend (Agile) and the CI/CD automation processes. It involves constantly monitoring, looking across teams, and constantly improving. Use experimentation to find better ways of doing things. Maybe use AI to assess areas and methods for improvement. Always use lead and cycle times as the actual indicators of improvement.

We can also use VSM techniques across all organizational value streams to determine the high priority/highest value improvement activities that can benefit from DevOp's rapid and efficient software delivery capabilities. The idea is that we can spend a lot of time, money, and resources building our DevOps pipelines, only not to see any real impact on the business if those new capabilities are not applied to the organization's most impactful value stream improvement initiatives. For example, we can use OKRs and **Weighted Shortest Job First (WSJF)** (a method used in the **Scaled Agile Framework (SAFe)**) to help teams prioritize a list of initiatives.

At this point, you have heard differing views on the potential pitfalls of DevOps implementations and recommendations on how to address the issues you might face. You've also learned about four different DevOps platform implementation strategies and the pros and cons of each. You then learned about the best approach to take when the organization's executive mandates the use of DevOps, and you've also learned why it is easier to automate the backend of the software delivery pipeline but not the fuzzy frontend. Now, we are going to dive into how to address a host of potential DevOps platform implementation issues.

Addressing the pitfalls of DevOps

In this section, you will learn strategies for addressing 18 scenarios that can present a challenge to your DevOps implementation plans. The list is not meant to be an all-inclusive discussion on situations you may face, but it is reasonably comprehensive. As you read through these subsections, begin to think about how you can apply the VSM concepts, methods, and tools you've learned about to discover issues and their root causes, as well as how to improve them.

Let's begin by recognizing and avoiding the consequences of Conway's Law.

Avoiding the pitfalls of Conway's Law

In 1968, Melvin E. Conway wrote an article for the **Harvard Business Review (HBR)** titled *How Do Committees Invent?* Unfortunately, HBR rejected it on the grounds that he had not proved his thesis (http://www.melconway.com/Home/Conways_Law.html). However, Conway persisted and submitted the paper to **Datamation**, who published it in April 1968. His persistence paid off, as one of his observations in the papers was that organizations tend to make systems (intentionally, broadly defined by Conway) that mirror the communications structures within the organization.

Here is the quote, verbatim:

Conway's Law (`http://www.melconway.com/Home/Conways_Law.html`):

> *"Any organization that designs a system (defined broadly) will produce a design whose structure is a copy of the organization's communication structure."*
>
> *— Melvin E. Conway*

Though Conway made his observation years ago, it is no less relevant today, including its application to systems that deliver software; even modern DevOps-based software delivery systems. So, let's use what we've learned about lean production systems to understand the consequences of Conway's observation.

Value stream management methods and tools help the organization streamline its value streams by eliminating waste and improving work and information flows. However, if the DevOps team is called to create an application that supports a critical business process, it would not make sense to construct its logic to mimic how it operates today. Instead, the business application needs to support the work and information flow improvements identified through a VSM initiative.

Conway's Law also applies directly to the software delivery team as a system. In fact, those are the most typical use cases when describing the impact of Conway's Law. Put most succinctly, any software application that's constructed will have as many layers or modules as there are discrete organizations participating in its build. In effect, the software will mirror how the teams separate their activities and communications.

AlanMacCormack, Carliss Baldwin, and John Rusnak discussed their findings relevant to Conway's Law in their 2012 HBR article titled *Exploring the Duality Between Product and Organizational Architectures: A Test of the 'mirroring' Hypothesis*. In their own words, they found the following correlation: *"The mirroring hypothesis predicts that these different organizational forms will produce products with distinctly different architectures. Specifically, loosely coupled organizations will develop more modular designs than tightly coupled organizations."*

Modern CI/CD and DevOps-based software delivery teams employ microservices, containers, and APIs, all of which support loosely coupled applications. Loosely coupled services are reusable and interchangeable and implemented without breaking existing interconnections.

Conway's Law describes the impacts organizational structures can have on software development. For example, large product teams that work as a disjointed collection of entities will create bottlenecks in the flow of their work, communications, and information flows. Looking at software delivery as a value stream, we know we need to eliminate these artificial barriers by aligning the teams horizontally around end-to-end value delivery flows. And we must also eliminate the waste that prevents continuous and synchronized flows.

Implementing a CALMS framework

Damon Edwards and John Willis initially coined the acronym **CAMS**, to stand for **Culture**, **Automation**, **Measurement** and **Sharing**. Later, Jez Humble added an L, to include Lean in the acronym, to make it **CALMS**. The **CALMS Framework** is a conceptual model for integrating DevOps teams, their activities, and the employment of their systems, tools, and toolchains. The elements within the CALMS acronym are further defined as follows:

- **Culture**: Requires a switch from command and control and hierarchical organizational business structures to collaborative work environments with shared responsibilities and organization around horizontal flows to support value-based deliveries.

  A DevOps culture welcomes change, uses feedback and information (metrics) to improve continuously, and is accountable for their work as a team. As with Lean, DevOps culture pushes decision-making as much as possible to those who perform or are responsible for the work.

- **Automation**: In DevOps, transformation includes automating manual tasks to the greatest extent possible. For example, recall the CI and test automation activities in the **Automated Delivery Pipeline** on the right of *Figure 15.1*.

  A DevOps-based software delivery pipeline eliminates repetitive and non-value-added manual work. IaC and CaC capabilities produce repeatable and high-quality processes and reliable systems. In fact, everything as code is the mindset behind DevOps automation, regardless of the tools you employ. Test automation (packaging builds and promoting them through test environments using automated deployments) implements CD capabilities.

- **Lean**: This involves making continuous improvements to streamline flows by eliminating waste that creates delays, waiting, and excess WIP. Lean seeks to achieve FLOW – smoothly transitioning work from one *work center* to the next – in the shortest amount of time, ideally with as few queues/buffers as possible. This is what this book is fundamentally about.

- **Measurement**: We can't fix something if we don't know what the problems are, their root causes, and what things most impact our ability to deliver value rapidly, frequently, and with high quality. For that, we need metrics and analytics. Identify your most critical Lean metrics, starting with the DORA Four: lead time (for change), change frequency, change failure rate, and **mean time to repair** (**MTTR**).

- **Sharing**: DevOps is fundamentally a collaboration strategy that aligns Dev and Ops activities. To be successful, Dev and Ops cannot be stovepipe silos. Instead, they must find common ground, and that common ground forms around delivering and sustaining software products customers will value. But collaboration is not enough; they must also share responsibilities for the success of the product across its life cycle.

Deciding on the appropriate DevOps platform strategy

Earlier in this chapter, you learned about four DevOps implementation options: build your own DevOps platform, purchase a DaaS license, use VSM tools, and build software factories. We do not need to cover the pros and cons of those four options again. However, we do need to address a few other issues, such as the use of containers and hybrid-cloud environments.

A container is a type of software that packages code and all its dependencies to deploy applications quickly and reliably, regardless of the target computing environment. However, if your organization is not operating at a very large scale, the use of container orchestration tools such as Kubernetes, Mesos, and others may be overkill. By a very large scale, we're talking about organizations the size of Google, Amazon, Netflix, most branches of government, and other businesses with huge volumes of constantly evolving internet-based services.

If your staff has no familiarity with the container orchestration tool, it can actually end up being a value-losing prospect. For example, even skilled developers find Kubernetes challenging to learn. Therefore, **Elastic Container Services** (**ECS**) or self-hosted Docker Swarm Mode are more appropriate for most organizations. Or even the use of traditional **virtual machine** (**VM**) environments may be sufficient to support your scaling needs. As a side note, even Kubernetes (also known as K8s) must run on a VM.

If you are committed to using containers, and you have a small shop that somehow managed to hire a couple of super K8s ninjas, they could make it work. But having that kind of talent on-hand in a small dev shop is rare and, likely, not cost-effective for the organization's application deployment needs.

If your team has plans to operate in one of the cloud service providers (AWS, Azure, GCP, and so on) but has no experience with those tools, it may make sense to take a **hybrid-cloud** approach initially. In other words, use the network and computing resources you have on-premises and slowly migrate to the cloud. This slow-roll strategy makes migration safer until your team formally decides they are ready to cut over to a 100% cloud architecture.

The hybrid-cloud approach does still require investing in new skills. For example, your developers need to learn the APIs and eccentricities of the selected cloud providers (that is, JSON or REST API syntax, Bash or Python for scripting in IaC applications, and automation servers such as Jenkins and Bamboo, which require specialized scripting knowledge).

Regardless of which DevOps platform implementation scenario you choose, the most effective or state-of-the-art tools may be too difficult to maintain if you don't keep a well-staffed team of experts on hand. Also, with more than 400 tools categorized as DevOps component solutions, which ones will you use, and why? Finally, what governance programs do you need to implement to evaluate the tools, handle licensing issues, and make informed budgeting decisions?

Finally, if you face a talent shortage in your workplace, your selection options will be constrained by your team's collective skills and experiences. So, how can you use the techniques of VSM to help your organization work through these issues? Once you have selected a DevOps implementation strategy, how can you use the metrics to make continued improvements to your software delivery flows?

Avoiding mandates

We spoke previously about DaaS being a viable option when the transition to implement DevOps-based software delivery capabilities is forced through executive mandates. The business drivers for such mandates may involve a burning platform situation or realizing that the organization is missing opportunities to compete effectively in our digital economy.

Regardless of the motivation, when supporting digital transformations, architect your DevSecOps solutions so that VSM roadmaps begin with your customer's current workflows and methods. Ripping away a development team's current practices and mandating a radically different one in short order will cause unexpected costs, reduce throughput, and lower team morale.

The bottom line is that people need to buy into change; it can't be mandated. However, suppose you encourage your Dev and Ops team members to participate in VSM value stream mapping and use a Kaizen-based approach to making lean-oriented improvements. In that case, those team members are more likely to buy into whatever change scenarios have been identified and help in the transitions.

Avoiding wasted time

Lean is fundamentally about eliminating waste, including those activities that take time away from our efforts to deliver customer-centric value. Some of the biggest time wasters are meetings instead of work. Yes, we must stay informed, but your organization's leaders must constantly ask whether specific meetings are essential. Are there better ways to keep people informed? And, if a meeting is necessary, they need to ask who really needs to attend.

Keep your daily standup meetings brief and laser-focused on identifying work that's been accomplished, specific issues or impediments, and determining action items. There's a reason they are called **Standing meetings**. It takes issues offline with only the appropriate people participating. In other words, you should conduct separate meetings for issue resolution.

Avoid long DevOps planning and implementation meetings. Big meetings have become popular, especially in SAFe with its large training classes and **program increments (PIs)**. Large meetings work when they are relevant, informative, and engaging. But large meetings never work for problem solving activities unless you can logically break the group into small teams, and then bring the groups back together to share their findings.

Whatever we do, we must ask ourselves, does this meeting make our team Leaner and more Agile? If you cannot precisely define a customer-oriented deliverable output for the meeting, chances are the meeting is not necessary. A common question to ask is whether your customer would see value in paying for the meeting – because that is the end result of every meeting you hold. In other words, your customers ultimately pay for those meetings through the price of your products and services.

Always look at meetings from a value-added perspective, just like you now know how to do with any other value stream activity. Ultimately, your meetings serve one purpose – to improve organizational value stream deliveries. Otherwise, they become a form of waste from a Lean-oriented perspective.

Eliminating silos and increasing cross-functional team collaboration

We've addressed this subject multiple times throughout this book. But fundamentally, this is what DevOps is about. Instead of having development and operations teams working in silos, we bring them together to collaborate and improve software value delivery.

But the term DevOps is actually limiting from a value-added perspective. This book mentioned DevSecOps, which includes collaborating with the security department to make our networks and applications safe. However, it's becoming more challenging in a digital economy to separate the work that's performed in other organizational and development value streams from the software delivery value streams. So, I would encourage you to use the term **BusDevSecOps** when referring to VSM initiatives operating as strategic transformations to compete in our digital economy.

The BusDevSecOps approach encourages cross-functional team collaborations to break down the hierarchical silos in the functional organizational model. The goal of BusDevSecOps is to promote the development of horizontal work, material, and information flows to improve the delivery of business value.

Suppose there is one important lesson we've learned in Agile: the volume of people is not a primary indicator of future success and may instead be a source of failure due to the increasing interconnections that come with scale. Instead, people work most efficiently in small teams.

Scaling is accomplished through various team-of-team concepts but best achieved when the teams integrate value streams to support the flow of work. In the end, the diversity of skills, relevant experience, and cross-team collaborations are what contribute most to an organization's success.

Upskilling becomes critical

VSM employs methods, tools, and metrics to improve an organization's value delivery capabilities continuously. We spoke in the previous subsection about the need to have a diverse set of skills in small teams to accomplish all the work that's been assigned. Agile and Lean both employ the concepts of putting all the necessary skills into small, self-directed teams.

Ideally, individual team members have multiple skills to provide more flexibility and fault tolerance. Still, those teams cannot continuously improve the way they work unless they are also continuously learning. Therefore, time and resources need to be made available for this, and the executives must instill the notion of continuous learning as part of the organization's desired culture.

Implementing pre-production testing

Fundamentally, CI/CD is a sequential flow of work activities, from ideation through delivery to customers. Modern software engineering practices that instill CaC, IaC, and test automation make it practical to streamline these activities with minimal, if any, human intervention.

As a result, it's possible to accelerate software delivery cycles by running CI and CD practices straight into production. However, it's usually better to build the CI/CD automation sequence but implement a pre-production stage before release. This approach allows application releases to be monitored in production-like environments before allowing the product to go to the customer. The reason for this is that it's better to find configuration problems in a pre-production environment than to have customers find it and having to roll back the release.

Here, again, the data capture and analytics capabilities of modern VSM tools make it easier to analyze and improve application performance in the pre-production environment, before allowing it to be released into a production environment.

Separating DevOps engineering from DevOps as a practice

DevOps engineers have the responsibility of helping install the integration, automation, and orchestration capabilities across CI/CD and DevOps pipelines. However, within those pipelines, the roles of developers and operations staff persist.

Now, we know that we cannot allow the folks to operate as siloed functions. So, instead, we need Dev and Ops to collaborate to break down the barriers that would otherwise reduce the organization's ability to deliver high-quality products rapidly and frequently, and minimize the potential for failed or suboptimal production releases.

In this context, DevOps engineering helps build automated pipeline capabilities. Still, DevOps, as a practice, is a strategy that brings Dev and Ops functions together to solve product delivery issues, both before and after each product release. Both capabilities are necessary to accelerate and improve value delivery.

Allowing flexibility in DevOps policies and procedures

Large enterprises have many value streams and often many products with unique value propositions. Therefore, IT must offer flexibility to address their customer's needs and ensure they are in tune with the delivery capabilities that bring competitive advantage for each product line. Moreover, requirements, practices, and technologies change over time. What works well today may not tomorrow. And we can always improve.

In the previous chapter, we discussed the importance of establishing a COE to develop governance policies around tools and practices during the initial prototype engagements, oversee the maturity of an organization's DevOps practices, and provide guidance to new teams and existing DevOps teams. The learning curve to acquire these DevOps skills and capabilities is quite steep, and the CoE reduces the impact of the organization's transitions.

Still, the CoE cannot be directive in nature. They fulfill mentoring, coaching, and servant leadership roles. They can help DevOps teams situationally analyze alternatives when the standard practices fall short in meeting internal and external customer needs. They also operate within the CALMS framework to assist the DevOps teams through their transformations and ongoing improvement initiatives. The role of the CoE is not to implement a command and control oversight mechanism that gets in the way of making informed and experiential improvements. The purpose of the CoE is to provide leadership, guidance, and support, but not through directives. They are servant leaders.

Now, let's move on and talk about how quality can be improved even while increasing delivery velocity.

Improving velocity with quality

A common term used among DevOps-oriented Agilists is **acceleration**. The idea behind the term is that the Lean flows of DevOps help us accelerate the delivery of software value. But the term **value** in that statement is just as significant as the term **accelerate**. Increased software delivery speed without improvements to quality only means delivering the wrong product more quickly and efficiently. Still, it's the wrong product – which means we might be going toward bankruptcy more quickly.

This concept applies across the software delivery value stream. When we decide to accelerate flow without putting equal consideration into improving the quality of the delivery, we create an opportunity for increased waste and failures.

CI with automated testing is a critical enabler for improving software quality. But so too are the fuzzy frontend activities associated with gathering requirements, writing associated acceptance criteria, and defining the tests that confirm the completeness or **Definition of Done** for each constructed work item. We can't get
the result right if we don't start right. Defects result from not getting the frontend right, which kills any velocity we might have had.

Building DevOps teams from within

We've noted that DevOps is a skillset that's not developed overnight. However, hiring dedicated resources to create a separate DevOps team is not the best way forward. Building dedicated DevOps teams from scratch will only create new siloes operating across your horizontal value stream.

Recall the issues of implementing horizontal value stream flows across the vertical functional silos in our discussions in *Chapter 13, Introducing the VSM-DevOps Practice Leaders*, in the *Defining values streams in DA FLEX* section. Refer to *Figure 13.3*. Instead, a better approach is to develop teams around value streams. This includes your DevOps engineers, plus existing **quality assurance (QA)**, operations, and development team members. This approach brings your existing people and processes into the work of organizing around value. There's no need to replace them. Instead, we need to bring them along.

Start with the people who enjoy being innovators and early adopters. Help them be successful and build on their success to establish the core foundations of your enterprise DevOps tools, policies, and procedures. Then, use the experience and success of those teams to bring in the early majority and, ultimately, the laggards.

This process does not have to take forever. However, large organizations with multiple product lines and multiple Dev and Ops teams can expect a multi-year journey. Therefore, a 3-year timeline to implement an organizational transformation on this scale is not unrealistic.

Automating database builds

Say what!? When building CI/CD pipelines, we are used to thinking about automating the execution of software builds, the standup and configuration of infrastructures for testing, and then executing the tests. However, we don't often think about how our application databases fit into these scenarios.

In CI, we pull a batch of files from specific branches within our source code repository and then allow the configuration scripts to execute the build and integration test process. The problem is that database code (stateful, order-specific, additive database structures) does not lend itself to merging code across branches. Ideally, database changes get merged into your batches before they are retrieved for processing. Also, database changes must be handled serially, and the order matters.

Data snapshots created in separate Dev environments will drift from each other over time, making it challenging to sync data for each build. Therefore, someone needs to be responsible for automating the databases alongside the application automation configurations.

Maintaining incident handling procedures

No matter how much time and effort we devote to building our automation scripts, something will inevitably go wrong. The purpose of our Agile retrospectives is to blamelessly review issues that occur and identify ways to avoid those failures in the future. And, when the failures are not entirely avoidable, we need to make sure we improve and document our recovery procedures.

The DevOps team needs to maintain a rigorous incident handling procedure to document how the configuration, testing, and deployment failures are handled. The best place to put this information is in the runbook documentation, which may be maintained in a source code repository such as Git or GitHub.

Integrating security with DevOps

The integration of security with DevOps is so important that many organizations refer to their automated software delivery pipelines as DevSecOps. Unfortunately, security is another potential silo within the IT organization. And, just as is true with the operations team, security folks tend to be risk-averse and may therefore be viewed as a bottleneck in the acceleration of software delivery.

However, a bigger mistake is to ignore or go around the security function to avoid delays. In the past year, while this book was written, we have seen first-hand the negative consequences of not paying attention to security. For example, the ransomware hack of the Colonial Pipeline Company shut down 45% of the oil deliveries to the East Coast of the United States for nearly a week. Another well-publicized event with potentially catastrophic consequences is the malware attached by hackers to a software update from SolarWinds. The malware allowed the hackers to monitor the computer networks of nearly 18,000 SolarWinds customers in both the government and the private sector and over four months.

Gaining knowledge of DevOps

It should seem obvious that having knowledge of DevOps is a requirement before initiating a DevOps mandate. But, unfortunately, it's much easier to understand the potential benefits of DevOps than it is to understand the issues involved with implementing DevOps on an enterprise scale.

It goes back to that statement made by my former Navy track coach, Al Cantello, about our wanting instant gratification. By now, you should fully appreciate the difficulties in establishing DevOps at Scale to support a digital business transformation. But it's much easier to dream about a better future state and yet quite another thing to do the work to achieve those desired goals. So we have to put in the work.

And that work has to start with the organization's executives as only they have the authority to drive and fund the transformation on an enterprise initiative.

Getting fatigued while implementing DevOps

The IT industry undergoes constant evolution. It's hard enough for IT specialists to keep up, let alone the rest of the stakeholders in an organization affected by their activities. Moreover, the complexity of DevOps makes it especially frustrating to implement at an enterprise scale.

It's easy to look at a DaaS-based DevOps platform solution and think we can stand up a new DevOps platform virtually instantaneously. At a limited scale, that's true – so long as you have the trained staff in-house who can immediately go to work.

But, on a larger scale, a series of issues will quickly arise, spanning budgets, training, mentoring, coaching, preferred and emergent tool integrations, unique configurations to support legacy applications, security, compliance, licensing, long-term supportability and sustainability, and value stream performance improvements. At times, it may seem like the organization takes two steps forward, only to fall back a step or two while executives and other stakeholders reassess previous decisions.

This is where value stream management comes into play. It's impossible to execute a game plan if you don't have one at the start. Yes, even football coaches make halftime adjustments. But those adjustments are tweaks to the original plans, and the goals and objectives remain the same.

DevOps implementation fatigue is another reason why executive support is so vital to a successful outcome. The organization's chief and line of business executives must keep the momentum going through the hard times. Clear and continuous communication from the expected OKRs is one way they help drive the implementations. Other times, they may need to be cheerleaders and coaches. But, in any event, they need to be informed, involved, and committed.

Coding secrets in source control

Joel Kruger mentioned this topic in his interview. Security must be a critical concern in all software delivery organizations. For example, DevOps-based software delivery systems use IaC and CaC to automate the execution of creating or updating the specified environments and application infrastructure configurations. But these configurations can be a security hole when access information is hardcoded into the instructions. As Joel notes, *"it's like posting your name and address and bank account information online."*

Another issue with hardcoding secrets is that each variation forces a new and unique configuration file to be constructed. However, instead of maintaining multiple copies of configuration files that do precisely the same thing, developers can use parameterized, reusable scripts alongside environment variables to reduce the sprawl.

For example, developers might write Ansible scripts to configure a server, but then have 50 separate instances to deal with unique but minor variables. It's much better to make one configuration and parameterize it so that development teams can simply change the parameters that affect their configurations.

The parameters code concept applies to configurations, human input, machine-to-machine interactions, web apps, and more. Everything needs to be modularized (open-ended), including IP addresses, hostnames, application names, resource configurations (CPU and RAM), default configuration files, certificates, and tokens.

> **Note**
> The need to audit configurations, such as in government and highly secure applications, can lead to hardcoding parameters and integrations within source code and tool scripts. However, tools such as AWS Secrets Manager, for example, allow you to parameterize your variable inputs but securely manage them and still allow auditing by authorized personnel.

This section concludes our chapter on defining the appropriate DevOps platform strategy. The next chapter is the final chapter for this book, where we will take what we've learned to use VSM and DevOps methods and tools to help affect digital business transformations. But before we move on, let's summarize what you've learned in this chapter and check your understanding of the concepts presented.

Summary

In this chapter, you had the chance to hear from five industry experts on their views about potential DevOps implementation pitfalls and various DevOps platform implementation strategies. These five individuals were selected to provide as broad a base of hands-on experiences as possible.

Next, you learned about four fundamental approaches to implementing DevOps platforms. This included building a custom DevOps platform, purchasing a cloud-based **DevOps as a Service (DaaS)** solution offering, employing VSM tools to integrate and orchestrate your DevOps toolchains, and building software factories by constructing self-service CaC, downloadable via Git or another SCM tool.

Finally, you reviewed 18 implementation scenarios that can create issues for your DevOps platform implementation program. As you read through these scenarios, you were encouraged to identify how you can leverage what you've learned about VSM and DevOps methods, as well as the tools to overcome these issues.

With this information, you are now ready to learn how to employ what you've learned to use VSM and DevOps methods and tools to digitally transform your business, which is the subject of the next and last chapter in this book.

Questions

1. Helen Beal instructs us not to create DevOps teams. What does she think we should do instead?

2. Scott Ambler suggests we can't limit our thinking to just Dev and Ops. What are the six key aspects of enterprise-class DevOps defined in PMI's DA toolkit?

3. Pramod Malhotra suggests we shouldn't even consider initiating a DevOps initiative unless we have what?

4. Al Wagner hears one common complaint from his customers. What is that complaint?

5. Joel Kruger identified **Configuration Management (CM)** as the means to protect an organization's IT assets. While he notes CM is not a new concept, what is relatively new about CM practices in a CI/CD and DevOps pipeline context?

6. What are the four fundamental DevOps implementation approaches an organization might take?

7. When corporate executives mandate a rapid transition to implement DevOps, what is usually the best strategy?

8. Jez Humble created the CALMS framework as a conceptual model for integrating DevOps teams, their activities, and employing their systems, tools, and toolchains. What does the CALMS acronym stand for?

9. This book suggests that it's better to build your DevOps teams from within to support your organization's value streams. Why is that?

10. Who is ultimately responsible for addressing issues of DevOps implementation fatigue?

Further reading

MacCormack, Alan, Carliss Baldwin, and John Rusnak. 2012. *Exploring the Duality Between Product and Organizational Architectures: A Test of the "mirroring" Hypothesis.* Research Policy 41 (8) (October): 1309–1324. doi:10.1016/j.respol.2012.04.011. https://dash.harvard.edu/bitstream/handle/1/34403525/ maccormack%2Cbaldwin%2Crusnak_exploring-the-duality.pdf. Accessed July 12, 2021.

16
Transforming Businesses with VSM and DevOps

In this final chapter, you will learn how to use **value stream management** (**VSM**) and DevOps tools and related implementation initiatives to transform businesses into viable entities to compete in our digital economy. But there are two parts to making digital transformations. In part one, we need to transform our software delivery capabilities to support the organization's business transformations at large. In part two, we use our transformed software delivery capabilities to improve the way we build and deliver products across our value streams.

In other words, we must connect the software delivery improvements achieved through our DevOps-related VSM initiatives to support the needs of our broader enterprise VSM initiatives. But such connections are not automatic. From the perspective of systems thinking, improving software development capabilities apart from the intersecting value delivery needs of the business is a form of local optimization. The only way an organization will see an adequate ROI from its VSM and DevOps tools investments is to use its enhanced software delivery capabilities to improve its value delivery capabilities across the organization.

In this chapter, you will learn how to align VSM and DevOps tool investments with corporate strategies and portfolio investments. We'll work through that topic in a stepwise approach. With that objective in mind, the topics covered in this chapter include the following:

- Uniting VSM initiatives
- Using VSM for DevOps improvements
- Connecting to enterprise VSM initiatives
- Using OKRs to drive business transformations
- Aligning VSM initiatives with strategies and portfolios
- Expanding the vision for the VSM tool industry

Note that the last topic will introduce a future vision for the VSM tool industry. It would be easy to read current documentation and press releases from VSM tool vendors and believe that their tools provide out-of-the-box solutions to have end-to-end visibility across all value streams. That's not really true today. Modern VSM tools provide end-to-end visibility of the activities that support software delivery pipelines. The VSM tool vision can be expanded to integrate all organizational development and operational value streams in the long run. I've included this topic as a call to VSM tool vendors to make that vision a reality.

Let's get started on understanding how to transform our businesses into competitive digital enterprises through VSM. We'll begin with a discussion on what it means to unite VSM initiatives, and why taking such actions are important.

Uniting VSM initiatives

Lean concepts are not new. For example, arguments could be made that Henry Ford's Model T production assembly lines embodied several of the concepts applied in modern Lean practices. For example, Ford created continuous and streamlined flows across automotive assembly lines and sequenced parts to arrive just before assembly. But it was the founder and future leaders of Toyota who took these concepts to the next level, led by these three individuals primarily:

- **Sakichi Toyoda** – Toyota's founder

    Developed and implemented the concepts behind **Jidoka** – *automation with a human touch* – as the means to facilitate quality at the source.

- **Kiichiro Toyota** – Sakichi Toyoda's son

    Founded the *Toyota Motor Corporation* and developed **just-in-time** (**JIT**) concepts for manufacturing.

- **Taichi Ohno** – Shop-floor supervisor, industrial engineer, and executive at Toyota

    Integrated Toyota's JIT system with its Jidoka System, defined the Kanban system, and established the principles behind Kaizen (continuous improvements). Ohno is also credited with defining many of the elements embodied in the **Toyota Production System** (**TPS**) such as pull-oriented production systems, the elimination of waste, **Quick Die changes** (**SMED**), non-value-added work, U-shaped work cells, and single-piece flows.

What eventually became known as *The Toyota Way* had such a profound impact on global competition in manufacturing that it was widely studied and duplicated as the means to survive in increasingly competitive global markets. The term **Lean** comes out of research conducted by the **International Motor Vehicle Program** (**IMVP**) at the **Massachusetts Institute of Technology** (**MIT**) under the direction of James P. Womack. John Krafcik, a researcher at IMVP, coined the term Lean Production, which is at the heart of VSM. Beyond these pioneers came many practitioners and experts who further expanded the use of Lean production practices.

The bottom line is that people who know about Lean already know about value stream mapping and VSM – but in a broader context across other organizational development and operational value streams. Moreover, they have been applying these methods for decades!

Diverging customer-centric development strategies

Still, Lean practices in software development and VSM are relatively new as mainstream software development concepts. While other domains and industries focused on Lean production practices to improve their customer-centric value delivery capabilities, the software community focused on implementing Agile-based strategies. Though Lean and Agile practices both focus on improving customer-oriented delivery of value and making continuous improvements, the early advocates of Agile set out to solve a different set of problems.

For example, Toyota sought to improve quality and efficiencies in an island nation, coming out of the Great Depression and then World War II, where access to resources was limited and expensive. Toyota's means of being competitive in its global markets was to build higher-quality products with fewer resources and simultaneously ensure they built only the products customers wanted when they wanted them. They became so good at this that the rest of the world's manufacturing industries had to respond in kind to survive. Other industries quickly followed the Lean trend.

In contrast, Agile came out of the software development community, and its advocates were solving a different set of problems. Specifically, the traditional project management model was not sufficiently responsive to address the evolving needs and priorities of businesses and their customers. So, Agile began as a set of values and principles to support the needs of small software development teams to become more responsive and adaptable. In the process, Agile evolved to implement iterative and incremental development practices that leveraged prototyping and empiricism to create working solutions with customer-directed inputs quickly.

But now, we see the concepts behind Lean and Agile beginning to merge, often characterized as implementing Lean-Agile practices. This topic is essential as Lean-Agile is the basis of the VSM Consortium's approach to implementing VSM tools as the means to improve DevOps-based software delivery capabilities. We'll discuss this in the upcoming section titled *Using VSM for DevOps improvements*. However, before we get to that topic, let's revisit what the modern VSM tool industry means when it uses the term VSM.

Defining VSM as a modern software tools category

In its modern contextual usage, VSM is a tools-driven strategy to support VSM practices to implement Lean-oriented improvements across CI/CD and DevOps pipeline activities. A casual search on the internet might lead us to think this is the only meaning behind VSM as the most recent information on VSM primarily came out of the VSM and DevOps tools industries.

For example, Forrester – in its New Wave™ article titled *Value Stream Management Tools Q3 2018*, defines VSM as follows:

> *VSM is an emerging tool category that connects an organization's business to its software delivery capability. VSM tools provide multiple roles — product managers, developers, QA, and release managers — a view into planning, health indicators, and analytics, helping them collaborate more effectively to reduce waste and focus on work that delivers value to the customer and the business.*

However, recall that *Section 1, Value Delivery*, and *Section 2, VSM Methodology*, of this book introduced the original concepts behind VSM as a generic Lean-improvement strategy and methodology. It's essential to distinguish between the traditional and modern VSM concepts here, as the fusion of the two VSM approaches is the best way forward to align our organization's resources to compete in a digital economy. With this understanding firmly in mind, we can now learn how and why we must fuse the traditional and modern VSM concepts.

Using VSM for DevOps improvements

In *Chapter 5, Driving Business Value through a DevOps Pipeline*, you learned how to apply a generic eight-step VSM methodology to any VSM improvement initiative. We used that same eight-step approach in our CI/CD pipeline improvement use case in *Chapter 6, Launching the VSM Initiative (VSM Steps 1-3)*, through *Chapter 10, Improving the Lean-Agile Value Delivery Cycle (VSM Steps 7 and 8)*. There is no reason we cannot use that same eight-step methodology to guide DevOps pipeline improvements.

Still, the VSM Consortium recommends a slightly different roadmap for VSM implementations related to making improvements across DevOps activities and toolchains, as shown in the following figure:

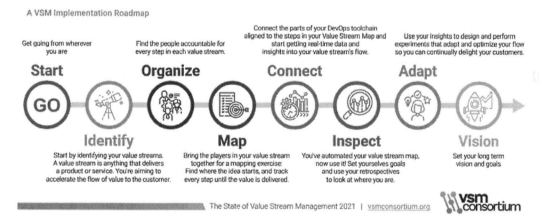

Figure 16.1 – VSM Consortium – A VSM Implementation Roadmap

In the VSM Implementation Roadmap, you can see similarities to both Lean and Agile improvement concepts. In fact, it's an amalgamation of both practices.

Implementing the Lean aspects of the VSM roadmap

The VSM Consortium's VSM Implementation Roadmap begins by identifying value streams, locating, and organizing the people who are accountable for each value stream activity, mapping both the current and desired future states, and connecting the DevOps toolchains to the activities in the value stream. Then, depending upon the selected **value stream management platform** (**VSMP**) in use, the DevOps toolchain integration can serve multiple roles, including integrating, automating, and orchestrating value stream activities spanning software development, security, and compliance.

However, the larger objective is to use the VSMP and its integrations with DevOps tools to capture real-time and end-to-end data across the identified software delivery value stream. Using a common and normalized data model, the value stream managers, team members, organizational executives, and other stakeholders have real-time visibility into software production flows, allowing them to observe and determine the cause of bottlenecks and waiting.

So, the primary difference between this part of the VSM Consortium's VSM Implementation Roadmap and the generic eight-step VSM methodology is the integration of software tools to capture end-to-end data in the value stream without the need for human intervention or manual data collection. Another key differentiator is the use of analytical tools, which we'll get into in the following subsection.

Implementing the Agile aspects of the VSM roadmap

The next two steps in the VSM Consortium's VSM Implementation Roadmap involve **inspection** and **adaption**. Scrum advocates will immediately recognize these two steps from Scrum's three empirical pillars of **transparency**, **inspection**, and **adaptation**.

In the previous subsection, you learned that VSMP products support the integration, automation, and orchestration of value stream activities. But the tools also give us visibility of work and information flows across our DevOps pipelines. So, though the term is not explicitly cited, the VSM Consortium has not ignored Scrum's pillar of *Transparency*. What is unique in the VSM tool industry is replacing the manual aspects of collecting and reporting data via its platforms and tools, which is enabled in the *Connect* step through the VSMP-DevOps toolchain integrations.

Now that we have real-time visibility across DevOps pipeline flows, the DevOps teams can *Inspect* the pipeline to inform their retrospective meetings with accurate and current information. We can use the insights gathered from the inspections and retrospectives to develop one or more hypotheses for potential solutions and perform experiments to evaluate the effectiveness of identified alternatives against our goals. Finally, we can *Adapt* our DevOps system based on our experiential findings.

So, from the *Start* through *Adapt* steps, the VSM Implementation Roadmap marries the best practices of both Lean and Agile into a seamless framework. This brings us to the last step, *Vision*. As it turns out, this is a critical step in Lean-Agile practices.

Establishing a business transformation vision

Recall that Agile evolved as a set of values and principles by software engineers and consultants to be more responsive to evolving customer needs and priorities. But Agile also evolved primarily as a small teams-oriented development philosophy where incremental changes are evaluated over each development iteration – based on the team's experiences from the previous Sprint. In other words, Agile-based improvements tend to be limited to very short planning horizons – measured in 1 to 4 weeks and limited to the budgets and authorities granted to the development team.

In contrast, Lean improvements often view changes across multiple planning horizons that span, potentially, several fiscal years and involve changes and budgets requiring executive-level sponsorship and commitment authorities. In fact, investments in both VSM and DevOps tools involve organizational investments and business operations, and cultural changes that small software development teams cannot authorize. Therefore, investments on this scale must support the strategies of the business, receive executive-level support, and fit within the organization's portfolio-level investments and priorities.

So, *Vision* as a VSM implementation step becomes vital to align the VSM and DevOps implementation objectives with the business strategies to gain executive support and prioritize budget allocations. And the only way that's going to happen is if the executives see how the improvements to software deliveries can improve the company's product deliveries across all organizational value streams.

Now that we understand how Lean and Agile concepts come together in the *VSM Implementation Roadmap* as a tools and DevOps-based software delivery improvement strategy, let's take a step back to look at the importance people play in the implementation and use of these tools.

Implementing tools is not a replacement for people

Having access to real-time data across your DevOps pipelines does not remove the need to have executives and managers performing *Gemba* walks, especially in large software development initiatives involving multiple teams. The people performing the day-to-day work across these DevOps pipelines have the greatest knowledge about how and why work is performed and the issues that interfere with their workflow. In a modern VSM tools context, Gemba walks are explorations that can involve both virtual and face-to-face data gathering and communication activities.

Similar to how Gemba was explained in the section titled *Going to see (Gemba)* in *Chapter 7*, *Mapping the Current State (VSM Step 4)*, the VSM members or VSM manager and executives can chat with the DevOps team members to ask the following questions:

- Ask the DevOps team members to describe the problems they experience with the way software development work is currently performed.

  - Note that most people tend to avoid discussing difficult subjects or express opinions they believe others don't want to hear.

  - Managers need to dive deeper to get past the superficial yet visible issues and get to the real problems that affect team performance and software deliveries.

- Next, ask the team members what they think are the root causes of the problems and show evidence to support their reasoning (**Transparency**).

- When the root cause is uncovered, next, ask the DevOps team members what should be done to resolve the issues and why.

- Then ask the DevOps team members how they will know if the problem is resolved.

  - What evidence will clearly indicate the problem is resolved?

  - What data and metrics can serve as indicators of successful outcomes and improvements?

- Finally, investigate the alternative recommended solutions through experimentation and inspection, and adapt to the approach that provides the most value.

You now understand the value of managers and executives going out to see what's going on and the kinds of questions they must ask of the DevOps team members. But, in many cases, the issues may require specialized skills and a team approach to resolve them. In those cases, the organization should establish a VSM team to conduct the analysis and manage the VSM initiative.

Creating a VSM team for DevOps transformations

Creating a VSM team, just as we would for any other type of VSM initiative, helps to guide DevOps-oriented software delivery value stream improvement investments and activities. Moreover, larger software products involving multiple development and support teams make it critical to stand up a dedicated VSM team to guide the overarching initiative.

It could be possible that a non-IT VSM team – one that's guiding an organization's development or operational value streams improvements – identifies the need to improve or align the software development delivery capabilities in support of their value stream. In such cases, the original VSM team can guide the DevOps-oriented improvements for their value stream, but their team must also include experts on DevOps activities and tools.

Regardless of which approach the organization takes, the VSM team takes on the responsibility for guiding the improvements in software delivery capabilities to meet the needs of the value stream. This alignment is easier to accomplish when the assigned VSM team supports one of the organization's development and operational value streams as its VSM initiative.

In contrast, a VSM team that supports DevOps as a standalone value stream must recognize that they must ultimately align the DevOps team to support high-priority improvements in other organizational value streams. By way of an analogy, it's hard to hit a target if you don't know what you are aiming at. So, the DevOps-oriented VSM team can take on that responsibility, working with the organization's portfolio managers, product owners, and other value stream managers to identify high-priority software development needs.

This subsection concludes our discussion on using VSM for DevOps-based improvements to software delivery capabilities. In the next section, we will look at how the DevOps VSM initiatives support an organization's digital business transformations.

Connecting to enterprise VSM initiatives

In this section, you'll learn how to connect traditional VSM methods with modern VSM tool applications and DevOps to support digital business transformations. You've learned throughout this book that organizations can use modern VSM tools to improve their DevOps-based software value delivery capabilities. However, organizations can and should also continue implementing traditional VSM initiatives to identify digital improvement opportunities across all other organizational value streams.

Let's look at *Figure 16.2 – DevOps pipeline providing digital improvements to manufacturing pipeline flows* to show how this strategy works. A traditional VSM initiative has identified three potential digital enhancements (Kaizen Bursts) within a manufacturing-oriented pipeline in this scenario. It doesn't really matter for this example as to what they might be, but they might include any of the following types of digital enhancements:

- Improved product order and materials information across manufacturing pipeline activities.

- Improved access to shop floor/manufacturing process information.

- Re-programming robotics and automated manufacturing systems to improve performance or reduce setup times.

- Implement automated quality inspection systems.

- Implement programming on an automated paint process.

- Improvements to align labeling and shipping instructions with products.

- Improvements to supply chain management systems to support JIT delivery requirements.

- Other digital enhancements.

The VSM team meets with the DevOps team to explain their requirements and priorities, informing their product backlog. The DevOps pipeline can technically be at any stage of maturity. Regardless, based on priorities, the approved digital enhancements make their way through the pipeline into production and must be supported and potentially modified over the life of the manufacturing product line:

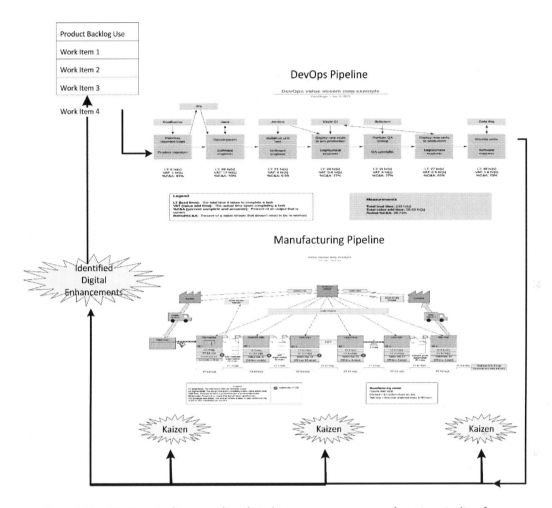

Figure 16.2 – DevOps pipeline providing digital improvements to manufacturing pipeline flows

The prioritized Kaizen Burst (improvement opportunities) identified in the organization's traditional VSM initiatives, working across all development and operational value streams, provide the information necessary to understand where digital transformations have the most positive impact on the business's operations. In this example, organizations use VSM methods strategically as a lean-oriented improvement technique to identify, assess, and prioritize where they can eliminate waste and streamline their value stream activities through digital transformations.

After reading this book, you should be fully aware that the strategic VSM initiatives identify many types of improvement opportunities to eliminate waste and streamline value stream flows, some of which may not require software-based solutions or enhancements. However, software and associated computing and network systems are at the heart of most product and value stream improvements in our digital economy. And we employ VSM tools to improve DevOps pipelines to support the digital improvement needs identified across all other organizational VSM initiatives.

We can direct our improved DevOps software delivery capabilities to eliminate waste and streamline flows across all organizational value streams. But, more often than not, it is those strategic VSM initiatives that help the organization identify strategic improvement opportunities – digital or otherwise. The recommendations ultimately require executive support and consideration for investment prioritization by the lean portfolio management function.

Suppose a software development team or a value stream manager takes shortcuts to circumvent the organization's budget approval processes. In that case, they will fail to obtain the management and financial support required for success. A small development team might find a way to fund their DevOps implementation as a standalone, but that's not a scalable process. And they might fail to deliver sufficient value to justify the effort or justify the expansion of their efforts.

As discussed in the introduction to this chapter, improving software delivery capabilities in isolation of other organizational value stream needs is a form of local optimization from a systems thinking perspective. We can expend a lot of time, effort, and money and not see a justifiable return on investment.

Here's an example of why this is the case. Measurements across a fully integrated, automated, and orchestrated DevOps pipeline have cycle times measured in microseconds – something your connected VSM tools will quickly point out. Much of the overall lead time delays come from the *fuzzy frontend* activities associated with product conceptualization, requirements, and design. But once the requirements, acceptance criteria, and design issues are sorted, and a feature moves into production, most of the cycle time events can be measured in minutes or less.

So, a mature DevOps-based software development pipeline is not going to be a bottleneck in an organization's value streams. The assumption, of course, is that the DevOps pipeline improvement activities have already resolved budgeting and approval issues for tools and created reusable configurations for standing up testing environments and executing CI/CD pipeline activities.

None of the initial DevOps pipeline improvement activities comes quickly or easily. The organization's IT function needs to invest time and resources in the effort. They will also need to obtain executive support and buy-in to scale DevOps capabilities across the enterprise.

There are three general scenarios in which DevOps enhanced software deliveries support an organization's business objectives, as shown in the list that follows:

- To produce standalone software products – for external customers

- Enhancements to physical products – such as the nav and control systems in modern automobiles

- Value stream improvements – to improve value delivery capabilities across operational value streams

It is not the objective of the previous list to conflate the use of software products with value streams. Instead, the objective is to note the ubiquitous nature of software across all types of development and operational value streams.

I've elaborated on this same point throughout this book to make it clear: I believe organizations must have two parallel VSM efforts going on at all times:

- VSM initiatives to improve software delivery capabilities

- VSM initiatives to support Lean improvements across the enterprise

Corporate-sponsored VSM initiatives operate across all development and organizational value streams to support continuous lean improvements – some/many of which will require digital enhancements to affect the desired value-added changes. So, while the VSM improvements for software delivery are vital, the real value of those improvements comes from aligning software delivery to support digital improvements across the enterprise. And those improvement opportunities are identified and prioritized across the organization's value streams through corporate-sponsored VSM initiatives.

Moreover, it should be a focus of VSM teams and their initiatives to identify areas where IT can improve product value, eliminate waste, and improve value stream flows – and the assigned DevOps team can help with these assessments. The software industry is becoming increasingly aware of the importance of aligning its efforts with product teams and value streams. For example, the VSM Consortium's initial report, due to be released in July 2021, found that nearly 40% (37.36%) of its respondents reported working in a product, feature, component, or stream-aligned team: https://www.vsmconsortium.org/.

You now know to align your DevOps-based VSM initiatives to support the organization's other value streams. In the following two sections, you will learn how to connect with those other value streams through the organization's strategic **Objectives and Key Results** (**OKRs**) and portfolio management. We'll start with the discussion on OKRs.

Using OKRs to drive business transformations

The concepts behind OKRs were created by Andy Grove, the former CEO of Intel, whose leader transformed the company into the world's largest semiconductor company. Early advocates of OKRs, first at Intel, followed by other technology companies, including Google. The employment of OKRs by Intel and Google was chronicled in the book *Measure What Matters*, by John Doerr (Doerr, 2017).

John Doerr learned about the use of OKRs from Andy Grove as an employee at Intel before he left to become a venture capitalist at Kleiner Perkins. During his tenure with Kleiner Perkins, he taught the principles behind OKRs to the companies he invested in, including Google.

OKRs are fairly simple in concept. **Objectives** state what is to be achieved by the organization, while **Key Results** are the targets we set and monitor as objective measures of successful outcomes. More than a set of goals and measurements, OKRs serve as a management methodology and a framework to focus the company's efforts.

Results must be quantifiable, measurable, and verifiable. In other words, we use real numbers for stating objectives, not fuzzy verbiage that can't be measured or proven. In short, with well-defined OKRs, there can be no doubt across the organization about whether we achieved our objectives or not.

OKRs are also time-bound, usually with quarterly objectives, though some organizations may implement monthly objectives. It's possible to have long-lived objectives, perhaps spanning a year or more in duration. Still, the key results may be monitored and rolled up over no more than a quarterly basis.

OKRs are not hidden from sight. They are made visible to all employees and stakeholders. If people don't know what targets the organization is shooting for, how will they know where they are going and if they get there? OKRs guide everyone's efforts.

The objectives of an OKR are not meant to be easy. Instead, they should be achievable and yet challenging. And, as noted above, the objectives need to be specific, clearly stated, quantifiable, and visible. The ideal is to set stretch goals that inspire the organization through its people to achieve great things.

By now, you may be wondering why we are discussing OKRs in a book about applying methods and tools for VSM and DevOps. The answer is that OKRs help drive corporate strategies, portfolio priorities and investment decisions, and ultimately VSM metrics.

For example, a corporate objective might be to deliver a new software product enhancement to support a niche market opportunity. Our measurable **key results (KRs)** might include the following:

- **KR #1**: Develop three required features over the next quarter.

- **KR #2**: Conduct a targeted marketing campaign to promote the product enhancements to 20,000 qualified prospects over the same period.

- **KR #3**: Sell 100 new software licenses in the first month of release and 400 total licenses by the end of the second quarter.

Did you notice that only *KR #1* has anything to do with software development? The other two dealt with sales and marketing support, which are part of the organization's operational value streams. That type of scenario will be typical in any strategic VSM initiative.

We might include other key results to describe reseller or other value stream improvement objectives and desired results. In general, an OKR will have between 3 and 5 key results.

Another important set of metrics used by organizations are **Key Performance Indicators (KPIs)**. It's essential to understand the distinction between KPIs and OKRs. For example, KPIs focus on performance measurements for individuals and teams or groups of people against their goals. As a result, KPIs tend to focus on tactical objectives, whereas OKRs support strategic goals.

Using the preceding example, we strategically introduced a new product variant to open up a new market niche. The key results help the organization understand the expectations. But they also provide an idea of which value streams are most affected. We can now use our VSM initiatives to guide the improvement efforts required to meet the objectives.

Aligning VSM initiatives with strategies and portfolios

VSM initiatives support strategic goals and objectives. This is true regardless of whether a VSM team is evaluating improvements to software deliveries through the implementation of DevOps pipeline capabilities or any of a myriad of other organizational value stream improvements. They are strategic because many of the improvement opportunities identified will involve investments and timeframes beyond what a small value stream team can authorize.

The chief executives will not support large investments that do not align with the business's mission, vision, and strategies. Larger enterprises will (or should) have more formal budgeting procedures than smaller entities. But regardless of size, the chief executives must have a mechanism to evaluate and prioritize investments. When viewed from this perspective, it should be apparent that VSM and DevOps tool investments compete against all the other potential investments under evaluation by the organization at large.

Since this is a book on VSM and not portfolio management, we will only touch briefly on this subject. However, the primary purpose of portfolio management is to centralize and control the budgeting and investments process so that organizations can evaluate all improvement opportunities and their priorities in the context of corporate strategies.

By their very nature, improvement opportunities tend to be project-oriented in nature. That is to say, they are characterized as having relatively short-term durations with defined beginning and end dates. The work is often relatively unique and standalone as one-off change endeavors. The executives make their budgeting and priority decisions based on return on investment criteria, so the improvement projects have precisely defined schedules, resources, and budget constraints.

As a result, portfolio management practices often spawned traditional projects and programs to manage the approved work. However, with the move to Lean-Agile practices, organizations move to implement Lean Portfolio Management concepts, such as those implemented by the Scaled Agile Framework® (SAFe®). Specifically, SAFe's Lean Portfolio Management process applies Lean and systems thinking approaches to strategy and investment funding, Agile portfolio operations, and governance.

You now have a general understanding of the portfolio management approach to evaluating, prioritizing, and approving budgets to support the improvement opportunities identified in the organization's VSM initiatives. You also know how to apply VSM methods and tools to improve value deliveries across the organization. Now let's move on to understand how the results of our VSM initiatives, no matter how successful, can fail over time without continued executive support, training, and Lean-oriented improvements over the organization's life.

Understanding how VSM initiatives can fail over time

While performing research for this book, I had a conversation with Todd Sperl – one of the founders of **LeanFITT**™, that I found both interesting and disturbing. He noted several examples where an organization makes investments in VSM initiatives and sees great and sometimes fantastic results, only to see the whole thing come apart a few years down the road. Moreover, he noted that when the organizations start to fail, they often fail harder and more quickly than it took to turn them into high-performing enterprises. In fact, they often end up performing below the levels they started at before moving to Lean. How does that happen?

I had discussions on this topic with Todd and later with Al Shalloway – the developer of PMI's FLEX. It's an interesting phenomenon and one that probably requires specific research to understand fully. But a common denominator appears to be new management coming in and not understanding how the organization changed its practices, behaviors, and culture to support improved horizontal flows of delivering value.

Sometimes the new management comes in through an acquisition. In other words, the success of the Lean company makes it an acquisition target. Still, the new executives fail to appreciate the Lean-oriented operations and structures that contributed to its success.

Instead, the new executives are often more familiar and comfortable managing the vertical silos that form around traditional business functions and domains, such as marketing, sales, manufacturing, HR, legal, accounting, transport, and warehousing. Moreover, the horizontal flow of value across domains is difficult to see; and seemingly much more difficult to manage than managing resources aligned with business domains and functions.

Figure 16.3 superimposes the horizontal flows of a value stream map against a traditional vertical organizational chart. Again, it's easy to see that there is no direct correlation between these incongruent views of managing an organization:

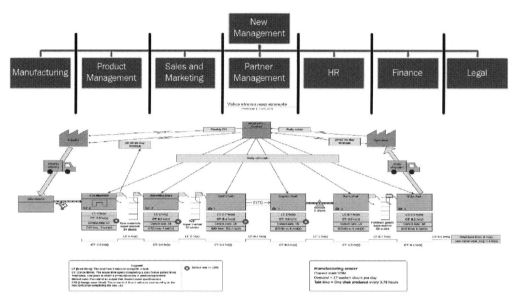

Figure 16.3 – Vertical organizational structures against horizontal workflows

As a result, the change back to managing vertical silos instead of managing product flows is an immediate killer for the organization's performance. First, barriers quickly build between the disparate groups that must work together to maintain the horizontal value delivery flows. Then, the processes that supported horizontal activity flows quickly dissolve and fail. At that point, the organization metaphorically finds itself back to fighting an endless series of fires it cannot put out. At that point, things are so broken that the organization begins to fail on a massive scale.

We can never fix value delivery problems within vertical silos. Instead, we must install horizontal collaborations and improve work and information flows, and that process takes time and effort to accomplish. But, appropriately executed, there is no rational reason to go back to managing vertical domains instead of continuing along the path of managing product-oriented horizontal flows.

By way of an analogy, though it may take many months or even years to construct a building, we can bring it down in a matter of hours with explosives and heavy equipment. Managers who go backward to implement traditional management practices and vertical functional silos bring the explosives and heavy equipment that quickly bring down our Lean production flows.

The bottom-line learning point for new executives, shareholders, and board members is to be careful when acquiring a Lean-oriented company that is already doing well. They must take the time to understand why and how it works before imposing new management structures.

This section completes our discussion on fusing traditional and modern VSM initiatives to support business transformations. However, before closing this book, let's address a potential future state for the VSM tool industry and the benefits all organizations would derive from this new and expanded vision to apply VSM tools.

Expanding the vision for the VSM tool industry

My ultimate vision for VSM is that the traditional VSM initiatives and modern VSM tool-oriented concepts come together. In fact, I think this could be a tremendous boon for the VSM tool industry. Instead of limiting their use to improve DevOps-based software delivery value streams, we could use the same integration, automation, and orchestration capabilities across all organizational value streams.

For example, how hard would it be to extend the VSM tools vision – which currently supports data capture and the normalization of data across software delivery pipeline activities, to also provide the same kind of end-to-end visibility and analysis across all value stream flows? Such a strategy would mean the VSM tool vendors create extensions to help their customers develop applications and integrations to monitor and capture data across other types of development and operational value streams and their activities.

Most manufacturing companies already employ commercial and custom software applications to control production flows. Process control systems are particularly important in highly integrated, automated, and high-volume production environments.

In *Section 2*, *VSM Methodology*, I questioned the need to have separate VSM methods for IT, conducted differently than the VSM initiatives supporting other development and operational value streams. I similarly question if we need a different set of tools for data capture, normalization, and analytics across disparate value streams. We need to apply VSM concepts and tool capabilities across all organizational value streams in our digital economy. The aggregation of tools will enable seamless and real-time access to data and provide end-to-end visibility and analytics from concept to value delivery/cash.

Summary

In this final chapter, you have learned how to unite the work of traditional VSM initiatives with the improvements made through DevOps-based VSM initiatives and tools to improve an organization's competitive posture in our modern digital world. While many VSM tool vendors make it appear that their VSM tools provide end-to-end visibility across all value streams, the reality is they are focused on IT-oriented value streams. That's not a bad thing because DevOps pipelines are complex and expensive, and time-consuming to build on an enterprise scale.

But you've also learned that improvements in any value stream in isolation of understanding their impact on the system as a whole are forms of local optimization. That means we can spend a lot of time and money on maturing our DevOps-based software delivery capabilities and not move the needle to help the organization improve its overall value-delivery capabilities and bottom line.

We must align our improved software delivery capabilities to support the needs across the organization's value streams. That is where much greater ROI lies. In fact, if that alignment does not occur, it's doubtful the IT organization will obtain executive-level support to sustain the initiative on a large scale across the enterprise. So, in this chapter, you learned that you must align VSM and DevOps tool investments with corporate strategies through the portfolio management process. And you must also align your improved DevOps pipelines to support the identified digital improvement opportunities across the organization's other value streams and their VSM initiatives.

Questions

1. What is a common use of VSM and DevOps tools and related implementation initiatives?

2. Ture or False: Lean and VSM are new concepts.

3. What problem did the leaders at Toyota face when they evolved the concepts that we describe today as Lean production?

4. What set of problems did the software community set out to address through the values and principles behind the Manifesto for Agile Software Development?

5. Which three steps of the VSM Implementation Roadmap correlate most closely with the generic eight-step VSM methodology introduced in this book?

6. Which step within the VSM Implementation Roadmap helps provide visibility across DevOps pipelines?

7. What are common improvement horizons and levels of authority for Agile and Lean?

8. Implementing a VSM or DevOps toolchain in isolation from evaluating improvements in other value streams is an example of what, and why do we care?

9. What is the purpose of portfolio management, and why do we care?

10. Why do at least some previously very successful Lean-oriented organizations fail over time?

Further reading

*   Doerr, John (2017), *Measure What Matters. OKRs – The Simple Idea That Drives 10X Growth*, The Bennet Group, LLC, Published by Portfolio Penguin, Random House LLC, London, UK.

Appendix A – VSM Charter

VSM Team Charter

Mission – Charter:
-

Strategic Alignment Factors:
-

Deliverables:
-

Timeframe/ Duration:
-

Expected Scope/ Approach/ Activities:
-

Team Resources:

Role	Name(s)	Participation Level	Skills Required

Team Process:

Process Item	Frequency	Audience/ Distribution

Company Name:

Expected Results:

Benefits: (Expected outcomes, results, or capabilities)	Metrics: (What metrics indicate a successful outcome?)

Key Customers & Suppliers:

Company Name or Function	Relationship		Level			Reviewer(s) Name
	Customer	Supplier	Economic	Operational	User/Tech	
External						
Cust. Name						
Internal						
Engineering						
IT						
Marketing						
Purchasing						
Quality						
Planning						

Assumptions:

-

Risks:

-

Internal issues:

-

External issues:

-

Appendix B – VSM Storyboard

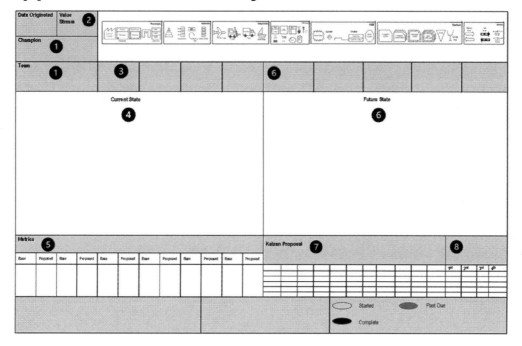

Assessments

You can find the answers to the questions at the end of all chapters here:

Chapter 1: Delivering Customer-Centric Value

1. Digitally enhanced technologies now allow organizations to conduct business on the internet, and via mobile technologies, while providing near-real-time global access to information and knowledge-based services. Plus, products communicate and obtain updates via the **Internet of Things (IoT)**.

2. The problem is that humans have an annoying habit of using the same terms among themselves, but thinking about the meanings of the words in very different ways. Different semantic meanings of terms make human-to-human and human-to-computer communications very challenging.

3. The combination of resulting experiences (including price) that an organization delivers to a group of intended customers in a given time frame, in return for those customers buying/using or otherwise doing what the organization wants instead of taking some competing alternative.

4. Everybody.

5. Because, in a competitive market, you will be quickly beaten by your competitors who are paying attention to the market and providing better customer-centric value for money.

6. Value streams are end-to-end collections of activities that create a result for a customer.

7. Features and functions are the instantiations of functional and non-functional requirements, while value streams are the activities that enable such deliveries.

8. VSM implements methods and tools that help organizations increase the value they deliver to customers by optimizing workflow across their IT value streams.

9. a. Strategy to portfolio – Drive an IT portfolio to business innovation.

   b. Requirement to deploy – Build what the business needs when it needs it.

   c. Request to fulfill – Catalog, fulfill, and manage service usage.

   d. Detect to correct – Anticipate and resolve production issues.

10. a. Table stakes to competing in a digital economy

   b. Accelerates the IT value delivery

Chapter 2: Building on a Lean-Agile Foundation

1. Scrum

2. Scaled Agile Framework

3. To link corporate strategy with portfolio, product, and architectural sustainment needs, and to determine funding priorities over multiple planning horizons.

4. Any two out of these four: Product Backlogs, escaped defects, failed deployments, Release **Net Promoter Score (NPS)**

5. a. Visualize the workflow

   b. Limit **Work in Progress (WIP)**

   c. Manage flow

   d. Make policies explicit

   e. Solicit feedback

   f. Generate ideas for continuous improvements

6. The ideal Lean production goal is to match each activity, and the overall production rates, to the rate of received customer orders or requirements.

   We can calculate this as the time taken to produce work items divided by the number of items requested over the interval, otherwise known as Takt time.

7. A linear-sequential process with no feedback loops.

8. We can accelerate value delivery by implementing streamlining, integration, and automation strategies.

9. a. Waiting – Delays in processing, including any time products spend waiting or in a queue

   b. Overproduction – Producing more of something than you need, or more than your customers currently want

   c. Extra-processing – Over-processing or conducting any non-value-added activity

   d. Transportation – Wasted time, resources, and costs from moving products and materials from one location to another

   e. Motion – Unnecessary movement, or activities by people

f. Inventory – Carrying and storing any materials and products not undergoing a value-added activity

g. Defects – Faults in the products or services produced

10. Agile methodologies often employ **iterative and incremental development (IID)** philosophies. Though minimal, the IID approach is still a form of batch processing. In contrast, Lean seeks to implement continuous flows, ideally as single-piece flows.

Chapter 3: Analyzing Complex System Interactions

1. Systems thinking is an approach to evaluate the complexity of large systems not as a collection of individual parts, but rather by evaluating the interactions between the elements that participate in the system.

2. Intentional and unintentional.

3. To determine the cause and effects of system interactions.

4. A modeling technique to evaluate complex interrelationships and interactions between elements in a system, to achieve reinforcing or balancing behaviors.

5. A linear-sequential process with no feedback loops.

6. $PC = \dfrac{n(n-1)}{2}$

Chapter 4: Defining Value Stream Management

1. **Value Stream Management (VSM)** is fundamentally about implementing Lean concepts within an organization and making the Lean development and delivery processes a way of life.

2. Materials and information flow mapping. The significance is that the identification and management of information flows are every bit as important as material flows across a Lean value stream.

3. Lean value always flows downstream towards the customer, and any preceding activity is upstream.

4. The same concept applies across each value stream. The activities furthest from the customer are always considered upstream from those that are performed closest to the customer.

5. True. Value streams include all value-creating and non-value-creating that an organization includes when bringing a product from concept to launch.

6. "An end-to-end collection of activities that creates a result for a 'customer,' who may be the ultimate customer or an internal 'end-user' of the value stream."

7. Development value stream – All of the actions, both value-creating and non-value-creating, required to bring a product from conception to launch.

8. Operational value streams – All activities from order to delivery.

9. Value streams include the activities required to process information from the customer, and actions to transform the product on its way to the customer.

10. They are:

    i. Commit to Lean

    ii. Choose value stream

    iii. Learn about Lean

    iv. Map current state

    v. Identify Lean metrics

    vi. Map future state

    vii. Map future state – customer demand

    viii. Map future state – continuous flow

    ix. Map future state – leveling

    x. Create Kaizen (continuous improvement) plans

    xi. Implement Kaizen plans.

11. Communications, management, setting up the proper starting conditions, sustainment, and tools.

12. The Pareto principle (also known as the 80/20 rule and the Pareto law) is a natural phenomenon that states that roughly 20% of the elements have 80% of the impact in any system. In the context of your VSM initiative, some value stream improvements will be more critical to the organization's immediate success than others. To make this kind of assessment, the VSM team needs to gather critical Lean-oriented metrics in production rates and waste across all value stream activities.

13. Identify and then name the value stream with the first and last activities. For example, common development-oriented value streams include Concept to launch, Raw material to finish product, and Order to cash.

Chapter 5: Driving Business Value through a DevOps Pipeline

1. DevOps began as a collaboration strategy in the context of Agile Systems Administration. The initial goal was to improve communications and collaborations between development and operations teams within an IT organization. Ultimately, CI/CD pipelines address the issues of mismatched velocities between development and operations teams.

2. Configuration Management, Task Management/Automation, Containerization

3. CI enforces a discipline of merging all developers' working copies of their code to a shared repository several times a day.

   The purpose is to verify each incremental code integration's functionality through software build and test processes as and when the code is developed.

   The goal is to ensure the main software code is always working and in a potentially deployable state.

4. Software developers thrive in a world of change, delivering new features and capabilities continuously. That's a good thing because customers and users want new features that add value. Systems administrators don't care for change all that much, as they are responsible for ensuring all networks, systems, and applications are running, stable, and secure. And that's a good thing too, as we need our networks and software to work and be secure.

5. Continuous delivery capabilities allow product teams to stand up to new environments and rapidly test new code updates with minimal, if any, manual labor.

6. CD's primary goal is to turn new updates into routine and high-velocity tasks that a development team can perform on-demand.

7. IaC allows developers to use a programming or scripting language to generate repeatable code or scripted instructions to provide IT infrastructure. Installed on a shared repository, IaC allows developers to stand up new servers on demand via a self-service model.

8. The purpose of CaC is to facilitate the versioned migration of application configurations between different environments.

9. The term "toolchain" specifies a scope of tools that support IT value stream activities. But the term "toolchain" by itself does not necessarily imply an integration or automation strategy.

10. The word "pipeline" connotes a flow. In the case of Lean-oriented production philosophies, we want streamlined and efficient flows of both work and information across our IT value streams.

11. SDLC and ITSM value streams, or CI/CD and ITSM value streams.

12. ITSM focuses on how IT teams deliver services. In contrast, ITOM focuses on the activities and tools used for event management, performance monitoring, and the operations processes depicted in the DevOps pipeline's Ops portion (*Figure 5.7*).

13. Project-based funding builds on projected future returns on investments.

14. Product-based funding models evaluate current costs and revenues to assess how much money to invest in development and operations support.

Chapter 6: Launching the VSM Initiative (VSM Steps 1-3)

1. Implementing Lean concepts within an organization and making Lean development and delivery processes a way of life.

2. Lean companies are more competitive than others because they continuously improve their business operations. Lean enterprises are more employee-friendly because they have respect for their work, and delegate responsibilities to the people doing the work. They also help to minimize the bureaucracy and hierarchical organizational structures that get in the way of productivity and ultimately cause employee stress and burnout.

3. Ask questions to determine the states of flow, order processing, lost sizes, customer demands, state of cleanliness and orderliness, inventory management, equipment setups, and product changeovers.

4. Demand, Flow, and Leveling

5. When you are just starting your VSM initiative, you may not yet know what good looks like in Lean performance and waste metrics.

6. Heijunka is a load-leveling tool that provides a better and more robust approach to level production schedules to deal with cycle time and batch size variances across production processes.

7. Heijunka uses the paced withdrawal method of production leveling based on Pitch. It does, however, break it out into Kanban units based on the volume and variety of production products.

8. VSM improves the flow of value across our organization.

9. The concept to launch value stream

10. The raw material to finished product value stream

11. The order to cash value stream

12. The cost reduction principle

    The seven wastes of Lean

    Two pillars of Lean – JIT and Jidoka

    The 5S system

    Visual workplace

    Three stages of Lean application: demand, flow, and leveling

13. Overproducing

    Waiting (Q time)

    Transport

    Overprocessing

    Inventory

    Motion

    Defects

Chapter 7: Mapping the Current State (VSM Step 4)

1. Without a current state value stream map, you may not be aware of the system-wide impacts associated with your current value stream activities.

2. We need to document our existing activity flows, order entry system, production control system, cycle times, equipment setup, and product changeover times, as well as our lot and batch sizes, quality levels, defects, and unsynchronized material and information flows.

3. Value stream mapping helps identify and eliminate waste that hinders productivity.

    Business process models are often used to support business process reengineering and improvement activities. They also serve to create business systems that automate those improvements.

4. We need to know the business process is efficient and value-adding, as automating a flawed process only exacerbates its inefficiencies with the rapid accumulation of non-value-added costs.

5. No, it's time to get to work. Just do it!

6. Without standards, communication and understanding quickly deteriorate among VSM team members and other stakeholders who review the maps.

7. The Gemba and current state mapping activities provide insights into the waste areas that hinder material and information flows.

8. **Go and see** – what's going on for yourself.

   Ask why – multiple times, to get to the root cause of an issue
   (using the 5 W's or 5 Whys)

   Respect people – your job is to help resolve problems, not find fault.

9. Start your current state mapping exercise from final customer deliveries and work your way upstream (backward) through the various processes.

10. It keeps the focus on the needs of the customer. It orients our minds to think in terms of pull-based flows. Moreover, we can better work our way through complex flows in production environments by having multiple assembly branches.

11. The VSM team must prioritize improvements in terms of the highest value impacts.

12. They are:

    Draw customers and suppliers.

    Draw the entry and exit activities.

    Draw all activities between entry and exit processes.

    List all activity attributes.

    Draw queue and waiting times between activities.

    Draw all communications that occur within the value stream.

    Draw push or pull icons to identify the type of workflow.

    Document all other collected data.

Chapter 8: Identifying Lean Metrics (VSM Step 5)

1. It's difficult to improve things without measures of the current state and desired future states.

2. CT is the timespan between starting and finishing a value stream activity. CT does not include **work in progress** (WIP) waiting times between value stream activities in this measure.

3. Not necessarily. There can be elements of non-value-added work within any activity in the form of waste. (For example, defects, inventory, motion, over-processing, overproduction, transport, and waiting.)

4. Six Sigma in Lean production processes provides measures of the desired quality goal. A Six Sigma quality goal is a measure of 3.4 defects per million opportunities.

5. Delivery Lead Time, Deployment Frequency, **Mean Time to Restore** (**MTTR**), Change fail percentage.

6. They are as follows:

- Time spent waiting.

- Time spent walking.

- Time spent entering data.

- Time spent retrieving files.

- Time spent sending and reviewing email or other messages.

- Value-adding work (processing time).

7. Change failure rates specify the percentage of time a change to the code results in a failure, usually detected in the form of a bug or a defect.

8. Lean Assessment Radar Chart

9. They are:

  - Continuous flows

  - Five S's of Lean

  - Order leveling

  - Quality

  - Training

  - Team member involvement

  - Visual controls

  - Work unit movement

10. The integration, automation, and orchestration of pipeline flows.

Chapter 9: Mapping the Future State (VSM Step 6)

1. The phases are:

    Phase 1- Customer Demand

    Phase 2 – Continuous flows

    Phase 3 – Leveling

2. To analyze customer demands for your organization's products or services to include quality objectives and lead time.

3. To improve flows so that our customers receive the right products or services, at the right time, and with the right features in the correct quantities.

4. To distribute work evenly across product lines, reduce waiting times, and eliminate batch processing (also known as working toward achieving single-piece flows).

5. Calculate Takt time by dividing net available operating time by the number of products required over time. Takt time is a measure of how often the value stream needs to deliver its products or service in order to meet customer demands. For example, a Takt time of 0.5 of a minute means the value stream must produce a new item every 30 seconds to keep up with customer demand.

6. Pitch equals the Takt time multiplied by the pack-out quantity. Pitch is the amount of time needed for a value stream to make one container of products.

7. Eliminating **work in progress** (**WIP**) leads to waste in the form of queues and waiting.

8. To produce and move one work item at a time, or at least the smallest practical number of items, through a series of value stream activities in as continuous a fashion as possible.

9. The objective of production leveling is to produce the same number of items consistently at exactly the Takt time rate.

10. Agile development teams aggregate selected work items from the Product backlog into Sprint backlogs, and then work those items as a single lot, from start to finish, across an iterative sprint duration (typically 1 to 4 weeks).

    Kanban boards employed with a traditional Agile or Scrum-based Sprint help the development team visualize and manage WIP. The Kanban boards implement a pull-oriented production control strategy from within the sprint backlog and across each sprint.

CI/CD and DevOps pipeline capabilities allow the Agile teams to pull work items directly from the product backlog and work them as single-piece flows across the IT value stream.

Chapter 10: Improving the Lean-Agile Value Delivery Cycle (VSM Steps 7 and 8)

1. When translated into English, *Kaizen* is a conjunction of two words – *kai* (to break apart) and *zen* (to make good). In other words, sometimes we need to break complex things apart before we can figure out how to put them back together as a better operating system.

2. DevOps is a business transformation activity that requires significant changes to the organization's business processes, as well as investments in new tools and technologies.

3. To visually display the planned improvement initiatives for each of the Kaizen Bursts across each of the three phases of future state improvements.

4. The purpose of this chart is to provide a highly visible display of improvement objectives, goals, and metrics for the VSM initiative. It also identifies risks and issues associated with each recommended improvement objective.

5. The purpose of this plan is to examine the details of the proposed VSM improvement activities. Specifically, the plan provides space to identify all improvement initiatives down to the task level.

6. Addressing customer demands.

   Improving the process flow.

   Leveling work.

7. With these initial Lean transformations completed and installed on an Agile-based framework, the IT-oriented value streams reform as Lean-Agile practices.

8. The technology and product adoption life cycle model.

9. VSM initiatives involve large-scale business transformations that may require months or even years to complete.

   The changes proposed by VSM teams may require restructuring organizations and significant financial investments.

   In short, VSM initiatives have a strategic impact, whereas Agile-based retrospectives tend to operate at the tactical level.

10. Product backlogs and Kaizen Boards.

Chapter 11: Identifying VSM Tool Types and Capabilities

1. The problem is that the data and metrics VSM tools have little practical use unless we first understand the goals, metrics, and activities behind Lean value stream improvements.

2. DevOps **value stream management platforms** (**VSMPs**) or, more simply, **Value Stream Management** (**VSM**) tools

    Value stream delivery platforms (**VSDPs**) or, more simply, DevOps toolchains and pipelines

    Continuous compliance automation (**CCA**) tools, also known as **Governance, risk, and compliance** (**GRC**) tools and platforms

3. Provides out-of-the-box connectors to integrate disparate DevOps toolchains and thereby facilitate the orchestration of IT activities across the plan, release, build, and monitoring activities.

4. VSMPs help to improve velocity, quality, and customer value by providing visibility and analytics across the IT value stream.

    They provide data and tools to monitor and assess strategic metrics, such as release velocity and the DevOps operational efficiencies.

5. To align IT with the organization's business objectives, while managing risks and meeting compliance requirements.

6. VSDPs provide integrated toolchains as out-of-the-box solutions, usually available as cloud-based CI/CD or DevOps platforms.

    VSDPs also include tools that support the visibility, traceability, auditability, and observability of activities across the software delivery value stream beyond the traditional platform capabilities.

7. VSDPs combine the capabilities of the DevOps platforms with VSM tool capabilities. You will find both DevOps platform vendors and VSM tool vendors merging in this shared space.

8. To measure the value delivery rate, including the four critical DevOps measures of deployment frequency, lead time for changes, mean time to restore, and change failure rates.

9. Eliminates waste in the DevOps value stream by coordinating and synchronizing data flows across the DevOps toolchain.

10. They help the DevOps or VSM team evaluate the impact of making a change on the DevOps value stream without affecting the actual system or data.

Chapter 12: Introducing the Leading VSM Tool Vendors

1. False. VSM as a discipline has been around for decades and is used to improve all organizational value stream flows.

2. True. VSM applies the principles of Lean production to make continuous improvements across all organizational value streams.

3. Defects, Inventory, Motion, Overprocessing, Overproduction, Transportation, and Waiting.

4. Thomas Davenport (*Process Innovation: Reengineering Work Through Information Technology*) and James Martin (*The Great Transition*).

5. Both Martin and Davenport evaluated process reengineering and process improvement initiatives from the lens of making value-based or value-delivery improvements, and with IT as a critical enabler to installing business process innovations.

6. **Artificial Intelligence** (**AI**) and **Machine Learning** (**ML**) help teams look inside organizational silos and aggregate data to form a holistic view of information, conduct analysis, and gain insights across sales, marketing, finance, development, operations, and technology teams.

7. Integration, automation, and orchestration.

8. VSM is a proven, effective, and disciplined step-by-step methodology for understanding and applying the principles and practices of Lean thinking.

9. VSM has its roots in the Lean production concepts employed in the **Toyota Production System** (**TPS**).

10. No, the DORA four metrics highlight the best performers among DevOps teams. However, VSM is a Lean improvement strategy that looks at many more metrics to determine how to improve an organization's value delivery capabilities across all value stream flows.

Chapter 13: Introducing the VSM-DevOps Practice Leaders

1. Its purpose is to help organizations worldwide deliver customer value by adopting and advancing value stream management tools and practices. The objective of the VSMC is to serve the whole VSM community by helping drive value stream management standards and innovation through leadership and community connectivity.

2. Structurally, the VSMC implements Lean practices and value streams as its operating model. In addition, its funding supports VSMC Research, Learning, and Outreach value streams.

3. The Consortium's initial research offering will be the *The State of Value Stream Management Report*, which will measure how teams apply value stream management principles, practices, and metrics to influence their value stream management outcomes.

4. PMI acquired **Disciplined Agile**, which focuses on implementing Lean and Agile practices in software development.

    PMI also acquired NetObjects, the developer of **FLEX (Flow for Enterprise Transformation)**, a framework based on systems-thinking, offering a comprehensive set of portfolio, Agile product management, executive/management, program, and team patterns for success based on Lean-Agile principles and practices.

5. DA provides a process-decision toolkit that helps individuals, teams, and enterprises optimize their **Way of Working** (**WoW**) in a context-specific approach.

6. Process Blades to help teams and organizations guide their selection of alternative techniques based on their unique software development needs. In turn, the process blades guide users on how to apply selected techniques to enhance critical organizational capabilities.

    Each process blade provides information on its philosophical underpinnings (or Mindsets), these being the roles and responsibilities of people applying the techniques or descriptions of streamlined business processes as Flows to improve business agility and employment options to address situational needs. Collectively, Mindsets, People, Flows, and Options represent four views about the DA toolkit.

7. The DA toolkit offers four levels of process blades, spanning Foundations, Disciplined DevOps, Value Streams, and DA Enterprise.

8. FLEX is PMI's approach to implementing value stream flows with the goal of improving value delivery using VSM techniques.

9. Value streams are the primary constructs for understanding, organizing, and delivering value in SAFe. SAFe introduced operational and development value streams, along with value stream mapping to their enterprise community of users. Understanding and continually optimizing value streams is key to practicing SAFe effectively.

10. Triggers, Steps, Value, People and Systems, and Lead Times.

11. Value Stream Management (VSM) is a leadership and technical discipline aimed at maximizing business value flow through the end-to-end solution delivery life cycle. VSM implements Lean, Agile, and DevOps values, principles, and practices across functions in the continuous operation, measurement, and optimization of value streams, from customer requests to solution delivery.

12. **Continuous Exploration (CE)**, **Continuous Integration (CI)**, **Continuous Deployment (CD)**, and **Release on Demand (RoD)**.

13. DevOps enables the Continuous Delivery Pipeline.

14. The **CALMR** acronym stands for *Culture*, *Automation*, *Lean flow*, *Measurement*, and *Recovery*.

    CALMR lies at the center of SAFe DevOps as a mindset that guides ARTs toward achieving continuous value delivery by managing simultaneous advancements in delivery.

15. VSM is the approach used to make Lean-oriented improvements across value stream flows. In SAFe DevOps, the goal is to increase the flow of business value from customer request to customer delivery.

Chapter 14: Introducing the Enterprise Lean-VSM Practice Leaders

1. James P. Womack, Ph.D. James Womack and his colleague, Daniel T. Jones, coined the term Value Stream in an article published in the Harvard Business Review magazine, titled "From Lean Production to the Lean Enterprise" (March–April 1994).

2. LeanFITT's founders were the original thought leaders in the early development of value stream management concepts and methodologies.

3. The issue is that those managers and executives have multiple value streams running through their functional departments, but the metrics and financial incentives drive department or facility-level improvements.

4. All of the actions, both value-creating and non-value-creating, are required to bring a product from concept to launch (also known as the development value stream) and from order to delivery (also known as the operational value stream). These include actions to process information from the customer and actions to transform the product on its way to the customer.

5. Lean Action Plans help reduce resistance, spread the right learning objectives, and engender the type of commitment necessary for a Lean enterprise.

6. The LeanFITT system offers methods, tools, and techniques to improve organizational processes, people, and profits.

7. The phases are:

   A. Getting people trained and engaged.

   B. Standardizing the improvement process.

   C. Energizing the team with active involvement and transparency.

   D. Making lean routine and sustainable.

8. The means and methods to *tell the continuous improvement story* logically and visually.

9. An informative measure of quality, a six sigma process is one in which 99.99966% of all opportunities to produce some feature or part are statistically expected to be free of defects.

10. Lean tools and quality tools

Chapter 15: Defining the Appropriate DevOps Platform Strategy

1. "Instill the mindset that DevOps is a cultural movement for the whole organization and design value stream teams that practice DevOps."

2. Solution delivery, DevSecOps, data DevOps, Multi solutions support, Common IT operations, and business operations.

3. Chief or line of business executives support the funding of the initiatives, allocate sufficient resources, and hold people responsible for achieving identifiable and measurable outcomes with timeframes, budgets, and ROIs that justify the effort.

4. How their IT managers and executives are tired of spending money on IT without showing value across the rest of the organization.

5. In CI/CD and DevOps pipelines, we can automate the deployment of new releases through configurations implemented as code in the form of **Infrastructure as Code (IaC)** and **Configuration as Code (CaC)**.

6. Building a custom DevOps platform, purchasing a cloud-based DevOps-as-a-Service (DaaS) solution offering, employing VSM tools to integrate and orchestrate your DevOps toolchains, and building software factories through the construction of self-service configurations as code, downloadable via GIT or another SCM tool.

7. Purchase a license to use commercial **DevSecOps as a service (DaaS)**.

8. Culture, Automation, Lean, Measurement, and Sharing.

9. Building a dedicated DevOps team from scratch is only going to create new silos operating across your horizontal value stream.

10. The organization's chief and line of business executives. They must keep the momentum going through the hard times.

Chapter 16: Transforming Businesses with VSM and DevOps

1. To transform businesses into viable entities to compete in our digital economy.

2. False. Outside of IT, where these concepts are relatively new, manufacturing and other industries have practiced Lean and VSM for decades.

3. Toyota sought to improve quality and efficiencies in an island nation, coming out of the Great Depression and World War II, when access to resources was limited and expensive. Toyota's approach to be competitive in its global markets was to build higher-quality products with less wasting of resources, while simultaneously ensuring they built only the products customers wanted when they wanted them.

4. Agile began as a set of values and principles to support the needs of small software development teams to become more responsive and adaptable. In the process, Agile evolved to implement iterative and incremental development practices that leveraged prototyping and empiricism to quickly create working solutions with customer-directed inputs.

5. Identify, Organize, and Map

6. Connect

7. **Agile** – measured in 1 to 4 weeks and limited to the budgets and authorities granted to the development team.

Lean – Often view changes across multiple planning horizons that may span several fiscal years, and involve changes and budgets requiring executive-level sponsorship and commitment authority.

8. Local optimization.

    Because we can expend much time, effort, and money on the initiatives but necessarily impact the value delivery capabilities of the organization as a whole.

9. The primary purpose of portfolio management is to centralize and control the budgeting and investments process so that organizations can evaluate all improvement opportunities and their priorities in context with corporate strategies.

    VSM and DevOps tool investments compete against all the other potential investments under evaluation by the organization at large.

10. Because new management comes in and cannot easily see the mechanism that supports horizontal value deliveries. They are more comfortable managing the vertical silos of traditional hierarchical business structures.

`Packt.com`

Subscribe to our online digital library for full access to over 7,000 books and videos, as well as industry leading tools to help you plan your personal development and advance your career. For more information, please visit our website.

Why subscribe?

- Spend less time learning and more time coding with practical eBooks and Videos from over 4,000 industry professionals

- Improve your learning with Skill Plans built especially for you

- Get a free eBook or video every month

- Fully searchable for easy access to vital information

- Copy and paste, print, and bookmark content

Did you know that Packt offers eBook versions of every book published, with PDF and ePub files available? You can upgrade to the eBook version at `packt.com` and as a print book customer, you are entitled to a discount on the eBook copy. Get in touch with us at `customercare@packtpub.com` for more details.

At `www.packt.com`, you can also read a collection of free technical articles, sign up for a range of free newsletters, and receive exclusive discounts and offers on Packt books and eBooks.

Other Books You May Enjoy

If you enjoyed this book, you may be interested in these other books by Packt:

Managing Software Requirements the Agile Way

Fred Heath

ISBN: 978-1-80020-6-465

- Learn how to communicate with a project's stakeholders to elicit software requirements
- Deal every phase of the requirement life cycle with pragmatic methods and techniques
- Manage the software development process and deliver verified requirements using Scrum and Kanban

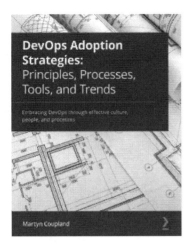

DevOps Adoption Strategies: Principles, Processes, Tools, and Trends

Martyn Coupland

ISBN: 978-1-80107-6-326

- Packed with step-by-step explanations and practical examples to help you get started with DevOps
- Develop the skills and knowledge you need to tackle the deployment of DevOps tools
- Discover technology trends such as FinOps and DevSecOps to get more value from DevOps

Packt is searching for authors like you

If you're interested in becoming an author for Packt, please visit `authors.packtpub.com` and apply today. We have worked with thousands of developers and tech professionals, just like you, to help them share their insight with the global tech community. You can make a general application, apply for a specific hot topic that we are recruiting an author for, or submit your own idea.

Share Your Thoughts

Now you've finished *Driving DevOps with Value Stream Management*, we'd love to hear your thoughts! Scan the QR code below to go straight to the Amazon review page for this book and share your feedback or leave a review on the site that you purchased it from.

`https://packt.link/r/1-801-07806-8`

Your review is important to us and the tech community and will help us make sure we're delivering excellent quality content.

Index

S

Made in the USA
Middletown, DE
24 September 2022